Values &
Public Policy

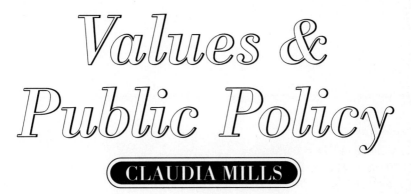

Values & Public Policy

CLAUDIA MILLS

University of Maryland

Under the general editorship of
Robert J. Fogelin
Dartmouth College

Harcourt Brace Jovanovich College Publishers
Fort Worth   Philadelphia   San Diego   New York
Orlando   Austin   San Antonio
Toronto   Montreal   London   Sydney   Tokyo

Acquisitions Editor: Bill McLane
Manuscript Editor: Kay Kaylor
Production Editor: Michael Ferreira
Designer: James Hughes
Production Manager: Mary Kay Yearin

Cover art: © Rafál Olbínski

ISBN: 0-15-594711-7
Library of Congress Catalog Card Number: 91-72171
Printed in the United States of America

PREFACE

The past two decades have seen the emergence of a new emphasis on the study of values in public policy. This is both an important development within the field of philosophy, as ethicists have begun to turn their attention to the real problems of real people in the real world, and a vital concern in the public arena, as the ethical considerations underlying public controversies receive increasing political and popular attention.

These developments are mirrored in the world of education. Applied ethics has become a staple of both introductory and upper-level philosophy courses. The curriculum of government departments and programs in public affairs frequently includes a strong normative component. Even high schools have begun to combine a renewed interest in the discussion of values with the desire to instruct young people in the skills of critical thinking.

This book responds to these needs. The articles in it range across the spectrum of live policy issues, probing the underlying value issues that make each controversial and important. We have aimed by and large to situate discussions in actual policy contexts, with examples drawn abundantly from policy issues that have continued to command public attention from year to year. Many are overview pieces, providing a balanced survey of the issues and arguments attending a contemporary policy controversy.

These articles have been distilled from those published in the Institute for Philosophy and Public Policy's quarterly, *QQ*, now ending its first decade of publication. The Institute for Philosophy and Public Policy at the University of Maryland has been a leading laboratory for research at the intersection of philosophical and policy issues. Established in 1976, the Institute has now devoted some fifteen years to conceptual and normative research into the structure of arguments and the nature of values relevant to the formation, justification, and criticism of public policy.

From start to finish this book has been a product of the Institute's ongoing work. All my colleagues over the years contributed through their research to the articles that form this volume. The intellectual substance of this collection owes everything to the shared efforts of Peter G. Brown, C. A. J. Coady, Robert Fullinwider, William Galston,

Mary Gibson, Amy Gutmann, Nancy Jecker, Steven Lee, Judith Lichten-berg, David Luban, Douglas MacLean, Richard Mohr, Bryan Norton, Thomas Pogge, Mark Sagoff, Ferdinand Schoeman, Jerome Segal, Henry Shue, Alan Strudler, Paul Vernier, David Wasserman, and Robert Wachbroit. Over the past decade, all of us received vital support from Lyndal Andrews, Elizabeth Cahoon, Louise Collins, Carroll Linkins, Susan Mann, Lori Owen, Rachel Sailer, Robin Sheets, Mary Ellen Stevens, and Kate Wiersema.

From this long list of colleagues and friends, two must be singled out for the special help they gave me in turning this massive amount of research and writing into an actual book. I want to thank Richard Mohr for his steady stream of nagging, nudging letters ("Hi! What's happening with the book?") and for his perceptive insights into how its eighty-three essays should be focused and organized. Most of all, I must thank Douglas MacLean for our weekly meetings at which the book began to take shape. It would never have happened without his steadfast encouragement and philosophical vision.

Claudia Mills

CONTENTS

Chapter 5   The Media   *197*

INTRODUCTION

W hy study the *values* underlying public policy? It might seem that values are abstract, while policy controversies are all too concrete; that values lie in the realm of theory, while policymakers struggle with practice; that values are timeless, while policy is crafted in the crucible of the here-and-now.

Yet in recent years increasing public attention has been focused on the values that underlie our public policies, and in the academic world "applied philosophy" has emerged as an important new field. Philosophers first began examining the values that animate policy debate of vital issues in the medical arena, issues such as abortion and euthanasia, for it was obvious that policy on such issues cannot be decided without exploring such basic philosophical questions as, What is it to be a person? What gives human life its meaning? Is there an important moral difference between killing someone and (merely) letting him or her die? Philosophers began to serve on hospital advisory boards, to staff national study commissions, and to testify before Congress; philosophy departments began to offer courses in contemporary moral problems, with a heavy emphasis on these life-and-death medical dilemmas.

As ethicists joined the debate about real-life moral problems, the issues garnering their concern have broadened. Medical policy is certainly not the only arena in which value questions prove critical. Can we discuss energy policy without close attention to our obligations to future generations? Can we talk about foreign policy without considering international justice? Can we discuss civil rights without seeking to establish grounds for those rights and their proper scope and application?

In their academic marriage, philosophy and public policy seem to bring to each other at least three pairs of complementary benefits. To the passions of policy debate, philosophy brings its characteristic emphasis on rigorous analysis and argument. Students exposed to a philosophical view of policy are trained to scrutinize unquestioned popular notions and to dismantle flawed arguments. In a complementary fashion, real-life policy cases breathe life into otherwise empty ethical abstractions. In this way, philosophy and public policy each provide what the other may lack: the trained exercise of reason and a necessary spark of passion to make the reasons matter.

A second pair of benefits that philosophy and public policy bring to each other in the classroom is philosophy's frank appeal to moral values, tempered by policy's pragmatic caution against easy moralizing. Rights, obligations, justice, autonomy, the nature of the good life—these are the stuff of moral philosophy. The philosopher is unabashed by arguments that rely heavily on these central ethical concepts. By importing philosophy into the study of policy, we learn to look beyond economics, beyond cost-benefit analyses and pollsters' tallies, to what is indeed just and right and good.

The temptation to preach is ever present, however, and a strong dose of policy considerations inoculates us against faith in moral platitudes and quick answers. Vague enthusiasm for human rights, for example, must be translated into policy. But are human rights best protected by strident denunciations of their violation or by "quiet diplomacy" that verges on silence? The danger that our actions may work against the very goals we hold most dear is one of the central perils of politics. Awareness of the risks moderates moral zeal.

The third pair of benefits goes to the heart of philosophy and public policy as an intellectual enterprise. In this field, ethical theories and actual policy conflicts are brought to bear on each other for mutual criticism and enlightenment. Consider energy policy. Our dependence on foreign oil and need for national energy self-sufficiency is an issue in international distributive justice. Our need for a transition from non-renewable fossil fuels to some renewable energy source such as nuclear or solar power raises in dramatic form our obligations to future generations, or intergenerational distributive justice. The choice between nuclear and solar power opens yet another set of issues: the analysis and evaluation of the risks posed by various energy alternatives and the values we attach to assorted ways of life. In all three cases, ethical questions must be addressed before policy questions can be resolved.

But in all three cases as well, the policy issues themselves signal limitations of the ethical theories involved to resolve them. Both international and intergenerational justice show the inadequacy of current contractual and consent-based theories of justice, since other nations and other generations are beyond any social contract in space and time. And in analyzing different energy risks, the very concepts of rights and justice may prove inadequate—certain energy choices may distribute risks fairly and evenly, without violating any rights, yet we may decide, from some differently grounded vision of our common good, that the risks posed are unacceptable. Thus policy and philosophy each extend the horizons of the other. Policy benefits by a sophisticated and careful examination of such concepts as rights, justice, liberty, and role morality, while at the same time it provides crucial tests of these common notions. Our goal is to establish some sort of "reflective equilibrium" between the two.

What if the result is not reflective equilibrium, however, but exponentially expanding confusion? Political scientists who turn to the study of values are struck by the lack of consensus on basic ethical principles, as common moral intuitions are challenged and often contradicted. Ethicists exploring issues in public policy are struck by widespread disagreement even among experts—on the risks and benefits of energy alternatives, for example, or the actual extent of human rights violations under repressive regimes.

This confusion has its dangers. Chief among them is the invitation to moral relativism—one might conclude glibly that no one really knows either what is going on or what principles ought to be guiding our responses to what is going on. Therefore, everyone should just do his or her best without worrying too much about getting anything right. But if this slide into relativism can be resisted, a new and deeper awareness of the moral complexity at the heart of our policy dilemmas may itself be the prime contribution of the marriage between the study of values and the study of public policy. That the answers are not easy or instantly available does not mean that the questions are not of perennial and enduring importance.

PART I

TECHNOLOGY, RISK, AND THE ENVIRONMENT

1

TECHNOLOGY
AND RISK

The closing years of the twentieth century bring with them mounting concern about how best to deal with the consequences of the manifold technological breakthroughs the century has wrought. We continue to grapple with air pollution and the risks of nuclear power; we worry whether we can fuel our energy-dependent industrialized economy without depleting dwindling reserves of nonrenewable natural resources; we look for new ways to store our staggeringly large stockpiles of hazardous wastes. As we face the next century, we despair of the legacy we may be leaving future generations, even as we wonder what, if anything, we actually owe to those who are born after us.

The first article in this chapter, "What Has Posterity Ever Done for Me?: Energy Policy and Future Generations," asks whether our generation does indeed have moral obligations as justice toward future generations. It may seem that we do not, that justice depends in some sense on reciprocity, while obligations to future generations would be completely one-sided. What kind of reciprocity does justice demand? Do future generations have any right to complain about their condition of existence, given that they are indebted to us for existing at all? Perhaps, the author suggests, we may find some way of understanding our interest in the well-being of future generations that bypasses talk of rights and obligations altogether.

The next article looks not at the grounds for our obligations to future generations but at their scope and content. Any use of nonrenewable resources involves leaving an irreversibly diminished inheritance, yet surely we are not obligated to forgo such use altogether. Nor is it possible to live contemporary life without passing on to our descendants certain long-lasting risks. "Are We Cheating Our Children?" explores the contours of our obligations to future generations and the ways in which these obligations constrain our current choices of energy policies.

In "Why People Fear Nuclear Power," Douglas MacLean examines what he calls "*the* technological debate of our time," the continuing controversy over the risks and costs of nuclear energy. MacLean suggests that the deep-seated public fear of nuclear power, despite the stated language of public debate, may have less to do with its risks and costs per se than with a host of other far-ranging concerns. Ultimately "people may fear nuclear power because of the kind of economic and political system—the kind of life—that they feel inescapably accompanies it."

This hardly means, however, that the risks associated with nuclear power are not all too real. One concern is the long-term storage of nuclear waste. Thousands of metric tons of high-level radioactive waste now crowd temporary storage facilities, awaiting permanent disposal—preferably in somebody else's backyard. In "Nuclear Waste Storage: Your Backyard or Mine?" MacLean discusses the difficulty of finding a fair procedure for choosing nuclear waste disposal sites, the nature of the compensation that should be offered affected communities, and the impact of present policy decisions on future generations.

Another unwanted byproduct of energy production is air pollution. Air pollution is plainly harmful to all who breathe—how, then, can polluters be permitted to emit airborne contaminants, given the familiar moral prohibition against causing serious harm to others without their consent? "Air Pollution: The Role and Limits of Consent" examines more closely the role the notion of consent plays in legitimizing—or condemning—current levels of air pollution. It focuses on three arenas: workplace air pollution, outdoor air pollution, and the dangers to nonsmokers posed by "secondhand smoke."

What Has Posterity Ever Done for Me?

Energy Policy and Future Generations

Claudia Mills

Scientists warn that our continued and increasing reliance on fossil fuels as a source of energy is causing a critical buildup of carbon dioxide in the atmosphere, leading to global warming and perhaps, in time, to the melting of the polar ice caps and widespread flooding of low-lying coastal cities, including Washington, D.C., Los Angeles, and New York. The alternatives? We could increase our reliance on nuclear power, but toxic nuclear wastes, unlike the world's diminishing oil reserves, are predicted to last a long, long time—at least several dozen centuries. Solar, wind, and water power seem less hazardous but perhaps more expensive possibilities, with conservation a safer bet still. But choosing these latter alternatives would mean that we, the present generation, would have to make major changes in how we now live—considerable sacrifices on behalf of generations to come.

Why should we make such sacrifices? Many would answer that we have no obligation to make any sacrifices at all. In 1909, Senator Henry Taller, former secretary of the interior, wrote: "I do not believe there is either a moral or any other claim upon me to postpone the use of what nature has given me, so that the next generation or generations may have an opportunity to get what I myself ought to get." After all, one might argue, we did not ask to be born now any more than they asked to be born later. While it is true enough that we arrived on the scene while air was breathable, water was drinkable, fuel was plentiful, and the nation's major cultural centers remained above sea level, that was just the luck of the draw. If others find themselves being born at a less auspicious moment, well, they took their chances in the generational lottery and lost fair and square: tough luck, guys. Our descendants may have reason to mourn their misfortune, but not to complain of any injustice.

But, of course, no such lottery exists. Philosopher Brian Barry points out that "all there really are are successive generations, some of which are potentially disadvantaged by the actions of their predecessors." Lady Luck may know nothing of fairness or unfairness, but *we do*, and if we grab and despoil, we are accountable, in the name of justice, for what we have done. Justice to whom? To those who inherit the earth after we have depleted and despoiled it.

Here, however, an objection can be raised. Justice cannot govern our relation with our descendants, because the requirements of justice, according to some popular theories, hold only among equals: the principles of justice are the rules by which those roughly equal in power and opportunity agree to cooperate for their mutual advantage. Realizing that all will be better off if each restrains himself within the bounds of the agreement, rational, self-interested individuals contract with one another to regulate their conduct accordingly. But among generations no such bargain is possible. Later generations have no bargaining power; they cannot threaten or offer anything.

Barry characterizes this view (which he rejects) by this metaphor: Each generation inhabits a single island, arranged along a current, with all the resources located on the island farthest upstream. The generation with the resources must decide what to use and what to float downstream to the later generations. What do the inhabitants of the upstream island gain by sharing resources with less fortunately situated islands? Nothing, it would seem. And so we can ask ourselves, in the words of Robert Heilbroner, "What has posterity ever done for me?"

If justice applies only in situations of reciprocal advantage, then justice cannot dictate our treatment of future generations. However, David A. J. Richards, professor of law at New York University, argues that a different kind of reciprocity is at the heart of our concept of justice. This notion of reciprocity involves not actual mutual advantage, but universalizability or role reciprocity: treating persons in the way one would reasonably like to be treated oneself. We have obligations of justice even to the weak and powerless, in this view, and these obligations are precisely to treat them as we would want to be treated were we weak and powerless. Applying these principles across generations, Richards concludes: "Insofar as the actions of one generation directly affect the interests of later generations, there is a relation among persons governable by moral reciprocity." What matters is not what future generations have done for us, but what we would have liked them to have done for us had our temporal positions been reversed.

Here another complication emerges. Philosopher Douglas MacLean points out that, whatever other rights potential future persons might have, they have no "right to be born." We have no obligation to bring as many future persons as possible into existence—if we did, the planet would rapidly get mighty crowded. But if potential persons have no right to be born, this seriously undercuts the claim of future generations to just treatment from us. For then the present generation can simply "solve" the problem of meeting its obligations to future generations by ensuring that no future generations exist in the first place. "You don't like living amid stockpiles of nuclear waste? Well, try not being born at all, and see how you like *that*."

To this challenge, two responses are possible. The first is simply to assume it away. The human race is *not* going to be deliberately exterminated; future generations *are* going to continue to exist—and so the fact that ending life on earth might be one solution to problems of intergenerational justice has no practical relevance for us in assessing our obligations to future persons.

The second response involves a radically different way of viewing intergenerational justice. MacLean proposes that, rather than looking at the rights and interests of future generations, we might do better to look at our own most deeply rooted interests and values. "A better proposal," he suggests, "is to argue that a concern for posterity is in our own interests—the interests of ourselves and our contemporaries. . . . Many of the interests we value most are directed not toward our own satisfaction, but toward the world." We value scientific research, political activism, and cultural monuments for their contributions to making a better world, a world that will endure long after we are gone. "The value of these things requires protecting them and passing them on, and this in turn requires creating an environment where culture and history can continue in ways we like to imagine they will. Alternatively, if we do not value posterity in this way, we undermine the value of these interests in our own lives."

Scientific warnings about environmental catastrophe alarm us not merely because we recognize an obligation to those who come after us, but because so much of what we ourselves value is directed toward the continued existence and flourishing of the human race. We do not want our monuments to be submerged by the rising waters unleashed by global warming because they are our *monuments*, our legacy to our descendants, the distinctive mark we have made on the universe. It is up to us, the members of the present generation, to see that this legacy is preserved and transmitted.

The views of Brian Barry, David A. J. Richards, and Douglas Maclean are taken from their essays in Energy and the Future, *ed. Douglas MacLean and Peter G. Brown, Maryland Studies in Public Philosophy (Totowa, N.J.: Rowman and Littlefield, 1983).*

Are We Cheating Our Children?

Claudia Mills

L ife in any form that we can imagine depends on energy, and life as we know it depends on an enormous amount of energy. Our highly industrial, technological, consumer-oriented civilization requires vast quantities of fuel to warm and cool us, feed and clothe us, drive our engines, and power our factories. The world's energy use has been increasing exponentially, with little sign of any imminent slackening; the last few generations have burned more fossil fuels than all previous generations combined. Even as the major industrial powers begin to question the desirability and possibility of limitless growth, Third World nations are hastening to build their own industrial plants and correspondingly accelerate their consumption of energy.

For how many more generations can this rate of energy use be sustained? Each generation cannot blithely burn more energy than the last and expect the generations that follow to be able to do the same. Viewed from a long-term perspective, the supplies of the most heavily relied on fuels are literally running out, while renewable sources of energy pose risks we are not yet able to predict or control, or have yet to be shown to be practicable for meeting the seemingly boundless energy needs of the contemporary world. Virtually all experts agree that supplies will continue to dwindle and risks will continue to mount, although there is far less consensus on workable alternative strategies.

Virtually everyone also agrees that it is wrong for the current generation to deplete exhaustible resources and produce inexhaustible hazards, bequeathing a future rich only in risk. Though philosophers debate the grounds for our obligations to future generations, few doubt the existence of the obligations themselves. Whether we explain them as obligations to respect the rights of future persons, or to maximize human happiness, or to produce a better world, the obligations limit our current range of energy choices, perhaps quite severely. No one takes seriously the view that the universe is ours to plunder and despoil as we will.

But what exactly is the scope of our obligations to future generations? What is it that we owe them? Any use of nonrenewable resources involves leaving an irreversibly diminished inheritance, yet surely we are not obligated to forgo their use altogether. Nor is it possible to live contemporary life without passing on to our descendants certain long-lasting risks. The future, furthermore, is in many respects unknown and perhaps even unknowable. What can we owe to those who may live unimaginably different lives in an unimaginably altered world? The answers to these questions constrain our current choices of alternative energy policies.

Supply and Opportunity

Two-thirds of the energy used in the world today draws on the resources whose future supplies are most uncertain: oil and natural gas. David Bodde, Assistant Director for Natural Resources and Commerce in the Congressional Budget Office, estimates that "world oil use [in 1980 was] about 64 billion barrels per day . . . which would suggest a seventy-year supply," given ultimate world oil resources "in the neighborhood of 1600 billion barrels." The outlook for natural gas is less certain, but no more optimistic. Bodde warns, "The transition away from oil and gas must certainly be completed within 100 years, and probably much sooner." The central question for designing a long-term energy policy is to determine how we will make this transition and who will pay the costs.

For our own generation, the question is not whether we should stop depleting the nonrenewable energy stock, since we could not abandon all use of these fuels, nor does justice require this of us. Earth's current inhabitants have rights, too, and if future generations can lay claim to a share of resources, so do we have our share. But what *is* our share, and how should we proceed in fairness both to ourselves and to our heirs?

Philosopher Brian Barry argues that all generations have an equal claim on natural resources: "From an atemporal perspective, no one generation has a better or worse claim than any other to enjoy the earth's resources. In the absence of any powerful argument to the contrary, there would seem to be a strong presumption in favor of arranging things so that, as far as possible, each generation faces the same range of opportunities with respect to natural resources."

Natural resources are valuable, however, only given adequate technology and capital to convert them into usable energy, and so each generation's share of resources must be determined in a fuller context. This means that our legacy to our descendants must include not only a decent share of the resources, but also a decent share of the technology and capital that make them valuable. For just as the present generation has no special claim to the resources, so it has no special claim to any but the incremental capital and technology it has contributed to its own vast inheritance. As Barry points out, "Most of the technology and the capital stock embodying it are not by any stretch of the imagination the sole creation of the present generation; we cannot therefore claim exclusive credit for it." Even if the current generation cannot avoid depleting the world's stock of resources, it can—and ought to—avoid depleting its inherited stock of capital and technology.

Indeed, we can—and ought to—enhance and increase the stock of capital and technology we pass on, for in this way we can compensate to some degree for unavoidable resource depletion. This idea of compensation provides the cornerstone of intergenerational distributive justice. Thus Barry proposes: "Future generations are owed compensation in other ways for our reducing their access to easily extracted and conveniently located natural resources. In practice, this entails that the combination of improved technology and increased capital investment should be such as to offset the effects of depletion." Law professor David A. J. Richards offers a similar proposal: Depletion of nonrenewable resources can be compensated if "concurrent with that depletion, a technology has been developed that will meet the depletion and make available to later generations . . . a technology that can secure from depleted resources at least as much (for example, energy) as would have been secured by the original resource." Barry's and Richards's proposals provide a minimal standard of fair resource allocation across generations.

Two questions arise:

(1) What if future generations have tastes and habits sufficiently different from ours, or develop sufficiently altered lifestyles or cultures, so that the resources we conserve for them do not give them the happiness or satisfaction they give us? For in some sense it is not the resources themselves that matter, nor even the energy they can be converted to, but how the quality of human life is enhanced by their use. What matters, in this view, is not what productive opportunities we bequeath our descendants, but how much utility they derive from those opportunities, and it is equality of utility for which we should strive.

But, in practice, Barry argues, it is enormously difficult to determine how individual persons "convert the means of happiness into happiness itself," and so these kinds of differences should be disregarded in determining public policy. Economist Talbot Page also opposes second-guessing the future in this way: "It seems sensible to focus on and limit our responsibility to what we can foresee and control. With some effort we can control the form of the heritage to be passed on to the next generation. It is beyond the control of the present generation to ensure that the next one will be happy or hard-working. . . . we can only assure them of certain opportunities for happiness that we foresee will be essential."

Barry maintains, moreover, that even if the practical difficulties of predicting future happiness were not insuperable, justice simply does not require equal distribution of enjoyment. "Justice consists in [everyone's] getting an equal crack at society's resources," not in everyone's getting the same measure of happiness from those resources. "We should not hold ourselves responsible for the satisfaction [future generations] derive from their opportunities." The opportunities are our concern; the satisfaction, theirs.

(2) But what if the world changes in such a way that the resources we carefully conserve and pass on no longer provide a viable source of productive opportunity? Page calls attention to the possibility that "a great deal of effort and sacrifice could be spent preserving some part of the resource base that no one in the future might want."

Although our radical ignorance about the future keeps this possibility in view, it can be all but dismissed, Page suggests, for "essential goods—conditions of basic health, alternative provision of energy sources, water, soil, space per capita, etc." It is extremely unlikely that such goods would ever be preserved for naught. And, "as an empirical matter, it appears that dependence on the physical resource base is growing, not shrinking." We may risk inefficiency by saving for our children, but by not saving we risk injustice. If we can avoid one only at the cost of the other—which is not at all certain—perhaps it is better to err on the side of behaving justly toward those who come after us.

What, then, does distributive justice across generations require of us? We should progress on the transition from nonrenewable to renewable resources, and develop technology to make our nonrenewables go further. But the renewable resources that are currently best developed to meet our burgeoning fuel needs also carry with them the greatest intergenerational risks, and new technologies to extend the nonrenewables may create risks of their own. Supply and risk are in some cases traded off against each other: Oil and natural gas are relatively benign in their health and environmental impacts, but their supplies are in greater danger of exhaustion; coal and uranium are more plentiful, but their attendant risks are greater. Any plausible principles of intergenerational justice must address questions of risk as well.

Risk and Neutrality

In ordinary cases we think it is wrong to impose harm on innocent persons, or to impose a significant risk of harm, without first obtaining their free and informed consent. We think it is wrong to impose risks on unconsenting others even when those put at risk receive as a result still greater benefits. Even less, of course, do we think risks can be imposed that benefit the risk-imposers at the risk-bearers' expense. At the very least, where harm is unavoidable and consent unobtainable, compensation is owed the sufferer, as a matter of justice.

These widely accepted principles governing risk imposition apply, if anything, with greater force when risks are imposed across generations. Although temporal distance does increase uncertainty about the possible consequences of our actions (who can say how likely it really is that radioactive wastes produced today will cause cancer five hundred generations hence?), two other factors heighten the moral seriousness of intergenerational risk imposition.

In the first place, it is obviously impossible to obtain the free and informed consent of future persons to risks created by current energy policies, so this basic condition for risk imposition cannot possibly be met in the intergenerational case. Second, the present generation reaps most of the benefits from the energy produced, while future generations bear most of the risks. Writes Barry: "With some examples such as nuclear power plants, the benefits and risks are asymmetrically distributed across time: the benefits disproportionately occur while the plant is producing electricity, and the risks continue in some form for thousands of years, until the radioactivity of the waste decays to a safe level." Richards adds: "This divergence of benefit and burden, combined with the future generation's lack of any voluntary choice in the matter, appears to make intergenerational cases of foreseeable risk imposition morally more questionable than comparable intratemporal cases . . . and any cost-benefit analysis that suppresses or ignores this moral feature is flatly unethical."

These considerations suggest a principle of intergenerational neutrality: A policy is considered neutral if the risks it imposes on future generations are not greater than the risks they would otherwise face if we did not adopt this policy. Applying the neutrality principle to the disposal of long-lasting toxic wastes from nuclear power plants, Thomas B. Cochran, staff scientist at the Natural Resources Defense Council, argues that risks of nuclear power are to be assessed by comparing the risks of the processed radioactive wastes with the risks of the unmined ore. He proposes, "Nuclear operations of all types should be conducted so the overall hazards to future generations are the same as those that would be presented by the original unmined ore bodies utilized in those operations." This standard could be met by emplacing wastes in an artificial "ore body" with characteristics identical to those of the original unmined ore. Unless Cochran's strict standard can be met in some such way, the risks otherwise imposed on future generations by nuclear power suffice to rule it out of consideration as an energy source.

Cochran's proposal for nuclear waste disposal may seem too narrowly focused, however, when we consider the perhaps equally grave and certainly shorter-term risks created by nuclear power's leading alternative. Although coal, unlike nuclear power, is nonrenewable, supplies are bountiful enough to provide energy for centuries. But the burning of coal and other carbonaceous fuels causes a dangerous buildup of atmospheric carbon dioxide (CO_2); the eventual global warming predicted if CO_2 buildup continues could ultimately melt the polar ice caps, causing major flooding and agricultural dislocation. Furthermore, CO_2 buildup may approach ominous levels even in some of our lifetimes. According to Bodde, "The range of uncertainty may be greater for CO_2 than for radioactive waste, but to the extent that a problem exists, it is likely to impinge upon us in the next fifty to two hundred years."

Thus Bodde argues that the risks from nuclear power cannot be assessed independent of the whole constellation of risks posed by alternate forms of energy use—or indeed, by the whole complex of technology that drives and sustains modern life. He replies to Cochran that "if our moral concern is the preservation of equal opportunity for future generations . . . then our duty is to create solutions to the disposal of radioactive waste in the context of the other threats to human existence, rather than in isolation. This implies a more holistic approach than has heretofore been taken."

Neither of the two leading alternatives to the most rapidly diminishing nonrenewables, then, provides an easy solution to the problem of intergenerational justice. It may be impossible to avoid leaving the world a substantially riskier place than we found it, though, again, we should apply our technological ingenuity to reducing the risks produced, and pass on added capital as a compensation fund for the future victims of our current choices.

Facing the Future

Bodde suggests three "necessary elements of any energy policy that would seek equality of opportunity for future generations":

- Resource-balancing strategies that assess the risks of nuclear power and carbon dioxide in the context of the overall energy picture

- Technological progress to ensure compensation for depletion of nonrenewable resources

- Nurturing of institutions, national and international, whose scope and capabilities match the nature of the social and technical problems before them

This last element of Bodde's program may be the most essential. He writes: "National institutions tend to select some problems (such as radioactive waste) for detailed attention while neglecting others (such as CO_2 buildup) . . . because we tend to work on that for which the societal instruments exist." National institutions are already in place to address, if not to resolve, the problem of nuclear waste disposal; atmospheric CO_2, by contrast, does not respect national boundaries and so cannot be handled by institutions on a national scale. "It seems clear that our obligation to future generations includes the building of institutions of sufficient scope to deal with the problems we bequeath them."

The way we produce and distribute energy has much to do with how we live the rest of our lives; it may have even more to do with how future generations live theirs. Energy is power, and oil power, coal power, and nuclear power can translate into economic and political power, as events of recent decades have made only too clear. Adequate institutions to control and contain this power may be the energy-related legacy that we should most endeavor to leave behind us.

The views of David Bodde, Brian Barry, David A. J. Richards, Talbot Page, and Thomas B. Cochran are drawn from their essays in Energy and the Future, *ed. Douglas MacLean and Peter G. Brown, Maryland Studies in Public Philosophy (Totowa, N.J.: Rowman and Littlefield, 1983).*

Why People Fear Nuclear Power

Douglas MacLean

The debate over nuclear power, in the United States at least, is *the* technological debate of our times. Deep and acrimonious controversy surrounds the complicated set of risks and costs belonging to the production of nuclear energy. Is nuclear power a comparatively cheap or expensive way to produce electricity? Massive public subsidies for nuclear-generated energy make clear assessment of comparative economic value difficult, and while operating costs of nuclear plants may be lower than those of coal plants, construction costs are far higher, and "back end" costs of decontamination and waste disposal have not even been calculated. Do the risks of future Three Mile Islands and nuclear weapons proliferation make nuclear power too dangerous to pursue? The estimates of these risks are hotly disputed.

Questions about the risks and economics of nuclear power are putatively empirical questions. But even if these were definitively settled, the public fear of nuclear power would be unlikely to go away. No new empirical facts or studies have much impact on public opinion in this area, nor do those involved in making or lobbying about nuclear policies think this impasse is likely to dissolve. Nuclear power is symbolic, and it has become a surrogate for a debate about some broadly social issues. In examining the possible reasons why people fear nuclear power, we raise a host of other concerns about the role of experts, the acceptance of risk, and the distribution of power in our society.

Leaving Nuclear Technology to the Experts

Defenders of nuclear power sometimes charge that people are afraid because they are hopelessly ignorant about the facts of nuclear technologies and are led astray by an almost equally ignorant and often irresponsible press. This account presupposes that the public opposition is basically technical, but misinformed.

It may be, however, that the contending parties have different political agendas in the dispute that centers on this technology. The nuclear power controversy is a political war, and the participants on both sides may be pursuing other goals on the battleground over health risks and safety standards, if this is where they think they can most easily achieve them. The perception of health and safety risks, by both experts and nonexperts, is strongly colored by these other factors. Someone who thinks that nuclear technologies have bad political implications will tend to see the health risks as worse than others see them. And someone who is acutely aware of the economic costs of safety equipment might tend to see the risks as lower than others see them. The experts are not without their own political axes to grind, and objective assessments are hard to identify.

Furthermore, any "expert" who wants to render some general judgment about nuclear power must address subjects beyond his or her area of special competence. The issues involved require a greater understanding of physics, engineering, medicine, epidemiology, geology, economics, systems analysis, psychology, management techniques, and so on, than any individual can muster. So, in a sense, there are no experts, no individuals who have special insight into all the technical areas, let alone the nontechnical ones.

Finally, rather than relying on experts to assess nuclear technology, people increasingly want a technology for which such blind reliance is unnecessary. One technology may be preferred to another because it allows those served by it to make their own autonomous decisions about its risks and costs. If nuclear power requires a surrender to the authority of experts, this may itself constitute a reason to reject that technology.

Technological Pessimism and Aversion to Risk

A second view is that people fear nuclear power because they are extraordinarily risk averse about nuclear power and basically pessimistic about new and sophisticated technologies.

The claim about technological optimism and pessimism can be dismissed as a red herring. Opponents of nuclear power are often quite optimistic about, say, the commercial feasibility of photovoltaic cells or sophisticated systems for converting biomass to fuel. Some nuclear engineers are paradigms of technological pessimism when they talk about solar power. Optimism and pessimism are technology-specific.

The risk-aversion charge is more serious. The public expresses fear about nuclear power far out of proportion to fear about other threats to their well-being. The risks of acid rainfall, for example, seem to inspire less general concern than risks of toxic radioactivity, even though the probability and magnitude of the former may make them no less threatening.

Nothing is necessarily irrational, however, about refusing a risk that is measurably lower than other risks one accepts. This would be clearly irrational only if the *qualities* of different risks (as opposed to the measurable balance of expected harms and benefits) were irrelevant to a rational decision to accept or reject them. This is at least counterintuitive.

The risks posed by nuclear power have several very special and disturbing characteristics. First, the risks and benefits are distributed differently across generations. The toxicity of nuclear wastes spreads risks over millennia, while the foreseeable benefits of using nuclear power are near-term in comparison. Thus the question of moral obligations to future generations is raised in dramatic form.

Second, the risks of nuclear power are in many cases catastrophic risks. These risks have a very low probability of occurrence, with nearly infinite costs should they occur. Apart from the real problem of assigning meaningful probability estimates to such catastrophes, it is difficult to know how we should evaluate them morally. One accident killing 50,000 people may be worse than a series of 50,000 single-death accidents.

Third, the risks of nuclear power include genetic mutations as well as cancer. Even if the dose-response relationships are similar for these two kinds of feared side effects, we might think one risk is a more serious concern. Women, for example, are significantly more likely than men to oppose nuclear power, perhaps primarily because of their more acute concern for the genetic effects of radioactivity on the unborn children of future generations. Some ill effects—including some ways of dying—are more dreaded than others. It matters to us not only when and where we die, but how, and the suffering we bequeath our children may matter to us still more. The nature and quality of these nuclear risks determine—and should determine—our judgment of their acceptability.

Choosing a Way of Life

Finally, people may fear nuclear power because of the kind of economic and political system—the kind of life—that they feel inescapably accompanies it. Following Amory Lovins, many people see our energy policy in the United States as embodying an exclusive choice between a nuclear future (the "hard" path of technological development) and a solar one (the "soft" path). Nuclear technologies are thought by these critics to be necessarily highly capital-intensive and highly centralized in their deployment as a system for producing and distributing the socially basic good of electricity. Solar, or soft, technologies, on the other hand, are thought to be compatible with, or even to encourage, a decentralized superstructure of deployment and production. Nuclear technologies, then, are likely to concentrate capital and power in the utility and oil industries (who own most of the uranium) to an even greater extent than they are concentrated today.

Some people believe that this path of development, like some other trends toward concentration of wealth and power in fewer and fewer hands, threatens the ability of individuals or even nations to control their own destinies. If the technology for producing energy requires centralized control, and if political power depends largely on energy, then technological development in the area of energy production can determine the distribution of social and political power in our world.

Fortunately, however, the dangers posed by the concentration of wealth and power can be resisted, for people can govern themselves and block this concentration. They can define individual rights and principles of distributive justice that they will act to defend. This is one of the primary purposes of government in a democratic society. We can make political decisions about the governmental and economic structures that our children will inherit.

This sociodynamic reason for fearing nuclear power calls our attention to the kind of society we will create by the economic and technological decisions we make. Like the fear about risks, it forces us to confront our moral requirements to future generations. Both these fears serve as reminders that economic considerations, though crucial, are not the only considerations. It is not only a level of welfare that is at stake in the nuclear power controversy, but also a kind of life.

Nuclear Waste Storage
Your Backyard or Mine?

Douglas MacLean

Nearly forty years after the United States began producing nuclear waste as a by-product of generating nuclear power, we still have not succeeded in disposing of any of it. Thousands of metric tons of high-level radioactive waste now crowd temporary storage facilities near the reactors that produce them. For twenty-five years the problem was virtually ignored, leading former South Carolina governor Richard Riley to remark, "There is a basic law of nuclear waste often overlooked: all waste remains where it is first put."

The issue became politically salient around 1975, and after much debate, Congress passed the Nuclear Waste Policy Act (NWPA) in 1982. The NWPA called for a waste site to be opened in a Western state by 1993 and a second site in the East by 2003; it also provided for extensive public involvement in the site selection process, and even allowed local authorities veto power over a selection. However, the reasonable provisions of this law soon came unhinged. Thus, in 1986, President Reagan selected three candidate sites—in Washington, Nevada, and Texas—from those already studied by the Department of Energy, and he cancelled plans to find a second site in the East. After further political maneuvering, the House of Representatives was left to select one site from the president's list. It may be a coincidence that the Speaker of the House at the time was from Texas and the majority leader from Washington, but the Yucca Mountain site in Nevada was chosen. Nevada was offered $10 million per year in compensation (rising to $20 million per year after the site opened), on condition that it forgo the right to disapprove the site.

Nevada actually received an amount greater than that from the federal government, and it used these funds to conduct technical research on the characteristics of the site, as well as research on the attendant social and economic impacts. The risks involved include eventual leaks, which might contaminate water supplies, and accidents while transporting wastes to the site. But Nevada's research also suggested that areas surrounding the site, including perhaps Las Vegas, would be economically stigmatized by a nuclear waste repository. Opposition to the site increased, and many Nevadans no doubt felt that they had not been treated equitably by decision-makers in Washington. Nevada spent some of its federal funds on lobbyists, hoping to persuade Congress to accept a different site. This annoyed some senators, who in 1986 reduced the federal funds given to the state. Then Nevada passed a referendum attempting to ban the site from the state, and the Senate responded by cutting federal funds to Nevada further in 1989, greatly hampering the state's ability to conduct such research. It is now certain that a waste site will not open in Nevada before the turn of the century, and it is far from clear that one will ever open there. Could this situation have been avoided?

When it comes to the siting of a nuclear waste repository, it is fairly easy to find reasons why somebody else's backyard is geographically, technologically, politically, and morally preferable to one's own. Nobody is thrilled at the prospect of a nuclear waste dump in the neighborhood; few communities would consider one a source of civic pride. But the wastes must be disposed of somehow and somewhere. In an ideal world, we could parcel out the risks of nuclear waste storage equally, so that we would each face the same chance of possible harm. But in our world, these risks must be distributed unequally. Those who live near the chosen sites are going to bear the risks, and if any harms eventuate, they will suffer the harms as well. How, then, should we decide: your backyard or mine?

Finding a Fair Procedure

In situations where we cannot distribute risks or harms *equally*, we can at least try to distribute them *fairly*. The procedures we use to assign such harms and risks will make a great deal of difference to how we feel about the ultimate distribution of outcomes. We might think them fair, even if unequal.

We can make a distinction between two different ways of appraising decision-making procedures. We can judge them on their tendency to produce the best outcome, where we have some independent way of assessing outcomes. Or we can judge them on their intrinsic merits: With intrinsically valuable procedures, whatever outcome results is ipso facto the best.

What are we looking for in a procedure for selecting a nuclear waste site? The political and social issues have become so dominant that no one seriously maintains that the site should be picked solely for its geological properties. A purely scientific procedure thus appears to be unsatisfactory, even if it identifies the "best" site in terms of the sheer physical safety of storage. The risks involved in transporting wastes, along with other problems, rule out selecting a densely populated site, even if its geological features are ideal. Nor would it be socially acceptable to pick a site in a sparsely populated area, if the state in which this site is located does not appear to benefit from nuclear power proportionately to other states. (Salt domes in Mississippi were eliminated from consideration for this reason.)

The reasons for not picking a site solely on its geological fitness are generally described as matters of equity, even though such a criterion would not obviously rely on any morally suspect considerations that discriminate against any particular population. If determining the site by geological criteria is unsatisfactory, then the procedures for site selection must be evaluated in part on their intrinsic merits, on their fairness, not simply on their instrumental value for picking an ideal physical location. Perhaps it shows something about the special nature of nuclear wastes that the procedure for picking a safe site must also satisfy political and democratic criteria. But the selection process cannot be evaluated strictly on intrinsic grounds of equity, either. We would not accept pure democracy here, for example, by using a random selection process that gives everyone an equal chance of avoiding proximity to a site, or by giving everyone an equal voice in opposing the site, which would in effect place it in the most sparsely populated area, regardless of geological suitability.

Geology, demography, and democracy are all relevant to the process of site selection. The procedure will have to be justified on scientific, political, and moral grounds. It is not obvious in advance that these criteria are simultaneously satisfiable. We have not yet found a procedure that is ideally equitable, reasonable, and socially acceptable.

Compensation for Risks

A fair procedure is one possible way to satisfy equity demands where harms, and the risk of harm, cannot be distributed equally. Compensation provides an alternative possibility for realizing equity. Given the difficulties of determining a fair procedure for siting a nuclear waste repository, the possibility of offering compensation for those risks takes on major importance, for when harms are offset by benefits this mitigates the need to distribute the risk of harm fairly.

How does a benefit compensate for a harm? The benefit must do two things: First, it must at least equal the harm in amount, and, second, it must *offset* the harm, so that the affected party is restored to something like a status quo ante. Attempts to compensate may fail if either condition is not met.

Some losses are so great that no amount of benefits can restore the balance. Death is one such loss, for the victim certainly, and perhaps also for the victim's family and loved ones. Other harms, especially mass disasters that create losses on a vast scale, may similarly exceed an individual's, a firm's, or even a society's ability to compensate. This is an important problem for many of today's risky technologies, and certainly for nuclear power.

Other losses may be difficult to compensate not because of the amount of harm suffered but because of the nature of the harm. Benefits do not necessarily "fall short," but they are inappropriate in a different way: They fail to offset the harm. The money offered might easily equal or exceed the economic value of, for example, a family heirloom, but its loss would not thus be offset.

These considerations are relevant to the selection of a nuclear waste repository site, for the choice may have profound impacts on local communities and their ways of life. The populations of these communities must bear some increased risk to their health and lives that the expected economic benefits of disposal activity might not be able to compensate. These people may also face fear and stigmatization, which we might have to compensate in different ways.

The economic impacts themselves might not be completely positive. Small rural towns, for example, may be converted to larger urban centers. The local economies may thrive, but the population's sense of its own identity—how people see themselves and their communities—may be altered forever. If it is necessary to compensate communities or individuals for siting a nuclear waste repository in their midst, then we need to ask what kind of values are threatened and whether the benefits in the compensatory package offered offset the nature as well as the level of the losses.

One way we might proceed in figuring out the appropriate kind and degree of compensation is to offer the affected parties some package of risks, harms, and benefits, and see if they accept it. Their consent determines whether compensation has been made, we might argue, for they will consent only if they regard our offer as making them ultimately better off.

While this method is frequently adequate, it can fail for several reasons. People may simply refuse to consent, especially if they see their losses as important and irreplaceable. Requiring explicit consent from all affected citizens may thus give each a veto power over public policy. Or the affected parties, such as future generations, may not be able to consent, yet it may be necessary nonetheless to impose risks or losses on them. If the parties lack the relevant information, or if they cannot process it rationally, as may well be the case with complex technological risks, then their consent can fail to be fully informed.

People also may be taken advantage of in ways we would consider morally unacceptable. It is generally beneficial to offer jobs to the unemployed, but people in need might accept an employment package even if the job was unnecessarily risky or other parts of the package were extremely harmful. Consent does not justify obvious exploitation. A depressed community will naturally have a greater incentive to bid for hazardous land uses if these bring needed benefits, but we must be wary of exploiting its needs.

Compensation packages must be designed in cooperation with affected communities, but local acceptance of an offer may not be sufficient to determine that fair and adequate compensation has been made. We have to evaluate the package directly and the conditions under which it is found acceptable. We need, therefore, to determine independently whether the consent is informed and free and whether the benefits are appropriate. If we are imposing particular health risks, for example, compensation might aim explicitly at reducing the overall level of health risks in other ways, through providing subsidized health plans, building hospitals and health care centers, and so on. Similar benefits are generally more likely to offset a harm than dissimilar benefits. But determining what counts as fair and adequate compensation may prove to be as thorny and intractable as determining what counts as a fair procedure for assigning risk.

Intergenerational Equity

Intergenerational equity is clearly one of the most important moral issues involved in selecting a permanent repository site for nuclear wastes. We seem to have a moral consensus that the costs of nuclear power should be borne by the generations that benefit most directly from it and that we do have a moral responsibility to protect future generations.

These concerns bear on a key decision regarding storage of nuclear wastes. We can store the wastes in a retrievable manner, or we can store them "permanently." Permanent storage generally has higher expected costs to our generation than retrievable storage, but although retrievable storage is probably less expensive today, it imposes some maintenance costs on future generations. The consensus we are assuming about our intergenerational duties might forbid this intergenerational transfer of costs, and in fact permanent storage appears to be the policy with the greatest current political support.

But retrievable storage also reduces an important risk to future generations, for if something does go wrong with a site, and radioactive material begins to escape into the biosphere, it will be far less costly to correct this problem if the wastes are stored retrievably. So the choice is between an alternative that is more expensive today and imposes a very high-cost risk on the future, or one that is less expensive today, imposing some maintenance costs on future generations but also eliminating the extremely costly risk.

Two normative considerations seem to be relevant. The first is an issue of fairness. It seems only fair that the present generation should be required to bear the higher costs, since we are the ones receiving the benefits. It is far from clear, however, how the benefits and their distribution should be measured. This issue arises relative to justice between generations and also among different populations in the same generation.

Should the benefits of nuclear power be seen as restricted to the less expensive electricity it directly generates? Or should we also include these more widely shared benefits: the lower indirect costs of electricity that result from the contribution of nuclear power to the nation's energy supply; the lower costs of products made from this cheaper electricity, which may be purchased far from the site of the original power plant; whatever technological insights gained from developing nuclear power that may prove beneficial, especially to future generations, and so on? It is far from easy to draw boundaries, either geographical or temporal, around the beneficiaries of this, or indeed any other, technology. The farther those benefits extend in time and space, the weaker the moral case for allocating the costs narrowly.

The second consideration is one of rationality. We can try to reach a decision here by asking what a reasonable individual living some time in the future would want for herself and would want us to decide if we were deciding on her behalf. It might seem more reasonable to bear some certain, fairly modest, costs in order to reduce the chance of a far more costly accident. This, at any rate, is the standard justification for buying insurance. Arguing from either the fairness of allocating costs or the rationality of paying to avoid risks, normative considerations would seem to favor retrievable storage, contrary to prevailing popular beliefs.

Conclusion

Nuclear power seems to be enjoying some resurgence in popularity today, in the wake of concerns about the global warming consequences of burning fossil fuels. This new awareness, however, does not address any of the problems that have plagued nuclear power in the past; at best, some people are beginning to think it may be less unacceptable than the alternatives. But this gives us greater reason to find socially acceptable solutions to nuclear power's traditional problems, beginning with disposing of the radioactive wastes we have already produced. We need to formulate—and then stick to—fair procedures for selecting a site; we must be willing to bear the costs of disposal, which will include carefully designed compensation packages to adversely affected communities; and, I have argued, we should rethink the wisdom of "permanent" disposal and seriously consider monitored retrievable storage instead. That would reduce the costs of accidents in the future and—who knows?—we may yet find a socially beneficial use for all that radioactive material. If nuclear power can regain popularity after decades of mismanagement and Chernobyl-like accidents, then anything is possible.

This article was based on research Douglas MacLean conducted while he was a consultant to the Equity Task Force of the Nevada Nuclear Waste Project office.

Air Pollution

The Role and Limits of Consent

Claudia Mills

A top-forty singer croons to his girl friend: "All I need is the air that I breathe and to love you." Like love, air is an essential human good: Wherever we go and whatever else we do or care about in life, we all must breathe. And like love, air is found everywhere: in a dimly lit bar, on a stroll in the park, on the factory assembly line, in the office copy-machine line, in cities, suburbs, farms, wilderness.

But, along with love and air, air pollution, too, turns up in all these places. In bars and restaurants, at work and at home, nonsmokers inhale what nearby smokers exhale: One cancer epidemiologist warns that breathing other people's cigarette smoke may bring early death to as many as 2,000 nonsmoking Americans every year. Airborne contaminants in the workplace (offices as well as factories) are responsible for the largest share of the 100,000 to 200,000 occupational disease fatalities in the United States every year. Even otherwise pristine wilderness is not untouched: The Office of Technology Assessment has estimated that "acid rain" currently threatens 9,500 lakes and 60,000 miles of streams. Some 50,000 deaths annually in the United States and Canada may be attributable to the effects of outdoor air pollution.

What moral judgment can we pass on air pollution in these different cases? In one common and persuasive moral view, it is simply wrong to cause a serious harm to another person without his or her consent, whatever the benefits—to you, to society generally, even to that person—of so doing. To cause disease or death, or to destroy another's property, is in this view to violate a moral right. Peter Railton, a philosopher at the University of Michigan, fleshes out this "Lockean" view with the image "of moral space as akin to a map at a registrar of deeds. Individual entitlements determine a patchwork of boundaries within which people are free to live as they choose so long as they respect the boundaries of others. To learn one's moral obligations one need only consult the map. Would a given act involve crossing another's boundary? If so it is prohibited; if not, permitted." Are pollution-caused injuries to persons or property, then, flatly ruled out?

The answer usually given is that such injuries may be permitted if those injured can be said to have given their consent to the polluting activity. Consent, as it were, opens up boundaries so that a border-crossing is no longer a moral offense. How adequate is this response in our three cases cited earlier: secondhand smoke, airborne hazards in the workplace, and outdoor air pollution? Can we say that the victims in these cases consented to the harms that befell them? What role does the notion of consent play in legitimizing, or condemning, current levels of air pollution—how much weight can we place on a consent requirement in setting our societal standards for air quality, and in deciding how these standards should be implemented? And where can we look instead if the concept of consent in some cases fails us?

Secondhand Smoke

Nonsmokers have always complained about having to breathe other people's smoke, but only in the past few years has the link between secondhand smoke and lung cancer been established. Suddenly the complaints have acquired a new seriousness. Most "passive smokers" don't actually contract cancer, of course, but are "merely" placed at a higher risk of contracting it. But risk levels are raised, Railton notes, because "some actual physical change has been wrought by [the smoker] in [the nonsmoker's] person or property. . . . each time I send some of my tobacco smoke your way you suffer some small physical change, not for the better." This counts as a harm, albeit a small one. And in the Lockean view what matters is whether or not a boundary was crossed, not the magnitude of its consequences: Shoplifters have been arrested for stealing a pack of chewing gum. Nor can the smoker's alleged "right to smoke" be placed in the balance here. While the smoker may have a right to smoke alone in her room, cheerfully contracting cancer if she likes, her right to smoke, like her right to swing her arm, ends where someone else's nose begins.

But doesn't the nonsmoking wife consent to the risk imposed on her by marrying a smoker and staying married to him? If she can't take the smoke, she can pack her bags and head for Rio. It can be argued, more generally, that the nonsmoker bothered by someone else's fumes is at liberty to walk away. But according to philosopher Mary Gibson, "this will not do. He or she must work, travel, eat, attend classes and meetings, and so on, like everyone else. . . . In a society in which a substantial proportion of the population smokes, avoiding involuntary exposure by eschewing all 'voluntary' associations where one might encounter secondhand smoke would make it impossible to lead anything like a normal life." She agrees that the more voluntary the association, the stronger the case for saying that the nonsmoker consents to the risk he undergoes. But we need to look long and hard at how voluntary the association really is.

In this first case, it seems, then, that the presence or absence of the nonsmoker's consent is critical in determining how much pollution the smoker is morally permitted to impose on those around him. Our societal goal should be to minimize the harms suffered by nonconsenting bystanders, to zero if possible.

How should this goal be achieved? Clifford Russell, an economist, identifies several dimensions on which we can compare different strategies for implementing air quality goals: how efficiently the goal is achieved; how achievement is monitored and enforced; what incentives polluters are given to reduce pollution still further; and whether the implementation plan is itself satisfactory on moral and political grounds.

To achieve our air quality goal in the secondhand smoke setting, Russell recommends outright prohibition of smoking in public places or the provision of segregated smokers' and nonsmokers' sections. Since "no social good is served by [smoking], and it is certainly not an inevitable result of any activity that does produce a social good," the only cost of prohibition is the discomfort experienced by the habitual smoker asked to refrain. Such discomfort can be intense, however, so where segregation can be inexpensively provided, it may be the preferred choice.

Better still would be for smokers to kick the habit altogether. The strongest antismoking incentives seem to be provided by growing public disapproval (fueled by Brooke Shields commercials calling smokers "losers"). Hefty taxes placed on cigarettes, to provide a financial disincentive to smoke, run into ethical objections, in Russell's view. "Any implementation system based on a tax . . . runs squarely aground on the distributional objection that the rich can pay to pollute. . . . The burden of achieving the social goal would be shifted to the least well off rather than shared on some appealing basis such as the initial contribution to the problem."

Workplace Air Pollution

It may seem more persuasive to argue that workers exposed to airborne contaminants on the job have consented to the risks they bear, particularly if they are paid additional wages in exchange for the additional risk. Gibson points to evidence, however, that a "wage premium" for risky work exists "in otherwise relatively desirable jobs, i.e., those that are relatively highly paid, secure, and unionized, but not in those jobs characterized by low pay, insecure employment, and lack of unionization." She concludes, "Inferring consent from labor-market behavior presupposes that workers are fully informed of the hazards they face before accepting (and while working at) jobs, that they have reasonable alternatives available to them if they find the risks unacceptable, and thus that they are satisfied with the wage/risk packages they currently get. Each of these assumptions is subject to serious question."

If we insist that airborne harms may not be imposed on workers without their consent, then in many cases workplace air quality will have to be considerably cleaned up, and at considerable expense. Enforcement of the consent requirement has a great deal more bite here than in the secondhand smoking case, since real social benefits derive from keeping production costs low. But our current societal consensus seems to be that workplace air pollution violates workers' rights. The Occupational Safety and Health Act mandates that permissible exposure levels for any toxic substance present in the workplace must ensure that "no employee will suffer material impairment of health or functional capacity," and this insistence on protecting worker health despite steep costs was upheld by the U.S. Supreme Court.

If we can achieve this same standard more cheaply, of course, so much the better. Russell believes that the most efficient route to attainment is for the regulator "simply to announce to each industry or plant the required ambient standard and then arrange to monitor its observance. . . . A simple announcement of the standard can bring about the least-cost solution, since each firm can be presumed to minimize its cost of compliance." A less efficient alternative is to specify, not a standard to be met, but a particular technology for meeting it, since this provides a firm with no incentive for developing cheaper and better means of pollution control. Some efficiency could be sacrificed, however, for ease of monitoring and enforcement. Russell notes that it is much easier to check that a certain piece of equipment is in place than to measure constantly fluctuating air quality. On the other hand, "installation does not guarantee operation, much less proper operation." In any case, the presence of the workers themselves, who can assume some on-the-spot monitoring responsibilities, makes enforcement less of a problem.

Implementing a workplace air quality standard through regulation backed with penalties for noncompliance also sends a clear message that we as a society morally condemn the practice of endangering worker health for corporate profits. Promulgation of the regulation itself, together with the rhetoric that accompanies it, signals that workplace health and safety have a high priority on the nation's agenda.

Outside Air Pollution

Perhaps there is no one who is not adversely affected by outdoor air pollution. Even those who live in low-risk regions have reason to care when wilderness lakes and forests are rained upon by showers with the pH of household vinegar, for wilderness—and, indeed, the air itself—is a shared resource owned jointly by all of us. Once again, in the absense of near-universal consent to current pollution levels, the "you stay within your boundaries and I'll stay within mine" view seems to entail very tight restrictions on polluting activity.

But this conclusion here seems unacceptable. In the previous two cases, it looked both feasible and fair to insist that no one be harmed by secondhand smoke or workplace air pollution without his or her consent. Where consent could not be obtained, pollution could not be justified. But how would one even begin to go about obtaining the actual explicit consent of every single individual affected by pollution in outdoor air? Nor does an appeal to "implicit" consent seem to be of any help, for what might initially appear as instances of implicit consent—such as buying a home in a polluted area—do not hold up under scrutiny. Railton maintains, "Someone who voluntarily moves into a high-crime (or high-grime) neighborhood may have acted unwisely, but he has not laid down his rights."

More crucially, an insistence on actual unanimous consent, even if feasible, seems unreasonably—and unfairly—strict. Should one individual, perhaps only marginally affected, be entitled to veto any polluting activity, however much it may benefit others? We may feel more inclined to scrap the consent requirement than to shut down all polluting industry. It seems that in the outdoor air pollution case, we have reached the limits of consent as a tool for setting air quality standards.

At this point Gibson suggests that we stop and ask ourselves what it was about consent that struck us as so important and look to this more basic, underlying notion to guide our policies. In her view, what lies behind consent requirements is a concern for autonomy, for self-determination, a concern "that one's life be one's own." Railton identifies the motivating factor behind the Lockean view as the Kantian idea of respect for persons as ends, not merely as means. If we look beyond consent to autonomy, or respect for persons' control over their own lives, what can we say about outdoor air pollution?

Gibson draws this conclusion: "There can be no substitute for actual, direct, informed, and meaningful participation in the formation, adoption, and implementation of public policy concerning air pollution by the persons whose lives, health, and values are potentially at risk." In particular, she rejects technocratic solutions that appeal to notions of "hypothetical consent"—speculations on the part of economists and bureaucrats as to what rational, well-informed individuals *would* consent to *if* they were consulted. "What we need, if we are to respect and promote autonomy," she argues, "are not more sophisticated algorithms for making decisions, but better ways of involving those whose lives will be affected by those decisions in making them." There is no magic formula, no neat cost-benefit analysis, for determining how much pollution we as a society can tolerate, given the clearly intolerable costs of achieving zero pollution. Gibson thus looks to democratic institutions and procedures to help us arrive at some kind of societal consensus.

Railton also sees the solution as lying in a process of social balancing and compromise. For him, the failure of the notion of individual consent to guide our public policies on outdoor air pollution shows that the Lockean conception of morality "that pictures individuals as set apart by property-like boundaries" cannot do justice to "the fact that we find ourselves situated in, and connected through, an environment." A workable policy on air pollution will not come from a rigid and narrow focus on individual rights, but from a fundamentally social dialogue.

Once we have arrived through democratic processes at a societal standard for outdoor air pollution—as we have through the Clean Air Act—by what strategy should it be implemented? The current approach, following the strategy for workplace pollution, again simply promulgates the standard, with penalties for noncompliance. But Russell argues that stronger incentives for technological innovation are provided by systems that, rather than flatly forbidding any pollution that exceeds the standard, set a charge or price on any excess discharges: "For any particular source, an incentive system that puts a fee on the discharge remaining after control will create a greater incentive to change than will a regulation specifying that same level of discharge." He believes there is little to choose between the two approaches as far as monitoring and enforcement are concerned, since accurate measurements are needed to assess both charges and fines.

The idea of emission charges has met with political resistance. It is felt that polluters already have a good enough reason not to pollute: that it is wrong. We do not let litterers pay to toss beer cans out of their cars; instead we post signs saying, "Littering is filthy and selfish so don't do it!" "By making pollution into an activity that one can pay to engage in," as Russell explains this objection, "the charge approach implicitly judges it to be ethically neutral—like buying a shirt. Those who judge pollution to be wrong in itself, as a crime against other persons, do not approve of that result."

In the Lockean view, of course, any amount of pollution, however small, is a wrong to which a clear moral stigma should be attached. But part of the reason for moving away from that view is the realization that a certain amount of pollution is inevitable in any production or consumption process. The fact that we set nonzero levels of pollution, Russell argues, sends the same ethical message as establishing a charge. So a case can be made for a charge approach, if it can receive democratic endorsement from those who will in the end be affected by the policy chosen.

Conclusion

Air pollution, as Railton concludes, makes us take seriously the fact that we exist not as isolated entities secure behind our fences, but as fellow creatures in a shared and threatened environment. While in some settings—when looking at secondhand smoke or workplace hazards—we can insist that individual consent remains fundamental, in others we may have to look beyond consent to autonomy and beyond the individual to a deeper sense of community. If anything is our birthright, it is the air that we breathe. The fervent outpouring of public support for the Clear Air Act suggests that we are serious about doing something to protect it.

The information in this article, and the quotes from Peter Railton, Mary Gibson, and Clifford Russell, are taken from essays in To Breathe Freely: Risk, Consent, and Air, ed. Mary Gibson, Maryland Studies in Public Philosophy (Totowa, N.J.: Rowman and Allanheld, 1985).

FOR FURTHER READING

Gibson, Mary, ed. *To Breathe Freely: Risk, Consent, and Air.* Maryland Studies in Public Philosophy. Totowa, N.J.: Rowman and Allanheld, 1985.

Grobstein, Clifford. *Science and the Unborn: Choosing Human Futures.* New York: Basic Books, 1988.

Lowrance, William. *Modern Science and Human Values.* New York: Oxford University Press, 1985.

MacLean, Douglas, and Peter G. Brown, eds. *Energy and the Future.* Maryland Studies in Public Philosophy. Totowa, N.J.: Rowman and Littlefield, 1983.

Mazur, Allan. *The Dynamics of Technical Controversy.* Washington, D.C.: Broadcasting Publications, 1981.

Regan, Tom. *Earthbound: New Introductory Essays in Environmental Ethics.* New York: Random House, 1984. See the sections titled "Ethics and Energy," by K. S. Shrader-Frechette, and "For the Sake of Future Generations," by Annette Baier.

2

NATURE, THE ENVIRONMENT, AND ANIMAL RIGHTS

L iving in harmony with nature, preserving and protecting our threatened environment, and respecting the rights of the fellow creatures who share with us planet Earth has become the creed of more than a small sect of environmental enthusiasts. Today concern for the natural world is coming to be taken for granted by all of us: Recycling programs proliferate, manufacturers design and advertise their products in environmentally conscious ways, and programs to combat environmental degradation top the national policy agenda. This chapter explores some of our reasons for caring about nature, the environment, and animal rights.

The Endangered Species Act mirrors popular concern for environmental protection by mandating stringent standards for protecting any plant or animal species that has been listed as threatened or endangered. However, the list of protected species is a short one, thus weakening the act's impact, and on a case by case basis we are often unsure whether one particular threatened species—the Tennessee snail darter, the horned owl—really warrants such a terribly big fuss, especially if preservation appears costly. "Preserving Endangered Species: Why Should We Care?" assesses leading rationales for caring about endangered species: the unknown economic potential of lost species, the cumulative danger posed by the loss of biological diversity, the intrinsic value, if any, belonging to the species themselves, and, finally, their potential for forming and transforming human values.

In "The Biotechnology Controversy," Mark Sagoff looks at the ways in which new developments in biotechnology are likely to affect how we think about the living world and how we understand our relationship to it. The environmental laws of the 1960s and 1970s, Sagoff writes, "did not regard nature as a congeries of raw materials fit for limitless human intervention and manipulation, but as a system of natural resources and communities that should be altered as little as possible." Biotechnology, of course, relies on diametrically opposed premises. Behind the conceptual difference between "raw materials" and "natural resources," Sagoff suggests, lies a fundamental distinction for evaluating new forms of biotechnology and justifying new regulations of it.

Environmental laws and regulations often impose duties on landowners to use and manage their lands in environmentally sensitive ways—to maintain habitat for endangered species, for example, or to refrain from filling wetlands. Do such laws and regulations interfere with property rights? Do they require that landowners be compensated for the costs of compliance? In "Property Rights and Environmental Law," Sagoff examines the central court decisions providing guidance in this area and offers an argument in defense of current environmental regulations.

Along with a concern for environmental protection has developed a concern for animal "liberation." A vocal movement protests the wearing of fur, the eating of meat, and medical and commercial experimentation on animals. What do the two movements have in common? Mark Sagoff answers: just about nothing. In "Animal Liberation and Environmental Ethics: Bad Marriage, Quick Divorce," Sagoff argues that the two movements proceed from such different premises and justify such different policies that, despite certain surface similarities between the two, "An environmentalist cannot be an animal liberationist; nor may animal liberationists be environmentalists."

In "Defending Human Chauvinism," however, C.A.J. Coady identifies a central assumption common to both "animal and nature liberationists," for both may be "plausibly viewed as calling for a new ethic" in rejection of the old "human centered" or "speciesistic" ethic. The arguments in support of such a new ethic strike Coady as seriously flawed, and he responds with a qualified defense of human superiority and a morality centered on human interests and concerns.

Both environmentalists and animal liberationists may have reasons to be concerned about patent No. 4,736,866, issued to Harvard University in 1988 for a genetically engineered, cancer-prone mouse—the world's first patent for an *animal*. In "Eight Worries about Patenting Animals," Robert Wachbroit surveys a series of intrinsic and extrinsic objections to patenting animals to determine which are easily dismissed, which sound and compelling.

Preserving Endangered Species
Why Should We Care?

Claudia Mills

When construction of the Tellico dam was temporarily halted because the project posed a threat to the endangered Tennessee snail darter, environmentalists were triumphant, economists relieved (the dam was an economic disaster in its own right). The general public seemed cheered by the triumph of such an improbable underdog, but uncertain that a lowly three-inch minnow was really worth the trouble of saving.

Surveys taken by Stephen Kellert of Yale University reflect this ambivalence in public attitudes toward species preservation. In a questionnaire modeled on the Tellico dam controversy, pitting an obscure fish species against various development projects, the fish species won out handily over recreational projects, tied with projects to divert water for industrial development, but was soundly defeated by projects to produce hydroelectric, agricultural, or drinking water improvements. As codified in the law of the land, the will of the people is expressed more strongly in favor of species preservation. The Endangered Species Act mandates stringent standards for protecting any plant or animal species that has been listed as threatened or endangered. However, the list of protected species is a short one, so the effect of the act is considerably weakened.

How much *should* we care about endangered species? Why, indeed, should we care at all? A first answer is that extinction is forever. It is irrevocable, the flung stone that cannot be called back. Still, we do irrevocable things all the time, sometimes half a dozen before breakfast. But our knowledge of the considerable benefits the human species has reaped from other species, together with our ignorance of what benefits we might someday glean from species currently threatened, make extinction particularly alarming. What if the *Penicillium* mold had gone extinct a century ago? Who knows what cure for cancer we would have discovered even a decade hence in some unknown species that went extinct yesterday? Thomas Lovejoy, executive vice president of the World Wildlife Fund, concludes, "Assuming that the biota contains ten million species, they then represent ten million successful sets of solutions to a series of biological problems, any one of which could be immensely valuable to us in a number of ways."

But this argument cannot bear a great deal of weight. It sounds too much like the reasoning of our old Aunt Tillie, who saves every bit of string or bottle cap on the off chance that it may someday come in useful. Clutter mounts up exponentially, and someday never comes. After all, philosopher Elliott Sober observes, "there are so many species. How many geese that lay golden eggs are there apt to be in that number?" For Sober, an argument from ignorance is no argument at all: "If we literally do not know what consequences the extinction of this or that species may bring, then we should take seriously the possibility that extinction may be beneficial as well as the possibility that it may be deleterious. . . . Ignorance on a scale like this cannot provide the basis for any rational action."

If we can't appeal to the possible future usefulness of species, what reasons do we have for preserving them? Put bluntly, what is it to us whether they live or die? But perhaps Aunt Tillie overlooked some benefits to preserving species. Do species have a value in their own right, independent of what value we place on them? Or can we, even within a human framework, find a noncommercial, nonscientific value to justify their preservation?

As Goes the Furbish Lousewort ...

Let us concede that only relatively few species are likely to prove of direct commercial or scientific use. Does this mean that the rest are therefore useless—expendable in the face of competing resource needs? That conclusion would surely be a hasty one, given the sheer magnitude of the species currently threatened. Extinctions that might not be worrisome viewed one by one take on a new seriousness when multiplied many thousandfold.

Lovejoy reports that hundreds of thousands to more than a million extinctions are projected to take place by the end of the century. The estimates vary widely (nobody even knows how many species exist, let alone how many are endangered), but "what is important," in Lovejoy's view, "is that every effort to estimate extinction rates has produced a *large* number."

Of course, almost every species that has ever lived has gone extinct, so extinction itself is natural, normal, routine. Even extinctions caused by human practices such as hunting and habitat fragmentation cannot be called unnatural: Humans are part of nature, too, as much as any other predators. But they are predators of matchless efficiency, and while all creatures in one way or another transform their environments, humans are currently transforming theirs on an unprecedented scale. The current rate of extinctions is extraordinary and exceeds the rate at which new species are evolving. This means that the planet is in the throes of a process of biotic impoverishment.

How alarming is this? What is lost with biological diversity? Lovejoy points out that "natural aggregations of species (ecosystems) are more than a large collection of genetic material; they also are involved in ecological processes, often of immediate public service value." These include watershed protection and moderation of climatic, hydrological, and nutrient cycles. With diminished diversity comes loss of clean and reliable water supplies and of soil fertility. Biological impoverishment weakens nature's regenerative power to resist human exploitation.

Lovejoy recognizes that "in any immediate sense it is hard to see how the loss of a single species will affect the day to day life of the average citizen who will probably not even know of the loss or that the species ever existed. Yet, when an ecosystem has been altered to the point that a public service benefit such as watershed protection is affected, it is not only quite obvious, but also, biological diversity will have by then suffered a significant reduction."

Lovejoy argues, in fact, that biological impoverishment may be directly responsible for human impoverishment. It is no accident, he suggests, that "those nations which are unsuccessful in maintaining their basic diversity of plant and animal life are also the ones least successful in protecting decent standards of living for their people." He blames heedless environmental policies in part for the fact that Haiti, the poorest nation in the Western Hemisphere, is in far more dire economic straits than its neighbor, the Dominican Republic, which has undertaken active initiatives to protect wildlife habitat.

Bryan Norton, an environmental ethicist, takes Lovejoy's argument to show that the preservationist does not need to document a specific present or anticipated commercial use for an individual species in order to justify saving it. Since "natural diversity, in and of itself, has utilitarian value," every species, as a unit of diversity, has prima facie utilitarian value as well. Rather than isolating a particular species and examining it for direct commercial or scientific potential, Norton views each species as a unit of diversity and looks at the total value we derive from living in a diverse world.

Granted, each species is only one tiny unit of the world's overall diversity, so perhaps Norton's argument leads in the end to our realizing that no one species matters very much. Speculations that the loss of any one species could trigger a chain reaction leading to some kind of environmental catastrophe are usually dismissed as fanciful. But if Lovejoy's and Norton's arguments do not support a heroic effort to preserve every threatened species, they provide a strong reason to preserve biological diversity generally, to protect the integrity of the natural world.

The objection can be raised, however, that the reasons given so far for preservation are the wrong kinds of reasons. We are doing what we can for other species because of what other species can do for us. We are taking a broader view of the benefits they provide, and a longer-term view, but still a view from the same vantage point, of human needs and interests. Species here are still *commodities*.

Intrinsic Value

Many environmentalists argue that species should be preserved, not for our sakes, but for their own. They claim that species have intrinsic, not merely instrumental, value. They are valuable, not merely in virtue of what else they are good *for*, but because they are good in *themselves*.

While these claims have considerable rhetorical force—compared, say, to discussions of the role of species in tertiary waste treatment—they raise more questions than they answer. *Why* do we think species have intrinsic value? In what is it grounded? What is it about species that makes them valuable?

One way to address these questions is to look at a case where the answers are clearer. We can disagree about whether species as such have intrinsic value, but nobody doubts that individual human beings are intrinsically valuable, if anything is. So what is it about human beings that grounds their value? Are species valuable in the same way?

If human beings are intrinsically valuable because we can *think*, then no helpful parallel between humans and other creatures can be drawn. Rationality seems an attribute exclusively human. But if we count morally because we can *feel*, because we can experience pleasure and pain, then a case can be made that other sentient creatures count, too. This is one rationale behind the animal liberation movement. Plants do not suffer, however, nor do lower life forms, and so the argument cannot be generalized to include them in its sweep.

A thornier problem is that no argument modeled on the intrinsic value of individual human beings can justify attributions of intrinsic value to whole groups—that is, to species, whether human or otherwise. Sober explains, "What is special about environmentalism is that it values the preservation of species, communities, or ecosystems, rather than the individual organisms of which they are composed. 'Animal liberationists' have urged that we should take the suffering of sentient animals into account in ethical deliberation.... But trees, mountains, and salt marshes do not suffer. They do not experience pleasure and pain, because, evidently, they do not have experiences at all. The same is true of species." Individual animals have individual experiences, of course, but a species does not have a collective "experience."

A more promising approach may be to say that ethical status derives not from having feelings or experiences, but from having needs or interests. A plant needs water, sunlight, and air, even if it does not consciously suffer from their deprivation. Likewise, we can say that a species needs to have its habitat protected, even if no conscious entity entertains such a want. Do "needs" of this sort have to be taken into account morally?

The problem, Sober points out, is that in this view of needs and interests almost nothing does not have moral standing. "If one does not require of an object that it have a mind for it to have wants or needs, what *is* required for the possession of these ethically relevant properties? Suppose one says that an object needs something if it will cease to exist if it does not get it. Then species . . . have needs, but only in the sense that automobiles, garbage dumps, and buildings do too. If everything has needs, the advice to take needs into account in ethical deliberation is empty." It is no help to the environmentalist if species turn out to be intrinsically valuable only in some sense in which just about *everything* is. We want a specific reason to value and preserve species, to hold their claims as counting for more than the claims—if any—of factories and junkyards.

It is more difficult than it might seem, then, to come up with a reason for granting intrinsic value to species that does not either piggyback illicitly on assignments of value to individuals or hand out attributions of value too indiscriminately. It looks as if the value of species is not intrinsic, but somehow dependent on the role species play in human lives and awareness.

Transformative Value

If the value species have depends on the value they have *for us*, does this make them into commodities for human use, like so many widgits? There are at least two reasons why we might be reluctant to draw this conclusion. First of all, something makes us want to put species of living organisms in a class apart from other resources, even resources that serve basic human needs. We debate whether species have intrinsic value, but no one argues for the intrinsic value of, say, tractors or ball bearings. Second, if the value of other species rests only on their ability to fulfill human desires, this seems to give them no secure claim *against* human desires. But it is the voracious desires fueled by human civilization that endanger species in the first place.

Sober responds to the first of these worries by drawing an analogy between objects in nature and works of art. The two have important similarities. "For both natural objects and works of art," he maintains, "our values extend beyond the concerns we have for experiencing pleasure. . . . When we experience works of art, often what we value is not just the kind of experiences we have, but, in addition, the connections we usually have with certain real objects." We value the existence of Michelangelo's *Pietà* beyond any value we derive from just seeing what it looks like. We value the process by which it was created, its history, its authenticity. The same is true, he suggests, of objects in nature.

Yet we are willing to concede that artistic masterpieces are not valuable in themselves, completely apart from any human consciousness of them: "What is valuable [in a work of art] is the relation of a valuer to a valued object. . . . when valuers disappear, so does the possibility of aesthetic value." That art objects—and natural objects—are not intrinsically valuable does not mean that their value is not of a special kind.

Norton characterizes this deeper element of value in nature and art by saying that both not only fulfill human desires but also transform them. Whereas commodities satisfy existing human preferences whatever these are, taken as given, experiences of works of art and study of the natural world lead us to question our values, to criticize and reform them, to alter them altogether. Where environmentalists have gone wrong, he feels, is in accepting a dilemma between either giving free rein to human wants and desires, in their present materialistic form (endangering vast tracts of wild habitat in the process), or else insisting that other creatures, other species, and the ecosystems they inhabit must have some value independent of human wants and desires altogether. But the dilemma is a false one, because "it unnecessarily contracts the range of human values to those founded on demands for given preferences. . . . This is to ignore the role of other species and varied ecosystems in forming and transforming our values."

According to Norton, wild species and undisturbed ecosystems provide occasions for experiences that allow us to rethink our place in the natural order. We learn from other species about the forms and limits of survival on a fragile planet; we learn about sharing the destinies of our fellows in the biotic community. "Appeals to the transformative value of wild species and undisturbed ecosystems thereby provide the means to criticize and limit human demands that threaten to destroy those species and ecosystems while at the same time introducing an important value that humans should place on them."

Conclusion

Where does this leave the snail darter and the furbish lousewort, the whole host of lowly species that we may never encounter in our lifetime and would not recognize if we did? How do these enlighten and uplift us? What transformative value do they possess? The answer, in the end, may be "not very much." They doubtless have some role in maintaining the natural order that we do not understand, and the handful of scientists who do know and study them may take aesthetic pleasure in doing so. Is this enough to save them? At what cost?

Norton's conclusion is that this may be the wrong question to ask. To examine species one by one is always to miss the value—commercial, scientific, aesthetic, transformative—in their interaction, in the whole interlocking system of nature in which human beings play only one small part. The lesson of the environmental movement is that nature is not best understood and protected piecemeal. To focus on each individual scrap of creation may distract us from the magnificence—and vulnerability—of the whole. It is nature itself, in all its diversity, that uplifts and sustains us. This is what we are bound to preserve.

The views of Stephen Kellert, Thomas Lovejoy, and Elliott Sober are quoted from their essays in The Preservation of Species, *ed. Bryan G. Norton (Princeton, N.J.: Princeton University Press, 1985). Bryan G. Norton's views are quoted from his chapter in* The Preservation of Species *and from his book* Why Preserve Natural Variety? *(Princeton, N.J.: Princeton University Press, 1987).*

The Biotechnology Controversy

Mark Sagoff

Biotechnology, according to most commentators, promises to revolutionize industry and everyday life. The British journal *The Economist* predicts that "biology will launch an industry as characteristic of the twenty-first century as those based on physics and chemistry have been of the twentieth century." Statements such as this express the sense of exhilaration and apprehension that, over the past few years, has produced screaming headlines, Promethean prospects, stockmarket fever, and all sorts of intellectual inflation. In even the most conservative view, however, new developments in biotechnology are likely to affect the way we think about the living world and the way we understand our relationship to it.

Nature and Society

Anthropologists, in describing the tribes they study, frequently emphasize the relation between the social structure of the tribe and its cosmology or view of nature. Among these anthropologists, Mary Douglas most prominently has argued that "the moral commitment of a community to a set of institutions" is secured by its view of what is natural and what goes contrary to nature, or in other words, "how the environment will react." The conception of nature implicit in social arrangements and institutions, according to Douglas, "exists as a structure of meaningful distinctions." The social order begins to come apart, she adds, when "separate voices claim to know about different environmental constraints" and different visions of nature contend for credibility.

It is commonplace to point out that the great social and cultural revolutions in society have been accompanied by—and are to an extent caused by—major changes in assumptions about nature and the place of humanity in it. The cosmology of pretechnological societies, for example, found in nature all sorts of omens and meanings by which people could explain natural events to themselves (e.g., as divine rewards and punishments) in order to give significance and importance to their own actions. The distinctions tribal societies drew between the pure and the polluted, the safe and dangerous, often served to legitimize power relationships and the rules and conventions that governed behavior in those societies.

After Galileo and Newton, a conception of the living world became dominant that reflected the order scientists had found in the physical world. The eighteenth century presented nature as a masterpiece of organic forms set together in a perfect design by a benign creator, a Great Chain of Being. A hierarchical and conventional order in society—where each group understood its station and its duties—reflected this idea of an immutable and static order in nature.

After Darwin, the nineteenth century experienced a reversal in its conception of the way the living world is organized. In the early days of evolutionary theory, Social Darwinists were quick to extend the ideas of competition, struggle, adaptation, fitness, and change from plant and animal communities to human societies, thus making "natural" the "great transformation" of land and labor into fungible, marketable commodities. It was only after a great deal of humane reconsideration—a battle still going on today in the arguments over sociobiology—that culture and nature were sufficiently distinguished to overcome some of the excesses of the Social Darwinist and eugenics movements.

By the 1960s, evolutionary theory had become established and with it a historical appreciation of humankind's origin and place in nature. In the United States, the environmental movement emphasized the importance of preserving the products of natural history, particularly biological communities, the "integrity" of which, so they argued, supported human survival. Environmental legislation enacted during the 1960s and 1970s called on the nation to preserve the "health" of ecosystems, the "integrity" of the nation's waters, and the "balance" of natural populations. These laws presupposed the idea that biological communities have a character or an identity we should preserve and respect. The environmental law of the 1960s and 1970s did not regard nature as a congeries of raw materials fit for limitless human intervention and manipulation, but as a system of natural resources and communities that should be altered as little as possible.

Growing interest in work on recombinant DNA during the 1970s challenged the idea that nature has boundaries (whether put there by God or by evolutionary history) that we should respect or that we cross at our peril. The "Recombinant DNA War" pitted two strong ideological positions against each other. On the one side, members of religious communities together with many environmentalists and members of the concerned public felt that there is something sacred about life, something about the identity of species we should respect, and that no good could come from crossing lines that either God or Nature had drawn. On the other side, many scientists and others considered fears such as these superstitious and regarded nature more as an object of endless manipulation, investigation, and use than as an object of ethical, religious, cultural, and aesthetic concern.

Debate over the risks and hazards posed by "designer genes" and recombinant DNA masks more fundamental differences concerning the extent to which we should preserve nature and the processes that are somehow "intrinsic" to it vs. the extent to which we may view the living world, quoting engineer Edward Yoxen, as "a vast organic Lego kit inviting combination, hybridization, and continual rebuilding."

Natural Resources versus Raw Materials

On college campuses during the 1970s, Hans Bethe, the eminent nuclear physicist, and Barry Commoner, the environmental activist, debated issues involving the dangers of nuclear power and pollution. In these debates, when Commoner spoke of the depletion of natural resources, Bethe would respond vehemently that there are no *natural resources* but only *raw materials*. Behind the conceptual difference between "raw materials" and "natural resources" lies a fundamental distinction for evaluating new technologies and justifying regulations.

For Commoner, natural objects come in natural kinds; form determines function. When we force or cross natural boundaries too often, as by an incautious and intrusive use of technology, we court environmental disaster. For Bethe, things do not have essences or forms determining their function. Rather, our cleverness in molding and manipulating materials to meet our needs determines what objects exist and the value they may have for us. Technology is the key to cornucopia, not the cause of catastrophe.

The distinction between natural resources and raw materials epitomizes the two sides in the debate over nuclear technology, but it also is relevant to the controversy surrounding biotechnology. Those on one side of the debate assert that the history of evolution has made natural species and ecosystems what they are and has given them forms or essences we ought to respect. We engage in manipulation at our peril. Those who inherit Hans Bethe's position, on the contrary, tend to see nature as a collection of materials that humankind manipulates to serve its interests and ends.

Two Concepts of Ecosystems

These two approaches motivate two different strategies for environmental management, such as in the Chesapeake Bay. In the past, the major emphasis in Chesapeake Bay management has been to clean up the bay or otherwise restore natural conditions so the species adapted to it, for example, striped bass and winter flounder, may thrive. Biotechnology presents an opportunity to work in the opposite direction. We may change the genetic structure of those species so they can better survive in the bay as it is or as it may become as a result of increasing pollution. This may be a more efficient strategy for fisheries management.

It is not unlikely that as a consequence of biotechnology two different trends will emerge in ecological research. One may be tied to natural history and will study systems like the bay as natural resources whose form is somehow "given" by events in the past. A second trend will investigate systems as independent of their histories, as reactions among raw materials, biotic and abiotic, of various sorts, all of which may be amenable to manipulation.

The question then may arise of which conception of the ecosystem we should use in formulating and enforcing environmental regulations. To insist on the first conception, which ties the ecosystem to its past, would lead us to limit the degree to which we can alter the makeup of bass, flounder, and other species to allow them to thrive in waters no longer fit to support them otherwise. We might require, indeed, that these fish be treated as indicator species, and believe that their disappearance suggests that pollution be reduced, not that they be altered to survive it. On the other hand, we may think of ecosystems completely in technical ahistorical terms. In that case, genetically engineered species, even if they bear little or no relation to "natural" ones, could form biological communities as interesting to study and as worthy of protection, prima facie, as any that have evolved over 10,000 or 100,000,000 years.

Two Mandates for Management

The Water Resources Council in 1973 stated in its *Principles and Standards* that the use of the nation's water and land resources should be "directed to improvement in the quality of life through contributions to the objectives of national economic development and environmental quality." It defined these objectives respectively as "to enhance national economic development by increasing the value of the Nation's output of goods and services and improving national

---

economic efficiency" and "to enhance the quality of the environment by the management, conservation, preservation, creation, restoration, or improvement of the quality of certain natural and cultural resources and ecological systems."

During the 1960s and 1970s, many environmentalists and others argued that the goals of *increasing the value of goods and services* and *preserving ecological systems* were generally consistent, since ecological systems support human life and provide all kinds of goods and services. Yet, with respect to specific resources and ecological systems, it is often hard to argue that protection rather than alteration and exploitation is the best way to maximize the flow of goods and services nature offers us. The Chesapeake's role as a liquid highway, for example, does not depend on the maintenance of a "natural" ecological system. What is more, the production of commercial fish and shellfish, it is often argued, would be far more efficient were the bay managed on aquacultural principles, as privately held aquacultural plots, rather than as a "commons."

Developments in biotechnology are likely quickly to force the question of whether we wish to regard the bay, for example, as a natural resource to be treasured and protected for its biological communities, or as a collection of raw materials to be managed to maximize the goods and services it may then produce. It seems that the development of marine biotechnology should be sensitive both to historical or aesthetic concerns and to economic concerns. We owe more to the history and beauty of nature—we value the grandeur of evolution too much—to regard nature simply as a material basis for economic exploitation, however far-reaching our biotechnological potential for exploitation may become.

The Mary Douglas quote is from "Environments at Risk," in Implicit Meanings *(New York: Routledge, Kegan, Paul, 1975). The Edward Yoxen quote is from* The Gene Business: Who Should Control Biotechnology? *(New York: Harper & Row, 1983).*

Property Rights and Environmental Law

Mark Sagoff

It is a commonplace that people are or ought to be free, in general, to use their property as they wish, as long as they do no harm to—and respect the rights of—others. Yet environmental laws and regulations apparently impose further duties on landowners, obliging them, for example, to maintain the integrity of landmarks and scenic areas, to refrain from filling wetlands, to preserve open space, to restore mined land to its original contours, to maintain habitat for endangered species, to allow public access to waterways and beaches, to leave minerals in place to support surface structures, and so on. State and local governments, in general, impose these duties on landowners by regulation rather than by exercising eminent domain. States prefer regulation to condemnation so they do not have to compensate landowners for the substantial losses in market value that often accompany statutory duties and restrictions. Governments may dedicate property to public use, then, not by taking property rights through eminent domain, but by regulating those rights away and, therefore, without compensating owners for the market value of those rights.

Courts are then called on to decide whether a statute that imposes public-spirited duties on property owners complies with the Fifth Amendment of the Constitution, which provides that "private property [shall not] be taken for public use, without just compensation." When courts sustain these statutes and ordinances, as they frequently do, local governments gain an important legal weapon for protecting the aesthetic, cultural, historical, and ecological values that often attract people and, therefore, subdividers and developers to a region. If the courts sheathed this legal weapon, however, society may have to kiss these values goodbye, since it cannot afford to exercise eminent domain to purchase the property in question, nor can it depend, except in a quite limited way, on private action in common law courts to protect these values.

When should a regulatory "taking" of property require the state to pay compensation, when not? I shall argue that compensation need not attend a regulation that takes property rights unless it also burdens some individuals unfairly to benefit other individuals. The "takings" question, in other words, may not depend simply on an analysis of property rights. Rather, it may also depend on a conception of justice.

Takings and the Police Power

In *Just* v. *Marinette County*, the Wisconsin Supreme Court sustained a local statute that prevented owners from using landfill and from building structures on coastal wetlands. The court held that the "takings clause" of the Constitution does not protect an interest, however profitable, in "destroying the natural character of a swamp or a wetland so as to make that location available for human habitation." Citizens have no claim for compensation, the court reasoned, when an ordinance restricts their use of property, "not to secure a benefit for the public, but to prevent a harm from the change in the natural character of the citizens' property."

The power to zone arises under the police power of the state, for which no precise definition exists, but which is often associated with the power to protect the health, safety, welfare, and morals of the community. The Wisconsin court argued that "it is not an unreasonable exercise of [police] power to prevent harm to public rights by limiting the use of private property to its natural uses."

In a remarkable book, *Takings: Private Property and the Power of Eminent Domain*, Richard Epstein castigates the *Just* court for its decision. Epstein observes that "the normal bundle of property rights contains no priority for land in its natural condition; it regards use, including development, as one of the standard incidents of ownership." Epstein concludes: "Stripped of its rhetoric, *Just* is a condemnation of those property rights, and compensation is thus required."

The argument Epstein presents has the form of a dilemma. First, Epstein argues that the government relies on a narrow conception of the police power to regulate private activities in order to prevent or to redress various wrongs and harms, including trespass, invasion, and injury. This use of the police power does not *take* but *protects* property; hence it does not require compensation.

Second, under a broader conception of the police power, the government may force the transfer of property rights to secure efficiency gains and increase social wealth. Transactions of this sort, Epstein reasons, diminish the property rights of some to benefit others; these forced transactions may be legitimate, he argues, but only if they are accompanied by just compensation.

In Epstein's view, coastal zone, critical area, landmark, and similar statutes typically do not prevent harm to individuals or to the public in any sense remotely cognizable in common law. Ronald Just, the plaintiff in the Wisconsin case, for example, might point out that by filling his wetland, he pollutes his own property, not that of others; no one would have an action against him in tort. The narrow conception of the police power, then, would not apply to him. The government might act under the broader conception of the police power, to be sure, to preserve the last vestiges of scenic and ecological amenity in the coastal region. When the government uses its broad powers in this way, however, it burdens people like Just, while it benefits those who have built houses and commercial establishments in the area and whose property will go up in market value as a result of regulations prohibiting further development. Regulations of this sort may be necessary, but the Constitution, in Epstein's view, insists that they be accompanied by just compensation.

If the state acts early enough, that is, while all landowners possess natural and aesthetic resources of which they may be made equally the trustees, then a zoning ordinance, which restricts uniformly the ways they may develop their property, may provide them implicit in-kind compensation, since it secures reciprocal advantage to all interested parties. Thus, an ordinance prohibiting *every* landowner in the District of Columbia from building a structure higher than the dome of the Capitol, for example, not only promotes the public good, but also benefits those it burdens, and thus implicitly compensates them.

The problem involved in most environmental zoning, however, is that it comes late in the day, when it makes winners of the many who have already subdivided and developed and losers of the few who have maintained the natural condition of their land. The Fifth Amendment, nevertheless, "prevents the public from loading upon one individual more than his just share of the burdens of government, and says that when he surrenders to the public something more and different from that . . . exacted from other members of the public, a full and just equivalent shall be returned to him" (*Monongahela Navigation Co.* v. *United States*).

Suppose this argument were sound; what would result if the courts accepted it? They may overturn statutes and ordinances that are the last hope of localities seeking to protect the character, ecology, amenity, and, one might say, the sanity of the social environment. What will replace these values? Mondo Condo. High Rise Heaven. Bungalow Bonanza. Move fast, 'cause they won't last. Let the courts adopt this vision of the Constitution—and the blitz is on.

Does the Right to Develop Imply a Right to Destroy?

The central incidents of property, however—the right to use, to exclude, and to alienate—do not include the right to destroy. The right to use a car one has borrowed or hired, for example, does not involve a right to destroy it; likewise, the right to use by consuming food does not entail a right to waste or spoil it. John Locke, to whom Epstein traces his theory of property rights, points out that spoiling or wasting is not an incident of use or possession. Locke reasons that a person can "heap up" as many resources as he or she can use or cause to be used economically—"the exceeding of the bounds of his just property not lying in the largeness of his possession, but in the perishing of anything uselessly in it."

To be sure, if an item is worthless, the possessor may have a right to toss it out. But the right to destroy does not attach to valuable property. For this reason, courts sometimes impose a "law of waste" to prevent property owners from destroying scarce resources of great value to others.

Just has no valid claim to compensation, according to this argument, because he is not entitled to destroy resources that have become scarce and are of great importance to society. The decision in *Just* is correct, in this view, because a regulation that prevents a landowner from destroying resources by filling a marsh does not take a right from him. He had no right to destroy those resources.

This result seems entirely consistent with a Lockean theory of property rights, which limits property not only to what can be possessed without waste, but also to what may be acquired from a commons [property owned and shared by all in common] without creating scarcity. As Locke put this thought, a person can rightfully acquire an unowned resource from the commons only if there be "enough and as good left in common for others."

One might argue that this famous Lockean Proviso covers aesthetic and ecological resources that belong as organic parts to larger systems and are destroyed when land is removed from its natural condition. Those who come to the commons early may legitimately appropriate these resources by consuming or destroying them, but when a common resource, such as natural beauty, becomes critically scarce, society may rule against further appropriations, because they significantly worsen the social situation from what it would be if the proposed "improvements" were not made.

We are now in a position to define a conception of harm to the public and, with it, a conception of the police power that lies between the horns of Epstein's dilemma. The *Just* court argued that a property owner may not validly claim compensation when he or she is prevented from "destroying the natural character of a swamp or a wetland . . . when the new use . . . causes a harm to the general public." The contention may be that the prohibited development would destroy resources the public owns in common, owing to "the interrelationship of the wetlands, the swamps and the natural environment of shorelands to the purity of the water and to such natural resources as navigation, fishing, and scenic beauty." In the past, an individual may have been free to appropriate these resources without depleting the commons unduly, but those times are gone. Mr. Just has come too late to the commons; there is no longer as much and as good for others. To destroy the ecological, aesthetic, cultural, and historical commons, in this view, is to cause a harm to the public that may justify statutes that restrict the ways property may be developed.

Not Property Rights But Justice

This argument, while relevant, is not decisive. Statutes that protect an ecological or an environmental commons may nevertheless restrict the use of property in ways that require compensation. The question whether compensation must accompany a regulation, as we shall see, need not turn on the relation between property and the police power. It may depend on whether the statute forces individuals to bear burdens that "in all fairness and justice, should be borne by the public as a whole" (*Armstrong* v. *United States*).

If Just were one of a very few landowners in the coastal area who had not yet developed their property, for example, he might reasonably argue that not he but his neighbors damage the ecological commons. The statute simply takes his land to buffer their pollution. Likewise, he may argue that he and other affected landowners constitute a minority too small to represent its interests fairly in the political process. He might argue the statute is unfair, moreover, if its primary effect is to promote the economic interests of those who have already developed their land.

Courts, in fact, generally will not uphold a land use restriction if its primary effect is to limit competition in an area or otherwise to benefit a few individuals at the expense of others. Regulations that restrict property to its "natural" uses may always be justified on ecological grounds and, in that sense, on the basis of protecting the public. But these statutes should not be sustained if their economic effects are grossly unfair to individuals.

How do courts determine whether these effects are unjust? They rely generally on rules of thumb; that is, they look out for particularly common injustices. They ask, is the economic loss imposed by the challenged statute terribly severe? Can the aggrieved property owner still make reasonable and profitable use of his land? Is the benefit to the public sufficient to warrant the burden the statute imposes on individuals? Are the restrictions reasonably appropriate and necessary to obtain the desired results? Does the regulation burden relatively few landowners—too few, perhaps, to represent their interests in the majoritarian political process?

Courts typically raise questions of these kinds—not theoretical questions about the nature and extent of property rights—in settling "takings" cases. The courts thus try to determine whether the plaintiff's interests have been treated equitably. This requires that the courts have a working concept of justice and fair play. It does not require that they apply a sophisticated theory about property rights and the police power. The Fifth Amendment bears on environmental policy, then, not by grounding a theory of property rights, but by assuring that the laws that protect the environment do not do so at the expense of justice.

Quoted in this article are Just v. Marinette County, *56 Wis. 2d 7, 201 N.W. 2d 761 (1972); Richard Epstein,* Takings: Private Property and the Power of Eminent Domain *(Cambridge, Mass.: Harvard University Press, 1985);* Monongahela Navigation Co. v. United States, *148 U. S. 312, 325 (1893); John Locke,* Second Treatise of Government, *ed. Thomas P. Peardon (Indianapolis: Bobbs-Merrill, 1952); and* Armstrong v. United States, *364 U. S. 40, 49 (1960).*

Animal Liberation and Environmental Ethics
Bad Marriage, Quick Divorce

Mark Sagoff

T he land ethic," Aldo Leopold wrote in *A Sand County Almanac*, "simply enlarges the boundaries of the community to include soils, waters, plants, and animals, or collectively, the land." What kind of community does Leopold refer to? He might mean a *moral* community, a group of individuals who respect each other's right to treatment as equals or who regard one another's interests with equal respect and concern. Leopold may also mean an *ecological* community, a community tied together by biological relationships in interdependent webs of life.

Let us suppose, for a moment, that Leopold has a *moral* community in mind; he would expand our *moral* boundaries to include soils, waters, plants, and animals, as well as human beings. Leopold's view, then, might not differ in principle from that of Christopher Stone, who has suggested animals and even trees be given legal standing, so their interests may be represented in court. Stone sees the expansion of our moral consciousness in this way as part of a historical progress in which societies have recognized the equality of groups of oppressed people, notably blacks, women, and children.

Peter Singer, perhaps more than any other writer, has emphasized the analogy between human liberation movements (e.g., abolitionism and suffragism) and "animal liberation," or the "expansion of our moral horizons" to include members of other species in "the basic principle of equality." Singer differs from Stone in arguing that the question whether animals have *rights* is less important than it appears: "What matters is how we think animals ought to be treated, and not how we employ the concept of a right." He also confines membership in the moral community to beings with the "capacity for subjective experience, such as the experience of pleasure or the experience of pain." But Stone and Singer agree that we have a moral obligation to minimize the suffering of animals and to balance their interests against our own.

Mother Nature versus Frank Perdue

What practical course of action should we take once we have climbed the spiral of moral evolution high enough to recognize our obligation to value the rights, interests, or welfare of animals equally with our own? In discussing the rights of human beings, Henry Shue describes two that are basic in the sense that "the enjoyment of them is essential to the enjoyment of all other rights." These are the right to physical security and the right to minimum subsistence. These, surely, are basic to animal rights as well. To allow animals to be killed, to permit them to die of disease or starvation, when it is within our power to prevent it, surely seems not to balance their interests with our own.

Where, then, shall we begin to provide for the basic welfare—the security and subsistence—of animals? Plainly, where they most lack this security, where their basic rights, needs, or interests are most thwarted, and where their suffering is the most intense. This is in nature. Ever since Darwin, we have been aware that few organisms survive to reach sexual maturity; most are quickly annihilated in the struggle for existence.

Consider this rough but reasonable statement of the facts, given by Fred Hapgood: "All species reproduce to excess, way past the carrying capacity of their niche. In her lifetime a lioness might have 20 cubs; a pigeon, 150 chicks; a mouse, 1,000 kits; a trout, 20,000 fry; a tuna or cod, a million fry or more; an elm tree, several million seeds; and an oyster, perhaps a hundred million spat. If one assumes that the population of each of these species is, from generation to generation, roughly equal, then on the average only one offspring will survive to replace each parent. All the other thousands and millions will die, one way or another."

The ways creatures in nature die are typically violent: predation, starvation, disease, parasitism, freezing. If the dying animal in the wild understood his condition, what would he think? Surely, he would prefer to be raised on a farm, where his chances of survival would be good, and to escape from the wild, where they are negligible. Either way, the animal will be killed; few die of old age. The path from birth to slaughter, however, is nearly always longer and less painful in the barnyard than in the woods. The misery of animals in nature beggars by comparison every other form of suffering in the world. Mother Nature is so cruel to her children she makes chicken magnate Frank Perdue look like a saint.

I do not know how animal liberationists, such as Singer, propose to relieve animal suffering in nature, but there are many ways we could greatly improve the situation at little cost to ourselves. It may not be beyond the reach of science to attempt a broad program of contraceptive care for animals in nature so that fewer will fall victim to an early and horrible death. One may propose, with all modesty, the conversion of our national wilderness areas, especially our national parks, into farms in order to replace violent wild areas with humane, managed environments. Animals and trees would then benefit from the same efficient and productive technology that benefits us.

My point in raising this argument is to suggest that the thesis that animals have important rights and interests that command our respect has little bearing on the policies it is supposed by some to support, in particular, policies intended to preserve and protect the natural environment. We must ask ourselves whether in fact the kind of policies environmentalists recommend would make animals better off in the long run. I see no reason at all to suppose they would.

Can Environmentalists Be Hunters?

In a persuasive essay, J. Baird Callicott describes a number of differences between the ideas of Aldo Leopold and those of Peter Singer—differences that suggest Leopold's environmental ethic and Singer's humanitarianism lead in opposite directions. First, while Singer and other animal liberationists deplore the suffering of domestic animals, "Leopold manifests an attitude that can only be described as indifference." Second, while Leopold expresses an urgent concern about the disappearance of species, Singer, consistently with his premises, is concerned with the welfare of individual animals, without special regard to their status as endangered species.

Third, wilderness, according to Leopold, provides "a means of perpetuating, in sport form, the more virile and primitive skills. . . ." He had hunting in mind. Hunters, since top predators are gone, may serve an important ecological function. Leopold was himself an enthusiastic hunter and wrote unabashedly about his exploits pursuing game. The term "game" as applied to animals, Callicott wryly comments, "appears to be morally equivalent to referring to a sexually appealing young women as a 'piece' or to a strong, young black man as a 'buck'—if animal rights, that is, are to be considered on a par with women's rights, and the rights of formerly enslaved races."

Hunting is what disturbs animal liberationists as much as any other human activity. Singer expresses disdain and chagrin at what he calls "'environmentalist'" organizations that actively support or refuse to oppose hunting, such as the Sierra Club and the World Wildlife Fund. I can appreciate Singer's aversion to hunting, but why does he place the word "environmentalist" in shudder quotes when he refers to organizations like the Sierra Club? Environmentalist and conservation-ist organizations traditionally have been concerned with ecological, not with humanitarian, issues. They make no pretense to improving the lot of individual animals; they attempt rather to maintain the diversity, integrity, beauty, and authenticity of the natural environment. These goals are ecological, not eleemosynary. They are entirely consistent with licensing hunters to shoot animals whose populations exceed the carrying capacity of their habitats.

I do not in any way mean to support the practice of hunting; nor am I advocating environmentalism at this time. I merely want to point out that groups like the Sierra Club, the Wilderness Society, and the World Wildlife Fund do not fail in their mission insofar as they devote themselves to causes other than the happiness or welfare of individual creatures; that never was their mission. These organizations, which promote a love and respect for the functioning of natural ecosystems, differ ideologically from organizations that make the suffering of animals their primary concern—groups like the Fund for Animals, the Animal Protection Institute, Friends of Animals, the American Humane Association, and various single-issue groups such as Friends of the Sea Otter, Beaver Defenders, Friends of the Earthworm, and World-wide Fair Play for Frogs.

I proposed earlier that Aldo Leopold views the community of nature as a *moral* community—one in which we, as members, have obligations to all other animals, presumably to minimize their pain. I suggested that Leopold, like Singer, may be committed to the idea that we should preserve and respect the natural environment only insofar as that promotes the welfare of the individual animals nature contains. This is plainly not Leopold's view, however. The principle of natural selection is not a humanitarian principle; the predator-prey relation does not depend on moral empathy. Nature ruthlessly limits animal populations by doing violence to virtually every individual before it reaches maturity. These conditions respect animal equality only in the darkest sense. Yet these are precisely the ecological relationships Leopold admires; they are the conditions he would not interfere with, but protect. Leopold, apparently, does not think an ecological system has to be a moral system in order to deserve our love. An ecological system has a beauty and an authenticity we can admire—but not on humanitarian grounds.

Animal Liberation and Environmental Law

Muckraking journalists, thank God for them, who depict the horrors that all too often occur in laboratories and on farms, appeal, quite properly, to our conviction that humankind should never inflict needless pain on animals, especially for the sake of profit. When we read stories about human cruelty to domestic animals, we respond, as we should, with moral outrage and revulsion. When we read accounts of natural history, which reveal as much suffering and slaughter, we do not respond with outrage or indignation. Why not? The reason is plain. It is not suffering per se that concerns us. What outrages us is human responsibility for that suffering.

Moral obligations to animals may arise in either of two ways. Our duties to nonhuman animals may be based on the principle that cruelty to animals is obnoxious, a principle nobody denies. These obligations, however, might rest instead on the stronger contention that we are obliged to prevent and to relieve animal suffering wherever it occurs and however it is caused; that we are obliged to protect the welfare of *all* animals just because they are sentient beings.

Animal liberationists insist, as Singer does, that moral obligations to animals are justified by their distress and by our ability to relieve that distress. Accordingly, the liberationist must ask: How can I most efficiently relieve animal suffering? The answer must be: by getting animals out of the natural environment. Starving deer in the woods might be adopted as pets; they might be fed in kennels. Birds that now kill earthworms may repair instead to birdhouses stocked with food—including textured soybean protein that looks and smells like worms. And to protect the brutes from cold, we might heat their dens to provide shelter for the all too many who freeze.

Now, whether you believe that this harangue is a *reductio ad absurdum* of Singer's position or whether you think it should be taken seriously as an ideal is no concern to me. I merely wish to point out that an environmentalist must take what I have said as a *reductio*, whereas an animal liberationist must regard it as stating a serious position. An environmentalist cannot be an animal liberationist; nor may animal liberationists be environmentalists. The environmentalist would sacrifice the welfare of individual creatures to preserve the authenticity, integrity, and complexity of ecological systems. The liberationist must be willing to sacrifice the authenticity, integrity, and complexity of ecosystems for the welfare of animals. A humanitarian ethic will not help us to understand or to justify an environmental ethic. It will not provide new foundations for environmental law.

This article is drawn from "Animal Liberation and Environmental Ethics: Bad Marriage, Quick Divorce," Osgoode Hall Law Journal 22, no. 2 (Summer 1984). The sources cited in this article are Aldo Leopold, A

Sand County Almanac *(New York: Ballantine, 1949); Christopher Stone,* Should Trees Have Standing? *(Los Altos, Calif.: William Kaufmann, 1974); Peter Singer, "All Animals Are Equal,"* Philosophical Exchange *1 (Summer 1974); Peter Singer, "Not for Humans Only: The Place of Nonhumans in Environmental Issues," in* Ethics and Problems of the 21st Century, *ed. K. E. Goodpaster and K. M. Sayer (South Bend, Ind.: Notre Dame University Press, 1979); Henry Shue,* Basic Rights *(Princeton, N.J.: Princeton University Press, 1980); Fred Hapgood,* Why Males Exist *(New York: Mentor NAL, 1979); and J. Baird Callicott, "Animal Liberation: A Triangular Affair,"* Environmental Ethics *4 (Winter 1980).*

Defending Human Chauvinism

C. A. J. Coady

My title is a little misleading. Although I shall be offering certain thoughts in defense of a position that some would regard as "human chauvinism" or "speciesism," I am really more concerned with clarifying just what is being said by those who use these terms in clamorous denunciation and what value their supporting arguments have.

The locus of my comments will be the moral concerns and outlooks that have fathered (or mothered?) two political movements—animal liberation and environmentalism. Despite points of tension between the animal and nature liberationists, both have in common that they may be plausibly viewed as calling for a new ethic. The characteristic move of the new ethicists is to declare that the traditional ethic is defective in its emphasis on the importance of human beings. This is its speciesism or human chauvinism. The old ethic was human-centered, the new will be . . . well, it will have some other center.

One Bad Argument

One bad argument against speciesism or a human-centered ethic consists in drawing attention to the fact that, just as we have come to realize moral concern cannot be restricted to the members of our own race ("racism") or of our own sex ("sexism"), so by a sort of analogical extension we come to see that it cannot be restricted to our own species ("speciesism"). But this argument gets things the wrong way around. It is clearly possible for someone who puts special moral importance on humankind to object to racist policies precisely because they treat their victims as being not human or, in Hitler's classic phrase, subhuman. When we consider that a common element in the usual moral consideration of racism and sexism is precisely that such outlooks ignore the fact that the members of the maltreated class are members of the human species like ourselves, then the condemnation of speciesism can hardly seem a simple extension of those other condemnations.

Justifying Human Superiority

Yet, at this point, it will be said that the idea something is specially morally important about human beings needs justification. I am of two minds about this demand for justification. I think it can be met but I am not sure that it has to be. There are various ground-floor considerations in ethics as in any other enterprise—for an animal liberationist such things as the "intrinsic good" of pleasure or interest satisfaction and the "intrinsic evil" of pain or interest frustration are usually ground floor. No further justification is given for them, or needed. It is not clear to me that membership in the human species does not function in a similarly fundamental way in ethics so there is as much absurdity, if not more, in asking "Why does it matter morally that she is human?" as in asking "Why does it matter morally that she is in pain?" Nonetheless, since justification is preferable to intuition where it can be given, I will try to provide it.

Before attempting such a justification let us be clear what it involves. We need some characterization, not necessarily a very precise one, of what it is about humankind that makes it worthy of more moral consideration than other known kinds, such as ants, dogs, pine trees, a strain of flu virus, or a type of rock. What we would thereby show, if successful, is that what environmentalists, such as Richard and Val Routley, call "the greater value assumption"—the assumption that human beings are of greater value, morally, than individuals of other species—is no mere assumption. We would also perhaps then vindicate a "human-centered ethic" in some sense of that confusing phrase.

A further caution is in order about what the task involves. We are trying to exhibit features of humankind that show that the human species is morally distinctive, but these need not show that no moral respect or even duty is owed to other species. The assumption to be vindicated is a greater-value assumption, not an exclusive-value assumption. An exclusive-value assumption would entail an attitude to nature that sees no value at all in either the animate or inanimate environment, except insofar as it subserves rather narrowly conceived human interests.

Intrinsic Values in Nature?

The issue of whether there are intrinsic values in the nonanimate world has become a point of serious division between the environmentalists and the animalists, because the former object to the latter's emphasis on pain, pleasure, and associated interests as the sole or primary deposit of value. The environmentalists object either that sentience is not a precondition for having interests or that it is not a precondition for having value. They accuse animal liberationists like Peter Singer of the dastardly sin of "sentiencism." I shall not venture to intrude on this domestic quarrel, but I want to look briefly at a few of the many examples produced by the environmentalists, responses to which are sometimes thought to support the view that there are intrinsic values to nonanimate nature. (I should say by way of cautionary note that the examples are sometimes intended to illustrate the quite distinct point that those who believe in intrinsic values in nature may well support different policies from those who do not). Of course the idea that there are intrinsic values, moral or otherwise, in nature is not by itself inconsistent with the greater-value assumption as I am understanding it, but the presentation of the stories sometimes suggests that such values will inevitably take precedence over human needs, interests, or goods. They therefore require some attention. Let me cite just three common examples.

The last-man example. This concerns the last man on earth, sole survivor of the collapse of the world system, who sets to work eliminating (painlessly) every living thing, animal or plant, and perhaps defacing mountains as well. If we think he has acted wrongly, presumably we are recognizing intrinsic value in nonhuman and even in nonanimate entities.

The river example. This is to illustrate the idea that natural phenomena can be damaged independently of any human- or animal-related damage in a way that calls for compensation. The idea is that pollution of a river involves more than damage to the humans affected by it, so compensation requires restoration of the river to its unpolluted state, and not merely monetary compensation to any people affected.

The noise in the forest example. This concerns an objection to "making unnecessary and excessive noise" in a forest. It is held that the believer in the new ethic's intrinsic values will avoid such noise even if no other humans are around to hear, and will so act "out of respect for the forest and its nonhuman inhabitants." Adherents of the traditional ethic will feel free to shout and howl as the mood takes them.

Before I leave these examples for your judgment, I will comment briefly because I have certain dissatisfactions with them. The river example is defective, as it stands, in placing so much weight on monetary compensation, since the people affected may need to have an unpolluted river in the future so that they do not suffer further damage. They may in any case prefer the appearance of a beautiful, clear, unpolluted stream in which they can catch healthy fish. If we remove these features by paying the people so much that they can move to the banks of another, clean river, and then so arrange things (noncoercively) that no humans or even animals are affected by the state of the river, is it so obvious that some moral wrong has been done by continuing to pollute the stream in a good (human) cause?

In the forest example we must, I think, exclude noise that might actually cause damage to a wild animal by, say, bursting its eardrums, but if we set that aside can it seriously be claimed that a moral issue about the noise arises? The last-man (or human) example may well go some way to showing that the lifestyles of various animals are valuable and should be respected by the last man; he would certainly not be entitled to engage in pointless slaughter of, for instance, the last surviving group of mountain gorillas. Nor should he engage in the pointless destruction of the naturally beautiful, such as a surviving forest. But this last case suggests not only that we may be dealing with aesthetics rather than ethics (though I do not propose too sharp a separation between them), but also that a strong component in our intuitive reaction may be the fact that pointless destruction ill becomes the nature of human beings. It remains unclear that there would even be an issue about the overriding of a value if the last man were to destroy several trees in order to build himself a hut, or, in extremis, to destroy a substantial part of the forest to protect himself from an approaching bush fire.

Speciesism Vindicated

Let me now return to my defense of the greater-value assumption. Insofar as the Routleys and other advocates of a new ethic rely on the deliverances of intuition about the morality of shouting in the forest, the last man on earth, and so on, it seems to me that humankind's greater moral importance over animals, ecosystems, trees, or whatever is far more obvious than any of the intuitions of the new ethic. Consider a small child being attacked by a rat. It is perfectly obvious to anyone not unbalanced by theory that it is morally right to injure or kill the rat if that is necessary to save the child. It makes no difference that the rat may be very smart (for a rat) and the child backward or that the child provoked the attack. Anyone who hesitated to act because of such considerations would be a moral idiot. Normally, at the level of intuition, serious human welfare clearly outweighs that of animals. I do not know how much we can rely on appeals to intuition, but they seem inescapable in these debates, and I think one should be wary of being bluffed out of one's pro-human intuitions. One should be particularly suspicious when marginal intuitions are used to construct an argument supposed to disenfranchise more robust intuitions.

As for a characterization of the superiority of the human species, my view is that we should not seek to uncover just *one* characteristic, such as rationality (though plainly rationality is important), but rather highlight a cluster of interconnected characteristics. So one could cite, in addition to rationality, the capacity for artistic creation, the capacity for theoretical knowledge of the universe and of oneself, the capacity for love including love of one's enemies, and very centrally the capacity for moral goodness. This last provides a crucial distinction between the inanimate, plant, and brute creation on the one side and humanity on the other, and makes talk of a moral community among humans, mountains, trees, lakes, fish, and kangaroos a bit one-sided. I should add that I do not here propose a particularly optimistic view of the human species, since I recognize that it is an essential concomitant of the capacities listed that they can be abused and that they imply the capacity for irrationality and wickedness. This is what human freedom, which is involved in all these characteristics, typically allows. Nonetheless, that humans have this complex of features makes them as a species more morally significant than the nonhuman world as we know it.

Objections Answered

There is a strategy employed by the Routleys and also by Peter Singer against claims of the form mine has taken. For any quality that is suggested as giving humans moral superiority, the strategy is to declare (a) that some nonhuman object or process or creature has it, too, (b) that not all humans have it, or (c) that some humans have it in different degrees to others. So in the case of rationality, for instance, we are told that some animals have it, that some defective or immature humans lack it, and that Einstein has more of it than others. In the case of the cluster of human properties I have proposed, however, it seems clear that our species is marked by these qualities, and being marked by them is deserving of moral respect, and it is merely delusional to suppose that the cluster is exhibited by any species in the nonhuman world as we know it. The wildest claims on behalf of Washoe, the talking chimpanzee, do not really establish him as an even moderately boring dinner guest. The passion to denigrate the human world has led to very extravagant and ill-founded claims for the linguistic and related achievements of chimpanzees and dolphins. Washoe's exploits have recently been subjected to much more sober and critical scientific assessment than they received at the hands of the original investigators, with alarmingly deflationary results.

As to the second and third parts of the strategy, it is of course true that immature, senile, and defective members of the species exist, but only an inordinately individualist ideology can hold that such members should be given treatment that takes no account of their species membership. We have a vital interest in the immature, the retarded, and the defective of our kind since, apart from anything else, we normal adults have been immature and may become damaged or handicapped. The focus of moral concern on isolated individuals and their present attributes rather than on species, groups, kinds, and types is not the only or, one might think, the sanest stance possible for moral theory. As to those members of the species who possess the featured capacities to an outstanding degree, a number of responses are possible. One is to note that it is very unlikely that many will possess the *complex* to a degree that raises problems of differential respect; a second is to distinguish issues to do with law, politics, and generally civil justice from those that concern other areas of morality—well-known reasons for not having legal and political inequalities exist, but these reasons do not necessarily apply in other areas of moral interest. Perhaps the saint is worthy of special moral respect and even more.

A final point about chauvinism. I wonder whether it would not be appropriate to say something here on behalf of artifacts and machines. Are the new ethicists in danger of sliding into a form of nature chauvinism?

This discussion is condensed from an unpublished longer paper given to a conference sponsored in Melbourne by the magazine Meanjin. *Peter Singer's theories may be found in his books* Animal Liberation *(New York: Avon, 1977) and* Practical Ethics *(Cambridge: Cambridge University Press, 1979). A good account of the "new ethic" from a more radical environmentalist perspective can be found in the chapter by Richard and Val Routley in* Environmental Philosophy, *ed. D. S. Mannison et al. (Atascadero, Calif.: Ridgeview, 1980).*

Eight Worries about Patenting Animals

Robert Wachbroit

In April 1988, the United States Patent and Trade-mark Office issued patent No. 4,736,866 to Harvard University for a genetically engineered cancer-prone mouse; the same patent would cover any species of transgenic mammal containing the patented recombinant cancer sequence. This, the world's first patent for an animal, has sparked intense controversy and aroused vociferous objections.

We may divide the objections to animal patenting into intrinsic versus extrinsic objections. An intrinsic objection finds patenting animals itself to be morally wrong; it refers to values or ideals associated with the very idea of an animal patent. Intrinsic objections turn more on what a patent claim symbolizes than on what power or control it confers, since most people who object to animals as *intellectual* property do not object to animals as *personal* property. Extrinsic objections concern the likely consequences of animal patents; these arguments are therefore based on empirical or contingent assumptions about what these likely consequences would be. Extrinsic objections often express broader worries about biotechnology in general.

The distinction between intrinsic and extrinsic objections can be related to the two standard justifications of the patent system. In one view, a patent is intended to reflect a property right: The product of mental labor by right belongs to the person who created it. In the other view, a patent is intended to encourage invention by offering as an incentive to inventors a limited monopoly on their inventions. Intrinsic objections to animal patents seem to be tied to the first view, since these objections are directed to concerns about the particular claim to property an animal patent would make. Extrinsic objections refer to the second justification of the patent system, since they express concerns about the consequences of animal patenting.

Here are the various arguments against patenting animals that have surfaced in public debate, first the intrinsic, then the extrinsic objections.

1. *Patenting animals is incompatible with the sanctity of life.* The paradigm of patentable subject matter is the mechanical invention. If life is seen along this dimension—and so, as Jeremy Rifkin, a noted critic of biotechnology, has suggested, an animal is seen to be little more than a complicated toaster—how can we attach any special value to life? Central to viewing life as having a sanctity is viewing the distinction between living and nonliving as having a moral component. If no *moral* difference between living and nonliving exists, how could the mere fact of life itself have moral value? According to the leading Supreme Court decision in this area, a living organism is no different from a "composition of matter," as far as patentability is concerned. Viewing organisms as "mere composites of matter" seems to deny a moral difference between living and nonliving.

It might be instructive to look at the controversies that surrounded Darwin's views on man. Darwin denied certain differences between people and other living things, and some people took this to be a denial of a moral difference between people and animals. But, plainly, it is not. No serious philosopher would argue that the fact of evolution undermines the moral difference between people and animals. Similarly, a materialist or a reductionist view of life need not be incompatible with there being a moral difference between living and nonliving.

Thus, insofar as this worry is about viewing life as having a material basis, it is not a serious moral objection. However, there is more to this objection. This has to do with the idea that patenting licenses our viewing these organisms as property that is made but not born. Some philosophers would argue that living things are distinguished by their having a certain kind of history, rather than by their having a certain kind of composition. In viewing transgenic animals as patentable subject matter, we are identifying them by their chemical makeup, rather than by their origin. The result is to force apart two concepts—of being alive and of being born (and not made)—that have been thought to be inseparable. The worry is that our understanding of the sanctity of life cannot be sustained if we divorce these two concepts.

This constitutes a serious objection to patenting animals, unless we can find some satisfactory way of reconstructing our understanding of the sanctity of life.

2. *Patenting animals encourages a disrespect for nature.* This objection can be understood in an intrinsic or in an extrinsic version.

The intrinsic version goes like this: Our relationship to nature is that of a caretaker or steward, not that of an owner; owners can do a lot more to their property than caretakers can to their trust. As caretakers, it is argued, our treatment of nature is subject to constraints against violating the integrity of the "natural order." A patent claim, as a claim of ownership, is thus a falsification of our proper relationship to nature.

The extrinsic version goes like this: It is a small step from thinking that existing species should be protected or that the integrity of a particular environment should be maintained to thinking that the *distinction* between species should be maintained. Patenting, however, will encourage the invention of creatures that undermine the integrity of the natural order.

The main problem for either version is that of extending environmental values and concerns to domestic and laboratory animals. It seems to me that the extension of environmental concerns to nonwildlife can only be based on false analogies. As they stand, these objections do not raise a serious moral problem for animal patents insofar as transgenic animals are understood as domestic or laboratory animals and not as "products of nature."

3. *Patenting encourages a dangerous technology.* A primary purpose of granting patents is to encourage technology and invention. Since doubts exist about the safety of biotechnology, this view is that we should establish a moratorium on animal patents until the risks of biotechnology are more fully studied and better understood.

Proponents of patenting are quick to reply that granting a patent does not certify safety. A patent does not grant a right to make, use, or market an invention; it confers only a right to *exclude* others from making, using, or marketing the invention. It is inappropriate to use the patent system for regulatory purposes.

This reply, however, may smack of legalism. While it might be important to separate agencies and offices whose mission is to promote or encourage technology from those whose mission is to regulate it, the effects of their actions are not so easily separated. A failure to regulate can be a form of promotion; a failure to encourage can be a form of regulation. The patent system has the *power* to regulate technology. Furthermore, there is a precedent for using the patent system as a regulatory tool: You cannot obtain a patent for an invention that is useful only in connection with atomic weapons.

All this suggests that a patent for a transgenic animal should not be granted *if* the animal poses a comparable kind of danger. Certainly the Harvard mouse does not fall into this category. Thus the objection may be a sound one, but only when applied on a case-by-case basis.

4. *Patenting animals will encourage inhumane treatment of animals.* Arguments over the ethics of animal experimentation have usually turned on whether the benefits to humans sufficiently outweigh whatever harm experimental animals suffer. If we weigh the good against the

bad consequences of using transgenic animals in biomedical research, the good consequences seem to dominate. At least this seems clear in the case of the Harvard mouse.

Transgenic animals introduce a further complication, however. Is humane treatment of a mouse humane treatment of a *transgenic* mouse? If we assume that what counts as humane treatment of an animal depends in part on the *kind* of animal in question, then at some point the genetic modification of the animal could be so great that the "parent" stock would no longer serve as a guide to what consists of humane treatment. To that extent, the objection makes the valid point that we should proceed cautiously—but as it stands, it does not support a blanket prohibition of animal patents.

5. *The patenting of animals will eventually lead to the patenting of humans.* Taken literally, this is an absurd objection. No one thinks that allowing animals as someone's personal property constitutes a slippery slope that ends in allowing people as personal property. Why should we think it is a slippery slope from the patenting of animals to the patenting of people?

Nevertheless, a deeper worry is at work here. While introducing human DNA into a mouse does not turn the mouse into a person, it does raise the question of the moral category in which transgenic animals belong, especially those containing human genetic material. What are we to think when such techniques are used on "higher" animals, such as monkeys? How ought we to regard such a "halfway" creature? As an augmented ape or as a diminished human?

Such decisions need not arise, as long as we restrict genetic manipulation so as not to result in any "halfway" animals. But as biomedical research demands better and better animal models, pressure will be increasing to produce halfway creatures as models for human disorders. Do the benefits of these accurate models outweigh the moral ambiguities and confusions that the creation of these animals would generate? This could become a serious worry. Thus while this argument does not raise an objection to the transgenic mouse, it does raise an objection to using the Harvard patent to create a transgenic primate.

6. *Patenting threatens the norms of scientific research.* The scientific community's search for truth involves the prompt dissemination of discoveries through publications and professional meetings. If scientists wait for patent approvals before announcing discoveries and if other researchers must obtain license in order to utilize and build on these discoveries, then research suffers. This objection seems especially relevant when, as in this case, the patented item has more value for research than for commercial use.

The usual approach on this topic is to draw a distinction between basic and applied research. The goal of basic research is knowledge; the goal of applied research is a commercial product. In basic research, it is important that scientists can replicate one another's results and build on them in order to advance our knowledge. In applied research, these concerns do not govern, and so applied research can be subject to proprietary concerns. Patenting basic research items is untenable: It does not generate any greater incentive to undertake basic research and could obstruct the flow of knowledge, slow down scientific progress, and undermine the cohesion and collegiality of the scientific community.

One could reply that although patents for basic research items may not increase the *incentives* to do basic research, they increase the *support* for such research. But does this extra benefit outweigh the costs—in particular, the accompanying loss of public support for basic research? Insofar as we value the traditional norms of basic research, there should be a research exemption for patents.

7. *The public should not pay twice for the products of publicly funded research.* When the basic research underlying a patent has been publicly funded, granting a patent in effect makes the public pay twice for an invention and allows private concerns to profit unfairly.

Those who defend current patent policy may respond that the public interest is not served by the mere existence of an invention. The invention must also be suitably manufactured, distributed, and marketed. A useful invention gathering dust on the shelf does no one any good. Thus, even if the public has funded research crucial to an invention, patent incentives may still be necessary to ensure that the invention reaches its market.

Yet insofar as a suitable market exists for a product, it seems that there should already be an incentive for private investment in it. The public should invest in research only when its benefits cannot be captured by the pricing mechanism. Perhaps, then, the public should not be supporting the kind of research that is captured so easily in market prices and, therefore, by private investors. Since the public has supported the relevant research, however, it has rights to the information that results.

8. *Patenting animals will have an unacceptable economic impact, leading to the economic downfall of the family farm.* Under this objection, owners of small and medium-sized farms will not be able to compete against the large agribusinesses that will use more efficient genetically engineered animals, or they will become caught in a technological treadmill, forced to invest more and more heavily in genetic technology simply to remain competitive.

This argument reflects more a political worry than an ethical one. What is wrong with allowing small farmers to go the way of the village blacksmith? There do not seem to be moral reasons for giving special economic protection to the small farmer, although other reasons having to do with our particular culture and history may exist. An assessment of these, however, would take us too far afield.

The objections thus far raised to the patenting of animals are a mixed bag of intrinsic and extrinsic objections, some easily dismissed, others sound and compelling. All need closer philosophical scrutiny as the wisdom and ethics of patenting higher life forms continue to be the subject of public debate.

FOR FURTHER READING

Callicott, J. Baird. "Animal Liberation: A Triangular Affair," *Environmental Ethics* 4 (Winter 1980).

Epstein, Richard. *Takings: Private Property and the Power of Eminent Domain.* Cambridge, Mass.: Harvard University Press, 1985.

Feinberg, Joel. "The Rights of Animals and Unborn Generations," in *Philosophy and Environmental Crisis*, ed. William T. Blackstone. Athens: University of Georgia Press, 1974.

Hargrove, Eugene C. *Foundations of Environmental Ethics.* Englewood Cliffs, N.J.: Prentice-Hall, 1989.

Norton, Bryan G., ed. *The Preservation of Species: The Value of Biological Diversity.* Princeton, N.J.: Princeton University Press, 1986.

Norton, Bryan G. *Why Preserve Natural Variety?* Princeton, N.J.: Princeton University Press, 1987.

Regan, Tom. *The Case for Animal Rights.* Berkeley: University of California Press, 1983.

Sagoff, Mark. *The Economy of the Earth: Philosophy, Law, and the Environment.* New York: Cambridge University Press, 1988.

Scherer, Donald and Thomas Attig, eds. *Ethics and the Environment.* Englewood Cliffs, N.J.: Prentice-Hall, 1983.

Singer, Peter. *Animal Liberation.* New York: Avon, 1977.

Singer, Peter, "Not for Humans Only: The Place of Nonhumans in Environmental Issues," in *Ethics and Problems of the 21st Century*, ed. K. E. Goodpaster and K. M. Sayer. South Bend, Ind.: Notre Dame University Press, 1979.

U.S. Congress, Office of Technology Assessment. *New Developments in Biotechnology: Patenting Life—Special Report, OTA-BA-370.* Washington, D.C.: U.S. Government Printing Office, April 1989.

Van De Veer, Donald and Christine Pierce, eds. *People, Penguins, and Plastic Trees.* Belmont, Calif.: Wadsworth, 1985.

Yoxen, Edward. *The Gene Business: Who Should Control Biotechnology?* New York: Harper & Row, 1983.

3

DECISION-MAKING ABOUT RISK AND TECHNOLOGY

Some of the hardest questions in deciding policy about the environmental risks posed by new technologies concern not the substance of the decisions but the further question of *how to decide*. Where risks are large-scale and of necessity imposed centrally, some mechanism is needed for making public choices about which risks are justified by the benefits they bring, which risks are plainly unacceptable. In the past few decades the leading policy approach in this area has been some variant of cost-benefit analysis—an elaborate mechanism for weighing and assessing the costs and benefits, as well as the risks, of new technologies. But some of the central assumptions of cost-benefit analysis have come under trenchant attack, as the articles in this chapter demonstrate.

"The Limits of Cost-Benefit Analysis" argues that cost-benefit analysis fails as a way of revealing and measuring our values. Cost-benefit analysis aims to measure our values about environmental protection by determining what we pay, or would pay if the opportunity were offered, as consumers putting a dollar value on wilderness experience. But Mark Sagoff counters, "It is nonsense to test the worth of an ideal or a principle by asking what people are willing to pay for it." Our values as citizens are not the same as our preferences as consumers, and therefore political questions cannot be decided by economic analysis, but only by political debate and argument.

Two economists reply to these and other objections to cost-benefit analysis in "Cost-Benefit Analysis Defended." They address the ways cost-benefit analysis treats those who lose out from a particular public policy, its attention to how the costs and benefits of various policies are distributed, its sensitivity to important social values, its alleged bias toward the easily quantifiable aspects of decisions, and special problems that arise when cost-benefit analysis is applied to decisions involving the imposition of risks. Richard Zeckhauser and Herman Leonard conclude that, within certain limits, cost-benefit analysis adds "a useful structure to public debate": "It is not perfect, but it is better than the alternatives."

Economists and policymakers are commonly faced with determining when it makes economic sense to invest in large-scale public projects whose investment costs are immediate, but whose benefits return only over a long period of time. In making these decisions, most economists make use of a positive discount rate that diminishes the value of costs and benefits as these occur further in the future—a project is worth undertaking if the discounted value of its benefits is greater than the discounted value of its costs. Reliance on such a discount rate provides one reason for believing that the present generation need not sacrifice on behalf of future generations. In "An Attack on the Social Discount Rate," Derek Parfit attacks six different arguments for using a discount rate in economic decision-making. He argues that while it is often morally permissible to be less concerned about the remote effects of our social policies, this is never *because* these effects are more remote. Rather, it will be for a number of other reasons that we would do better to address directly.

Many government agencies promulgate regulations aimed at saving lives, but by law some agencies balance gains in safety or health against the costs of achieving them; others must act to reduce risks in whatever ways are technologically feasible. This leads to some startling differences in standards, so that the median cost of saving a life in one agency may be $50,000, while in another it is $12 million. How do we determine what we should spend on saving a life? How much uniformity in standards is appropriate or desirable in this area? "Risk Analysis and the Value of Life" examines cost-benefit analysis as a tool for setting what has been called "the social value of life." It concludes that efficiency in lifesaving must be balanced against our interests in expressing the special value of human life.

Still discussing risk-cost-benefit analysis, Langdon Winner, in "The Risk of Talking about Risk," suggests that decision-making techniques that set out to ascertain and evaluate *risks* per se have an element of bias built in at the outset, for the very language of risk carries with it problematic assumptions lacking in more traditionally worded discussions of "hazards" and "dangers." What do we do with a hazard? We generally avoid it or seek to eliminate it. What do we do with a risk? Sometimes we decide to take it. Winner concludes that "a number of important social and political issues are badly misdefined by identifying them as matters of risk"—misdefined, and accordingly, mishandled.

A reliance on risk analysis has led to a belief that understanding of technically intensive policy problems can be broken down into two distinct components: an "objective" technical component, in which the scientific experts tell us the facts, what the risks *are*, and a "subjective" policy component, in which the rest of us take those objective facts and make decisions about them. "Faith in Science" suggests that the two-stage model of policymaking is flawed, as well as the ideal of science it presupposes. Values permeate the first "objective" stage; scientists are no more detached and bias-free than the rest of us. We cannot hope to solve the problems of new technologies by deferring to a scientific priesthood.

In a democracy, public policies toward risk should reflect public attitudes toward risk. But what if the latter can be shown to be irrational and confused? "Rethinking Rationality" examines the seeming irrationality of our entrenched attitudes toward risk, and the alleged inconsistencies researchers have found there. Its authors conclude that, while some of our troubling attitudes toward risk are striking examples of human fallibility, others show rather good sense, albeit in defiance of "expert" assessments of risk. "Our irrationality shows the need for expert guidance in risk management, but the complexities in our values also suggest that the expert's analytic techniques for revealing public values may be flawed." Once again, expert techniques of risk-cost-benefit analysis turn out to be in some measure inferior to the alternative of "muddling through" unaided.

The Limits of Cost-Benefit Analysis

Mark Sagoff

In 1981 President Reagan ordered all federal agencies to refrain from major regulatory action "unless the potential benefits to society from the regulation outweigh the costs." Executive Order 12291, published in the *Federal Register* on February 10 of that year, was intended to help reform the nation's cumbersome regulatory process. Its critics have contended, however, that it has only added another layer of bureaucratic paperwork. The concepts of "benefit" and "cost" are too vague to lead to useful reform; one could only expect "paralysis by analysis" to result.

Who is right? Does cost-benefit analysis offer a neutral and rational approach to sound regulatory policy? Does it bias or delay hard choices instead?

Economists in the 1940s and 1950s, who developed cost-benefit analysis, did so to apply the theory of the firm to the government. They thought that public investments should return a profit to society as a whole. These economists compared the market value of irrigation and hydroelectric power, for example, with the capital costs of building dams. The Flood Control Act of 1938 insisted on this weighing of economic pluses and minuses. It permitted the government to finance water projects only when "the benefits to whomsoever they accrue [are] in excess of the costs."

The environmental and civil rights legislation of the 1960s and 1970s dramatically changed this situation. Congress passed these laws—as it had earlier approved child labor legislation—for political or ethical rather than for primarily economic reasons. Even if child labor were profitable for society as a whole we may still want to outlaw it. Similarly, the Clean Air and Clean Water acts were passed to improve air and water quality and not necessarily to achieve economically "optimal" levels of pollution. We may insist on a cleaner environment as a matter of pride, even if the resulting economic benefits would not balance the costs.

The Occupational Health and Safety Act of 1970 requires that the exposure of workers to toxic substances be set at standards as low as are "feasible." In two leading cases—one involving benzene and the other cotton dust—industries opposing stringent safety standards argued before the Supreme Court that regulations are "feasible" or "reasonable" only if they are cost-beneficial. Critics of this view say that if it were adopted workers would be maintained as machines are—to the extent that is socially profitable. Workers would then not be treated as ends-in-themselves, but as mere means for the production of overall social efficiency or utility.

The same debate arises with respect to the protection of wildlife and the preservation of wilderness. In 1969, for example, the Forest Service approved a plan by Walt Disney Enterprises to develop a vast resort complex in the middle of the Sequoia National Park. This would have attracted 14,000 paying visitors a day—far more than go there now. What could be more cost-beneficial? Yet Congress, in response to ethical and cultural arguments, outlawed this profitable scheme.

The Department of Interior constantly faces a choice between preserving the integrity and historical authenticity of wilderness environments or selling them off to entrepreneurs who are willing to pay a great deal for their use. These entrepreneurs know how to market a park—to turn unprofitable and often inaccessible wilderness areas into money-making golf courses, motels, bars, discos, swimming pools, restaurants, gift shops, and condominiums. These are things we Americans want and are willing to pay for as consumers—no matter what we might think of them as citizens. A free market calls for these things; they sell, and consumer benefits outweigh consumer costs.

The problem, as many people point out, is that although markets reveal our consumer interests, they may fail to measure our countervailing ethical or aesthetic principles and our convictions and concerns as citizens. Markets exist for bowls of porridge but not for birthrights. Must we, then, act only as consumers, to turn every arcadia into an arcade and all our free natural beauty into money-making commercial blight?

Economists respond to this question in two ways. Some recognize that cost-benefit analysis simply cannot be used to settle ethical or political controversies. Others are developing a "new" economics to create surrogate or imaginary markets to "price" ethical values and political convictions.

Economists of the first sort allow that Americans are not just consumers with interests they want satisfied in markets; these economists recognize that we are also citizens who have opinions legislatures are supposed to represent and rights courts are supposed to protect. These economists concede, therefore, that pollution, health, and safety standards should be determined through moral persuasion and political compromise. Economic factors are important, of course; they may not be decisive but they should be taken into account. These economists contend, moreover, that regulatory agencies should do the will of the legislature at the least social cost. These agencies should be beholden to the political institutions of our democracy. They should not, therefore, use the findings of market or cost-benefit analysis as a substitute for the results of the legitimate political process.

Economists of the second kind believe that cost-benefit analysis can take the values, arguments, and convictions of citizens into account. These economists sometimes try to estimate the worth of moral and ethical values on the basis of market data, for example, by looking at prices paid for property in the range of protected areas. They may judge the value of preservation by the amounts people are willing to pay to visit a wilderness. The primary technique, however, is to ask citizens how much they are willing to pay for the satisfaction of knowing that the government has acted consistently with some principle, to save endangered species, for example. Even if citizens would pay only a few dollars each for these moral "satisfactions," the aggregate sum might be very substantial.

This approach to cost-benefit analysis—which regards the ideals and aspirations of citizens as "externalities" consumer markets have failed to "price"—rests on three mistakes. First, it allows economists to justify virtually any policy at all or its opposite, for it is easy to find "fragile" values, "intangibles," and "moralisms," to support almost any position.

This ambitious approach to cost-benefit analysis rests also on what philosophers call a category-mistake. This is the mistake of describing an object in terms that do not appropriately apply to it, such as saying the square root of two is blue. It is nonsense to test the worth of an ideal or a principle by asking what people are willing to pay for it. As well try to establish the truth of a theorem by asking what it is worth, in economic terms, to mathematicians. Nobody asks economists how much they are willing to pay for their view that cost-benefit analysis should form the basis of regulatory policy. No, the views of economists are supposed to be judged on the merits, not priced at the margin. Why shouldn't this courtesy extend to the opinions of other people as well?

Third, cost-benefit analysis, insofar as it "prices" our convictions as citizens in the same way as our interests as consumers, confuses economic exchange with the political process. Political decisions have to be cost-conscious; they need to take economic factors into account. But this does not reduce them to economic decisions. To think otherwise would be to suggest that economic "experts" should take the place of elected representatives as interpreters of the public interest. This would replace democracy with a kind of technocracy. It would deprive us of our most cherished political rights.

These three mistakes arise from a fundamental confusion concerning what values are. According to many economists, values are simply wants or preferences; thus David Pearce, for example, writes, "Economic values are what people want. Something has economic value—it is a *benefit*—if it satisfies individual preferences." It follows from this view that all desires—even those that are racist, malevolent, self-destructive, nasty, or just silly—are equally legitimate, equally worthy of being satisfied. The only way outside of force to settle conflicts among "values," then, might be via cost-benefit analysis, in other words, by finding out which preferences are backed by the most money.

Many of us believe another, better way exists to deal with social controversies than to imagine hypothetical bidding games to solve them. We believe that intelligent adults, or their representatives, can discuss political questions on the basis of reason and argument. At the end, if they vote, the outcome will represent not so much what a majority prefers, but what it believes, all things considered, represents what is right, good, or consistent with our culture and heritage.

Conflict in our society involves ideological contradiction as well as economic competition. The one cannot be understood in terms of or reduced to the other. Cost-benefit analysis may be used to give us information about those wants and preferences for which markets exist and are appropriate. But this use is limited. We must otherwise rely on political argument and compromise in Congress ending in a vote, and not resort to cost-benefit analysis terminating in a bottom line.

David Pearce is quoted from his essay "Environmental and Economic Values," in Towards an Ecologically Sustainable Economy, *ed. Britt Aniansson and Uno Svedin (Stockholm: Swedish Council for Planning and Coordination of Research, 1990).*

Cost-Benefit Analysis Defended

**Herman B. Leonard and
Richard J. Zeckhauser**

Cost-benefit analysis, particularly as applied to public decisions involving risks to life and health, has not been notably popular. A number of setbacks—Three Mile Island is perhaps the most memorable—have called into question the reliability of analytic approaches to risk issues. We believe that the current low reputation of cost-benefit analysis is unjustified, and that a close examination of the objections most frequently raised against the method will show that it deserves wider public support.

Society does not and indeed could not require the explicit consent of every affected individual in order to implement public decisions that impose costs or risks. The transactions costs of assembling unanimous consent would be prohibitive, leading to paralysis in the status quo. Moreover, any system that required unanimous consent would create incentives for individuals to misrepresent their beliefs to secure compensation or to prevent the imposition of relatively small costs on them even if the benefits to others might be great.

If actual individual consent is an impractically strong standard to require of centralized decisions, how should such decisions be made? Our test for a proposed public decision is whether the net benefits of the action are positive. The same criterion is frequently phrased: Will those favored by the decision gain enough that they would have a net benefit even if they fully compensated those hurt by the decision? Applying this criterion to all possible actions, we discover that the chosen alternative should be the one where benefits most exceed costs. We believe that the benefit-cost criterion is a useful way of defining "hypothetical consent" for centralized decisions affecting individuals with widely divergent interests: Hypothetically, if compensation could be paid, all would agree to the decision offering the highest net benefits. We turn now to objections commonly raised against this approach.

Compensation and Hypothetical Consent

An immediate problem with the pure cost-benefit criterion is that it does not require the actual payment of compensation to those on whom a given decision imposes net costs. Our standard for public decision-making does not require that losers be compensated, but only that they *could* be if a perfect system of transfers existed. But unless those harmed by a decision are *actually* compensated, they will get little solace from the fact that someone is reaping a surplus in which they could have shared.

To this we make two replies. First, it is typically infeasible to design a compensation system that ensures all individuals will be net winners. The transactions costs involved in such a system would often be so high as to make the project as a whole a net loss. But it may not even be desirable to construct full compensation systems, since losers will generally have an incentive under such systems to overstate their anticipated losses in order to secure greater compensation.

Second, the problem of compensation is probably smaller in practice than in principle. Society tends to compensate large losses where possible or to avoid imposing large losses when adequate compensation is not practical. Moreover, compensation is sometimes overpaid; having made allowances *ex ante* for imposing risks, society still chooses sometimes to pay additional compensation *ex post* to those who actually suffer losses.

Libertarians raise one additional argument about the ethical basis of a system that does not require full compensation to losers. They argue that a public decision process that imposes uncompensated losses constitutes an illegal taking of property by the state and should not be tolerated. This objection, however strongly grounded ethically, would lead to an untenable position for society by unduly constraining public decisions to rest with the status quo.

Attention to Distribution

Two distinct types of distributional issues are relevant in cost-benefit analysis. First, we can be concerned about the losers in a particular decision, whoever they may be. Second, we can be concerned with the transfers between income classes (or other defined groups) engendered by a given project. If costs are imposed differentially on groups that are generally disadvantaged, should the decision criteria include special consideration of their interests? This question is closely intertwined with the issue of compensation, because it is often alleged that the uncompensated costs of projects evaluated by cost-benefit criteria frequently fall on those who are already disadvantaged.

These objections have little to do with cost-benefit analysis as a method. We see no reason why any widely agreed on notion of equity, or weighting of different individuals' interests, cannot in principle be built into the cost-benefit decision framework. It is merely a matter of defining carefully what is meant by a benefit or a cost. If, in society's view, benefits (or costs) to some individuals are more valuable (costly) than those to others, this can be reflected in the construction of the decision criteria.

But although distribution concerns could be systematically included in cost-benefit analyses, it is not always—or even generally—a good idea to do so. Taxes and direct expenditures represent a far more efficient means of effecting redistribution than virtually any other public program; we would strongly prefer to rely on one consistent comprehensive tax and expenditure package for redistribution than on attempts to redistribute within every project.

First, if distributional issues are considered everywhere, they will probably not be adequately, carefully, and correctly treated anywhere. Many critics of cost-benefit analysis believe that project-based distributional analysis would create a net addition to society's total redistribution effort; we suggest that is likely, instead, to be only an inefficient substitution.

Second, treating distributional concerns within each project can only lead to transfers within the group affected by a project, often only a small subset of the community. For example, unisex rating of auto insurance redistributes only among drivers. Cross-subsidization of medical costs affects only those who need medical services. Why should not the larger society share the burden of redistribution?

Third, the view that distributional considerations should be treated project-by-project reflects a presumption that on average they do not balance out—that is, some groups systematically lose more often than others. If it were found that some groups were severely and systematically disadvantaged by the application of cost-benefit analyses that ignore distributional concerns, we would favor redressing the balance. We do not believe this is generally the case.

Sensitive Social Values

Cost-benefit analysis, it is frequently alleged, does a disservice to society because it cannot treat important social values with appropriate sensitivity. We believe that this view does a disservice to society by unduly constraining the use of a reasonable and helpful method for organizing the debate about public decisions. We are not claiming that every important social value can be represented effectively within the confines of cost-benefit analysis. Some values will never fit in a cost-benefit framework and will have to be treated as "additional considerations" in coming to a final decision. Some, such as the inviolability of human life, may simply be binding constraints that cannot be traded off to obtain other gains. Nor can we carry out a cost-benefit analysis to decide which values should be included and which treated separately—this decision will always have to be made in some other manner.

These considerations do not invalidate cost-benefit analysis, but merely illustrate that more is at stake than just dollar measures of costs and benefits. We would, however, make two observations. First, we must be very careful that only genuinely important and relevant social values be permitted to outweigh the findings of an analysis. Second, social values that frequently stand in the way of important efficiency gains have a way of breaking down and being replaced over time, so that in the long run society manages to accommodate itself to some form of cost-benefit criterion. If nuclear power were 1000 times more dangerous for its employees but 10 times less expensive than it is, we might feel that ethical considerations were respected and the national interest well served if we had rotating cadres of nuclear power employees serving short terms in high-risk positions, much as members of the armed services do. In like fashion, we have fire fighters risk their lives; universal sprinkler systems would be less dangerous, but more costly. Such policies reflect an accommodation to the costs as a recognition of the benefits.

Measurability

Another objection frequently raised against cost-benefit analysis is that some costs and benefits tend to be ignored because they are much more difficult to measure than others. The long-term environmental impacts of large projects are frequently cited as an example. Cost-benefit analysis is charged with being systematically biased toward consideration of the quantifiable aspects of decisions.

This is unquestionably true: Cost-benefit analysis is *designed* as a method of quantification, so it surely is better able to deal with more quantifiable aspects of the issues it confronts. But this limitation is in itself ethically neutral unless it can be shown that the quantifiable considerations generally push decisions in a particular direction. Its detractors must show that the errors of cost-benefit analysis are systematically unjust or inefficient—for example, that it frequently helps the rich at the expense of the poor, or despoils the environment to the benefit of industry, or vice versa. We have not seen any carefully researched evidence to support such assertions.

We take some comfort in the fact that cost-benefit analysis is sometimes accused of being biased toward development projects and sometimes of being biased against them. Cost-benefit analyses have foiled conservation efforts in national forests—perhaps they systematically weight the future too little. But they have also squelched clearly silly projects designed to bring "economic development" to Alaska— and the developers argued that the analysis gave insufficient weight to the "unquantifiable" value of future industrialization.

In our experience, cost-benefit analysis is often a tool of the "outs"—those not currently in control of the political process. Those who have the political power to back the projects they support often have little need of analyses. By contrast, analysis can be an effective tool for those who are otherwise not strongly empowered politically.

Analyzing Risks

Even those who accept the ethical propriety of cost-benefit analysis of decisions involving transfers of money or other tangible economic costs and benefits sometimes feel that the principles do not extend to analyzing decisions involving the imposition of risks. We believe that such applications constitute a *particularly* important area where cost-benefit analysis can be of value. The very difficulties of reaching appropriate decisions where risks are involved make it all the more vital to employ the soundest methods available, both ethically and practically.

Historically, cost-benefit analysis has been applied widely to the imposition and regulation of risks, in particular to risks of health loss or bodily harm. The cost-benefit approach is particularly valuable here, for several reasons. Few health risks can be exchanged on a voluntary basis. Their magnitude is difficult to measure. Even if they could be accurately measured, individuals have difficulty interpreting probabilities or gauging how they would feel should the harm eventuate. Compounding these problems of valuation are difficulties in contract, since risks are rarely conveyed singly between one individual and another.

The problem of risks conveyed in the absence of contractual approval has been addressed for centuries through the law of torts, which is designed to provide compensation after a harm has been received. If only a low-probability risk is involved, it is often efficient to wait to see whether a harm occurs, for in the overwhelming majority of circumstances, transactions costs will be avoided. This approach also limits debate over the magnitude of a potential harm that has not yet eventuated. Creators of the risk have the incentive to gauge accurately, for they are the ones who must pay if harm does occur.

While in principle it provides efficient results, the torts approach encounters at least four difficulties when applied to many of the risks encountered in a modern technological society. The option of declaring bankruptcy allows the responsible party to avoid paying and so to impose risks that it should not impose. Causality is often difficult to assign for misfortunes that may have alternative or multiple (and synergistically related) causes. Did the individual contract lung cancer from air pollution or from his or her own smoking, or both? Furthermore, the traditional torts requirement that individuals be made whole cannot be met in many instances (death, loss of a limb). Finally, paying compensation after the fact may also produce inappropriate incentives, and hence be inefficient. Workers who can be more or less careful around dangerous machinery, for example, are likely to be more careful if they will not be compensated for losing an appendage.

Our normal market and legal system tends to break down when substantial health risks are imposed on a relatively large population. These are, therefore, precisely the situations in which the cost-benefit approach is and should be called into play. Cost-benefit analysis is typically used in just those situations where our normal risk decision processes run into difficulty. We should therefore not expect it to lead to outcomes as satisfactory as those that evolve when ordinary market and private contractual trade are employed. But we should be able to expect better outcomes than we would achieve by muddling through unsystematically.

We have defended cost-benefit analysis as the most practical of ethically defensible methods and the most ethical of practically usable methods for conducting public decision-making. It cannot substitute for—nor can it adequately encompass, analyze, or consider—the sensitive application of social values. Thus it cannot be made the final arbiter of public decisions. But it does add a useful structure to public debate, and it does enable us to quantify some of the quantifiable aspects of public decisions. Our defense parallels Winston Churchill's argument for democracy: It is not perfect, but it is better than the alternatives.

An Attack on the Social Discount Rate

Derek Parfit

It is now widely believed that, when we are choosing between social policies, we are justified in being less concerned about their more remote effects. All future costs and benefits may be "discounted" at some rate of n percent per year. Unless n is very small, the further future will be heavily discounted. Thus, at a discount rate of 10 percent, effects on people's welfare next year count for more than ten times as much as effects in twenty years. At the lower rate of 5 percent, effects next year count for more than a thousand times as much as effects in 200 years.

Such a "Social Discount Rate" seems to me indefensible. The moral importance of future events does *not* decline at n percent per year. A mere difference in timing is in itself morally neutral. Remoteness in time roughly corresponds with certain other facts, which are morally significant. But since the correlation is so rough, the Discount Rate should be abandoned.

Why was it adopted? I am aware of six arguments.

(1) The Argument from Probability

It is often claimed that we should discount more remote effects because they are less likely to occur. This confuses two questions: (a) When a prediction applies to the further future, is it less likely to be correct? (b) If some prediction is correct, may we give it less weight because it applies to the further future? The answer to a is often "Yes." But this provides no argument for answering "Yes" to b.

We ought to discount predictions that are more likely to be false. Call this a "Probabilistic Discount Rate." Predictions about the further future are more likely to be false. So the two kinds of Discount Rate, Temporal and Probabilistic, roughly correlate. But they are quite different. It is therefore a mistake to discount for time *rather than* probability.

One objection is that this misstates our moral view. It makes us claim not that more remote bad consequences are less likely, but that they are less important. This is not our real view. A greater objection is that the two Discount Rates do not always coincide. Predictions about the further future are not less likely to be true at a rate of n percent per year. When applied to the further future, many predictions are indeed *more* likely to be true. If we discount for time rather than probability, we may thus be led to the wrong conclusions.

(2) The Argument from Opportunity Costs

It is sometimes better to receive a benefit earlier, since this benefit then can be used to produce further benefits. If an investment yields a return next year, this is worth more than the same return ten years later, since the earlier return can be profitably reinvested over the ten years. Once we have added in the extra returns from this reinvestment, the total returns over time will be greater. A similar argument covers certain kinds of costs. The delaying of some benefits thus involves "opportunity costs," and vice versa.

This is sometimes thought to justify a Social Discount Rate. But the justification fails, and for the same two reasons. Certain opportunity costs do increase over time. But if we discount for time, rather than simply adding in these extra costs, we will misrepresent our moral reasoning. More important, we can be led astray. Consider benefits that are not reinvested but consumed. When such benefits are received later, this involves no opportunity costs. Consider this example. If we build a proposed airport, we will destroy some stretch of beautiful countryside. We might try to estimate the benefits that we and our successors would then lose. If we do not build the airport, such benefits would be enjoyed in each future year. At any discount rate, the benefits in later years count for much less than the benefits next year. How could an appeal to opportunity costs justify this? The benefits received next year—our enjoyment of this natural beauty—cannot be profitably reinvested.

Nor can the argument apply to costs that are merely "consumed." Thus it cannot show that a genetic deformity next year ought to count for ten times as much as a deformity in twenty years. The most that could be claimed is this. Suppose we know that if we adopt a certain policy, some risk of causing such deformities will occur. We might decide that for each child so affected, the large sum of k dollars could provide adequate compensation. If we were going to provide such compensation, the present cost of ensuring this would be much greater for a deformity caused next year. We would now have to set aside almost the full k dollars. A much smaller sum, if set aside and invested now, would yield in twenty years what would then be equivalent to k dollars. This provides one reason for being less concerned now about the deformities we might cause in the further future. But the reason is not that such deformities matter less. The reason is that it would now cost us less to ensure that when such deformities occur, we would be able to provide compensation. This is a crucial difference.

Suppose we know that we will not in fact provide compensation. This might be so, for instance, if we would not be able to identify particular deformities our policy had caused. This removes our reason for being less concerned now about deformities in later years. If we will not pay compensation whenever such deformities occur, it becomes irrelevant that, in the case of later deformities, it *would* be cheaper to ensure now that we *could* pay compensation. But if we have expressed this point by adopting a Social Discount Rate, we may fail to notice that it has become irrelevant. We may be led to assume that, even without compensation, deformities in twenty years matter only a tenth as much as deformities next year.

(3) The Argument that Our Successors Will Be Better Off

If we assume our successors will be better off than us, two plausible arguments exist for discounting the costs and benefits we give to them. If we are thinking of costs and benefits in a purely monetary sense, we can appeal to diminishing marginal utility. The same increase in wealth generally brings a smaller real benefit—a smaller gain in welfare—to those who are better off. We may also appeal to a principle of distributive justice. An equally great benefit, given to those who are better off, may be claimed to be morally less important.

These two arguments, though good, do not justify a Social Discount Rate. The ground for discounting these future benefits is not that they lie further in the future, but that they will go to people who are better off. Here, as elsewhere, we should say what we mean. And the correlation is again imperfect. Some of our successors may not be better off than us. If they are not, the argument just given fails to apply.

(4) The Argument from Excessive Sacrifice

A typical statement runs: If we did not use a discount rate, any small increase in benefits that extends indefinitely in time could demand any amount of sacrifice in the present, because in time the benefits outweigh the costs.

The same objections apply. If this is why we adopt a Social Discount Rate, we shall be misstating what we believe. Our belief is not that the importance of future benefits steadily declines. It is rather that no generation can be morally required to make more than certain kinds of sacrifices for the sake of future generations. If this is what we believe, this is what should influence our decision. If instead we take the belief to justify a Discount Rate, we can be led quite unnecessarily to implausible conclusions. Suppose that, at the same cost to ourselves, we could prevent either a minor catastrophe in the nearer future or a major catastrophe in the further future. Since preventing the major catastrophe would involve no extra cost, the Argument from Excessive Sacrifice fails to apply. But if we take that argument to justify a Discount Rate, we can be led to conclude it is the major catastrophe that is less worth preventing.

(5) The Argument from Special Relations

According to common-sense morality, we ought to give some weight to the interests of strangers. But there are certain people to whose interests we ought to give some priority, people to whom we stand in certain special relations. Thus each person ought to give some priority to his or her children, parents, pupils, patients, constituents, or fellow compatriots.

Such a view naturally applies to the effects of our acts on future generations. Our immediate successors will be our own children. According to common sense, we ought to give special weight to their welfare. We may think the same, though to a reduced degree, about our obligations to our children's children. Such claims might support a new kind of discount rate. We would be discounting here, not for time itself, but for degrees of kinship. But at least these two relations cannot radically diverge. Our grandchildren cannot all be born before all our children. Since the correlation here is more secure, we might be tempted to employ a Standard Discount Rate.

Here, too, this would be unjustified. When applying a Standard Discount Rate, more remote effects always count for less. But a discount rate with respect to kinship should, I believe, level off. When we are comparing the effects of two social policies, perhaps effects on our children ought to concern us more than effects on our grandchildren. But should effects on the fifth generation concern us more than effects on the sixth?

Nor should the rate apply to all kinds of effects. Thus, if our acts may inflict severe harms, the special relations make no moral difference.

(6) The Argument from Democracy

Many people care less about the further future. Some writers claim that, if this is true of most living Americans, the U.S. government ought to employ a Social Discount Rate. If its electorate does care less about the further future, a democratic government ought also to do so. Failure to do so would be paternalistic, or authoritarian.

This argument need not be discussed here. We should distinguish two questions: (a) As a community, may we use a Social Discount Rate? Are we morally justified in being less concerned about the more remote effects of our social policies? (b) If most of our community would answer "Yes" to question *a*, ought our government to override this majority view? The Argument from Democracy applies only to question *b*. To question *a* it is irrelevant.

Conclusion

I have discussed six arguments for the Social Discount Rate. None succeed. The most they could justify is the use of such a rate as a crude rule of thumb. But this rule would often go astray. It may often be morally permissible to be less concerned about the more remote effects of our social policies. But this will never be *because* these effects are more remote. Rather, it would be because they are less likely to occur, or will be effects on people who are better off than us, or because it is cheaper now to ensure compensation—or it would be for one of the other reasons I have given. All these different reasons need to be judged on their merits, separately. To bundle them together in a Social Discount Rate is to blind our moral sensibilities.

Remoteness in time roughly correlates with a whole range of morally significant facts. But so does remoteness in space. Those to whom we have the greatest obligations, our own family, often live with us in the same building. Most of our fellow citizens live closer to us than most aliens. But no one suggests that, because such correlations exist, we should adopt a Spatial Discount Rate. No one thinks that we should care less about the long-range effects of our acts, at a rate of *n* percent per yard. The Temporal Discount Rate is, I believe, as little justified.

Risk Analysis and the Value of Life

Claudia Mills and Douglas MacLean

One of the chief mandates of government is to protect the lives of its citizens. It does this through providing military defense against foreign attack and criminal sanctions against domestic assault. But death comes not only through war and bloodshed, and in this century, government, via its regulatory agencies, has protected people as well against various more diffuse threats to life and health; death from any cause leaves its victims just as dead. We believe it falls within the jurisdiction of government to protect its citizens with equal vigilance against many threats to life.

But if we look at the mandates of different regulatory agencies that share the common goal of protecting life, we see that they pursue this goal with differing degrees of zeal. Some agencies must balance gains in safety or health against the costs of achieving them; others must act to reduce risks in whatever ways are technologically feasible. This leads to some startling differences in standards. A review of the cost effectiveness of some proposed lifesaving programs has shown that the median cost of saving a life was $50 thousand at the Consumer Product Safety Commission and $64 thousand at the National Highway Traffic Safety Commission, while the same median value was $2.6 million at the Environmental Protection Agency (EPA) and $12.1 million at the Occupational Safety and Health Administration (OSHA). Surely this comparison suggests that we are spending too much in some areas, too little in others, or both.

The estimated cost of saving a life should no doubt be brought more into line across different programs, not only for reasons of equity, but also for reasons of efficiency. We could save more lives for the same total regulatory budget if we allocated these funds differently. But which inequalities should we accept? How should other values weigh against the number of lives we could save? And what should the overall median value be anyway? How do we decide?

The Social Value of Life

Policy analysts have been trying to answer these questions for some years now. One of their practical goals is to bring more order and coherence to the piecemeal approach to health and safety regulation of the 1960s and early 1970s. The methods they have developed—different specific techniques for analyzing and comparing risks, costs, and benefits—are intended to help us think clearly and comprehensively about all these issues.

One way to do this is to calculate what risk-analysts call "the social value of life." They look at consumer choices that reveal preferences for safety, as opposed to other goods, and at social decisions to accept some level of risk when the cost of reducing it further would be too great. Measures such as these can be used to establish a systematic, consistent benchmark for deciding what we should spend on lifesaving policies.

A justification for being explicit and analytic about what we are willing to spend to save lives is that by allocating our risk budget more efficiently, we can reduce everyone's risk of early death. Equally important, since every dollar we spend on increased safety is a dollar diverted from enhancing our lives in other ways, we can make better comparisons between improving life's quality and increasing its longevity. Living longer, after all, is a poor substitute for living well.

But many find the prospect of setting a social value for life a chilling one. This may be partly because they fear entrusting such decisions to a technocratic elite that might abuse its powers. Even setting aside this fear, however, it seems unconscionably cold and calculating to tote up the dollar value of individual human lives in an accountant's ledger. If, for example, we decide to forgo certain safety measures in coal mines, because we have coolly estimated that their costs do not justify their benefits, this will almost certainly mean some miners' deaths will not be prevented. It means, that is, some real flesh-and-blood human beings will die in order to save what may amount to only a few pennies on a dollar. Likewise, if we decide certain pollution control measures in a larger power plant are not worth their cost, numerous deaths can be expected to result. Isn't this killing to save money?

The risk-analyst's response is that, like it or not, trade-offs between safety and other goods do have to be made. We could always spend more—perhaps a good deal more, to make the world safer—perhaps a little bit safer. At some point, as a society, we have to strike a balance. Risk analysis helps us do this in an orderly, rational way. According to Allan Gibbard, professor of philosophy at the University of Michigan, "'Killing to save money' is a tendentious way of describing the operation of a power plant with substantial pollution controls. . . . The phrase would allow us to dismiss a thousand man-years of sweat and toil as mere 'money' while underlining diffuse effects on health as 'killing.'" Impassioned rhetoric will not let us off the hook of making hard choices.

Furthermore, a sufficiently sophisticated risk analysis, one that in Gibbard's terms addresses "the expected total intrinsic reward" of our lives, will not ride roughshod over our actual feelings about safety and health, or anything else. Even if our feelings are not rational or consistent, they matter, Gibbard explains, because they are ours: "They determine much in the way we experience our lives and the ways we experience each other." Frustrating them has costs of its own, to be counted in with all the rest: "A risk-cost-benefit analysis that takes into account all contributions to expected total intrinsic reward must count things other than lives saved, injuries and illnesses avoided, and resources diverted to do these things. It must count effects on the ways people who stand ready to carry out a policy experience their lives."

Suppose, for example, we could save more lives if we spent our budget for mine safety on preventing accidents rather than on heroic, extremely expensive rescue efforts for trapped miners. Nevertheless, Gibbard recognizes, it may be "dehumanizing to stand idly by when strenuous, expensive effort has a substantial chance of saving lives." An ideal risk analysis would count the benefits of saving more lives but also the costs of forfeiting some of the psychological rewards of human fellowship.

But can risk analysis take account of all our other values, throwing them in one gigantic hopper with the number of lives saved and the dollar costs of saving them? Is risk analysis just a neutral way of structuring our decisions, incorporating all our values, whatever they are, and giving them whatever weight we determine to be important? Or do some values resist treatment in this way?

Many people are uncomfortable with the suggestion that risk analysis should be a decision procedure for making choices that seem important both for their consequences and for the real and symbolic value that attaches to how they are made. For this reason, decisions about life and death are decisions we might especially resist consigning to the risk-analyst's decision machine.

Human life, we might say, has a sacred or priceless value. This is often taken to mean that life has infinite value, but this is not the correct interpretation of what it is for something to be held as sacred. Certainly we are not willing to spend infinite sums of money to save lives; we have other competing priorities. Indeed, many of the things we regard as priceless may have perfectly well-determined market values.

To call something priceless may only mean it is not for sale, not that no one could afford it.

The mark of a sacred object lies less in how much we value it than in how we express that value. In every culture, sacred values are attended by special ceremonies and rituals. We might characterize rituals as irrational or nonrational behavior, actions in which the relationship between means and ends is deliberately inefficient. This aspect of rituals indicates their symbolic meaning and draws the attention of the community to objects, relationships, or roles that have a special place in the life of the group.

Our culture, too, has its own rituals for expressing the sacred value of life. These include saving crash victims, fliers lost at sea, or astronauts; retrieving the wounded or dead in battle; diverting resources used for making mines safer in order to mount rescue missions for trapped miners; or even supporting individual medical treatment rather than more public health measures. These defy economic sense—they are intended to defy economic sense. They are intended to show that life has a value that cannot be cashed out in purely economic terms.

We can conclude from this that the value of life is complex. It has at least two aspects that can conflict with each other. First, human life has intrinsic value: Saving lives or preventing early deaths is good, and the more lives saved the better. Risk analysis is an important tool for furthering this value. Second, human life has a sacred value, which must be expressed through rituals and other special actions. Setting acceptable levels of risk must be guided by both aspects of this value, even though they may have to be balanced and traded off against each other. We might reasonably choose to accept certain inefficiencies—to save fewer lives than we might otherwise save—in order to maintain the sacredness of human life. Risk-analysts insist that we are willing to accept some risks as a trade-off to improve life's quality; why should we not also accept some risks, some localized inefficiencies, in order to maintain the integrity of the value of human life?

For these reasons we might resist across-the-board applications of risk analysis. But Gibbard responds that a sensitive form of risk analysis can meet these objections. In the end, he argues, we can still look at the various rituals we engage in to show the sacred value of life and ask whether on balance they contribute, in the deepest sense, to the intrinsic reward of our lives. We can ask: Does the existence of this or that ritual—however passionately we are attached to it in the press of daily life—really make our lives more worth living? "In a cool hour," Gibbard maintains, "we should be willing to reflect on what we regard with reverence in normal life." This is the kind of detachment involved in relying on ideal risk-cost-benefit analysis, which tries to remain sensitive to all the values and procedures that contribute to intrinsically rewarding lives.

Muddling Through

Can sacred values, personal commitments, and the important but subtle conventions and practices that characterize a culture be treated in this way? What would it mean to incorporate even these deepest values into some grand risk-cost-benefit analysis that aims at maximizing the intrinsic reward of our lives, in the broadest sense?

We might be skeptical that any formal system of analysis could ever capture all our values and concerns with the requisite sensitivity, since these depend so much on details of the concrete contexts in which they arise. Moreover, it is not clear what the yardstick for measurement is to be. If all our values are to be compared and assessed on one single scale, what is that scale? Most risk-analysts have taken the common currency to be money, the amount we as individuals or as a society are willing to pay to satisfy our preferences and promote our values. But Gibbard rejects this standard, since, given the vast differentials in income, different amounts of money mean different things to people differently situated. His measure is the far broader notion of the intrinsic reward of a person's life. But is this too vague to be of any practical application?

We might be better off giving up the search for a sensitive, yet workable metric, consigning risk analysis to a more limited and less inclusive role. We might focus our attention on directly examining our values more closely, without presupposing that we can ever find a method that will make them orderly and systematic. Why should we, after all, think we would be better off allowing our judgments and intuitions to be corrected by some general analytic method?

Conclusion

What should we conclude from this about how systematic and coherent our government agencies should be in tackling risks to life and health?

Annette Baier, professor of philosophy at the University of Pittsburgh, gives one reason why it may make for more systematic and coherent policy not to aim at a standard across-the-board policy for preserving life. She suggests that our traditional approach has its own rationale that may make more sense and achieve better results than the alternative presented by risk analysis. Traditionally, we have divided the responsibility for facing various dangers not on the basis of what interests or rights are threatened, but instead by the source of the threat. Thus, the judicial system protects security of life, liberty, property, and contract—all against threats by individual offenders; the Environmental Protection Agency protects many of our vital interests and rights against threats to the environment—furthermore, not against all threats to the environment, only those "that come from thoughtless or ruthless human policies." Different public authorities, on Baier's view, "take on different public 'enemies,' each of which may threaten several vital interests." Should we worry that under this division of labor no one is thinking about *all* the threats to security of life, or coordinating all measures to protect it?

Baier thinks not: "To try to deal in one budget (the total lifesaving budget) with the threat to human life posed by a rise in terrorism, and to deal with the threat terrorism poses to liberty in a different budget (the total liberty-saving budget) would lead to less, not greater, coordination. Doubtless there are better ways to partition our public labor than we have yet devised, but . . . 'rationalizing,' if that amounts to identifying some abstract common goal in several areas and then adopting an efficient total plan to reach it, aiming at consistency in all the areas affected, may be one of those rational strategies that it is even more rational to restrict."

Thus, it would be a mistake for federal regulatory agencies to aim in a coordinated way at maximizing the overall efficiency of how government resources for lifesaving are expended. Regulatory agencies like EPA and OSHA are not invisible bureaucracies established to duplicate the work of the Office of Management and Budget and bring efficiency and coherence to regulatory policies. They are, rather, very public institutions that the public expects to vocalize the ideals of a society that cares deeply about the lives and health of its citizens.

Although we now realize how important it is to the nation and to its economy for these agencies to be cost-conscious, nevertheless, when the administrator of EPA appears at a press conference to announce a regulatory decision, people are not primarily concerned with knowing that the agency has found the ideal cost-benefit ratio. People want to know that things they value deeply—our health, the environment, and our natural resources—are being guarded and protected by the agency we have created to be the trustee of these values.

In sum, the actions of such agencies have symbolic and expressive significance. This may help us to understand the "rituals" that have been forced on some of these agencies, like the taboos against looking at cost-benefit analyses or establishing a social value of human life. It might help us to understand why modest inconsistencies in achieving our lifesaving goals may be less worrisome than certain efforts to correct them. If life is indeed sacred, we may not always choose to protect it in the most efficient way, but in a way that recognizes—and expresses—its special value.

The median lifesaving costs cited are taken from John D. Graham and James W. Vaupel, "Value of a Life: What Difference Does It Make?" Risk Analysis, *vol. 1, no. 1 (1981). The views of Allan Gibbard and Annette Baier are taken from their essays in* Values at Risk, *ed. Douglas MacLean, Maryland Studies in Public Philosophy (Totowa, N.J.: Rowman and Littlefield, 1986).*

The Risk of Talking about Risk

Langdon Winner

Contemporary discussions of risk contain a fruitful possibility. Addressing ways the broader effects of industrial production can damage environmental quality and endanger people's health and safety, such inquiries have the potential to raise one of the most important questions that face modern society: Are there justifiable limits to the application of today's scientific technology? But this potential will be difficult to realize, for the very introduction of risk as a common way of defining policy issues is far from a neutral development. Self-conscious risk assessment adds a distinctively conservative influence to public policy debate. It seems to me that under any foreseeable conditions where this new art will be practiced, its primary effect will be to delay, complicate, and befuddle issues in a way that will sustain an industrial status quo relatively free of socially enforced limits.

Risks versus Hazards

With the rise of risk assessment in the 1970s, questions previously talked about in such terms as the "environmental crisis," "dangerous side effects," "health hazards," and the like were gradually redefined as questions of "risk." The difference is of no small importance.

If we declare ourselves to be identifying, studying, and remedying hazards, our orientation to the problem is clear. First, we can assume that given adequate evidence, the hazards to health and safety are fairly easily known. Second, when hazards of this kind are revealed, agreement on what to do about them is readily found among all reasonable people. Thus, if we notice that a deep, open pit stands along a path where children walk to school, it seems wise to insist that the responsible party, be it a private person or public agency, either fill the pit or put a fence around it. Similarly, if we have good reason to believe that an industrial polluter is endangering our health or harming the quality of the land, air, or water around us, it seems reasonable to insist that the pollution cease or be strongly curtailed.

If, on the other hand, we declare that we are interested in assessing risks, a number of changes tend to occur in the way we proceed. What otherwise might be seen as a fairly obvious link between cause and effect, air pollution and cancer, for example, now becomes something fraught with uncertainty. What is the relative size of that risk, that chance of harm? And what is the magnitude of the harm when it does take place? In answering these questions, the risk assessor is constrained to acknowledge what are often highly uncertain findings of the best available research. Prudence becomes not a matter of acting effectively to remedy a suspected source of injury, but of waiting for better research findings. Although toxic chemicals themselves may have been disposed of in reckless fashion, scientific studies on the consequences must be done with scrupulous care. Action tends to be postponed indefinitely.

Frequently augmenting these uncertainties about cause and effect are the risk-assessor's calculations on costs and benefits. How much is it reasonable to spend in order to reduce a particular risk? Is the cost warranted as compared to the benefit received? Once we are informed about how the cost of reducing environmental risks is likely to affect consumer prices, taxes, industrial productivity, and the like, our desire to act decisively with respect to any particular risk has to be weighed against these economic priorities.

A willingness to balance relative costs and benefits is present in the very adoption of the concept of risk to describe a situation. In contrast, this disposition to weigh and compare is not announced by the concepts of danger, peril, hazard, and threat. Such terms do not presuppose that the source of possible injury is also a source of benefits. What does one do with a risk? Sometimes one decides to take it. What, by comparison, does one do with a hazard? Usually one seeks to avoid it or eliminate it.

The use of the concept of risk in business dealings, sports, and gambling reveals how closely it is linked to voluntary undertakings. An investor risks his capital in the hope of making a financial gain. A football team in a close game takes a risk when it decides to run on fourth down and a yard to go. A bettor at a Las Vegas blackjack table risks money on the chance of a big payoff. In contrast to the concepts of danger, hazard, or peril, the notion of risk tends to imply that the chance of harm is accepted willingly in the expectation of gain.

Noticing that everyday life is filled with risky situations of various kinds, contemporary risk assessors focus on a set of psychological complications that further compound the difficulties offered by scientific uncertainty and the calculations of risk-cost-benefit analysis. Do people accurately estimate the risks they actually face? How well are they able to compare and evaluate such risks? And why do they decide to focus on some risks rather than others? Psychological research tends to show that people have a fairly fuzzy comprehension of the relative chance of harm involved in their everyday activities.

This research is often used to discredit the claims of those who focus on the chance of harm from some particular source. Why should a person who drives an automobile, a notorious cause of injury and death, be worried about nuclear power or the level of air pollution? Invidious comparisons of this kind are sometimes employed to show that people's fears about technological hazards are completely irrational.

This drift in some scholarly writings on risk assessment finds its complement in the advocacy advertising of corporations in the oil, chemical, and electric power industries. A typical advertisement from Mobil Oil's "Observations" series illustrates the way in which popularized risk psychology and risk-cost-benefit analysis can work in harmony with corporate goals. "Risky business," the ad announces. "Lawn mowers . . . vacuum cleaners . . . bathtubs . . . stairs . . . all part of everyday life and all hazardous to your health. The Consumer Product Safety Commission says these household necessities caused almost a million accidents last year, yet most people accept the potential risks because of the proven benefits. . . . Risk, in other words, is part of life." Its text goes on to evoke a string of psychological associations linked to the experience of risk in economic enterprise. "Cold feet. What America does need are more companies willing to take business risks, especially on energy, where the risks are high. . . . We're gamblers. . . . Taking risks: it's the best way to keep America rolling . . . and growing." Poker anyone?

A deep-seated tendency in our culture is to appreciate risk-taking in economic activity as a badge of courage. People who have qualms about occasional side effects of economic wheeling and dealing can easily be portrayed as cowardly namby-pambies just not up to the rigors of the marketplace. Our culture embraces risk-taking as one of the warrior virtues. Those who do not possess this virtue should, it would seem, please not stand in the way of those who do.

Avoiding the Risk Debate

The risk debate is one, then, that those with certain kinds of social interests can expect to lose by the very act of entering. Deliberations about risk are bound to have a strongly conservative drift. The conservatism to which I refer upholds the status quo of production and consumption in our industrial, market-oriented society. This status quo is supported by a long history of economic development in which countless new technological applications were introduced with scant regard to the possibility they might cause harm. Because industrial practices acceptable in the past have become yardsticks for thinking about what will be acceptable now and in the future, attempts to achieve a cleaner, healthier environment face an uphill battle.

One path through the mass of issues that characterize the risk debate is to take each one separately in its own right. For example, one might question how reasonable it is to apply the very strict standards of certainty used in scientific research to questions that have a strong social or moral component. Must our judgments on possible harms and the origins of those harms have only a 5 percent chance of being wrong? Doesn't the use of that significance level mean that possibly dangerous practices are "innocent until proven guilty"?

But for those who see issues of public health, safety, and environmental quality as fairly straightforward matters requiring urgent action, these exercises in methodological refinement are of dubious value. It is sensible to ask, why get stuck in such perplexities at all? Should we spend our time working to improve techniques of risk analysis and risk assessment? Or should we spend the same time working more directly to find better ways to secure a beautiful, healthy, well-provided world?

Fortunately, many issues talked about as risks can be legitimately described in other ways. With any cases of past, present, or obvious future harm, it is possible to discuss that harm directly without pretending you are playing craps. A toxic-waste disposal site placed in your neighborhood need not be defined as a risk; it might appropriately be defined as a problem of toxic waste. New Englanders who find acid rain falling on them are under no obligation to begin analyzing the risks of acid rain; they might retain some Yankee stubbornness and confound the experts by talking about "that destructive acid rain" and what is to be done about it. A treasured natural environment endangered by industrial activity need not be regarded as something at risk; one might regard it more positively as an entity that ought to be preserved in its own right.

My point is, then, that a number of important social and political issues are badly misdefined by being identified as matters of risk. Whenever possible, such misdefinitions ought to be resisted, along with the methodological quagmires they bring in train. This is not to say that there are no issues of broad-scale social policy where the concept of risk is legitimately applied. In some applications of modern science and technology, the uncertainty that surrounds suspect practices and their possible effects is so great that risk is an entirely suitable name for what is problematic. Recent worries about possible mishaps from the use of recombinant DNA techniques in scientific research and industrial applications seem to me a case where the term was accurately applied. But there is, in our time, a willingness to cluster an astonishingly large range of health, safety, and environmental problems under this one rubric.

Two kinds of issues in particular strike me as territory that ought to be reclaimed from this cluster. First is our understanding of cases of actual harm—cancer, birth defects, other illnesses, deaths, damaged environments, and the like—obviously connected to profit-making industrial practices, yet sometimes treated as if their reality were merely probabilistic. We may visit the hospitals and gravesites if we need to. We may wander through industrial wastelands and breathe deeply. But let us not pretend our troubles hinge on something like a gentlemanly roll of dice, or that other people's sickness and death can be deemed acceptable from some august, supposedly neutral standpoint. That only adds insult to injury.

Finally, at times an issue that urgently needs to be addressed is poorly described (or not described at all) by being subsumed under the category of risk. A technology recognized as an example of true risk in one context, recombinant DNA research and development, will be badly misconstrued if it is seen as nothing more than a risk question in another emerging context: public policy on genetic engineering. It is one thing to think about the prospect that a lethal bug might escape from the laboratory, quite another to ponder what it means to assume direct control of the evolution of the human species. Possibilities made available by the new biotechnologies are profound ones. But they are not questions of risk. It may happen, nevertheless, that because risk was the focus of discussion for the first decade of thinking about the ethical dimensions of recombinant DNA research and development, it will continue to shape discussions on this topic for years to come. We could see, for example, the application of moral rules of the following kind: Unless the development of a new genetic configuration can be shown to involve substantial quantifiable risks, the development will be sanctioned for speedy implementation. If that happens, the shortcomings of today's discussions about risk will return to us with a vengeance.

Faith in Science

Claudia Mills and Douglas MacLean

America is in love with scientists. The personal prestige of research scientists is high, and science consistently ranks toward the top of the list in polls surveying the esteem we hold for various institutions (with government consistently trailing behind). The Apollo space program remains, for many, the crowning American achievement, the standard of success against which other aspects of American life are judged—and found wanting. (As in: "If they can put a man on the moon, why can't they fix the potholes on my street?")

We tend not to blame scientists and engineers for the social and environmental problems that are the by-products of new technologies. Instead, we rely on the scientific community to tell us what the problems are and what can be done to remedy or prevent them. Increasingly, the most pressing contemporary problems seem irreducibly technical and scientific. What should we do about acid rain? The answer depends on what combination of pollutants can be pinpointed as its cause. What technological advance can prevent future industrial disasters like the one in Bhopal or future famines like the one in Ethiopia? Even the most urgent question of all, how to avoid nuclear war, is seen to be scientific at its core. Are strategic defenses technologically feasible? How bad would nuclear winter be? What do the weapons do, and what will be left after they have done it?—technical questions all.

We have extraordinary faith that science can provide the needed answers, due perhaps to a picture of scientists as detached from the world of conflicting values and competing interests. Science seems a touchstone of objectivity; whereas politicians are accountable to their constituents, and often to powerful interest groups, scientists are accountable only to the truth. Small wonder that opinion polls show that on technically intensive policy issues, most people believe that the final say should be left to the experts.

Many of the thorniest controversies involve scientific uncertainty, however, where it is not difficult to find scientists who will defend claims that lend support to opposing positions. Scientists and policy-makers, often hoping that scientific progress will in the end dissolve the disputes, are concerned in the meantime that our faith in the objectivity of science and the ultimate emergence of truth remain unshaken. Their goal is to separate facts from values in these debates as much as possible, to isolate the scientific elements from the value questions, which are then left to the political process to resolve.

According to this understanding of the issues, technically inten-sive policy problems can be broken down into two distinct compo-nents: an "objective" technical component and a "subjective" policy component. The scientific component is the province of the scientific experts, who lay out the facts—the nature of the problem and how it might be solved. The policy component is where we assess rival inter-ests and struggle to formulate common values.

This faith in scientists might be unwarranted, however, and the model of science it presupposes—science as the detached quest for truth—has itself been challenged. Perhaps scientists are more like the rest of us than we have been willing to admit, and science more kin to the rest of human intellectual endeavor. If this is so, perhaps scientists should play a different role in helping to resolve policy controver-sies—different, but no less essential.

Overconfidence

A large body of literature in the psychology of judgment and decision-making shows that people are strikingly overconfident in their judgments. Over 95 percent of us, for instance, think we are better-than-average drivers. While the same literature shows that scien-tists and engineers, particularly those skilled in dealing with risk and probability, are somewhat more likely than the rest of us to realize these mistakes and correct for them, scientific experts by and large tend to be subject to the same biases as the rest of us.

In one study on dam safety, a group of seven engineering experts was asked to estimate how high the water level would have to rise for a given dam before the dam would fail. They were asked to give a range of estimates such that they were 90 percent confident the true failure height fell within that range. The surprising result was not only that the seven estimates did not agree, but also that when the dam later failed, not one of the experts' ranges of estimates included the actual failure point. Such studies exhibit dramatically how the confidence of experts—and our confidence in experts—can be exaggerated and misplaced.

It is perhaps natural that technical experts should be especially prone to overconfidence in the area of their expertise, and in their own faith in science. Harvey Brooks, a professor of technology and public policy, argues that scientists, of all people, can hardly be expected to be objective about the implications of their own research: "In practice, if an expert has any qualifications to deal with an issue at all, he or she cannot really have a completely open mind. . . . An engineer who has chosen to devote his or her career to the perfection of a particular technology is more likely to be skeptical of any evidence of possible adverse effects of this technology than somebody less expert in that particular field."

The Intrusion of Values

Scientists are like the rest of us in other important respects as well. Unavoidably they filter their scientific judgments through their other attitudes, beliefs, and values. Brooks points out that even when experts agree on the facts, they can disagree on what the facts can be taken to prove. Some experts view a single finding of possible danger as sufficient to trigger alarm; others defend new technology as safe until proven otherwise. Where the burden of proof is lodged often depends on a submerged policy agenda. Brooks observes, "Experts have their own political preferences, and if experiments or analyses point to conclusions or policies different from those with which the experts entered the discussion, they tend to demand a higher standard of proof than they would have if the available new evidence supported their starting position."

William D. Ruckelshaus, former administrator of the Environmental Protection Agency, agrees that "values appear as important influences on the outcomes of risk assessment." He cites as an example a National Academy of Science report, which estimated that over the next 70 years the number of cases of bladder cancer caused by saccharin would be somewhere between 0.22 and 1,144,000! Since, as Ruckelshaus comments wryly, "This sort of range is of limited use to the policymaker," scientists are under pressure to opt for some narrower point on the spectrum. "Such choices," according to Ruckelshaus, "are influenced by values, which may be affected by professional training, or by ideas about what constitutes 'good science,' and, of course, by the same complex of experience and individual traits that gives rise to personal values in all of us."

A different and more troubling problem is that "the facts" cannot be lifted directly from the scientific journals and plugged into the policy debate. They must first be expressed in a way the public can understand, and how they are expressed can affect—and distort—the policy outcome. No matter how "neutral" the scientific work is, there may be no neutral description of it that can be incorporated into policy discussions. The psychological literature on decision-making shows that people's preferences are often determined by the way a choice is described to them and can change under different descriptions that appear to be equivalent. For example, lung cancer patients face the option of treatment by surgery or radiation. In one study, statistics about the effects of these two treatments were presented to different groups of people, including lung cancer patients, students, and physicians. In all groups, the choices changed markedly according to whether the expected results of the treatments were described in terms of the chances of living or the chances of dying. (And the most significant preference reversals were recorded among the physicians!) The seemingly trivial choice of terminology significantly influenced the life-and-death choice of treatment.

In policy debates, how the experts present the facts often has a good deal to do with what they want the policy outcome to be. Brooks gives a classic example: ". . . the debate, just prior to the atmospheric test ban treaty of 1963, over the effects of nuclear bomb testing fallout. Those who favored testing expressed health damage estimates in terms of the increased chances of cancer for an individual exposed to fallout. Expressed as a fraction, such increases were minimal. The critics of testing, however, often expressed the identical facts in terms of the extra deaths that would occur worldwide within a period of fifty years . . . as a result of current fallout. Such figures were very high and could be especially intimidating when quoted without comparison to other types of fatalities that occur randomly in large populations. How commentators presented the same objective hazard often depended on how they valued the societal benefits of the activity causing it."

Situations also might occur where any description of the facts is value-laden, and in such situations the bias might come in the very detachment sometimes associated with the model of science just described. Simply knowing that some action or policy will result in the deaths of some people who would not otherwise have died does not tell us whether the act is murder, killing, allowing some people to die, or even saving some lives. Many factors enter into the proper description of "the facts," and so the language, say, of physics might be an utterly inappropriate way to describe the choice between two policy options. Thus some redescriptions of a choice situation, although equivalent in the sense of not altering the probabilities or outcomes, will nevertheless be rejected for social or even psychological reasons, because they are inappropriate and distort the problem. The two-stage model—first the "objective" facts, then the "subjective" policy context—cannot deal with cases where our understanding of the facts cannot be separated from the policy context in which they are embedded.

The Objectivity of Science

The deepest objection to this model, however, challenges not the ability to separate the two stages of scientific input and policy output, but rather the objectivity imputed to the first stage. What do scientists do, we may ask, that is so much more objective than what the rest of us do as social "scientists," humanists, ordinary citizens?

The standard answer, so frequently assumed it is seldom explicitly stated, is that scientists are in the business of discovering truth—in the words of philosopher Richard Rorty, "truth as correspondence to reality, the only sort of truth worthy of the name." The idea is that there is a way the world is "out there," independent of human thought and desire, and this provides an objective standard against which scientific progress can be measured. Scholars in "softer" fields, and policymakers in the midst of the political fray, have no such clear and unbending standards against which to measure themselves. In ethics, politics, and literature, there is no independent "way the world is." *We* make the ethical rules, work out the social contract by which we enforce them, create the works of art that illuminate them.

Rorty, an influential critic of this view, suggests that, in our secular culture, science understood in this way acquires a religious dimension. "The scientist replaces the priest. The scientist is now seen as the person who keeps humanity in touch with something beyond itself. . . . truth is now thought of as the only point at which human beings are responsible to something non-human."

But this attitude and the underlying view that inspires it are, according to Rorty, both mistaken. There is no "way the world is" independent of our investigations into it and by which we measure their success—or at least it is not helpful to talk as if there were. For we have no way of ever getting beyond our own constructed system of theories and beliefs to check the correspondence. We have no way of standing back from our view of the world and matching it against how the world "really" is. All we can do is compare certain portions of our worldview with other portions, and compare our worldview with possible alternatives. The triumph of science, in Rorty's account, is not that it agrees with reality, but that scientists have managed to agree with one another: "The presence of unforced agreement . . . gives us everything in the way of 'objective truth' which one could possibly want: namely, intersubjective agreement." But in this view, "'truth' applies equally to the judgments of lawyers, anthropologists, physicists, philologists, and literary critics." The scientist can boast, then, of no special objectivity.

The Role of the Scientists

What follows from our defrocking of the scientist as priest? Where will the scientist now fit into the policy-making process? One promising answer is that we should rely less on scientists to work alone dredging up and neatly packaging the facts—and rely more on scientists to work together with the rest of us formulating and articulating our shared values.

Historian Barton J. Bernstein has looked at early research into the feasibility of the artificial heart as an example of misplaced reliance on unaided and untempered technological expertise. Scientific and medical consultants speculating in the mid-1960s reached extraordinarily optimistic conclusions about the prospects for developing a totally implantable artificial heart. Almost thirty years later the most conspicuous success of the $200 million research expenditure is the artificial heart implanted, with great media fanfare, in Barney Clark. Clark, Bernstein reports, "struggled through 112 painful days linked up to [a 350-pound] console before he died—hardly a testament to technology triumphant."

The experts' speculations were noteworthy for ignoring the possible psychological and social effects of the artificial heart on the recipient, the family, and the community, and the economic strain on the nation's health care system. More surprisingly, they also "did not adequately explain four serious technological problems: those of developing appropriate biomaterials, a pump, and a power source, and of stimulating the autonomic nervous system."

In 1972 a second committee appointed by the federal government considered the same set of problems—and came to very different conclusions. "This committee," Bernstein argues, "composed of people in fields such as law, sociology, ethics, and political science, proved more realistic, more probing, and less optimistic about the artificial heart." It defined "the profound ethical, economic, personal, and social problems" the first committee sidestepped; moreover, it showed greater sensitivity to the technical problems as well. Bernstein concludes: "The contrast suggests the danger of allowing medical experts almost exclusively to shape policy."

But if we give a less free hand to scientific experts in "objectively" defining our policy options, at the same time we may be meting out a greater freedom. The scientist's priestly garb doubles as a straitjacket,

---

and traditional notions of the scientist's role may limit the contribution the scientist can make in the policy process.

An instructive example is drawn from the relatively youthful science of ecology. Philosopher Mark Sagoff presents a dilemma ecologists face as consultants on environmental policy. Most ecologists believe they have an important role to play in shaping policy by providing arguments and reasons for why we should respect and protect the integrity and health of functioning ecosystems. But they feel that as ecologists they can promote environmental goals only by dredging up "hard," "objective" findings that show why these goals make good policy (i.e., economic) sense.

Thus ecologists have felt driven to marshal every available scientific hypothesis that uncovers quantifiable benefits to be derived from preservationist policies. Two that Sagoff cites as having been particularly influential in mobilizing public support are the "outwelling" hypothesis—that salt marshes support an abundance of marine life by pumping a rich supply of nutrients into coastal waters—and the diversity/stability hypothesis—that a diverse collection of species contributes to community stability, and, conversely, that a loss of any individual species increases the risk of ecosystem collapse. Unfortunately, both hypotheses are highly dubious, and counterexamples to both abound. But ecologists have been reluctant to disavow these hallowed creeds for fear of forfeiting all leverage in lobbying for environmental protection.

A way out of the dilemma is available, however, which Sagoff endorses. It is to realize that the task of ecologists is not just to draw up scientific-sounding arguments for the economic benefits ecosystems can produce. As ecologists, as scientists, their task is also to find "a vocabulary or conceptual framework . . . that helps us to *evaluate* not simply *control*, to *appreciate* not simply to *manipulate*, to *protect* not just to *manage*." Our society recognizes—and has codified into law— ethical, cultural, and aesthetic reasons for protecting the natural environment, and Sagoff's point is that scientists—*as scientists*—have something to say about these as well. Ecologists' professional expertise gives them a special vantage point for making sense of notions such as the "health" and "integrity" of ecosystems, and they can participate in the policy process by helping us to define and interpret these goals. This task is just as objective, and just as properly scientific, as the task of collecting data and making predictions.

Conclusion

We might do better, then, to both retrench and enhance the scientist's role in policy-making and to make room for the fuller participation of social scientists, humanists, and the lay public at all stages in the policy process. Brooks concludes, "Perhaps the principal lesson from our experience with the interaction of experts and laymen in public policy decisions of high technical or scientific content is the need for greater introspection into the nontechnical values and preferences that affect both the selection of evidence and its interpretation by all the participants, both laypersons and experts." We need a frank, open, public discussion of these values and preferences, in which both experts and the public can participate. We will be better citizens for such a debate, and the policies that emerge from it will be better policies.

The sources used in preparing this article are Harvey Brooks, "The Resolution of Technically Intensive Public Policy Disputes," Science, Technology, & Human Values, *vol. 9, no. 1 (Winter 1984); M. Hynes and E. Van Marcke, "Reliability of Embankment Performance Prediction," in* Proceedings of the ASCE Engineering Mechanics Division Specialty Conference *(Waterloo, Ontario: University of Waterloo Press, 1976); William D. Ruckleshaus, "Risk in a Free Society,"* Risk Analysis, *vol. 4, no. 3 (1984); Barbara J. MacNeil et al., "On the Elicitation of Preferences for Alternative Therapies,"* New England Journal of Medicine, *vol. 306 (May 27, 1982); Richard Rorty, "Science as Solidarity," manuscript, n.p., n.d.; Barbara J. Bernstein, "The Misguided Quest for the Artificial Heart,"* Technology Review *(November/December 1984); and Mark Sagoff, "Environmental Science and Environmental Law,"* Institute for Philosophy and Public Policy Working Paper FE-2 *(College Park, Md.: Institute for Philosophy and Public Policy, 1985).*

Rethinking Rationality

Claudia Mills and Douglas MacLean

Just when you were getting used to the idea that alfalfa sprouts cause cancer and exercise causes infertility, word came about the possible threat posed by radon in your home. Every night local news stations advertised their evening report by a teaser promising more information on the threat of this invisible form of indoor air pollution. The estimated chance of death by radon, even in the most pessimistic accounts, is far smaller than the chance of dying in a car accident; yet few news broadcasts try to attract viewers by headlines promising defensive driving tips. Likewise, everyone is afraid of getting AIDS; far fewer dread diabetes, a much more prolific killer.

It is well known that people's worries about various risks correlate poorly with the actual dangers they pose. Our judgments are seriously flawed, and it seems that at the very least, our attitudes about risk are often inconsistent, if not perverse.

Of course, those charged with inconsistency in such matters are free to respond, "So I'm inconsistent. Big deal!" Many would join with Ralph Waldo Emerson in holding that "consistency is the hobgoblin of little minds," or with William Allen White that "consistency is a paste jewel that only cheap men cherish." We may have our own reasons to pick and choose our own fears, whether or not our choices line up with somebody else's dispassionate assessment of what is truly fearsome.

Yet consistency in some form defines what it is to be rational, and we are less complacent about the charge of irrationality. Certain principles of consistency in our choices—so obvious, on first reflection, that they hardly need stating—have been taken to constitute what rationality is. If risk is what you care about, and automobiles are riskier than radon in the home, isn't it irrational not to adjust your concerns about the two accordingly?

If it turns out that people are indeed irrational in their attitudes toward risk, this has troubling implications for many of our public policies governing risk. In a democracy, public attitudes are the cornerstone for policies; they are embodied in the laws we pass and reflected in regulations that give those laws substance. If public opinion on regulatory issues is shaped by frivolous or confused considerations, this bodes ill for our prospects of establishing rational public policies.

Perhaps, however, apparent inconsistencies in our attitudes about risks can be given some other explanation. Perhaps people focus concern on certain risks because they are responding to factors researchers are simply failing to measure. Or perhaps the standard model of rationality cannot accommodate the complexities of human reasoning. How rational or irrational *are* we? And how much does this matter?

Who Cares about Risk Anyway?

A first, sympathetic explanation of why people worry disproportionately about certain risks—out of proportion to the riskiness of the risk—is that the category of *risk* hardly exhausts the full range of what most of us care about in our daily lives. People talk about risk and experts talk about risk, but the two groups may be talking past each other, for "risk" often seems just a convenient label to slap on a broad family of other concerns.

Risk-analysts compute the chance of dying from a given activity, but most people care not only about their chance of dying but about what life is like while they are living it. Trade-offs between quality and quantity of life are made all the time in personal decisions about health and safety. Mark Twain, told that he could add five years to his life by giving up smoking and drinking, reportedly quipped that five years without smoking and drinking weren't worth living. Similar trade-offs are relevant in the policy arena as well.

Thus people may prefer one technology to another for reasons other than the actual risks to life and health associated with it. They tend to care about the form of social organization it encourages (solar power lends itself to decentralization, while nuclear power is by its nature highly centralized), about the control they feel they have over its risks (one, perhaps specious, reason for worrying less about driving than flying), about whether the risks are assumed voluntarily or imposed by others, about whether these occur now or later, affect many or few, and so forth.

These factors help to explain some of the results experts find so puzzling. If risk-analysts are preoccupied exclusively with risk, while our concerns are more diverse and wide-ranging, it is not surprising that their research should deliver a verdict of irrationality. But here the fault lies not in how human beings think about risk, but in an overly narrow and restrictive focus of measurement.

Other findings are less easily explained, however, by pointing to a richness in our values overlooked by risk-analysts. They suggest that people are often driven by indefensible cognitive processes—at least some of the time we simply process information in crazy ways.

Failing Grades in Probability

Measurements of risk have two components: an assessment of the probability of some outcome and an assessment of whether that outcome would be good or bad (and how good or bad it would be). Thus opportunities arise for people to make two different kinds of mistakes.

First, we can make erroneous judgments about probabilities. Many of the laws of probability have a counter-intuitive flavor, and temptations to fallacy are common. Most of us have to struggle to resist the so-called gambler's fallacy, the wistful belief that after enough successive losses the odds have to favor a win. Only reluctantly do we abandon our gut feeling that after five coins in a row have come up heads, surely the next coin will come up tails, despite the mathematician's insistence that the odds on any fair coin toss remain fifty/fifty.

The gambler's fallacy is an obvious and familiar example of a cognitive failure. More interesting is research on how poorly people do at probabilistic reasoning even when they appear to be doing it quite well.

Most of us, who can hardly balance our checkbooks without a pocket calculator, wisely eschew complicated calculations of probabilities in favor of simple rules of thumb, or heuristics, that help us assess probabilities in a rough-and-ready way. Pioneering psychologists Daniel Kahneman and Amos Tversky have studied many of these heuristics. One is "salience," or the ease with which we can call examples of a certain kind of occurrence to mind. Salience is a generally reliable guide to likely patterns in the world around us: We can think of fewer redheads than brunettes in our acquaintance because brunettes indeed outnumber redheads in the population. But such heuristics can lead us to make mistakes, as when the salience of some risk is reinforced by undue media attention (another possible reason why airplane crashes are more feared than automobile accidents). On balance, however, the heuristics Kahneman and Tversky identify, unlike the gambler's fallacy, are promising strategies for coping efficiently with the uncertainties we face. It is not surprising that even the best heuristics will not always give the same results one would get if one took the trouble to figure in the specifics of the case, but it is surely reasonable to sacrifice some accuracy for convenience.

What *is* surprising, however, is the extent to which these heuristics dominate even obviously relevant countervailing information. Tversky and Kahneman have shown that when heuristics are triggered, people let themselves completely ignore information that may be far more important but less salient. In one study, Tversky and Kahneman asked people to judge whether an individual selected from some population was more likely to be an engineer or a lawyer, where the population consisted of 70 percent engineers and 30 percent lawyers. Such "base rate data" about the background population is crucial to assessing probabilities correctly. They found that in the absence of any description of the individual's characteristics and traits, people's judgments were based on what they knew about the percentage of lawyers and engineers in the population, but "prior probabilities were effectively ignored when a description was introduced, even when this description was totally uninformative." When asked to decide if some undescribed Tom was more likely to be a lawyer or an engineer, subjects guessed he was 70 percent likely to be an engineer, but when they were asked about Dick, who was described simply as a "30 year old man, married with no children," these subjects opted for a fifty/fifty probability.

The conclusion to draw from such research seems fairly straightforward. We not only rely on heuristics but are dominated by them, even when we should not be. When it comes to judging probabilities, people are, with some frequency, simply wrong.

Knowing What We Value

A more controversial and troubling realm of error lies in the way people value outcomes. We may expect people to be poor at assessing probabilities, but we want to give them credit for at least knowing their own minds when it comes to assigning values to the outcomes of their choices. They can confidently judge which of two alternatives is the more attractive.

Or can they? Another striking finding of Kahneman and Tversky is that people's value-judgments are notoriously influenced by the way in which various choices are framed. Every retailer knows that customers consider $99 a far more attractive price than one a mere dollar higher, while the difference between $97 and $98 makes no difference at all. Similarly, customers tend to be delighted by a discount for cash payment, but bristle at a surcharge for using credit cards—although such policies can usually be described either way.

Tversky and Kahneman thus have described the systematic nature of how preferences are affected by the way a problem is framed. They have scientifically grounded the suspicion that people prefer the "half full" cup over the "half empty" cup, showing the extent to which framing does indeed affect judgment, even on some important policy issues.

Kahneman and Tversky ask us to suppose that the United States is preparing for the outbreak of an unusual Asian disease, which is expected to kill 600 people unless action is taken. Two alternative programs to combat the disease have been proposed. If program A is adopted, 200 people will be saved. If program B is adopted, there is a 1/3 probability that 600 people will be saved and a 2/3 probability that no people will be saved. When the alternatives were posed in these terms in a test survey, 72 percent of respondents opted for program A, only 28 percent for program B. A second group was given the same options, but described in this way: If program A is adopted, 400 people will die; if program B is adopted, there is a 1/3 probability that nobody will die, and a 2/3 probability that 600 people will die. This time only 22 percent opted for the first program, while 78 percent opted for the second—a clear preference reversal. The framing of the question proved decisive in eliciting a response. When program A was seen as involving a gain of 200 lives, it was rated far more favorably than when it was seen as involving a loss of 400.

This research, moreover, reveals not only the extent to which framing affects what is perceived as a loss or a gain, but also a deep and abiding asymmetry in how losses and gains are regarded. In study after study, people show more concern about avoiding a loss than receiving an equivalent gain. In one experiment, for example, researchers Jack Knetsch and J. A. Sinden gave half their subjects tickets to a lottery and the other half $3. When the first group was given an opportunity to sell their tickets for $3, 82 percent kept them, but when the second group was allowed to buy lottery tickets for their $3, only 38 percent wanted the tickets. Human beings seem strongly disposed, for whatever reason, to defend their own personal status quo, to hang on to what they've got. Tversky and Kahneman call this tendency "loss aversion."

Framing effects and loss aversion together explain an important class of preference reversals. People value gains and losses differently, and the framing of a problem determines a "reference point" for viewing outcomes as gains or losses. In the Asian disease example, the description of the problem determines whether people see the alternatives as lives saved or lives lost, which in turn determines preferences among the alternatives.

Is loss aversion irrational? In one popular model of economic rationality it is. According to this conception, what matters is the bottom line, where you end up, whether you got there by avoiding a loss or forgoing a gain. But for others, the choice process itself may legitimately matter to us, as well as its ultimate outcome. We have a common set of reactive attitudes, like regret and reproach, which are often provoked by the decisions or choices we make and not just by the choiceless outcomes that result from our decisions. The very same outcome might provoke delight in one context—some small gain you were lucky to realize—but regret in another, for example, if you could have done far better by choosing differently.

It is not always reasonable to be affected by such attitudes, of course, but given their persistence and pervasiveness, we may do well to factor them into our decisions. For example, if your acquaintances, your boss, or your constituents are more likely to hold you responsible for the losses that result from your risky decisions than for the lost opportunities that result from choosing to avoid risks, then choosing to avoid a loss rather than to maximize the expected outcome would seem to be an eminently prudent strategy. An adequate conception of rational choice should assess the value of decision processes them-selves and our reasonable reactive attitudes and aversions. This would involve a more complex understanding of alternatives than exclu-sively focusing on outcomes in the measurement of risk.

We might accept loss aversion, but what about our susceptibility to framing effects? Surely preference reversals in cases like the Asian dis-ease example are irrational. After all, the two programs of disease con-trol remain the same, however described. Nevertheless, the issue of framing effects might be more complicated. If two different descrip-tions cover the same choices, rationality requires that we make the same decision in each case. Stated in this way, the principle seems hardly exceptionable. But the problem is that there may be no clear way to determine what counts as a redescription of the same prospect, rather than descriptions of different prospects. Is the situation of some-one who gained some money and lost it gambling the same or differ-ent from that of someone who never had any money to begin with? While framing can determine the reference point for viewing different possible outcomes as gains or losses, there may be no general way to determine what the correct reference point should be. One's current position is not always an appropriate benchmark. A raise in salary, for example, might trigger delight by comparison to one's actual salary, but disappointment compared to one's legitimate expectations.

Much of the moral fabric of our lives depends on finding the appropriate descriptions of objects and events that, from some detached perspective, could equally well be described in some other way. A person's arm can be seen as a human limb or as meat and bones. Assessments of guilt and responsibility, in law and in morality, often turn on what description of an event is true or most appropriate. And our culture is currently divided deeply on whether a human fetus is a person or merely a human organism.

Finally, some recent research in this area suggests further complexities, that people's value judgments apparently depend not only on how the outcomes of a choice are framed, but also on the framing of the choice itself, the process for eliciting the judgments of gain or loss. Paul Slovic of Decision Research, Inc., has shown that we will get a different picture of the value people place on, say, tea or coffee, according to whether we ask them whether they *prefer* tea to coffee, whether they judge tea to be *better* than coffee, or whether they would be *willing to pay more* for tea than for coffee. This research also reveals some remarkable preference reversals. Some of Slovic's examples focus on a choice between two bets with roughly equal expected payoffs: One has a higher probability of winning, while the other involves a smaller chance of a larger gain. People prefer to take the higher probability bet, but they are willing to pay more for the chance to take the other. Again, according to one popular conception of rationality, values, preferences, and choices should reflect the same consistent ordering, so these reversals would be irrational. But some of Slovic's results might be taken instead to show how values can be expressed in importantly different ways. We might value some things deeply, for example, but think it inappropriate or wrong to pay for them at all.

What Should We Conclude?

The conclusions from this research are mixed. We find some striking examples of human fallibility and some clear limits to human rationality. But other cases show plain folks exhibiting reasoning that may not square with expert assessments of risk but nonetheless does not seem obviously faulty. On the one hand, people do poorly at judging probabilities and are persistently led astray by framing effects. On the other hand, their reasoning often shows both good sense and a sensitive appreciation of the complex nature of difficult choices.

In any case, it is doubtful people will ever change to become more fully rational. Tversky and Kahneman's research findings, confirmed in countless studies over many years, show that people's patterns of choice are amazingly tenacious and persist at all levels of education and technical sophistication. In a country where most adults would be hard-pressed to find a least common denominator between two fractions, education in the laws of probability and in the subtleties of risk analysis is going to produce limited results. We are going to have to deal with people as they are.

Nor does increased reliance on expert risk analysis seem to provide a better foundation for public policy. Our irrationality shows the need for expert guidance in risk management, but the complexities in our values also suggest that the expert's analytic techniques for revealing public values may be flawed. Nobody ever said that democracy, with its reliance on the popular will, would produce the best results all of the time, but only results that were preferable on balance to those generated by alternative arrangements. We seem to be more rational than animals, less rational than angels, or computers. In other words, human.

The sources quoted in this article are Amos Tversky and Daniel Kahneman, "The Framing of Decisions and the Psychology of Choice," Science, *vol. 211 (1981); Tversky and Kahneman, "Rational Choice and the Framing of Decisions,"* Journal of Business, *vol. 59 (1986); Jack L. Knetsch and J. A. Sinden, "Willingness to Pay and Compensation Demanded: Experimental Evidence of an Unexpected Disparity in Measures of Value,"* The Quarterly Journal of Economics *(August 1984); and Paul Slovic, "Preference Reversals,"* Institute for Philosophy and Public Policy Working Paper RR-2 (College Park, Md.: Institute for Philosophy and Public Policy, March 1987).*

FOR FURTHER READING

Kahneman, Daniel, Paul Slovic, and Amos Tversky. *Judgment Under Uncertainty: Heuristics and Biases.* New York: Cambridge University Press, 1982.

Kelman, Steven. "Cost-Benefit Analysis: An Ethical Critique," *Regulation* 5 (January/February 1981).

MacLean, Douglas, ed. *Values at Risk.* Maryland Studies in Public Philosophy. Totowa, N.J.: Rowman and Allanheld, 1986.

Page, Talbot. *Conservation and Economic Efficiency.* Baltimore: Johns Hopkins University Press, 1977.

Tversky, Amos, and Daniel Kahneman, "The Framing of Decisions and the Psychology of Choice," *Science* 211 (1981).

PART II

ETHICAL ISSUES IN THE LAW, THE MEDIA, AND MEDICINE

4

THE LAW

Nowhere are our values exposed more clearly, nowhere do they clash more directly, than in the domain of the law. Lawyers and judges face a tangle of ethical issues on a daily basis, knowing that the answers they give will have concrete consequences for the human beings whose lives are at stake in the legal case unfolding. This chapter explores a few of the ethical issues faced by lawyers, judges, and society at large in determining the shape of the legal structure under which we all live.

In "Why We Mistrust Lawyers," David Luban quotes Carl Sandburg's lines: "Why is there always a secret singing when a lawyer cashes in? Why does a hearse horse snicker hauling a lawyer away?" The answer he gives is that the *role morality* of lawyers— what lawyers do, and indeed are professionally obligated to do, in representing their clients—may be at odds with the dictates of *ordinary morality*, the ethical standards that govern our behavior, and the lawyer's too, in everyday life, once professional roles have been left behind. Thus according to the dictates of their professional code of ethics, lawyers may be expected to shield morally reprehensible individuals, zealously assist in morally dubious projects, and keep immoral confidences, sometimes at a terrible cost to third parties. These three examples—involving immoral clients, adversary zeal, and confidentiality— are treated separately in the next three articles. Here Luban looks at the conflict between role morality and ordinary morality more generally. He considers various justifications for maintaining a distinction between the two, but concludes that in the end "role morality grants the lawyer no moral privileges or immunities. It may turn out that anything morally wrong for a nonlawyer to do on behalf of another is morally wrong for a lawyer to do as well."

The next three articles each treat in further detail particular conflicts between ordinary and legal role morality. "Representing Immoral Clients" asks whether a lawyer is under a moral obligation to take on a repugnant client—or is the lawyer under a moral obligation to send such a client away? Are lawyers like butchers and bakers, selling their services to any and all customers, whatever their moral character? The analogy seems strained, for the lawyer acts in a far more direct way to further a client's morally dubious projects, and the law, dealing as it does in rights and justice, is an area of especially vital concern. But if lawyers refuse to represent immoral clients, they essentially preempt the full judicial process, setting themselves up as extra-judicial tribunals. If every lawyer refuses a case, some individual will be left without representation, perhaps with urgent legal needs unmet. Lawyers, then, must weigh their obligations to promote justice, to respect human dignity, and to preserve their own moral integrity.

"The Zealous Lawyer: Is Winning the Only Thing?" considers the lawyer's professionally mandated duty of adversary zeal on behalf of a client. The ABA Code of Professional Responsibility dictates, "The duty of a lawyer, both to his client and to the legal system, is to represent his client zealously within the bounds of the law." The article examines this duty of zealous advocacy in the arenas of criminal justice, civil litigation, business law, administrative law, and public interest law. It concludes that zealous advocacy is appropriate and justified in criminal defense, but "in civil law, business law, administrative law, and public interest law, zeal must be tempered by a respect for truth and justice, and adversariness must often give way to a thoughtful and sensitive attempt to explore large and difficult questions about where the public interest lies."

"To Tell or Not to Tell: Conflicts about Confidentiality" looks at the ethical conflicts lawyers and other professionals (doctors, priests, company employees, government workers) face when asked to keep secrets that concern threats to third parties or the public welfare. How do we balance special duties of confidentiality against the possibly grave harms that a breach of confidentiality might avert? Two guidelines are suggested: Obligations of confidentiality vary with the kind and degree of harm threatened to others, and they are weaker as the secrets concealed belong to large collectivities rather than lone individuals.

The next two articles concern further issues about legal practice. David Luban in "Should Lawyers Advertise?" examines arguments for and against restrictions on legal advertising and solicitation. He considers the objections that advertising helps to fuel a litigation explosion and compromises lawyers' professionalism, but concludes that advertising and solicitation are more than justified in leading to lower costs and improved access for citizens in need of legal services. In "Should Legal Services Rise Again?" Luban raises and responds to four common objections to "impact" or class-action lawsuits filed by publicly funded lawyers: It is wrong to use the tax money of people opposed to liberal aims and programs to further them; impact cases divert legal attention from the lower-profile legal needs of numerous poor clients; lawyers bent on law reform sometimes recruit clients as plaintiffs, using the legal system to achieve ends the lawyers have chosen independently of the wishes of the people they ostensibly represent; and it is wrong for groups unable to get what they want through ordinary democratic means to frustrate the democratic will by obtaining their aims in court. Luban concludes, however, that class-action suits as a tool of law reform have provided "a service to democracy, not an assault on it."

Two articles address the judge's role in the legal process. "Judicial Activism versus Judicial Restraint" by David Luban takes on the continuing controversy over the role of judges in interpreting and shaping the law. The terms "judicial activism" and "judicial restraint" are usually used as all-but-empty slogans, or as euphemisms for "liberal" and "conservative," respectively. But Luban, submitting the pair to closer scrutiny, finds at least seven different ways judges can play a more or less activist role in interpreting the law. In some, legal activism is plainly unjustified; in others, it is precisely what judges, as judges, are supposed to do.

"Settling out of Court" takes on a different question about a judge's responsibilities: whether and to what degree judges should encourage the parties to a legal case to settle their dispute out of court. Most filed lawsuits—upwards of 85 percent—do not reach trial; if they did, our legal system, on all accounts, would collapse under their weight. The imperative toward settlement is defended on other, less purely expedient grounds as well; it increases participant satisfaction with the legal process, producing a voluntary compromise rather than a coercive winner-take-all judicial verdict. But reasons exist—most notably, a concern with the quality of justice provided the parties as well as with the effects of settlement on third parties and the public at large—for thinking that the current enthusiastic trend toward settling cases out of court should be discouraged rather than encouraged, and at the very least regulated more carefully.

The last three articles in Chapter 4 round out the examination of the law by considering, in turn, jury awards of large punitive damages to plaintiffs, the current crisis facing the insurance industry and tort system, and, finally, the nature and special wrong of entrapment. In "Two Cheers for Punitive Damages," David Luban examines punitive damages in light of the staple justifications offered for punishment more generally: particularly deterrence, retribution, and what Luban calls "norm projection." In "Confronting the Insurance Crisis," Alan Strudler looks at the staggering rise in insurance premiums, held to be a direct effect of the soaring costs of lawsuits under our tort system. Clearly the tort system could stand to be reformed, but "what one counts as an attractive tort reform depends on what one regards as the proper goal of the tort system." If the principal goal is compensating victims, Strudler suggests, a broad no-fault approach might serve this goal more efficiently and more fairly as well. In "What Is Wrong with Entrapment?" John Kleinig raises the thorny questions of what constitutes legal entrapment of a criminal defendant and why exactly entrapment ought to function as a legal defense to the charge of criminal wrongdoing. Kleinig examines both the traditional "subjective" approach (placing the emphasis on the defendant's prior disposition to commit a crime) and the contrasting "objective" approach (which focuses on the character of the state's involvement in the commission of the crime in question). Kleinig finds problems with both approaches and recommends an alternative occupying a middle ground between the two.

Why We Mistrust Lawyers

David Luban

People sometimes wonder about lawyers. The legal profession enjoys enormous prestige and respect, yet we also view it with suspicion. Folklore says lawyers are smart, but they are sharpers. They are pragmatic, useful, but unprincipled. Every attorney knows he or she is not a folk hero. Carl Sandburg's lines reflect the popular attitude: "Why is there always a secret singing/When a lawyer cashes in?/Why does a hearse horse snicker/Hauling a lawyer away?"

Attorneys are indignant, justifiably, at the suggestion that their general run of honesty is lower than that of the common run of humanity. Thoughtful lawyers are apt to suggest that the public confuses the morality of a lawyer with that of his or her client; it assumes that a profession willing to counsel dishonest and unworthy clients is itself unworthy and dishonest. But the public is wrong, for if lawyers were to do otherwise, they would be setting themselves up as private gatekeepers of the legal system, usurping the functions of judge and jury. For this reason it is the essential condition of advocacy that the attorney's morals and the client's are totally distinct.

A lawyer, then, may have a moral duty to assist in an immoral case. Yet we think that no one is morally bound to assist immorality. We may describe this as a conflict between *ordinary morality* and the *role morality* of lawyers. These do not always conflict, of course; for example, both ordinary morality and role morality would condemn a lawyer who swindles a client. But cases will arise where the conflict is quite pointed, and these entitle us to ask how the demands of a professional role can override ordinary moral requirements that we thought were binding on everybody.

Lawyers' codes of professional responsibility do not always address these problems. They ignore many of the morally problematic situations lawyers face in the course of their professional lives. This is not surprising, since these codes specify only the role obligations of lawyers. The course of action they dictate may be inappropriate for cases where these obligations and ordinary morality come into conflict.

Examples of Conflict

There are examples aplenty of genuine conflicts between ordinary morality and lawyers' role morality:

> The client is the prosperous president of a savings-and-loan association. In leaner days he had borrowed almost $5,000 from a man working for him as a carpenter. He now wishes to avoid repaying the debt by running the statute of limitations. He is sued by the carpenter and calls his lawyer [*Zabella* v. *Pakel,* 242 F. 2d 452 (1957)].

The ABA Code of Professional Responsibility is unambiguous about the lawyer's duty in this example: "A lawyer shall not intentionally fail to seek the lawful objectives of his client through reasonably available means permitted by law." Role morality demands that the lawyer assist his client in this project. From the point of view of ordinary morality, however, it is morally wrong to assist someone in reneging on his legitimate debt.

> The client has raped a woman, been found guilty by reason of insanity, and institutionalized. He wishes to appeal the decision by asserting a technical defense, namely, that he was denied the right to a speedy trial. [*Langworthy* v. *State,* 39 Md. App. 559 (1978), *rev'd,* 284 Md. 588 (1979)].

In this example, the client is not attempting to do something immoral, but it is, nevertheless, clearly contrary to the general interest to loose a mad rapist on the public. From the point of view of ordinary morality, the lawyer who asserts this defense is acting irresponsibly. As in the previous example, however, the ABA Code specifies an adamantine duty to assert the client's legal rights, including the technical defense.

> A youth, badly injured in an automobile wreck, sues the driver responsible for the injury. The driver's defense lawyer has his own doctor examine the youth; the doctor discovers an aortic aneurism, apparently caused by the accident, that the boy's doctor had not found. The aneurism is life-threatening unless operated on. But the defense lawyer realizes that if the youth learns of the aneurism, he will demand a much higher settlement. [*Spaulding* v. *Zimmerman,* 116 N.W. 2d 704 (1962)].

The lawyer's role responsibilities are again unambiguous. He must keep the client's secrets unless the client is contemplating commission of a crime. Secrets are, according to the Code, "information gained in the professional relationship . . . the disclosure of which . . . would be likely to be detrimental to the client." Thus, the knowledge of the aneurism is a secret. Nevertheless, it is plain that ordinarily, without the special duty of confidentiality, it would be incumbent on a person to tell the youth. An innocent life is at stake.

One says in discussions of examples like these: The lawyer is free to refuse the case. Indeed, if the lawyer's outrage is great enough to prejudice his judgment, he is required to do so. Now, it must be admitted that refusal or withdrawal from a morally troublesome case may be the most practical method to relieve a lawyer of an otherwise intolerable conflict. But that such a strategy is available does not resolve the moral issue itself, for our adversary system is based on the proposition that *some* lawyer should take the case. If it is morally *obligatory* for the "last lawyer in town" to do so, it must be morally *permissible* for him. But of course, what is permissible for the last lawyer in town is permissible for any lawyer, else legal ethics become a matter of musical chairs where the last lawyer to opt out of the role is the loser. Thus, the possibility of opting out does not yield a strategy for reconciling the lawyer's role with ordinary morality. Nor does it resolve the examples to note that in each the problem arises from a law that permits morally dubious outcomes. It is too simple to blame the law rather than the lawyer, for in every case the lawyer must decide to be the agent who brings about the outcome. It is the lawyer who pushes the red button.

Resolving the Conflict

We may want to resolve conflicts between ordinary morality and role morality by denying that any meaningful distinction exists between the two. If it is morally wrong to harm an innocent person gratuitously, then how can going to law school, being admitted to the bar, and taking money for the action make it right? The distinction might also be denied by defending the universality of role morality. Sociologists suggest that we always act in some social role or other. Every role carries with it its own behavioral norms. By this reasoning, all moralities must accommodate to roles, and we should be skeptical of the notion of an ordinary morality that fails to make these accommodations. Thus, the distinction seems doubly suspect.

If we allow the distinction, we must explain exactly how an appeal to role morality is supposed to justify an action that would otherwise seem morally unacceptable. An obvious move is to claim that (1) moral responsibility for the action falls on the role itself and not on the role agent, and (2) the role itself is morally desirable. The first of these, however, is simply false. We would not allow a torturer to evade moral responsibility by saying, "I personally would never pull out your toenails, but that's my job." If the role is immoral, its immorality accuses, not excuses, the person who holds it. Thus, the whole burden of the argument falls on the claim that the role is a morally good one.

But even the goodness of the role itself may not turn out to matter. In the second example, for instance, we might find ourselves inclined to say, "Who cares about the role? All that matters is that this lawyer is loosing a mad rapist on the city." However desirable the lawyer's role might generally be, the act it requires in this case certainly leads to an undesirable result. The goodness of the role matters only if we do not evaluate role-derived actions as isolated cases, but think of them instead as instances of policies that are morally good. If we describe what the lawyer is doing as "defending the right of an improperly tried individual to his freedom" rather than "loosing a mad rapist on the city," his act seems to promote the public interest, because the general policy is a beneficial one.

The question, then, is whether the individual action or the general policy that requires it is the proper subject of moral evaluation. The appeal to role morality assumes that the evaluation of policies rather than individual acts is the right approach—that, for example, if the policy of zealous advocacy is on balance a good one, the lawyer should follow it even on occasions when he or she knows it will result in harm. And indeed, a good reason for putting policies over acts is that it leads to greater predictability and regularity in social behavior. If we could not count on persons occupying certain social roles to act according to the expectations of the roles, we would live in a very capricious society indeed.

A strong case can be made, however, in favor of directing moral evaluation to individual acts instead. An agent confronts decisions one at a time: If, after balancing the wrong done by breaking role against the wrong done by acting in role, the agent sees that an action is morally unacceptable, it cannot be correct to sweep this insight under the rug by saying that the individual action is not the proper subject of moral evaluation. But if acts rather than policies are the object of moral judgments, it may not be possible to justify behavior by appealing to social roles.

An Analogy to Public Officials

The conflict between role obligations and ordinary morality is a familiar one in politics, where the risk of "dirty hands" is especially acute. Moral compromise is the risk if one is to act in the public realm: To try to keep clean hands is self-indulgent. The morality of clean hands is the morality of private life; it is superseded by a role morality when one becomes a public official, because the community interest is more important than one's own private interest, even one's private *moral* interest. That, at any rate, is the most plausible justification of political morality.

Now, the lawyer resembles the public official in certain obvious respects. Like the politician, the lawyer seeks to promote certain interests through verbal and persuasive means, in a situation frequently marked by maneuvering and threats. Most importantly, the lawyer, like the politician, is acting on behalf of someone else; both lawyer and official represent a constituency.

But there's the rub. The conflict between political and ordinary morality is resolved in favor of the former only because of the importance of the public interest. The lawyer, however, typically represents private and not public interests. Even so-called public interest lawyers treat the public interest they hope to represent through the persons of private clients. How can the attorney claim to be bound by the "dirty hands" morality of public officials when he or she is acting on behalf of a merely private interest? How can a lawyer ever be permitted to do for a private client what neither would be permitted to do for himself?

Conclusion

This is not intended to deny that overriding role obligations may justify otherwise suspect legal practices. But if the notion of a role morality that can at times supplant ordinary morality is to be made coherent, a sophisticated account must be offered of this distinction, an account that spells out exactly how role morality is to be appealed to in offering justifications for action. If the analogy to public officials is to be pressed, similarities between the concept of legal and political representation must be carefully explored.

If such clarification is not forthcoming, it may turn out that role morality grants the lawyer no moral privileges or immunities. It may turn out that anything morally wrong for a nonlawyer to do on behalf of another person is morally wrong for a lawyer to do as well. The legal profession may have to find another exculpating plea to offer Sandburg's hearse horse.

Representing Immoral Clients

Claudia Mills

When the Nazis wanted to march through the neighborhoods of Holocaust victims in Skokie, ACLU lawyers defended their right to march. When Charles Manson, the Boston Strangler, and the Midtown Slasher went to trial, they all had lawyers by their side. Powerful corporate conglomerates hire armies of lawyers to assist them in crowding out any struggling competition. Anyone in our country who wants to welch on any debt or weasel out of any obligation can probably find a lawyer ready to take on his case.

Under our judicial system, every criminal defendant who so wishes must be represented by legal counsel. However heinous the offense, however frank the avowal of guilt, some lawyer undertakes the representation. In unsavory suits as well, many lawyers are willing to make their services available. Often it seems clear to many of us in these cases which side is the "good" side, which side ought, in the name of justice, to prevail. Yet some lawyer is dedicating the full measure of his professional devotion to furthering the cause of the other side.

Both lawyers and philosophers have raised difficult moral questions about the representation of "repugnant" clients. Is a lawyer under a moral obligation to take on a repugnant client, or under a moral obligation to send the client away? Or is the decision to represent properly left to the lawyer's own professional discretion? Is the lawyer damned if she takes the case, damned if she doesn't, or neither?

The Lawyer as Butcher and Baker

The current ABA Code of Professional Responsibility leaves the decision to represent largely up to the individual lawyer. While the Code is not particularly clear or explicit on these matters, it seems to state that lawyers have no duty to represent any given client, aside from duties imposed by court-ordered appointments, or generalized duties of pro bono service. "A lawyer is under no obligation to act as advisor or advocate for every person who may wish to become his client." A lawyer has a duty to refuse representation only "if the intensity of his personal feeling . . . may impair his effective representation of a prospective client."

This position acquires initial plausibility from an analogy between the legal profession and many other sorts of jobs. The butcher and baker, it is argued, may sell their goods or services to whomever they please, within fairly broad limits. (They may not discriminate against customers on the basis of race, for example.) The butcher does not have to sell his pork chops to every Tom, Dick, and Harry who happens along. Nor, on the other side, must he refuse to deal with customers who show themselves less than morally upright. The choice belongs to the butcher.

This account requires some qualification, however. We might criticize the butcher on moral grounds for sending a poor and starving customer away empty-handed. Or suppose that the butcher knew that one of his frozen lamb chops would be used as a murder weapon, with the evidence conveniently cooked in a post-crime supper. Would he have the right to avert his eyes as he rang up the sale?

Furthermore, the butcher-lawyer analogy may itself be questioned on two counts. First, the lawyer interacts with clients far more extensively and intimately than the butcher does. The lawyer acts in a more direct way to further their morally dubious projects. Second, the legal profession may be argued to have a special moral dimension many other lines of work do not. The butcher deals in ribs and steaks—the lawyer deals in rights and justice. Defending rights and promoting justice are not incidental components of what lawyers do in carrying out their professional tasks. Justice and rights are at the heart of what the legal profession is about.

Refusing the Immoral Client

Philosopher Virginia Held of the City University of New York argues that a lawyer's decision to accept or reject a prospective client should be heavily influenced by a concern for justice and individual rights. The lawyer must ask whether a prospective client has a moral (as well as legal) right to press his or her claim, and whether the interests of justice will be best served by representing such a client.

In criminal cases, of course, every defendant has a constitutional right to counsel, and usually also a moral right to defend himself against the awesome power of the state. In civil cases, however, there is no constitutional right to counsel. There may be a moral right to *some* legal representation, but not to representation by any *particular* lawyer. In Held's view, "A lawyer must first of all exercise responsibility in considering whether he or she is morally permitted to sell legal services to people exercising legal rights they should not, on moral grounds, be permitted to have." Lawyers in our society wield a great deal of power; they are able, for good or for ill, to help alter our judicial system and strengthen or weaken its respect for political and economic rights. In exercising this power responsibly, the lawyer's choice of clients is extremely important.

Even for criminal cases, Held maintains that lawyers have an obligation to choose clients carefully. Here, too, "those most deserving of an outcome favorable to them in a legal controversy ought to have the strongest legal talent on their side. Lawyers should . . . employ their talents in behalf of those clients who most clearly deserve them." Unless she is the "last lawyer in town," the lawyer should refuse to sell her services for a morally repugnant cause.

Representing the Immoral Client

On the other side of this dispute are those who argue that the lawyer has instead an obligation to *withhold* independent moral judgment. The lawyer does not serve justice by heeding but by muffling the still small voice of his private conscience. Judge George Sharswood, in his 1854 treatise on professional responsibility, wrote that "The lawyer, who refuses his professional assistance because in his judgment the case is unjust and indefensible, usurps the functions of both judge and jury." In both civil and criminal cases, the final decision is to be reached through the full judicial process, and not preempted by the lawyer's personal verdict.

Does this mean that a criminal lawyer should defend even the known guilty? Charles Wolfram, professor at Cornell Law School, identifies this as the traditional lawyers' reply: "Defense of the known guilty is appropriate in order that the established governmental system, and not private legal perceptions, determine guilt and innocence." Even in cases of seemingly cut-and-dried guilt (and guilt is rarely if ever *that* cut or *that* dried), lawyers should not set themselves up as extrajudicial tribunals.

In civil cases as well, Alan Donagan, philosophy professor at the California Institute of Technology, argues for the right of individuals to pursue, so far as the law permits, what they take to be reasonable and justifiable ends. In a complex and complicated society like our own, one person's ends may very well come into conflict with another's, and "persons of honor in a free society" may disagree about what would count as a just resolution. Frequently such conflicts will be carried into the courts.

According to Donagan, "A society fails in respect to the human dignity of its citizens if it fails to allow them a fair opportunity to raise such questions about what is due to them under the law before properly constituted courts, and to defend themselves against claims upon themselves or charges against themselves; it would so fail if it denied them the opportunity to hire legal advisors whose professional obligation would be . . . to represent them in doing these things."

Now, "whatever a lawyer may believe about his client's case, [typically] he cannot deny the possibility that his client may be morally as well as legally in the right." It behooves the lawyer, therefore, to reserve his private judgment and, by accepting some morally dubious cases, assist in maintaining a legal system in which the human dignity of all claimants is equally respected.

Wolfram suggests a different justification for a limited duty to represent even disreputable clients. Just as the butcher may be under an obligation to give a piece of meat to someone who is starving, the lawyer is sometimes under an obligation to represent "a necessitous client who has a compelling need for legal services. . . ." The underlying duty here is "a fundamental moral duty to rescue," qualified by consideration of "the capacities of the lawyer, the risk that may be incurred by the lawyer or caused to others, and the nature of the client's legal needs." This duty to rescue extends to the rescue of morally disreputable clients if "the client's claim is legally just, the client's claim is a socially important and morally compelling one, and the need of the client for this particular lawyer's services are truly pressing."

In Wolfram's view, the duty to represent does not arise for minor legal matters, but only to vindicate some legal right to an essential human need. Thus, some lawyer might have an obligation to defend an innocent Nazi erroneously accused of a serious crime. But for Wolfram, a Nazi's right to march through Skokie is not an urgent enough legal matter to generate an obligation to represent Nazi clients, at least not on grounds of *rescue*.

The Last Lawyer in Town

The "last lawyer in town" may be obligated to represent immoral clients if refusing means that human dignity will go unrespected or urgent legal needs will be unmet. But what about everyone else? Do the arguments for a duty to represent mean only that *some* lawyer will have to accept an unsavory case, or that no lawyer can justifiably refuse?

Held suggests that, while everyone may be entitled to counsel, not everyone is entitled to the *best* counsel. First-rate lawyers may—and in Held's view should—pick their cases with care, while mediocre lawyers, and all lawyers sharing the burden of representing unpopular clients, will occasionally get stuck representing clients with unjust or immoral ends. Likewise, Donagan's argument from human dignity does not seem to imply that every lawyer has an obligation to take every case, but that lawyers should be on guard that their private judgments do not conspire to leave any claims unrepresented. Wolfram specifies that his duty of rescue does not apply if many other lawyers are available and willing to handle the necessitous client's case.

It does seem, however, that if the last lawyer in town is *obligated* to represent a disreputable client, it is at least *permissible* for other lawyers to do so as well. It does not seem necessary to have in hand a certificate of unanimous refusal before accepting a morally problematic case.

Lawyers, like everyone else, are morally accountable for their actions, both private and professional. They are morally accountable for representing disreputable clients and morally accountable for refusing. In the absence of clear instructions from the professional code, it is left up to individual lawyers to weigh their obligations to promote justice, to respect human dignity, and to preserve their own moral integrity. Each lawyer must face the hard question: Will he be known for the company he keeps, or for the company he turns away?

The views of Virginia Held, Charles Wolfram, and Alan Donagan are taken from their essays in The Good Lawyer: Lawyers' Roles and Lawyers' Ethics, *ed. David Luban (Totowa, N.J.: Rowman and Allanheld, 1984).*

The Zealous Lawyer

Is Winning the Only Thing?

Claudia Mills

Famous football coaches have given us proverbs like "Winning's not the best thing, it's the only thing" and "Show me a good loser and I'll show you a loser." Sports fans are by and large not impressed by the putative distinction between winning and some other sense of "playing well" (as in the lame parental adage, "It's not whether you win or lose but how you play the game"). Playing the game better than the other team is precisely how you win and, more, the team that plays enough better than its opponents to score that extra point deserves to win. "May the better team win" is at some level a tautological wish universally granted, since winning can be thought of as defining the better team. Now, on any given occasion a generally excellent (i.e., winning) team may disgrace itself with sloppy, shoddy playing. But over time the best team will be the team that wins the most. Thus, Vince Lombardi and Woody Hayes have a point when they tell us nothing else counts.

Lawyers within an adversary system of justice such as ours have been thoroughly schooled in the Lombardi-Hayes philosophy of competition. They are steeped in it in law school and held to its standard by their codes of professional obligation. For the cornerstone of the adversary system is the lawyer's duty of zealous partisanship on behalf of his client. The ABA's Code of Professional Responsibility dictates, "The duty of a lawyer, both to his client and to the legal system, is to represent his client zealously within the bounds of the law." Murray L. Schwartz, professor of law at the University of California, Los Angeles, explains the lawyer's zeal in this way: "When acting as an advocate, a lawyer must, within the established constraints upon professional behavior, maximize the likelihood that the client will prevail." Prevail, as in *win*.

To ensure that the lawyer's zeal is undiluted by any personal moral scruples, our legal system also holds, in Schwartz's words, that "a lawyer is neither legally, professionally, nor morally responsible for the means used or the ends achieved" in his adversary representation of the client. Whatever the client's (arguably legal) ends, the lawyer must employ all (arguably legal) means to achieve them. He cannot bribe the jury, just as the coach cannot bribe the referees. But the lawyer can, and on some accounts *should*, dazzle the jury with every dubious trick in a bulging bag of legal shenanigans, from humiliating truthful witnesses under the guise of cross-examination to unleashing a torrent of frivolous objections whenever his opponent tries to address the court. In our legal system, as in "Monday Night Football," playing well is playing to win, and lawyers are not permitted to play any other way.

At least two things seem disturbing about this analogy between zealous legal advocacy and no-holds-barred athletic competition. First, we do not think winning defines legal merit the way winning defines excellence in sports. We have an independent standard of legal merit and just desert—imprecise though it may be—that allows us to ask whether the side that did win *should* have won. The client who *should* prevail is the client with truth and justice on her side, and it disturbs us that lawyers are supposed to defend with equal zeal both deserving and undeserving clients, as if the merits of the client's cause were irrelevant.

Second, legal battles are not games where everybody plays hard for two hours and then goes home to a "real life" unaffected by the results of the competition. People's lives—the lives of actual human beings—can be radically changed by what happens to them in courts of law. People do not usually wind up in court unless something of value to them is at stake. So it matters whether zealous partisanship by adversary attorneys is a good way of uncovering truth, defending legal rights, or upholding human dignity. It matters greatly.

Is zealous advocacy by lawyers on behalf of their clients a good way of serving these goals? What is zealous advocacy good for and what limits, if any, should be placed on it? In what arenas does the lawyer's zeal serve legal justice? In what arenas is such zeal inappropriate or even destructive of the values our legal system is intended to protect and promote?

Criminal Justice

Most justifications of zealous advocacy center on the defense attorney's properly (we feel) heroic efforts on behalf of the criminal accused. In most criminal cases a lone individual faces an extremely serious charge brought by the impersonal and powerful state, a charge that carries with it severe and stigmatizing sanctions. The attorney's zeal may be all that stands between the defendant and a wrongful conviction that will exact irrevocable penalties: to lose one's liberty is to lose a part of one's life. Even where the defendant is guilty, the attorney's zeal may be the only check on the state's abuse of its massive powers in administering justice, and great power, as we all know, is subject to great abuse.

The vast majority of lawyers in our adversary system, however, are not involved in criminal defense, and the vast majority of those who seek legal services are not accused of any crime. Can a justification of zealous advocacy in criminal justice be extended to cover lawyerly zeal applied elsewhere in the legal system?

It seems not. David Luban, a philosopher at the University of Maryland Law School, argues that "criminal justice is a very special case in which the zealous advocate serves atypical social goals. . . . The goal of zealous advocacy in criminal defense is to curtail the power of the state over its citizens. We want to handicap the state in its power even legitimately to punish us. And so [zealous advocacy] is justified, not because it is a good way of achieving justice, but because it is a good way of hobbling the government and we have political reasons for wanting this. . . . Criminal defense is an exceptional part of the legal system, one that aims at protection rather than justice."

These atypical goals of criminal justice are embodied in certain unique features of the criminal trial that create an asymmetry between the two parties—the defense and the prosecution—not found anywhere else in American law. Numerous provisions are designed specifically to curtail the zeal of the prosecution, so that full-steam adversary advocacy is limited to one side. The state must appoint counsel, at its own expense, to assist unrepresented opponents in preparing a criminal defense; the defendant is presumed innocent until proved guilty; and the burden of proof placed on the prosecution is the heaviest one found in the law, proof beyond a reasonable doubt. Moreover, public prosecutors are held to a standard of candor in dealing with their adversaries not mirrored in the duties of defense counsel. The prosecuting attorney is required to turn over to the defendant evidence that he or she has uncovered and does not intend to introduce; the defense has no comparable obligation.

Murray Schwartz concludes, "These functional and structural differences between criminal and civil trials and between the roles of the opposing advocates seriously undermine holding out the criminal defense lawyer as the archetype of the advocate within the adversary system. . . . What emerges from this analysis is the surprising conclusion that the model of the adversary system is significantly different from the very proceeding most often referred to as its prime illustration: criminal trials." A defense of zealous advocacy in other arenas of the law, then, can draw little support from its defense in the very special arena of criminal justice.

Civil Litigation

In civil cases, where one private party brings suit against another, no systematic asymmetry in wealth and power occurs between the two parties that would require rules curbing the zeal of one side for the sake of the other. Furthermore, what one side gains as the outcome of a civil contest, the other side loses—every dollar awarded to A comes right out of B's pocket. Thus lawyers for both sides, it seems, should be equally zealous. Does this mean that both lawyers should press their case with zeal unabated? To answer this question, we again must look at the ends this area of law is intended to serve.

Two of the ends of civil law, certainly, are to uncover the truth and to vindicate legal rights. These are of course not unrelated. As Schwartz points out, "The judicial answer to the question, 'What should now happen?' depends on and is often resolved entirely by the answer to the question, 'What did happen?'" So our question becomes: Is zealous partisanship by two adversary attorneys a good way of achieving truth and justice?

Defenders of zealous advocacy argue that truth is best sought by a wholehearted dialectic of assertion and refutation: If each side attempts to prove its case as energetically as possible, with the other side trying as energetically as possible to assault the steps of the proof, it is more likely that all of the aspects of the situation will be uncovered than in a less adversarial investigation.

However plausible such a theory may be, Luban observes that its empirical validity is, in fact, impossible to assess. "One does not, after a trial is over, find the parties coming forth to make a clean breast of it and enlighten the world as to what *really* happened. A trial is not a quiz show with the right answer waiting in a sealed envelope." The arguments for—and against—zealous advocacy as a means to finding out the truth are merely "untested speculations from the armchair."

But Luban doubts whether zealous advocates themselves seriously believe their own justificatory theory. "No trial lawyer believes that the best way to get at the truth is through the clash of opposing points of view. If a lawyer did believe this, the logical way to prepare a case for trial would be to hire two investigators, one taking one side of every issue and one taking the other." Indeed, the rival investigators should be urged to prevent the introduction of evidence unfavorable to their side of the issue, to minimize the importance of any unfavorable facts that do come to light, and to turn all their rhetorical skill to swaying and preying upon the trial lawyer's sympathies. "That no lawyer would dream of such a crazy procedure should tip us off" that something is amiss with zealous partisanship as an investigative technique.

Nor have we any reason to think that the clash of two zealous adversaries is the best way to guarantee that a client's legal rights are protected. "Every skill an advocate is taught is bent to winning cases no matter where the legal right lies," Luban reminds us. "If the opponent manages to counter a lawyer's move with a better one, this has precisely nothing to do with legal rights." The wordplay of two fast-talking modern attorneys is hardly more relevant to the establishment of legal rights, in Luban's view, than the swordplay of two fast-stepping medieval duelers sent out to settle suits on behalf of their employers. Luban concludes, "We have no reason at all to believe that when two overkillers slug it out the better case, rather than the better lawyer, wins."

Murray Schwartz recommends that the rules governing the scope and limits of adversary advocacy be revised to circumscribe lawyerly zeal by a greater commitment to finding out the truth, since any determination of legal right must be grounded in the facts of the case. A good start in this direction, he suggests, would be to adopt rules that "would require a lawyer to report to the court and opposing counsel the existence of relevant evidence or witnesses the lawyer does not intend to offer; prevent or, when prevention has proved unsuccessful, report to the court and opposing counsel the making of any untrue statement by client or witness or any material omissions; and question witnesses with the purpose and design to elicit the whole truth." Such revised rules, he believes, would serve the ends of civil justice better than current exhortations to pursue the client's interest to the farthest legal limits.

Who Is the Client?

Unbridled zeal appears even less justified when we look beyond litigation to other areas of legal practice. In business law, for example, the lawyer's duty of undivided loyalty to the client grows not out of any crusade for truth and justice, but from the less lofty fear that lawyers as employees may divert some of their zeal to benefitting themselves at the employer's expense. The worry motivating the duty is that agents will compete with their principals, thus defeating the purpose of agency. But the agent competing on behalf of the principal seems bound to keep his competitive zeal within the recognized moral constraints that govern economic competition generally in our society.

In administrative law and public interest law, the problem is not that the lawyer may compete with the client, but that it is not clear who exactly the client is supposed to be. Attorney Daniel Schwartz, observing the administrative law bar, points out that you cannot advance the client's cause until you know who the client *is*. "For the government attorney, this question may receive a variety of responses. Various candidates for the 'client' role include the agency employing the attorney and/or its administrators, the federal government, or the 'public interest.' . . . In many cases, the lawyer is the client; that is, he or she is at least an initial decision-maker concerning what kind of cases to bring and what issues to raise."

Even lawyers practicing before administrative agencies on behalf of private-sector clients face the same problems to a large extent. Although the client may be clearly defined, the client's interests often are not. Schwartz explains that the "client's perception of its interests may be shaped to a more-than-usual extent by the expert advice of its 'specialist' law firm, whose expertise consists in large part in its ability to 'read' the regulatory climate within the agencies." Thus, "administrative lawyers are not constrained by independent clients; [and] clients are not constrained by the judgment of independent lawyers." Zeal in administrative proceedings is therefore subject to few moderating influences.

Public interest lawyers, who bring litigation aimed at righting institutional wrongs and making far-reaching changes in the law, are also unable to maintain a strictly adversarial role. Like the administrative lawyer, the public interest lawyer cannot take a client's interests as given and proceed straightforwardly to further them with zeal. Furthermore, the interests of the parties, once defined, may conflict with one another, and it falls to the lawyer to decide which of the conflicting interests should be represented. Thus, philosopher Andreas Eshete argues, "the [public interest] lawyer cannot sidestep a deliberation on the merits of the interests at stake in the specific institutional wrong he aims to correct."

The best remedy for righting the institutional wrong of racial discrimination in schools, for example, is a matter of deep and divisive controversy, even among its victims. Parents of minority children in some districts would prefer to see the schools improved, rather than integrated—their goal is a decent education for their children, and this may be hindered rather than furthered by disruptive and bitterly contested busing programs. But the interests of future generations of schoolchildren, and the future of American society generally, may not be best served by perpetuating racially divided educational institutions. "Hence, in deciding what institutional reform to advocate," Eshete concludes, "the lawyer does not have ready-made interests to champion. And a responsible lawyer must look beyond the conflicting interests to the underlying public values of the legal system."

Beyond Adversariness

We have been asking what zealous advocacy is good for; the answer seems to be that it is good for criminal defense, but that in civil

---

law, business law, administrative law, and public interest law, zeal must be tempered by a respect for truth and justice, and adversariness must often give way to a thoughtful and sensitive attempt to explore large and difficult questions about where the public interest lies.

Murray Schwartz and Daniel Schwartz both criticize current codes of professional responsibility for holding up adversarial zeal as the dominant standard of lawyerly excellence. They recommend amending the codes to show a clearer recognition of the limits of such zeal. But Eshete asks whether lawyers trained and drilled in adversarial techniques and attitudes will be *able* to move beyond these to meet the broader demands of the lawyer's role. Education, professional training, and years of practice, in Eshete's view, "must leave their trace on a person"; the adversarial lawyer develops an adversarial character that he cannot shed at will when placed in situations where aggressiveness and combativeness are no longer appropriate.

Robert Condlin, professor at the University of Maryland Law School, argues that law schools should be conducting a rigorous reexamination of their educational practices. Adversarial skills certainly have their place in law practice, and so students do need to be trained in techniques that will allow them to go out and win cases without agonizing over whether every case should be won. They need to learn how to manipulate clients, witnesses, and decision-makers, how to think on their feet, how to get their clients what they want. But Condlin worries that in law schools today these behaviors are "learned unselfconsciously, as a set of disembodied means, not as part of a larger moral system that includes constraints on the use of such means. . . . The problem is one of teaching habits with limited and specific uses as if they are appropriate responses to all legal practice relationships."

Law schools do not and cannot simply teach students law. They also inescapably teach their students what kind of lawyer they should become, and what kind of person. And it seems that the kind of lawyer they should *not* become is one who wins any case at any cost. For when lawyers like that win, the rest of us lose.

The views of Murray Schwartz, David Luban, Daniel Schwartz, Andreas Eshete, and Robert Condlin are drawn from their essays in The Good Lawyer: Lawyers' Roles and Lawyers' Ethics, *ed. David Luban, Maryland Studies in Public Philosophy (Totowa, N.J.: Rowman and Allanheld, 1984).*

To Tell or Not to Tell
Conflicts about Confidentiality

Claudia Mills

"**T**hree can keep a secret," Benjamin Franklin once wrote, "if two of them are dead." The urge to tell secrets is a powerful one, and pervasive practices of confidentiality have accordingly developed to keep it in check. The duty to keep secrets is a principal part of what friends owe one another, a cornerstone of most codes of professional ethics, and a charge placed on workers and citizens in the name of loyalty to their employer and their country.

Philosopher Bruce Landesman suggests that our ordinary duties of confidentiality are based in part on respect for the need all of us have at one time or another both to express information to others and to keep control over how that information is subsequently used. We need the reaction and response of another person—and so share a secret—but also need to retain a proprietary hold on the secret, and so swear our audience to confidentiality. Sissela Bok, author of *Secrets: On the Ethics of Concealment and Revelation*, likewise justifies confidentiality in terms of our respect for individuals as capable of both *having* and *sharing* secrets, our respect for both personal autonomy and interpersonal intimacy. Furthermore, once a promise of confidentiality is given, the duty to keep promises provides an additional reason not to tell.

Some secrets ought not to be kept, however. One has a prima facie duty to reveal certain sorts of information to the proper authorities: information about crimes committed or contemplated, for example, or concerning impending harm to innocent third parties. The obligation to keep a secret may have to be balanced against the obligation, in certain circumstances, to tell a secret, and Landesman argues that appeals to confidentiality provide no easy way out of such moral dilemmas. The confidante "remains an autonomous moral being and thus free to deliberate about what to do with the information once it has been received. That it has been revealed in confidence is a powerful reason for keeping it secret, but cannot settle the issue. The hearer cannot remain a moral agent without retaining the right to consider the information in light of other factors that may, all things considered, provide even stronger reasons for revealing it."

This kind of moral conflict is heightened when the ordinary duty of confidentiality is buttressed by additional professionally grounded obligations to keep secrets. Doctors and lawyers, for example, are bound by the canons of their profession not to reveal the confidences of patients and clients. But when these confidences concern threats to third parties or to the public welfare, the professional duty of confidentiality clashes with the ordinary moral duty not to stand by as serious wrongs are committed. Employees are often under a special obligation to guard company secrets. But when these secrets threaten the health and safety of consumers or workers, private enterprise warrants public concern, and employees have to wrestle with the difficult decision of whether—and how loudly—to blow the whistle. Those who work in national defense matters face these dilemmas in their most extreme form. A certain degree of secrecy is essential for national security, but some secrets can be kept only by endangering the democratic values that in the end are all that make national security matter.

What secrets should be kept? What secrets should be told? How do we balance these special duties of confidentiality against the possibly grave harms a breach of confidentiality might avert?

Client Confidentiality

Many codes of professional ethics are built around a principle of confidentiality. Doctors, lawyers, psychiatrists, social workers, accountants, and priests all assure those who come to them for assistance that their communications will be kept in confidence. Making good on that assurance is a matter both of professional obligation and professional pride. The confidentiality promised clients is not absolute, however, and there are broader and narrower restrictions on what falls within its scope: Lawyers, according to the ABA's new code of ethics, are permitted—though not required—to reveal a client's intention to commit a criminal act resulting in imminent death; psychiatrists have been required to reveal a serious danger of violence posed by their patients. But even given such restrictions, professionals bound by a duty of confidentiality may be obligated to keep secrets they would otherwise be obligated to disclose.

What considerations justify a professional obligation of confidentiality and dictate its appropriate scope? Practitioners in many professions argue that success in achieving the underlying goal of their profession depends on how forthcoming the client is with confidences, which in turn depends on the professional's promise of confidentiality. In evaluating the case for confidentiality in any profession, then, three questions need to be answered: (1) How important is the purpose to be achieved by that profession? (2) To achieve this purpose, is it necessary the client tell all to the professional? (3) How strict a promise of confidentiality is needed in order for the client to feel free to tell all?

Psychiatrists claim, for example, that psychic healing takes place when their patients' darkest secrets are brought to the light of conscious rational scrutiny. Confidentiality is promised so that no hidden guilt or trauma will be withheld. But how extensive should such a promise be? Bok points out that "no evidence suggests that therapy will be imperilled if patients know that therapists have the duty to reveal . . . plans of violence." Some patients even hope their plans will be thwarted.

Nor does the end achieved by psychotherapy seem weighty enough to justify the failure to breach confidentiality where serious harms to third parties are at stake. Thus the California Supreme Court held in *Tarasoff* v. *The Regents of the University of California* that the psychotherapists whose patient murdered Tatiana Tarasoff breached a duty overriding confidentiality in failing to warn the victim of the patient's violent threats against her. The "public interest in effective treatment of mental illness" is outweighed by "the public interest in safety from violent assault," the court concluded. "The protective privilege ends where the public peril begins."

The end sought by the legal profession, however, may seem to be a weightier one: justice for all. If lawyers can make a case that confidentiality is necessary to secure this end, the duty of confidentiality within the legal profession will have a stronger justification. Accordingly, lawyers argue that they cannot represent their clients effectively if clients withhold any relevant information from them. And in our highly complex legal system, justice requires that all parties to a proceeding be represented effectively by counsel. Confidentiality is, then, a means to justice.

Or is it? Philosopher Jeremy Bentham objected in 1827 that justice in criminal cases is not in fact served by holding lawyers to a pledge of confidentiality. Justice is done when the innocent are acquitted and the guilty are convicted, and confidentiality assists neither goal. The innocent have no reason to fear that disclosure of their secrets will lead to conviction; the guilty have no right to hope that concealment of their secrets will lead to acquittal.

Bentham's argument faces two challenges. The first questions the assumption that innocent clients will be able to tell all even if no promise of confidentiality is given. Innocent clients may not be legally sophisticated enough to be aware they are innocent. Monroe Freedman, author of *Lawyers' Ethics in an Adversary System*, gives the example of a battered wife who shoots her husband in self-defense: She may falsely believe herself guilty of murder and so deny the shooting altogether—thus jeopardizing her lawyer's best defense strategy. Such extremely ignorant and timid clients are likely to be rare, however, and it can be argued that confidentiality protects this very special subset of innocent clients at the cost of letting a far greater number of guilty clients go free.

A deeper challenge to Bentham's argument denies that the fundamental goal of providing defendants with legal representation is to maximize the number of correct verdicts rendered. More important even than justice is respect for individual rights and human dignity. Freedman writes, "Before we will permit the state to deprive anyone of life, liberty, or property . . . we require that certain processes be duly followed which ensure regard for the dignity of the individual, irrespective of the impact of those processes upon the determination of truth." No defendant, innocent or guilty, is required to stand alone against a hostile world without a legal advocate as his or her champion.

But the question now arises: How much confidentiality must be promised in order to ensure respect for every client's human dignity? Freedman argues that a client who cannot trust his lawyer to keep confidences can enjoy his right to effective counsel only at the cost of jeopardizing his right against self-incrimination. For if he tells all, he risks incriminating himself through his own lawyer's testimony against him. But Alan Donagan, a philosopher at the California Institute of Technology, objects that respect for human dignity cannot license a sweeping duty of silence. It is true that a society that respects human dignity will recognize a legal right against self-incrimination. "But a legal right, even one that society is morally obliged to grant, is not necessarily a moral right. A murderer has no moral right whatever to escape incrimination by concealing the victim's body, although it would be wrong to compel him to reveal where it is." And what the defendant has no moral right to do, he has no moral right to enlist professional help in doing—and no one has a moral right to provide that help.

Proposals to weaken the scope of confidentiality have been forcefully resisted by the legal profession, however. Take away the right of confidentiality in the name of social utility, caution many lawyers, and you open the way to totalitarianism. (Under Nazism, lawyers were authorized to reveal client confidences on behalf of goals supported by "healthy folk feeling.") As a society we have so far been willing to err on the side of respecting the confidences of the accused individual, and to pay the costs of providing that respect.

Individuals versus Groups

The arguments we have been considering so far concern obligations of confidentiality owed to individuals—both simply as persons and as clients, patients, and so on. Sissela Bok takes as one of our bedrock assumptions that individuals should have a certain amount of control over how private to keep their own private lives. "Without a premise supporting a measure of individual control over [the degree of secrecy and openness about] personal matters, it would be impossible to preserve the indispensable respect for identity, plans, action, and belongings that all of us need and should legitimately be able to claim." This presumption of the legitimacy of individual control underlies our ordinary moral duties of confidentiality and lends additional plausibility to professional duties of confidentiality owed to vulnerable human beings in need of assistance. It is an argument based on human dignity.

But when confidentiality is instead owed to a group that wields any considerable amount of power over individual lives, Bok believes the presumption shifts. "When those who exercise power of [this kind] claim control over secrecy and openness, it is up to them to show why giving them such control is necessary and what kinds of safeguards they propose."

What reasons support practices of collective secrecy and place on individuals an obligation to keep group secrets? In general, it would be difficult for most groups to function cohesively if members felt no bonds of loyalty to one another to keep group secrets. Within specific group contexts, additional rationales for secrecy apply, which generate corresponding obligations of confidentiality.

Corporations often ask their employees to promise not to reveal trade formulas to competitors—without some such protection, it is argued, businesses would have no incentive to invest their resources in technological innovation. Some measure of secrecy is justified in the administrative and bureaucratic context as well. "If administrators had to do everything in the open," Bok notes, "they might be forced to express only safe and uncontroversial views, and thus to bypass creative or still tentative ideas." It is neither fair nor fruitful to expose early stages of planning to the glare of publicity. The case for military secrecy is particularly powerful, since every state requires considerable secrecy in order to defend itself against enemy forces, and so to ensure its very survival.

Thus a battery of reasons supports some extent of collective, as well as individual, confidentiality. But collective confidentiality can derive no support from most of the arguments that proved persuasive at the individual level. David Luban argues, for example, that lawyers who represent corporate clients cannot justify keeping shady secrets by appeal to the human dignity argument. "A corporation does not have human dignity, because it is not human. It is an abstract entity which is considered a person only in a technical sense. Corporate personality is a legal fiction." Nor will it work to argue that while the corporation itself is not human, the particular employees who manage its affairs are. Such maneuvers, Luban charges, "attempt to blur the distinction between corporate entities and the people who work for them; to transfer the human individuality of the latter to the former. . . . We are rightly skeptical when Madison Avenue describes a mammoth multinational as 'People building widgets to help people.'"

Bok provides a particularly egregious example of the fallacious transposition to the collective level of the confidentiality rightly owed to individuals. "Consider . . . the prolonged collaboration between asbestos manufacturers and company physicians to conceal the risks from exposure to asbestos dust. These risks were kept secret . . . even from those workers found in medical checkups to be in the early stages of asbestos-induced disease. When a reporter approached a physician associated with the concealment as consultant for a large manufacturer, the physician turned down his request for an interview on grounds of confidentiality owed as a matter of 'the patient's rights,' and explained, when the astonished reporter inquired who the 'patient' was, that it was the *company.*"

Where appeals to human dignity, or patient and client rights, are inappropriate, as they are here, it is more difficult to justify keeping secrets that pose serious harms to innocent third parties. The arguments for collective secrecy and confidentiality may be persuasive enough to warrant a good amount of individual inconvenience, or even hardship, in their service. But by and large they will not be able to outweigh counter-balancing moral considerations. Employees entrusted with knowledge of corporate practices that endanger workers' or consumers' health or pollute the environment may find themselves obligated to betray that trust and become whistle-blowers.

Bok cautions, however, that whistle-blowing, with its destructive repercussions, is not a first-resort solution to group malfeasance, nor a course to be taken lightly. "Potential whistleblowers must first try to specify the degree to which there is genuine impropriety and consider how imminent and how serious the threat is which they perceive. [They must] consider whether the existing avenues for change within the organization have been sufficiently explored. It *is* disloyal to colleagues and employers, as well as a waste of time, to sound the loudest alarm first." Further, "openly accepted responsibility for blowing the whistle should . . . be preferred to the secret denunciation or the leaked rumor" to provide those accused a fair opportunity to defend themselves. But when these conditions are met, Luban concludes that employees must follow actress Lauren Bacall's instructions: "You know how to whistle, don't you? Just put your lips together and blow."

Military secrecy is obviously more strongly justified than corporate or administrative secrecy. When it comes to national security, the values at stake in guarding secrecy may seem weightier than anything that can be put in the balance against them. If disclosing military secrets jeopardizes national security—or even national survival—then a powerful case can be made against disclosure, even to avert some grave harm.

Too seldom noticed, however, is that secrecy can also *endanger* national security. Bok observes that the failure of the 1980 hostage rescue mission in Iran has been blamed on overly restrictive secrecy measures that prevented participants from coordinating plans and cooperatively reassessing those plans when conditions deteriorated.

We must also ask what all our defense efforts are supposed to be defending—presumably our system of democracy, whose highest ideal is active citizen participation in all vital issues. With excessive military secrecy, Bok holds, "citizens lose ordinary democratic checks on precisely those matters that can affect them most strongly." She doubts that "democratic processes *can* persist in the face of current amounts of secrecy, of public ignorance about what should be the public's business above all else."

One striking breach of confidentiality regarding military matters in recent years was the decision of Daniel Ellsberg and Anthony Russo to give the classified Pentagon Papers to *The New York Times*, thereby exposing the record of ineptitude, deceit, and concealment that told the story of U.S. involvement in Vietnam. Bok applauds their very difficult decision: "The information about the origins and conduct of the war in Vietnam should never have been kept secret in the first place. This information was owed to the people, at home and abroad, who were bearing the costs and the suffering of the war; keeping them in the dark about the reasons for fighting the war is an abuse of secrecy. The extent of the secrecy could be justified neither on military nor administrative grounds. It demonstrated, rather, the extraordinary danger to society that endemic secrecy represents."

Conclusion

Each of us owes respect to the secrets others confide to us, because we all recognize in ourselves the need to confide secrets to others. But obligations of confidentiality are weaker as the secrets concealed belong to large collectivities rather than lone individuals, and as concealment threatens danger to others. Here, as elsewhere in ethics, individuals may face hard choices that no law, code, or promise can settle for them.

The views of Bruce Landesman and Alan Donagan are taken from their essays in The Good Lawyer: Lawyers' Roles and Lawyers' Ethics, *ed. David Luban, Maryland Studies in Public Philosophy (Totowa, N.J.: Rowman and Allanheld, 1984). Sissela Bok's views are quoted from* Secrets: On the Ethics of Concealment and Revelation *(New York: Pantheon Books, 1982). Monroe Freedman is quoted from* Lawyers' Ethics in an Adversary System *(Indianapolis: Bobbs-Merrill, 1975) and "Wrong? Silence Is Right,"* The New York Times, *February 14, 1983. David Luban's views are quoted from* Lawyers and Justice: An Ethical Study *(Princeton, N.J.: Princeton University Press, 1988).*

Should Lawyers Advertise?

David Luban

In the second week of June 1988, newspaper front pages reported two apparently unrelated, but in actuality deeply connected, decisions. In *Shapero v. Kentucky State Bar*, the Supreme Court struck down bans on targeted direct mailings by lawyers interested in rounding up clients who may have suffered a specific kind of injury. In this way it continued a line of decisions relaxing bar-imposed restrictions on advertising and solicitation.

The same day, a jury awarded $400,000 in damages to the widower of Rose Cipollone, a smoker who had sued the Liggett Group for purveying the cigarettes that had caused her lung cancer. At first glance it seems that the two cases have nothing in common. But a few days later, the *Washington Post* ran a story entitled "Who Will Be the Next Rose Cipollone? Lawyers Search for 'Perfect Plaintiff' to Widen Gains of Tobacco Liability Trial." The story explained that Cipollone's lawyers would begin to search for other tobacco plaintiffs—a search that would amount to a kind of solicitation that is clearly a first-cousin to targeted direct mailings.

Another interesting aspect links the *Shapero* decision to the tobacco litigation. The law firm representing Cipollone invested $500,000 in direct expenses and $2 million in lawyers' time and recouped only a tiny fraction of the amount; nevertheless, it clearly believed that the preparation it had put into the case is an investment that will pay off. Now the firm has drawn blood, gotten the first cigarette victory ever onto the books, and acquired vast expertise in the workings of the cigarette industry. All this amounts to a kind of legal and intellectual capital that will pay dividends in future litigation. And, like any similar investment, it must be advertised in order to attract the customers. In *Zauderer v. Office of Disciplinary Counsel of the State of Ohio*, the *Shapero* decision's immediate Supreme Court predecessor, lawyers specializing in Dalkon Shield legislation had mass-mailed advertisements providing explicit information about the shield. Targeted direct mailings could be an even more efficient means of gaining clients who fit a law firm's litigation-acquired experience.

Decisions such as *Shapero* and *Zauderer* permit lawyers to take specialty cases that are unlikely to be profitable in the short run, in order to train and prepare themselves in the specialty for the long run. Lawyers cannot engage in such a practice unless they can get the word out to potential clients, and highly targeted advertising is the best way to do so. Tooling up for a long-run specialty should be encouraged, for it may help the individual client even in the short run. It is doubtful, for example, that a law firm would have invested $2.5 million in Rose Cipollone's highly risky case if it did not see the possibility of developing a lucrative specialty. Cipollone would not have had her day in court.

Solicitation and advertising are lineal descendants of the old common-law crime of barratry—in Blackstone's words, "the offence of frequently exciting and stirring up suits and quarrels between his majesty's subjects." In the baldest form, worries about lawyer advertising and solicitation are worries about shysters—about lawyers who don't give a fig for professionalism and who are all-too-eager to contribute to the current litigation crisis. Fear of the shyster expresses itself in those two staples of current debates over the legal profession: the litigation explosion and loss of professionalism. In her *Shapero* dissent, Justice Sandra Day O'Connor worries explicitly about the demise of professionalism and the advent of the professional sleazeball. I suggest, on the contrary, that the developments presaged by *Shapero* are to be welcomed. Advertising and solicitation are important components of professionalism, fulfilling some of its basic goals.

The Litigation Explosion

Let us begin by reviewing some of the assumptions underlying critics' worries about the litigation explosion. At the heart of litigation phobia is an idealization of social relationships, which sees a legalistic society as a falling-off from a prior organic society. Implicit is a comparison with an allegedly less litigious, less rights-conscious, more harmonious yesteryear. But when was that? Data from the St. Louis Circuit Court since 1820 show a litigation rate in the nineteenth century twice as high as in the 1970s, while Accomack County, Virginia, had a litigation rate in 1639 that was more than four times as high as any contemporary county for which data exist. Judge Richard Posner's careful analysis of federal court caseloads shows a genuine litigation jump around 1960, but we must not forget that the federal courts handle only about 2 percent of American litigation. In state courts, data from 1960 do not exist, but more recent data suggest that whatever the extent of the litigation explosion may have been, it has leveled off or stopped. For example, from 1981 to 1984, population rose 3 percent, but total filings in tort, contract, and real property actually declined 4 percent; from 1978 population rose 8 percent and tort filings rose just 9 percent. Moreover, much of the novel federal tort litigation—most notably asbestos product-liability filings, which in 1985 amounted to 31.3 percent of all federal products-liability cases—is perfectly explicable as a response to genuine and important grievances, rather than touchiness and truculence. If the litigation crisis is really not an inexplicable itch to sue, then perhaps the prospect of lawyers spreading the disease through advertising should not fill us with so much alarm.

Legal Professionalism

Indeed, one person's "stirring up litigation" is another's "informing people about their injuries and legal rights." This thought underlies the Court's advertising and solicitation decisions.

Consider *Shapero*. Its argument is neither problematic nor complex, and even Justice O'Connor's dissent agrees that "the reasoning in *Zauderer* supports the conclusion reached today." Earlier Court decisions had protected truthful advertising by lawyers in the mass media and extended the protection to mailed announcement cards; *Zauderer* extended it further to mass mailings of specific information such as Zauderer's Dalkon Shield advertisement. In *Shapero* the Court notes that mass mailings, unless done "ineptly," will reach the same people as targeted mailings, along with others for whom the information is inapplicable; thus, the targeted mailing is merely a more efficient mass mailing, and "the First Amendment does not permit a ban on certain speech merely because it is more efficient." The possibilities of high-pressure sales tactics and overreaching are ruled out by the print medium, and this distinguishes the case from the in-person solicitation the Supreme Court earlier had agreed could be banned. As the *Shapero* decision amusingly puts it, "A letter, like a printed advertisement (but unlike a lawyer), can readily be put in a drawer to be considered later, ignored, or discarded." Thus, bans on any mode of truthful written advertising are unconstitutional.

Justice O'Connor, joined by Chief Justice William H. Rehnquist and Justice Antonin Scalia, dissents not from the reasoning in *Shapero* but from the entire "line of cases built on defective premises and flawed reasoning." She explains: "The roots of the error in our attorney advertising cases are a defective analogy between professional services and standardized consumer products." The arguments on behalf of lawyer advertising all concern its economic efficiency, but "The economic argument against these [advertising] restrictions ignores the delicate role they may play in preserving the norms of the legal profession." Membership in a profession requires one to "temper one's selfish pursuit of economic success by adhering to standards of conduct that could not be enforced either by legal fiat or through the discipline of the market." The privileges and advantages of professional life are "means to a goal that transcends the accumulation of wealth. That goal is public service."

I certainly agree with the latter proposition, though many lawyers will not. The public service tradition of the bar is real, admirable, and essential if law practice is to contribute, in Justice O'Connor's words, to "a legal system that is both reasonably efficient and tolerably fair." But Justice O'Connor mistakes the import of the economic arguments on behalf of lawyer advertising. They are not self-interested arguments that lawyer advertising will lead to additional emoluments *for the lawyer.* Some lawyers will benefit from advertising, while others who may be forced to lower their rates to compete will suffer economic harm. Rather, the argument on behalf of advertising is that it will lead to lower costs and improved access to law *for the citizen.* Zauderer's advertisement may well have alerted women who had been sterilized by the Dalkon Shield that they could obtain compensation; Shapero's targeted mailing may have saved the homes of legally untutored individuals threatened with foreclosure.

Advertising and targeted mailings serve the same purpose as notification of class members in a class action: letting people who share a problem know that they may have a legal remedy. In a mass society such as ours, it is increasingly likely that large groups of people will share the same problems and situations. Mass toxic torts such as Dalkon Shield are merely the most graphic example of what may well be the archetypal legal problem of the future. Highly specific yet group-wide advertising is probably the only way significant numbers of people who have suffered damage from the ever-larger economic and technological forces at work in contemporary society will learn the true nature of their problem and what the law can do for them. In one sense this is "stirring up litigation." But in a more real sense it is our technologically adventurous and conflict-ridden society itself, not lawyer advertising, that stirs up the litigation. It was not Zauderer who was ultimately responsible for Dalkon Shield litigation; it was the manufacturer of the Dalkon Shield. Zauderer's advertisement, like Shapero's, was a form of professionalism in the modern world: It attempted to fulfill the worthwhile goal of responding to the evolving legal needs of the public. The fact that successful advertising would be good for

Zauderer's and Shapero's incomes does not diminish their profession-alism, unless indifference to income is taken to be a component of professionalism. Unfortunately, Justice O'Connor comes close to say-ing this.

Justice O'Connor argues that "imbuing the legal profession with the necessary ethical standards is a task that involves a constant strug-gle with the relentless natural force of economic self-interest." Now, this is true inasmuch as lawyers can always find unethical ways to eke out a few additional bucks—but how do bans on solicitation or adver-tising contribute to imbuing ethical standards in the legal profession? Here one wants an argument that exhibits in a concrete and practical form the "delicate role [bans on advertising] may play in preserving the norms of the legal profession." Justice O'Connor's argument offers nothing of the kind, as she herself is compelled to admit: "While it may be difficult to defend this role with precise economic logic, I believe there is a powerful argument in favor of restricting lawyer advertising and that this argument is at the very least not easily refuted by eco-nomic analysis."

Her claim, in brief, is that restrictions on advertising serve a sym-bolic function, signaling to attorneys that their services are not a mere commodity, and thus changing the way attorneys think about their practice: "Such restrictions act as a concrete, day-to-day reminder to the practicing attorney of why it is improper for any member of this profession to regard it as a trade or occupation like any other." Small wonder that "this argument is at the very least not easily refuted by economic analysis"; it is built on assertions that can scarcely be tested at all.

But even as a speculative argument this one is full of holes. First and foremost is that it ignores the many ways the practice of law *is* a trade or occupation like any other. Lawyers charge fees, issue itemized bills, worry about their incomes or where the next client is coming from, choose "growth" areas of practice, and fret that time is money. Clearly, nothing is wrong with this: *c'est la vie.* Confronted as lawyers are with overwhelmingly potent signals that their practice is indeed a trade—signals like a firm's balance sheet—the symbolism of advertis-ing restrictions will surely be swamped. Moreover, if the point is to send purely symbolic messages of professionalism to attorneys, other symbols might do the job as well as advertising restrictions. Restric-tions on commercial speech are scarcely well-tailored to the substan-tial government interest in a high-quality legal profession if their function is merely to serve as "reminders."

It makes much more sense to evaluate professionalism not in a lawyer's indifference to the trade aspects of practice, but in her other

---

attitudes and actions: pride in her craft, honesty, participation in law reform activity, and pro bono work. These are fully consistent with attempting to drum up business by informing people of their legal possibilities and of their legal rights.

Should Legal Services Rise Again?

David Luban

The Legal Services Corporation (LSC), founded by Congress in 1974 to provide legal services for poor people, has been reduced since 1980 to a shell of its former self. Conservative critics from Spiro Agnew to Ronald Reagan charged that LSC lawyers were abusing their charter to enact a liberal agenda. Under the Reagan administration, the LSC's budget was slashed and funds redirected to ideologically conservative causes. An unsympathetic board and several scandals have harmed morale among legal-aid lawyers— indeed, in 1987 the LSC's chairperson publicly called for its abolition. Finally, strict limitations have been imposed on the kind of activities in which LSC-funded lawyers could engage, chief among these being very stringent requirements on filing class actions against the government.

Class-action suits have become an emblem of everything opponents find objectionable about the LSC. In such suits (it was believed), lawyers recruit a purely nominal plaintiff-of-record representing a class of litigants who have never heard of the case and who may very well oppose the litigation. On behalf of this class, the lawyers proceed to demand widespread restructuring of social institutions or extravagant damage awards, thereby enacting their own social agenda through the courts in subversion of the democratic will as expressed through legislatures or executive action.

So goes the argument. In reply, LSC supporters point out that only a small percentage of the litigation entered by legal-aid programs has involved class-action suits or attempts to restructure institutions. (In the legal-services vernacular, such cases are called "impact" cases.) The overwhelming bulk of the LSC caseload has been individualized service—divorces, child abuse or neglect cases, landlord/tenant cases, Social Security, and so forth. (In the vernacular, this kind of work is sometimes called "handing out Band-Aids.")

Both sides of such a debate presuppose that there is something suspicious about impact work. I wish to argue that this presupposition is wrong—that absolutely nothing is illegitimate about impact work by legal-services lawyers, even highly politicized ones. On the contrary: law reform of this sort is at once an admirable attempt to further social justice and a professional responsibility to help more clients rather than fewer. It is precisely what lawyers ought to be doing.

Let me answer four objections to it in turn.

The Taxation Objection

To be sure, there are strong arguments for the presupposition that (too much) impact work is illegitimate. First of all there is the argument that it is wrong to use the tax money of people opposed to liberal aims and programs to further them.

This objection seems at first glance to be merely a stupid gripe. People don't like to pay taxes; they do like to complain about them, and about how revenues are spent. As a matter of fact, however, no one can seriously class the dollar-a-year per capita that goes to legal services as an "incredible taxpayer rip-off."

Rather, talk of taxes is a stand-in for a less frivolous argument, based on the ideas that (1) governmentally funded agencies in some sense "stand for" public values and decisions, (2) such agencies should as a consequence not take sides on hotly contested political issues, and (3) impact litigation does take sides. The phrase *how my tax dollars are spent*, that is, is a surrogate for *what my government stands for.* And the Taxation Objection then amounts to the claim that the government should not stand for anything as controversial as LSC-funded impact work.

If, however, it is wrong to spend the tax dollars of opponents of integration on attempts to enforce it, it is equally wrong to spend racial minorities' tax dollars to support discrimination. In fact, anything that government does or fails to do about a controversial issue implicates it in values antagonistic to one side or the other; anytime the government is a party in a lawsuit it is "taking sides" against those who hold its adversary's values. As it stands, then, the Taxation Objection fails to show that governmentally funded legal-service work, even when politically controversial, is illegitimate.

The Equal-Access Objection

Insofar as impact work diverts legal-aid lawyers from handing out Band-Aids, it might be thought that it is actually inimical to the ideal of equal access to the legal system. For then legal-aid officers will turn away clients with "Band-Aid" problems because the lawyers are too busy filing class-action suits, or whatever. If a legal-aid office makes a decision to target, for example, public housing cases at the expense of others, legal problems not "on target" will not receive counsel; this in effect denies these problems equal consideration by the legal system. Targeting, to put the point another way, treats clients aggregatively rather than individually—a client's problem is addressed only if enough other clients share the same problem. What, then, has become of the ideal of equal access to the legal system, the *raison d'être* of legal aid?

The answer is that the ideal had its budget cut. Had enough money existed to maintain a larger staff, the office could have taken all cases; as is, some sort of selection or triage principle must be applied. The decision to target a goal like public housing can be justified by considerations such as the importance of shelter as a basic need and the benefitting of a greater number of people. At this point the ball is in the objector's court: What is her candidate for a triage principle?

If the Equal-Access Objection is taken seriously, the only candidate for a triage principle is first-come-first-serve or even a "lottery," for nothing about a potential client's case can be taken into account except the bare fact that the client has requested legal services. First-come-first-serve treats everyone's problem as of precisely equal worth to everyone else's. Never mind that it may lead to a very inefficient allocation of scarce legal resources. Never mind that the total service thus rendered to the indigent population has little to do with its net needs and desires. Never mind that it's crazy—it may be crazy, but it's fair.

Clearly, however, it is too crazy to be fair. By ignoring differences in urgency among cases, first-come-first-serve ignores the connection between access to the legal system and the people's reasons for wanting access to it. And once their link with human projects and values is broken, it becomes hard to see why legal services should exist at all. A woman faced with court-ordered sterilization needs a lawyer faster and more desperately than her neighbor who wants to make Montgomery Ward honor the warranty on her dryer; first-come-first-serve, however, in effect puts both their names in the hat. It disconnects demands for legal aid from needs for legal aid, and thus abdicates the very judgment on which the importance of legal aid rests.

If urgency can be taken into account, however, it is difficult to see why a legal-aid office's decision to target an issue such as public housing is ruled out. One dimension of urgency—"intensive urgency"— concerns the importance of the interests at stake; another dimension of urgency—"extensive urgency"—concerns the number of people affected. Targeting by a legal-aid office usually means going after cases that are urgent in both these senses. The purpose for seeking law reform or high impact, instead of handing out Band-Aids, is that the former will help more poor people in more important ways. This, I submit, is quite a reasonable ground for choosing cases.

The Client-Control Objection

A third objection is that in impact work lawyers rather than clients are calling the shots, using the legal system to achieve ends the lawyers have chosen independently of the wishes of the people they ostensibly represent. Let me begin by conceding the accusations that are the basis of this objection: Public interest lawyers bent on law reform sometimes recruit clients as plaintiffs; they occasionally pressure their clients on behalf of The Cause; and they may even file class actions when a large part of the class—maybe even a majority—opposes them.

What I do not concede is that anything is wrong with this.

This is clearly so regarding lawyers recruiting clients for law-reform activities. It does not matter whose idea the project is; all that matters is that the client, like the lawyer, becomes committed to the project. For obvious reasons a plaintiff might have to be recruited by lawyers in a law-reform case. Potential plaintiffs might not know that what is being done to them is illegal or may assume that action against it is out of the question. It takes guts to litigate against an institution that has its thumb poised over your eye.

The accusation that lawyers rather than clients seize control is more troubling. Consider an example. Ms. P belongs to a tenants' organization and agrees to be the plaintiff in a suit against D Real Estate ("unhealthiest tenements in town"). P is represented pro bono by L, a committed tenants' rights lawyer who hopes that *P* v. *D* will set an important precedent. D does not want the precedent and tries to "buy out" P with a cash settlement before the trial. It is clearly in P's personal interest to accept the offer. Should L counsel her to do it? If P wants to accept it, should L nevertheless try to pressure her into going to trial? Who is L representing—P or The Cause?

Similar problems can arise in class-action suits. When the "class" in such a suit is itself divided on the issue at hand, lawyers will be acting in opposition to the wishes of some—perhaps even a majority—of the very people whose interests they claim to represent. In several cities, for example, NAACP attorneys' commitment to racially integrated schools has led them to file class actions even though black parents preferred upgrades in the quality of education in all-black schools over integration.

In terms of the bar's ethical codes, both problems involve forbidden conflicts of interest between lawyers and their clients. I want to suggest, however, that lawyers and their clients can engage in a political mode of action that differs significantly from the ordinary lawyer-client relationship.

When a client engages the services of a lawyer for everyday business, they enter a contractual relationship where the element of reciprocity consists in the client's promise to pay the lawyer in return for services. At that point, however, the lawyer becomes the client's *agent*, and the duties are no longer mutual. An agent has a primary one-way commitment to his or her principal, and a derivative one-way commitment to successfully carry out the various pieces of business transacted on behalf of the principal.

When attorney and client are engaged in politicized public-interest law, by contrast, their relationship is one of mutual political commitment. Political allies have a primary one-way commitment to the political cause and a derivative *mutual* commitment to each other, undertaken freely and reciprocally by people who regard each other as political equals.

Return now to Ms. P, the member of the tenants' organization who now wishes to settle her precedent-setting case against D Real Estate because D has made her an offer she doesn't want to refuse. Ms. P engaged in the suit to further the goals of the tenants' organization, and lawyer L represented her pro bono because of his commitment to those goals. At this point, Ms. P is on the verge of betraying L, her other allies in the tenants' organization, and the cause for which they were all working. Since L's relationship with her is one of mutual political commitment, of primary commitment to the cause and only secondary commitment to Ms. P, it is entirely appropriate for L to pressure her to decline the settlement even though doing so is not in her personal interest.

Problems of class conflict in class-action suits can be resolved by a closer look at what it is for a lawyer to represent the will of a political group. Who is the NAACP's client class in the earlier example? Is it the black parents in the city the lawyers are trying to desegregate, or is it all American blacks, whose interests in racial integration may be adversely affected if large local pockets of segregation are left undisturbed? More importantly, the NAACP may have to take into account the interests of future generations of blacks in and out of the city. If this uncovers an intergenerational conflict of interest, the demand for representativeness cannot require the lawyers to conform their actions to the wishes of only the parents.

Yet the NAACP lawyers must side with one class or the other, since if they do nothing they are doing exactly what one class wants them to do. It seems to me they have only one recourse, and that is to do what, in their considered judgment, is best. We must not forget that many black parents in Topeka wanted school improvement rather than integration and opposed the NAACP's suit in *Brown* v. *Board of Education*. Had the NAACP lawyers refused to act in cases of class conflict and division, segregated schools would still be legal today.

The Objection from Democracy

The Objection from Democracy says it is wrong for groups to frustrate the democratic will by obtaining in court what they cannot obtain in the political rough-and-tumble. In a democracy, law is to be made by majoritarian legislatures, and the role of courts is restricted to protecting the rights of minorities, not making law themselves.

But in reality legislatures themselves do not work on majoritarian principles. Democratic control over the action of elected individuals is exercised only indirectly, through pressure groups or interest groups, which need not represent the viewpoint of electoral majorities. The most effective pressure groups are often the best organized, best connected, and most affluent special interests, and these are not likely to reflect the majority point of view. The costs for majorities to organize are prohibitive; it is simply too tempting for each individual to "free-ride" on the time and energy invested by others. Between 80 and 90 percent of public television watchers make no voluntary contribution to its funding, even when they agree it is a bargain at the price. Political organization is less of a bargain and the price is higher.

Critics often lose sight of the fact that the class-action device was introduced precisely to overcome such economic blocks to organization. Its use can enhance democratic decision-making by allowing courts to police legislative failures based on the free-rider problem. It gives a voice to the silent majority. And if it is democratically appropriate for the courts to intervene in the political process because it has failed to be democratic, then it is appropriate for lawyers to advocate such intervention. It is a service to democracy, not an assault on it.

Judicial Activism versus Judicial Restraint

David Luban

The terms "judicial activism" and "judicial restraint" have been staples of our political vocabulary for decades. They are used frequently, sloppily, and in a sloganeering fashion, and the first question that confronts us is whether they still mean anything at all (assuming they ever did). One cynical answer is that their meaning is all too clear: In current political discourse "judicial activist" is a euphemism for "liberal," "judicial restraint" for "conservative." Perhaps that is so, but such a narrow and partisan political reduction of the debate should be condemned. Talk of judicial activism and judicial restraint pretends to be about principle, not party politics. If the "principles" one appeals to are merely code-names for partisan positions, however, the aspiration to principled argument is a sham, a charade of high-mindedness.

It is, moreover, a charade that can hope to succeed only if the key terms "activism" and "restraint" at one time possessed some other relatively nonpartisan and explicitly jurisprudential meaning the current political debate is aping. It is that other meaning we urgently need to understand.

The basic problem is that the terms do not have just one meaning; in our recent history alone it is possible to find at least seven different, only partially overlapping, uses of the term "judicial activism."

1. Particularly in the 1960s and 1970s, accusations of judicial activism were hurled in connection with the broad use by federal trial judges of their injunctive power to effect so-called "structural remedies" for constitutional violations. The most notorious and divisive structural remedy was court-ordered school busing and (more generally) court-supervised school desegregation. But structural remedies were also used to implement prison reform as a cure for Eighth Amendment violations, as when federal Judge Frank Johnson took over the entire Alabama prison system, and for other purposes as well.

2. This first sense of judicial activism is commonly confused with overeagerness to strike down legislation on constitutional grounds. Actually these are very different. Structural remedies do not respond just to unconstitutional legislation, but also to other illegal practices officials are unwilling to reform, and conversely, aggressive constitutional review implies nothing about the kind of remedy a judge chooses.

3. Aggressive constitutional review of legislation is itself frequently confused with judges creating new constitutional rights. The latter charge is a particularly bitter one, often leveled against the Warren Court by its critics. Yet of all the meanings commonly attached to the term "judicial activism," this is the least useful and coherent. The reason is that talk of "new rights" simply begs the question. Any time a novel legal question appears before the Supreme Court, the winner emerges with a right that has never been explicitly declared before. If that is all that is meant by "new rights," the Court could avoid creating them only by going out of business. "New rights" must therefore mean something more like new general rights, such as the right to privacy. But the Court's opinion would attempt to show why even the "new" general right was implicit in prior law, and hence was *not* a novelty.

   Thus, the criticism claiming that a court has engaged in creating new rights must simply be a confused way of saying that these rights were not implicit in the law, that the judge interpreted the law incorrectly. If that is what is meant, why not just say so? It should be clear, moreover, that mistaken interpretation of the law is a danger any judge can stumble into, including proponents of judicial self-restraint.

4. In public debates about the Supreme Court, the most prominent meaning of "judicial activism" involves the theory of constitutional interpretation. A judicial activist in these terms is a judge who engages in making constitutional law that cannot be firmly tied to clear constitutional language or to the intent of the Framers. In his best-selling book *The Tempting of America*, former Judge Robert Bork insists that judicial restraint requires justices to refrain from doing this; a restrained judge must interpret the constitution by appealing to original intent. The debate between non-originalism (or as lawyers call it, "noninterpretivism") and originalism is thus another meaning of judicial activism versus judicial restraint, clearly distinct from the three we have just canvassed.

5. Non-originalism is in turn often confused with substituting the judge's own morality for the law. Clearly they are different. To say, as the non-originalist does, that constitutional interpretation must appeal to information or values not explicit in the language or the Framers' intent in no way suggests that those values must come from the judge's own morality. Some non-originalists tell the judge to look to community morality, or tradition, or to the evolving state of the law, all of which might be alien to the judge's own morality.

6. Seventh Circuit Judge Richard A. Posner has proposed another meaning for judicial activism/judicial restraint in his award-winning book *The Federal Courts*. For Judge Posner, judicial restraint should be defined as the attempt to limit the power of the courts over other governmental institutions, while judicial activism is the attempt to increase the power of the courts vis-a-vis the other branches. Non-originalism and "the judge's own morality" can be pressed into the service of either activism or restraint as Posner understands these.

7. Last (and least), some critics equate judicial activism with result-oriented judging, that is, tailoring legal principle to fit the judge's prior convictions about how he wants the case to come out. But this is simply abusive: It equates judicial activism with prejudice or with infidelity to law.

Evaluating Judicial Activism

Is activism a bad thing? As our discussion so far should make clear, that will depend on what you mean by "activism." We can simplify the problem by considering just three principal meanings of "activism": Judge Posner's notion of courts increasing their own power over other governmental institutions, non-originalist constitutional interpretation, and moralistic judging.

Judge Posner thinks we need judicial restraint today because activist decisions, in his sense, cannot meet a "publicity test" he proposes: "A decision is principled if and only if the ground of decision can be stated truthfully in a form the judge could publicly avow without inviting virtually universal condemnation by professional opinion." And, Judge Posner believes, no judge could come right out and say he or she was attempting to increase the power of the courts over other governmental institutions.

Here Posner appears to have blurred the distinction between the *aim* of a decision and its *side effects*. It is true that no judge could publicly avow he had decided a case *in order to* enhance the power of the courts—we do not easily tolerate judicial empire-building. But more typically the enhancement of judicial power over other institutions is not the aim or ground of decision—it is an incidental side effect. Judge Johnson did not run the Alabama prison system for the sake of running the prison system, but because officials refused to correct constitutional violations: That, not a desire to grab power, was the ground for Johnson's decision. And so in the end it is unclear whether judicial activism emerging merely as a by-product of the courts' decisions fails the publicity test after all.

While other stronger arguments on behalf of judicial restraint could be offered, Posner himself is quite convincing in rebutting many of them. He points out that judicial activism does not make big government bigger, since the courts' extra power comes at the expense of other governmental branches; that even though courts are not majoritarian or representative institutions, this shows only that it is a mistake to think of our constitutional system as majoritarian and representative, since the Constitution obviously created the courts; and that while courts are not very good at running institutions such as prisons, other branches of government may not be any better. At best, "judicial self-restraint is a contingent, a time-and-place-bound, rather than an absolute good," because in some historical situations the other branches of government are badly in need of checks and balances, while in others they are not.

Original Intent

What of the debate between non-originalism and originalism? Originalists, recall, insist that vague constitutional provisions be filled in by appealing to the intent of the Framers, whereas non-originalists will appeal to values or information found elsewhere, for example in our present-day moral understanding.

At first glance, originalism seems very persuasive, little more than insisting that when you read an eighteenth-century novel and come across an unfamiliar word, you should look it up in an eighteenth-century dictionary rather than a contemporary *Webster's*. For what is a document other than the concrete expression of its authors' intentions?

Nevertheless, there are powerful objections to appealing to Framers' intent. The primary problem is an obvious one. Even if we can find out what individual Framers intended, how can we figure out the "group intention" of the Framers as a collective body? There is no such thing as a group mind, and we may suspect that there is no such thing as a group intention either. To construct a group intention out of information about individual intentions, we will need some rule of combination. Do we count the intentions of Framers who opposed a measure? What of those who supported it but only as a regrettable compromise? Or because of log-rolling? As philosopher Ronald Dworkin points out, moreover, it seems up for grabs whether to count a Framer's *intentions* as his *hopes* or his *expectations* about how a clause will be interpreted. The moral is that "Framers' intent" can be determined only by making a lot of conventional or even arbitrary choices. But that proves that the originalist, no less than the non-originalist, is incapable of answering a constitutional question without importing a lot of contemporary theoretical baggage into the enterprise. And we are likely to be a lot more confident about the values the non-originalist appeals to, such as our contemporary moral understanding, than we are about how to answer the various questions concerning group intentions. So the originalist may well turn out to be marching us onto a shakier and more controversial limb than the non-originalist.

An even more devastating problem for the originalist arises from the fact that Framers' intentions can be concrete or general, and these may be incompatible. Take a simple example based on the Seventh Amendment guarantee of a jury trial for civil matters involving more than $20. On its face, nothing could be clearer. But suppose we ask whether we should interpret this in eighteenth-century dollars or today's dollars. In today's dollars the amount of money would be much higher.

Let us try to answer the question by appealing to Framers' intent. Their *concrete* intent could not be clearer: to guarantee jury trials if more than $20 was at issue. But their *general* intent might have been this: to make sure that jury trials would be available when the amount at issue was significant, but to permit courts or legislatures to deny jury trials for trivial disputes. For at the close of the eighteenth century, $20 was a significant amount of money. Nowadays, however, a $20 litigation is almost too trivial even for small claims court; so if we respect the Framers' concrete intention, we violate their general intention, and vice versa.

If this sounds farfetched, please remember that even Judge Bork, the best-known proponent of originalism, invoked the same argument at the confirmation hearings over his nomination, which the Senate rejected, to the Supreme Court. Senator Arlen Specter asked whether, given his commitment to originalism, Judge Bork would have had to vote against the *Brown* decision, since the historical evidence suggests that the framers of the Fourteenth Amendment did not intend it to preclude school segregation. Judge Bork replied that their *general* intention was to ban race discrimination; their *particular* belief was that separate-but-equal was not invidious race discrimination, but, since we are convinced that they were wrong about the particular belief, we respect their general intention by rejecting their concrete intention.

Now, in fact this line of argument amounts to abandoning originalism—first because it picks and chooses among the historical views of the Framers, taking some seriously while rejecting others, but second because it seeks a general intention, an overarching idea largely independent of the historical minutiae. How do we determine the general intention of a provision? The best evidence, it seems, is in the language of the provision itself, understood in such a way as to yield a plausible general principle. We reconstruct the Framers' general intention, that is, by finding the most reasonable reading of their language we can, but at this point originalism has simply become non-originalism, and the debate is over. For now we see that even the originalist must interpret ambiguous constitutional language in such a way that it seems most reasonable.

Most reasonable to whom? Isn't this simply smuggling in the judge's own values? A first reply to this ultimate objection of "moralistic judging" is that the alternative to the judge interpreting vague language according to his or her own standards of what is most reasonable is the judge interpreting vague language according to his or her own standards of what is *less* reasonable—and that seems merely perverse.

A more satisfactory reply is that it is indeed wrong for judges simply to cite some value as though it were an authority like a statute or prior case: That would be usurpation. Rather, a judge shows that a principle is reasonable by reasoning to it rather than from it—by argument rather than by fiat.

Can values be established by argument, by reason? Well, we do argue with others about questions of value, and sometimes we even persuade or are persuaded. That suggests the answer is yes. Some, however, including Judge Bork, deny that values are susceptible to reasoned discourse. In his best-known work of constitutional theory, Bork wrote: "There is no principled way to decide that one man's gratification is more worthy than another's or that one form of gratification is more worthy than another. . . . [T]he judge has no basis other than his own values upon which to set aside the community judgment embodied in the statute. That, by definition, is an inadequate basis for judicial supremacy."

Can value judgments be the conclusions of reasoned arguments, or are they simply expressions of "gratification," the brute fact that one thing pleases me and another does not? This is the oldest, and perhaps still most unsettled, question of moral philosophy. It is a surprising yet reassuring fact that the issue of judicial activism, on its surface an intensely practical matter of public concern, may ultimately turn on this subtle and disturbing question of moral theory. Surprising, because we do not often expect theory to matter so much; reassuring, because it convinces us that even apart from its undeniably crucial political aspect, the public debate over judicial activism turns on a matter of perennial importance.

Settling out of Court

Claudia Mills

"**I** would rather lose my vineyard," wrote Montaigne, "than go to court for it." Many Americans feel otherwise. Whether or not we are, as many have charged, the most litigious nation in human history, our civil litigation rate is certainly among the highest in the world.

Most lawsuits that are filed—upwards of 85 percent—do not reach trial. The great majority are settled out of court by the parties' attorneys before a formal jury verdict or judicial decision is rendered. This is a matter of sheer necessity. "It is a given," according to U.S. District Court Judge H. Lee Sarokin, "that if cases did not continue to settle in roughly the same percentages, our system of justice would come to a standstill." For reasons of cost and speed, "in rare exceptions, it must be conceded that the preponderance of settlements in the judicial system is a worthy goal."

The imperative toward settlement rather than trial is defended on other, less purely expedient, grounds as well. Settlement is claimed to leave participants more satisfied with the resolution of their case. It is lauded as representing a voluntary agreement between the parties, rather than a coercive court order, a give-a-little, get-a-little compromise, rather than a lopsided black-and-white judgment in which the winner takes all. And what Harvard's president Derek Bok has called the "gentler arts of reconciliation and accommodation" involved in negotiating a settlement are, well, kinder and gentler than the aggressive rough-and-tumble of hardball litigation in the adversary system. Insofar as the so-called litigiousness of the American public is decried, a trend toward resolving rather than trying suits seems an impulse in the right direction.

This favorable attitude toward settlement shows itself in the growing willingness of judges to use the power of the bench to put considerable pressure on the parties to settle. It has inspired a movement within the legal community for alternate dispute resolution (ADR), resolution of disputes either through mandatory mediation or outside the court system altogether, in neighborhood dispute-resolution centers. ADR is supported by such odd bedfellows as the establishment bar association, which views ADR as a way of easing the current crisis of the courts, and liberal-left reformers who welcome it as a more participatory and less bureaucratic approach to dispute resolution of the people, by the people, and for the people.

Certainly settlement will continue to be the destiny of most civil cases brought in American courts, just as most criminal cases will continue to be disposed of through plea bargaining. But we can ask whether this trend should be encouraged or insofar as possible resisted. Should judges actively promote settlement as a core judicial function or should they concentrate their efforts elsewhere? Settlement is cheaper and swifter—is it *better*?

Participant Satisfaction

One criterion for comparing settlement with judgment is to look at the participants' own satisfaction with the process. For all that people sue, apparently they don't *like* to sue. When asked in one study how they felt in general about suing people, 77 percent of respondents thought one should settle without suit if possible or always settle without suit. What people seem to want, by and large, is just to get their problem solved (put crassly: to get some money from somebody else), rather than to achieve a legal victory for its own sake. In a survey of Detroit area residents, for example, the proportion of respondents reporting serious problems who sought "justice" or legal vindication (as opposed to a satisfactory adjustment) was tiny in all areas other than discrimination. Moreover, in a study of small claims courts in Maine, parties whose cases were mediated reported themselves satisfied with their experience more often than those whose cases were adjudicated (66.6 percent to 54 percent).

Marc Galanter, professor at the University of Wisconsin, Madison, Law School, reminds us, however, that "significant numbers of those who settle are not very happy with the outcome." The difference in levels of reported satisfaction between settlement and trial survey groups is not all that great. And satisfaction with the entire process does not run very deep. Galanter cautions that "the choice of settlement (or trial) is a choice in a context of limited knowledge, strategic exigency, and a limited set of perceived alternatives." Thus he is wary of equating the "choice to settle or to litigate with an informed affirmation of the quality of the process."

Reviewing the research on levels of participant satisfaction with settlement, philosopher David Luban argues that "participants aren't necessarily satisfied because the process has been a good one; they can be satisfied simply because their expectations have been illegitimately lowered." And, Luban points out, "attorneys interested in facilitating a settlement are great client-expectation lowerers." Galanter agrees: "Lawyers may spend a great deal of effort 'educating' their clients about the virtues of settlement compared to the cost, uncertainty, and arbitrariness of adjudication." The fox decides the grapes are sour once he knows (or has been led to believe) he cannot have them anyway; the client who has been convinced he cannot win at trial is then convinced to take what he can in settlement. When preferences have been carefully crafted to be easily satisfiable, their subsequent satisfaction proves little.

Moreover, although both parties may declare themselves satisfied with their settlement—at least satisfied enough to avoid trial—significant inequities between the parties may make the rest of us question whether satisfaction in itself is an adequate index for justice. The biblical dictum that "for whosoever hath, to him shall be given, and he shall have more abundance: but whosover hath not, from him shall be taken away even that he hath" (Matt. 13: 11-12) is reflected in the dynamics of the negotiating process. Both the cost savings and the satisfaction resulting from settlement tend to be unevenly distributed, for reasons that have more to do with the parties' initial endowments than with the merits of the case.

Legal scholar Owen Fiss, of Yale University Law School, explains that "settlement is (in part) a function of the resources available to each party to finance the litigation, and those resources are frequently distributed unequally. . . . In these cases, the distribution of financial resources, or the ability of one party to pass along its costs, will invariably infect the bargaining process; and the settlement will be at odds with a conception of justice that seeks to make the wealth of the parties irrelevant." Quite simply, the poorer party may be so desperate to get anything at all that he accepts whatever payment his adversary is willing to give. The more powerful and affluent party, on the other hand, already comfortably situated and with the resources to finance a protracted trial, has the luxury of choosing to bide his time, holding out for terms to his advantage.

Of course, the weaker party is disadvantaged in a trial as well. But, Fiss argues, in a trial "we count . . . on the guiding presence of the judge, who can employ a number of measures to lessen the impact of distributional inequalities." And "there is . . . a critical difference between a process like settlement, which is based on bargaining and accepts inequalities of wealth as an integral and legitimate component of the process, and a process like judgment, which knowingly struggles against those inequalities."

It turns out, then, that what we care about is not so much satisfaction as justice. Is there any reason to think settlements are more likely to lead to just results than trials? It may be hoped that as each side in a settlement proceeding has the opportunity to hear and consider the other's point of view, each will be led to appreciate the merits of the other's case. The resulting agreement may then be more just and fair, more decent and humane, than what might otherwise emerge. But Luban suggests that any advantage ADR has in this respect will be modest at best. The parties are, after all, adversaries, which is why they took each other to court in the first place. The party in a stronger bargaining position is seldom likely to accept a settlement that diverges greatly from what she could hope to get at trial.

Public Effects of Settlement

So far we have been considering whether settlement works to the interests of the disputing parties themselves. But the plaintiff and defendant are not the only ones affected by the outcome of their altercation and how it is reached; the choice between settlement and judgment may have vital ramifications for third parties as well as for the public at large.

Returning to the issue of participant satisfaction, the satisfaction of those parties present to a settlement may be achieved at the expense of other individuals or groups whose concerns their agreement flagrantly ignores. Luban, arguing that "an ADR process may well succeed because the participants are able to pass the losses and downside risks on to third parties," gives this example. "A hospital plans to build a halfway house for convalescent schizophrenics in a well-to-do neighborhood; the neighborhood's residents object and initiate legal action to prevent the construction; the hospital persists; the mayor sends in a mediator; and the disputants solve their problem by the hospital agreeing to erect the halfway house in a poor neighborhood instead." Such a "nimby" (Not in My Back Yard) problem is solved to the satisfaction of both contesting parties by thrusting it conveniently into the backyard of a third.

Civil litigation has a public as well as a private dimension. Once it enters the court system, a dispute between two private citizens raises issues that rightly concern the public at large. Of course, the taxpaying public, who foots the bill for the nation's administration of justice, has an interest in reducing costs, and all of us have an obvious stake in maintaining an efficient and orderly judicial system. These interests may be well served when cases settle out of court. But we have other values that the trend toward settlement may jeopardize.

Settlement frequently goes hand in hand with secrecy. Judge Sarokin reports that "judges routinely . . . seal settlements at the request of the parties. Indeed, defendants frequently impose such secrecy as a condition of consummating the settlement and make disclosure a ground for rescinding it." Cases abound in which such "gag orders" have seriously compromised the public welfare. In recent years, reports *The Washington Post*, General Motors settled a rash of lawsuits filed by victims of fiery car crashes and then used court secrecy procedures to keep company documents about auto safety from becoming public. In another, hardly atypical case, McNeil Pharmaceutical, a subsidiary of Johnson & Johnson, was able to seal the records of hundreds of lawsuits involving fatal and life-threatening allergic reactions caused by its painkiller Zomax, thus preventing a public debate on its risks and permitting other Zomax users to continue to be jeopardized. The *Post* series concludes, "Every day, someone gets into a car, takes a drug, sees a doctor, or wakes up near a toxic site that has been the subject of a lawsuit covered by a confidentiality order."

When cases settle, the judge is also deprived of the opportunity to deliver an opinion that would otherwise have added to the body of legal precedent that constitutes our "common law." Indeed, Judge Sarokin charges, "some settlements are consummated for just that very purpose—namely to preclude the establishment of a precedent which might affect other cases or establish requirements for future conduct." But, according to Fiss, the tasks of the judge are "not simply to maximize the ends of private parties, not simply to secure the peace, but to explicate and give force to the values embodied in authoritative texts such as the Constitution and statutes: to interpret those values and to bring reality in accord with them. This duty is not discharged when the parties settle." Where would we be today, what progress would we have made toward making good the Constitution's pledge of racial justice, if Linda Brown had settled her case against the Board of Education of Topeka, Kansas, rather than taken it to trial?

Cost Arguments

Setting cost aside, then, it is difficult to defend settlement of civil cases as demonstrably superior in some other way to trial. In facing the problems posed by our overloaded civil court system, concerns about the sheer quantity of cases pending may have to be traded off against concerns with the quality of justice provided. Judges who pride themselves on being "settlement judges" rather than "trial judges" may earn kudos for cost-cutting, but that is all.

And even those kudos, it turns out, may be undeserved. While it is incontrovertible that settlement expedites the processing of cases, it is not clear that judicial efforts to facilitate settlement end up reducing costs or speeding dispositions. The vast majority of cases will settle out of court anyway; little is apparently gained by judges actively attempting to initiate or to broker settlements. Galanter observes, "That judicial participation increases the number and speed of dispositions is, for its proponents, an article of faith. But the few studies that have undertaken systematic observation have found little evidence that judicial efforts bring about production gains." The dynamics of settlement, then, seem to be relatively independent of judicial intervention.

Sarokin warns, moreover, that the trend toward settlement, while easing court dockets in the short run, may actually work to increase judicial caseloads in the long run. While it "obviously reduces the number of pending cases . . . it may simultaneously encourage the filing of new ones. The settlement mode of litigation makes it unnecessary to be certain of one's defense to the claims asserted. Tenuous suits may be instituted and weak defenses interposed with the confidence that neither is likely to be tested. The knowledge that the court will undertake to resolve the matter before trial may be adding to the number of cases instituted and defended." Thus is spawned a spate of nuisance suits, long decried by insurance companies—cases filed simply to settle.

Even granting the cost arguments, however, it may be that the balance between quantity and quality is being wrongly struck. Sarokin fears that "the court's interest in disposing of cases, of reducing its calendar, is becoming obsessive. Quantity has begun to compete with quality." He charges that the practice of issuing judicial "report cards," published statistics on each judge's total of dispositions and speed in rendering decisions, encourages a judicial "assembly line." Interestingly, he observes, "there are no published statistics on the number of opinions written, the number of reversals or affirmances, and obviously no analysis of the quality of a judge's performance. . . . To be careful, thorough, thoughtful and reflective are not characteristics which the statistics reveal or encourage. The reports reveal pressure to do a lot and do it quickly."

Fiss expresses an even stronger opposition to settlement, stating, "I do not believe that settlement as a general practice is preferable to judgment or should be institutionalized on a wholesale and indiscriminate basis. It should be treated as a highly problematic technique for streamlining dockets. . . . Although dockets are trimmed, justice may not be done. Like plea bargaining, settlement is a capitulation to the conditions of mass society and should be neither encouraged nor praised."

Conclusion

The fact that most cases settle, and must settle, out of court will continue to characterize our civil court system. We need to ask not whether it should continue, but how it should be regulated and the extent to which judges should actively intervene to encourage it. Sarokin, for one, recommends removing judges from the settlement process, leaving mediation and negotiation to specialists in that field and thereby freeing judges to concentrate on the task of judging. Other needed reforms might include legislation curbing the guarantee of secrecy as a condition of settlement; such legislation is currently under consideration in a number of states.

The general and mounting enthusiasm for out-of-court settlement has obscured the imperative to subject it to critical scrutiny and regulatory controls. At the very least, we need to ask some new and different questions. After all, as Galanter writes, "most remedy-seeking in the vicinity of courts is going to eventuate in settlement. Ensuring the quality of these settlements is a central task of the administration of justice."

The sources used in preparing this article are Judge H. Lee Sarokin, paper prepared for the Institute for Philosophy and Public Policy Working Group on Judicial Ethics, at Washington, D.C., May 1987; Marc Galanter, "Judges and the Quality of Settlements," Institute for Philosophy and Public Policy Working Paper JJ-1, (College Park, Md.: Institute for Philosophy and Public Policy, March 1989); David Luban, "The Quality of Justice," Denver University Law Review 66 (1989); Owen Fiss, "Against Settlement," The Yale Law Journal 93 (1984); and Benjamin Weiser and Elsa Walsh, "Public Courts, Private Justice" (four-part series), The Washington Post, October 23, 24, 25, 26, 1988.

Two Cheers for
Punitive Damages

David Luban

Punitive damages are awarded to a plaintiff in a civil suit when the defendant's injurious behavior was not merely illegal but also morally offensive—when a tort was intentional, for example, or the defendant was negligent to the point of recklessness. The aim of such awards is explicitly to punish the defendant over and above compensating the plaintiff's present and future losses from the injury.

Many critics suspect that juries use punitive damages simply in order to pick deep corporate pockets, giving an undeserved windfall to plaintiffs. Such critics believe this encourages unscrupulous plaintiffs' lawyers to bring weak or frivolous cases that don't belong in court; the result is a litigation explosion, increased insurance premiums, and a brake on innovative new technologies for fear they will spawn expensive lawsuits. For this reason, many tort reformers propose capping or even eliminating punitive damages.

The evidence does not substantiate the charges, however. State courts—where 98 percent of litigation occurs—report that tort filings have grown only slightly faster than the population over the last decade, and the most extensive study of punitive damages finds that they are awarded in a mere 1.5 percent of personal-injury cases.

Critics also believe, however, that high punitive damages are unprincipled and indeed unconstitutional. "Let the punishment fit the crime" expresses the principle of proportionality, and punitive damages are often grossly disproportionate to compensatory damages. It is this criticism, based on philosophical principle, that concerns me here.

In its 1988–1989 term the U.S. Supreme Court heard a case entitled *Browning-Ferris Industries (BFI)* v. *Kelco*. Kelco was an independent garbage-hauler in Burlington, Vermont, which set itself up in competition with the only other garbage-hauler in town, a subsidiary of BFI (a large Houston-based corporation). Kelco—owned by a man named John Kelley—soon attracted more than half the market, and BFI responded badly. A BFI executive ordered its local franchise to put Kelley out of business, using the expression "Squish him like a bug." BFI slashed its prices and soon won back a sizable portion of the market. Kelco sued for predatory pricing, and the jury awarded $51,000 in compensatory damages. However, presumably impressed by "Squish him like a bug," the jury proceeded to impose $6 million in punitive damages on BFI.

BFI appealed, claiming that punitive damages so far in excess of the compensatory damages amounted to "excessive fines," prohibited by the Eighth Amendment along with "cruel and unusual punishment." The Supreme Court ruled seven to two in favor of Kelco, but based the decision on grounds having nothing to do with proportionality. [In the spring of 1991, the Supreme Court resoundingly upheld the constitutionality of large punitive damages in *Haslip* v. *Pacific Mutual Life Insurance Co.*] I agree with tort reformers that unlimited punitive damages violate the principle of proportionality, but I also want to argue that there is nothing at all disproportionate about punitive damages of a magnitude bigger than the injuries actually suffered by the plaintiff.

Norm Projection and Deterrence

First, consider the staple justifications of punishment: deterrence, retribution, incapacitation, rehabilitation. The latter two—incapacitation and rehabilitation—are unlikely to be at issue in punitive-damage cases. Typically we think of rehabilitation as a process of retraining, education, therapy or whatever that occurs during a term in prison, and it is hard to imagine a corporate entity being "rehabilitated" by paying money. Similarly, incapacitation usually means prison, and is pertinent to punitive-damage cases only in the rare situation when a jury decides to put the defendant out of business. Thus, discussion of punitive damages should focus on deterrence and retributivist theories.

Not only on these two, however; punishment may prevent offenses in other ways besides deterrence. Deterrence suggests that people will disobey the law unless they fear punishment. But this is a gross caricature of our political psychology. Many of us will willingly comply with law once we know it is seriously intended, and sociologists point out that an important aim of punishment is to highlight in a public way the serious intent behind legal norms.

This said, consider the complaint about punitive damages raised by BFI. It claims that $6 million is disproportionate because it so far exceeds the $51,000 compensatory damages. BFI thinks punitive damages should be scaled to compensatory damages, which measure the bad consequences of the tort to its victim. BFI's proposed scaling principle thus scales punishment to the bad consequences of an offense. But, as we shall see, this idea makes no sense under any of the three remaining rationales for punishment—norm-projection, deterrence, and retribution.

Under the norm-projection rationale, the purpose of punishment in this suit is to emphasize that the law against predatory pricing is a serious one. And I believe this can be done *only* if the punitive damages are grossly disproportionate to compensatory damages. Kelco lost $51,000 worth of business to BFI because of its predatory pricing. If the punitive damages were roughly commensurable with compensatory damages—say, $150,000—BFI might well be tempted to treat this as a mere cost of doing business and to play what is called the "enforcement lottery": continue its predatory practices hoping it will be successfully sued only one time out of four, so it will still turn a profit.

That is, with lenient punitive damages companies will be more likely to treat the law not as a norm demanding compliance but merely as a kind of tax on predatory pricing. The difference is fundamental. A serious norm prohibiting conduct is *categorical*: It says "Don't do X!" By contrast, a tax on conduct is *disjunctive*: It says "Either don't do X or else pay," thereby presenting the norm in merely optional form. My contention here is that only by imposing punitive damages of a different order from compensatory damages can a jury convey the message that a norm is categorical, that it demands compliance and not cost-benefit analysis. The point is to make the numbers on the balance sheet so ridiculous that the offender stops looking at the balance sheet.

Similarly, to fully deter would-be offenders from engaging in morally outrageous behavior, the price tag must be high enough to make playing the enforcement lottery an unattractive proposition. We have seen that this requires punitive damages that far outweigh the gains from committing the tort, weighted by the likelihood of being sued successfully: The lower the chance of being caught, the higher the punitive damages. In the BFI case, BFI's gains roughly equaled Kelco's losses—the compensatory damages. Since predatory pricing schemes are not easy to detect, deterrence requires setting BFI's punitive damages well in excess of its gains, and thus well in excess of compensatory damages.

Retribution

The heart of my analysis arises on retributivist theories of punishment, and the basic point is simply stated. A retributivist scales punishment to the heinousness of the offense, and that is not measured by the magnitude of harm. A moment's negligence behind the wheel, of the sort each of us has been guilty of many times, may result in horrible consequences, while cold-bloodedly throwing a child out of a skyscraper window may result in very little harm because the child's suspenders miraculously catch on a flagpole.

The hard question is what scaling principles make retributivist sense, and to answer this, we must know what makes retributivism plausible. In *Forgiveness and Mercy* philosopher Jean Hampton explains that culpably harming another person or being culpably negligent expresses a false view of the wrongdoer's value relative to that of the victim. Implicitly it says that the victim is a low person, the sort of person one can do this kind of thing to. Or it says that the wrongdoer is an especially valuable and high kind of person, the sort of person entitled to take liberties with the well-being of others. Or it says both.

It is crucial to Hampton's analysis of retributivism that the wrongdoer has implicitly asserted a kind of undeserved mastery and superiority over the victim: in different words, the wrongdoer has expressed a falsehood about the world of value. The purpose of punishment is to reassert the truth about the relative value of wrongdoer and victim by inflicting a publicly visible defeat on the wrongdoer. And the magnitude of punishment must reflect the magnitude and if possible the nature of the asserted inequality between wrongdoer and victim. A more heinous act expresses more contempt for the victim's value relative to the wrongdoer's, and so a more decisive defeat must be visited on the wrongdoer to reassert our public judgment of the victim's worth. If the punishment is too lenient, the society as a whole implicitly ratifies the view that the victim is the sort of person it is all right to do these things to. (Hampton offers a telling example: If sentences for forcible rape are low, the legal system is expressing a contemptuous view of the value of women relative to men.)

This still does not tell us how a retributivist would scale punitive damages. And of course there can be no formula for punitive damages, since heinousness cannot be assigned a straightforward dollar value. But once we begin to focus on the requirement that the punishment express, as transparently as possible, the true scale of values in the moral world, we have a rough-and-ready yardstick for assessing punitive damages (and, in some cases, for capping them). Let me illustrate what I mean with an example.

In 1981 a California jury heard a case involving Grimshaw, a boy who had been hideously burned in an explosion of his Ford Pinto. The plaintiff presented evidence that Ford had known of the Pinto's defective gas tank, but had decided against recalling it after a cost-benefit analysis showed that the company could save $125 million by leaving the unaltered cars on the road. The jury awarded the boy $125 million in punitive damages, later reduced by the judge to $6.6 million. The case has been cited by critics of the tort system as a classic example of a jury run amok, but I believe the jury's award was a perfect case of "letting the punishment fit the tort."

Under a deterrence rationale the jury's decision makes obvious sense: Ford's reliance on cost-benefit analysis indicates that it could be deterred only if it lost money through its decision, and the jury's punitive damages were calculated precisely to annihilate Ford's profit. But in a retributivist view it also makes sense to take the outcome of Ford's cost-benefit analysis as a measure of wrongdoing. Ford had displayed contempt for Grimshaw's value, but more importantly it had displayed a certain *kind* of contempt for Grimshaw's value. In Immanuel Kant's famous words, it treated Grimshaw as possessing merely a price, not a dignity. For this reason, inflicting a monetary defeat on Ford was an especially expressive form of punishment. Moreover, Ford had affixed its customers' prices through the technique of cost-benefit analysis. Therefore, the jury chose to impose a monetary defeat on Ford that incorporated within it a reference to Ford's own cost-benefit analysis—a defeat Ford could not help but understand because the jury held up the cost-benefit analysis as a kind of mirror in which we would all recognize the moral truth of the situation.

Obviously, the medium of monetary damages has limited expressive power, and in many instances of high punitive damages we will be unable to infer anything from the amount beyond the message that the jury thought the tortfeasor had been a real schmuck. Nevertheless, high punitive damages are often adequate expressions of the tortfeasor's wrongdoing. Punitive damages arise most often in the context of economically motivated wrongdoing: corner-cutting in manufacturing or recalling products, as in *Grimshaw,* or ruthless business practices, as in *Kelco.* High punitive damages hit *homo economicus* where it hurts: an eye for an eye, a tooth for a tooth, and a bottom line for a bottom line.

The Practical Reason for Punitive Damages

This brings me to one of the most important points about punitive damages. It is the nature of the beast that punitive damages are sought only against white collars, because only white collars have deep pockets. I want to contend that punitive damages are the only practical method of exercising social control on white collars, because criminal penalties are no substitute. For even if egregious and morally shocking torts were criminalized, the cases would never be prosecuted, because it is very hard to determine that an accident was brought about by such torts. Consider the Pinto cases once again. The only objective event in each is a car crash and subsequent burning. The repeated pattern of such crashes indicating defective design emerges only when we do a statistical analysis of all the evidence from many different states and jurisdictions, and then investigate the company to discover culpable negligence. No federal agency has or could have the resources to carry out such massive investigations across the entire range of accidents and products. Nor would we want such an omniscient federal agency.

The punitive-damages system remedies this problem in the most obvious way: It provides injured parties and their lawyers with financial incentives to do the investigation themselves. Typically, a tort lawyer works on a 30- to 40-percent contingency fee and invests thousands of dollars of her firm's resources in investigation, hoping to recoup the investment by winning big-ticket punitive-damages cases. She is a bounty hunter. She may not be a "nice person," for bounty hunters are mainly out for the buck. This is the grain of truth in critics' suspicions about personal-injury lawyers. But in a world of scarce public resources for law enforcement, the private bounty hunter does an important and worthwhile job. Viewed in this light, the punitive-damages system exists not to provide plaintiffs with windfalls, but to induce the bounty hunter to do her job. And this provides an important practical argument against slashing punitive damages: If we cut back on the bounty hunter's reward too much by limiting punitive damages or contingency fees, we will lose out on needed law enforcement.

For as we have seen, government is incapable of controlling white-collar wrongdoing, though it may work to control the villainous poor. That leaves the punitive-damages system, which—warts and all—stands out as our best hope for protection from the villainous rich.

This article was condensed and adapted from Marc Galanter and David Luban, "Poetic Justice: Legal Pluralism and the Jurisprudence of Punitive Damages," manuscript, n.p., n.d. Sources cited in this article are Kelco v. BFI, *845 F. 2d 404 (2nd Cir. 1988); Jean Hampton, "The Retributive Idea," in Jeffrie G. Murphy and Jean Hampton,* Forgiveness and Mercy *(Cambridge: Cambridge University Press, 1988); and* Grimshaw v. Ford, *119 Cal. App. 3d 757 (1981).*

Confronting the Insurance Crisis

Alan Strudler

T he insurance industry confronts an antagonistic public. California voters, who pay high insurance premiums and suspect that insurers are gouging them, passed an initiative that limits the right of an insurer to choose the price at which it can offer to sell a policy. According to the president of the National Insurance Consumer Organization, "more than 40 consumer organizations, from well-known national groups to small state-oriented groups, are seeking changes in insurance laws and regulations" based on the California initiative. In one form or another, then, the California initiative threatens to spread across the nation.

The California incident cannot be understood simply in terms of a desire among voters for cheaper insurance. Voters have fastened on the insurance industry and not on other businesses that sell expensive products. Consumers believe insurance premiums are *unfairly* expensive.

Insurers, on the other hand, maintain that inefficiencies in the tort system rather than their own greed best explain increases in premiums. To defend this view, they invoke the work of social scientists who have compiled evidence of inefficiency and waste in the tort system. They then argue that the tort system must be reformed.

Evidence of inefficiency or waste, however, does not in itself justify changes in regulations that govern tort and insurance. The public tolerates some inefficiency where the alternative would be to sacrifice moral decency and rights, and it apparently regards the tort system as a device for vindicating the individual's right not to be unfairly harmed. Proposals for tort reform must, therefore, square with the public goals and values that underlie the tort system.

However important these goals and values may be, the approach most states now take in aiding accident victims, an approach that relies heavily on the tort system, grows more expensive each year. Until recently, stable and hence inconspicuous insurance premiums have hidden the costs of the American response to accidents, but as insurance prices soar, we no longer avoid social decisions about how to pay for these costs. If Americans continue to endorse the tort system as the primary vehicle for protection against accident costs, then insurance premiums—which ultimately pay for that protection—will increase. On the other hand, if we find that this system is not an appealing way to provide the kind of protection we want, then it is time to consider mechanisms that are less expensive and more efficient than those found in the current tort system.

The Tort System as a Compensation Device

The public blames a variety of social woes—including corporate bankruptcies, the refusal of municipalities to provide needed services, and the withdrawal of useful pharmaceuticals from the market—on escalating tort and insurance costs. Certainly one cannot deny that the prospect of tort liability has a chilling effect on the provision of many goods and services—especially the products of modern technology, including pharmaceuticals, chemicals, and nuclear power. Why does the tort system seem to hound these products?

One explanation stems from the nature of the products involved. While many of these products improve health and contribute to social welfare, they also expose some individuals to increased risk. Use of a vaccine, for example, might decrease the incidence of a particular disease and thus diminish morbidity, but in many instances the vaccine might itself cause serious side effects. The vaccine might produce a net benefit in lives saved, then, but cause paralysis, disfigurement, or death to some who would have been better off without the vaccine.

When jurors are asked whether the manufacturer of such a vaccine should be liable for the harm it does, their sympathies tend to lie with those who suffer, and juries therefore may find against the manufacturers. As the law stands, however, a manufacturer may be liable for a harm only if it was negligent or its product was defective. While legal scholars still debate the precise interpretations of negligence, strict liability, and other standards of liability in tort cases, most commentators agree that these standards ultimately implicate a cost-benefit test: Decisions about manufacturer liability require weighing the social costs and benefits of the manufacturer's product or conduct.

Juries, however, seem reluctant to weigh costs against benefits. The reasons for this reluctance are various. First, a jury may be moved by compassion or sympathy for the injured person, and thus refuse to put the interest of society as a whole before that of the individual. Second, juries may doubt the relevance of riskiness in life—they may suppose that for every accident anyone suffers, someone else is probably responsible and should pay to make the victim whole. Third, juries may look for "deep pockets," treating the legal system as a substitute for social insurance. Finally, society, whether expressing itself in jury decisions or in statutes, is willing to spend far more to prevent "artificial" than "naturally" occurring hazards, thus buying much less overall safety than it would if concerned solely with cost and so implicitly rejecting an efficient balancing of costs against benefits.

Jury bias against synthetic risk, if it exists, may create a disincentive for the production of risky but socially useful technologies, and it may prompt manufacturers to withdraw some useful products from the market. It may also cause insurance prices to escalate, along with the price of insured products. Some commentators maintain that to avoid the impact of these jury biases, we should take decisions about product liability out of the hands of juries and turn these over to regulatory agencies, which are better equipped to engage in "unbiased" cost-benefit analysis.

Clearly this suggestion makes most sense on the assumption that the aim of the tort system is to create incentives that encourage manufacturers to sell only products whose social benefits exceed their costs—including the costs of accidents. But one might, instead, believe that the goal of tort law is to aid victims, to redistribute risk, or to redistribute wealth. What one counts as an attractive tort reform depends on what one regards as the proper goal of the tort system.

In any case, juries act on their preference that the tort system be used as a device for compensating accident victims. Unless those of us who wish to improve the tort system learn to accommodate or work around the jury preference for compensation, we risk the prospect that jurors will use the tort system to serve aims it cannot efficiently serve.

Assessing the Tort System
As a Compensation Device

No matter how attractive the compensation function of the tort system may seem, one must take seriously the strong reasons against social reliance on tort as a device for paying all claims for compensation. One reason, already noted, is that the threat of paying such compensation may serve to discourage manufacturers and others from engaging in socially valuable but risky activity.

Tort actions are now so expensive, moreover, and involve so many transaction costs that any good they achieve is bound to be vastly overpriced. Successful tort claimants get merely 30 to 40 percent of the money that enters the tort system. The rest goes to pay administrative costs, including legal fees, court costs, and the salaries of insurance company employees who devote their time to seeing claims through the legal process. As a vehicle of compensation the tort system compares poorly with one of its main competitors, first-party insurance, in which 70 to 80 percent of money that enters the system eventually goes to accident victims.

Typically, money paid for "pain and suffering" constitutes the largest portion of an accident victim's tort recovery. When the tort system requires payment for pain and suffering, the potential tortfeasor then in effect purchases insurance (or self-insures) for protection from the prospect of paying these kinds of damages. The cost of this insurance passes on to consumers through higher product prices. Yet it seems doubtful that people think insurance against pain and suffering would be worth buying. In fact, no demand exists for first-party insurance against pain and suffering. Thus, in paying the price of a product that includes a judicially imposed premium for insurance against pain and suffering, consumers are compelled to purchase insurance few would purchase freely. This adds another reason to believe that the tort system, as it currently exists, requires the public to spend money on items it does not want to buy. While the idea of the tort system as a device for vindicating common-law rights against "pain and suffering" may express admirable sentiments, it is an open question whether these are sentiments we can afford to vindicate in so inefficient a way.

The tort system, of course, ignores the enormous number of accident victims who have no good prospects for recovery in court. But there may seem to be no morally relevant difference between a person who suffers an illness through exposure to natural elements in the environment and a person who suffers the same illness when caused by human activity: Both are equally needy and may deserve our help. Through the tort system, we apparently express a social preference in favor of those whose injuries or illnesses have been caused by human activity. From the perspective of the accident victim, this seems arbitrary. Why should a person be penalized because nature or chance, rather than a human being, caused his illness or injury?

In response to the charge that the tort system perversely fastens upon the misery of those whose accidents were caused by human activity, one may say that the system's sole function is to take money from those who wrongly cause harm and then give it to victims of that harm, and that this function bears no relevance to the scope of social duty to provide aid in other circumstances. In this view, tort law is a matter of correcting a moral imbalance between a tort victim and his injurer, and nothing more.

Proponents of this "corrective justice" interpretation of the tort system must recognize, however, that funds will exist to pay legitimate claims only if society does not preempt the tort system by providing, for example, through a mandatory insurance scheme, aid to victims of accident or illness regardless of causation issues. Adoption of such a scheme would express a social judgment that the interests of victims of natural accidents and the interests of tort victims are equally worth protecting. It remains an open question whether such preemption would compromise the rights of tort victims under the "corrective justice" approach.

Alternative Approaches to Compensation

Many commentators suggest, as a way to cut through the Gordian knot, that society institute a broad no-fault approach to insurance and tort reform. In two well-known instances, attempts have been made to supplant or supplement tort law through insurance schemes that pay for injuries regardless of fault: workers' compensation and no-fault auto accident programs. In each instance, the prospective accident victim makes a mandatory trade in which he forgoes the common-law right to damages and, in exchange, receives the right to prompt recovery of economic loss, along with payment of his attorney's fees. The victim then receives relief from the common-law requirement that he prove his accident was someone else's fault. The virtue of no-fault, at least in theory, is that it provides the important compensation benefits we associate with the tort system, but avoids the enormous transaction costs and unpredictability of the tort system. It is time to consider seriously whether the morally legitimate aims of the tort system could be well-served by reshaping that system so it more closely resembles a no-fault regime.

In many jurisdictions no-fault auto compensation programs have succeeded in providing quicker and more certain coverage than that provided through traditional tort liability systems. Nobody, however, regards no-fault as a complete success. Too often, no-fault represents an unstable legislative compromise. Many no-fault programs, for example, limit an accident victim's common-law rights only minimally; "add on" programs of this sort, of course, increase insurance costs rather than lower them. And many no-fault programs deprive the accident victim of any meaningful recovery.

Strong arguments can be made that workers' compensation programs provide payment that is both cheaper and better than compensation provided through comparable components of the traditional tort system. Inadequacies in workers' compensation awards, however, apparently contribute to the recent explosion in products liability suits. Injured employees, dissatisfied with the puny recovery available from their employers for on-the-job injuries, look elsewhere—that is, to those who manufacture the products they use at work—to get compensation for their injuries. Legislators and judges, who sympathize with the plight of industrial accident victims, see little reason to limit such circumvention of the workers' compensation system.

Whatever the merits and shortcomings of no-fault regimes, one might suspect that they do not have a rosy future. In a recent California election, a no-fault initiative was decisively defeated, and in legislatures, momentum for no-fault plans has virtually disappeared. The current political unpopularity of no-fault may be a short-term consequence of poorly designed no-fault systems and voter anger at insurers: Often the public regards no-fault proposals as mere reductions in accident victims' rights, as nothing more than a boon for insurers and business.

Nevertheless, as the tort and insurance crises worsen, the possibility of defensible and workable no-fault programs must be taken seriously. A huge variety of no-fault plans exists. A careful analysis of the ways such plans can be structured, coupled with attention to the ethical and social goals they must serve, can show no-fault to be a plausible alternative to the present impasse.

What Is Wrong with Entrapment?

John Kleinig

Police are often tempted to use deceptive tactics in investigative work, and indeed are sometimes justified in doing so. Many offenses could not be successfully prosecuted without the use of deceptive tactics—for example, white-collar crime, organized crime, and crimes, such as blackmail and extortion, where the victims are inhibited about reporting. In all these cases, the traditional reliance on testimony of the victims is likely to be inadequate, and evidence needs to be gained in other ways. Unless deceptive tactics are used to detect crimes like these, criminal charges are likely to be concentrated on crimes more commonly associated with the poor and minorities, giving the criminal justice system a class bias. And even for more commonplace crimes, the use of deceptive tactics may be an efficient means of collecting evidence and ensuring the conviction of wrongdoers, given opposition to the excessive use of coercion in law enforcement and constitutional constraints on the gathering of evidence by the police.

In the United States, entrapment constitutes a legal limit on the use of deception in investigation. It is a defense that, if established, will result in the acquittal of a person charged with a criminal offense. But it is not always clear what makes for entrapment or why it ought to function as a defense.

What exactly is entrapment? Why does it constitute a defense against criminal accusations?

The Subjective Approach

Discussions of entrapment have generally taken the form of a comparison between "subjective" and "objective" approaches.

The subjective approach places the emphasis on the defendant's mental state—on whether or not, prior to the inducements offered by state officials, the defendant was disposed to commit a crime of the particular type with which he or she is charged. Thus, in *U.S.* v. *Russell,* Justice William H. Rehnquist argued that the defense of entrapment can be made "only when the Government's deception actually implants the criminal design in the mind of the defendant." What lies behind the subjective approach is a desire to protect innocent defendants. The purpose of the defense, according to Chief Justice Earl Warren, is to draw a line "between the trap for the unwary innocent and the trap for the unwary criminal." Where the "disposition" to commit the alleged offense has been "implanted" in the mind of an "innocent" person, the line separating permissible deception and entrapment has been crossed. The defendant is no longer culpable.

But what is involved in "implanting," such that it should diminish culpability? Suppose Abel is reluctant to commit a crime of a certain type, say to embezzle funds; however, Agent Baker plays on Abel's sympathies and persuades him to engage in the embezzlement. Under the subjective approach this counts as entrapment, for Agent Baker "implants" the intention to embezzle in Abel's mind. Now suppose Abel has a general inclination to embezzle, but has not formed any specific intention to do so; Agent Baker gives Abel the opportunity to embezzle, and Abel responds affirmatively. In the latter case, the subjective approach claims that Baker does no more than provide the water that will determine whether or not the fertile seeds of criminal conduct are already there.

However, if the issue is one of *culpability* for the crime, isn't Abel just as culpable in both cases? Suppose in the first case Baker had been a private citizen rather than a government agent. Then Abel could not have claimed in his defense that Baker "implanted" the intention in his mind, rendering him non-culpable. At the very most what Baker did would be a mitigating factor. So the issue does not seem to be a simple one of culpability. Why should the fact that Baker is a government agent make all the difference? This the subjective approach fails to explain.

The Objective Approach

In contrast to the subjective approach, the objective one focuses on the character of the state's involvement in the commission of the offense with which the defendant is charged. As the court in *Russell* put it, "The question is whether—regardless of the predisposition to crime of the particular defendant involved—the governmental agents have acted in such a way as is likely to instigate or create a criminal offense." Or again, in the words of Justice Felix Frankfurter, the question is "whether the police conduct revealed in the particular case falls below standards, to which common feelings respond, for the proper use of governmental power."

This concern with the government's conduct has manifested itself in a number of different ways. Sometimes the issue has been whether excessive persuasion was used to induce the defendants to commit the crime—not whether the persuasion was excessive in relation to the particular defendant, as in the subjective approach, but whether it was excessive in relation to some objective standard. As the California Supreme Court posed the question: "Was the conduct of the law enforcement agent likely to induce a normally law-abiding person to commit the offense?" Other times, what seems to have been at issue was the fact that the government had supplied something essential to the commission of that kind of crime. All cases seem to have had a further, supervenient point of concern—that in acting as it did the government operated in an unseemly manner.

But if the subjective approach's terminology of "implanting" is problematic, the objective approach's talk of "creating" crime is no less so. For how does entrapment differ in this respect from the use of decoys or other methods of undercover detection? If the point is to charge the government with being the crime's "precipitating cause" or sine qua non, then in any case where the crime would not have occurred but for the government's involvement, a defense of entrapment will be sustainable.

If the point is to charge the government with having made the crime "easier," there does not seem to be any particular problem with the government's action unless, in creating the opportunity, it has brought about the formation of a specific intent where none previously existed. And the objective approach eschews any concern with the defendant's specific intent. If the point instead is to charge the government with having played "the major part" in the crime's occurrence, then determining whether entrapment has occurred will again need to take account of the subjective factors that play a central role in the subjective approach. Otherwise, how could it be established that the government has played a major part? Since the objective approach explicitly excludes from consideration the mental state of the individual concerned, it is to be wondered whether it is seriously concerned with the issue of "creation" (i.e., causation).

An Alternative

The difficulties confronting both subjective and objective approaches should at least raise the possibility that they do not offer productive alternatives for characterizing entrapment. At the same time, the strong support existing for each suggests that each captures something of importance.

To set up an alternative approach, it may be helpful to start with a major (though not exclusive) concern of the objective approach—a distinction between acceptable and unacceptable ways for governments to control crime. Proponents of both traditional approaches hold that it is unacceptable for governments to operate so as to induce defendants into committing crimes they would not otherwise have committed. It is only when the defendants are charged with offenses of a type they would have committed without the government's involvement that the government does not overreach itself. The point is not that the *particular* offense would have been committed had the government not been involved, but that an offense *of that kind* would have been committed had the government not been involved. (It would be much too demanding to insist, as a rule, that the particular offense would have occurred in the absence of government involvement—that would severely and unnecessarily handicap undercover work.) From this starting point, where the traditional approaches differ is over the means for determining when the government has behaved unacceptably. Subjectivists believe that if the person was predisposed to commit a crime of that particular type, the bounds of acceptability will not have been crossed. Objectivists believe that if the government has played too substantial a role in the crime's creation, the bounds of acceptability will have been crossed.

We may do better if we do not focus on whether this or that responsibility-establishing or responsibility-defeating factor is present, but on whether the situation enables us to *tell* whether the defendant would have acted in such a way had the government not been involved in the way it was. Sometimes the government's involvement bulks so large that we may no longer be able to have any confidence that, absent its involvement, the individual concerned would have committed an offense of the kind in question. When that is so, the defense of entrapment should be available to the defendant.

If, then, what makes for entrapment is the government's involvement in criminal activity in a manner that *either* draws into it those who would not otherwise have engaged in conduct of that kind *or* leaves it unclear whether those who engaged in it would otherwise have done so, we can resolve the stalemate between the subjective and objective approaches. The fact that a defendant was not—in some reasonably full-bodied sense—predisposed to criminal conduct of the kind charged will constitute a strong reason for believing that entrapment occurred. For it provides a fairly clear indication that without the government's involvement the defendant would not have engaged in that kind of criminal activity. This is the burden of the subjectivist approach. But even if the defendant is predisposed to engage in criminal conduct of the kind charged, a defense of entrapment may be available. For the government's involvement may bulk so large it is no longer possible to tell, from the participant's behavior, whether he or she would otherwise have actually engaged in conduct of that kind. In recognizing this, we acknowledge a point emphasized by objectivists—the excessive involvement of government in the creation of a crime.

What Is Wrong with Entrapment?

The position I have taken so far is that entrapment does not give us any reason for thinking those entrapped are criminals. It is a structuring of circumstances such that the outcome possesses questionable evidential value. Justice Frankfurter, however, puts the point more positively and moralistically: "The power of government is abused and directed to an end for which it was not constituted when employed to promote rather than detect crime and bring about the downfall of those who, left to themselves, might well have obeyed the law."

I think this is right, but overstates the objection to entrapment. Sometimes the effect of entrapment will be that crimes are committed that would not otherwise have occurred. But that will not always be the case. Sometimes a crime of that type would have been committed anyway; however, because of the government's involvement, we would be left without sufficient reason for knowing whether that would have been the case.

Behind Frankfurter's moralism lies the further belief that the government, in conducting itself in a certain way, offends the standards of decent behavior. But this, I would suggest, is an issue distinct from that of entrapment. Certainly the police sometimes engage in undercover tactics that, however successful, are so egregious, outrageous, or abhorrent that they should be outlawed by the courts and their evidential yields not be allowed to count. However, I am not convinced the entrapment defense is what is required to outlaw such tactics. The entrapment defense is probably best left as it is—as a defense that challenges the connection between the defendant's involvement in a particular crime and the claim that the defendant would anyway have committed a crime of that type. The claim that certain government activities are in themselves improper should, I believe, be addressed as a separate issue—perhaps as a violation of due process.

However it is addressed, the issue of abhorrent government conduct is problematic. At what point does government conduct go beyond the pale? Does it vary with the kind of offense? Some objectivists argue that it becomes unacceptable when it is sufficient to induce the average, normally law-abiding citizen to commit a crime. But this may be to pitch the limits too low—especially if it can be argued that more can be demanded of those in positions of greater trust and responsibility than of the average, law-abiding citizen. A reasonable flexibility may be needed, not only to take account of the differing expectations we have of people, but also to avoid a situation where only inexperienced criminals are caught.

Philosopher Gerald Dworkin offers a plausible test for determining when the government has overreached itself. The criminal law, he argues, is not a pricing system indifferent to the choices made by citizens—whether they obey or choose instead to disobey and pay the penalty. It is meant to be obeyed. Government goes too far when its actions have the effect of saying not "Do not do X," but "Do X." When it does the latter, it not only violates the *telos* of criminal law, but also deals unfairly with citizens. It becomes a tester of virtue rather than a detector of crime.

In any case, my point is not to deny that in entrapment the government may be left with the stain of crime on its hands, but to deny that this is what makes entrapment a proper defense. What makes it a proper defense is its evidential bankruptcy. Entrapment is an inappropriate investigative technique, not only or primarily because it traps the innocent or manifests substandard behavior on the part of governmental agents, but because it leaves us without adequate grounds for establishing the *guilt* of those whom it succeeds in ensnaring.

This article was condensed and adapted from John Kleinig's lecture materials on police ethics.

FOR FURTHER READING

Bayles, Michael. *Professional Ethics*. Belmont, Calif.: Wadsworth, 1981.

Freedman, Monroe. *Lawyers' Ethics in an Adversary System*. Indianapolis: Bobbs-Merrill, 1975.

Fried, Charles. "The Lawyer as Friend: The Moral Foundations of the Lawyer-Client Relation." *Yale Law Journal* 85 (1976).

Goldman, Alan. *The Moral Foundations of Professional Ethics*. Totowa, N.J.: Rowman and Littlefield, 1980.

Kipnis, Kenneth. *Legal Ethics*. Englewood Cliffs, N.J.: Prentice-Hall, 1986.

Luban, David, ed. *The Good Lawyer: Lawyers' Roles and Lawyers' Ethics*. Maryland Studies in Public Philosophy. Totowa, N.J.: Rowman and Allanheld, 1983.

Luban, David. *Lawyers and Justice: An Ethical Study*. Princeton, N.J.: Princeton University Press, 1988.

Postema, Gerald J. "Moral Responsibility in Professional Ethics." *New York University Law Review* 55 (1980).

Simon, William H. "The Ideology of Advocacy: Procedural Justice and Professional Ethics." *Wisconsin Law Review* 1978 (1978).

Wasserstrom, Richard. "Lawyers as Professionals: Some Moral Issues." *Natural Law Forum* 5 (1975).

5

THE MEDIA

Few institutions shape our society more powerfully than the mass media. Their political coverage and commentary provide the cornerstone of our democracy; their boundless capacity to entertain creates our culture; their tireless advertising fuels our consumer economy; their death-grip on our children molds the next generation. This power raises questions about regulation of the mass media, as well as questions about the ethical standards that should govern the profession of journalism.

We cherish the ideal of a press free from government interference—but the growing power of the mass media means, as one author notes, that "we need protections *from* the press as well as protections *for* it." The article "Freedom and Fairness: Regulating the Mass Media" examines arguments for and against regulation of the mass media, based both on the principles underlying our commitment to freedom of speech and on the practical successes and failures of regulatory activity to date. It considers the alternatives of "self-regulation" by the press's adherence to strict norms of professional accountability; reliance on market mechanisms to ensure that the press serves the public interest; and, finally, the hotly contested issue of some degree of actual governmental oversight. It concludes that governmental regulation may serve a legitimate function as a counterweight to powerful economic interests: "The question we should be asking is not whether regulation of the press is permissible, but what kinds of regulation work most effectively to enhance the diversity and quality of public debate in our democracy."

In "Deregulating the Electronic Media," Judith Lichtenberg focuses on the asymmetry between the extensive First Amendment protection afforded newspapers and other print media and the closer regulatory supervision given radio and television broadcasting. She considers various rationales for treating the two differently—scarcity, the need for governmental licensing, the nature of the respective news products, and the effects of different media on their audience. In the end, however, her argument against deregulating the electronic media turns not so much on these differences as on the underlying rationale for freedom of speech itself.

The media have long been charged with printing an undue amount of "bad news"—in recent years, in particular, critics have complained that media coverage of technological and other health risks is overly pessimistic. "Is Good News No News?" examines this charge more closely, with attention both to claims about the content of media reports on technological issues compared to "reality" and about the impact of media reporting on public beliefs and attitudes.

In the late twentieth century, no mass media would exist without the economic prop of advertising. Advertising itself has cultural effects as powerful as anything in the publishing and broadcasting it supports. "Is Advertising Manipulative?" responds to some common worries about the ways advertising exerts its power over us: by playing on our emotions, by playing on our weaknesses, and by catching us somehow unawares. While much advertising does not seem to be subject to moral criticism on these grounds, advertising certainly can be manipulative in all three of these ways.

Advertising is especially suspect when it targets vulnerable audiences, such as children. Children aged six to eleven watch an average of twenty-seven hours of television a week, for a total of fourteen hundred hours a year; preschool children watch even more. Much of what they watch is saturated with advertising. "Children's Television" asks how worried we should be about what our children are watching—and what is being sold to them as they watch. And what, if anything, should we do about it?

Just as advertising can be manipulative, so can journalism proper. And journalists can manipulate not only their audience, but also their subjects, preying on a subject's vanity and ignorance only to betray it, as Janet Malcolm charged in a famous *New Yorker* piece on the relationship between journalist and source. In "The Dilemma of the Journalist/Source Relationship," Judith Lichtenberg examines the ever-present temptation for journalists to betray their sources—and suggests that the alternative may be even more troubling.

Freedom and Fairness
Regulating the Mass Media

Claudia Mills

Freedom of the press is the cornerstone of America's image of itself, par excellence "what we have that the Russians don't." Compare the striking difference between Soviet press (non)coverage of the Chernobyl disaster and the searing, exhaustive U.S. press coverage of the Challenger explosion. Until the day of the funeral, the ill health of a Soviet leader is denied by government-owned newspapers; American papers embarrass the first lady by emblazoning the front page with elaborate diagrams of the president's colon and prostate gland. Even when we feel that the press goes too far, jeopardizing national security for the sake of a scoop, we often find in the end that its vigilance was justified—most recently, when reporters' unwillingness to "back off" from investigating the release of hostage David Jacobsen led to the uncovering of the Iran-Contra affair. We cherish the ideal of a press free from government interference.

Of late, however, the shining armor of the press has become tarnished. The increasing number of libel suits and the size of punitive judgments against the press show public wariness about its trustworthiness. Critics charge that reporters are not, indeed cannot be, impartial spokespersons for the Truth, but necessarily represent the interests of entrenched power groups, inspiring the quip that the only way to have freedom of the press is to own one.

According to philosopher Judith Lichtenberg, the growing power of the mass media means that we need protections *from* the press as well as protections *for* it, and both, she argues, are consistent with the ideal of freedom of speech. Our commitment to freedom of speech has two different strands: The first is an opposition to censorship, based on a belief that "one should not be prevented from thinking, speaking, reading, writing, or listening as one sees fit"; the second, equally fundamental, is our conviction that "the purposes of freedom of speech are realized when expression and diversity of expression flourish." We want no voice to be silenced; we also want many voices to be heard. While "government intervention seems to intrude upon the first principle, . . . it may advance the second."

Both principles are codified in landmark Supreme Court cases. In *Miami Herald* v. *Tornillo* the Court struck down a Florida statute requiring newspapers to provide politicians, attacked in the course of an electoral campaign, with a free opportunity to reply. Freedom of the press here was equated with editorial autonomy. But the second strand in our commitment to free speech is represented by *Red Lion Broadcasting* v. *FCC*, in which the Court upheld the Federal Communications Commission's (FCC) requirements that radio and television stations provide free reply time to those attacked in station broadcasts. Unlike their print counterparts, the broadcast media, which are federally licensed, were required (until 1987) by the "fairness doctrine" to devote a reasonable amount of time to the coverage of controversial issues of public importance and to do so fairly. While the asymmetrical treatment of the print and broadcast media is troubling to many, it is not clear whether the discrepancy should be resolved by treating the press more like broadcasting or treating broadcasting more like the press.

Proposals for heightened regulation of the press raise goosebumps in many, however, who view governmental intervention in the mass media as a last resort. They would rather implement the goals of broadening access to the press and stimulating robust wide-open debate of public issues by allowing the press itself to exercise professional responsibility, or by relying on market forces. Only if these fail can government regulation be considered—and even then perhaps not. Whether or not we turn to the state to implement our commitment to a diversity of voices may depend crucially on how well it has been shown to work—what kinds of regulation work best, what kinds work at all.

Self-Regulation of the Press

Many journalists maintain that external regulation of the press is unnecessary, because the press itself is its own severest critic. Reporters, at least in popular imagery, are by nature independent and skeptical, delighting in controversy and muckraking, even when some of the muck to be raked lies close to home. In numerous ways the various organs of print and broadcast journalism bend over backwards to achieve fair and balanced coverage of thorny issues. A casual reading of the ombudsman's column in the *Washington Post* and of a week's worth of letters to the editor shows the willingness of a major paper to print inside accounts of its own failures and hostile outside criticism. Thus journalism professor Carl Sessions Stepp argues that "journalism is a craft peculiarly suited to internal reform. . . . Journalists are propelled by the First Amendment syndrome, a set of beliefs (maybe even a mythology) that, via broad acceptance, assumes a self-fulfilling power that can drive the profession."

Several recent trends, however, which Stepp himself notes, undermine the journalistic heritage on which his hopes for reform are founded. The first of these is intensified concentration of media ownership. Twenty corporations control more than half the 61 million daily newspapers sold every day; twenty corporations control more than half the revenues of the country's 11,000 magazines; three corporations control most of the revenues and audience in television, ten corporations in radio, eleven corporations in all kinds of books, and four corporations in motion pictures. Continuing concentration drastically centralizes control over the forum in which voices are heard and likely limits access to it.

A second troubling development is the increasing intrusion of nonnews corporations into the news enterprise. As Stepp points out, "The press is part of big business, and increasingly, it is owned and operated by big business corporations that may have only incidental interest in journalism and that may be controlled by individuals without grounding in journalistic principles." Finally, the proliferation of broadcast and cable outlets forces the news media to compete incessantly for consumer time, thus driving public-affairs coverage further toward entertainment.

Even in the face of these challenges, Stepp still calls for a renewed commitment to professional responsibility on the part of the media themselves, rather than government regulation. In his view, regulation would only make matters worse: "The system is animated by the ideal of First Amendment freedom from government interference; government intrusion would necessarily subvert that ideal and demolish the fundamental assumption on which the press operates. It is hard to imagine that the ensuing system would be an improvement."

But legal scholar Owen Fiss fails to see an inevitable tension between government regulation and professional accountability: "Why is it assumed that state regulation of the media and professional independence are necessarily inconsistent? It seems to me that it all depends on the nature of the regulation. Indeed, the fairness doctrine can be seen as strengthening and perhaps even generating the resolve of reporters and editors to act in a way that furthers the democratic aspirations of the First Amendment. As we saw from *Brown* v. *Board of Education* and the civil rights movement of the sixties, exemplary 'folkways' can sometimes be nourished—and maybe even created or legitimated—by strong exercise of state power." He concludes that professional norms alone are "frail and weak, compared to the challenge."

Let the Market Do It

If self-regulation cannot give us the kind of media we require in a democracy, what about letting the people themselves decide what kind of media they want by what kind of media they watch and read? Let them vote, so to speak, with their remote control buttons. Originally, regulation of broadcasting was justified by appeal to scarcity of broadcast frequencies; the fairness doctrine was devised to correct the "market failure" produced by the physical limitations of the electromagnetic spectrum. Now, with the advent of cable and satellite technology, scarcity has given way to abundance, oligopoly to cornucopia. With this impediment to a freely functioning market removed, market forces should ensure that if people in fact want a certain kind of news coverage, it will be provided; if in fact they do not, then in one view of democracy the loss is not to be regretted. By allowing the media to be driven by ratings and advertising, we will at least be giving the people the media they want, indeed the media they deserve. By accurately mirroring the state of popular tastes, ratings are a way of empowering the people to have the final say on television programming.

We might find ourselves appalled, however, at what popular sovereignty in this context really means. Fewer people watch the news every night than watch *Wheel of Fortune.* The ratings wars among network news programs have been blamed for further crumbling of the time-honored wall of separation between news and entertainment and the resulting replacement of hard news coverage with fluffier "lifestyle" stories. (As one network news executive asked, "Do people in Lubbock, Texas, really need to know about the latest vote in Ways and Means?") Unless the nation is faced with a war or major disaster, interest in events of the day gives way to interest in what sweater Dan Rather is wearing and what sign-off phrase he uses.

According to Jeffrey Abramson, a political scientist, the "democratic" defense of ratings-driven news misunderstands what democracy really requires; it assumes that "the only news democratic citizens need is news that pleases them—news that they watch for the same reasons that they watch a situation comedy. But this is to treat viewers not as democratic citizens at all but only as consumers tuning in to be amused. . . . [Such news] can flatter the culture but not examine it; it can please viewers but not make them think."

Abramson also objects that the only audience that matters to Nielsen ratings is the mass audience, measured in forty or sixty million persons. "All power goes to that audience and even a show that attracts, say, thirty million persons in a time slot where competitors are bringing in forty million persons is in danger of cancellation. A television documentary such as PBS' upcoming history of the civil rights movement is expected to hold an audience of 1 million persons per segment; but this is a virtual no-show as far as commercial television is concerned."

Each network thus pursues the same mass audience with the same fare in each time slot. As a result, Abramson concludes, "The nation can for the most part conduct its business on television only on borrowed time; the economics of commercial television are pushed solely by the imperative to capture the largest possible audience for advertisers. This imperative typically stands against the realization of democratic ideals we commonly associate with diversity in programming or access to the marketplace of ideas for the widest possible array of contending voices."

Is Regulation the Answer?

Considerations such as these lead us to turn to the state for a remedy, for government, via such provisions as the fairness doctrine, can mandate broader access to the media and enhance the quality and breadth of public debate. But now the question arises: How can we trust the government to be a watchdog of the media when a chief function of the media is to be a watchdog of the government? If the government is empowered to tell the media how to run their business, won't this compromise the fundamental adversary relationship between the two?

The appropriate response here, according to Lichtenberg, "is not that we can trust government more than opponents of regulation believe, but that we can trust others less. Regulation is needed just because private power poses a grave threat to the independence and integrity of the press." Lee Bollinger, a law professor, states simply: "Our concern is with power—that is, the ability to command an audience more or less exclusively—and that is a concern that is not diminished by the way in which that power is achieved. It should make no difference to us, in other words, whether the power is the consequence of physical limitations associated with the use of that medium. . . or the result of limitations of the economic system (concentrations of economic power) or the result of clear market success in solidly appealing to a segment or majority of the community. It is the risks associated with power over access to the marketplace that raise the sense of alarm and not the source of that power."

But isn't the state equally subject to the influences of social and economic power that it would seek to control? A democratic government is responsive to the public will, which often means to private money, and hence to privileged power groups. Stepp argues, "If one defines the problem of access and diversity as seeking voice for perspectives other than those of a privileged and powerful minority, then government seems an ironic place to turn for help. Government is by definition integrated with the power class in American society and it is axiomatic that the press already gives greater voice to the 'outs' than the government does or is likely to."

Fiss concedes the danger that the state "will be the victim of the very same forces that dominate public debate and not counteract the skew of the market but rather reinforce it." He maintains nonetheless that "there is still a difference worth observing between a public official and a program manager of one of the networks (or an editor of a newspaper). However imperfect the systems of accountability are in the public sphere, at least they exist." Fiss concludes, "We turn to the state because it is the most public of institutions and because it alone has the power . . . to counteract, or modulate, the influence of the market and the constraint that it imposes on our politics."

Does Regulation Work?

The final question is a pragmatic one: Does regulation work? If no objections arise in principle, objections still may occur in practice. Does regulation in reality enhance or stifle robust, wide-open debate? Does it foster or chill discussion of public issues?

How successful—and how intrusive—regulation is depends on the form it takes. Two broad approaches to regulation of the media are usually distinguished. *Content regulation* makes specific demands of press institutions to cover certain kinds of issues, to cover them in a certain way, or to provide access to certain points of view. (The fairness doctrine is the most prominent example.) *Structural regulation* instead builds rules and constraints into the structure and organization of the media taken as a whole.

Most press resistance has been mounted against content regulation, as both dangerous and ineffective. Sara Engram, deputy editorial page editor for the Baltimore *Evening Sun*, reflects the sentiments of many journalists in arguing that the fairness doctrine ended up working against the goals it was designed to achieve: "Instead of encouraging enlightening discussion of matters of public interest, the fairness doctrine provides a crutch for the kind of journalism that can be described as, at best, terminally bland." In her view, the fairness doctrine "can—and does—encourage a constricted notion of fairness that ultimately limits the public debate. . . . I suspect that in practice 'each side' quickly becomes 'both sides' and the broadcaster can move on to the next 'issue' satisfied that he has gotten the FCC off his back."

Bollinger replies, however, that evidence for the alleged "chilling effect" of the fairness doctrine rests largely on broadcasters' own testimonial claims, which are likely to be self-serving. He points out that the often overlooked first provision of the fairness doctrine, which requires broadcasters to provide coverage of public issues, could be used to overcome any chilling tendencies of the requirement of fairness. Finally, he insists that any amount of chilling must be balanced against the enhancement of speech provided by the expanded number of voices heard.

But did the fairness doctrine, as it was enforced, enhance public debate significantly? Henry Geller, director of the Washington Center for Public Policy Research, charges that the FCC "failed miserably" in requiring broadcasters to devote a reasonable amount of time to issues of public concern: "In a half-century of regulation, it has never denied a license for failure to deliver sufficient news or public affairs. . . . The comparative renewal process is just as great a charade. The incumbent always wins, no matter what its past record." The fairness doctrine shaped broadcasters' concern more by the shadow it cast than by the stick it wielded.

We might do better, then, to rely on structural approaches to regulation, such as rules prohibiting multiple ownership of news organizations or designating certain cable channels for public access. Economic incentives can be offered to news organizations to promote diversity or provide services unlikely to be offered in the unrestricted marketplace. Instead of returning to the concept of broadcasters as public trustees, bound by a fairness doctrine, Geller proposes exacting from station owners a modest "spectrum fee," to be used to subsidize public affairs and similar programming by public radio and television stations, who are willing and able to provide the high-quality broadcasting other stations eschew. This proposal faces the objection that only a miniscule proportion of the population tunes in to public stations and so the majority would still lack exposure to thorough, thoughtful treatment of the issues of the day. But at least their deprivation would be self-chosen.

Conclusion

The press has had a long history of resisting governmental regulation and defines itself by its adversary role to government. But as the media grow more powerful, the government may be needed as an adversary to them, and, in the late twentieth century, both government and media may be needed as adversaries to powerful economic interests. The question we should be asking, then, is not whether regulation of the press is permissible, but what kinds of regulation work most effectively to enhance the diversity and quality of public debate in our democracy.

The views of Judith Lichtenberg, Carl Sessions Stepp, Owen Fiss, Jeffrey Abramson, Lee Bollinger, Sara Engram, and Henry Geller are taken from their essays in Democracy and the Mass Media, *ed. Judith Lichtenberg (New York: Cambridge University Press, 1990).*

Deregulating the Electronic Media

Judith Lichtenberg

One is bound to have mixed feelings about the role of the mass media in our society. On the one hand, a strong and independent press is crucial to a well-functioning democratic society; it is a cornerstone of the American political system. The press provides access to information citizens need to make informed choices about the development of public policy; it allows them to influence and participate in the decision-making process. On the other hand, the power of modern mass communications—to persuade or propagandize, to grant or deny access to the ears of America—makes them potentially dangerous and gives us some reason to fear them. We are led to conclude that, at the same time we need protections *for* the press, in the late twentieth century we may need protections *from* it as well.

No one doubts that radio and television count as "press" and that they are forums for speech and expression. But the electronic media have never enjoyed the extensive First Amendment protection afforded newspapers and other print media. Radio and television stations are licensed at the discretion of the Federal Communications Commission, and they are subject to a variety of regulations, including equal-time rules and, until 1987, the fairness doctrine, which required that they devote a reasonable amount of broadcast time to controversial issues of importance to the public, and that they offer "reasonable opportunity for opposing viewpoints."

What explains the deeply entrenched asymmetry between the government's treatment of print and broadcast media? The standard explanation is that opportunities for broadcasting are—or at least were in the years when communications policy was being formulated—scarce in a way that opportunities for expression through print are not. The electromagnetic spectrum is limited not only in the sense that more wish to use it than space is available, but also because the total absence of regulation would result in electromagnetic chaos, so no one could succeed in communicating. And so it seems, just as the chairperson of a town meeting can, consistent with First Amendment freedoms, set some limits on participants' speech, government, too, may and indeed must make decisions about who can broadcast, and when and where, on the spectrum.

Today, however, new communications technologies—cable television, satellite broadcasting, videodiscs, and so on—make opportunities for electronic broadcasting less scarce and less expensive. Not only can cable bring a hundred channels to the ordinary household, but increasingly that same household is served by only one newspaper. The printed word, it seems, is scarcer nowadays than the broadcast word. Calls for the deregulation of broadcasting have accordingly become common in the last few years.

Yet the inference that the electronic media are ripe for deregulation proceeds too quickly. From the premise that opportunities for expression in the electronic media are no more scarce than in print media, we may conclude that electronic and print media ought to be treated alike. But should we abandon regulation for broadcasting, or impose it on newspapers? The symmetry argument does not by itself tell us.

Scarcity aside, other differences may exist between print and electronic media that provide grounds for different treatment. Even though cable television can easily provide many channels, cable operators must be granted, by a municipality or other local government, the privilege of laying cable through public property. That alone seems to have implications for which requirements are legitimate to impose on cable operators. Cable companies necessarily depend on public decisions and on the public's granting of privileges; newspapers do not. It is important to remember also that cable operators own their cable; despite the multitude of channels, without regulation it would be entirely their decisions what goes over the wire. The mere existence of a hundred channels does not by itself ensure either variety or quality.

Another question relevant to mass media regulatory policy is whether the "products" of the electronic and print media differ significantly. Both, of course, produce news (among other things), but it is obvious they do this in different ways. Perhaps the nature of the news products of television and newspapers has a bearing on the regulations appropriate to each.

Making and Taking the News

In *1984* (written in 1948, during the infancy of television), George Orwell created a powerful emblem of the future: the telescreen. The telescreen existed in every Party member's house (and everywhere else a Party member might go), and it enabled Big Brother to watch you. People sometimes compare today's real-life, nearly omnipresent television with Orwell's telescreen. Yet such comparisons seem to misfire, partly because there is no Big Brother, but also for a less happy reason. A lesson of modern communications technology may be that Big Brother doesn't *have* to watch us, as long as we are watching him.

We have reason to be concerned about the economic and political power of the mass media. But what is perhaps more disturbing is their ability to influence public opinion—if they do not tell us what to think, one writer has said, they at least tell us what to think *about*. The relevant questions here are questions of human psychology. Does exposure to television affect people differently from exposure to print, thereby justifying the separate treatment of print and electronic media? Widespread concern about this problem seems to date only from the age of television, suggesting that electronic media have greater manipulative power. Certainly the sheer pervasiveness of television—compared with newspapers—in most Americans' lives is cause for concern. But the issues are complex.

On the one hand, seeing violence on television has an immediacy print cannot achieve. Some people attribute the strength of the Vietnam antiwar movement to the nightly exposure of the American public to scenes of war. Yet exposure to violence may also have the opposite effect; it almost inevitably seems stylized, and we get used to it. Does television make things seem more real, or less?

Another relevant difference between print and electronic media is the extent to which the television audience is captive. The viewer can, of course, turn the machine off, but if he does not, he is more subject to what passes before him than the reader of a newspaper, who must actively and continually pursue information.

Finally, limitations of time and space impinge differently on television and newspapers. Even leaving aside considerations of television's "telegenic" nature, which clearly affects what is shown, the severe constraints of time and space under which television operates must make its reporting more partial than what is possible in a newspaper. Of course, all reporting, in every medium, is a matter of selection and adaptation from the countless happenings in the world that might in some view be considered important. Indeed, this realization might be said to mark the beginning of the end of the naive belief that the press can bring us "all the news that's fit," and that there is a way that is, in Walter Cronkite's phrase, "the way it is." To what extent is this process of selection and adaptation influenced by the nature of reporting itself? To what extent is it influenced by the nature of a given medium?

How we answer these questions will influence our view of the regulations appropriate to different media.

Freedom of the Press

It is interesting to note that both advocates and opponents of deregulation of the electronic media invoke the First Amendment and the ideal of a free press. Advocates of deregulation argue that the original rationale for government control—scarcity—no longer holds, and so electronic media should get the same extensive First Amendment protection as newspapers. They understand freedom of the press to mean that government has no business interfering with one's freedom to speak or publish. Freedom of the press is the press's freedom from interference.

But those who defend regulation of the electronic media also rely on the ideal of a free press. They focus on a different aspect of that ideal: not the absence of government interference, but the multiplicity of voices, the ability of as many as possible to express their opinions and have those opinions heard by as wide an audience as possible. The fulfillment of this ideal might sometimes require not governmental restraint, but governmental insistence on someone's right to speak and be heard.

How can we decide between these two strands in the doctrine of freedom of the press? Is the conflict between them genuine? Perhaps a better understanding of the justification of a free press will clarify what freedom of the press is, and what it requires.

A standard justification for a free press appeals to the metaphor of "the marketplace of ideas." In the unfettered competition of conflicting views, it is said, truth will more likely emerge victorious. In a democratic society, the best government is one based on informed choices; the electorate must therefore have access to information, and freedom of the press is the best way to ensure it. This argument justifies freedom of the press in terms of its assumed beneficial effects: A free press is a means to certain desirable ends.

Although such reasoning is perfectly familiar in this context, it seems at odds with another standard justification of such constitutional protections: that freedom of speech or expression is a personal *right*. The significance of the difference seems clear: If the justification for a free press is in terms of public benefits, then if it is more beneficial to society to regulate (or deregulate), so be it; if the justification is in terms of rights, then our policies will have to reflect the ideal of freedom of the press that best fulfills these rights. We need, then, to look more closely at what these rights are.

Why, one might ask, should people have a right to self-expression? Two reasons seem clear. One is that a person's beliefs are integral to her; to refuse to allow a person to express those beliefs is to cut her off from herself and others and to deny her political worth. But this idea would probably not convince us of a right of self-expression if we did not at the same time believe that in some sense speech is innocuous. If words alone *could* break your bones, rights of free speech would be problematic; we have no patience with someone who says *he* expresses *himself* by cutting off other people's ears. But this seems paradoxical: Freedom of speech and press is rooted in the importance of words, but also in their harmlessness.

So far we have been focusing on the rights of speakers to express themselves, rather than on the rights of audiences or of "society" to have available a variety of voices and opinions. Analysts usually assume that public-benefit justifications focus on audiences or society at large; justifications in terms of rights focus on speakers.

This assumption is challenged in the claim, heard increasingly often, that "the public has a right to know." When stated in this bald and unqualified way, it seems naive and implausible to think the public has any such right. The public has no business sticking its nose in many personal and private matters. Certainly the public cannot have a right to know everything (whatever that would mean). Perhaps, though, it has the right to know the sorts of things relevant to the proper and effective functioning of a democratic society. Now, if the public has a right to know something, then someone has an obligation to tell it, or at least not to stand in the way of its being told. The latter seems the more plausible formulation in the case of the public's right to know.

Isn't it likely, however, that something stronger is at work than the public's *right* to know or hear? Doesn't the public in a democratic society sometimes have an *obligation* to know or hear minority viewpoints or nonstandard interpretations whether it likes it or not? While a right to express oneself would not by itself imply a right of access to a public forum, like a newspaper or television station, a public right—not to mention an obligation—to hear minority viewpoints and nonstandard interpretations might imply such a right of access.

The primary argument against such rights of access to the mass media seems to be that implementing them requires government intervention, and that this is itself an infringement of press freedom. The model of government interference on which this argument relies is censorship. The wrongness of censorship can be argued on several grounds: It deprives a person of the right of self-expression; it deprives the public of important information or opinions; it undermines the press's watchdog function. But it is not clear why in principle these arguments should stand in the way of the government's regulating the press only to the extent of ensuring that more voices and opinions are heard.

The founding fathers framed the First Amendment before the advent of the modern newspaper; today newspapers are often relegated to the status of antiques. To decide the constitutional, political, economic, and moral issues raised by the new communications technology, we will have to look at freedom of the press in correspondingly new ways; we will have to answer questions the founders would not have been able even to ask.

Is Good News No News?

Judith Lichtenberg and Douglas MacLean

No news is good news, the saying goes, carrying with it the suggestion that most news, at least as it is reported in the news media, is bad news. The charge is commonly leveled that the media place an undue emphasis on the negative, hawking papers with screaming headlines of gloom and doom, attracting television viewers with color footage of guts and gore. In recent years, in particular, critics have complained that media coverage of technological and other health risks is overly pessimistic, savoring of sensationalism.

By far the most ambitious and provocative research documenting this view is the twenty-five-year study by German sociologist Hans Mathias Kepplinger and his colleagues of coverage of technology in the German print media. Kepplinger's claim, for which he has amassed a great deal of evidence, is that media coverage of a variety of technological issues—in particular air, water, and forest pollution, radioactive fallout, and fatal traffic accidents—has become increasingly negative over the last twenty years, while the objective indicators for those issues have shown improvement or at least have not declined. For example: "The press hardly reported water pollution at all during the period of the greatest pollution of the Rhine in the late 1960s and early 1970s. . . . The press only emphasized water pollution when the pollution of the Rhine had receded and the regeneration ability of the river in terms of bio-chemical oxygen requirements had increased considerably. In relation to the Rhine there is a contradictory development between the real pollution and reported pollution." Thus, Kepplinger concludes, the media do not convey an accurate picture of reality. And, furthermore, "This new portrayal of reality by the media leads to a fundamental change in the public's views."

This view involves two claims: one about media content (a claim about the content of media reports on technological issues compared to "reality") and one about media effects (a causal claim about the impact of such reporting on beliefs and attitudes). Let us examine each of these, beginning with the second.

Media Effects

The evidence for the view that the media's (inaccurate) portrayal of reality changes public opinion is unclear. It is never posssible to be certain, and rarely possible to be even confident, that an effect was caused by media coverage rather than by something else. Part of Kepplinger's evidence for his conclusions seems to be that public opinion lags behind media coverage by about a year; that is, negative coverage of an environmental or technological risk is followed by negative public opinion about it. But this may be a case of *post hoc, ergo propter hoc* reasoning (the fallacy of thinking that because an event follows another, it was caused by it). Journalists and the public may both be responding to some third factor, with journalists quicker to react to events. In that case journalists would appear to be in the vanguard of opinion change, without actually wielding much influence themselves.

Another possible explanation is that as media coverage of a controversy increases, public opposition to the controversy increases—irrespective of whether the coverage is predominantly negative or not. Allan Mazur, author of *The Dynamics of Technical Controversy*, surmises that exposure in the press to the disagreements among experts makes a technology seem dangerous; even if pro- and anti-technology sentiments are well-balanced, the public is inclined to conclude that it is better to be safe than sorry. If this is so, then it is not the negativity of coverage that contributes to negative public opinion; the mere increase in coverage, whether negative or positive, will bring about this effect.

Mazur's view is supported by the conclusions of the *Report of the Public's Right to Information Task Force* of the President's Commission on the Accident at Three Mile Island. At least part of the impetus for the task force's content analysis was the belief among many critics that American press coverage of Three Mile Island had been unduly alarmist or sensationalist. The content analysis found that, overall, reassuring statements reported by the press far exceeded alarming ones (56 to 39 percent). One way to reconcile the impression of alarmism with this finding is via Mazur's view that the mere increase in press coverage of an event or technology contributes to intensifying the sense of danger, even if coverage is not particularly negative. Perhaps people believe that those who speak on behalf of a technology "protest too much."

The idea that the public tends to react negatively to media coverage of environmental and technological risks even where coverage is not predominantly negative suggests that people process negative and positive messages differently. This suggestion is confirmed by the find-ings of Amos Tversky and Daniel Kahneman, two psychologists study-ing risk perception. Their work shows that people adopt a reference point from which outcomes or choices are seen as positive or nega-tive, and they tend to react more strongly to negative options relative to their reference point than to positive options. We tend to be more eager to avoid losses than to secure comparable gains. Thus, if people see a technology as possibly saving lives but also as risking some loss of life, they will weigh the losses more heavily than the gains in decid-ing whether to support or oppose the technology.

These findings are reinforced by work done by German re-searchers Elisabeth Noelle-Neumann and Wolfgang Donsbach on what factors influence the newspaper reader's selection or retention of infor-mation. The flood of information grows continually, and the question arises: What filters do we use to let some of this information in and leave some out? Noelle-Neumann and Donsbach concluded that peo-ple are more receptive to negative information in the press than to positive. Supporters of a technology, for instance, are more likely to be affected by critical information about it than are critics likely to be affected by positive coverage.

These findings—which come from a variety of social scientists in different fields and research areas—all support the view that people process negative and positive information differently. What follows from this? An important conclusion is that, even where people's views are formed largely on the basis of news coverage, it is a large leap from the claim that people have predominantly negative views about an environmental or technological issue, or are unduly alarmed about a given risk, to the view that the media have covered the issue in a sen-sational or predominantly negative way. And even where news cover-age contains more negative than positive messages, it may be the amount and prominence of coverage, rather than the slant, that has the greater impact on public opinion.

Media Content

What of the charge that the media do not portray an accurate pic-ture of reality because press coverage is unrealistically negative? This view invites difficult questions about the proper role of the media, for it contains an implicit accusation: It suggests that the media *ought* to be attempting to reflect reality. But this assumption needs to be exam-ined critically.

Indeed, looking at what the media do in communicating risks reveals a deep tension in our expectations of what the media ought to do. From one angle, the criticism that the media do not accurately reflect reality seems a perfectly legitimate and natural one. Of course the media should reflect reality. What, after all, is the alternative? Bias. Distortion. One side of the story. But the view that the media ought at least to strive to mirror "the way things are" conflicts with much of what we know about about how the news media do in fact operate. More important, it neglects how they must necessarily operate.

It would be absurd to expect your daily newspaper to give an accurate picture of "reality" full-stop. There is altogether too much reality: subatomic reality, chemical reality, astronomical reality, psychological reality, political reality, economic reality, and lots of other realities, too. At the very most a newspaper can select from among these—omitting, say, subatomic reality as irrelevant to its readers' concerns and concentrating on political and economic reality. But even this is too vast an area. Journalists must find further ways of lopping off large chunks of reality. We begin to draw close to the standard criteria for what is newsworthy, familiar to students of journalism. What is news is what is new, unusual, interesting, important, dangerous, controversial, a change from the norm.

Seen in this way, news coverage is inherently "unrealistic"; it gives us a "distorted" view of the world; it aims, and *should* aim, at nothing else. Yet it is difficult to reconcile the necessary selectivity of the news media with our interests in truth and objectivity. How do you select a small sample of subjects, events, and trends in the world from the teeming multiplicity without distorting their significance?

Often you don't. Journalists can always be criticized for the criteria they employ in choosing news stories. We may well object to the prevailing practice summarized by a memo said to have hung in the newsroom of a British daily: "One Englishman is a story. Ten Frenchmen is a story. One hundred Germans is a story. And nothing ever happens in Chile." But an objection to the particular principles implicit in a given case leaves untouched the wider principle that *some* criteria must be employed to select from the mass of possible news stories. So we can ask: Is the media's presumed emphasis on negative aspects of risk-issues justified?

To take Kepplinger's example, assume that water pollution in the Rhine has declined over the last fifteen years, while media coverage of the pollution has increased. Does this indicate a defect in press coverage that ought to be remedied? Not necessarily. First of all, people (journalists or the general public or both) may not have been aware of the Rhine pollution at its peak. What you don't know can hurt you, but it cannot scare you. Since the environmental movement only began to gather momentum in the late sixties, it is perfectly plausible that water pollution was greater before people were disturbed by it.

Even if people were aware of the pollution before extensive media coverage (surely they saw it and smelled it), they may not have viewed it as an alterable part of the environment. It is a commonplace that people rebel against their circumstances when they begin to see the possibility of something better, and that this happens not when their circumstances are most dire, but when they have begun to improve. So it is very plausible that those who lived near the Rhine in the early sixties saw its filth as one of the unfortunate but inevitable consequences of civilization.

These points may go some way toward explaining and justifying negative media coverage of pollution even in the face of improving conditions. Pollution may still be excessive, even less exists today than twenty years ago. We may appreciate its risks more now than when they were greater. And we may hold different values because of previous successes in pollution control, which lead us to demand further improvements in the environment. Nothing is obviously irrational about this process. In covering such issues, journalists can be registering public dissatisfaction with a state of affairs despite its improvement over some previous state. They may be reflecting social values, engendering them, or both, but this need not indicate a failure to see "reality" as it is. For the reality at issue here includes people's values and expectations.

Of course the question remains: Are journalists partly responsible for increased awareness of pollution and changing values among the public, or are they simply responding to popular trends? No doubt more research in this area can shed some light on this question, but like other chicken-and-egg questions it remains largely unanswerable. Common sense suggests that both factors play a part: Journalists, as members of the larger society, respond to social trends (although perhaps more quickly than the typical citizen); at the same time they act as catalysts, speeding up those trends.

Conclusion

That negative news coverage of an issue increases, while the objective indicators of "negativity" (pollution or other damage) remain the same or even improve, in itself indicates no defect in the media's treatment. Deciding what is newsworthy and what "reality" news reporting ought to capture is intrinsically difficult and controversial, and reporters must grapple with these questions every day. We can perhaps blame reporters and editors if they simply wrap themselves in First Amendment justifications, as though the social consequences of their decisions were of no importance. But as they try to decide the exact scope and limits of "all the news that's fit to print," they are entitled to be Cassandras as well as Pollyannas; other charges must be brought against their natter beyond that of negativism.

This article was condensed and adapted from "The Role of the Media in Risk Communication," a paper presented at the International Workshop on Risk Communication in Julich, the Federal Republic of Germany, October 17–20, 1988. The sources cited are Hans Mathias Kepplinger, "Artificial Horizons," manuscripts, n.p., n.d.; Allan Mazur, The Dynamics of Technical Controversy *(Washington, D.C.: Communications Press, 1981);* Report of the Public's Right to Information Task Force *of the President's Commission on the Accident at Three Mile Island (Washington, D.C.: U.S. Government Printing Office, 1979); Amos Tversky and Daniel Kahneman, "Prospect Theory: An Analysis of Decisions under Risk,"* Econometrica *47 (1979); Kahneman and Tversky, "The Framing of Decisions and the Psychology of Choice,"* Science *211 (1981); and Elisabeth Noelle-Neumann and Wolfgang Donsbach, "Selective Exposure to Newspaper Content," presented at the International Communication Association Conference, May 21–25, 1987, Montreal.*

Is Advertising Manipulative?

Claudia Mills

One common charge brought against advertising is that it is manipulative: Even when it is not outright fraudulent, it works on us sneakily and inexorably, getting us to want what somebody else wants us to want, persuading us to buy what somebody else wants us to buy. But surely people try to get us to want things all the time and exercise all different kinds of persuasive—not to mention coercive—power over us. What in particular is meant by the charge of manipulation, so that people are bothered when they feel they have been its victim? It is not easy to specify exactly what makes some sorts of advertising cross the line from morally acceptable persuasion to morally suspect manipulation. The charge of manipulation, we shall see, can be used to carry several quite different accusations that may or may not be validly addressed to advertising.

Manipulation As Covert Persuasion

Sometimes we mean by "manipulation" any attempt at persuasion that is in some way covert, where the person doing the persuading wants to hide from his targets the fact that that is indeed what he intends. The manipulator does not lie about any facts about the external state of the world; instead he deceives others about the internal state of his own desires and intentions. A classic example here is Tom Sawyer's persuading his friends to take on his chore of whitewashing Aunt Polly's fence by pretending that he himself thinks whitewashing is glorious fun.

We might object to attempts at covert persuasion on two grounds. First, they might lead people to make substantively worse decisions and to take substantively worse actions than they would otherwise have done. Certain exceptions aside, covert processes in general are not as reliable as open attempts at persuasion. The suspicion will be ever-present that if the program someone is selling were so wonderful, she would not have to resort to covert tricks to sell it. As often as not, one thinks, this suspicion will be well-founded.

A second worry about covert persuasion is that it may make us feel we have been led to undertake some action less than voluntarily. Tom's friends would not have whitewashed the fence if they had known he wanted them to do it; they could claim, therefore, to have been misled about some crucial feature of the circumstances and so to have failed to give their fully informed consent to the enterprise. But whether we think covert persuasion makes us act involuntarily depends on whether we think other people have an obligation to exercise persuasion overtly. If they have done nothing wrong by hiding their intentions from us, we cannot complain they have violated our autonomy in the process.

Do we want to condemn the deception involved in covert persuasion? One might think, after all, that deception about one's own desires and intentions is more acceptable than deception about some external fact of the matter; we are not dealing here with the bold-faced lie. My own desires and intentions are paradigmatic of the private; isn't it my business whether or not I want to make them public?

Whether covert persuasion counts as morally wrong will depend in the end on the extent to which we think one has an obligation to be open and straightforward with others, on the degree to which transparency is expected in human relationships. The answer will vary according to the kind of relationship in question—intimate, friendly, business, frankly adversarial—and the presuppositions and assumptions governing that kind of relationship.

Relatively little advertising counts as manipulative in this first sense. For one, most adults recognize advertisements for what they are: usually straightforward—indeed, blatant—attempts by manufacturers to persuade consumers to buy their products. (Many children, however, do not, raising special worries about advertising targeted at such a vulnerable audience.) For another, in commercial settings one would presumably have fairly minimal obligations to broadcast one's intentions to others. But if we are worried about advertising that deliberately and successfully conceals its persuasive intentions, we can take steps to address specific problematic practices.

Certainly some ads try to manipulate by dressing themselves up as something other than advertising, by disguising themselves, for example, as magazine feature articles (a ploy undertaken frequently with travel ads) or as journalistic essays (a favorite advertising strategy for Mobil, which buys space for its ads on newspaper op-ed pages). Presumably readers apply more relaxed standards of scrutiny to straight reporting or opinion pieces than to advertising, a fact advertisers hope to turn to their own use. Here it seems reasonable to require explicit labeling of advertisements as such.

A related advertising technique involves disguising the commercial intent behind a message by feigning intimacy with the audience or invoking the consumer's genuine loyalties. This approaches the ridiculous in computer-personalized, direct-mail appeals that mention the recipient's name a dozen times on a page. Celebrity endorsements belong in this category as well, for to the extent that viewers like and trust celebrities, they feel that these admired figures would not be endorsing a product just to make money. We feel betrayed when we find out that Olympic champions don't endorse Wheaties out of a missionary zeal to share their training secrets with us, their fans—and indeed don't really eat Wheaties for breakfast at all. And would that nice, fatherly Bill Cosby say he liked Pepsi if it wasn't truly his favorite soft drink? The proper remedy here would seem to be heightened educative measures to raise the level of consumer savvy.

Manipulation As Appeal to Emotion

A second account of manipulation starts with the idea not of covert persuasion, but of emotional persuasion, involving not deception but distraction by powerful feeling. The charge of manipulation is leveled against an attempt to persuade someone to believe or do something that appeals to her emotion rather than to her reason.

It is difficult to make out a case, however, that emotion-based persuasion is any less likely to produce true beliefs and good desires than purportedly rational persuasion. Suppose, for example, that I am trying to understand the problem of homelessness in America. I could study sociological data on the causes of homelessness and the demographic profile of this population. But I could also go to see a film that vividly portrays the day-to-day life of a family living in a squalid city shelter. That the latter appeals directly to my emotions, to my heart rather than my head, should not make it count as manipulative in any morally troubling way. In fact, it may very well be a superior vehicle for persuasion.

The danger is always, of course, that emotion-based appeals can lead us astray or can be invoked to distort the real and relevant issues. "Anecdotal evidence" may tug at our heartstrings while nonetheless putting forward a false and distorted view of the broader reality. But so-called rational arguments can mislead us in just the same way. They, too, can be partial and incomplete. Consider the ease with which people can lie with statistics and make numbers seem to say anything they want them to say. Both rational and nonrational persuasion, then, can be legitimate means of influence and both can be manipulative.

Advertising uses both reason-based and emotional persuasion to capture its customers. That it tends to rely on emotion-based persuasion cannot in itself be used to mount a case against it. We have to judge advertising here by asking whether it uses image-oriented *or* informational ads to lead us to buy a product we for whatever reason *should not* buy.

It certainly seems that advertising can lead us to favor a product for no good reason. For many categories of products, no objective differences exist among brands. One advertiser noted of beer brands, for example, that "The many competitive brands are virtually identical in terms of taste, color, and alcohol delivery, and after two or three pints even an expert couldn't tell them apart."

Two points can be made here. First, the kind of subjective difference introduced by advertising itself may well count as a legitimate reason to buy something. An advertising campaign can give a product an "aura" that it is not bizarre to consider in making a purchase. As Eric Clark notes in his recent book *The Want Makers*, in some cases the image that helps to sell the product now *is* the product. If Coke and Pepsi taste the same, cost the same, and work in the same way to quench thirst, this does not make them the same if their image is different, for, Clark says, "Pepsi-Cola, like its arch rival Coca-Cola, is primarily its image."

Second, it is one thing to act without a good reason for acting where we are otherwise indifferent between two choices; it is quite another thing to act in the face of good reasons against so doing. After all, like Buridan's ass, when standing thirsty in front of the pop machine, we have to buy *something*. Why not, on the basis of its advertising, buy a Pepsi? It is far more worrisome when advertising leads us to favor, not a virtually identical product, but an inferior product (or an equivalent product at a higher price—priced to cover its advertising costs!), or, worse still, a dangerous product, such as cigarettes.

Manipulation As Playing on a Weakness

A third account of manipulation involves playing not on emotions generally but on certain emotions or emotional states, such as fear, lust, greed, sorrow, loneliness. Manipulation can involve playing on another's weakness, taking advantage of some kind of power one has over another. Numerous charges of manipulation, in this sense, have been brought against advertising for the extent to which it exploits the fears and anxieties of consumers, as well as their ignorance and gullibility.

It is not easy, however, to make out the idea of manipulation as playing on a weakness in some meaningfully narrow and specific way. How do you get anybody to do anything except by finding some button to push, some lever to operate? As an advertiser, how would I get anyone to buy anything without appealing to some want, some need, some hope, some longing, some lack that my product is claimed to remedy? We can hardly condemn any and all profiting from others' weaknesses. Surely what is wrong is not that I profit from a product designed to help others lose weight, correct bald spots, cure impotence, and so on; objections should arise only if I make an excess profit, more than I would on a product for which the need is not so desperate. Even here it is hard to know what counts as excess benefit without looking at what people are actually willing to pay for a product that speaks to their heart's yearnings.

At least some of what bothers us about advertising based on fears and vulnerabilities is that the products advertised are often worthless. The weight-loss nostrum is not going to make pounds melt off in hours, nor is the special scalp cream going to regrow a full head of hair, nor is the aphrodisiac going to cure sexual impotence. But if we had a product that did indeed give reliable results in weight loss, hair growth, and sexual potency, and these were advertised without undue exaggeration, our objections would be much diminished. Can an advertiser dwell on the misery of obesity, baldness, or impotence? The answer here seems to be that whether or not she does this is immaterial. We don't need advertising to tell us we don't want to be fat or bald or impotent. We knew that already. While advertising can contribute to a culture in which thinness, youth, and sexual prowess are made into fetishes, the desires to be thin, young, and sexually attractive are more powerful than any advertising. We were searching for the fountain of youth long before Madison Avenue existed.

Other ads, however, do not play on already existing needs and fears; they are charged with creating new ones. It has been suggested that personal concerns, say, with body odor and bad breath, have been manufactured to a large extent by advertisers. We otherwise might have been content just to smell the way human beings smell. I myself doubt this; I think I would notice—and mind—body odor even if I hadn't been exposed to commercial after commericial for Sure, Ban, Right Guard, and the like. But it is safe to say that until advertisements for Wisk, no one ever dreaded the taunting jeer of "Ring around the collar!" In any case, it seems that the creation of new fears to be played upon is morally worse than playing upon existing fears.

Conclusion

The charge of manipulation can mean many things. Here we have examined three: manipulation as covert persuasion, manipulation as persuasion based on emotion rather than reason, and manipulation as playing on another's weakness. Although much advertising does not seem to be subject to moral criticism on these grounds, it certainly can be manipulative in all three of these senses. We will want to be on our guard against advertising that conceals its persuasive intent, advertising that misleads through specious emotion-based or rational argument, and advertising that seeks to create and then to exploit consumer fears and weaknesses. Of course, this list does not exhaust the possibilities for moral and aesthetic objections to advertising— one might argue, for example, that it is a kind of cultural pollution, or that it contributes to the creation of a crassly materialistic culture. Here I have only sought to understand one common objection more clearly.

Children's Television

Claudia Mills

A fternoon in America, and millions of kids are sprawled on the floor watching television. On one station, the Masters of the Universe (available from Mattel at $4.97 each) triumph over the forces of evil; on another, the Defenders of the Universe (sold separately for $3.97 apiece) do the same. Turn the dial, and an animated rubber Gumby figure (in two sizes: $2.99 and $1.50) attempts to tug on viewers' heartstrings ("If you've got a heart, then Gumby's a part of you"), his adventures punctuated by commercials for Circus Fun cereal (featuring chocolate-covered marshmallow animals) and Snickers bars. It is hard to resist the conclusion that commercial children's TV is a wasteland.

Yet children aged six to eleven watch an average of twenty-seven hours of television a week, for a total of fourteen hundred hours a year; preschool children watch even more. By the time the average American child graduates from high school, he or she will have logged more hours in front of the TV than in the classroom. How worried should we be about what our children are watching—and about what is being sold to them as they watch? And should we be trying to do something about it?

It's Not What You Watch

It seems obvious that it is better to have children learning their alphabet on "Sesame Street" than watching shoddy, violence-packed cartoons. But against this position it has been suggested that the medium of TV itself dominates any message, for good or ill, it might seek to convey.

British critic Cedric Cullingford argues that it doesn't matter what children watch because, "even at its most intense moments," television "can appear as little more than background." Children "associate the pleasures of television with a mild form of boredom," which they nonetheless turn to fondly because "boredom is so little trouble." Like adults, kids watch TV for "entertainment without demands," and what they watch makes very little impression on them, emotionally or intellectually: "Of all the information that children will have seen over an evening's viewing, of all the hours of action, children remember very little. They know that they have *seen* the programmes but can say almost nothing about them." Thus Cullingford turns a skeptical ear to stories of TV's supposed great dangers to the minds and hearts of youth: TV doesn't *matter* enough to pose any real threat.

Marie Winn, author of *The Plug-in Drug*, agrees that it doesn't matter what children actually watch on TV, but for the opposite reason: not because watching TV is so harmless, but because it is so harmful. Winn sees television-watching as essentially a passive experience, a "one-way transaction" that induces in children a zombie-like state: "The child's facial expression is transformed. The jaw is relaxed and hangs open slightly; the tongue rests on the front teeth . . . The eyes have a glazed, vacuous look . . ." Winn also claims that TV, far from powerless, is addicting. She concludes that it doesn't matter what children watch any more than it matters whether an alcoholic drinks Jack Daniels or moonshine. In fact, Winn goes so far as to say that the interests of children are better served by simply broadcasting junk, "since conscientious parents are more likely to limit their children's television intake if only unsavory programs are available." How children of less conscientious parents would fare under unrestrained industry indifference Winn does not say.

The most vociferous advocates of improved content in children's programming have targeted two key areas of concern: on the positive side, the educational potential of television; on the negative side, its pervasive violence. The educational promise of television has so far blossomed best in "Sesame Street," launched in 1969 by the Children's Television Workshop with lavish budgets and extraordinary participation by educators. Early studies by the Educational Testing Service in 1970 and 1971 indicated that the young watchers of "Sesame Street" made great gains as a result of their viewing experience, but later studies attributed these rather to concerted parental involvement in the viewing. Teachers report that "Sesame Street" has helped young children to recognize numbers and letters, but this early boost has not translated into improved language skills later in school. Certainly disadvantaged children, however long and hard they stare at the tube, have not caught up academically with children of educated parents. But that television has not been strikingly successful at imparting factual knowledge or teaching language skills does not mean that it teaches nothing. "Sesame Street" may be as important for elevating children's aesthetic tastes or for fostering nonracist attitudes, as for drilling the alphabet. Even Cullingford concedes that children pick up from TV such amorphous things as "tone, gestures, and attitudes" that may shape their worldview.

By now it is hardly news that American television is violent: By age five the typical child in the United States has viewed more than two hundred hours of violent images, and the average fourteen-year-old has witnessed the televised killings of some thirteen thousand human beings. The number of violent incidents on TV is rivaled only by the number of studies of their effects. The prevailing view seems to be, to quote the conclusions of the National Institute of Mental Health's 1982 report: "Violence on television does lead to aggressive behavior by children and teenagers who watch the programs." Many studies have been criticized, however, as relying too heavily on laboratory simulations; others show a correlation between television viewing and aggressive behavior without proving any causal connection. And definitions of "violence" in television are so elastic that conclusions about its frequency must be drawn with some care, lest a comedian slipping on a banana peel be classed as an incident of violence. It seems fair to say, nonetheless, that violence on children's television, and on television generally, should be monitored vigilantly.

For the rest, does it matter what children watch or not? Philosopher Judith Lichtenberg likens the charge that program content does not matter to the frequent claim that it does not matter *what* children read, only *that* they read. But, just as few are convinced that comic books are as good for young readers as the enduring classics of children's literature, so it is hard to accept that beautifully produced television dramas are as bad for children as their present alternatives.

A final issue concerns children's advertising. A National Science Foundation (NSF) study estimates that on average children are exposed to some twenty thousand commercial messages each year, most for toys, cereals, candies, and fast-food restaurants. (Few tout, say, the importance of eating spinach.) The NSF report cites evidence that children under eight years of age have substantial difficulty in comprehending the difference between commercials and programs. Younger children also express a greater belief in commercials and request advertised products more frequently than more mature youngsters do. This raises special questions about the appropriateness of advertising to children in this age group, particularly when so many of the products advertised (e.g., highly sweetened products) are arguably harmful for them.

Funding Public Television

These concerns about children's television can be addressed via two chief avenues. One is to increase the support given to public television, which generally has superior programming for children and no commercials. According to Edward L. Palmer, vice president and senior research fellow at the Children's Television Workshop, our Public Broadcasting System (PBS) lags far behind the British Broadcasting Corporation, which airs 840 hours of at-home children's television each year, representing one-eighth of the total program schedule carried on its two stations. Of these, 630 hours (75 percent) are newly produced programs. By contrast, PBS carries about 150 hours a year of new children's programming, with repeat programming hovering just short of 90 percent. Palmer sees investment in children's television as a singular bargain: The cost of "Sesame Street" averages among the more than nine million preschoolers who tune in to the show to less than a penny per day per original program. Even a children's programming budget adequate to provide daily programming for all age groups (which Palmer puts at $62.4 million) is, he points out, but a tiny fraction of the more than $100 billion we spend each year in this country on public education.

The implied analogy is that the same reasons that lead us to support public education should lead us to support public television. We support public education because we have a common interest in preparing future citizens to participate intelligently in our democracy and because we want, both for prudential and for moral reasons, to help children grow up into capable, employable adults. If some cold water is dashed on television's hopes as an educator, these arguments cannot directly translate into support for publicly funded programming. But much of the curriculum of our schools is not specifically designed to turn children into future voters and workers, but to enhance their lives, and our collective life, in other ways. The rest of us have a stake in how young minds and hearts are formed and how America's children spend the better part of their waking days. Improving the quality of television seems as important an objective as, say, offering art and music appreciation classes, or physical education, in the schools.

Public television is often criticized as coercively elitist. Aren't some select groups taxing the majority to provide programs catering only to their highbrow tastes? Whatever their general merits, such arguments fail to convince when the issue is children's television. No one denies that paternalism is justified with children or that adults—parents, teachers, society at large—are entitled, indeed obligated, to shape and mold children's preferences and values. We cannot appeal to children's existing tastes to determine what should be offered to them, since their tastes are in flux and will be determined largely by what in fact we offer.

Regulating Commercial Television

However rich the offerings on public television, the audience for it seldom exceeds 5 percent of the population. If we are to have any significant effect on what children are actually watching, we must consider mandating certain levels of quantity and quality for children's programming on commercial stations and regulating children's advertising—or banning it altogether.

Regulation of the broadcast media always has been more stringent than regulation of the print media, based partly on the argument that since broadcast outlets are licensed by the government, it is appropriate for government to allocate them in a way that serves the public interest. But regulation of the media, and of advertising as well, raises charges that it conflicts with freedom of expression.

Lichtenberg replies that measures to give neglected groups greater access to the media do not conflict with the objectives underlying freedom of expression, but indeed support them. We want freedom of expression in part because we oppose censorship: We should not be prevented from thinking, reading, writing, listening—or broadcasting—as we see fit. But opposition to censorship does not exhaust our interest in freedom of expression, in Lichtenberg's view. We also want diversity of expression to flourish; we want to hear a multiplicity of voices. And this can include the voices of children and voices speaking directly to their concerns and needs. Freedom of expression rests on both the rights and interests of speakers and the rights and interests of listeners. Certainly the rights and interests of children as speakers have traditionally been ignored ("Children should be seen and not heard"); they are an all but voiceless group in the public sphere. But their rights and interests as listeners have been neglected as well, and improving children's programming would work to redress this imbalance.

Advertising, too, is a form of expression, and free speech arguments can be given for protecting commercials. However, courts have not extended to commercial speech the full range of First Amendment protections. The Federal Trade Commission requires that advertisements be truthful and that their factual claims be substantiated, requirements that would not be tolerated in other realms of discourse. And, according to philosopher Alan Goldman, any moral right to advertise "does not include a right to defraud, or moral license to mislead people into buying harmful products."

Goldman suggests that we need to consider "first, the audience to whom the advertisement is addressed, and second, the degree of increased risk of serious harm from being misled into use or misuse of the product. If a specific audience is addressed, typical members of that audience ought not to be misled. But as the risk of serious harm increases, the prohibition against deception must become more strict in order to prevent deception of less circumspect consumers."

Both considerations are crucial in assessing advertisements targeted to children. With adults the standard presumption, perhaps mistaken, is that the typical consumer is able to recognize the persuasive intent of commercials and discount their claims accordingly. But with young children at least, the *typical* viewer is far more susceptible to the manipulations of Madison Avenue. With adults we can say, "If people are gullible or careless enough to fall for *that*, so much the worse for them." But the vulnerability of children cannot be dismissed in this way, and when children are deliberately or inadvertently misled by commercials, standards of truth in advertising are compromised.

How much harm is done to children by their naive trust in advertisements? It might be argued that any harm is relatively minor, since final purchasing decisions are made by adults, who should be able to assess the merits of the coveted products more wisely. Of course, a whining child can wear away many a parent's better judgment, but the purchase is still mediated through an adult's judgment. (Children's vitamin ads were removed from the air because they were directly consumed—eaten—by children in toxic quantities.) Children may in the end be worse off, of course, if they wheedle their parents into feeding them junk food and straining the family budget by foolish toy purchases. And if we are concerned about the effects of television on children's values and attitudes, we have to worry about the relentless materialism that bombards young viewers via the constant stream of commercial messages.

What Should We Do?

Budgetary constraints at present make any increase in funding for public television unlikely. Congress has taken action, however, in passing the Children's Television Act (similar to a bill vetoed in 1988 by President Reagan), which limits commercials on children's shows to twelve minutes per hour on weekdays, and ten and half minutes on weekends. While this curtails children's advertising to some extent, the level of advertising permitted still exceeds what is found during most adult-oriented programs. Tougher guidelines for advertisers and program directors have yet to be enacted. In the meantime, parents can take advantage of a technological marvel called the *off* button. It may be the most potent weapon parents now have against low-quality children's television.

Sources quoted in this article are Cedric Cullingford, Children and Television *(New York: St. Martin's Press, 1984); Marie Winn,* The Plug-in Drug, *rev. ed. (New York: Viking, 1985); Edward L. Palmer, "Providing Quality Television for America's Children," in* The Future of Children's Television: Results of the Markle Foundation/Boys Town Conference *(Boys Town, Nebr.: The Boys Town Center, 1984); Alan Goldman, "Ethical Issues in Advertising," in* Just Business, *ed. Tom Regan (New York: Random House, 1984); and Judith Lichtenberg, "Foundations and Limits of Freedom of the Press,"* Philosophy & Public Affairs *16 (1987), reprinted in* Democracy and the Mass Media, *ed. Judith Lichtenberg (New York: Cambridge University Press, 1990).*

The Dilemma of the Journalist/Source Relationship

Judith Lichtenberg

Is every journalist "a kind of confidence man, preying on people's vanity, ignorance, or loneliness,
gaining their trust and betraying them without remorse"? So charged
journalist Janet Malcolm in a widely discussed two-part article in *The
New Yorker* that aroused anger and controversy among journalists and
other writers. Malcolm accused writer Joe McGinniss of betraying Jeffrey MacDonald, convicted of brutally murdering his wife and two
children in 1970. McGinniss, originally sympathetic to MacDonald,
undertook, with MacDonald's cooperation, to write a book about his
case. Ultimately McGinniss became convinced of MacDonald's guilt;
his best-selling book, *Fatal Vision*, depicts MacDonald as a cold-
blooded sociopath. MacDonald sued McGinniss for breach of contract; a mistrial was declared after the jury became deadlocked five to
one in favor of MacDonald, and the case was settled for $325,000.

The Malcolm/McGinniss/MacDonald affair brings to light a
pointed moral problem faced by journalists seeking information from
sources. But it leaves in the shadows the other side of this problem,
which is probably more damaging to daily journalism. For every journalist who has betrayed a source's trust, many more have been bought
by it. If betrayal worries us, so should the failure to betray. Both problems derive ultimately from the same root.

It does not take great insight into human character to see why people should be reluctant to share information with those who show
hostility toward them or assume an adversarial stance. When the information is highly personal or for some other reason makes a person
vulnerable, it stands to reason that she is most likely to share it with
those she thinks she can trust. Even when the information is not so
volatile, the sophisticated source knows that she has something the
journalist wants. She is likely to expect sympathy, at the very least, in
return for divulging valuable information.

These facts put journalists in an awkward position. If the price of getting information is the appearance of sympathy, journalists have essentially two choices. They can *appear* sympathetic, while not really *being* sympathetic, in which case they confront the problems of deception and betrayal that Malcolm vividly describes. Not only is this practice morally questionable, it is likely to produce psychic discomfort. It is, moreover, a poor strategy for encouraging others to trust one in the future.

The alternative is for journalists to appear sympathetic by actually *becoming* or being sympathetic, in which case they are at enormous risk of losing the critical distance necessary for telling a story accurately or impartially. The problem is particularly acute for journalists with regular beats who must depend on long-term associations with sources. (Elite Washington journalists who attend parties with the people they write about are at special risk.)

Although the journalist has very strong self-interested reasons for maintaining cordial relations with sources, being sympathetic is not a choice one makes in a calculating or fully conscious way. For one thing, to choose to befriend someone for the sake of some further end is psychologically difficult. For another, it is quite natural for a journalist—or for anyone studying another person, group, or culture—to become sympathetic to the perspective of his or her subject. As a philosopher observing the journalistic culture, I find myself confronting precisely the same dilemma. The closer you get and the more details you see of someone's situation, the more likely you are to sympathize and the less likely to criticize. You come to learn that she is a wonderful mother and a fine person, that he jokes with the press and always returns phone calls. And as you understand why things have happened or are done in a particular way, the more natural, logical, or inevitable they come to seem. The more you can *explain*, the less urge you feel to *justify*.

But to understand all is to forgive too much. In getting closer, we acquire the wisdom of seeing that things are more complicated than they seem from afar. The trick—an extremely difficult one—is to strike the right balance: to be close enough to understand, yet distant enough not to be taken in; close enough to appreciate the subject's point of view, yet distant enough to appreciate other points of view. Too must distance and you wrong an individual, not enough and you wrong the public.

Between the two horns of the dilemma—too much sympathy, or not enough—the first is the path of least resistance for journalists. When morality is conceived simply in terms of personal relations, this approach has moral purity on its side, in addition to psychic painlessness and expediency. The result, I believe, is that political news often hews too closely to the views of offical sources.

This dilemma will persist as long as journalists needs sources, and as long as sources exhibit the natural human preference for allies over adversaries. Journalists will be tempted either to betray their sources, or to befriend them.

FOR FURTHER READING

Klaidman, Stephen, and Tom L. Beauchamp. *The Virtuous Journalist.* New York: Oxford University Press, 1987.

Lichtenberg, Judith, ed. *Democracy and the Mass Media.* New York: Cambridge University Press, 1990.

Malcolm, Janet. *The Journalist and the Murderer.* New York: Alfred A. Knopf, 1990.

Pool, Ithiel de Sola. *Technologies of Freedom.* Cambridge, Mass.: Harvard University Press, 1983.

Schauer, Frederick. *Free Speech: A Philosophical Inquiry.* Cambridge: Cambridge University Press, 1982.

6

MEDICINE

We live in an age where the medically miraculous has become the medically routine. Physicians today can transplant hearts, kidneys, and livers; they can keep extremely premature infants alive for months and even lifetimes; with new techniques of genetic screening, they can detect the genetic makeup of unborn children; in time, they will be able to alter genetic destiny as well. Yet certain diseases stubbornly refuse to yield their secrets to medical research, most notably AIDS, reminding us of the stark limits to the powers of our most acclaimed miracleworkers. This chapter explores some of the ethical issues raised by the latest innovations in medical research and treatment, and by the dread disease, unknown a decade ago, that promises to be the scourge of the last years of this century.

The growing success of human organ transplants raises a host of questions about what the government should do, promote, permit, or prohibit to meet the mounting need for transplantable organs. In "Against Selling Bodily Parts," Samuel Gorovitz examines several proposals for government intervention in this area, warning against both the dangers of government coercion and the equal dangers of government laissez-faire. "The question of how to close the gap between the demand for and the supply of transplantable organs," he writes, "is no less than the question of what sort of society we wish to advocate, endorse, and nurture."

Dan Brock, in "Life-Support Decisions for Newborns," reviews some of the moral issues that haunt decisions to provide or terminate life-sustaining treatment for seriously handicapped infants, including the special status of newborn persons, the proper role of quality-of-life considerations, the relevance of costs borne by families and society at large, the distinction between killing and "merely" letting die, and the dangers of well-intentioned misuse or ill-intentioned abuse of policies permitting nontreatment.

The next two selections—"What Is Wrong with Eugenics?" by Robert Wachbroit and "The Genetic Adventure" by Stephen Stich—evaluate the various sources of our collective unease with the kinds of genetic manipulations that now lie on the medical horizon. Wachbroit dismisses worries that genetic engineering would fail to serve the interests of children or the interests of society, narrowly construed. Instead he suggests that, say, choosing the sex or race of one's child is worrisome for the insult it poses to the dignity of the sex or race not chosen. "Eugenics," he writes, "involves saying that whatever the value of the child's original condition, that value is second-rate." For his part, Stich rejects worries concerning the equitable distribution of the advantages brought by genetic engineering, as well as arguments that it violates God's plan or the "evolutionary wisdom" embodied in millions of years of natural selection. For Stich, genetic engineering is potentially troubling because it raises the possibility that "the age-old presumption of a more or less fixed human nature may begin to dissolve," and with it the shared background assumptions to which we appeal in resolving moral disputes. "How shall I reason with a Moslem fundamentalist or a Marxist or a Moonie if what divides him from me is not merely his traditions and his convictions, but also his genetics? The prospect is at once so staggering and so unprecedented that we hardly know how to begin thinking about it."

New genetic discoveries and technologies in medicine also challenge our understanding of the traditional obligations of the physician. In "Who Is the Patient?" Robert Wachbroit considers cases where the physician's duty of confidentiality is tested by her awareness of the genetic basis of her patient's disease, and thus its implications for crucial life choices of others sharing those same genes. "As our scientific understanding of diseases improves," Wachbroit suggests, "our moral responsibilities will become more complex."

Chapter 6 closes with two articles on AIDS. AIDS is special both because it is to date incurable and because its victims in this country are predominantly gay men. In "AIDS: What to Do—And What Not to Do," Richard Mohr argues against quarantine of AIDS patients and paternalistic interference with gay institutions, and in favor of preventive funding and state-funded hospice care. Central in his argument is the need for government to respect gay citizens as "autonomous and independent beings" and to provide compensatory justice to gays systematically and legally thwarted in the establishment of their own gay families. In "Mandatory AIDS Testing," Mohr examines marital testing programs and those for military recruits and immigrants. He charges that the flagrant inefficiency of such testing exposes its dominant aim: the establishment of compulsory heterosexuality as a sacred value.

Against Selling Bodily Parts

Samuel Gorovitz

The transplantation of a human kidney is no longer a rare or highly uncertain process. More than five thousand patients receive transplanted kidneys annually, and their prospects for lasting success are bright. Because improved immunosuppressant drugs like cyclosporin have greatly increased the survival rate for transplant patients, the primary barrier to successful transplantation for thousands of patients with end-stage renal failure is now the lack of an adequate supply of transplantable kidneys. Patients often wait years after being listed as prospective transplant recipients, and those years are filled with the discomfort and constraint of dependence on dialysis—each year of which is as costly as the $40,000 transplant operation. Because of the sharp recent increase in our capacity to transfer living tissues of various kinds successfully from donors to recipients, the large shortage of transplantable materials is growing even larger. Controversial economic, political, and moral issues swirl around our efforts to respond to this new situation.

How can we best meet the vital needs of patients who require transplant surgery, while respecting the various related interests and concerns that come into play? We are faced here with choices that, in the words of Richard Titmuss, author of *The Gift Relationship*, "lead us, if we are to understand these transactions in the context of any society, to the fundamentals of social and economic life." The question of how to close the gap between the demand for and the supply of transplantable organs is no less than the question of what sort of society we wish to advocate, endorse, and nurture.

The Role of Government

What should the government do, promote, permit, or prohibit in respect to organ transplantation? The range of possible responses is great. Proposals have been made to presume consent by prospective donors in the absence of clear evidence to the contrary, to establish commercial markets in organs, and to increase the efficiency of present approaches through devices ranging from tax incentives to public education. I am not aware of any proposal yet that organs should be made available regardless of the wishes of the person whose organs are at issue—but at this point it would not surprise me.

Any position on the role of government here must rely on a broader conception of the proper role of government generally. It is not the responsibility of government to be the solution of first resort to the problems of contemporary society; rather, the private sector is our best hope for meeting a broad range of needs. The government has a responsibility to step in only where it must, to safeguard the public interest. Further, the government should exercise great caution in enacting prohibitions on behavior. Only where it can sustain a persuasive justification may it properly constrain the behavior of citizens; it has no business prohibiting actions merely because they are offensive to the sensibilities of a portion of the citizenry, or because they could conceivably lead to more serious abuses in the future. Nor may it require actions simply because they would be in the public interest. Requiring actions (such as the payment of taxes or participation in national defense in wartime) or prohibiting actions (such as violation of the civil liberties of citizens) requires strong justification indeed.

For this reason, the appropriate role for the government in respect to the shortage of organs is catalytic rather than coercive. To require the donation of cadaver organs would be to ride roughshod over the rights of individuals to exercise discretion over the disposition of their bodily parts. Even to presume consent in the absence of dissent would be to place the burden where it does not belong. Those who prefer not to donate organs, for reasons of religion, superstition, or squeamishness, or for no reason at all, would be cast into a defensive position in which they might feel hard pressed to protect themselves and their families against intrusions of a most intimate sort.

Yet the problem remains and grows, so something must be done. An ideal solution would lie in a massive shift in national sentiment about transplantation—a shift that would greatly increase participation in voluntary donation plans and would also greatly diminish the barriers, psychological and economic, to participation by the medical profession in efficient collection and distribution of organs.

The American Council on Transplantation may become an effective instrument for rationalizing our methods of collecting and distributing organs and for increasing public participation in donation plans—but that will require it to have significant financial and institutional backing, a firm and energetic resolve to meet its objectives, and a fair bit of good luck. Its prospects of success were greatly enhanced by the passage of HR5580 in 1984, which, without being coercive or intrusive, fosters a major increase in our structural capacity to achieve an adequate solution based on a voluntary and altruistic response to the plight of potential transplant recipients.

This bill amends the Public Health Service Act to authorize financial assistance for organ procurement organizations; to establish a United States Transplantation Network; to establish a Task Force on Organ Transplantation to "conduct comprehensive examinations of the medical, legal, ethical, economic, and social issues presented by human organ procurement and transplantation"; and to prohibit a commercial market in transplantable organs. This last provision is my present concern.

The approach represented by HR5580 must be given every reasonable chance of success, for the alternatives are grim indeed. One of the worst would be governmental takeover of the whole domain, responding to national shortages with national criteria, supported by mandatory and intrusive processes of collection. The disadvantages of such a scheme, I trust, need no elaboration here. However, a comparable peril exists on the other side. For another alternative is to allow a commercial market, linking supply and demand through the mechanisms of free enterprise. And the disadvantages of *that* scheme do require some elaboration.

Kidneys for Sale

This is no idle speculation. H. Barry Jacobs of Virginia has established a business for the commercial brokering of kidneys. He has proposed to commission the sale of kidneys from persons in the Third World, for whatever price is needed to induce them to sell, and then to broker the kidneys to affluent Americans. The brokerage fees will make the enterprise, in Jacobs's own words, "a very lucrative business."

This plan raises many questions that go beyond the immediate need to increase the supply of kidneys. The demand for transplantation will continue to increase, as will the variety of transplantable tissues. Today we focus mainly on kidneys, corneas, and livers, knowing that lungs and hearts are also transplantable. But skin, bone and muscle are transplantable, too, and recent successes in the reattachments of digits and limbs foreshadow the transplantation of such parts in response to major trauma. It would be naive not to realize we are at the beginning of the problems associated with our newly developed capacities of medical and surgical intervention.

Jacobs defends his scheme by appeal to humanitarianism, public service, and the American way. He points out that his plan will deliver kidneys to people who need them, and cash to people who need it, quite possibly to their mutual benefit. And with the traditionally admirable flexibility of the free-market system, the scheme can function long before the catalytic efforts of the government or the American Council on Transplantation can take effect. If, as Jacobs claims, all related transactions are to proceed by the voluntary actions of fully informed and uncoerced adults, we must pause before concluding that a legitimate public interest lies in prohibiting such exchanges.

Many assumptions in the Jacobs scheme are open to challenge. The risks to donors are greater than he has admitted. The scheme makes a mockery of informed consent, as is evident to anyone familiar with federal regulations protecting human research subjects—regulations that reflect a sensitive awareness that desperate circumstances can be implicitly coercive and that the provision of excessive inducements to the oppressed can constitute a violation of their autonomy. And problems of quality control might be insuperable. But we miss the most fundamentally important issues if we focus on such weaknesses in the proposal. At stake are important features of the distribution of vital resources in the challenging years ahead.

Various standards exist for judging the greatness of a society—by the peaks of its achievements in the arts and culture, or in technology, by the average material standard of living of its people, by the scope of its territorial authority, and so on. I have always thought one appropriate standard for making such judgments is how a society treats those whom it treats least well. The analogue at the level of the family is compelling, at least. No matter how we admired the talented, affluent, accomplished family next door, our judgment of them would plummet if we discovered that they had one family member whom they abused, whose interests they ignored, whose needs left them unmoved, and whom they exploited to their own maximum advantage. That discovery would teach us much about their character and integrity—about their sense of justice within a social structure. By the analogous criterion, American society still falls short of its loftiest ideals.

Another criterion for judging the greatness of a society is the way it treats its most seriously disadvantaged. (This criterion is related to, but not the same as, the previous one.) People beset by grinding poverty, malnutrition, and ignorance, like those beset by life-threatening illness, are clearly in highly disadvantaged circumstances. Surely one aspect of the Jacobs scheme is that it is profiteering on the desperation of these two groups. But what better societal response to their plight is there to endorse?

A free-market model is based on the values of competition, individual initiative, and the elasticity of supply and demand in response to market forces. But medical need is no respecter of success in the world of commerce. The poor are more likely, not less likely, to be seriously ill, and their ability to obtain medical care is seriously compromised by their poverty.

To distribute vital resources according to ability to pay is to set aside all concern for medical need as the primary determinant of access. It is to set aside considerations of compassion and cooperation, and abandon efforts to fashion a society where mutual supportiveness is our response to desperation. It is to sanction the expansion of unfettered commercialism into dimensions of life that could provide the opportunity for a greater sense of community and of national purpose.

The argument for a commercial market in kidneys might have greater force had we put ourselves to the test, and failed. But we are just now acknowledging a new national need and fashioning a constructive governmental response to that need. It is far too soon to judge that response a failure.

The only adequate barrier to the commercialization of life in the proposed manner is a legislative prohibition. I support such a prohibition, and I do so as one reluctant to endorse any unnecessary restriction on individual liberty. Such a prohibition, however, is necessary to test our capacity as a nation to meet the present shortages, and to find ways to deal with future shortages, with due regard for the dictates of liberty and social justice. We are well advised to temper our passionate and worthy defense of liberty with consideration of the social context without which our liberty would be a tragically empty achievement.

An additional reason for supporting the prohibition derives from the symbolic significance of the proposed market in organs. At a time when we urgently need to nurture good relations with the Third World, our international credibility would be dealt a severe blow by our tolerance of a plan whereby the poor in underdeveloped countries were exploited as a source of spare parts for rich Americans.

In the Third World, it is unlikely that strong restrictive action will effectively prevent the plundering of poor people's parts for profit. Their public health concerns still center on problems of sanitation, nutrition, and infectious disease. Any effective controls must be at our end. But it is no surprise, nor inappropriate, that the world's most highly developed nation should bear the burdens of exercising responsibility over medical science's most advanced capacities. If we want the world to be inspired by our example as a humane and just society, we must be prepared to provide that example.

I am not concerned merely with the prospects for international exploitation and the damage it threatens to our image abroad. I pressed Barry Jacobs in debate to explain why he proposed to seek organs elsewhere, rather than from among America's downtrodden—the street people in New York, the unemployed migratory farm laborer, the inner-city destitute, the most impoverished of our Native Americans on reservations. He replied, changing his stance, that he will go abroad for kidneys only if these American sources are inadequate to meet the demand. Thus would he have us turn on our own poor to seek relief for our well-to-do.

I am concerned, of course, with what such a scheme would do to those whose destitution and desperation might move them to sell bodily parts in the hope of gaining a foothold for the climb out of poverty. But I am concerned even more about what such behavior would do to the rest of us, and what it would reveal about our compassion, our commitment to equality, our capacity to make voluntary efforts in the public interest, and our willingness to face common problems with collective resolve.

That the poor are exploited is unarguable. That their poverty seems intractable is a continuing tragedy of our unprecedentedly affluent society. I hope history will be able to judge us as a society that never abandoned its struggle to eliminate that poverty, that strove always to enhance its respect for individuals and for their capacity for mutual aid, and that faced the problems of an awesome new technology with humanity and efficiency both, rather than as merely another commercial opportunity. I believe there is a legitimate public interest in striving to bring this about.

This article is based on testimony presented to the Subcommittee on Investigations and Oversight, Committee on Science and Technology, United States House of Representatives, November 9, 1983. HR 5580 was passed by the House on June 21, 1984, and was subsequently signed into law. The complete testimony, a critical discussion of it by James M. Humber, and Samuel Gorovitz's rejoinder may be found in "Buying and Selling of Human Organs," in Biomedical Ethics Reviews, 1985, *ed. James M. Humber and Robert F. Almeder (Clifton, N.J.: Humana Press, 1985).*

Life-Support Decisions for Newborns

Dan W. Brock

The Baby Jane Doe case of 1984 was in many respects typical of the extraordinarily difficult and troubling cases about life-sustaining treatment for seriously handicapped newborns to gain the attention of the courts, the media, and ultimately the public. Baby Jane Doe was born with spina bifida, a condition in which the spinal column is exposed, commonly resulting in lack of bowel and bladder control, paralysis below the waist, and mental retardation. The degree of disability can vary widely. Her parents decided, together with their physician, not to provide maximally aggressive treatment that might have permitted the infant to live to perhaps age twenty and without which she was likely to die by age two.

Public and government attention had been focused on this area nearly two years earlier in the "Baby Doe" case in Bloomington, Indiana, when an infant who suffered from Down's syndrome was allowed to starve to death after its parents refused to permit surgery to repair its esophagus. The Reagan administration, in an initially heavy-handed response to the very real problem, put hospitals on notice that withholding nutritional sustenance or medical or surgical treatment needed to correct a life-threatening condition in an infant because the infant is handicapped is unlawful and in violation of Section 504 of the Rehabilitation Act of 1963. The notice was accompanied with threats of loss of all federal financial aid to the hospital, with the establishment of a hotline for confidential reporting of purported violations, and with Baby Doe squads to investigate possible violations.

These regulations were successfully challenged in court, but meanwhile substantively similar regulations were promulgated based on the 1984 amendments to the Child Abuse Prevention and Treatment Act. These regulations essentially require that all infants with life-threatening conditions be treated unless in the distinguishing physician's or (physicians') reasonable medical judgment any of the following circumstances apply: (i) The infant is chronically and irreversibly comatose; (ii) The provision of such treatment would merely prolong dying, not be effective in ameliorating or correcting all of the infant's life-threatening conditions, or otherwise be futile in terms of the survival of the infant; or (iii) The provision of such treatment would be virtually futile in terms of the survival of the infant and the treatment itself under such circumstances would be inhumane.

The exceptions do not, however, permit withholding appropriate nutrition, hydration, or medications. These guidelines, as well as their interpretation in particular cases, remain controversial and have not stilled the ethical debate.

More consensus has arisen about the desirability of Congress's recommendation that hospitals establish ethics committees to review such decisions. The President's Commission for the Study of Ethical Problems in Medicine also recommended in its report, "Deciding to Forgo Life-Sustaining Treatment," that hospital ethics committees be established to review decisions to forgo life-sustaining treatment for defective newborns. Neither the Reagan administration, nor the President's Commission, nor Congress wished such committees to replace parents and physicians as decision-makers about care. But because of the significant potential for conflict of interest between such infants and their parents, who commonly will assume the often enormous burdens of care involved, the President's Commission believed that regular review of such decisions was desirable. While recent years have seen a great increase in the proportion of hospitals with ethics committees, our experience with them remains limited and their potential effectiveness in this area uncertain. Nevertheless, experience over the last twenty years with the establishment of the Institutional Review Boards charged with reviewing the protection of human research subjects suggests that ethics committees might successfully play a similar review role here. Thus, I believe the administration and Congress's recommendation for ethics committees to review these decisions, unlike some other aspects of their response to this problem, is basically sound. Improving procedures by which such difficult and important decisions are made is surely to be welcomed, perhaps especially where no consensus exists regarding the proper decisions to appeal to in responding to public concern.

Nevertheless, I believe it would be a mistake to expect that either substantive federal guidelines or improved procedures, with review of decisions by hospital ethics committees, will put the controversy to rest. It should be emphasized that most decisions to stop life support for newborns do not raise troubling moral issues. Most involve infants who are known at birth to be nonviable, incapable of living beyond a few weeks or months, or who in the course of treatment, usually for conditions associated with extreme prematurity and low birth weight, reach a point where they have become nonviable. In each of these cases, a point comes at which further life support is futile.

But questions arise about providing life support that will result in a life of seriously diminished quality. This kind of case, exemplified by some instances of Down's syndrome, spina bifida, and extreme prematurity, touches areas of deep moral uncertainty and disagreement in our society. Some of the controversy concerns appropriate decision-making procedures—most importantly, the legitimate role, if any, for government and the courts, and the degree of decision-making discretion properly accorded to the parents—but the controversy extends beyond these. I want to mention briefly some of the issues that make these decisions so morally intractable, whatever our confidence in decision-making procedures.

First is the fundamental question of whether it is as seriously wrong morally to allow a newborn infant to die, or to kill it, as it is with a normal adult human. The law in general gives the same legal protections regarding life as it gives an adult. But there are reasons to believe the moral issue is not as straightforward. One reason is familiar from the abortion controversy. Birth is a problematic point at which to draw a great moral difference in the wrongness of killing. Newborns may be seen as occupying a moral status somewhere between that of unborn fetuses and adults. And unborn fetuses are often considered replaceable; if amniocentesis indicates a fetus is defective, for example, many believe it is permissibly destroyed in order to try again for a normal pregnancy. A second reason lies in one plausible account of why killing a normal adult human is a serious moral wrong: In doing so we deprive that person of most of what he or she desires—to have a future and to pursue his or her aims in that future. But a newborn infant is probably unable to conceive of having a future and so is unable to have any desires about its future that might be frustrated by its being killed. This first question, then, concerns whether infanticide might be morally permissible in some circumstances in which killing and adult person would not be.

Second is the question of what role quality-of-life considerations properly have in decisions about sustaining life. One interpretation of the federal legislation is that the expected quality of the infant's life may play no role in such decisions. However, such a view is morally problematic. Competent adults do commonly weigh the expected quality of their lives in deciding whether to accept or reject life-sustaining medical treatment. Some competent adults also say they would want their lives ended if they should ever be in conditions similar to those of many handicapped newborns. Of course, these adults have a normal life behind them and experience these new reduced circumstances as a loss, whereas a handicapped newborn may never know a different quality of life and so may adjust to the life it is given in a way adults might choose not to do.

On the other hand, a powerful moral tradition is that all human lives are equally valuable and equally to be protected. But this is a difficult view to sustain with the most defective newborns, such as those born anacephalic, that is, missing all or most of their brains. And if considerations of the quality of life are relevant, which ones and in what way? Do we weigh prospects for pleasure and pain, capacities for social interaction, possibilities for eventual self-sufficiency? Sometimes an appeal to the likely quality of these infants' lives represents an unjustified discrimination against the handicapped, but it need not always be that. Sometimes it represents genuine moral uncertainty about the relevance of quality of life to decisions about sustaining or taking life.

A third general difficulty is what role hardships and costs to others, in particular to other family members and the larger society, should be allowed to play in these decisions. The hardships are real and often overwhelming, and it would be callously insensitive to deny their existence. The limited availability of continuing support services for seriously handicapped children exacerbates the burdens placed on family members.

And the general societal costs for supporting such persons are often very high, with many handicapped unable ever to make normal social contributions. In utilitarian moral views such considerations are not in principle irrelevant to whether life must be sustained or may be taken. On the other hand, many believe there is a serious moral right not to be killed, or in these cases not to be allowed to die. Where a serious moral right is at stake, such effects on others, whether family or society, are morally irrelevant to these decisions.

Fourth is that several controversial distinctions concerning the moral permissibility of forgoing life-sustaining treatment generally arise also in the case of newborns. Let me illustrate with the case of turning off a life-sustaining respirator. Is doing so killing the infant, or is it "merely" allowing it to die? In the usual circumstances under which this occurs, many would characterize turning off the respirator as allowing the infant to die. Yet if the very same action were done for a different reason, say to protect an inheritance instead of to end the infant's suffering, it would be understood as killing. So whether such decisions result in killing or allowing to die is controversial because it is unclear just what the difference is. But it is also unclear whether it matters morally if this is killing or allowing to die. Many believe that killing is, in itself and apart from any other features of the action, morally worse than allowing to die. Others, myself included, hold this view to be mistaken. And so this moral controversy, too, intrudes itself into the general debate about sustaining the lives of handicapped newborns. But matters are worse still, for problematic decisions abound in this area, such as the distinctions between not starting and stopping treatment, between ordinary and extraordinary or heroic treatment, and so forth. In my view, none of these distinctions, as they are usually understood, are in themselves morally important, but whether my view is correct further complicates decisions about life-sustaining treatment for handicapped newborns.

Throughout all these issues lurk concerns about the possible well-intentioned misuse or ill-intentioned abuse of public or legal policies permitting nontreatment of handicapped newborns. Even if one believes that considerations of quality of life or burdens to others could sometimes justify forgoing treatment, one might consistently oppose public policy permitting nontreatment on these grounds, because of worries that such policies would be misapplied more often, or in more serious ways, than not. But of course no one knows to what extent any changes in policies would actually lead to more abuse, that is, to what extent the "slope" from here to an overall worse situation is indeed sufficiently slippery to warrant not moving onto it at all.

I should emphasize that I have not sought to defend any particular view here about when forgoing life-sustaining treatment for handicapped newborns is justified. On the contrary, if I am correct that the issues to which I have drawn attention are deeply implicated in this controversy, then a far more detailed and lengthy argument than could be attempted here is needed. Hospital ethics committees are, I believe, a step in the right direction in providing regular review and continuing discussion of these decisions. But some decisions not to treat seriously handicapped infants raise such complex and controversial issues that they will undoubtedly remain deeply troubling and tragic.

What Is Wrong with Eugenics?

Robert Wachbroit

Eugenics, as traditionally understood, was an effort to improve the human race by applying the wisdom of animal breeders. If people of good quality were to mate with each other and people of bad quality were not to reproduce, the result would be more people of good quality. As Harvard economist Thomas Schelling nicely puts it, traditional eugenics was an effort to select parents. Of course this effort encountered a number of problems. Illusions about what is inheritable and a failure to calculate how slowly gene frequencies would change by this method are two straightforward problems. Above all, one would like to say, eugenics is morally objectionable since any effective method of selecting parents would involve objectionable intrusions in a private matter if not downright coercion. No one questions the horror of the Nazi eugenic programs so there is no need to labor the point.

Traditional eugenics was an effort to select parents. Modern eugenics is an effort to select children. Or better yet, to design them. Biotechnology opens up the possibility of directly altering the genetic makeup of our descendants. This is not a mere possibility: The technology is expected to be available within a couple of decades. When that time comes, a child's genetic makeup will no longer be limited to that of his or her parents and the natural lottery. Parents with Huntington's chorea, beta thalassemia, or sickle cell anemia will be able to stop the inheritance of these diseases and have healthy children. But we need not stop there. Short people can have tall descendants, black people can have "white" descendants, and bald people can have hirsute descendants. Is anything wrong with this?

While some of us might think so, articulating that thought is by no means easy. Certainly the problems with traditional eugenics offer no guidance. No one need be coerced. Indeed, eugenics might appear to be just a part of reproductive and parental autonomy. If we do not object to couples deciding when to have children and how many children to have, should we object to their designing their children?

Two Side Worries

In order to focus the discussion, I would like to mention two worries concerning eugenics only to set them to one side. Eugenics, like any medical therapy, involves some risks. Not only might an actual genetic manipulation fail, causing injury to the patient, sterility, or deformed progeny, unsuspected linkage among genes might have undesired consequences. For example, suppose memory capacity were genetically manipulable, but it was sadly discovered that such manipulation resulted in, say, mentally unstable children. Such worries, by no means unimportant, are worries over cases where eugenics *fails*. Unless we think eugenics is impossible, such worries do not guide us in thinking about cases where eugenics *succeeds*.

A different worry about eugenics concerns its connection with abortion. As things look now, the likely gene therapy techniques would involve detaching a few cells from the embryo within the first week before any cell differentiation occurs, analyzing their genetic composition, and then performing the desired therapy on the remaining cells. As a result of the analysis, the detached cells would be destroyed. Because these detached cells are undifferentiated, they could have developed into a complete fetus on their own. Thus, the procedure of human gene therapy could involve techniques that some people would find morally equivalent to abortion, and they would object accordingly. But the worry here is not so much over eugenics as over a side effect. It is by no means clear that eugenics will have to use such procedures.

The Interests of the Child

How should we think about modern eugenics? If we think about it in one way, eugenics is always in the interests of the child, or at least always believed to be so by the parents. This is plain for the case of removing uncontroversial genetic defects, but it also holds for the so-called enhancement therapies. Given studies showing that 6'3" males do better in our society than 5'3" males, it would clearly seem to be in a male child's interest to be the taller height. In general, any property that is a plausible candidate for eugenics is one that prospective parents reasonably believe confers an advantage to the child. Any advocacy of eugenics will start with this thought.

This thought hardly needs to be argued, for it follows from the definition of "eugenics"—which is, having as its object "the production of fine offspring" (OED). Of course, with developing technology this leaves open the possibility of directly altering the genetic makeup of a child for *non-eugenic* reasons. A couple might want a boy for no other reason than that they have a girl and they want to experience something different, or they might just want to ensure that their child has eyes to match the bedroom walls. These are cases where genetic manipulation is being performed to meet the parents' interests or desires, not the child's. In some cases the manipulation might strike us as innocuous, in others as foolish and irresponsible. But in any case, the reasons behind non-eugenic manipulation will seem weak when compared with the reasons behind eugenic manipulation.

Claiming that eugenics is nearly always in the child's interest may seem too quick. Who is to say what is in that child's interest? How do we know it would not be better for that child to be short and weak or even handicapped with a genetic disease? Despite these shortcomings, perhaps because of these shortcomings, he or she may have a happier life. In fact, what we regard as shortcomings may be no more than local prejudices. After all, it was not that long ago that being left-handed was regarded as a handicap. How can this generation presume what is good for later generations?

Taken out of context, these questions can easily be overwhelming. But placed in their proper context, they are quite mundane. We typically empower parents with the authority to decide what is in their child's interest. For the most part, this authority rests on the belief that parents are the best judges of their child's interest. As an epistemic judgment, parents are held to know, on the basis of presumed intimacy and concern, what is in their child's interest. As a regulative judgment, parents are held to have the authority, derived from the institution of the family, to inform if not determine some of their child's interests. Although parental authority is not absolute and has often been challenged, these challenges are usually against the parents' competency—they have false beliefs about what is in their child's interest—and not against the idea such authority should exist. Even radical challenges to the family question only the placing of this authority, not its legitimacy. Consequently, individual exceptions aside, a eugenic decision on the part of parents is fully in keeping with how we think a child's interests should be acknowledged.

Nevertheless, although eugenics is always in the child's interest, a number of people have tried in various ways to dismiss or deny its benefits. For example, some have objected that eugenics amounts to "playing God." However, without making some controversial assumptions in theology, this protest does not distinguish eugenics from any other medical intervention. Who would object to modern public health efforts, such as the elimination of smallpox, on such grounds? While at various times some people have claimed that an epidemic was God's judgment and that trying to control the disease, by inoculations or other preventative measures, was wrongly trying to avoid God's punishment, such claims are no longer taken seriously.

The secular or naturalistic counterpart of the "playing God" objection is that eugenics amounts to tampering with the wisdom of evolution. The result of millions of years of natural selection is a delicate balance of fragile structures and processes, which direct gene manipulation would upset. The reply to this objection is the same. Under this Panglossian reading of evolution, any attempt to eliminate a disease or affect morbidity rates would be objectionable. Medicine must be viewed as an unnatural and destructive interference. It is difficult to believe that this accurately articulates what worries people about eugenics.

The Interests of Society

Up till now I have tried to present the case for eugenics—eugenics is typically in the interest of the child. Consequently, if we wish to find a way to identify the sort of considerations that oppose eugenics, we need to look beyond the child's interest. A frequent thought has been to point to the consequences of everyone, or at least most people, designing their children. To fix ideas, let us consider choosing the sex of children. If people were allowed to determine the sex of their children, so the worry goes, the result would be a catastrophic sex-ratio imbalance, favoring males.

The reasoning in this worry is weak. The claim that more male children would be born if a choice were available is based on surveys reporting that people prefer their first child to be male. Of course, it does not follow that if someone prefers A over B, then that person would actively bring about A if he or she could. But, for the sake of argument, let us swallow this assumption. Since surveys report that couples prefer having an equal number of boys and girls, the source of sex-ratio imbalance would be from couples who have an odd number of children, with single-child couples having the greatest impact on the imbalance. To get some sense of the numbers involved, suppose that *all* single-child couples use sex-selection techniques and all decide on male children. The resulting sex-ratio imbalance would then be approximately 60 percent males to 40 percent females. What is the harm in that?

One reply might be that, making the obvious assumptions, the number of families would decrease by 10 percent, with the population decreasing accordingly by 10 percent. This is not clearly a bad consequence. Indeed, people who worry about overpopulation would have to regard this result as a good thing.

A different reply might be that having an equal number of men and women is simply an important value for us. But I doubt this is true. Even a casual look at population statistics shows we tolerate all sorts of sex-ratio imbalances. Consider all of the people over the age of 65. Here the sex-ratio imbalance is 60 percent to 40 percent, but of women over men. In fact, if we are looking for striking sex-ratio imbalances, we need only consider the group of single people over the age of 45, for there the sex-ratio imbalance is not 60 percent to 40 percent but rather 80 percent to 20 percent: a four-to-one ratio of women to men! Nevertheless, no one, I think, would suggest that these imbalances should be corrected by direct compensatory actions such as having preferred health care, better Medicare coverage, or even major research specifically in the health problems of elderly males.

I do not wish to suggest that nothing is wrong with choosing the sex of one's children. However, I do not think that what is wrong with it lies in some harmful consequence of the sex-ratio imbalance itself. Rather, what is prima facie wrong with determining that the sex of a child be male is that it insults the dignity of women; it demeans the value of being female. The designer by his or her actions is saying, in effect, that whatever the value of being female is (or whatever the value of the child's original sex is), that value is second-rate.

This objection does not turn on any hypotheses regarding the popularity of eugenics. The other two objections do not identify anything wrong in a single case of sex selection; their worries turn on the consequences of how it could be used and an assumption that its use would likely be widespread. This invites the defender of eugenics to reply that these worries show only that eugenics efforts can be abused, but this hardly distinguishes eugenics from any other technology. Consequently, the most these worries can recommend is that eugenics efforts should be regulated to prevent any harm that might occur from their aggregate use. But if sex selection for male children denigrates the value of being female, then it does so even in a single case.

This objection can be easily generalized to cover cases of genetically altering the racial or ethnic features of one's progeny, and, so generalized, it identifies what we would find troublesome about such cases. This suggests we might generalize even further: Eugenics involves saying that whatever the value of the child's original condition, that value is second-rate.

We can thus see the problem of eugenics as a conflict between two values. On the one hand, we have the value of benefiting the child's interests by altering certain of his or her characteristics; on the other hand, we have the value of the original, untreated condition. How the matter will resolve depends on the particulars. Suppose the original condition were a generally recognized disease, such as Huntington's chorea. Since presumably little if any value can be attached to such conditions, the interests of the child would be decisive. However, in cases where we hold that it is important not to treat the value of the original condition as second-rate, such as sex or racial selection, the interests of the child, unfortunately real though they may be in our society, may not be decisive. We do not want to treat those conditions as being of little value, as if they were diseases. The coherence of our values might not tolerate it.

Old Eugenics versus New Eugenics

Despite the differences, the new eugenics involves the same kind of conflicts that underlay the old eugenics, but with the positions reversed. The old eugenics pitted an alleged state interest in the quality of the genetic composition of the community (the gene pool) against individual rights and liberties over reproduction, that is, the value of improving the gene pool versus the value of individual reproductive autonomy. The case for the old eugenics foundered on false empirical assumptions. Wild claims were made regarding what sort of conditions are inheritable, such as "nomadism," "shiftlessness," and "thalassophilia" (love of the sea). In addition, false claims were made about how much gene frequencies are affected by selective breeding. A standard calculation from population genetics shows that reducing the frequency of a recessive gene from 5 percent to 2.5 percent, even with a vigorous eugenics program, would take more than two hundred generations! I wish I could say that the violation of individual rights was decisive in the downfall of the old eugenics, but neither history nor the courts support that view. When the public health is at stake, individual rights are seen as luxuries. Exposing the false empirical assumptions contributed to the view that the quality of the gene pool is not a public health problem, and so contributed to the repudiation of the old eugenics.

In contrast, the new eugenics pits the alleged interests of an individual against the value the state would find in not having certain human conditions manipulated—against a concern for the stability and harmony of the community. Admittedly, the ways a particular case of eugenics could constitute a threat to that concern will not always be entirely clear. Indeed, when the genetic condition to be altered is unquestionably defective, the state's interest will coincide with the child's interest, since reducing the frequency of such genes is in the interest of public health. There is a danger here, however. If genetic diseases are once again held to constitute a public health *problem*, modern eugenics could very well share the moral collapse of the old eugenics.

The Genetic Adventure

Stephen P. Stich

Humankind is embarked on an extraordinary adventure, an adventure promising rewards that could barely have been imagined as recently as a generation ago. But human genetic engineering poses moral and social dilemmas every bit as daunting as the rewards are enticing.

It seems clear that in the decades ahead research yielding knowledge relevant to human genetic engineering will continue and accelerate. What is more, I think the acceleration of research in this area is to be welcomed. The medical, industrial, and agricultural applications of genetic engineering research will transform our society in ways even more profound than the computer revolution now well under way. I am enough of an optimist to believe most of these changes will be for the good. However, as we learn more about the mechanisms of human genetics, it is also inevitable that we will start learning how to manipulate the human genome to suit our tastes, or what we perceive to be our needs, in domains far removed from those that traditionally have been the concern of medicine.

At first this ability will be restricted to characteristics under the control of a single gene or a small number of genes. But as our knowledge progresses, we will learn more and more about how to manipulate those characteristics of beings—both physical and mental—under the control of many separate genes. In our current state of knowledge we simply do not know the extent to which aspects of intelligence and personality are under genetic control and thus susceptible to genetic manipulation. But as I read the evidence we now have, there is every reason to think that a substantial component of our mental and moral lives is influenced by our genetic endowment. It would be remarkable indeed if we did not all come genetically equipped with mental strengths and weaknesses just as we come equipped with innate physical strengths and limitations.

As our ability to manipulate the genetic composition of our own offspring grows in sophistication in the decades ahead, the social pressures to use this new technology will become intense. During the last decade we have seen an explosion of interest in home microcomputers; many of the people who buy these wonderful, expensive machines do so in the hope they will give their children a competitive edge in a technologically competitive world. Closer to the fringes of our society we have seen that some women are prepared to have themselves impregnated with the sperm of a Nobel Prize winner in the hope of bearing an intellectually gifted child. Both of these phenomena underscore the fact that the desire to help one's children excel is a powerful and widespread motivational force in our society. When, via genetic engineering, we learn how to increase intelligence, memory, longevity, or other traits conveying a competitive advantage, it is clear that there will be no shortage of customers ready to take their place in line. Moreover, those who are unwilling or unable to take advantage of the new technology may find that their offspring have been condemned to a sort of second-class citizenship in a world where what had been within the range of the normal gradually slips into the domain of the subnormal.

Obviously if history unfolds more or less along the lines I have been predicting, plenty of social problems will be generated. Ensuring equitable access to the new technology and protecting the rights of parents and children who have chosen not to utilize the technology are two that come quickly to mind. These issues, however, are variations on a familiar theme. We already have analogous problems with equal access to high-quality education for children. And in the decades ahead we will increasingly have to worry about the technological illiteracy of people from deprived educational backgrounds. I do not mean to suggest these are unimportant concerns—far from it. Still, I am inclined to think that if problems of equity and discrimination were the only problems human genetic engineering generated, most people would welcome it as an almost unmixed blessing. Given the enormous increase in knowledge required to function in our increasingly technological society, it might well be argued that the capacity to improve our learning and reasoning abilities by genetic engineering had arrived just in the nick of time.

As we gradually map and learn to manipulate the human genome, however, it will become possible to alter or enhance many traits, not merely those, like intelligence and memory capacity, that are generally desirable and convey an obvious competitive advantage. It is a good bet that tastes, character traits, and other aspects of personality have a substantial genetic component. I do not think it is beyond the bounds of realistic possibility that in the next generation or two—and perhaps very much sooner—prospective parents will be able to choose from a library of genes in redesigning their own offspring. Nor is there any reason to suppose that all people or all societies will make the same choices. However, if different societies, or different groups within our own society, make systematically different choices for several generations, we may begin to see the genetic fragmentation of the human species. The divisions that separate cultural groups may come to include genetic differences so profound that members of different groups will no longer be interfertile.

The Western tradition of moral philosophy has left us unprepared to deal with the dilemmas posed by genetic engineering. Consider first the quandaries that arise when we try to think about such central ethical questions as the nature of the good or moral life, against the background of the emerging genetic engineering technology. From Socrates down to the present, just about everyone who has pondered the question of how men and women ought to live their lives has presupposed that human nature is in large measure fixed. Of course, profound disagreements have arisen about what human nature is like. However, the moral issue has always been conceived of as attempting to determine what sort of life a person should lead, given that a human being is a certain type of creature. This tradition leaves us radically unprepared to think about the questions forced on us by the prospect of human genetic engineering. Sometime within the next century, and perhaps much sooner than that, the age-old presumption of a more or less fixed human nature may begin to dissolve. It will no longer suffice to decide what constitutes the good or moral life for the sort of creature we happen to be; we shall also have to decide what sort of creature (or creatures!) humankind ought to *become*.

A worry of a rather different sort arises when we turn our attention to the processes of moral dialogue and the attempt to resolve ethical disputes. The Western philosophical tradition offers many views about the nature of rational moral dialogue and the quest for ethical agreement. But, I think, a common strand runs through just about all theories on this subject. In one way or another the notion of a shared human nature is rung in to explain how it is possible for people to reach a meeting of the minds on moral matters. When we are able to transcend our cultural and ideological differences, and agree on some ethical principle or judgment, it is because, despite our manifest differences, we share our humanity in common. However, human genetic engineering threatens to undermine the foundations of rational ethical dialogue by fragmenting our common nature along social and ideological lines. How shall I reason with a Moslem fundamentalist or a Marxist or a Moonie if what divides him from me is not merely his traditions and his convictions, but also his genetics? The prospect is at once so staggering and so unprecedented that we hardly know how to begin thinking about it.

Many people are inclined to think that the proper course of action is to put on the brakes in an effort to avoid ever reaching the point where these hard choices will have to be made. Many find it deeply distressing that we should even contemplate significant alterations in the human genome. Others worry that the power quite literally to remake our species is a power humankind will not use wisely, and because of this worry, they urge that we take steps now to ensure that this power will not be acquired. I have considerable sympathy with some of the concerns that underlie the recommendation to put on the brakes, though that is not the recommendation I would make.

I think two rather different arguments have led people to think we ought not to acquire the capacity to manipulate the human genome. One of these arguments is theological. God, it is said, designed humans as He wished them to be, and humans alter God's plan at their peril. Now, I am no theologian, but it seems to me this argument should evoke deep skepticism. For even if we grant for the sake of argument that God has a design or plan for the human species, we must take account of the overwhelming weight of evidence indicating He chose to unfold this plan via the mechanisms of evolution and natural selection. Species are not fixed over time, and each of us alive today had distant ancestors who were far more genetically different from us than we are likely to be from any imaginable genetically engineered descendants. The fallacy of the theological argument is to equate the divine plan with the status quo. Since the Renaissance, this sort of argument has been used repeatedly in an effort to oppose technological or social innovations that threatened to have a major impact on the structure of societies and the way people live. None of us, I would venture, are tempted to think that the technological, social, and economic patterns of the late Middle Ages reflected God's plan for how we should live. Nor do we think anything is sacrosanct about the genetic endowment of our Cro-Magnon forebears. I see no more reason to think God's ultimate genetic plan—if He has one—is reflected in the genetic composition of late-twentieth-century humankind.

The second argument against acquiring the capacity to manipulate the human genome rests not on a theological premise but on a scientific one. The current constitution of the human gene pool, it is argued, is no accident. We became the sort of creatures we are as the result of millions of years of natural selection. During those millions of years, many genes disappeared from the gene pool because the characteristics they impart to the organism were less adaptive than the surviving alternatives. Thus in a sense the current genetic makeup of humankind stores a great treasury of information about the sort of design that can flourish in our environment. It is folly, this argument concludes, to fiddle with the hard-won "evolutionary wisdom" bequeathed to us in our gene pool.

Now, although I ultimately disagree with this argument, I have considerable sympathy with the central insight it is urging. Human beings—indeed all currently existing species—are highly evolved, extraordinarily complex, and marvelously well-adapted to their natural ecology. We should be very wary indeed about altering components of this system until we have a good understanding of what role the components play in the overall organization of the system. However, it is one thing to suggest we act cautiously, keeping in mind that there are generally good evolutionary reasons for an organism's genome being the way it is. It is quite another thing to suppose natural selection cannot be improved on. To accept that view is to accept the Panglossian assumption that the status quo is the best of all possible worlds. And that assumption is simply not true. A single example may serve to make the point. It now appears that the gene for sickle cell disease survived and flourished because an individual who carries only one such gene is better able to cope with malaria. In an area where malaria is endemic, the sickle cell gene conveys a selective advantage. However, when the swamps are drained and the mosquito population declines, the sickle cell gene is no longer worth having. What this example illustrates is that genes that may have been useful in the environment in which the species evolved may cease to be adaptive when the species finds itself in a new environment. But, of course, the environment in which humankind now exists is radically different from the environment that shaped the genome of our hunter-gatherer forebears. Thus we have every reason to think that the results of natural selection *can* be improved on.

Let me close with some brief observations on the policy implications of these reflections. As I have already indicated, I think it would be a serious mistake to adopt policies aimed at preventing the development of a technology capable of making major modifications in the human genome. However, it is certainly an area that cries out for ongoing, informed monitoring. Thus I endorse with enthusiasm proposals for an independent body, made up of scientists, ethicists, religious leaders, educators, and lay people whose function would not be to regulate but to study issues as they appear on the horizon. However, I am inclined to urge an even stronger role for education in dealing with the challenge of genetic engineering and other new technologies. Unless the public and the political leaders who represent them come to have a better understanding of the basic science underlying these new technologies, we have little hope that our social decisions will be wise ones. This understanding does not come easy, and it will be expensive. But in the long run the distressingly low level of scientific understanding in our society will be more expensive still.

Who Is the Patient?

Robert Wachbroit

New genetic discoveries and technologies in medicine have raised a host of profound ethical questions. One of the most prominent concerns our understanding of the traditional obligations of the physician, in particular, his obligation regarding confidentiality. As we learn more and more about the genetic basis of many diseases, questions such as "To whom does the physician owe a duty of confidentiality?" are becoming increasingly difficult to answer. Part of this difficulty can be traced to a transformation in our understanding of who is the patient, and a corresponding change in our understanding of the physician-patient relationship.

Let me illustrate this transformation with an example, based on a true case recently told to me. A young boy has been diagnosed as having hemophilia A. Since this is an x-linked, recessive disease, there is good reason to believe the boy inherited the defective gene from his mother, who in turn inherited it from her mother. (Because it is a recessive disease, these women are under no risk of contracting any symptoms or suffering the disease themselves, even though they carry the harmful gene.) The physician learns that the boy's mother has two sisters. Given the available information, each of these sisters has a 50-percent probability of also being a carrier of the harmful gene. The physician wishes to inform these sisters of their condition, since it might affect their reproductive plans, but the boy's mother, who has had a terrible falling out with her sisters, forbids it. Bent on withholding information as a way of getting revenge on her sisters, she insists that the boy's right to confidentiality be respected.

Admittedly, articulating the ethical question raised by this sort of case as "Who is the patient?" is not the usual approach. A more common one would be to frame the ethical question in terms of the scope and limits of the physician's duty of confidentiality to the patient. Thus, if the medical condition may (or must) be disclosed to others, this is because the duty of confidentiality here is outweighed by other obligations. By presenting the issue instead in terms of who the patient *is*, I am trying to underscore a shift in how such cases should and will be seen. If the physician must disclose the information to others, this does not reflect a duty or consideration that competes with the integrity of the physician-patient relationship. Rather, it grows out of that very relationship. Disclosures in these cases are not "news leaks." If and when they are justified, they arise from the physician's loyalties and obligations as a *physician* to the patient. The physician's disclosure, if it is to have this kind of justification, must be to his patient. The crucial question, however, is who is the patient.

We can get a better understanding of how this question will become increasingly significant by analyzing the hemophilia example. I will begin by examining three different models of health care that might be invoked to frame the ethical dilemma raised.

The Private Health Model

The most familiar model is what we could call the *private health model*. Its clearest applications are to cases of physical injury or non-communicable diseases. In such cases, the question "Who is the patient?" has an obvious answer: The patient is the particular individual suffering the disease or accident. According to this model, the physician's mission is to care for his patient and treat the medical condition. This mission, however, is constrained by a respect for the autonomy of the patient. This respect is generally taken to mean that the physician must have the patient's informed consent before performing any major medical intervention. Furthermore, the physician owes a duty of confidentiality to the patient.

In this model two arguments arise for the physician's duty of confidentiality. One argument looks at the consequences of assigning such a duty. By binding the physician in this way, we encourage the patient to provide the physician with any information that might help in providing medical care, regardless of how embarrassing or awkward the information might be thought to be. Without this duty, people might withhold information or even fail to seek medical care because they fear their broader interests might be jeopardized. The other argument looks at the rights of the patient, in particular the right to privacy. Insofar as the patient has a right to privacy, the physician has a corresponding obligation to respect that right, which is expressed in a duty of confidentiality.

Of course, the duty of confidentiality in the private health model is not absolute. The most notable exception is when disclosure would prevent the occurrence of serious harm. That exception, however, does not arise in the hemophilia A case. Disclosing the genetic information would at most succeed in preventing the birth of possible harmed individuals, but that is quite different from preventing any actual harm. (If this is not clear, imagine that the aunts are informed, but they decide nevertheless to have children. Given that the children, including any who are born with hemophilia A, might not otherwise have been born, can we say any of them have been harmed?) Thus, we should conclude that, whatever the physician's own feelings in this case, he is ethically obligated to keep the information confidential. Since the two sisters are not the physician's patients and no harm is threatened to any actual, identifiable party, he has no special duty toward them.

It might be thought this problem could be avoided by the physician's simply announcing in advance that his duties of confidentiality have several exceptions. Among these exceptions are cases where the physician believes disclosing medical information to a patient's relatives could result in a direct benefit to them. The patient is thus told that access to health care services is contingent on his consenting to these exceptions.

This approach, however, faces several problems. First of all, what is the moral justification for this modification in the duty of confidentiality? Can it be reconciled with the arguments for confidentiality identified in the private health model? Or does this modification represent a new exception to that duty, requiring its own justification? Second, suppose the patient does agree with this restriction. Is the physician then obligated to inform relatives in cases such as the one given? If obligated, is it because he is a *physician* or would anyone who learned the relevant information have the same obligation to inform the relatives? Finally, what happens if the patient refuses to consent to these restrictions? If the physician refers the patient to some other physician who does not place such restrictions, then the potential problem is simply passed to someone else. From the standpoint of the medical community, the problem remains. If the physician does not refer the patient to anyone else, does this mean the patient is to be abandoned? This hardly seems to be a satisfactory result since the point of placing these restrictions was, in effect, to ensure the physician is not forced to ignore important health concerns.

The Public Health Model

A different approach to the problem of disclosure is the *public health model*. Its clearest application is to cases of highly contagious diseases. In such cases, the patient is the public, and the physician's mission is to promote the public's health. Concepts such as autonomy or informed consent are to be understood in terms of the political will and decision-making process of the public. This model, however, includes no duty of confidentiality since it plainly makes no sense to talk about such things with respect to the general public.

Because the public's will does not always reflect a consensus, the mission of the public health model may, at times, conflict with a respect for the autonomy of some individuals. As cases of quarantine or mandatory vaccinations illustrate, public health measures may require restricting some people's liberty or ignoring some people's choices. While these conflicts point to regrettable costs in this model, they do not give rise to any constraints on the physician's mandate, given the sheer magnitude of the serious harm that would be avoided. The public's health cannot be sacrificed for the sake of the rights of some individuals. Because of this decisive normative feature in the public health model, identifying anything as a public health problem is a significant matter. Some of the darker moments in our history arose from incorrectly characterizing some problems as public health problems. In many cases, for example, state sterilization laws enacted in the early part of the twentieth century were based on the view that "feeblemindedness" was a public health problem. Unchecked, it would undermine the quality of the race. In a famous Supreme Court decision, Justice Oliver Wendell Holmes said, "The principle that sustains compulsory vaccination is broad enough to cover cutting the Fallopian tubes. . . . Three generations of imbeciles are enough."

Let us suppose hemophilia A is taken to be a public health problem. Then, according to this model, the physician has no duty of confidentiality in this matter; instead he has a duty to inform not only the sisters of their possible medical condition, but also anyone else responsible for controlling the spread of this disease.

While both the private health and the public health models have some legitimacy, neither perfectly fits the facts of this example. The private health model is not entirely appropriate, because we are dealing with a *transmissible* disease. We should not see the disease as confined to isolated individuals, for how we treat the disease in one individual will affect the likelihood of its appearing in another individual. But neither is the public health model entirely appropriate because we are dealing with a *noncontagious* disease. The general public is not at any special risk because some individuals have this disease. Indeed, as we noted, no actual people are at risk; only the possible offspring of women carrying the relevant gene could be affected. If we regard incurable genetic diseases, such as hemophilia A, as public health problems, then we are in effect regarding the birth of certain kinds of individuals as public health problems, a view that is as ominous as it sounds.

The Family Health Model

Finally, let us consider what we could call the *family health model*. As the name suggests, the physician's patient is the entire family, where "family" is understood to refer to a genetic network rather than a social institution. The physician's duties are to the family as a whole. While his respect for the family's privacy obligates him to refrain from disclosing any information to unrelated third parties, this obligation does not extend to the family itself. The family's privacy is plainly not violated by disclosing information to other family members.

The family health model seems to acknowledge that genetic diseases are often family diseases, and therefore it appears tailored to fit some of the ethical problems arising in this area. It also seems to fit the current practice of some physicians, since members of a family typically see the same physician. Nevertheless, this model has problems as well. First, if the family is the patient, the physician would seem to be ethically obligated to ensure that all its adult members are informed of the medical situation. But many families are scattered, with some members completely out of touch with others. Without a radical change in the profession, the physician does not have the resources to track down distant family members. Moreover, many families are divided. Who, then, speaks for the family? Who decides some piece of information should be kept confidential? Rather than clarifying the ethical issues, the family health model may simply shift them.

I do not wish to suggest that the options I have surveyed are the only options or that the problems I have raised with them are insoluble. We have only begun to reflect on these matters. But as we learn more and more about the genetic basis for various common diseases, such as cancer, Alzheimer's disease, manic-depressive psychosis, diabetes, and others, this kind of case will become progressively familiar. As our scientific understanding of diseases improves, our moral responsibilities will become more complex. A diagnosis will not only identify a disease; it may also thereby indicate the medical condition of other individuals. Thus, physicians from a wide range of specialties will increasingly find themselves confronting situations where it is unclear who the patient is, and consequently, unclear what their responsibilities and obligations are.

This article was adapted from "Who Is the Patient? A Moral Problem," Maryland Medical Journal *38 (1989).*

AIDS
What to Do—And What Not to Do

Richard D. Mohr

Of those dead and dying from AIDS, two-thirds are gay men. Tens of thousands have been felled by the disease. As things stand, government funding for patient care is virtually nonexistent, and preventive funding has risen significantly only as AIDS has come to be perceived as a threat to the dominant, nongay culture. What should the government be doing—and not doing—to meet the mounting crisis?

What Not to Do: Quarantine

The aim of preventing harm to potential innocent victims is largely noncontroversial. The defense of individuals from substantial harm from others is on any account a chief warrant for governmental action, and for governmental coercion. But care must be taken in how that aim is realized.

Already, state-mandated discrimination against groups at risk for AIDS has begun with employment and access to services—allegedly on medical grounds, but in pointed contradiction to judgments of the Department of Health and Human Services, the Centers for Disease Control, and the National Institutes of Health. This trend takes on alarming proportions when coupled with the recognition that prisons and quarantines are distinguishable neither in terms of the harms from which society would protect itself, nor in terms of the harms they inflict on "offenders." As leper colonies have shown, it is silly to suppose internment of the innocent does not stigmatize them.

The current hysteria about AIDS on the part of the general public, when not simply a manifestation of already existing antigay prejudices, is based on the presumption that the disease is spread indiscriminately. But the most important fact about AIDS for public policy purposes is not that it is deadly, but that it, like hepatitis B, is caused by a blood-transmitted virus. This means that for the disease to spread, bodily fluids of someone with the virus must directly enter the bloodstream of another. The virus is not transmitted casually. And not just any bodily fluid will do. Only blood, semen, and vaginal fluids have been implicated in the transmission of AIDS. In consequence, you get the AIDS-causing virus from what you do with people who already have the virus.

The case for general, indiscriminate contagion cannot be made out. Therefore government policy based on that fear—in particular quarantines of AIDS-exposed persons—is unwarranted.

What Not to Do: Paternalism

The mode of contagion for AIDS ensures that those at risk are those whose actions are a contributing factor to their risk of infection—chiefly through intimate sexual contact and shared hypodermic needles. (A small exception is newborns of infected mothers. For this set of cases, social policy should be whatever it already is for parents who pass fatal congenital diseases to their children.) It is the general feature of self-exposure to contagion that makes direct government coercive efforts to abate the disease particularly inappropriate.

If independence—the ability to guide one's life by one's own lights to an extent compatible with a like ability on the part of others—is, as it is, a major value, one cannot consistently with that value prevent people from putting themselves at risk through voluntary associations. For mutual consent guarantees that the "compatible extent" proviso of the independence principle is satisfied. The important question then becomes whether the medical circumstances of AIDS are so severe as to warrant paternalistic protection of those not exposed, either through banning or highly regulating the means of possible transmission.

Paternalistic interference, in one justification, is warranted when a person is operating at risks he or she is unable to assess due to diminished mental skills or lack of information. The solution tailored to such incapacities, though, is chiefly education. This line of argumentation at most justifies labeling dangerous products, in the way such labels are placed on cigarettes.

But far from justifying major paternalistic coercion of gay institutions, say by closing gay baths, this argument suggests that paternalistic arguments surrounding AIDS are not even being advanced in good faith. Five years of the AIDS crisis passed before the federal government even put out bids for *studies* of ways programs of AIDS education might be effected. And even now federal strings attached to federal funds prevent safe-sex literature from being sexually explicit enough to be sexually effective.

Another legitimate way of justifying paternalistic coercion is to argue that one should be protected from ceding away the very conditions that enable one to be an independent agent. One is not allowed to contract to become a slave. Do these grounds warrant state-imposed bars to putting oneself at risk for AIDS?

Admittedly minimally good health—indeed, life—is a necessary condition for being viewed seriously as an independent agent. So the AIDS case might seem relevantly similar to the contracting-to-slavery case. It differs, though, in two significant and decisive ways.

First, slavery *by definition* is a condition of lost independence. However, as with other venereal diseases, not every sexual encounter with an AIDS-exposed person exposes one to the virus. The risk is high but not invariably catastrophic, so putting oneself at risk for AIDS becomes less like contracting for slavery and more like being a race car driver or a mountain climber. In cases like these the considered standard of our society is that the assessment of risk ought to fall to the individual.

Second, in the slavery case we are unable to imagine what momentary gain could be reasonably balanced against the value to the individual of independence permanently lost. However, sex, like health, is in general a central personal concern, and addressing sex as central and appropriating it to oneself in some way or another is probably necessary to meaningful life: as the chief portal to ecstasy; as a recurrent natural need; and as the near occasion of, undergirding for, and necessary prompt to marital love.

The centrality of sex to life means that it may have to be balanced with the value of continued independence—independence is not our only value or prior to all other values. Striking a balance surely is not a decision the state could reasonably make across the boards for all. Individuals, not the state, must make the difficult choices where values centrally affecting the self come in conflict. This principle is generally recognized when health and religious values come in conflict: The state ought not to force a lifesaving blood transfusion on a patient who believes it will eternally damn him.

Governments that have written off the value of gay sex altogether—making it illegal largely on religious or other grounds that do not appeal to the causing of harms to others—should be viewed as especially suspect when they make paternalistic arguments on behalf of gays. For by this very course they have already shown that they do not respect gays as autonomous and independent beings.

What to Do: Preventive Funding

The centrality of sex to individual lives, though, points the way to a chief justification for state funding of preventive AIDS research.

People ought not to be in the position where they have to make trade-offs among the central components of a complete life. Ending the conflict among central personal values will be especially attractive when the means to it place no nearly comparable burden on others. What is required in the case at hand is tax dollars for basic immunological research and applied viral research. Yet, given the ends likely to be achieved and assuming an equitable tax system, taxation places no comparable burden on those taxed.

A second argument for preventive AIDS funding is that no one should have to live in a condition of terror. Imagine a prisoner who is not actually ever tortured but who daily witnesses the torture of others in adjacent cells. Not only the torture victims themselves, but he too has experienced cruel and unusual punishment. Constantly expected but uncertain destruction seizes up the mind and turns it against itself, destroying the equanimity necessary for thinking, deciding, and acting.

Gays now live in such a condition of generalized terror. As the number of AIDS cases has risen exponentially, leaving nearly everyone with lost acquaintances, gays are experiencing—at a minimum—the equivalent of the V-2 bombings of London. Quite independent of any view held on moral guilt or innocence in the spread or acquisition of AIDS (the prisoner in our example was, say, a murderer), no one deserves the terror that has filled the everyday reality of gays. Indeed, everyone exposed to terror has a positive claim that it be ended.

What to Do: Tending the Innocent

Though AIDS is normally contracted in a situation where one has put oneself at risk, the disease ought not to be viewed in general as a case of paying the piper, as one might claim suffering from a mountain-climbing accident ought to be viewed, where the effects of negligence to oneself are to be borne by oneself.

Consider, first, that the incubation period for the disease is indeterminately long. AIDS first came to light anywhere in the United States only in mid-1981, when it was shrouded in mystery, its nature unknown. This means that even people who totally swore off sex on first hearing mention of the disease would still be coming down with it now.

Second, as mentioned, educational material that would make people aware of their risks has been largely mishandled by government. And the mass media have been more than a little chary to provide details of safe-sex practices. So many people have been taking risks in situations of constrained information. Even under conditions of complete information, furthermore, it turns out that most individuals are not very good at making judgments of risk management. That this is so makes a big difference in assigning fault to individuals.

Nor is sex drive something over which one has absolute control. One thing that seems likely to be confirmed by the AIDS crisis is that sexual orientation is not a matter of choice, or else every gay man cognizant of the health crisis would have attempted to switch orientations long ago. If orientation is fairly fixed, the only question becomes how much sex is okay. The Surgeon General recommends that gay men simply be celibate—unless they have lived in decades-long, completely monogamous relationships. This advice seems little rooted in an understanding of the cussedness of sexual and cultural reality. On the one hand, the recurring and intrusive nature of sexual desire guarantees that in general gay men, as others, will not be celibate. On the other, long-term gay relations have been a rarity, and necessity is a particularly poor forge for working the most delicate of human bonds. Those who espouse safe-sex guidelines also seem to bump up against reality. Safe-sex is poor sex—as likely to frustrate as satisfy.

Equally important, sex is virtually the only mode in which gays in our culture are allowed to identify themselves to themselves. So the gay person's sexual orientation is the chief facet of his existence, just as for blacks, being black, due to cultural realities, is the chief facet of their existence. As a result something more than just pleasure and the fulfillment of need is wrapped up in sex for gays. Identity itself is at issue.

In light of these facts, it looks as though the chortling "we told you so" of some conservatives is, at the least, unjustified.

What to Do: Hospice Care

AIDS has no cure. Tendance for AIDS patients chiefly requires routine nursing and hospice care. Historically, routine nursing and hospice functions have been performed by family members. Even now the standard nursing home carries out this tradition in its own unsatisfactory way: It falls to the patient's family to arrange for the "home," pay the bills, and provide whatever emotional support the patient is to receive. I wish to suggest that hospice and nursing care from the state are due to gay patients as a matter of compensatory justice for society's and government's destruction of the possibility of the creation of gay families.

Fifty percent of nongay marriages fail even when they are given the highest imprimatur society has to offer and luxuriate in substantial attendant material benefits. It is surprising, indeed amazing, therefore, that any gay relationships survive. If society will not let you be gay by ones, it certainly will not let you be gay by twos.

Hatred of gays as internalized by gays—a condition magnified and darkened by the AIDS crisis—is probably the leading cause of the failure of gay relations to materialize and mature. If matrimonial love entails unqualified acceptance of the beloved, the taint of self-hatred will vitiate gay love. Furthermore, where discrimination against gays is widespread, it is unlikely gay couples will flourish. For acting as a couple tends to cast one's affectional preferences into the public realm and so makes one a target of discrimination.

It perhaps goes without saying that attempts by gays to create blood and extended families of their own have been blocked at every turn by society and now increasingly by the state. Many states have recently been codifying into statute and regulation what has been the reality in practice all along—the exclusion of child custody, adoption, and fostering by gay couples. These policies systematically block the creation of gay familial units and indirectly contribute to the decay of gay relations by appealing so directly to an alleged wickedness of gays as corruptors, and an alleged worthlessness of gays as role models.

Compassion would suggest and compensatory justice should require that the day-to-day care of the final-stage AIDS patient be provided in lieu of the care he would have likely had but for society's blocking his creation of his own family.

This article is condensed and adapted from a paper, "AIDS, Gay Life, State Coercion," which became Chapter Eight of Gays/Justice—A Study of Ethics, Society, and Law *(New York: Columbia University Press, 1988).*

Mandatory AIDS Testing

Richard D. Mohr

Well after *Brown* v. *Board of Education*, Jackson, Mississippi, maintained racially segregated public swimming pools, claiming that only through segregation could violence and social chaos be avoided there. The federal courts saw through this strategem, noting that it was a variant of the heckler's veto, thinly masking racial animus. But did Jackson integrate its pools? No. The city council voted instead to close them all. This time out, the courts were not so wise.

In 1971, the Supreme Court upheld the constitutionality of the pool closings. The Court was snookered by the surface similarity of the policy's treatment of blacks and whites—neither could, after all, use the swimming pools. The practice appeared to treat similar cases similarly. And indeed the pool-closing statute did not refer in any way to blacks. However, shallow formalism aside, the pool closing was an even more inequitable treatment of blacks than was the original policy of segregation. Segregation merely perpetuated social custom, but the closings were a social ritual that elevated pervasive custom to the level of a sacred value. For the white city council's action told blacks that whites view them as so disgusting and polluting that white social solidarity will be maintained even if to do so requires of whites the loss of comfort, joy, and the pleasures of the season. Happiness is as nothing when social identity is challenged. The Court could not see that the point of the legislative act of closing the swimming pools was to stigmatize blacks, even though the act made no mention of them.

Similarly, I will argue that the significance of mandatory AIDS-antibody testing is the degradation of gays and the reconsecration of heterosexual supremacy as a sacred value, even though mandatory testing, to date, has not been directly aimed at gays nor, indeed, has made any mention of them. AIDS-testing legislation should not be understood as business-as-usual public policymaking aimed at the social good of protecting public health—it can adequately be understood only in terms of the nature and function of social rituals, in particular, purification rituals.

Purification Rituals

Six years into the AIDS crisis President Reagan gave his first and only speech on AIDS. Without ever mentioning gays, the president called for mandatory testing for AIDS antibodies among certain segments of society: marriage-license applicants, prisoners, and immigrants applying for permanent U.S. residency. Subsequently, the latter two forms of testing were formally instituted at the national level through administrative rule, and Illinois and Louisiana enacted (and later revoked) mandatory marital testing laws. Other groups already subject to mandatory federal AIDS-testing are military recruits and active-duty personnel, Foreign Service officers, and employees of the Job Corps.

The public health community has done a passable job in showing that mandatory testing is not justified on traditional public health grounds. In particular it has shown that coerced testing is unlikely to do much to stop the spread of the disease, is likely to drive the disease underground, is a very poor investment of public dollars incapable of justification on a cost-benefit analysis, and will have consequences both tragic, in the case of false test results, and absurd, when the funds for the tests' administration could be going into desperately needed research and patient care.

However, the public health community, in showing this, has completely missed the social point of the statutes and rules mandating antibody testing. Indeed, in its very claims (though true) that the laws are inefficient, it actually sustains the evil of the laws' real purpose. For governmental actions mandating AIDS testing are not merely miscalculations, misdirected attempts to maximize utility. Rather, they are part of the social rituals through which the nation expresses and strengthens its highest values—the values, that is, for which it will pay any price.

Such rituals and their values are the means by which and the forms in which the nation identifies itself, and through which it maintains, largely unconsciously, its group solidarity. But group solidarity comes with a price—or, as social theorist Mary Douglas has summarized: "Solidarity is only gesturing when it involves no sacrifice." The social inefficiency of AIDS testing demonstrated by the public health community is the sacrifice society has accepted to express and reconfigure its solidarity around its central sacred value. An examination of cases will show that the chief sacred value wrought by various AIDS-testing laws is what Adrienne Rich has called compulsory heterosexuality.

Typically, when all goes well, a society does not have a foreground cognition of what its highest values are. They are not the object of its active social concern, but a filter through which all social structures are projected and, in turn, through which social behavior is perceived. Because compulsory heterosexuality is so pervasive in society as to be its persistent and uniform background phenomenon, it goes as unnoticed in our thinking about society as air at a constant skin temperature goes unnoticed as we walk around a room. Though we are completely engulfed in it, we are completely oblivious to it. No one looking at the cavalcade of wedding and engagement pictures in Tuesday's newspaper thinks, "Gosh, what a slew of heterosexuals." Paradoxically, then, in AIDS-testing legislation what is most degraded—the gay person— goes entirely unmentioned.

Marital Testing

The most obvious case for my general thesis is mandatory testing as a condition of getting a marriage license—remember, gays need not apply.

Courts have done backflips in order to uphold the legal existence of marriages, even when the formal requirements (like age) and procedural requirements (like solemnization) for entry into the marriage have been wholly absent or blatantly violated. They have done so to such an extent as to draw into doubt the rule of law in this area. The one spot, though, where they have balked at allowing access to marriage is access for gays. The courts have used every legal contrivance to block the recognition of gay marriages. These paired legal patterns showing a systematic and uniform warping of judicial judgment clearly suggest that here we have reached the bedrock and fundamental stuff of society— the thing that will not be budged, the thing that cannot be remade.

When absolutes are challenged, beware. And that is what is happening in the AIDS crisis, in part because it has thrown gays more prominently and more threateningly into social consciousness than ever before, and in part because of the transfiguration of sexual values wrought by it. AIDS has caused people to confuse the merely instrumental virtue of prudence with the final goods acquired through prudence. AIDS has certainly upped the ante on the means to a robust sex life; promiscuity unguarded is not now prudent. But rather than seeing AIDS as merely raising prudential concerns, weak minds, including many gay ones, have unwittingly transferred the badness of the means—high costs—to sex as an end. Sex is now a final bad, to be tolerated and redeemed, if at all, only within an abiding relation for which it serves as a token or symbol, a relation of exclusive marriage. For all the wrong reasons, AIDS has applied conceptual pressures to the going social definition of marriage—a definition that gives heterosexuals an exclusive purchase on marriage.

Now, marriage is the central institution of heterosexuality. If, under pressures exterior to the institution of marriage, but interior to the society it is supposed to epitomize and valorize, the institution is to be maintained in its traditional form, it must be purified and re-anointed. Simply perpetuating the old bar to gay legal marriages is not sufficient to new circumstances. A new ritual is called for and it is handily supplied by the AIDS crisis itself, since, as shown by AIDS jokes and graffiti, a virtual identification in the mind of America exists between AIDS and gays. The new ritual that, within the configuration of marriage, will do the requisite work is to test those who are to be married to make sure they are not polluted with the very stigma that challenges the institution itself. Here a social policy, perfectly absurd when viewed in terms of social utility, makes perfect sense when viewed as a social purification ritual. Marital AIDS-testing reconsecrates the temple of marriage and the cosmic canopy of heterosexuality—largely by the careful exorcising of demons.

Immigration and the Military

Other categories of mandatory AIDS-antibody testing can be treated in shorter compass. Immigration and military policies are nominally designed to defend the nation, but the history of both institutions—their racial histories, for instance—shows that their chief function is not so much defending but determining and defining what the nation is. This is the real reason that mandatory AIDS-testing has been instituted in these two areas.

The military has offered various paternalistic and strategic rationalizations for testing. But what tips the military's hand to reveal its true motives is its practice. Even though Congress has barred the armed forces from using a soldier's antibody status as a reason for ousting him, in practice the military simply badgers the antibody-positive soldier until he admits he is gay and then discharges him on that ground. Antibody testing is the physical correlate for homosexuality that the armed forces have long been seeking in order to purge themselves of pogues. Recent empirical studies have found that the military's past record of discovering even its sexually active gay males has been very poor indeed. With AIDS testing the army now thinks it has found the tool for which it has long hankered.

Since 1952, federal law has barred gays from becoming resident aliens and so also naturalized citizens. Yet gays are notoriously difficult to identify at the borders—they look just like people. The purpose of AIDS antibody-testing in immigration and in its twin, military policy, is the barring of gay people from the institutions by which the nation defines itself, in order to keep the nation pure.

Of Walls and Vampires

Prison testing is a convoluted yet particularly telling case. The real reason for prison testing is provided by a remark, cryptic on its surface, made by then Attorney General Edwin Meese. As reported in the June 9, 1987, *New York Times*, Meese claimed that prison testing is necessary because when prisoners are released many of them gravitate toward jobs in day-care centers. I take it that this dense remark, when unfolded, entails something like the following concatenation of ideas: One, homosexuality is a corruptive contagion, so that even if one was not queer going into prison, one likely is when coming out; and two, all gays are child molesters.

A corruptive contagion is a disease that reproduces itself from one person to the next simply and sufficiently through its symptoms. The myth that homosexuality is a corruptive contagion—that one gets it from someone performing homosexual acts on or near one—runs very deep in our culture. In 1978, Associate Justice (now Chief Justice) William H. Rehnquist, while protesting the Supreme Court's declining to hear a successful gay student case, went out of his way to hold that a gay student organization's claim to campus recognition is "akin to . . . those suffering from measles [claiming they] have a constitutional right, in violation of quarantine regulations, to associate together and with others who do not presently have measles, in order to urge repeal of state law providing that measles sufferers be quarantined."

AIDS, too, is mistakenly thought to be a corruptive contagion. Irrational fears of casual contagion and the mistaken but popular comparison of it to airborne diseases like influenza suggest that it is a disease whose symptoms are the proximate cause of its transmission. In fact, since it is a blood-borne disease, the actions of the person who gets the disease are (virtually always) the proximate cause of its transmission. It is the clustering of these two errors of taking gays and AIDS as each a vampire-like corruptive contagion, together with a statistical overlap between the two on a par with that of poverty and color, that has led to the virtual identification of AIDS and gays in the mind of America. They are taken as a tandem of invisible lurking evils, lying in wait to get you.

The real rationales for antibody testing in prisons (and the isolation there of those testing positive) apply just as well to all gays in non-prison settings, whether testing positive or not. The ritualistic purpose of prison testing is to assert the social validity of purging gays from the general population. Gays might do well to remember that the 1942 immurement of the Warsaw Ghetto was promulgated as a public health measure—to stop the spread of typhus. It made no reference to Jews. And gays might well remember, too, that Franklin D. Roosevelt's executive order 9066, which set up America's concentration camps, made no mention of Japanese-Americans. Rather, it authorized the military to exclude "any and all persons" from designated areas to protect national defense.

Conclusion

Testing discovers and divides. Testing discovers the invisible and mysterious and it divides "us" from "them." It is the perfect vehicle for a civilization reasserting its most basic values under challenge. It casts lurking threats into the light so that they may be exiled or committed to the flames. At the same time, testing regroups the dominant culture by showing it is willing not only to sacrifice others to its values but to sacrifice itself for the sake of them as well. Thus the more the public health community points up the irrationality of mandatory testing by its own criteria, the more it underscores and contributes to the true function of the testing, which is the assertion of group solidarity through self-sacrifice. In this crisis, the public health community is the lone lit candle in Franz Kafka's cathedral: Its singular flame simply makes the darkness darker.

This article is drawn from a paper that became Chapter Ten of Gays/Justice—A Study of Ethics, Society, and Law *(New York: Columbia University Press, 1988).*

FOR FURTHER READING

Panem, Sandra. *AIDS Bureaucracy.* Cambridge, Mass.: Harvard University Press, 1988.

Pierce, Christine, and Donald VanDeVeer, eds. *AIDS, Ethics, and Public Policy.* Belmont, Calif: Wadsworth, 1988.

President's Commission for the Study of Ethical Problems in Medicine and Biomedical and Behavioral Research. *Screening and Counseling for Genetic Conditions.* Washington, D.C.: U.S. Government Printing Office, 1983.

President's Commission for the Study of Ethical Problems in Medicine and Biomedical and Behavioral Research. *Splicing Life.* Washington, D.C.: U.S. Government Printing Office, 1982.

Singer, Peter, and Deane Wells. *Making Babies: The New Science and Ethics of Conception.* New York: Charles Scribner's Sons, 1985.

PART III

FOREIGN POLICY AND NUCLEAR DETERRENCE

7

FOREIGN POLICY ISSUES

Even as this book goes to press, the world is changing, and with it some of the basic presuppositions of U.S. foreign policy. The division of the political sphere into East (Communist) and West (capitalist and democratic) no longer represents reality; ideological boundaries are being redrawn even as political boundaries themselves are shifting. But despite the stunning events of recent months and years, other global realities remain. The crushing poverty of much of the Third World shows no sign of abating, and the questions of international justice it poses have yet to be addressed, let alone answered. And global politics is still very much an exercise in power—covert and overt, economic and military, terrorist and conventional—by one nation attempting to assert its national interest against another. The articles in this chapter focus largely on the relationship between the United States and the less developed nations of the world—the ways we aid and abuse them, the ways they fear us and cause us to fear them.

In "Income and Development," Jerome Segal pushes the ongoing debate over Third World development to its deepest level by asking the often overlooked question: What *is* development? He examines several different approaches to economic growth and development, and argues that development is best measured by looking at, first, the extent to which the basic human needs of a population are met, and, subsequently, the extent to which individuals in that population are encouraged to develop their full human potential. His argument has implications for the design of U.S. foreign aid programs; it also has some surprising implications for the course we, as a supposedly "developed" nation, should choose for ourselves.

What form of government is best suited for developing nations? While most of us would answer "representative democracy," many political theorists have argued that developing societies are not ready for democracy. Charles R. Beitz, in "Should All Countries Be Democracies?", examines the cultural, economic, and institutional factors that cast doubt on the appropriateness of democracy to the Third World. He concludes that the antidemocratic arguments fail to make a strong enough case for authoritarian over democratic regimes.

Several articles deal with ways the United States uses the political and economic vulnerability of other nations to further its own policy objectives. "Plowshares into Swords: The Political Uses of Food" surveys some of the issues arising from the use of American food aid and sales as an instrument of U.S. foreign policy. Is the political use of food a legitimate means for pursuing social, economic, and political justice and a stable world peace—not to mention other less lofty and more self-serving policy ends? Or is it wrong to use as a weapon or bargaining chip something that is the object of so central and universal a human need? Certainly no policy of food aid can be entirely nonpolitical in its effects—if, indeed, we can even predict with any confidence what those effects will be. The article concludes with several caveats to those who would try to use food aid as a building block toward a better world.

Food is not the only thing shipped across U.S. borders to further various U.S. policy objectives. Hazardous products, materials, and jobs are routinely exported as well, often with the explicit endorsement of the U.S. government. "Exporting Hazards" discusses possible justifications for subjecting foreign nationals to hazards deemed too dangerous for American consumers and workers—for example, that it is the responsibility of foreign governments to issue their own health and safety regulations, or that on balance the export programs bring sufficient economic benefits to Third World nations to outweigh their harms. It concludes, however, that current practices cannot ultimately be justified, in either moral or prudential terms.

The U.S. government has used not only its export programs but also its human rights policy as a means toward achieving other policy objectives. In "Playing Hardball with Human Rights," Henry Shue argues emphatically against selective enforcement of human rights violations in pursuit of other policy goals. Rights are not means to another end, nor are they ends in themselves. Rights, instead, function as constraints on both means *and* ends. Are there any cases where rights must be violated or rights violations overlooked? Shue offers three guidelines for "playing hardball" with human rights—guidelines that suggest not only that tolerance of human rights violations is usually unjustified, but also that it is usually counterproductive and in fact detrimental to long-term American policy objectives.

In "The Ethics of Covert Operations," Charles R. Beitz examines the three potentially controversial features of the U.S. government's covert interventions into another nation's internal affairs: the ends for which they are undertaken, the means used to pursue those ends, and the constitutional process they at times seem to subvert. Moral questions can be raised in each of these areas, leaving doubts whether most covert actions, in practice at least, can be successfully justified.

But all intervention in another sovereign nation's internal affairs cannot be ruled out, at least in theory. This, David Luban suggests in "The Legacy of Nuremberg," is what we learned, or should have learned, from the trial of the major Nazi war criminals almost half a century ago in Nuremberg. The legacy of Nuremberg is complex and self-contradictory, however, for the Nuremberg Charter both outlaws "crimes against humanity," thus providing the impetus for the human rights movement, and outlaws aggressive war that violates state sovereignty, thus blocking most attempts to intervene against states that themselves violate the human rights of their citizens. Luban suggests we abandon Nuremberg's defense of state sovereignty in favor of its insistence on vigilant prosecution of human rights violations.

As we attempt to intervene in the affairs of other states, so they attempt to intervene in ours. For relatively powerless states and revolutionary movements, the only available lever for affecting U.S. policy is some form of terrorism. Is terrorism "a criminal activity that no political cause can justify," as the State Department has charged? Or can it be a legitimate and effective tactic of political change? "Terrorism" addresses these questions, as well as the seemingly hopeless question of what can and should be done to combat terrorist activity.

Income and
Development

Jerome Segal

T he term "development" and terms such as "less developed," "undeveloped," and "underdeveloped" are universally used in talking and thinking about change in the Third World. There are journals of development economics, textbooks on the process of development, organizations devoted to development. It is therefore striking that for all that has been written about development and how to achieve it, relatively little attention has been given to the basic question: What is development?

The notion of development suggests something of a natural process an entity goes through. Thus we might speak of the development of an acorn, or of a child, but not the development of a stone or of a bookshelf. Moreover, the process envisaged is not a matter merely of change, but involves the working out of an entity's *potential*. When an acorn develops into an oak tree, the change comes from within; outside elements serve only as an environment within which the oak can develop into itself and in so doing fulfill its potential. The notion of development, then, carries within it the complementary notions of actualization, growth, maturity, fullness of being.

Given these particular features of the concept of development, it is striking that we speak of nations, economies, and societies as developed and undeveloped. Just what we mean by "potential," "maturity," or "fullness of being" when discussing economies and societies is elusive. Thus, economists, planners, and decision-makers typically turn to some notion that is more easily articulated and more readily used as a guide to policy choices. The notion of economic growth is appealing in this way. An economy has grown if and only if the pile of goods and services produced by that economy (the total or per capita output) in a given time period is larger than the pile it produced in the previous time period.

But we cannot equate development with growth. Simply growing larger carries with it no notion of maturity. In principle, a mature elephant could get larger and larger, yet we would not say the giant elephant was more advanced or had more fully realized its potential than had normal-sized elephants. Similarly, economic growth does not necessarily imply that the society is becoming more developed, or even that the economy is becoming more developed.

Economic *development*—as an ideal Third World countries are supposed to be striving toward—must depend on something broader. An economy is more developed, not if it produces an ever-larger pile of goods and services, but if it more fully contributes to the development of the society as a whole. And a society is developed insofar as it makes possible the development of the human beings within it. It is the notion of human development that is our central concept.

Income versus Basic Needs

How is one to link an appraisal of societies to judgments about the kind of human beings they give rise to? Almost all modern thought about development is egalitarian in the sense that concern is with the *breadth* of human development rather than the *depth*. It does not measure development by the heights of human greatness achieved in a given society, but by the general level of human well-being. But within a general egalitarian framework, the distinction is made among three broad approaches to economic development that go under the rubrics "trickle down," "equitable growth," and "basic needs." These three views adopt different understandings of what counts as development progress, of what it is for an economy or a society to *be* developed. They also differ with respect to *how* to achieve development—but that is not our immediate issue.

For both the equitable-growth and trickle-down conceptions the central good to be attained is higher income levels. Moreover, while it is clear that equitable-development advocates care about the distribution of income, the trickle-down conception is also concerned with distribution. The point of arguing that higher levels of overall Gross National Product (GNP) *will* trickle down through the society is to attempt to show that aggregate economic growth benefits everyone.

The two views have a fundamental difference with respect to the goals of development, however. The claim that economic benefits trickle down contains an implicit suggestion that so long as everyone, or almost everyone, ends up benefiting, all is well. The question of *how much* trickles down to *how many* is generally not raised by trickle-down advocates. It is sufficient that most people have higher incomes, whether or not some broad increase in inequality occurs.

In the equitable-growth orientation, an increase in most people's— or even everyone's—income does not automatically constitute progress. Whether or not progress has occurred is a matter of the balance between the gains in income and the loss of equality. If a broad increase in inequality of income occurs, then the growth in income for the poorer classes would have to be significant; not just any increase is adequate.

Now let us compare these income-based orientations to the basic-needs approach. The basic-needs theorist make two observations. First, having more income is not a good in itself; what is important is satisfying basic needs. And second, we cannot assume that needs are better satisfied at higher income levels. A great deal depends on the composition of output, on the quantities and prices of the goods and services available for purchase with private income, and on the extent and quality of a wide variety of goods and services typically provided by the government (health services, education, water quality).

Both the trickle-down and the equitable-growth orientation are prepared to accept income and its distribution as adequate indicators of developmental progress. They argue that income allows people to satisfy their preferences, and that no valid basis exists for giving priority to some other pattern of consumption than that actually chosen by the individual (and the public sector to which he or she is subject). The basic-needs orientation is unwilling to take income as an index of developmental progress. It insists on looking at the extent to which basic needs have actually been met, at the extent to which problems such as hunger, malnutrition, illiteracy, infant mortality, and disease have actually been overcome.

Earlier I maintained that a concept of societal development rests on the more fundamental notion of human development. What basis is there for going from the claim that people have a higher level of income or basic-needs satisfaction to the claim that they have achieved a higher level of development?

Orientations that view income as ultimately significant regardless of the extent to which it results in need satisfaction will be hard pressed to establish the connection. But it is logical to link the notion of needs with the notion of development. To see this, consider how we distinguish between something someone *needs* and something he or she *wants*. People want all sorts of things; they need only a limited set of things. Moreover, they need these things whether or not they want them. Basic needs are no mystery, consisting essentially of food, shelter, clothing, health care, and education. To call something a basic need is to say that in its absence the individual's most basic physical and intellectual development will be blocked. Thus, a basic-needs conception of development understands developmental progress as the elimination of conditions of mass deprivation that prevent the fuller development of the individual. Income approaches to development can make this connection only insofar as income is taken to be a reliable indicator of basic-need satisfaction, and this, of course, is a highly questionable assumption.

The Case against Getting Richer

Once basic needs have been taken care of, however, what is the relationship between human development and increasing wealth? One school of thought is that beyond a certain point the relationship is antithetical: Accumulation leads to greater taste for accumulation, appetite merely begets further appetite, and in the end human development suffers as we become further engaged in the processes of accumulation and consumption. Few of us in the rich societies have not, at least for some brief moment, paused to wonder if in fact our involvement with "things" has not gone too far, has not in some ways taken us away from some undefined pursuit that is more important.

The case that can be made for economic progress well beyond the level of pure subsistence does not have to do with the value of things, but with the value of time. The greater value of higher levels of productivity is not that they make possible higher levels of consumption, but that they make possible lower levels of labor. The impoverished are forced to spend an enormous amount of time in activities that are ultimately destructive of their human potential. What the rich have, at least potentially, is the time to devote themselves to those things worth doing for their own sake. Their time—that is, their life—is no longer a means to the attainment of the means of staying alive.

If persons spend a major part of their waking hours engaged in activity that fails to serve as a vehicle for personal expression, that does not embody their values, that does not provide either the esteem of others or self-esteem, and that is not a vehicle for personal growth, then their participation in economic life is destructive of their development, except insofar as it provides them with the resources and leisure time to pursue that development in other spheres of life.

Put in different terms, two possible notions of a developed economy exist. In both, a developed economy is one that contributes to the development of the human beings who participate in it. The distinction is between extrinsic and intrinsic impacts on human development. The primary extrinsic impact on human development is the provision of income and financial security. The intrinsic impacts have to do with the wide range of direct effects economic activity has on psychological, intellectual, and moral development.

Human health is precarious—activity that is not intrinsically healthful cannot be undertaken for long before it harms the individual. A developed economy that rests primarily on the extrinsic contribution of economic activity is possible only if work time is reduced to a relatively minor portion of a person's time. An extrinsically developed economy would provide the economic resources and financial security that allow individuals to pursue what is worthwhile in itself with only, say, ten hours of work a week. The wealthiest economies today have this potential. In fact, however, these economies operate within a broader social life that does not permit individuals to avail themselves of this potential. The central dynamic is that at the income and consumption levels that would correspond to ten hours of work a week, the individual can rarely achieve self-esteem or the esteem of others. A person who works ten hours a week and lives on the average income that ten hours provides would be a misfit in our society. Periodically certain subcultures attempt to free themselves from material attachments—to develop an alternative shared understanding of the bases of personal and social esteem. But without cultural change that redefines the meaning of income and consumption, only isolated individuals can take advantage of the potential for extrinsic economic development that wealthy societies provide.

The other notion of a developed economy is one that provides for human development intrinsically, through forms of work and organization that are inherently enriching and thus promote rather than stunt human development. On a mass basis no such forms have yet emerged. Indeed, many have argued that we have moved toward forms of economic life that are intrinsically destructive of human development.

In general, over the last fifty years, Americans have taken most of the increase in labor productivity in the form of higher income rather than in the form of less labor time or more self-developing forms of labor. *Our economic life is neither extrinsically nor intrinsically developed.* And just as we have been undone by the rising level of income and consumption all around us, which has changed the social meaning of lower levels of income, so today the world is being enmeshed in our consumption styles. Every Third World country today knows the life-style of the rich countries, and the tastes of the poor are shifting toward appetites for what they do not have and will never attain. The implications here are horrifying. The following table shows the number of years it will take various developing nations, at recent growth rates, to catch up to the income levels of the rich countries.

What we need is an egalitarian concept of development that will function to advance the genuine development of the poorer nations. The notion of equitable growth will not do this. Even at rapid rates of equitable growth, the vast masses of humankind will be engaged indefinitely in pursuit of the income levels of the rich countries. We need a type of development that will allow these masses quickly to overcome the most debilitating aspects of their poverty and then to avoid transforming themselves into a mere means for the advancement of their incomes. In short, we need a notion of development that will permit

The GNP Race

Country	$ GNP per Capita 1983*	Annual Growth Rate GNP/Capital 1965–83*	Years until Gap Closes if 1965–83 Rates Continue
Industrial Market Economies	11,060	2.5	
Korea, Rep. of	2,010	6.7	42
Brazil	1,880	5.0	73
Syria	1,760	4.9	79
Yemen Arab Rep.	550	5.7	98
Ecuador	1,420	4.6	101
Indonesia	560	5.0	124
Egypt	200	4.2	167
China	300	4.4	196
Philippines	760	2.9	687.5
Morocco	760	2.9	687
Sri Lanka	330	2.9	902
Cameroon	820	2.7	1334.7
Costa Rica	1,020	2.1	Never
Kenya	320	2.3	Never
India	260	1.5	Never
46 other developing countries (e.g., Bangladesh, Zaire, Burma, Tanzania, Haiti, Pakistan, Bolivia, Peru)			Never

*Source: The World Bank, *World Development Report*, 1985. Gap calculations are by author.

overcoming the worst poverty-induced obstacles to human development and at the same time will articulate what it is to have a developed society and to be a developed human being at low levels of income. I have argued that a basic-needs conception of development is a central part of this notion. Basic needs can be satisfied at relatively low levels of income, but only if a society deliberately seeks a development path that will allow it.

It may be objected that this is all very nice for those in rich countries to espouse because it leaves them at the top and tells the rest of humankind to settle for less. This objection misses the point. The prescription of low incomes and high leisure levels is not offered merely to the poor. It also represents the direction that we in the rich countries should go in, if we are to become not just rich, but truly and fully developed.

Should All Countries Be Democracies?

Charles R. Beitz

International declarations of human rights pro-
claim that all societies, regardless of level of development, should be political democracies. In all societies, however
poor and economically backward, public decisions are to be made by
citizens expressing their preferences in open and free elections, and
the right to participate in the political decision-making process is to be
universally respected. Many political theorists and economists argue,
however, that developing societies are not fully ready for democracy;
democratic institutions presuppose certain economic, social, and
political conditions that are simply not present in many poor nations.
In their view, democracy may be the ideal against which the governments of the wealthy, industrial nations are to be judged, but it is neither appropriate nor fair to hold the political institutions of developing
societies to the same standard.

This debate has considerable importance for contemporary political practice. The conduct of foreign policy by a great power such as
the United States may decisively influence the prospects of democratic
movements or regimes elsewhere, even when this influence is unintended, and particularly in developing societies whose domestic
affairs are especially vulnerable to outside events. Democratic regimes
might be destabilized as a result of International Monetary Fund-
imposed austerity measures; authoritarian regimes might be reinforced by favorable aid and credit policies; military assistance
intended to strengthen a friendly regime threatened from the outside
may provide hardware and training for domestic repression. In
morally appraising the consequences of its foreign policy, the United
States cannot ignore the question of whether democratic institutions
are or are not desirable in all societies.

We can take it as a settled part of our moral outlook that relatively
developed industrial societies should be politically democratic.

Democratic institutions are justified by appeal to a fundamental principle of political equality: Political institutions should be arranged so all
members are treated as equals. Democracy promotes equality by
affirming citizens' respect for themselves and others as persons capable of making and carrying out their own political choices: Each individual is regarded by others as a person whose choices deserve to be
taken into account. And democratic procedures seem more likely
than others to yield policies and practices that take equal account of
everyone's legitimate claims. The interests of all are more likely to be
furthered under democratic rule.

Such is the traditional justification for democracy in advanced
societies. If this justification does not hold for the developing countries
of the Third World, the reasons should emerge in a comparison of the
social, economic, and political characteristics of developed and
developing societies. Do the different circumstances of the world's
poorer nations lead to different conclusions about what form of government is morally best for them?

Cultural Differences

Many contemporary developing societies lack certain cultural features that are present in the Western democracies and appear to be
related to their political stability and efficiency. These include widely
held attitudes of citizens that political decisions are indeed significant
determinants of social welfare, and that citizens generally can and
should influence these decisions. Strong political cultures encouraging
broad citizen participation are not found in most developing societies.
On the contrary, active interest and participation in political events is
unusual. If a flourishing political culture is a necessary condition for
the development of political democracy, these cultural differences tell
decisively.

Assuming for the moment that these observations about the political cultures of developing societies are true, what is their relevance?
The mere fact that a civic culture is present in democracies and absent
in nondemocracies does not show that it is a necessary condition of
democracy. But the political-culture argument does undercut the traditional justification for democracy. Democracy does not affirm self-
respect if political activity is not viewed as an important means of
control over one's life prospects. In traditional cultures self-respect is
secured in other ways—for example, by willingly carrying out one's
assigned role in a social hierarchy. Furthermore, democracy is likely to
produce legislation that takes account of all interests only if political

rights are exercised by all segments of the population. In nonpartici-
pant societies, democratic institutions are unlikely to ensure that all
interests will be taken into account.

Even if the political culture argument is valid, however, it does not
follow that authoritarian institutions are to be preferred, from a moral
point of view, to democratic ones. The important question is whether a
particular authoritarian government will fare any better at sustaining
self-respect and taking account equally of all citizens' interests.

There is controversy as well about whether the political-culture
analysis of nonparticipation in developing societies is accurate. Peasants struggling along in subsistence agriculture may decline political
participation for reasons that have little to do with the presence or
absence of a strong political culture. If a peasant's main concern is
bare survival, political passivity is simply a risk-minimizing strategy.
Lack of political participation need not be a sign that political rights
have little value in securing self-respect. It may be merely a rational
response to the structure of opportunities and costs grimly presented
in day-to-day subsistence.

Institutional Weakness

Another important difference between developed and developing
societies lies in the strength of their political institutions. The political
institutions of developing societies tend to be weaker and comparatively inefficient and unreliable. They perform their principal functions
poorly and they do so at great cost.

According to Samuel P. Huntington, well-known for his work in
this area, the political institutions of developing societies must be
strengthened before widespread political participation can be encouraged. Huntington holds that the creation of political institutions is
undermined by the premature expansion of opportunities for political
participation. In his view, the costs of democracy at early stages in the
process of political modernization are excessive: Premature creation
of participatory institutions will endanger other human rights, such as
the right to security of the person, and reduce the efficiency with
which government performs its other functions.

Huntington's position can be questioned on several grounds. One
might wonder, for example, if experience bears out the hypothesis that
political institutions of prematurely participatory societies tend to
decay rather than to develop. More fundamentally, Huntington's view
invites the conclusion that institutional stability is to be valued regardless of who wields power within those institutions. As institutions are
strengthened, the political power of the underlying coalition of social

forces is strengthened as well. Huntington's view might justify a government's suppressing personal liberties in order to protect the most regressive of underlying social interests.

Thus, even if widespread political participation does hamper institutional development, democratic institutions would be inappropriate in a developing society only if alternative institutions would be more likely to promote the development of eventual social justice. Huntington's claims provide no reason to fall back on uncritical support for authoritarian institutions, regardless of their social bases and their tendency to enhance or hinder the prospects of liberty.

The Dynamics of Growth

By definition, the developing societies have production capabilities vastly below those of developed societies. At the same time, their rates of population growth are comparatively high. For both reasons, economic growth is extremely important. A common view is that democratic politics tends to reduce the rate of growth, both in developed and developing countries. What might be called the "growth first" argument holds that rapid growth is the more urgent goal in developing societies, justifying the suppression of political rights on its behalf.

The argument runs as follows. Growth is primarily a process of capital formation, and the rate of capital formation is a function of the rate of savings. Since the rich have a higher propensity to save, the larger share of national income should be channeled to the wealthy. Democratic institutions tend to work against this pattern of income distribution, depressing the rate of savings below its optimal level. Thus economic growth can best be promoted by authoritarian regimes.

This argument may well point to a trade-off between growth and democracy. It is less clear, however, that this trade-off should be resolved in favor of economic growth. It is certainly *not* clear unless the goal of economic growth is qualified by distributive considerations. Development strategies designed to maximize growth have in fact often resulted in absolute declines in the well-being of the poorer half of the population. The "growth first" argument as it stands fails to recognize that what is important is not promoting growth per se, but promoting equitable growth: growth that helps to alleviate and prevent the worst forms of poverty. If the "growth first" argument gives us a reason to reject democracy in developing societies, it must be because authoritarian governments are likely to be more successful in fostering *equitable* growth.

Democratic institutions operating in poor societies can fail to promote the economic interests of the least well-off in two ways. First, political rights, even where available to all, benefit some more than others. Inequalities in education and wealth result in unequal abilities to take advantage of such rights in pressing effective claims. Second, electoral mechanisms among uninformed and frequently illiterate peasants are particularly prone to manipulation by traditional elites. In both cases inequalities in social background are reflected in large inequalities of political influence, and those most in need of protection are least able to obtain it through political means. A nondemocratic regime may be preferred to a democratic one if (and this is a large "if") it more adequately satisfies the requirements of genuine political equality.

Conclusion

None of the antidemocratic arguments support the general conclusion that democracy is inappropriate in developing societies. All suffer from an unwarranted a priori belief that authoritarian regimes can be expected to govern more successfully than democratic ones. But all authoritarian governments are not created equal: Some are competent and some are incompetent; some respect personal rights and some are ruthlessly repressive; some have the support of disadvantaged groups and some represent privileged interests. Surely these differences matter.

Circumstances may occur under which democratic governments may be less likely to treat all their members as equals. Initial inequalities in the distribution of material resources may permit advantaged social groups to exploit the machinery of democracy at the expense of those less advantaged. This could not be a sufficient reason, however, to reject democratic forms of government. In addition there must be some reason to believe that an alternative regime would be more successful in these respects, without being morally deficient in other ways—for example, by turning to brutal and repressive means for securing the compliance of the population. These are both tall orders, and it is, to say the least, most unlikely that very many actual authoritarian regimes would pass these tests.

This article is drawn from "Democracy in Developing Societies," in Boundaries: National Autonomy and Its Limits, *ed. Peter G. Brown and Henry Shue (Totowa, N.J.: Rowman and Littlefield, 1981).*

Plowshares into Swords
The Political Uses of Food

Claudia Mills

The United States produces and exports more food than any other nation, in a world where more than a billion people are chronically malnourished and half a billion eke out an existence on the edge of starvation. Only a handful of nations produce more food than they consume, and the United States is chief among these, dominating the world's food supply to a greater extent than all the combined nations of OPEC dominate the world's oil. Such a vast productive capacity set against the rest of the world's desperate poverty places the United States in a position of awesome power to determine whether its neighbors eat adequately or go hungry.

In recent years, the United States has freely wielded its "food weapon" to further both its own security and economic interests and the broader goals of world prosperity and peace. Presidents from Dwight Eisenhower through Jimmy Carter, Ronald Reagan, and George Bush have used American food aid and sales to achieve their own foreign policy objectives, whether rewarding anti-Communist regimes for capitalist solidarity or punishing repressive regimes for human rights violations. Food exports have been manipulated to stifle criticism of the American military intervention in Vietnam, to chasten the Soviet Union for its military intervention in Afghanistan, and to forge peace accords for the embattled Mideast. The frankly political use of food aid is sanctioned by American law: Title I of Public Law 480 authorizes the use of food aid to develop foreign markets for American agricultural commodities and to complement U.S. foreign policy objectives; Title III links food aid to development programs (in contrast to Title II, which grants aid almost exclusively on humanitarian grounds). And Section 116 of the Foreign Assistance Act provides for cessation of aid to nations whose governments engage in gross violations of human rights. Thus the use of food as a policy instrument has received legislative legitimation.

Some observers urge that food exports should become still more politicized, recommending that the United States join with other food producing and exporting nations to form a "FOPEC" (Food Producing and Exporting Countries) cartel similar to OPEC. Food has been hailed as "America's secret weapon." But others recoil from using food in this way, insisting that the starvation of millions of innocent persons—half of them children—must not be ignored or exploited to achieve political or economic ends.

Is the political use of food a legitimate means to promote our military security and increase the export profits of our producers? Is it an acceptable tool for pursuing social, economic, and political justice and a stable world peace? Or is it wrong to use as a weapon or bargaining chip something that is the object of so central and universal a human need?

Food As National Property

The most extreme advocates of the politicization of food exports take the view that food is fully the property of the nation whose soil it is grown on, just as oil is fully the property of the nation whose territory it lies beneath. America's abundant harvests were grown on American soil; therefore they are ours, to distribute as we choose. In this view, it is both our right and our obligation to use the power food represents; to reject or ignore the possibilities of using food to enhance our own position in the world and to increase the world's peace and justice is to squander a valuable opportunity bequeathed to us. Just as individuals are given talents and abilities they are expected to use wisely and well both for self-improvement and for bettering the world around them, so are nations given natural resources they are to exploit both in their own national interest and in the interest of the global community. Thus, commentator Lowell Ponte, defending the political uses of food, writes, "Should we consider food as a weapon? It is a power that destiny has put in our hands. Rather than reject it, we must consider the best and wisest ways to use this power to prompt development in other nations, to encourage cooperation, to discourage aggression."

Against this view it can be argued, however, that the fertile soil and long growing season that make possible America's agricultural bounty are not gifts of "destiny," but benefits arbitrarily parceled out by nature, to which their beneficiaries have no special moral entitlement. That oil lies beneath the sand of Saudi Arabia and wheat grows well in the soil of Kansas are arbitrary facts of nature, to which no moral significance should be imputed. As political philosopher Charles R. Beitz argues in *Political Theory and International Relations*, "The fact that someone happens to be located advantageously with respect to natural resources does not provide a reason why he or she should be entitled to exclude others from the benefits that might be derived from them." The accidents of nature do not provide a secure foundation for morally decisive ownership claims.

Of course, a great deal of our agricultural productivity can be attributed to American technology, to our free-enterprise system, and to the hard work of American farmers. These considerations do establish a special American claim to the fruits of our own labor. But this claim must always be set in the context of the original natural endowments that allowed technology, free enterprise, and hard work to be as spectacularly successful here as they have been.

Furthermore, food is not just one commodity among others, some random stuff the United States has a lot of. Food is an essential requirement of every human being on earth. As such, it is the object of a basic and widely recognized human right. Even were America's claim to the surplus produce of its farms more secure, it would still have to be weighed against the urgency of this universal human right, which is at present so tragically unfulfilled.

The view that food is national property to be disposed of as we please, then, is unsatisfactory. At the very least this means America is not free to use food as a weapon for promoting just any of our own national interests, at the expense of the more pressing needs of others. Nor are we free to use food to multiply the profits of American producers and distributors, at least not while millions suffer from chronic malnutrition.

It may be difficult to separate out cases where food aid and sales are used merely to promote our own national interest from cases where a broader set of goals is furthered; even highly politicized Title I food aid is directed only to countries with an evident use for imported food. Daniel E. Shaughnessy, former deputy coordinator of the A.I.D. Office of Food for Peace, points out, "Even the most humanitarian program has a political element to it, and conversely even the most political program has its humanitarian aspects."

But we are nonetheless able to identify certain political or economic uses of food that are ruled out once we reject the view that American-grown food is simply *ours*. Clearly, food aid that harms its recipients while benefiting American agricultural concerns is illegitimate. It would be impermissible to encourage a taste for American wheat in foreign rice eaters, with the goal of creating a dependency on American exports. Such an economic program has no redeeming humanitarian benefits. Nor would it be permissible to cut off badly needed food exports simply to curb expressions of anti-American sentiment in receiving countries. These are the kinds of political and economic uses of food that must be rejected as unacceptable.

Politics-Blind Food Aid?

These considerations may suggest that *all* political uses of food are illegitimate, that food *aid*, at least, should be awarded strictly on non-political grounds, directed solely to those most in need. Food should be allocated to the hungry, period, not to hungry anti-Communists or hungry consumers of American exports, or even to hungry human rights activists. Philosopher Thomas Nagel writes that truly humanitarian aid "should be directed at the impoverished purely in virtue of their humanity. . . . Aid which simply lifts people off the absolute bottom and helps them to a minimally adequate diet addresses a need so general and basic that it is an inappropriate vehicle for the expression of political preference. . . . A humanitarian food aid policy would therefore base allocation solely on nutritional needs."

In at least two ways, however, all food aid is and must be inherently political. In the first place, it is individual persons who suffer from hunger, while food aid is often awarded on a national level. Problems thus arise in making sure the neediest individuals in any country are indeed those who benefit from food aid granted to their government. Political and economic considerations are relevant here in ensuring that food aid accomplishes what it sets out to do—that it relieves the hunger of the hungriest. Second, all major food sales and grants have political, economic, and social consequences that go beyond the immediate relief of hunger. "No aid," Nagel recognizes, "can be entirely nonpolitical in its *effects*," and no responsible food export policy can refuse to take these into account.

Food policies directed toward national governments must pay attention not only to a recipient nation's aggregate wealth or food supply, but to how wealth and food are internally distributed. In countries where wealth is greatly concentrated, as it is in much of the Third World, food and development aid may do little or nothing to relieve the misery of the poorest people, and may even aggravate distributional inequities by channeling additional income and influence to the already better off. Likewise, food aid directed impartially toward the hungry of all countries, regardless of their political systems or the human rights records of their governments, may serve only to prop up tyrannical regimes or stave off revolutionary reforms. Thus, politics-blind food aid can work against the welfare of those it is designed to help most.

Among the most important ancillary consequences of food aid are its impact on Third World development and population growth. Food aid may work either to encourage or discourage development, and development may be either beneficial or harmful to the worst-off in an underdeveloped country. Food aid may perpetuate dependency, stalling programs to boost domestic production and to achieve self-sufficiency; food aid directed at stimulating development may disrupt local patterns of subsistence and undermine traditional cultures. Anthropologist Norge Jerome calls attention to "the tragic and costly effects of public and private economic development programs on millions of individuals throughout the world. The demands of economic development programs have often triggered rapid changes in the traditional system of food production, processing, distribution, and consumption, and a decline in . . . nutritional status." Currently a great deal of debate among economists and anthropologists centers on what sorts of development our food aid should be targeted to stimulate or avoid. Food aid cannot be given out without some sensitivity to these debated consequences.

Food aid also has complicated and disputed implications for a nation's population growth. Opponents of food aid often claim that it pits the present poor against the future poor, by allowing the current generation of parents to continue to produce too many future children. In their scenarios, food aid averts a smaller famine today only at the price of creating a larger famine tomorrow. These critics recommend that food aid be channeled only to countries making a good-faith effort to control their rate of population growth, by linking food aid to contraceptive practice.

But such linkage might well be counterproductive. In the developed industrialized countries population curves have fallen off only *after* a certain level of prosperity was achieved. Population control seems to be itself dependent on the availability of adequate supplies of food. One leading explanation of this phenomenon is that parents limit family size once child mortality rates have lowered sufficiently to assure them that what children they do have are likely to survive. As explained by Michael F. Brewer, former president of the Population Reference Bureau, this "child survival hypothesis . . . suggests significant changes in the content and staging of U.S. aid programs," with family-planning efforts carefully coordinated to follow programs of food aid and development. If aid levels are too low, or family-planning programs ineffective, food aid may exacerbate the very problems it aims to alleviate. Once again, food aid cannot be parceled out with an oblivious eye to its other implications.

Food for Peace and Prosperity

The use of food aid to control population growth raises the question of the moral legitimacy of using the promise of food or the threat of its withdrawal to manipulate the behavior of individuals and nations. To make population control a condition of receiving food may seem a coercive interference in the internal affairs of sovereign nations, as well as in the very private and personal decisions individuals make about the size of their families. Shaughnessy dismisses efforts to link food aid with population control by asking, "Would the United States accept any foreign proposal that carried with it the caveat that we would have to meet birth control criteria?"

In the case of population control, food is used as an incentive to behavior that will end up reducing future hunger. Food is used, at least indirectly, to ensure the adequacy of future supplies of food. The same might be said of food programs designed to encourage or discourage various development patterns: The end goal of the manipulative pressures is to establish a solid agricultural base to feed future generations.

In other cases, however, food has been used manipulatively to achieve ends much less clearly related to the reduction of world hunger. President Jimmy Carter, for example, cut off PL 480 food aid to Augusto Pinochet's Chile and Anastasio Somoza's Nicaragua as part of his campaign against human rights violations. Both Henry Kissinger and Carter used promises of increased food aid to bring about an Egyptian/Israeli peace settlement, dramatically increasing food aid to Egypt after Anwar Sadat's signing of both the Sinai peace agreement and the later Camp David accord. Some have suggested that U.S. grain sales to the Soviet Union might operate as a possible deterrent to any future nuclear exchange.

Is food an appropriate diplomatic tool for protesting human rights violations and giving peace its best chance? Despite the worthiness of the goals in these instances, it may still seem that food is a singularly inappropriate instrument of behavior modification—that, although the consequences of food aid and sales must be carefully weighed and assessed, it is wrong to use food to apply deliberate manipulative pressure on the governments of hungry people. The offer of food or the threat of its withdrawal can have an irresistible coercive force. It may seem unfair to use food as a diplomatic lever, however high the stakes.

It seems overly fastidious, however, to refuse to make make *any* distinctions among the ends for which food aid or sales may or may not be manipulated. To use food exports as a tool for ultimately improving world nutrition levels, or to dampen the nuclear arms race, is very different from using them to punish developing countries for trade with Cuba or the Soviet Union. That food is a central human need and the object of a basic human right does not make food exports sacredly immune from diplomacy and negotiations that may even work to ensure greater satisfaction of that need and protection of that right. Nor is the right to food the only right we care about protecting. Rights not to be tortured and not to be killed are weighty as well, and manipulation of food to secure these rights may be fully justified.

How, then, do we sort out acceptable from unacceptable uses of food? One first try at a principle is this: Food exports may be used politically with the objective of reducing world hunger or preventing conditions equally grave and distressing, such as imminent war and widespread and egregious violations of human rights. It is not wrong to withdraw food aid or sales from repressive regimes to punish their systematic violation of international human rights; it is not wrong to promise food aid or sales to belligerent regimes on the condition they abstain from the horrors of war.

Two caveats are in order, however. The first is that the political use of food carries with it the ever-present danger of self-deception and outright dishonesty. It is all too easy to convince ourselves that U.S. economic and security interests just happen to coincide with the needs of the hungry. Those who believe, or pretend to believe, that the menace of spreading communism is an evil on a par with mass starvation will feel justified in diverting food from those who may need it most. Thus shipments of food to famine-stricken Bangladesh were delayed in 1974 when the United States discovered that nation had sold jute to Cuba. Good practical reasons may well exist for a near-universal ban on such overtly political manipulations of food. Otherwise we may find ourselves filtering food aid and sales through the blinders of our own self-interest.

Second, even the most sincere efforts at making the world better may tragically misfire. Thus Jerome points to the dangers of well-intentioned development programs that work only to increase poverty and powerlessness; Brewer warns that the child-survival hypothesis is only weakly supported by available evidence, so that inadequate food aid programs may contribute to inadvertent population crises. Perhaps in the face of such widespread uncertainty we should harbor no grand schemes for using food to bring about any major international improvements. Our only sure truth seems to be that a quarter of the world's people are severely malnourished, and half of these are young children, innocent if anyone in this world ever is. Thus all we can do is to act, as sensitively and sanely as possible, minimizing whatever inevitable damage we unwittingly cause, remembering that in the final analysis, food is for eating and not for waging even the noblest political and ideological crusades.

The views of Daniel E. Shaughnessy, Thomas Nagel, Norge W. Jerome, and Michael F. Brewer are taken from their contributions to Food Policy: The Responsibility of the United States in the Life and Death Choices, *ed. Peter G. Brown and Henry Shue (New York: The Free Press, 1977). Lowel Ponte is quoted from his essay in the May 1982 issue of* Readers' Digest. *Charles R. Beitz is quoted from* Political Theory and International Relations *(Princeton, N.J.: Princeton University Press, 1979).*

Exporting Hazards

Claudia Mills

It has been common practice for U.S. firms to market in the Third World products and materials that have been banned or restricted in the United States. Pesticides and chemicals too dangerous for American use are shipped to developing countries, where regulatory standards are absent, weak, or poorly enforced. Such banned consumer goods as children's pajamas treated with cancer-causing chemicals have found their way into the cradles of Third World infants.

It also has been common practice for U.S.-based transnational firms to establish factories in Third World countries when minimum-wage requirements and health and safety codes in the United States make the move economically attractive. A striking example is the processing of the pervasive product asbestos, long identified as a cause of asbestosis (cousin to "black lung" and "brown lung") and various cancers. Standards covering asbestos processing have been issued by the Occupational Safety and Health Administration, and cleaner technologies have become available. But rather than installing the new technologies in U.S. facilities, some corporations are moving the more hazardous (but cheaper) methods into poorer countries, such as Mexico. Thus dangerous jobs are exported as well as dangerous products.

Such exports have been restricted and facilitated by differing U.S. government policies. Five days before leaving office, for example, President Jimmy Carter issued an executive order restricting the export of some U.S. products whose use is banned or severely restricted in this country. A month later, that order was revoked by President Ronald Reagan. Current administration policy appears to facilitate the export of hazards across our borders.

The result is that products and jobs deemed too dangerous for American consumers and workers are deemed acceptable for consumers and workers in other countries. Yet few would want to claim, straightaway, that the welfare of foreigners counts for less than the welfare of fellow citizens, that different moral standards govern how foreigners and citizens may be treated. Few would say that it does not matter, after all, if *foreign* workers are exposed to asbestos, or if *foreign* children contract cancer from their sleepwear. Certainly few would say it out loud. How, then, can this clear application of lower standards to foreigners be justified?

It's Their Responsibility, Not Ours

A first justification of current practices goes like this. The reason certain substances or manufacturing processes are banned in the United States is because the United States government banned them. The reason they are not banned in the Third World is because Third World governments have not banned them. If our government permits the export of hazardous products or facilities, this does not show a disregard for foreign welfare on the part of *our* government. It is not our government's business to look out for the interests of foreign workers and consumers. That is the business of foreign governments, and if they do not act to protect their own citizens, it is not for the U.S. government to intervene on their behalf—especially when such intervention puts American industry at a competitive disadvantage. An argument like this one seems to underlie recent shifts in executive policy.

This implicitly assumes, however, that governments in the underdeveloped and desperately poor Third World are able to defend themselves against the powerful corporations of the advanced, industrial nations. *Ought* implies *can*, and to say that Third World governments ought to protect their workers and consumers is to assume they are able to do so.

Political scientist Thomas Biersteker casts doubt on this assumption. He argues that the global balance of power remains heavily tilted toward affluent nations and their transnational corporations. Third World governments have little political and economic autonomy in the face of international corporate might.

In the past decades nations of the Third World have made significant efforts toward greater independence. Third World governments have launched massive programs of nationalization and embarked on ambitious agendas of economic self-reliance. These developments have led political scholars to talk about a "resurgence of state power" among the world's poorest nations. In Biersteker's analysis, however, despite strides toward greater autonomy and self-sufficiency, "transnational corporations are still able to constrain the exercise of state power in the Third World."

Biersteker's point is well illustrated by nationalizations. The frequency and scope of nationalizations increased dramatically during the 1970s, as states sought to take control of foreign enterprises by acquiring the assets of industries operating within their territory. "In theory," Biersteker explains, "once national control has been attained, exploitative practices of the past can be halted, and an increase in the state's revenues can be anticipated." In practice, however, wealth and control have remained in the hands of the transnationals. "The defensive capabilities of transnational corporations and the structure of the world economy have constrained and effectively neutralized the assertion of state power through nationalization."

It indeed may be that American corporations are put at a competitive disadvantage if they are required to upgrade foreign factory safety or notify foreign governments of hazardous shipments. But foreign governments are at a far greater competitive disadvantage, struggling among themselves to attract, and then to control, some portion of international investment and trade. They are hardly in a position to dictate health and safety standards to the multinationals. Responsibility for imposing and enforcing standards must be borne by those better able to bear it.

We Can't Help Out the Whole World

It might seem, therefore, that the responsibility for protecting the interests of foreign workers and consumers should fall on the U.S. government. If foreign governments cannot effectively look after their own, let us look after them.

Unfortunately, however, the world is filled to overflowing with the hungry, destitute, repressed, and unprotected. It cannot be up to us to take on all the manifold tragedies crowding every corner of the globe. We cannot legislate regulatory standards for pesticide use in every field in Latin America. We cannot lay down codes of workplace safety for every factory in Africa. Our obligations cannot extend so far.

According to philosopher Judith Lichtenberg, it is a widely held view that nations do not have positive obligations to look out for the welfare of other nations or extranationals. Special treaties or agreements might generate such obligations, but, in the common view, one nation does not ordinarily have any duties to actively protect the citizens of another.

But this does not mean, Lichtenberg points out, that "nations and their members are thought to have no obligations to extranationals. The common view is rather that . . . such obligations are entirely negative: they are obligations to refrain from interference in extranationals' affairs." Citizens of one country certainly do have obligations not to harm foreign citizens; they are duty-bound to leave them alone.

The moral principle "It is wrong to inflict avoidable harm on other people" is almost universally accepted. Few would assert that this "no-harm principle" makes an exception of foreigners. Yet Lichtenberg observes that the implications of this principle for international policy seem largely unrecognized. Even setting positive obligations aside, the no-harm principle itself requires that current practices be amended.

For corporations are bound by the no-harm principle, as well as individuals and nations. They have no special license to inflict harm on foreign nationals. It seems to follow that even if corporations have no direct responsibility to promote the interests of their workers or those who consume their products, they do have an obligation not to subject their employees to excessive workplace hazards or to market products that endanger the health and lives of those who use them. Whether or not the governments of Third World countries act to protect their citizens from corporate harm, the corporations ought not to inflict it. That foreign workers and consumers are unprotected does not serve as an excuse to place their safety and health in jeopardy.

Furthermore, even if our government has no duty to actively protect foreigners from harm, it has a duty not to facilitate the infliction of harm by corporations based within its jurisdiction. If it is wrong for corporations to export hazards, then it is wrong for any government to facilitate their export. Governments ought not serve as accomplices to corporate wrongdoing.

It is true that our government cannot solve the problems of the entire world. This follows as well from "*ought* implies *can*." But our government can avoid causing further problems by doing what it can to prevent the infliction of harm by corporations that bear its name. And insofar as corporations and governments do inflict harm, they are bound by the no-harm principle to make appropriate restitution to those who suffer from their policies.

Are Hazardous Exports Really So Bad?

A final attempt to justify these current practices suggests that the export of hazardous products and jobs does not really violate the no-harm principle. Philosopher Henry Shue examines the plausibility of standard arguments for this position.

Hazardous exports do not violate the no-harm principle, it is argued, because they are not, on balance, *harmful*. Costs to Third World people may take the form of new dangers to health and safety, but new benefits are also part of the same package. Banned pesticides exported to insect-infested nations may provide agricultural benefits that outweigh any other risks. In countries with severe unemployment, hazardous jobs may be preferable to no jobs at all. "Money for food, plus some asbestos fibers in the air," Shue notes, "can be better than clean air and an empty plate."

This defense, however, Shue emphatically rejects. It can sometimes be acceptable to impose on others costs that are greatly outweighed by concomitant benefits. But the costs of the hazards exported are costs of a special kind. Consider the costs faced by asbestos workers in foreign plants using the banned technology. They involve physical damage that is serious and irreversible: Lost lungs do not grow back; malignant tumors continue to spread. Furthermore, the health risk posed to foreign workers is undetectable and unpredictable without a level of medical knowledge and care to which they generally have no access. And this undetectability and unpredictability are avoidable at the choice of the firm's management: The damage can often be detected from a simple X ray exam. Finally, the probability of receiving the damage risked is very high. These central features are shared by pesticide poisoning and chemically caused cancers as well. When all these conditions hold, Shue concludes, the cost in question is prohibited by the no-harm principle. Such costs are *harms*, if any costs are, and they cannot be imposed on other human beings without their free choice.

A second line of defense is therefore to claim that foreign nationals consent to the new dangers—the harm is not inflicted on them, since they voluntarily accept it. But this defense is legitimate only if the workers and consumers are indeed fully informed of the severity and probability of the harm they face. Consent based on ignorance and false information does not provide any excuses. Yet the current administration dispute is precisely about whether or not manufacturers should be required to *notify* foreign governments of harmful shipments before proceeding with their export. It is the effective transmission of information that is under attack. Likewise, many firms with operations abroad have not informed their workers of health and safety hazards. Shue asks: "Why is informed consent not more appealing when it does in fact relieve a firm of the responsibility of having inflicted harm upon unsuspecting people? I believe that the real explanation . . . has a great deal to do with . . . the discounting of the welfare of people across national boundaries, especially when the boundaries also mark cultural, ethnic, or racial differences. Harm to foreigners is simply not taken as seriously."

Coming Full Circle

The question underlying the export of hazards concerns the moral significance of national boundaries. The map of the globe is crisscrossed with dotted lines, sometimes seemingly arbitrary, changing with colonizations and rebellions and wars. Yet those lines determine the extent of national sovereignty and the limits of citizenship. Frequently they determine how poor or rich those living within them will be and how able their governments will be to protect their rights and interests.

At one time, when nations were far more isolated and self-contained, national boundaries may have set limits to moral obligation. They do not limit our obligations today. According to Lichtenberg, a person's, corporation's, or nation's obligations extend as far as the actual or potential effects of their actions. In an ever-increasingly interdependent world, the effects of actions are not easily contained. Our obligations no longer terminate at a nation's borders, because the consequences of our actions do not cease there. Through technological progress, international trade, and codependence on dwindling natural resources, all nations have come to form one moral community. And so, Lichtenberg writes, "the limits of the planet are the limits of our [moral] world."

This interdependence provides self-interested as well as moral reasons to look after the welfare of other nations and their citizens. Lichtenberg suggests that by furthering the interests of other countries, we may in the end further our own interests as well. "Recent world developments have begun to show the extent to which a nation's long-term self-interest may dictate much greater attention to the interests of other nations. Interdependence means that our wrongs come back to haunt us, and not just others."

This may be especially true for the exporting of hazards. Advanced and developing nations are increasingly bound together in one interdependent world economy. The United States imports food from some of the same countries to which it exports poisonous pesticides. The Food and Drug Administration reports that "nearly half of the green coffee beans imported into the United States contain various levels of pesticides that have been banned in the United States." The coffee we drink, therefore, may contain substances intended for consumption only by unprotected foreigners. Our wrongs may come back to haunt us rather sooner than we had expected.

The views of Thomas Biersteker, Judith Lichtenberg, and Henry Shue are taken from their essays in Boundaries: National Autonomy and Its Limits, *ed. Peter G. Brown and Henry Shue (Totowa, N.J.: Rowman and Littlefield, 1981).*

Playing Hardball with Human Rights

Henry Shue

The U.S. government often acts as if each government should be allowed to pick and choose its own favorites among established human rights and attend exclusively to these. Such an attempt at selective enforcement of human rights was authorized, for example, by a formal policy memorandum adopted by the Department of State on October 27, 1981, which states: "'Human rights'—meaning political rights and civil liberties—conveys what is ultimately at issue in a contest with the Soviet bloc. The fundamental distinction is our respective attitudes toward freedom. . . . We should move away from 'human rights' as a term, and begin to speak of 'individual rights,' 'political rights,' and 'civil liberties.'"

Such a narrowing of human rights to political rights and civil liberties would omit rights to physical security, like the rights against torture and "disappearance" explicitly listed in the laws controlling U.S. foreign assistance. It also dismisses the third general category of internationally recognized human rights, the right to fulfillment of vital needs such as food, shelter, health care, and education. The supposition seems to be that a nation can simply focus on the rights "at issue in a contest" with its principal adversary and relegate all the other rights to the periphery.

Human rights, under such a policy, seem primarily to be used as a means toward other ends of foreign policy, specifically as a weapon against the USSR. This manipulative attitude reveals a deep incomprehension of human rights and of how human rights actually function.

Human rights are inconveniences—grit in the gears. Due process is a pain in the neck; torture gets quicker answers. Dissidents disrupt the war effort; the disappeared cause no further problems. Human rights are supposed to be nuisances and obstacles, especially for governments. They are not designed to allow the smooth execution of policy, but to force policy to take twists and turns around individuals whose insistence on their own claims is a most unwelcome complication for people with bigger fish to fry.

Rights have a different logic from almost all other considerations that go into policy. To fail to see this is to fail to understand how rights work. Most of the time reasoning about policy appropriately takes a means/ends form. We decide what consequences we want to produce—we choose our ends—and then we select our means accordingly. Or we look at the means at our command—we examine our resources—and then select our goals accordingly. Sometimes we let our means dictate our ends, sometimes we let our ends dictate our means, and, of course, we usually do quite a bit of both.

Nothing is wrong with the mutual adjustment of means and ends. But *rights do not fit*. Rights cannot be accommodated within this pattern, because *rights are neither means nor ends*. Instead, rights are constraints on both.

Since rights are not means, it is unacceptable to pick and choose among them as best serves your ends. To notice that within the Soviet Union there are no free elections but relatively few people are "disappeared," while within allied states people are "disappeared" right and left but partly free elections are held, and then to decide *for this reason* to keep talking about the absence of elections but to say as little as possible about disappearances, is to fail to respect the integrity of authentic rights. It is to respect only the limits that are no obstacle to the pursuit of one's goals and to ignore the limits that are in the way. Yet the purpose of rights is to get in the way of politics as usual.

I take it that a reply might be that a selective enforcement of human rights is not undertaken in pursuit of just any old goal. The goal of such policies is to stop the spread of communism. Since Communist regimes to a unique extent irretrievably, systematically, and severely violate human rights, any manipulation of rights along the way by the United States is for the sake of the ultimate triumph of human rights. Or so the argument goes.

The policy seems to be Machiavellianism in the pursuit of human rights—ruthlessness now for the sake of rights later. But it doesn't wash, even in theory. *Rights are not ends either*. To defend against the charge that rights are being treated as means by replying that they are instead being pursued as ends would still fail to respect rights for what they actually are. Ends or goals may be deferred, especially if the deferred fulfillment will be greater than the immediate fulfillment would be. But rights—even those that must be pursued gradually and progressively—may not be optionally deferred until other projects are completed.

Lenin is supposed to have said: "A revolution is not a dinner party." The U.S. government seems to want to say: "Neither is the defense of democracy." But this spirit of you-can't-make-an-omelet-without-breaking-eggs is precisely what human rights are intended to thwart. Even in war there are things civilized people do not do in order to win.

Surely, it will be suggested, the preceding is a bit harsh, especially if it assumes human rights may never be violated or that it is never necessary to violate one right in order to fulfill another. We need to stake out a plausible position that lies between Machiavellianism and moralism in the realm of rights, to discuss the ethics of second best: "dirty hands," messy compromises, tragic choices. Will U.S. policy fare any better in this light?

First, a wet blanket. It is very dramatic to believe one faces tragic choices, thrilling to think one must do evil to achieve good. But ruthlessness is not always so wonderfully effective—the Nazis, for example, did lose in the end. Since necessary evils can be so bracing to perform, we should be quite certain they are actually necessary. Fighting fire with fire can be very satisfying, especially if you really hate your enemies. We should always first be sure that water would not work equally well—or, sad thought, even better.

Still, sometimes rights must be violated—or, at the very best, violations of rights must be overlooked. Can we formulate any "Guidelines for Hardball"? I think so.

First, if you are playing dirty because you are determined to win, be sure the dirty playing is actually helping you win. I am, of course, not suggesting the principle, do it *if* it helps you win. The principle is, do it *only* if it helps you win. If the justification for indulging—or subsidizing with aid or supplying with weapons, technology, advice, and political endorsement—violations of fundamental rights is that the violations are contributing over the long run to U.S. national security, at least be sure that the U.S. position is in fact being strengthened.

Much of our allegedly "realistic" swashbuckling seems not merely ineffectual but extremely counterproductive. After Ferdinand Marcos eliminated traditional democracy from the Philippines in 1972, we doubled security assistance in the name of making Clark and Subic Air Bases more secure. But our main accomplishment seems to have been to attract the hatred for the dictator's corrupt opulence and brutal repression onto ourselves as his foreign sponsor, just as we concurrently did in Iran. A generation ago it would have been difficult to find two more passionately pro-American societies than the Iranian and the Filipino. U.S. diplomacy succeeded in alienating the one and came close to alienating the other. To trade the long-term goodwill of a whole society for the short-term cooperation of an individual dictator, now long since deposed, was in both cases a poor trade.

The second "Guideline for Hardball" is *proportionality*. The marginal contribution to, for example, U.S. national security of our indulgence of rights violations must be significantly greater than the harm done by the violations. Try to imagine that it was somehow to the advantage of U.S. interests in Guatemala to have a murderous fanatic like Rios Montt on our team. Did it contribute *enough* to U.S. interests to have been worth the slaughter of so many Indians?

Part of the difficulty of sensing any approximation of proportionality in such cases is that the supposed benefits to U.S. society tend to be speculative and hypothetical, while the violations of rights are concrete and actual. Consider the gentleness of U.S. criticisms of South Africa, one of the most totalitarian dictatorships in the world today, which is justified in terms of South Africa's supposed contribution to U.S. national security by such means as potential ready access to strategic minerals. *If* the U.S. Air Force quickly needed a large number of planes of a certain sort, and *if* those planes could only be built using certain strategic minerals, and *if* we had forgotten to stockpile the minerals even though the USSR remembered to, and *if* Zimbabwe did not also have the minerals in question (or would not sell them because of the U.S. alliance with South Africa), and *if* South Africa was still under the control of the current rulers, and *if* they would not sell the minerals simply for the money involved but only out of goodwill, then we might need their goodwill. Would you invest in the stock of a company whose success depended on the conjunction of so many different factors? Meanwhile, millions of South Africans are being herded into the poorest regions of their country, where it is very difficult to earn enough money to feed their children, and deprived of self-government. Are these stunted and shortened lives worth less than the *increment* in U.S. national security that might depend on the goodwill of the South African regime?

The third "Guideline for Hardball" is closely related: The violations of rights must be the *least evil alternative*. To continue with our example of South Africa, why couldn't we have gone ahead and stockpiled the strategic minerals and then aggressively supported an end to apartheid? Well, it would be expensive, it would add to the deficit. But now we are talking about indulging apartheid in order to save money, not in order to defend our national security. We can obtain the strategic minerals either way—it is simply cheaper to do it by deferring our purchases of strategic minerals until we actually need them and meanwhile staying on the good side of the regime.

In sum, I am willing to concede that in foreign policy the tolerance of rights violations by allied governments can be morally justified—but *only if* these three conditions are met. Undoubtedly other conditions in addition to those I have specified must also be met. But how many cases satisfy even these three, leaving aside others I have failed to specify?

For example, I have used U.S. indulgence of South Africa's systematic racism to illustrate the difficulty of satisfying the condition of proportionality. In fact, I do not think U.S. indulgence of apartheid even satisfies our first condition. I think we are creating conditions where we will be hated and despised by the regime that overthrows the regime we now support.

The practical difficulty about playing hardball with human rights is that people do not appreciate being subjected to malnutrition, torture, arbitrary imprisonment, and other severe violations of basic rights. It is not easy to cultivate the favor of the violators without incurring the hatred of the violated, who in many cases are likely to form the next government whenever it comes. This is not a moral argument—it is an appeal to national interest—but it is highly relevant for those self-styled realists who want us to deal with the world as it really is.

The Ethics of Covert Operations

Charles R. Beitz

" **C**overt action" has been used to describe many different kinds of activities in U.S. foreign policy since World War II. The most controversial of these include the U.S.-backed coups d'etat in Iran and Guatemala in the 1950s, the Central Intelligence Agency (CIA) assassination plots against foreign leaders such as Fidel Castro and Patrice Lumumba in the 1960s, the attempts to prevent the election of Salvador Allende as president of Chile in 1970 and then to subvert his government after he was elected anyway, and, of course, the contra war in Nicaragua during the 1980s. A larger number of covert operations have met with general, if not unanimous, public approval—for example, financial and political support for moderate parties and labor organizations in Italy and France in the late 1940s and 1950s, and military aid for the anti-Soviet guerrillas in Afghanistan in the 1980s.

These operations had certain elements in common. Each involved interference in the internal affairs of another state. In each case efforts were made to conceal the involvement of the United States. Each was carried out without public congressional scrutiny or review. Yet the differences among the cases are more striking. They encompass diverse kinds of activities, in pursuit of disparate political objectives, undertaken covertly rather than overtly for a variety of reasons. This should make us hesitate to draw categorical conclusions like those that occur so often in discussions of the ethics of covert action (e.g., that it is always wrong).

It seems fairly clear that the issues of principle arising for controversial cases of covert action fall into three groups: Sometimes we argue about the *ends* of covert action, sometimes about the *means* used to pursue these ends, and sometimes about the constitutional *process* through which the operations in question were (or were not) authorized and overseen. Let us consider each in turn.

Ends

Covert action is interventionary in a broad sense: In almost every case, it aims at influencing the course of political life in the target state by inducing or preventing a change in government or policy. Interference typically risks several kinds of harm, reflected in the three most prominent general arguments against intervention: It offends the political sovereignty of the state being interfered in; it disrupts a people's common life; and it upsets the international order.

Some people think its interventionary character is enough to show why *all* covert action must be illegitimate. But this is too quick. All the prevailing views about ethics in international affairs recognize exceptions to the general prohibition of intervention, such as self-defense, counter-intervention, and intervention to prevent gross violations of human rights. Thus, we must confront the question of whether (and how) the exceptions might apply to covert action.

A CIA official suggested one answer when he described "covert actioneers" as "the 'do-gooders' of the clandestine business" because their aim is usually to lend help to "people and institutions legitimately in need of such assistance." Covert action, this official was claiming, has a paternalistic, other-regarding rationale: Its goal is to serve the interests of the residents of the state where it takes place.

Although few cases of covert action appear to have been motivated by this kind of rationale, we should not dismiss it altogether. It reflects a long tradition in American foreign policy of justifying intervention on the grounds that it is good for those whose societies are being intervened in. The Reagan Doctrine of support for "freedom fighters" is only the most recent formulation of this idea. So it is worth observing that paternalistic considerations could justify intervention, if at all, only if there were good reasons to believe its consequences really would be in the interests of the target population. This is no small matter. One needs to know enough about the culture and values of the target society to make informed judgments about its welfare, and enough about its politics and history to calculate the likely consequences of the kind of intervention contemplated. Any review of the history of intervention in U.S. foreign policy would quickly conclude that in few cases could the principal decision-makers honestly have claimed sufficient knowledge to make these judgments responsibly. *Covert* interference encompasses additional difficulties arising from the constraints of secrecy. For example, a special problem of operational control occurs when intermediaries are employed to carry out the interference—partly because their aims may differ from ours, and partly because the chain of command is more ambiguous and less reliable. This leads to greater uncertainty in predicting the costs of the operation and increased chances of unintended results.

The more common justification of covert intervention, of course, is that it advances the security interests of the nation. But the ambiguities of the idea of the *national interest* are well known, and the bare invocation of this idea, without more, can hardly justify any potentially costly venture. For one thing, it may refer to values of varying degrees of urgency or moral significance: Although both protecting a population against unprovoked attack and protecting access to raw materials or markets for goods could be said to be in the national interest, for example, they represent concerns of dramatically different levels of importance. In addition, the national interest may be invoked in response to threats of differing degrees of immediacy: Compare the imminent threat of a military invasion with the long-term threat that a nonaligned but left-leaning and strategically located regime might come to be a Soviet ally. From a moral point of view, these differences matter. Those who would justify a policy of covert intervention on the grounds that it could help avert threats to U.S. interests must explain what values would be advanced by the policy in question, how these are threatened under the status quo, and why these threats are important enough to justify the harms that interference would impose on its victims.

Advocates of covert action often point out its desirability as an instrument of foreign policy, in comparison to the alternative of regular military force, which does more damage and intrudes more deeply on the rights of other states and peoples. Covert action provides a "third way" between diplomatic pressure and overt economic or military aid, on the one hand, and direct military intervention, on the other. But the familiar tendency to rationalize adventuristic foreign policies by invoking vague and overblown conceptions of national interest suggests that the relatively less damaging character of covert action might be more a liability than an asset. For the low-risk, quick-fix aspect of covert action almost certainly encourages decision-makers to commit national power more widely than they would otherwise find it advisable to do. It also reduces the incentives to reach diplomatic solutions.

Means

Covert operations can employ a wide variety of means, each of which raises different ethical questions. These include the acceptability of techniques of noncoercive interference such as propaganda and corruption of the integrity of domestic political procedures, the justifi-ability of political assassinations, and the legitimacy of supporting forces that use indiscriminate military and paramilitary tactics in their efforts to destabilize a government.

I would like to concentrate on issues surrounding covert action as a form of manipulation. Covert action is often manipulative. The meaning of this, and of the evil connected with it, is not as obvious as it may seem, especially in the context of international relations.

On the level of individual relations, manipulation is a form of power that employs deception of those over whom power is exercised. It is a way of getting what you want despite the possible resistance of others. Manipulation occurs when you exercise power over other peo-ple, inducing them to behave according to your wishes, in a way intended to conceal from them that power has been exercised. For example, you might induce people to do one thing rather than another by providing them with skewed or incomplete information or by alter-ing their preferences in ways they are unlikely to detect (as in simili-nal advertising). The distinctive evil of manipulation derives from the fact that by attempting to hide the exercise of power, manipulation seeks to enlist a person's capacity for self-determination in the service of goals that are not, or not necessarily, the person's own. Because manipulation interferes with the normal process of selecting goals and deciding how to pursue them, it is an invasion of a person's autonomy. And because it operates invisibly, manipulation leaves a person pecu-liarly defenseless against this invasion.

A clear analogy exists at the international level. Consider, for exam-ple, the CIA's attempts to manipulate the Chilean elections of 1964 and 1970 by funneling funds to conservative forces in order to prevent vic-tories by leftist parties. These activities were not coercive in any strict sense; individuals were not forced to act against their will. Nor were constitutional procedures crudely set aside (as they were in the coup of 1973, for example). Rather, constitutional procedures were *used*, in the pejorative sense of that term. The United States acted in ways calcu-lated to cause the normal processes of social decision-making to pro-duce outcomes that might not otherwise have occurred. Because the U.S. role was kept secret, the Chilean people were defenseless against it; for example, in deciding how to vote, they were unable to compen-sate for the influence on their attitudes and beliefs of U.S. interference in their domestic political life. This is just as much an assault on the autonomy of those affected as is manipulation of individuals. Indeed, it is worse. The offense to individual autonomy is compounded at the social level by an offense to democracy, whose integrity depends on the capacity of its people to participate knowledgeably and rationally in political deliberation. This, of course, is precisely what manipulation subverts.

Constitutional Processes

Covert operations have to be kept secret to be effective, but this means they cannot be subjected to the usual processes of public consideration and review. Political scientist Gregory Treverton refers to this as "the paradox of secret operations in a democracy." On the one hand, Treverton is ready to agree that on some occasions covert action would be justifiable on grounds of national security. On the other, he does not see how covert action, even if justifiable on these grounds, can be reconciled with democratic principles.

The difficulty in this way of seeing things can be explained in two connected points. First, democracy is not some sort of mechanical device designed to harness individual political decisions to the popular will, so that any decision not approved by the people must be suspect. Democratic institutions are the means for ensuring the responsiveness of policy to the interests of the people and for deterring the unauthorized use of power by those who hold public office. We need not deny that democratic citizens could have good reasons for removing certain categories of decisions from popular control or even popular review. Indeed, a wide range of existing practices in such disparate areas as the administration of justice and macroeconomic policy suggest exactly this. These practices limit opportunities for public review of executive decisions, yet we do not usually regard them as contrary to democratic ideals.

But this does not mean (and this is the second point) that there is nothing more to be said about how the democratic idea constrains the role of secrecy in government. We need to tell a story connecting any provisions for secrecy with the underlying aims of democratic institutions, showing in each case why those aims are likely to be achieved more successfully with secrecy than without it. This story would also suggest the limits of secrecy—where to draw the line between decisions that may be made secretly and those that must be publicly acknowledged, and what procedural safeguards would be desirable to deter negligence and malfeasance among those officials who operate behind the shield of secrecy.

The real issue is not whether we make a logical or conceptual mistake in thinking covert action is compatible with democracy. The serious question is practical, not conceptual: It is whether ways exist to organize the planning and execution of covert operations so they serve rather than subvert the aims of democratic government.

The new covert-action regime instituted in the mid-1970s employs a form of limited accountability whereby the executive branch is required to inform certain members of Congress about the planning and execution of covert operations. The proponents of the new regime were moved by the hope it would help deter several kinds of abuse of executive authority. Chief among these was the danger that covert action would fail to be the servant of official policy. They also hoped to deter transgressions of domestic law and the Constitution, and to guard against violations of international law and human rights.

This new emphasis on accountability has ethical as well as political significance. It reflects a judgment about the conditions under which it could be reasonable for U.S. citizens to risk depriving themselves of information important to the conduct of democratic political life—in other words, about the practical conditions under which democracy and covert action can coexist.

The question before us today is whether the judgments reached almost two decades ago were sound. Events of the Ronald Reagan years suggest that the formula worked out in the mid-1970s was a step in the right direction, but that it contained loopholes enabling zealots in the CIA and the National Security Council to repeat the same kinds of abuses of authority the formula was devised to deter. Certainly efforts should be made to close these loopholes.

But as a matter of political ethics, our emphasis should be on a deeper question. This is whether any form of accountability is likely to be sufficient to bring the unauthorized use of executive power under control. If the answer to that question is no, then our democratic principles compel us to consider whether the capacity to conduct covert operations in peacetime should properly belong to the executive branch at all.

This article was adapted and condensed from "Covert Intervention As a Moral Problem," Ethics & International Affairs *3 (April 1, 1989).*

The Legacy of Nuremberg

David Luban

More than forty-five years ago, on November 20, 1945, the trial of the major war criminals of the Third Reich began in the ruined city of Nuremberg. It is a commonplace that the trial was a "historic" occasion, that it left a legacy for future generations. The men who conceived and conducted the trial understood it that way; they intended it to be epoch-making and viewed their own words and deeds (not, perhaps, without a touch of self-aggrandizement) through a reverse telescope from the eyes of a distant and more pacific age.

It is impossible for us to read accounts of the Nuremberg trial without realizing it signifies something much different to us than to those who conceived it. For us, Nuremberg is a judicial footnote to the Holocaust; it stands for the condemnation and punishment of genocide, and its central achievement lies in recognizing the category of *crimes against humanity*: "murder, extermination, enslavement, deportation, and other inhumane acts committed against any civilian population . . . or persecutions on political, racial or religious grounds . . . whether or not in violation of the domestic law of the country where perpetrated." For those who conceived the trial, on the other hand, its great accomplishment was to be the criminalization of aggressive war, inaugurating an age of world order. For this reason, its decisive legal achievement lay in recognizing the category of *crimes against peace*: "planning, preparation, initiation or waging of a war of aggression or a war in violation of international treaties, agreements or assurances. . . ."

This idea that Nuremberg was to be the Trial to End All War seems fantastic and naive forty-five years (and 150 wars) later. It is also a dangerous and mistaken idea that has done much to vitiate the real achievements of the trial, in particular the condemnation of crimes against humanity. The Nuremberg Charter incorporates an intellectual confusion, leaving us, as we shall see, with a legacy that is at best equivocal and at worst immoral.

Aggression and Sovereignty

At neither the Nuremberg nor the Tokyo trials was the crime of aggression defined. But in 1974 the United Nations offered the following definition: "Aggression is the use of armed force by a State against the sovereignty, territorial integrity or political independence of another State. . . ." Though it was not until 1974 that aggression was linked explicitly with the violation of sovereignty, this definition is clearly in the spirit of Nuremberg. But what, then, is sovereignty?

The concept was formulated in the early modern era, as the nation-state began to emerge in Europe. It signified that only one ultimate source of law exists in a state, namely the state's sovereign. From this follows the notorious doctrine of *act of state*, which exempts sovereigns from legal liability for their depredations against other states, on the theory that prosecution of the sovereign of one state by the court of another state amounts to one state's exercising jurisdiction over another.

Historically, the doctrine of sovereignty was formulated to secure the dominance of secular authority over the Church; the doctrine, however, had the additional consequence that so-called "natural law"— constraints on the content of law ascertainable by reason alone—had no place in the theory (since in practice the Church claimed the right to announce natural law—despite the fact that it was supposed to be a matter of reason and not revelation). Nothing constrained the sovereign: From the fact that the king was the sole lawmaker, it followed that he was the highest lawmaker as well. No domestic legal standards existed to which he himself could be held responsible, unless these were self-imposed. Conjoined with the act-of-state doctrine, this conclusion implies that sovereigns are liable under neither domestic nor international law, that "the king is above the law."

It was this doctrine that Article 7 of the Nuremberg Charter assaulted: "The official position of defendants, whether as Heads of State or responsible officials in Government departments, shall not be considered as freeing them from responsibility or mitigating punishment." By making even sovereigns legally liable for their deeds, Article 7 denies that the sovereign is the sole source of law in his state; it thus denies the doctrine of sovereignty itself.

Similarly with Article 8: "The fact that the defendant acted pursuant to order of his Government or of a superior shall not free him from responsibility. . . ." By criminalizing acts that are legal according to the positive law laid down by the sovereign, Article 8 thus denies that the sovereign is the sole source of law for his subjects.

And similarly, Article 6(c) outlaws crimes against humanity even when committed by a state against its own subjects and "whether or not in violation of the domestic law of the country where perpetrated." Article 6 (c), the most enduring moral achievement of Nuremberg, is irreconcilable on its face with the classical doctrine of sovereignty. Together with Articles 7 and 8, then, it perforates or even destroys the doctrine in the name of "humanity" and individual responsibility toward it.

This is an important achievement, and nothing to regret. As Robert Jackson, the chief prosecutor at Nuremberg, pointed out, the act-of-state and superior-orders doctrines taken together would imply that no one could be held responsible for the crimes the Tribunal was trying: The former would exempt those exercising sovereign authority, while the latter would exempt their subjects. Yet it would be a moral absurdity (and political impossibility) to punish nobody for Auschwitz. The plain fact of the matter is that the Third Reich was a criminal state in every moral sense the word "criminal" possesses, and the law had to reach those who carried out its crimes.

Two Problems with Sovereignty

It is an unhappy fact of human existence that we never forget how to commit a crime once we have been taught. The Third Reich may well be the first state whose criminality was virtually its defining feature; it will not be the last. In this regard, the framers of Nuremberg understood very well the importance of their endeavor. Since the Nazis had set dark precedent for criminal states, had invented new forms of evil-doing, had made the unthinkable real (after which it is only a matter of time until it becomes routine), it was necessary to restructure our moral imaginations in order to fortify ourselves for a world of criminal states. If this meant exploding time-honored propositions and concepts, then so be it.

The trouble was that the propositions and concepts reflected a political reality—the system of nation-states—no one was prepared to condemn. And so, just at the moment Articles 6(c), 7, and 8 of the Nuremberg Charter undermined the doctrine of sovereignty, Article 6(a) fortified it by making aggressive war—violation of sovereignty—a crime.

This proved in the event to be a moral problem even more than a conceptual one. If the law is to be anything humane, it must guide our moral imaginations; and since it is now imperative that our moral imaginations include the awareness of criminal states, the law must also include the awareness of criminal states. For this reason alone, the classical doctrine of sovereignty, which acknowledges the authority of criminal states, is no longer feasible. And so, Article 6(a)—which protects the sovereignty of all states, even criminal states, so long as they do not launch wars—should be seen as a mistake.

In any case, the doctrine of sovereignty bears little relevance to the modern world; it is an old-European concept, meant for nation-states—literally, states whose boundaries correspond with those of homogeneous linguistic and cultural communities. Outside of Atlantic Europe, and particularly in the Third World, we find at best limited correspondence between states and homogeneous communities. For this reason, "statist" politics implies perpetual ferment and instability, as contending ethnic or tribal groups vie with each other for control of the apparatus of sovereignty.

Article 6(a) is Eurocentric in another way as well. The European nation-states (and the United States) exercised economic and often political control over much of Asia, Africa, and Latin America, and at Nuremberg this state of affairs was assumed by all to be fitting and uncontroversial. (It is startling to our ears to hear Jackson refer to the acquisition of colonies as a "legitimate objective" for Germany.) By criminalizing any breaches of sovereignty, Article 6(a) criminalized anti-imperialist struggle as well. This was noted by Indian Judge R. M. Pal in his famous dissenting opinion in the Tokyo war-crimes trial: "I am not sure if it is possible to create 'peace' once for all, and if there can be status quo which is to be eternal. At any rate in the present state of international relations such a static idea of peace is absolutely untenable. Certainly dominated nations of the present day status quo cannot be made to submit to eternal domination only in the name of peace." Pal is not attacking a straw man, for in his opening address at Nuremberg, Jackson had stated: "Our position is that whatever grievances a nation may have, however objectionable it finds the status quo, aggressive warfare is an illegal means for settling those grievances or for altering those conditions."

Statism versus Human Rights

These theoretical confusions and practical misfortunes are, unhappily, an enduring legacy of Nuremberg. Articles 6(c), 7, and 8 are founding documents of the modern human rights movement, and of the form of politics that favors intervention on behalf of human rights, even when violations occur within the boundaries of sovereign states. Article 6(a), however, has been a major moral enemy of the human rights movement, inasmuch as attempts at sanctions or interventions against human rights offenders are inevitably denounced as violations of their sovereignty. It is the tension between statism and human rights that renders the legacy of Nuremberg equivocal; the human rights movement and human rights violators are vying for the contested legacy of Nuremberg.

Jackson saw this point all too clearly. To arguments that humanitarian intervention in a country's internal affairs was a traditional legal principle that would be contravened by Article 6(a), he countered that nonintervention was sacred to Americans, who had no intention of letting other countries interfere in our own policies of racial discrimination: "It has been a general principle of foreign policy of our Government from time immemorial that the internal affairs of another government are not ordinarily our business; that is to say, the way Germany treats its inhabitants, or any other country treats its inhabitants, is not our affair any more than it is the affair of some other government to interpose itself in our problems. . . . We have some regrettable circumstances at times in our own country in which minorities are unfairly treated." Jackson, in other words, argued for subvening Article 6(c) to Article 6(a) partly in order to enclose American human rights violations within a wall of state sovereignty. By contrast, the other horn of the Article 6 dilemma was seized by Thurgood Marshall and his colleagues in the NAACP in their brief in *Morgan* v. *Virginia*, a transportation desegregation case; they argued that Americans had not spilled their blood in a war against "the apostles of racism" abroad only to permit its flourishing at home.

Let me be clear: I am not claiming that Articles 6(a) and 6(c) are logically or legally contradictory. They can be reconciled simply by making an exception to the doctrine of sovereignty when crimes against humanity are at issue: One allows humanitarian intervention in a sovereign state's affairs, but only when the humanitarian issue has risen to the horrific level of crimes against humanity.

But I am asking about the *legacy* of Nuremberg. That means the potential of its principles for growth and development, for extension and precedent-setting, for adaptability to changed political circumstances, for underlying moral commitments that are not so much the logical implications of the principles as they are their "deep structure." Philosopher Ronald Dworkin speaks of precedents exerting a "gravitational force," and we must ask what the gravitational force is of reconciling Articles 6(a) and 6(c) in this fashion.

Article 6(a) tells us that we cannot intervene in the affairs of a sovereign state on behalf of human rights until—here Article 6(c) enters the picture—the violations rise to the level of horror of crimes against humanity. This means that in each case we must indulge in a grotesque and blood-curdling calculus of murder, torture, and enslavement to determine which clause of Article 6 controls. This is the price we pay for making Article 6 consistent.

If, on the other hand, we abandon the attempt to reconcile Articles 6(a) and (c), we must choose one of them. The choice of 6(c) is a fecund one: When the condemnation of crimes against humanity is allowed to develop as a principle of law and morality, it flowers into the politics of human rights. For the condemnation of "inhumane acts committed against any civilian population" and "persecutions on political, racial or religious grounds" need not be restricted to Holocaust-size events in its gravitational force. It extends to human rights violations in general.

By contrast, Article 6(a), as Justice Pal predicted, flowers into a deification of the status quo and allows the notion of state criminality to slip through its conceptual net. The choice between the two should not be a difficult one.

Terrorism

Claudia Mills

In Enniskillen, Ireland, a bomb explodes during a memorial service, fatally injuring eleven civilian mourners gathered to honor their dead. Explosives detonated in the crowded Rome and Vienna airports kill tourists heading home for the holidays. A cruise ship is held hostage in the Mediterranean, and an elderly, wheelchair-bound passenger slain. Ordinary people going about their ordinary business are subjected to violent assaults carried out not by any legal authority or warring army, but by secret groups motivated by some political grievance. This is terrorism.

Terrorism horrifies almost all of us, even, sometimes, its perpetrators: The IRA issued an apology after the Enniskillen bombing. International terrorism is "the cancer of the modern world," says one commentator, "a dynamic organism which attacks the healthy flesh of the surrounding society." The U.S. State Department calls terrorism "a criminal activity that no political cause can justify." President Ronald Reagan made the battle against terrorism a rhetorical cornerstone of his foreign policy.

Why does terrorism inspire such revulsion? Why do acts of terrorism horrify us more than other acts of political violence? Fewer than 200 Americans died in terrorist incidents abroad in all the years between 1973 and 1982; the Central Intelligence Agency (CIA) estimates that about 3,300 people worldwide were victims of terrorism between 1968 and 1980. These figures pale by comparison with the 200,000 reported killed on East Timor island by Indonesians between 1980 and 1984; the more than 30,000 killed in El Salvador between 1979 and 1982; the 20,000 murdered in Chile in the two years after General Augusto Pinochet's 1973 coup—not to mention the civilian casualties in the last dozen of this century's bloody wars. Yet terrorism grips our collective consciousness in a way far out of proportion to the numbers involved.

Philosopher Judith Lichtenberg suggests we react this way in part because the horror of terrorism is simply more telegenic: The dramatic nature of many terrorist incidents lends itself to intensive media coverage, which focuses our fear and outrage on one particular kind of violence. "A hijacking is ready-made news: it occurs *here* and *now*"; the seizing of American hostages is "a breaking story, an ongoing crisis providing the press with a continual flow of action, suspense, and new information."

It is also, Lichtenberg notes, only human nature to care more about violence when we can imagine ourselves in the place of its victims. Violence targeted at ordinary people makes ordinary people everywhere feel uneasy. When American tourists are gunned down on a holiday abroad, other Americans find themselves thinking, "That might have been me"—however minute the chance of such an occurrence. But while this facility in identifying with victims of terrorism helps to explain our greater preoccupation with this kind of violence, it provides no guidance, Lichtenberg argues, for how we should evaluate terrorism in *moral* terms.

What is distinctively wrong or evil about terrorism compared with other forms of political violence? How wrong or evil *is* terrorism? Is terrorism always beyond the moral pale, or can it ever be justified? What can and should be done to combat it?

Who Is Innocent?

The evil laid at the door of terrorism is that it harms or menaces innocent people to achieve its political ends. Those attempting to justify a given terrorist act (or to deny it deserves the morally loaded label of "terrorism") argue either that its victims are not innocent in some deeper sense or that the violence is nonetheless justified as the only means to a greater good.

Terrorist acts target civilians; do they target the *innocent*? Philosopher Robert K. Fullinwider points out that who is "innocent" is often precisely the question at issue between terrorist groups and their opponents. Terrorist acts are often directed against political leaders, government officials, civilian agents of occupying powers, or the police—who at least bear some responsibility for the policies that draw the terrorist's ire. Nor are guilt and innocence strictly legal matters. Where the law itself is corrupt or violates our moral standards, we can sympathize with the desire to "take the law into one's own hands," to redress injustices to which it is obdurately blind. The terrorist, in Fullinwider's view, sees himself as appealing to a "higher law," to morality itself.

In many cases, however, it is difficult to claim that terrorists' victims are connected in any clear way to the alleged crimes redressed by terrorist violence. What reasonable connection did Leon Klinghoffer, the passenger slain by the *Achille Lauro* hijackers, have to Palestinian grievances against Israel? His only "crime" was to be American and Jewish—an offense against neither law nor morality. According to Fullinwider, "If this is enough of a connection to make [someone a] fair target, then no one is innocent. The 'immunity of the innocent' is emptied as a moral notion." If terrorist violence of this sort is to be justified, some other strategy will be needed to do it.

"You Can't Make an Omelet without Breaking Eggs"

A second avenue for justification is to argue that violence against even the truly innocent is a regrettable but necessary means to achieve some greater good. At least some revolutionary groups are seeking to resist oppression and to promote justice; violence may seem to be their only viable option for advancing these goals in the face of the greater might—and hostility—of their oppressors. The claim here is, quite simply, that terrorism works and it is the only thing that works.

Does terrorism work? According to Walter Laqueur, author of *The Age of Terrorism*, terrorist violence has been strikingly ineffective at producing political change. Individual terrorist campaigns have tended in fact to produce "violent repression and a polarization which precluded political progress." Seen in historical perspective, Laqueur observes, "terrorism has been effective only in very specific circumstances. . . . In most cases, terrorism, in the longer run, made no political difference one way or another—in some, it caused the exact opposite of what the terrorists hoped and intended to achieve." Even if violence against the innocent were an effective tactic of political change, it is almost never the only option available for political transformation, not for a movement with the widespread popular support needed for political legitimacy. Laqueur's historical analysis of terrorism bears out the conclusion that "terrorism frequently occurs where there are other, non-violent political alternatives."

Nor is it clear that most terrorism, even if successful, would actually result in securing greater justice. Today's revolutionary movements, according to Laqueur, often aim at "domination, not liberation; this kind of terrorism is simply one form of nationalist or religious strife." Even where terrorists have been fighting dictatorships for greater political freedom and social justice, success might "well mean the replacement of one type of dictatorship by another, more effective or more charismatic, but more severe; the case of Iran provides a great deal of food for thought."

The Moral High Road

Finally, whatever the claimed efficacy of terrorism, one wants to say there are some means we just *don't use*. Civilized people have renounced some means as morally indecent, among them attacks against the truly innocent. Even in warfare, limits are drawn beyond which we will not go.

But in this century, as in all centuries before, even the most civilized states with the most robustly moral rhetoric have repeatedly crossed these uncrossable moral lines. Terrorism is hardly the only example of violence against the innocent for political ends. Attacks on the innocent, 'just war' theory notwithstanding, are a staple of modern-day warfare. The fire bombing of Dresden, Germany, and the London Blitz were deliberate attempts to raise the toll of civilian casualties, and 120,000 men, women, and children perished in Hiroshima and Nagasaki. These military decisions were defended as hastening the end of the Second World War and so reducing the ultimate costs in human suffering: A noble end was held to justify ignoble means. If Harry Truman could make such a claim, why not Yasser Arafat?

Philosopher C. A. J. Coady argues that the moral justifiability of terrorist violence should be assessed in the same way as the moral justifiability of violence committed by organized states. But in fact it is not. Coady suggests that "many condemnations of terrorism are subject to the charge of inconsistency, if not hypocrisy, because they insist on applying one kind of morality to the state's use of violence in war . . . and another kind altogether to the use of violence by . . . the revolutionary. For one's own state a utilitarian standard is adopted which morally legitimates the intentional killing of non-combatants so that such acts of state terrorism as the bombing of Dresden are deemed to be morally sanctioned by the good ends they supposedly serve. The same people, however, make the move to higher ground when considering the activities of the rebel or the revolutionary and judge his killing of non-combatants [as intrinsically wrong]." Coady resolves the inconsistency by objecting to the "technique of terrorism as immoral wherever or whenever it is used or proposed."

If this standard is adopted, state violence against the innocent may end up looking worse than terrorist violence. Certainly the figures cited earlier suggest that state violence is responsible for a vaster quantity of human misery. If terrorism contains some special evil, then, it cannot lie in the fact that it alone targets the innocent or wreaks a terrible toll in human misery. The special horror of terrorism cannot be simply that, as Coady quotes a modern-day jingle, "throwing a bomb is bad, dropping a bomb is good."

The Distinctive Wrong of Terrorism

What, then, makes terrorism special? Does our present preoccupation with it have any rational grounding? Certainly the preoccupation with terrorism is intensified by the special frustrations in trying to deal with it. Recent administrations have been consumed with the practical problems of terrorism: Desperation to obtain the release of American hostages led to the humiliating recourse of an arms deal with the Ayatollah Khomeini. There seems to be no straightforward way to avenge terrorism without endangering still more innocent bystanders—and without making ourselves into terrorists in the process, since terrorism typically offers no clear target for retaliation and we do not want to be guilty ourselves of indiscriminate violence.

This last may contain the key to what is not only the distinctive frustration but also a distinctive evil of terrorism. It is this: Terrorism preys on the special vulnerability of those who try to live by a moral code that invests vast moral significance in ordinary, individual persons. First, the terrorist counts on the fact that an adversary will indeed be devastated by the death or kidnapping of even a single citizen and will be willing to jeopardize any number of foreign-policy concerns to return one captured journalist to his or her family. And, second, the terrorist gambles that the same moral code will tie an adversary's hands in responding to terrorist provocation.

We ourselves may violate our own moral code, may stand guilty of war crimes or other monstrous moral wrongs, but insofar as we try to live up to a moral vision that places value on every individual person, terrorism can be said in effect to hold us hostage just to what is best in us. It achieves its results by exploiting our most deeply held moral convictions. It differs in this respect from the violence states perpetrate in warfare—warfare is carried on by a sheer exercise of raw power, intended to compel the adversary's surrender by brute force alone. A warring army aims to leave the adversary no choice but to surrender, by destroying any power to resist. Terrorist violence needs no nuclear bombs, but only crudely made car bombs, for its most potent weapon is not its military might, but its adversary's moral sensibilities, moral conscience, and moral code.

Responding to Terrorism

How can we respond to terrorism? One commonly proposed first step is a simple one: Insofar as terrorism capitalizes on the media coverage it attracts, we can take steps to deny it any publicity. John O'Sullivan, deputy editor of the London *Times*, argues that by their front-page coverage of terrorism the media "help the terrorist spread an atmosphere of fear and anxiety in society, they provide him with an opportunity to argue his case to the wider public, and they bestow an undeserved legitimacy on him." But Lichtenberg counters that, if anything, media coverage "promotes not terrorism but Rambo-like responses to it." First, "by emphasizing terrorist incidents . . . to the neglect of other political violence, it exaggerates the significance of terrorism and promotes the view that it constitutes the greatest threat to world peace, civilization, and the rule of law. In addition, the style of most media coverage—long on drama and slogans (America Held Hostage: Day 412), short on analysis and explanation—encourages the view that terrorists are irrational psychopaths to whom the only appropriate response is force." And as long as hostage dramas sell newspapers and boost ratings, the media in a free society are not likely to limit coverage of them.

The natural response when struck with terrorism, of course, is to strike back, as the United States has tried to do overtly in the raid on Libya and covertly in various CIA maneuvers and machinations. As we have seen, attempted retaliation can be morally problematic. Political theorist Michael Walzer reminds us that "counter-terrorism can't be excused just because it is reactive," for "every new actor . . . claims to be reacting to someone else, standing in a circle and just passing the evil along." Repression and retaliation, Walzer cautions, "must not repeat the wrongs of terrorism, which is to say that they must be aimed systematically at the terrorists themselves, never at the people for whom the terrorists claim to be acting. . . . The refusal to make ordinary people into targets, whatever their nationality or even their politics: this is the only way to say no to terrorism." Lichtenberg agrees that "our claim to moral superiority lies in our refusal to adopt the tactics of terrorism. The outrage we reserve for it is mere hypocrisy if in our zeal to destroy it we become near enough to terrorists ourselves."

Benjamin Netanyahu, permanent representative of Israel to the United Nations, insists that a policy of restraint would leave the West at the mercy of terrorism: "In practical terms, an inflexible rule against risking civilian casualties would make any military action virtually impossible. . . . Responsible governments seek to minimize civilian casualties. But they do not grant immunity to an aggressor simply because their response might endanger civilians. . . . An absolute prohibition on civilian casualties affords the terrorist an invincible shield."

The risks—moral and otherwise—that the United States should be willing to run in responding to terrorism depend greatly on what exactly is placed at risk by terrorism. Here Laqueur argues that the threat posed by terrorism seems to be exaggerated. He rejects the metaphor of terrorism as "the cancer of the modern world," pointing out that it is neither fatal to society ("there has not been so far a single case of a society dragged down to destruction as a result of terrorism") nor spreading (the number of terrorist bombings has remained fairly constant over the last twenty years). If this is so, we should perhaps err on the side of protecting innocent human life, wary of eroding the moral difference between perpetrating terrorism and responding to it.

Another approach is to attempt to respond not to terrorism itself, but to its underlying causes—in Walzer's words, "to address directly, ourselves, the oppression the terrorists claim to oppose." Laqueur rejects the view, however, that terrorism and oppression are tightly correlated or that "the only known means of reducing the likelihood of terrorism is a reduction of the grievances, stresses and frustrations underlying it." Even if a reduction of grievances would quench terrorist ardor, often the grievances simply cannot be eliminated. Where the demands of national and religious groups are mutually exclusive, for example, "acceding to the demands of one group may mean injustice to another."

Some would even argue that attempts to prevent terrorism by reducing the oppression that animates it are not only unlikely to be successful but in fact aid and abet the terrorist. "There is an argument," Walzer notes, "that we should refuse to acknowledge any link at all between terrorism and oppression—as if any defense of oppressed men and women, once a terrorist campaign has been launched . . . would give terrorism the appearance of effectiveness, and so increase the likelihood of terrorist campaigns in the future." But, in Walzer's view, this kind of argument just goes the terrorist one better at his own game: "First oppression is made [by the terrorist] into an excuse for terrorism, and then terrorism is made [by the anti-terrorist] into an excuse for oppression." We cannot let the terrorist intimidate us from acting justly.

The greatest danger terrorism poses for the United States may lie in a double-edged temptation: On the one hand, to overreact, to respond in kind, with equally indiscriminate violence; on the other, to become so jaded by repeated terrorist incidents that threats to innocent human life no longer seem worth resisting. In both cases we violate our moral convictions and compromise our moral vision. In both we make ourselves more like the terrorist.

The sources quoted in this article are Judith Lichtenberg, "Beneath the Rhetoric of Terrorism," manuscript, n.p., n.d.; Robert K. Fullinwider, "Understanding Terrorism," in Problems of International Justice: Philosophical Essays, *ed. Steven Luper-Foy (Boulder, Colo.: Westview Press, 1988); Walter Laqueur,* The Age of Terrorism *(Boston: Little, Brown, 1987); C. A. J. Coady, "The Morality of Terrorism,"* Philosophy 60 *(1985); John O'Sullivan, "Deny Them Publicity," in* Terrorism: How the West Can Win, *ed. Benjamin Netanyahu (New York: Farrar Straus Giroux, 1986); Michael Walzer, "Terrorism: A Critique of Excuses," in Luper-Foy,* Problems of International Justice; *Benjamin Netanyahu, "Terrorism: How the West Can Win," in Netanyahu,* Terrorism: How the West Can Win.

FOR FURTHER READING

Beitz, Charles. *Political Theory and International Relations.* Princeton, N.J.: Princeton University Press, 1979.

Beitz, Charles, et al., eds. *International Ethics.* Princeton, N.J.: Princeton University Press, 1985. See especially the debate between Michael Walzer and David Luban.

Brown, Peter G., and Henry Shue. *Boundaries: National Autonomy and Its Limits.* Maryland Studies in Public Philosophy. Totowa, N.J.: Rowman and Allanheld, 1983.

Brown, Peter G., and Henry Shue. *Food Policy: The Responsibility of the United States in the Life and Death Choices.* New York: The Free Press, 1977.

Hoffman, Stanley. *Duties Beyond Borders: On the Limits and Possibilities of Ethical International Politics.* Syracuse, N.Y.: Syracuse University Press, 1981.

Luper-Foy, Steven. *Problems of International Justice: Philosophical Essays.* Boulder, Colo.: Westview Press, 1988. See especially the essays on terrorism by Robert Fullinwider and Michael Walzer.

Shue, Henry. *Basic Rights: Subsistence, Affluence, and U.S. Foreign Policy.* Princeton, N.J.: Princeton University Press, 1980.

8

NUCLEAR
DETERRENCE

The Cold War may be ending, but the legacy of its nuclear arms race will long be with us, as are some tens of thousands of nuclear warheads, as well. This chapter considers some of the moral issues arising out of the policy of nuclear deterrence, either against the Soviet Union or against some new enemy as yet unknown.

"Not with a Bang: The Moral Perplexities of Nuclear Deterrence" surveys some of the classic issues that define the nuclear deterrence debate: the choice between so-called countervalue and counterforce strategies (the one targeting weapons against cities and civilian populations, the other restricting the targets to military installations and missile sites); the likelihood that deterrence of either kind will indeed achieve its objective; the moral legitimacy of declaring an intention to kill millions of innocent civilians, albeit an intention one fervently hopes never to have to carry out; and, finally, the alternatives to be faced should deterrence fail.

In "Does Nuclear Deterrence Work?" Steven Lee approaches his question by looking at the conditions necessary for deterrent threats in general to be effective. If we examine how these conditions are satisfied in a paradigmatic case of effective deterrence, such as legal deterrence, this can help us understand how the comparison between conventional military deterrence and nuclear deterrence should be made.

David Lewis, in "Buy Like a MADman, Use Like a NUT," focuses on the choice between two different nuclear strategies: MAD (Mutual Assured Destruction—the policy of targeting and threatening cities, that is, of making a nuclear threat so terrible that the other side will take it seriously and so be deterred from its own nuclear strike) and NUTS (Nuclear Use Theorists—the policy of developing and procuring nuclear weapons capable of actually fighting a nuclear war, that is, of making a nuclear threat so credible that the other side believes it and so, again, is deterred from striking first). Lewis argues that, rather than accepting the choice between these two "rival package deals," we should select certain elements of each, buying the relatively few and cheap weapons required for MAD, but, if deterrence should fail, using our weapons in counterforce rather than countervalue warfare, like a NUT.

It has been suggested, by Ronald Reagan among others, that nuclear deterrence is morally inferior as a military posture to some form of nuclear defense. Reagan's Strategic Defense Initiative (popularly known as Star Wars) thus proposed developing technology to destroy enemy missles mid-flight. "Wouldn't it be better," Reagan asked, "to save lives than to avenge them?" In "Are Nuclear Defenses Morally Superior?" Henry Shue argues that enthusiasm for the moral superiority of nuclear defenses is, however, unwarranted: "Defensive weapons are not inherently more moral than offensive weapons—it is purposes, not weapons, that count."

The final article in this chapter, "Banning the Bomb: A Few Decades Too Late," reviews a number of approaches toward moving away from present levels of nuclear deterrence, including the Strategic Defense Initiative, deep reductions in nuclear arsenals, unilateral disarmament, and attempts at global cooperation—such as, of course, the stunning changes in East-West relations that have taken place since this article was written and that continue to astonish us still.

Not with a Bang
The Moral Perplexities of Nuclear Deterrence

Claudia Mills

In this century, poets have wondered whether the world will end in fire or ice, in a bang or a whimper. But in the almost five decades since the first atomic bomb was detonated over Hiroshima, eschatological questions have no longer seemed the poet's special province. Fears of global nuclear holocaust have occupied millions of ordinary human beings who, though more or less resigned to living with the bomb, remain determined not to die by it.

No goal could be more widely shared than the goal of having human life on earth continue and flourish, of not destroying human life or—perhaps even worse—altering it beyond recognition. Do the thousands of nuclear warheads the superpowers currently point at each other place human life as we know it in peril? It is a commonplace to observe that each side possesses ample nuclear capability to destroy the other side many times over. Those who build and deploy these massive arsenals maintain, however, that unlike all previous weapons known to man, nuclear weapons, precisely because of their terrifying destructive potential, exist not to *be used*, but to *deter* their ever being used. They serve the ends of peace, not of war, by making nuclear war too terrible to contemplate.

Philosopher George Sher of the University of Vermont finds these claims about the deterrent role of nuclear weapons radically perplexing: "Any policy which is seriously thought necessary to maintain peace, yet which may end by extinguishing all human life, must raise moral perplexities on an unprecedented scale." Certainly our current deterrence policies raise a battery of urgent moral questions. Does deterrence work? Which policies work better, deter more surely? If policies of deterrence work, do we need to know anything else to assess their moral acceptability? What other human concerns could possibly weigh in the balance against the need to avert nuclear war? And what if deterrence fails?

Counterforce and Countervalue

Two dominant positions have defined themselves in the nuclear strategy debate among those who can bring themselves to deploy nuclear weapons at all: One camp would target the warheads against cities and civilian populations; the other would restrict the targets to military installations and missile sites, with the primary aim of disarming, rather than decimating, the other side.

The latter, *counterforce* strategy embodies the long-standing military tradition that, in the words of University of Maryland political scientist George Quester, "To attack the enemy of the same cut of uniform is fair game. To bomb civilians is not. . . . The most honorable note of military training anywhere is that the only legitimate target will be people in uniform on the other side." Civilian immunity is a cornerstone of "just war" theory, which condemns waging war against the "innocent."

In the nuclear age, however, *countervalue* strategy has come into its own. In the early years of nuclear weapons design, indeed, technology was insufficiently developed to permit aiming at specific military installations. Accuracy extended only to targeting enemy cities, raising the specter of the indiscriminate slaughter of civilians. Deterrence theorists have turned this very crudeness of nuclear weapons to advantage in justifying their existence, however. Unsuited for waging and winning a war, these new and terrible weapons were suited instead for ensuring that such a war would never be fought. Counterforce strategy, these theorists claim, however humane it might sound, is actually far more dangerous, for it destabilizes the fragile peace that countervalue strategy can preserve.

Quester explains: "When either side has the ability to disarm the other's military, it will be tempted to do so, lest it lose this ability later on, lest the other side attain it afterward. . . . Victory may simply go to whoever strikes first, with a result that each side will race to strike in crisis, shooting first and asking questions later, producing a war which neither side may have wanted." Strategists must consider not only how to wage war fairly and effectively, but how not to let the war begin in the first place. It may not matter if counterforce strategy makes war somewhat less deadly if it also makes war more likely.

If each side pursues a counterforce strategy, targeting its missiles against civilian population centers instead of missile sites, then neither side has any incentive to strike first. Neither is led to the brink of "use them or lose them" trigger-happiness, for each side's arsenal will survive the other side's attack. But their cities, and their vital life as a nation, will not survive. If A destroys B's cities, B's weapons will be launched in retaliatory destruction against A's cities as well. Countervalue strategy raises the stakes of war by ensuring that everyone, including any side that gambles on starting a war, will lose utterly. This approach of Mutual Assured Destruction (MAD) is argued to be a powerful peacekeeper.

Strategies like MAD escalate the magnitude of the possible horror but seek above all to deter it. In the traditional counterforce strategy, the horror is less horrible, but considerably more likely to befall. Since the consequences of nuclear war in either case will be horrible enough, and only dubiously contained, it may be most important that the war not begin. As Sher notes, "The consequences of nuclear war will count against deterrence only if that policy runs an appreciable risk of failure. . . . If there is no appreciable risk of failure, then the consequences of failure become irrelevant." In the final analysis, it seems, what counts is whether deterrence *works*.

Does Deterrence Work?

What does it mean for deterrence to work? McGeorge Bundy, adviser on major elements of U.S. foreign policy over the past twenty-five years, remarks that in one sense our deterrent policies have obviously worked: No nuclear war has taken place. In the same sense, he reminds us, the deterrent policies of Finland, Austria, Canada, and Mexico have worked as well. These nations possess no nuclear weapons. But they have a concept of deterrence, "a view of what is necessary to prevent the use of nuclear weapons against them." And these nations can equally well claim on behalf of their policies that "there has been no war against them, and no coercion that has prevented their citizens from living lives decisively better than those of the generation before them." Clearly, Bundy says, "the judgment that deterrence has worked is not a judgment that any particular form of deterrence was the best available—or even that it was necessary. . . . It is only an assumption, and one not open to proof, that the nuclear weapon [is] indispensable to [deterrence]."

These considerations imply that other policy elements may work to deter as much as the balance of terror does—or perhaps more. Bundy suggests that detente itself may be a "reinforcement to deterrence, in the sense that clear agreements can be more stable, more reliable, more costly to challenge, and more reassuring than tension caused by open disagreement."

Such considerations also imply that the vast economic costs of the MAD strategy are not unimportant in its assessment. When no one can empirically prove or disprove that a massive arsenal effectively safeguards peace, it is not clear how many additional trillions of dollars should be earmarked for the military. But Bundy, for one, thinks "prudent modernization" should suffice to maintain a credible deterrent, so the monetary costs of deterrence perhaps need not be as staggering as Pentagon estimates might suggest.

Mutual Assured Destruction carries with it moral as well as economic costs, however, and some have argued that these may be great enough to count decisively against MAD, *whether or not it works.* Some means may be flatly ruled out as morally unacceptable, even if they are necessary to achieve important ends. We ordinarily don't believe that "It works" gives a full answer to the question, "Is it morally acceptable?" Of course, most ends are not as vital as deterring nuclear war. What moral reasons tell against MAD, and how much weight should we give them?

Intentions, Innocence, and Immunity

The original objection to MAD was that targeting nuclear warheads against cities violates the principle of civilian immunity. To this it was replied that MAD is not a strategy for fighting a nuclear war, but for deterring a nuclear war, so the carnage that *could* result if a war *were* fought under this strategy need not count against it.

It is true, nonetheless, that the warheads are in fact pointed at civilian populations and that each nation has threatened to launch them if attacked. Our leaders even now declare their firm intention to launch such a retaliatory assault, knowing full well the resultant slaughter. Suppose we believe that it is always wrong to kill the innocent, and that the ordinary citizens of any country are by and large innocent of any acts of war. Is it any less wrong to *intend* to kill them than to commit the killing itself?

Gregory Kavka, philosopher at the University of California at Irvine, explains our usual reasoning for thinking it is not. "We regard the man who fully intends to perform a wrongful act and is prevented from doing so solely by external circumstances (e.g., a man whose murder plan is interrupted by the victim's heart attack) as being just as bad as the man who performs a like wrongful act." (Kavka notes that the principle also holds if I intend to kill my neighbor *if he insults me* and fail to kill him only because he happens to refrain from insult.) We tend to treat the intention to perform an act as the beginning of the act itself.

However, Kavka rejects the principle that if an act is wrong, intending to perform it is also wrong. The principle fails precisely when applied to deterrent intentions, to "intentions adopted solely to prevent the occurrence of the circumstances in which the intention would be acted upon." In the usual case, an agent forms an intention to do something because he or she desires to do that thing, and thus the moral evaluation of intention and act are fused. But in the case of deterrent intentions, the intention is formed independently of any desire to carry out the act intended and is indeed compatible with desiring *not* to carry it out. The intentions driving the MAD strategy, Kavka concludes, may be evaluated on their own merits.

Furthermore, Kavka casts doubt more broadly on the supposed immunity of innocent civilians. Generally we believe that "persons have moral immunity, and it is impermissible to deliberately impose significant harm or risk on them, unless they are themselves morally responsible for creating relevant harms or dangers." But the degree of moral responsibility necessary to annul this immunity may be construed more or less strictly in different situations. "Our beliefs about dangerous situations are complex enough," according to Kavka, "to take account of the fact that there are various kinds of connections an individual may have to a given danger, and that these may hold in various combinations and degrees. . . . When there is a significant present danger, and control of that danger *requires* loosening the conditions of liability, our inclination is to regard some loosenings as justified."

Thus, we feel more justified in stopping a knife-wielding madman by shooting him than in achieving the same result by shooting an uninvolved third party, although the madman is not strictly responsible for what he does. Or, Kavka suggests, compare deterring country Y from attacking by threatening retaliation against its cities, with deterring it by threatening retaliation against the cities of uninvolved nation Z. In the case of collective action by an organized group, individual contributions are typically indirect and insignificant, and to insist on a tight causal connection to establish responsibility "would be to let too many people (in some cases perhaps *everyone*) off the hook, and largely lose the ability to influence group acts by deterrence."

Finally, we may not want to accept the moral prohibition against killing the innocent in its most absolute form. Even those who believe that certain acts are wrong regardless of what good they may produce or what evil they may avert are reluctant to rule out *all* attention to consequences. If the fate of the world hangs in the balance, acts that would otherwise lie beyond the moral pale may be countenanced.

It seems, therefore, that this objection against Mutual Assured Destruction strategies of deterrence fails. If nuclear deterrence works to avert a great evil—and of course no one can know that it does— then these moral costs it involves do not seem weighty enough to tip the scales against it.

If Deterrence Fails

Suppose, however, that deterrence fails. Despite nation A's declared intention to retaliate against any nuclear attack launched by nation B, B pushes the button. Millions of A's citizens are killed; untold millions more are horribly maimed and burned. The threat of retaliation having accomplished nothing, should A retaliate nonetheless? *May* A retaliate? For retaliation could accomplish nothing more, it might seem, than sheer, pointless vengeance, butchery for butchery, with no human good to be gained.

The one thing we can know about what *would* happen if deterrence failed is that we can know nothing. Bundy writes: "No one can have or hope to have any clear idea of what would in fact happen 'if deterrence failed'—that is, if nuclear war began. This difficulty is not escaped by any theory, because no theory can predict with any confidence the behavior of any government, friend or foe, in such a situation." How would heads of states react in a situation of "unprecedented stress and danger, . . . in the midst of already appalling destruction"? Would credible communication among the superpowers still be possible? Which weapons would function with what efficiency? Which intentions would be read into what actions? "Would the impulse to stop the slaughter be stronger than the impulse to kill the killers, and would it be the same or opposite on the two sides? Who can tell?"

Philosopher David Lewis of Princeton University argues that in situations of such vast and overwhelming ignorance we can also know next to nothing about what we *should* do. In the early stages of a major nuclear war, no strategist could know what course of action could help to save his or her country—or if a country was left to save. Where no one can possibly know what retaliation could or could not accomplish, moral evaluation of the decision to retaliate is on extremely shaky ground.

Lewis points to the radical uncertainty under which generals and soldiers of all ranks would be groping toward a decision. "It might indeed be true, if deterrence failed, that our retaliation would accomplish no good purpose, would accomplish nothing but dreadful and off-target vengeance. It might also be false. What is preposterous . . . is to imagine that anyone could *know* that there was nothing left but vengeance. . . . I say that it might well be right to launch the counterattack: instrumentally rational and morally right, all things considered. As right, that is, as any choice could be in so desperate and tragic a predicament."

It might, of course, be wrong. Retaliation might do nothing more than to complete the devastation already begun, gratuitously incinerating additional millions and rendering huge portions of the earth unfit for human life—if the extensive genetic damage that would also be wreaked did not preclude the possibility of future generations' enjoying anything that could be called "human" life. And it *would* be wrong, by Lewis's account, for our strategists to *intend* to launch a counterattack massive beyond any military necessity, massive beyond any consideration of what could possibly be right.

Wrong and pointless. For Lewis believes that "no such intentions are necessary to provide deterrence. The intention to launch a counterattack only if, and only to the extent that, it is right provides deterrence galore. . . . The sort of counterattack that might serve a good purpose would be a dreadful retaliation as well."

We need not worry that anything less than the vastest devastation imaginable will not be sufficiently terrifying. In a world such as ours, with arsenals such as ours, we have no shortage of fear, just a shortage of hope.

The views of George Sher, George Quester, McGeorge Bundy, and David Lewis are taken from their essays in The Security Gamble: Deterrence Dilemmas in a Nuclear Age, *ed. Douglas MacLean, Maryland Studies in Public Philosophy (Totowa, N.J.: Rowman and Allanheld, 1984). Gregory Kavka's views are drawn from his essay in* The Security Gamble *and from his article, "Some Paradoxes of Deterrence," in* The Journal of Philosophy *75, no. 6 (June 1978).*

Does Nuclear Deterrence Work?

Steven Lee

Does nuclear deterrence work? This is the central question in any examination of the fundamentals of nuclear weapons policy. If nuclear deterrence works well, there is strong prudential reason, in terms of national self-interest, to retain it, and if it does not, there is strong prudential reason to abandon it. But this question is central to a moral appraisal of nuclear deterrence as well, in any moral view that takes the consequences of our actions and policies seriously.

The question of whether nuclear deterrence works well can be asked in at least two different ways. The broader question is about the *absolute* deterrent value of nuclear threats, that is, their effectiveness in comparison with a policy of no military threats at all; the narrower question is about the *marginal* deterrent value of nuclear threats, that is, their effectiveness in comparison with nonnuclear military threats. The latter question is the one most of us care about in asking whether nuclear deterrence works.

How should this question be answered? Most commonly, it is argued that nuclear deterrence must work well because there has been no war between the United States and the Soviet Union since 1945. But such an argument exhibits the same error made by the person who is sure the amulet she wears keeps elephants away because she has not seen any elephants since beginning to wear it. No effort is made to show any connection beyond mere concurrence between nuclear deterrence policy and the absence of war.

A comparison between nuclear deterrence and conventional military deterrence might better be made not empirically, but by a closer look at the nature of deterrence itself. After all, deterrence is a pervasive relation among persons and institutions at all levels of social groupings, from the family to the nation to the world order. If we try to analyze what conditions are necessary for deterrent threats in general to be effective, and then examine how these are satisfied in a paradigmatic case of effective deterrence, such as legal deterrence, this can help us understand how the comparison between general military deterrence and nuclear deterrence should be made.

Legal Deterrence

Effective deterrent threats satisfy two conditions. First, they create the belief in the minds of the parties threatened that should they fail to conform their behavior to the required standards, it is likely that the threatened harm will be imposed on them; that is to say, that the threatening party has the capability and the willingness to carry out the threats. Second, these beliefs result in the threatened parties conforming their behavior to the required standards.

How do legal deterrent threats satisfy these conditions? For legal deterrent threats, the general ability of the state to carry out its threats is not in doubt, given the state's effective monopoly on the use of force. But some room for doubt exists about the state's ability to impose the threatened harm for particular cases of nonconforming behavior, since it is often difficult to detect who is responsible for such behavior. Thus the grounds for the belief that the state is able to carry out its legal deterrent threats are not completely firm; particular potential violators may have some reason to doubt the state's ability to punish them.

What about the basis for the belief that the state is willing to carry out its legal threats? Mere declarations of an intention to carry out a threat are normally not a sufficient basis for a belief that the threat will be carried out. Rather, the basis for the belief that the state is willing to carry out legal threats is to be found in the state's past behavior of legal threat executions. To create the belief that it is willing to carry out legal threats, the state must have a history of having done so. It must be able to point to cases where those who were not deterred by the threat then suffered the consequences threatened. To put the point paradoxically, the general success of legal deterrence is dependent on its occasional failure. Legal deterrence does not merely tolerate failures, maintaining its overall success despite them, but it actually makes use of them, and even requires them, for its overall success.

Now, if the belief that the threatener is able and willing to carry out its threat is to lead the threatened parties to conform their behavior to the required standard, they must be assured that if they do so conform, the harm threatened for nonconformity will not be inflicted on them; otherwise they would have no incentive to conform in order to avoid this harm. Moreover, the harm threatened must be sufficiently severe in relation to the expected gain from nonconforming behavior: Nonconforming behavior must not pay. Our system of legal deterrence generally satisfies these conditions.

Finally, for a threat to work, the party threatened must know what behavior will avoid the infliction of the threatened harm, which means that the required standards of behavior, in addition to being public, must be sufficiently clear and precise. Legal systems make use of devices, in addition to careful legislative drafting, to minimize vagueness in the law, devices such as relying on precedent in judicial interpretation of laws. But vagueness in the standards, coupled with the fear of the threatened harm, may actually lead the threatened parties to restrict their behavior more than they would if the standards were clear and precise, to "err on the side of safety." Vagueness in the required standards of behavior may then enhance deterrence effectiveness, but it also may undercut it.

Military Deterrence

General military deterrence differs from legal deterrence in several important respects bearing on its effectiveness.

For military deterrence, the belief that the threatener has the general ability to carry out its threat comes less easily. Military deterrence, in most cases, is mutual: Each party is both the threatener and the threatened. As opposing states approach parity in military force levels, the ability of each to carry out its military threats against the other becomes more and more doubtful.

Military deterrence has important implications as well for the belief that the threatener is willing to carry out its threats. The history of particular nations executing their military threats is usually short and sometimes nonexistent. Engaging in military action, whether by challenging a threat or executing a threat, is usually very costly. In addition, any history of threat executions is likely to be ambiguous. The earlier threat executions may have been by different regimes, against different states with different military capabilities and different relations to the threatener, and in response to different sorts of challenges.

Since history is largely inadequate to provide a demonstration of a state's willingness to carry out its military threats, the alternative is to find a measure for attributing a presumption of willingness. In the absence of evidence to the contrary, it may be presumed that a state is willing to execute its threats if and only if it would be in its perceived self-interest to do so. The main reason for the execution of a military threat, and hence the main factor in assessing its rationality, is the military prospect for denying the opponent his objective in aggression, considered in conjunction with an appreciation of what is at stake for the state subject to the aggression.

The mutuality of military deterrence also undermines the assurance that the threatened party can avoid harm through conformity to the threatener's standards, since mutuality creates motivations for, and consequent fears of, preemption. The possibility of a preemptive attack means that neither side can be assured that conforming behavior on its part will make it immune from attack. But military deterrence is made more robust by the fact that if two states are at least close to parity in military capability, the threatened harm is certainly severe enough to outweigh whatever the aggressor might hope to gain. (States are notorious, however, for their lack of foresight about the cost of war.)

The threats and standards in military deterrence are, finally, more vague than in legal deterrence. The threatened party will be uncertain about what range of aggressive behavior on its part would lead to threat execution, because this depends, in the context of military deterrence, on a highly speculative assessment of what responses to its aggression the threatener would then perceive to be rational. While such uncertainty might lead the threatened party to be especially cautious, it may also weaken deterrence by fostering risk-taking behavior.

The purpose in comparing legal and military deterrence is not to show that military deterrence is not effective, but to show what factors are relevant to the assessment of its effectiveness. Military and legal deterrence are not alternatives to each other, since they operate in different realms, one at the domestic level and the other at the international level. To show that legal deterrence is more effective than military deterrence does not show that anything is more effective than military deterrence at the international level (short of the domestic law of a world government). Our purpose is simply to set the stage for drawing some conclusions about a specific form of military deterrence, namely, nuclear deterrence.

Nuclear Deterrence

How does nuclear deterrence fare in comparison with general military deterrence in terms of the factors just discussed?

Nuclear deterrence, like general military deterrence, is mutual, but as the label "mutual assured destruction" suggests, it is mutual in a stronger sense. In the nuclear situation, each side has the military ability to destroy the other side no matter who strikes first. Thus, it is a form of mutuality that should raise no doubts about the ability of the threatener to execute its threat, unlike the mutuality of other forms of military deterrence. The mutuality of nuclear deterrence thus should promote rather than undermine the effectiveness of deterrence. As a result, nuclear deterrence has the additional advantage of increasing assurances that the party threatened can avoid the threatened harm by conformity to the standards. Motivations for preemption should be eliminated under nuclear deterrence, because with each side able to destroy the other no matter what, nothing would be gained and much lost by striking first. (Doctrines of nuclear war fighting, however, bring this into question.)

Even more clearly for nuclear deterrence than for conventional military deterrence, the willingness of the threatener to execute its threats must be attributed presumptively; the history of nuclear deterrence provides no instances of threat executions. But such a presumption fails completely for nuclear deterrence. No reasons are sufficient to make rational the execution of a nuclear threat between the superpowers in the context of the nuclear situation. No interest can be of sufficient importance to outweigh the potential losses from military conflict when these losses carry a serious risk, including the destruction of the society.

The severity of the threatened harm is a distinctive feature of nuclear threats that would seem to have a strong impact on their effectiveness. Combined with the certain ability each side has to carry out its threat, the severity of the threat creates what has been called "the crystal ball effect." Any leader of a superpower contemplating aggression against the other can foresee clearly, as if in a crystal ball, the likely outcome of total ruin. This may, as well, influence whether the vagueness inherent in nuclear threats (as in other military threats) increases or decreases their deterrent effect. The crystal ball effect may lead to a decided tendency toward greater caution.

Our comparison shows that nuclear deterrence has both striking advantages and striking disadvantages when compared with general military deterrence. On the one hand, nuclear threats seem superior in deterrent value due to the distinctive character of the mutuality of nuclear threats and to the special restraining potential of the crystal ball effect. On the other hand, the deterrent value of nuclear threats seems to suffer considerably due to the failure of the presumption of willingness to execute nuclear threats. Focusing on the advantages would lead one to be very optimistic about the effectiveness of nuclear deterrence, while focusing on the disadvantages would lead one to extreme pessimism. Attempting an overall comparative evaluation taking into account both sets of factors, given their significance and the sharpness of the opposition between them, may well leave one in a great state of uncertainty.

An argument remains, however, that may show that nuclear threats do *not* have marginal deterrent value. Threats cannot have marginal deterrent value, however much they may appear to, unless they also have some absolute deterrent value. If some special feature of nuclear threats, distinct from other military threats, raises the possibility that they have *no* absolute deterrent value, then whatever marginal deterrent value they may seem to have would be illusory.

There is such a special feature of nuclear threats. The point is often made that nuclear deterrence can tolerate no failures, that is, no instances of nonconforming behavior (assuming such an instance would be or would lead to nuclear war). If there was an instance of nonconforming behavior, the likely result of destroying society would mean that the system of deterrence as a whole had failed. The system would have proved ineffective in an *absolute* sense, because, as one might put it, it would not have brought about fewer instances of nonconforming behavior than what is necessary to allow the social order to continue. (Likewise, a system of legal deterrence would have no absolute deterrent value if it did not succeed in avoiding complete social chaos.) For nuclear deterrence to have absolute deterrent value, we may say, the probability of its failing to deter (say, per year) must be so low that it is very unlikely a failure would occur over decades or even centuries. If nuclear deterrence cannot guarantee that it is very unlikely to fail over an extended number of years, it must be regarded as ineffective in an absolute sense. Unless nuclear deterrence can do a substantially better job at deterring aggression than history has shown conventional military deterrence has been able to do, then nuclear deterrence is *absolutely* ineffective, because conventional military deterrence can tolerate a much higher rate of failure without social breakdown (or destruction) than nuclear deterrence can.

If nuclear deterrence is to be considered substantially more effective over the long haul than conventional military deterrence, then it must have a substantial, not merely minimal, *marginal* deterrent value in comparison. But our argument does not support this; the advantages in effectiveness of nuclear deterrence over conventional military deterrence are matched by its disadvantages. As a result, we have reason to believe that nuclear deterrence has no absolute deterrent value and so no marginal deterrent value over conventional military deterrence. Having nuclear deterrence would then be worse than having no system of military deterrent threats at all.

This article is drawn from "The Logics of Deterrence," a chapter of Steven Lee's Morality, Prudence, and Nuclear Weapons *(New York: Cambridge University Press, forthcoming).*

Buy Like a MADman, Use Like a NUT

David Lewis

Author's Note: This article was written in 1986 and has not been revised since.

When theoreticians think about nuclear deterrence, often they focus on a nasty choice between two rival package deals. The two have gone by various names over the years, but let me take the paired epithets: MAD (Mutual Assured Destruction) versus NUTS (Nuclear Use Theorists). Each package is a bundle of policies: centrally, policies for the procurement of strategic nuclear forces and conditional intentions about how to use those forces in case of war.

In a debate between MAD and NUTS, each side may say that the other's policies involve a twofold risk: a grave moral risk of committing massacres and a grave prudential risk of inviting and undergoing massacres. If they say so, they are right. The contest between these two repugnant alternatives gives nuclear deterrence itself a bad name. How does the very idea of nuclear deterrence turn into the nasty choice between MAD and NUTS? Does it have to happen? Is there no way around it?

MAD: If You Can't Be Credible, Be Dreadful

To trace the reasoning that drives us MAD, start with a simple conception of nuclear deterrence. We deter the enemy from doing X by threatening that if he does, then we will punish him by doing Y. But the enemy might notice that if he does X, we will then have no good reason to do Y. What's more, he may be able to give us a reason not to: He may threaten that if we do Y, then he will punish us by doing Z. Of course we may threaten that if he does Z then we will . . . but he might doubt that as well. In short we have a credibility problem: Our deterrence is apt to fail because our threats are not believed.

How to resolve it? One way is to make the threatened retaliation very, very severe. Then even if the enemy thinks we would have excellent reason not to retaliate, still he would not dare to call our bluff. If he evaluates risks as he should, multiplying the magnitude of the harm by the probability, we can make up in the first factor for what is lacking in the second. We can threaten a vast nuclear massacre, on an altogether different scale from the ordinary horrors of war. Destruction on this dreadful scale needn't be credible to deter. Although it could serve no good purpose to fulfill the threat, the risk that we might do so in blind anger suffices.

The MADman thinks it obvious that deterrence requires a solution to the credibility problem, and obvious that the only solution is to find a threat so dreadful that it needn't be credible; and he expects the enemy not to overlook the obvious. Therefore he thinks that for the enemy, as for us, an assured capacity to destroy cities will be seen as the *sine qua non* of nuclear deterrence. Further, he thinks it would take no great effort for the enemy to counteract any steps we might take to protect our cities. Therefore he thinks such steps would be, at best, costly and futile. We buy the means to reduce the enemy's strategic forces by counterforce warfare; the enemy buys enough more missiles to assure himself that enough of them will survive. We buy expensive defenses, the enemy buys enough more missiles to assure himself that enough of them will get through. We spend money; he spends money. Afterward there are many more nuclear weapons in the world, and each of them is one more place where an accident could happen. In case of war, not only does the world get fallout and smoke from the destroyed cities, but also it gets fallout (and smoke and dust) from preliminary counterforce attacks and intercepted warheads. And still our cities are subject to vast and intolerable destruction. What have we gained?

The MADman boasts that his goals for deterrence are "finite." If each side can count on having enough surviving weapons to meet the standard of assured destruction, that is all that either side has reason to want. Neither side has an incentive to expand or improve his forces, for all that would happen is that the balance would be reestablished at increased cost, increased risk, and increased danger to the rest of the world.

Thus the MADman's policy for procurement of nuclear weapons is as moderate and benign as can be, short of renouncing nuclear deterrence altogether. But his policy for conduct of nuclear war is quite the opposite. What is the commander in chief supposed to do if deterrence fails? He is not supposed to do anything to protect the country entrusted to his care; he cannot, since it was thought futile to provide the means for limiting damage. Rather he is supposed to fulfill the threat to destroy cities—a vast massacre, serving no good purpose whatever. There is nothing else he can do. Thus MADness carries a grave moral risk. What is raised is the chance of the most wicked act that it is possible for anyone in our time to perform.

NUTS: The Credible Warning

To trace the reasoning that drives us NUTS, we start as before. The NUT agrees with MADman that it is essential to solve the credibility problem, but he favors a different solution. His plan is to find some sort of nuclear attack that would not only be a retaliation, but also would serve some vital purpose. Our threat would be credible because we would have, and we would be seen to have, a compelling reason to fulfill it. The retaliation we could have compelling reason to deliver is counterforce warfare. It is worthwhile to destroy the enemy's forces, especially his strategic nuclear weapons. This reduces the risk to ourselves and our allies if war continues.

Thus we solve the credibility problem, and thereby we make it possible to succeed in nuclear deterrence—so says the NUT. But note a consequence of his argument: It has to be ambitious counterforce. If we want a highly credible warning that we would resort to counterforce warfare, there has to be little doubt that we expect its gains to be worth its risks.

But the drawbacks of an excellent counterforce capacity are these. First, and worst, an excellent counterforce capacity demands preemption. If our excellent counterforce capacity has been attacked, it may still be some sort of counterforce capacity, but it will no longer be excellent. The highly credible warning is, alas, not a warning of retaliation, but of preemption. Further, it gives the enemy his own incentive to preempt. His forces are under the gun: Use them or lose them. Whatever use he may have in mind had better be done before it is too late.

This pressure to preempt is probably the gravest risk that the NUT embraces in his quest for credibility. But it is not the only one. Besides short-term instability in times of crisis, there is a second, long-term instability. The MADman could boast that his goals for deterrence are finite. Not so for the NUT. If we need enough capacity for counterforce warfare that we can credibly warn of our strong incentive to undertake it, then what we need is an increasing function of what the enemy has. In fact, we need superiority. For reasons the MADman has already given, a risk of arms racing is indeed a grave risk, both moral and prudential.

The third grave risk, this one primarily a moral risk, concerns the collateral damage from ambitious counterforce warfare. Given the proximity of missile fields to Moscow and Leningrad, it makes little difference whether we target the population of Moscow per se, and so the NUT runs a grave moral risk of committing vast massacres, just as the MADman does. Not an equally grave risk: The MADman's attack is useless, whereas the NUT's is meant to destroy weapons that menace us. Further, the NUT's attack kills many fewer people. Too many people live downwind from the enemy's missiles, but not as many as live in the enemy's cities. Yet though the numbers that measure the NUT's moral risk are much better than those that measure the MADman's, even the better numbers are far from good.

The MADman proposes to run grave moral and prudential risks so that a none-too-credible threat can be made very dreadful. The NUT proposes instead to run grave risks so that a somewhat less dreadful threat can be made very credible. His risks are different—most importantly, lesser massacres but more chance of inadvertent war—but no less grave overall.

Existential Deterrence

But what else can we do? How could the enemy be very powerfully deterred by a none-too-credible threat of a none-too-dreadful outcome?

This is how. Compare two ways a burglar might be deterred from trying his luck at the house of a man who keeps a tiger. The burglar might think: "I could do *this*, and then the tiger would do *that*, and then I could do *so-and-so*, and then the tiger would do *such-and such*, and then. . . ." If all such plans turn out too low in their expected payoff, then he will be deterred. But if he is a somewhat sensible burglar, his thoughts will take a different turn. "*You don't tangle with tigers.* Especially when you've never tried it before. Not even if someone (someone you don't trust) claims that these tigers have somehow been tamed. Not even if you carry what the salesman claimed was a surefire tiger stopper. You just never know what might happen."

The hypothesis of existential deterrence is that it is through thoughts like these that our nuclear arsenal deters our somewhat sensible enemy. Existentialism says that the credibility problem more or less solves itself. Given an enemy who, like ourselves, is risk averse, pessimistic, skeptical, conservative, deterrence is easy. To deter such an enemy, it is our military capacities that matter, not our intentions or incentives or declarations. If we have the weapons, the worst case is that somehow—and never mind why—we use them in whatever way he likes least. Of course he is not at all sure that the worst case will come about. But he mistrusts arguments to the contrary, being skeptical; and he magnifies the probabilities of the worst case, being pessimistic; and he weighs it in deliberation out of proportion to the probability he gives it, being averse to risk. In short: He will be deterred by the *existence* of weapons that are *capable* of inflicting great destruction. And we are the same way.

If existentialism is true, then the package deals of MAD and NUTS fall apart. We can borrow ideas from the MADman and the NUT and have the best of both. But we can leave behind the parts of their reasoning that require us to run grave risks in order to solve the credibility problem.

Buy Like a MADman, Use Like a NUT

The MADman's policy for procurement of weapons was as moderate and benign as can be. The forces he requires are comparatively small and cheap. He creates no temptation to preempt. His standards of adequacy are finite, in the sense that both sides at once can meet them. We could be well content—if it were not for his abominable policy about what to do in case of war. But if existentialism is true, we can buy like a MADman if we like, but that implies nothing about what we ought to do in case of war, or what we ought to intend beforehand. We needn't strive to give some credibility to our dreadful threat to destroy the enemy's cities. We needn't threaten it at all. We have weapons and war plans that give us the assured capacity to do it, and their very existence is deterrent enough.

So far, so good; but a big question remains. What if we buy the MADman's finite deterrent, but it lets us down? What if deterrence fails after all, and in a big way? In that case, I say, we ought to use like a NUT. We ought to engage in counterforce warfare with what remains of our forces, hoping thereby to limit further damage to us and to our allies. We should not retaliate by destroying cities; on the contrary, we should compromise the efficacy of our attacks so as to reduce collateral death and destruction. We should proceed as if we valued the lives of the enemy's civilians and soldiers—simply because we *should* value those lives—but less than we value the lives of those on whose behalf we are fighting.

If we use like a NUT, but with nothing more than what remains of a MADman's forces, then our aims in counterforce warfare cannot be too ambitious. We cannot hope to reduce the enemy's remaining forces to the point where he no longer has the capacity to do dreadful damage to whatever remains of our population and our resources for recovery. But the numbers count; they are not infinite, and not incomparable. If tens of millions are already dead, doubtless that is quite enough to exhaust our stock of adjectives and saturate our capacity to feel horror.

But that is no reason why it is not worthwhile to save the lives of tens of millions more.

Limitation of further damage is worthwhile. Counterforce warfare, even of a modest sort, is a way to limit further damage. Therefore using our remaining nuclear weapons for counterforce warfare is the right thing to do. It is, of course, a better thing to do than destroying the enemy's cities. That alternative is easy to beat. But also, I say, it is a better choice than doing nothing, and waiting to see what sort of follow-on attack we suffer from the enemy's remaining forces.

It may be objected that it seems senseless to build forces designed for one mission when all the while we intend to use them only for another. If we buy like a MADman, we buy a force that is just right for retaliating against cities; but if the time comes to use like a NUT, we will wish the forces had been made more suitable for their only truly intended use: modest, second-strike counterforce warfare with avoidance of collateral damage.

Now it is the NUT's turn to have his package deal broken up. His policy about what to do in case of war—counterforce warfare meant to limit damage—is comparatively moderate and benign, at any rate, compared to the MADman's. We could be well content—if it were not for his dangerous policy for procurement of weapons. Because he wants damage limitation not only for its own sake but for the sake of credibility, he requires weapons capable of meeting ambitious goals. Then the very same strength that supports the credible warning makes dangerous incentives to preemption in the short term and arms racing in the long term. Our solution is to buy suitable weapons, but limit their numbers.

Even a MADman's finite deterrent gives some significant capacity for counterforce. But all agree that the MADman's forces create little temptation to preemption or arms racing. They are not yet above the danger line. Then let them set a benchmark: Let us have forces suited for counterforce warfare, but let us have only enough of them to match the counterforce capacity of the MADman's finite deterrent. In that case, they should be no more destabilizing.

For finite counterforce, whatever enhances second-strike capacity without enhancing first-strike capacity is all to the good. Excellent post-attack command and control, for example, would be extremely advantageous. But it would not increase first-strike counterforce capacity in the least—because peacetime command and control is already excellent. Likewise, any improvement that holds capacity fixed while reducing collateral death and destruction is all to the good. If we aim our warheads more accurately and reduce their explosive yield (a trend that is already well under way), we can hold capacity fixed while we reduce the fallout, both local and global. And improved accuracy can mean that we need fewer warheads altogether.

If we trade numbers for accuracy, this reduces our capacity to destroy cities. Of course we do not have reason to want to destroy cities, but we do want the enemy to be deterred by the thought that somehow we might anyway. If the capacity is what deters, dare we reduce the capacity? I suggest that we can reduce it a lot without making existential deterrence any less robust. Any second-strike force that could accomplish something worthwhile in counterforce warfare, even with lower yields than we use today, would *a fortiori* be capable of enormous destruction.

Conclusion

As theoreticians, we want an understanding of nuclear deterrence that is neither MAD nor NUTS. We don't want to be committed to wickedness, and we don't want to fuss over credibility. We don't want deterrence through damage limitation—we want damage limitation for its own sake, and deterrence can look after itself. We don't want to think that damage limitation is worthless unless it is wonderful. We don't want to put adjectives in place of numbers, shirking the responsibility to save tens of millions of lives just because the outcome is dreadful either way.

Are Nuclear Defenses Morally Superior?

Henry Shue

When President Reagan launched his Strategic Defense Initiative (SDI) in 1983, he asked the simple rhetorical question: "Wouldn't it be better to save lives than avenge them?" SDI, which proposes to destroy Soviet missiles in flight, packs a powerful *moral* appeal, compared to our traditional policies of deterrence through the threat of assured destruction. For what is more moral than self-defense, less moral than massive retaliation against civilians? I want to argue, however, that enthusiasm for the moral superiority of nuclear defenses is unwarranted. But first I want to take note of three more obviously flawed arguments that have been offered of late on their behalf.

Three Bad Arguments

The first bad argument proceeds by equating the right to bear arms with the right to wear armor. Lewis Lehrman, chair of Citizens for America, includes in his moral case for SDI the argument that since the American president takes an oath to "preserve, protect, and defend" and individual Americans have a "natural right of self-defense," the pursuit of the Strategic Defense Initiative "would satisfy both the requirements of our Constitution and our consciences." This is merely semantic conjuring, which confuses means with ends. The right to self-defense is the right to take measures toward the end of defending yourself. It in no way follows that defensive measures are the only or the most appropriate means to the end of self-defense. If the right to self-defense had meant the right to adopt strictly defensive measures, we would probably not have the National Rifle Association but the National Bulletproof Vest Association. Obviously, an offensive weapon can be used for defensive purposes, and many of the technologies being developed under SDI can be used in attacking satellites. The real debate, then, is about the relation of means to ends: What purposes is SDI technology intended to serve and what purposes would it in fact serve?

The second bad argument takes the form of a rhetorical question: If SDI is such a bad idea, how come the Soviets are so much against it? There are quite a few difficulties with the general rule of always doing the opposite of what the Soviets say they want. One is that the Soviets are well aware of knee-jerk anti-Soviet tendencies and may try to use them. Some Reagan administration officials defended the current U.S. offensive buildup partly as a good way to cause the Soviets to spend their economy into the ground while trying to keep ahead of us in offensive systems. Maybe some clever Soviets are hoping we will spend our economy into the ground on defensive systems (plus offensive systems). In any case, we should probably think for ourselves. As President Dwight Eisenhower said, "We need only what *we* need."

The final argument to be set aside is that, after all, the Strategic Defense Initiative is just research—and who can be against research? For a start, we should be clear that the issue is not research or no research. The choices are research at public expense now, research at private expense now, or no research now. And the research part of SDI, which is projected to surpass the Apollo program, is research on a vast scale indeed.

Two further considerations seem to me to be decisive. One is momentum. Science writer William Burrows commented in *Foreign Affairs* that the program manager is yet to be born who can walk into a room and say, "General, the $30 billion is all gone now, and we have decided that this initiative was a bad idea, sir." Much more important, the Soviet response will come to the research and development—they are not going to wait and see how the field testing turns out. A major research commitment is a major political act in American/Soviet relations.

The Moral Argument

Let me turn now to the argument that SDI will be morally superior to alternative policies regarding nuclear war. The moral problem to which SDI is proposed as the solution is, quite simply, the unprecedented and literally unimaginable destruction that offensive missiles used in retaliation do themselves and invite in return. The two most obvious ways of avoiding this barbaric devastation are the direct route of the elimination of the offensive missiles themselves and the indirect route of the construction of defenses so effective that they would be the technological equivalent of disarmament.

It is not surprising that the same people who, in the debate over offensive weapons systems, have been proponents of "war-fighting"

counterforce weapons and critics of assured destruction are also proponents of SDI. The moral thread in the argument is perfectly consistent: In both cases, the point is to minimize the risk of destruction. The
counterforce offensive weapons are supposed to diminish the risk of
nuclear war by a reduction in the *magnitude* of destruction through
increased accuracy and (allegedly) reduced yields, if deterrence fails,
and by a reduction in the *probability* that deterrence will fail through
their increased effectiveness as deterrents. The first goal, then, is to
produce the most moral (or least immoral) possible offensive nuclear
weapons. SDI then would simply finish the job and take us completely
away from offensive weapons—or anyhow, as far away as we can get.

Now, the difference between "completely away from offensive
weapons" and "as far away as we can get" highlights the chief difficulty
facing those who want to provide a moral defense for strategic
defense. The hope that seems to be winning whatever public support
SDI is garnering is that we can move beyond U.S. retaliatory deterrence and make offensive weapons impotent and obsolete. The trouble seems to be that SDI would not begin with population defense. The
"intermediate deployment" of SDI would be missile defense, designed
to enhance, not eliminate, U.S. retaliatory deterrence. But as long as
SDI enhances the invulnerability of U.S. retaliatory forces, it seems
utterly unresponsive to the moral arguments against retaliation. We are
keeping the offensive missiles, which are what the moral argument
condemns.

However, a rationale for the temporary continuation of reliance on
retaliation as a decisive step toward the elimination of retaliation has
been given by policy analysts Keith Payne and Colin Gray in *Foreign
Affairs*, as follows. Even if the technology for a population defense
were available, we might not want to move directly to it. The construction of a highly effective population defense for the United States
would tend to eliminate the Soviet capacity for retaliation (and first
strike). This prospect could create instability as we moved out of the
situation where the Soviet Union could still retaliate (strike first) into
the situation where it cannot. The Soviet Union, that is, would have an
incentive to go ahead and take what might be its very last opportunity
for all time to attack. The strongest deterrent to that last-chance attack,
until the invulnerable defenses are completed, is the same old deterrent as always: a survivable retaliatory force.

The purpose of missile defenses is, then, in the persuasive phrase
of Payne and Gray, "to guard the transition" to population defenses.
The moral position implicit here is this: During the intermediate
deployment of missile defenses, SDI will rely no less (and no more) on
retaliatory offensive weapons than we do now and so will be no less

(and no more) immoral than it is now; however, intermediate deployment is the best means to full deployment, at which point we can satisfy the requirements of morality by eliminating the offensive missiles altogether.

A Skeptic's Reply

Although the rationale of guarding the transition seems the best justification available for continued reliance on offensive missiles, it has its weaknesses. What is to be said about the fact that the means to the end of the elimination of retaliation is the enhancement of retaliation (for an indefinitely long transition period)? A first answer would be, in effect: The end justifies the means. Here we fight fire with fire— we cross beyond retaliation on a bridge of retaliation. But as a defense of the moral superiority of SDI (over alternatives like assured destruction), the argument that this end (eliminating retaliation) justifies the means (enhancing retaliation) faces a dilemma: If the argument works, it works just as well for assured destruction as for strategic defense; and if it does not work, it does not work.

For both SDI and assured destruction, the fundamental question remains: Are there any circumstances under which we intend to retaliate? In both cases, the answer is, *yes, if deterrence fails*. The defender of SDI can add, Yes, if deterrence fails before we have eliminated our offensive missiles, to which we think this is the best means. But the defender of old-fashioned retaliation can add the same vague qualification: Advocates of both forms of deterrence quite sincerely hope to get beyond retaliation somehow someday. The simple fact of having a worthy ultimate goal does not, however, deal with the moral problem of what retaliation would entail if it were to be unleashed.

To rid himself of this unwanted parallel with justifications of assured destruction, the advocate of the moral superiority of SDI needs to argue not that the end is so noble or urgent that it justifies the means, but that the connection between the end and *this* means is much tighter than the connection, if any, between the end and alternative means.

Can the advocate of SDI make good on this claim? The thesis that offensive missiles will guard the transition to the defensive revolution raises worries endemic to all transitions: They have a nasty way of never ending. We need to be given strong grounds for confidence that the offensive missiles will, if not "fade away," somehow or other be negotiated away or go away. Otherwise the moral argument does not work. It is planning to retaliate, not being retaliated against, that a long tradition of 'just war' morality requires us to eliminate.

Proponents of SDI have not yet spelled out a convincing account of how or why the transition is going to occur. The contention, for example, that our construction of population defenses will give the Soviets a positive incentive to switch from offensive missiles to defenses of their own is unpersuasive. Why should they respond to our defenses with defenses rather than with enhanced offenses, which would almost surely be cheaper? In response to Soviet work on defenses, the U.S. Air Force has stepped up work in the Advanced Strategic Missile Systems program and other secret programs to develop penetration aids, highly maneuverable warheads, and other defense-defeating technology. We have no reason to expect that the Soviet Air Force would simply give up on offensive innovations because on a given day our defenses seemed to swing the advantage to us.

We have more positive grounds, however, for doubting that enhanced retaliatory offensive missiles will ever be the bridge beyond retaliation. Here I want to distinguish my argument from the argument that on technological grounds an adequate population defense can simply never be built. According to that argument, the SDI would not be worth building even if (a big if) we thought we had solved all the individual technical problems, because all the different aspects of all the different layers must work well together in an extremely hostile environment (direct attack) the first time it is used. The first and only test of the extraordinarily complex system will be the one and only time it is used in battle.

I, however, do not want to say that it cannot be done. What I do want to suggest is this: Never in a million years would we develop such certainty and confidence in an untested defense that we would dismantle the retaliatory deterrent, which would otherwise be our only backup. If this is correct, the moral defense of enhanced deterrence as guarding the transition to the elimination of deterrence fails.

The U.S. Air Force's manual, *Military Space Doctrine*, begins with the sentence, "Space is the ultimate high ground." With the Strategic Defense Initiative the president has tried to seize the moral high ground within space. I have suggested, however, that we are still in the swamps we have inhabited for some time. Defensive weapons are not inherently more moral than offensive weapons—it is purposes, not weapons, that count. The president's purpose is lofty, but it is the same goal shared by defenders of assured destruction, advocates of the freeze, and lots of others who disagree about the means. The moral case for SDI will not have been made until it has been shown why it will lead to the elimination of retaliation rather than to a spiral of offensive/defensive arms races, and will lead to the elimination of retaliation more surely than all the alternative routes, like the build-down. If not, SDI will fail to alter the moral scene, and it will fail at phenomenal expense. Its cost, given the uncertainty of its promise, may be the ultimate moral argument against SDI. At that level of budgeting, it competes with all the other good we could certainly do, not least of which would be to recapture control over wild budget deficits. Actually to accomplish a few good things seems morally better than to attempt something so grand and revolutionary, but so uncertain of good effect.

Sources cited in this article are Lewis Lehrman, "A Moral Case for 'Star Wars,'" New York Times, February 19, 1985, p. A23; William Burrows, "Ballistic Missile Defense: The Illusion of Security," Foreign Affairs (Spring 1984); and Keith B. Payne and Colin S. Gray, "Nuclear Policy and the Defensive Transition," Foreign Affairs (Spring 1984).

Banning the Bomb
A Few Decades Too Late

Claudia Mills

For close to half a century, we have lived in "the shadow of the bomb," and as nuclear arsenals multiply, the shadow lengthens. That nuclear holocaust would be an unspeakable catastrophe requires no argument. As the bumper sticker reminds us, "One nuclear bomb can ruin your whole day." But the present state of nuclear deterrence, in which the superpowers aim tens of thousands of warheads at each other, is viewed by many as a nightmare in its own right, and a moral abomination.

In *The Abolition*, Jonathan Schell argues that by consenting to live under the doctrine of deterrence, "we bear responsibility not only for the lives of the people whom 'we' may kill but also for the lives of those whom 'they' would kill; namely, our families, our friends, and our other fellow-citizens. . . . Our acceptance of nuclear weapons is in that sense a default of parenthood, of love, of friendship, of citizenship. . . ." Quoting Nikita Khrushchev's remark following the Cuban missile crisis, that the smell of burning flesh was in the air, Schell observes, "in truth, that smell is never far from our nostrils now."

Of course vast numbers of people carry on with their daily business for the most part oblivious to the realities of nuclear deterrence, giving little thought to the weapons targeted against them, less to the weapons their government targets against others. If this is so, then, according to Australian philosopher C.A.J. Coady, so much the worse, morally, for them. He likens those who avert their noses from the threat of nuclear incineration to those good German burghers who failed to notice preparations for the Nazi death camps.

Coady holds nuclear deterrence to be immoral. He also recognizes, however, that it is not clear exactly what follows from that admission. The issue is not whether we should bring nuclear weapons into existence. The weapons are with us, and our policy is in place. The difficulty arises, in Coady's view, because "the matter of retreating from the policy of threat has pragmatic and moral aspects itself," leaving "room for a gap to arise between the judgment that [nuclear deterrence] is seriously immoral and the decision what to do about avoiding or abandoning [it]."

Nuclear deterrence—the promise to punish any nuclear transgression with the "assured destruction" of the enemy and, maybe, of oneself and the rest of the world as well—is hardly, on the face of it, a palatable alternative. But, Schell suggests, "there is nothing wrong with the doctrine of deterrence which is not wrong simply with the possession of vast nuclear arsenals." So-called war-fighting strategies to employ those weapons in some "limited" nuclear exchange are, if anything, less reassuring still. The problem lies not in doctrine, he argues, but in "existential features" of the weapons themselves. Thus the hope is to "ban," not deterrence, but the bomb—in Schell's words, to get rid of the bomb before it gets rid of us.

The Strategic Defense Initiative

One way to escape from the bomb, short of eliminating nuclear weapons altogether, is to construct defenses effective enough, in the hope of Ronald Reagan, to render ballistic missiles "impotent and obsolete." In March 1983 the president unveiled his "Strategic Defense Initiative (SDI)," calling on the scientific community, which gave us nuclear weapons in the first place, to develop new technology to save us from them. The image conjured by the imagination is of a huge bulletproof bubble arching over the Earth, sheltering allies and adversaries alike. (Reagan vowed to share defensive technology, once developed, with the Russians.) Against such an impenetrable shield, nuclear weapons, as in a Saturday morning cartoon, bounce off and fall away, harmless. With a defensive system in operation, innocent civilians on both sides would no longer be held hostage to the threat of nuclear war. And, once useless, swords could be beaten to plowshares, or simply forgotten.

In reality, the "bulletproof bubble" is to be a vast network of laser interceptors, coordinated with split-second timing and perfect precision by a computer program of unparalleled complexity. Will it work? Will it work well enough to make nuclear weapons "impotent and obsolete"? Leon Sloss, a leading spokesperson for strategic defenses, cautions, "At this stage in our knowledge of advanced defensive technologies, it seems unlikely that we can create a perfect defense or eliminate nuclear weapons at any time in the foreseeable future. Even if SDI is successful, it will not provide defense against all nuclear weapons." Sloss recommends, not supplanting offense by defense, but a mix of offensive and defensive forces: "Defense should not be seen primarily as defending specific targets, but rather as providing one of several layers of protection which will add greater uncertainty and ambiguity to the calculations of Soviet planners." Defense, then, is one more tool for us to use in maintaining deterrence against the Soviets, not a protective umbrella shielding us both.

For this reason, philosopher Henry Shue argues, the pursuit of SDI cannot be construed as the moral high road, for "We are keeping the offensive missiles, which are what the moral argument condemns. . . . It is planning to retaliate, not being retaliated against, that 'just war' morality requires us to eliminate." Other critics charge that, far from demonstrating the futility of further developments in offensive weapons, SDI will spur yet another escalation in the arms race. According to Harold Feiveson, of Princeton University's Center for Energy and Environmental Studies, "defense of population is likely to sabotage efforts to restrain the arms race and to provoke an offensive response by the adversary which could well result in still greater damage in the event the arsenals were actually used." We build defenses, they build offenses to counter them. They spend money; we spend money. And in the end?

Deep Reductions

A second way to back off from the bomb is through deep and dramatic reductions in the number of nuclear weapons. Feiveson advocates a 90 percent reduction in superpower arsenals, arguing that "essentially all the roles claimed for today's absurdly bloated nuclear arsenals could be achieved as well with drastically reduced numbers of weapons." The foundation of nuclear deterrence is the relationship of mutual vulnerability, where one side deters the other from a nuclear attack by threatening nuclear retaliation and is itself deterred by leaving its own population unprotected against retaliation for any transgression of its own. "Certainly," Feiveson maintains, "both superpowers have far more weapons than needed to hold hostage the adversary. . . . In fact, the mutual hostage relationship is clearly a very hardy one. No disarmament (short of virtually complete disarmament), no offensive buildup, no defensive umbrella, appears likely to upset it in the slightest."

In *The Abolition* Schell takes the argument for reduction one step further, pressing to the conclusion that "in the nuclear world the threat to use force is as self-cancelling at zero weapons as it is at fifty thousand nuclear weapons." Schell advocates abolishing nuclear weapons altogether, keeping only the factories for manufacturing them, and, most important, the knowledge of how to do so—"knowledge that nations are powerless to get rid of even if they want to." This alone—the fact that nuclear weapons can never be uninvented, nuclear innocence never regained—keeps deterrence sufficiently robust that the weapons themselves become superfluous. "It has often been said," Schell notes, "that the impossibility of uninventing nuclear weapons makes their abolition impossible. But . . . the opposite would be the case. . . . Once we accept the fact that the acquisition of the knowledge was the essential preparation for nuclear armament, and that it can never be reversed, we can see that every state of disarmament is also a state of armament. And, being a state of armament, it has deterrent value."

One considerable advantage of deep reductions in nuclear arsenals, according to Feiveson, would be a savings in money and resources: "It cannot be denied that the arms race, as now constituted, involves an abhorrent waste of resources in a world stained by hunger and poverty." This advantage would be eroded, however, if money were lavished instead on building up even more expensive conventional forces. Both Feiveson and Schell defend their plans as also leading to greater stability in times of crisis. As Schell puts it, "We sometimes say that we live on the brink of nuclear destruction. But . . . it would be more accurate to say that we are hanging by one arm from a branch that sticks out over the brink." Abolition, he argues, would at least return to us to the brink again.

Sloss replies, however, that it is at best a "tenuous proposition" that the degree of danger is directly proportional to the size of the arsenals. "One can argue that very small arsenals are more unstable than large ones, because of the potential risk from cheating on the size of the arsenals; the increased temptation with a limited force to attack limited numbers of high value targets (i.e., cities); or the added leverage given to a small power to threaten a large power." Critics speculate that we might do better to leave the missiles slumbering in their silos than to pace the floors of the factories feverishly anticipating a signal to race into production.

A second objection is that shrunken arsenals might nevertheless be targeted at innocent women, men, and children (though Feiveson emphatically rejects direct targeting of cities); even in Schell's proposal, as he himself admits, "we would still be implicated in the intention—somewhere, someday, perhaps—of slaughtering millions of people. Instead of rejecting nuclear deterrence categorically, we would still be relying on it." Both Feiveson and Schell defend their proposals, nonetheless, as decisive steps in the right direction. Feiveson hopes that reduced nuclear forces would lead to scaled-down notions of what nuclear weapons can be used for and mark the beginning of serious detente. Schell hopes that abolition of nuclear weapons would at least succeed in pushing nuclear terror "into the background of our affairs . . . thereby clearing a space into which the peaceful, constructive energies of humanity could flood."

A final problem—or challenge—for both proposals is that both depend critically on bilateral, mutual reductions. The United States and the Soviet Union are to join together in deeply cutting—or abolishing—their nuclear stockpiles. But Sloss comments, "The post-war record of limiting and controlling armaments offers little promise that negotiation is the route to security. . . . arms control negotiations are the product of an adversarial relationship which, if it changes at all, will only change gradually." Indeed, economist Thomas Schelling lambastes arms control negotiations as themselves driving the arms race. He charges that the purchase of, for example, MX missiles seems to be "an obligation imposed by a doctrine that the end justifies the means—the end something called arms control and the means a demonstration that the United States does not lack the determination to match or exceed the Soviets in every category of weapons." Of late, investment in SDI has been championed, not as contributing to defense for its own sake, but for its usefulness as a bargaining chip, and as a threat to lure the Soviets to the bargaining table.

Schelling holds out hope, however, that "something that deserves to be identified as arms control can come about informally and without being recognized as arms control by the participants." For example, with no formal Soviet acknowledgment of the principle that a war in Europe should be kept nonnuclear, both sides have proceeded to some extent to pursue that objective de facto by purchasing and installing appropriate weapons. However, it seems that the kind of reciprocal restraint Schelling describes aims at maintaining a robust status quo of deterrence rather than trying to achieve any radical overhaul of the nuclear balance.

Unilateral Disarmament

If it seems unlikely that the superpowers can cooperate on any significant initiative toward bilateral disarmament, the option remains for the United States to lay down its arms unilaterally. The United States could decide simply that the deadly game of nuclear terror is one that it declines to play. While the American political climate at present is hardly conducive to such a proposal, it remains in our power to adopt, and some might argue that its adoption is morally incumbent on us.

As Shue outlines one rationale for unilateral disarmament, "Avoiding the commission of a wrong yourself takes moral priority over preventing even very bad things, for which you are not responsible, from happening." We threaten nuclear attack against the Soviets to deter them from attacking us, or our allies. If deterrence works, then, it serves to prevent the Soviets from inflicting terrible harm. But if the threat itself is immoral, we have ourselves committed a grievous wrong, and it is our job to look after our own conscience and let the Soviets look after theirs.

Shue emphatically disagrees with this reasoning. If our withdrawal from the nuclear brotherhood would be destabilizing (for example, by alarming allies like Germany and Japan, who then might begin their own, perhaps more threatening nuclear buildup), that increase in risk must be on our conscience as fully as our own continuing participation in deterrence would be. "If the choice to abandon deterrence unilaterally would in fact create an unstable situation in which nuclear war would occur, that choice can hardly be described simply as letting other people kill each other. It is contributing knowingly to the occurrence of great harm. In a situation of interdependent decisions, what you *do*—not a distant *consequence* of what you do—may be to increase danger with which others must deal."

On a small, crowded planet, after so many mistakes have already been made, it may be that we cannot preserve our moral purity singlehandedly. Progress toward peace and stability may have to come through international cooperation, not by our own isolated action, however high-minded it might be.

Conclusion

In a more perfect world, nuclear deterrence would be no one's first choice for how to conduct the world's business. That we aim tens of thousands of warheads at the Soviets as they aim tens of thousands of warheads at us is, at best, a peculiar premise for global harmony. But that nuclear deterrence is morally flawed unfortunately need not mean that any other course of action now open to us is any better. As Shue points out, "It may well be that all the options toward nuclear deterrence still available now are wrong, but that some are more deeply wrong than others. Nowhere is it written that in every situation there is a right way out—indeed, nowhere is it written that in every situation there is any way out." But that all options are flawed does not mean that any choice is as good as any other. It means we must choose the least bad—that is to say, the best available. If this turns out to be a continued reliance on some kind of deterrence, then that may be the choice that now lies before us.

Maybe the first steps we can take to retreat from the nuclear brink will not be major policy initiatives, but more humble, homely measures: a shift away from inflammatory rhetoric, an encouragement of friendship between Soviet and American communities, families, children. If the bomb cannot be "banned," perhaps it can be moved from the center to the periphery of human affairs—a last resort made progressively more remote. If we cannot get rid of the bomb, perhaps we can rid ourselves of the kind of politics that relies on it, by abandoning the illusion that nuclear missiles create political power.

In the meantime, Schelling reminds us, "Most of what we call civilization depends on reciprocal vulnerability." A balance of deterrence doesn't have to mean a balance of terror: "People regularly stand at the curb watching trucks, buses and cars hurtle past at speeds that guarantee injury and threaten death if they so much as attempt to cross against the traffic. They are absolutely deterred. But there is no fear. They just know better."

The views of C.A.J. Coady, Leon Sloss, and Harold Feiveson are quoted from their essays in Nuclear Deterrence and Moral Restraint: Critical Choices for American Strategy, *ed. Henry Shue (New York: Cambridge University Press, 1989). Henry Shue's views are quoted from "Are Nuclear Defenses Morally Superior?" (this volume) and from "Redistribution of the Risk of Nuclear War," manuscript, n.p., n.d.*

FOR FURTHER READING

Holmes, Robert. *On War and Morality*. Princeton, N.J.: Princeton University Press, 1989.

Lee, Steven. *Morality, Prudence, and Nuclear Weapons*. Cambridge Studies in Philosophy and Public Policy. New York: Cambridge University Press, forthcoming.

Luttwak, Edward. *Strategy: The Logic of War and Peace*. Cambridge, Mass.: Belknap, 1987.

MacLean, Douglas, ed. *The Security Gamble: Deterrence Dilemmas in the Nuclear Age*. Maryland Studies in Public Philosophy. Totowa, N.J.: Rowman and Allanheld, 1984.

Shue, Henry, ed. *Nuclear Deterrence and Moral Restraint: Critical Choices for American Strategy*. Cambridge Studies in Philosophy and Public Policy. New York: Cambridge University Press, 1989.

PART IV

CIVIL RIGHTS, CITIZENSHIP, AND POLITICAL LIFE

9

CIVIL RIGHTS

The passage of the Civil Rights Act of 1964 marked a new or renewed commitment to upholding the civil rights of all citizens in this country. Yet almost three decades later, blacks are still struggling to claim the promise of equal participation in American political and economic life held out by that landmark legislation. The first article in this chapter, on affirmative action, addresses this struggle. Other articles deal with a broadening of a concern for civil rights to include not only racial minorities but women and gays, and cover two further civil rights issues regarding privacy and drug testing.

In "A Defense of Affirmative Action," Thomas Nagel takes seriously three central objections to what he calls "strong affirmative action," an actual policy of active preference for minority-group members (or women) over white (or male) job candidates. Given the strength of these objections to affirmative action, in terms of inefficiency, unfairness, and damage to self-esteem, strong affirmative action "should be undertaken only if it will substantially further a social goal of the first importance." While this condition is not met by all programs of affirmative action, Nagel argues that it *is* met by those that address deep-seated patterns of racial discrimination and injustice.

The next three articles examine issues involving discrimination against women. "Paying Women What They Are Worth" discusses the policy known as "comparable worth"—that women and men should be paid the same not only for equal work, but for work equal in *value*, for work of *comparable worth*. The National Academy of Sciences summarized its findings on the persistent wage gap between men and women in this way: "Not only do women do different work than men, but also the work women do is paid less, and the more an occupation is dominated by women, the less it pays." This seems a clear indication that something has gone wrong in how our society values the work women do. But what exactly *has* gone wrong? Are there serious moral problems in the way wage scales and pay rates are determined? Or do the problems arise external to the labor market, in some morally troubling features of the larger society?

Segregation of men and women takes place not only in the workplace, but in the clubhouse—indeed, segregation in the clubhouse has ramifications in the workplace. In "Private Clubs and Public Values," Deborah L. Rhode looks at a number of questions surrounding access to gender-segregated institutions: questions about public and private, sameness and difference, and formal versus substantive equality.

Perhaps the most symbolic arena for the exclusion of women has been the military; while recent years have seen steady growth of female participation in the armed forces, women are still barred from combat. "Women in the Military" looks at military service for women as both a right and a duty of full citizenship, concluding, "If the right to fight is a citizenship right, it is a right qualified women share with qualified men. If citizenship carries with it an obligation to serve, women, as full and equal citizens, will have to accept their portion of the military burden."

While the 1964 Civil Rights Act extends its protections to both women and minorities, gay Americans are virtually denied any protection of their civil rights and liberties. As Richard Mohr writes in "Gays and Civil Rights," "Gays are now at about the same place blacks were in 1945." In that article, Mohr argues that the general justifications for civil rights legislation apply with particular force to gays.

Discrimination is not only a matter of law, of course, but also of custom and attitude—even of the jokes we tell one another. "Racist and Sexist Jokes: How Bad Are They (Really)?" discusses humor as a vehicle of discrimination, whether racist, sexist, ethnic, or homocentric. Are such jokes "just jokes"—or do they affront the dignity of oppressed groups and individuals?

The concluding two articles in this chapter examine two civil-liberties issues special to our time. The first investigates the threat posed to privacy by the vast memory storage and omnipresent reach of the computer. The databases of the federal government alone contain some four billion separate records about American citizens, seventeen items apiece, making the odds alarmingly good that some computer somewhere knows something about you that you would rather it didn't. "Privacy in the Computer Age" explores the questions of what privacy is and why we value it personally and as a society, asking how we weigh the threatened value of privacy against the vast array of other benefits brought to us by computer technology.

Finally, "Drug Testing in Sports," by Douglas MacLean, looks beyond the objections that drug testing programs are inaccurate and invite abuse, focusing on the more fundamental question of whether such invasions of privacy can be morally justified. MacLean surveys drug testing of student and professional athletes, and in the workplace generally, with attention to the special features that affect the justifiability of drug testing in each arena.

A Defense of Affirmative Action

Thomas Nagel

The term "affirmative action" has changed in meaning since it was first introduced. Originally it referred only to special efforts to ensure equal opportunity for members of groups that had been subject to discrimination. These efforts included public advertisement of positions to be filled, active recruitment of qualified applicants from the formerly excluded groups, and special training programs to help them meet the standards for admission or appointment. Close attention was also paid to procedures of appointment, and sometimes to the results, with a view to detecting continued discrimination, conscious or unconscious.

More recently the term has come to refer also to some degree of definite preference for members of these groups in determining access to positions from which they were formerly excluded. Such preference might be allowed to influence decisions only between candidates who are otherwise equally qualified, but usually it involves the selection of women or minority members over other candidates who are better qualified for the position.

I will call the first sort of policy "weak affirmative action" and the second "strong affirmative action." It is important to distinguish them, because the distinction is sometimes blurred in practice. It is strong affirmative action—the policy of preference—that arouses controversy. Most people would agree that weak or precautionary affirmative action is a good thing, and worth its cost in time and energy. But this does not imply that strong affirmative action is also justified.

I shall claim that in the present state of affairs it is justified, most clearly with respect to blacks. But I also believe that a defender of the practice must acknowledge that there are serious arguments against it, and that it is defensible only because the arguments for it have great weight. Moral opinion in this country is sharply divided over the issue because significant values are involved on both sides. My own view is that while strong affirmative action is intrinsically undesirable, it is a legitimate and perhaps indispensable method of pursuing a goal so important to the national welfare that it can be justified as a temporary, though not short-term, policy for both public and private institutions. In this respect it is like other policies that impose burdens on some for the public good.

Three Objections

I shall begin with the argument against. Three objections to strong affirmative action are that it is inefficient, that it is unfair, and that it damages self-esteem.

The degree of inefficiency depends on how strong a role racial or sexual preference plays in the process of selection. Among candidates meeting the basic qualifications for a position, those better qualified will on the average perform better, whether they are doctors, police officers, teachers, or electricians. In some cases, as in preferential college admissions, the immediate usefulness of making educational resources available to an individual is thought to be decisive because of the later use to which the education will be put or because of the internal effects on the institution itself. But by and large, policies of strong affirmative action must reckon with the costs of some lowering in performance level—the stronger the preference, the larger the cost to be justified. Since both the costs and the value of the results will vary from case to case, this suggests that no one policy of affirmative action is likely to be correct in all cases, and that the cost in performance level should be taken into account in the design of a legitimate policy.

The charge of unfairness arouses the deepest disagreements. To be passed over because of membership in a group one was born into, where this has nothing to do with one's individual qualifications for a position, can arouse strong feelings of resentment. It is a departure from the ideal—one of the values finally recognized in our society—that people should be judged so far as possible on the basis of individual characteristics rather than involuntary group membership.

This does not mean that strong affirmative action is morally repugnant in the manner of racial or sexual discrimination. It is nothing like those practices, for though like them it employs race and sex as criteria of selection, it does so for entirely different reasons. Racial and sexual discrimination are based on contempt or even loathing for the excluded group, a feeling that certain contacts with them are degrading to members of the dominant group, that they are fit only for subordinate positions or menial work. Strong affirmative action involves none of this; it is simply a means of increasing the social and economic strength of formerly victimized groups and does not stigmatize others.

An element of individual unfairness exists here, but it is more like the unfairness of conscription in wartime, or of property condemnation under the right of eminent domain. Those who benefit or lose out because of their race or sex cannot be said to deserve their good or bad fortune.

It might be said on the other side that the beneficiaries of affirmative action deserve it as compensation for past discrimination, and the compensation is rightly exacted from the group that has benefitted from discrimination in the past. But this is a bad argument, because as the practice usually works, no effort is made to give preference to those who have suffered most from discrimination, or to prefer them especially over those who have benefitted most from it, or been guilty of it. Only candidates who in other qualifications fall on one or other side of the margin of decision will directly benefit or lose from the policy, and these are not necessarily, or even probably, the ones who especially deserve it. Women or blacks who do not have the qualifications even to be considered are likely to have been handicapped more by the effects of discrimination than those who receive preference. And the marginal white male candidate who is turned down can evoke our sympathy if he asks, "Why me?" (A policy of explicitly *compensatory* preference, which takes into account each individual's background of poverty and discrimination, would escape some of these objections, and it has its defenders, but it is not the policy I want to defend. Whatever its merits, it will not serve the same purpose as direct affirmative action.)

The third objection concerns self-esteem and is particularly serious. While strong affirmative action is in effect, and generally known to be so, no one in an affirmative action category who gets a desirable job or is admitted to a selective university can be sure he or she has not benefitted from the policy. Even those who would have made it anyway fall under suspicion, from themselves and from others: It comes to be widely felt that success does not mean the same thing for women and minorities. This painful damage to esteem cannot be avoided. It should make any defender of strong affirmative action want the practice to end as soon as it has achieved its basic purpose.

Justifying Affirmative Action

I have examined these three objections and tried to assess their weight, in order to decide how strong a countervailing reason is needed to justify such a policy. In my view, taken together they imply that strong affirmative action involving significant preference should be undertaken only if it will substantially further a social goal of the first importance. While this condition is not met by all programs of affirmative action now in effect, it is met by those that address the most deep-seated, stubborn, and radically unhealthy divisions in the society, divisions whose removal is a condition of basic justice and social cohesion.

The situation of black people in our country is unique in this respect. For almost a century after the abolition of slavery we had a rigid racial caste system of the ugliest kind, and it only began to break up a generation ago. In the South it was enforced by law, and in the North, in a somewhat less severe form, by social convention. Whites were thought to be defiled by social or residential proximity to blacks; intermarriage was taboo; blacks were denied the same level of public goods—education and legal protection—as whites, were restricted to the most menial occupations, and were barred from any positions of authority over whites. The visceral feelings of black inferiority and untouchability this system expressed were deeply ingrained in the members of both races, and they continue, not surprisingly, to have their effect. Blacks still form, to a considerable extent, a hereditary social and economic community characterized by widespread poverty, unemployment, and social alienation.

When this society finally got around to moving against the caste system, it might have done no more than to enforce straight equality of opportunity, perhaps with the help of weak affirmative action, and then wait a few hundred years while things gradually got better. Fortunately it decided instead to accelerate the process by both public and private institutional action, because there was wide recognition of the intractable character of the problem posed by this insular minority and its place in the nation's history and collective consciousness. This has not been going on very long, but the results are already impressive, especially in speeding the advancement of blacks into the middle class. Affirmative action has not done much to improve the position of poor and unskilled blacks. That is the most serious part of the problem, and it requires a more direct economic attack. But increased access to higher education and upper-level jobs is an essential part of what must be achieved to break the structure of drastic separation that was left largely undisturbed by the legal abolition of the caste system.

Changes of this kind require a generation or two. My guess is that strong affirmative action for blacks will continue to be justified into the early decades of the next century, but that by then it will have accomplished what it can and will no longer be worth the costs. One point deserves special emphasis. The goal to be pursued is the reduction of a great social injustice, not proportional representation of the races in all institutions and professions. Proportional racial representation is of no value in itself. It is not a legitimate social goal, and it should certainly not be the aim of strong affirmative action, whose drawbacks make it worth adopting only against a serious and intractable social evil.

This implies that the justification for strong affirmative action is much weaker in the case of other racial and ethnic groups, and in the case of women. At least, the practice will be justified in a narrower range of circumstances and for a shorter span of time than it is for blacks. No other group has been treated quite like this, and no other group is in a comparable status. Hispanic-Americans occupy an intermediate position, but it seems to me frankly absurd to include persons of Asian descent as beneficiaries of affirmative action, strong or weak. They are not a severely deprived and excluded minority, and their eligibility serves only to swell the numbers that can be included on affirmative-action reports. It also suggests a drift in the policy toward adopting the goal of racial proportional representation for its own sake. This is a foolish mistake, and should be resisted. The only legitimate goal of the policy is to reduce egregious racial stratification.

With respect to women, I believe that except over the short term, and in professions or institutions where their absence is particularly marked, strong affirmative action is not warranted and weak affirmative action is enough. This is based simply on the expectation that the social and economic situation of women will improve quite rapidly under conditions of full equality of opportunity. Recent progress provides some evidence for this. Women do not form a separate hereditary community, characteristically poor and uneducated, and their position is not likely to be self-perpetuating in the same way as that of an outcast race. The process requires less artificial acceleration, and any need for strong affirmative action for women can be expected to end sooner than it ends for blacks.

I said at the outset that people tend to blur the distinction between weak and strong affirmative action. This occurs especially in the use of numerical quotas, a topic on which I want to comment briefly.

A quota may be a method of either weak or strong affirmative action, depending on the circumstances. It amounts to weak affirmative action—a safeguard against discrimination—if and only if independent evidence shows that average qualifications for the positions being filled are no lower in the group to which a minimum quota is being assigned than in the applicant group as a whole. This can be presumed true of unskilled jobs most people can do, but it becomes less likely, and harder to establish, the greater the skill and education required for the position. At these levels, a quota proportional to population, or even to representation of the group in the applicant pool, is almost certain to amount to strong affirmative action. Moreover, it is strong affirmative action of a particularly crude and indiscriminate kind, because it permits no variation in the degree of preference, whatever its social and economic cost. For this reason I should defend quotas only where they serve the purpose of weak affirmative action. On the whole, strong affirmative action is better implemented by including group preference as one factor in making appointment or admission decisions, and letting the results depend on its interaction with other factors.

I have tried to show that the arguments against strong affirmative action are clearly outweighed at present by the need for exceptional measures to remove the stubborn residues of racial caste. But advocates of the policy should acknowledge the reasons against it, which will ensure its termination when it is no longer necessary. Affirmative action is not an end in itself, but a means of dealing with a social situation that should be intolerable to us all.

Paying Women What They Are Worth

Claudia Mills

In Montgomery County, Maryland, a liquor clerk with a high school diploma and two years experience draws a higher salary than a schoolteacher in the same county with a bachelor's degree, specialized teaching training, and the same amount of experience. Almost all the liquor clerks are male; two-thirds of the teachers are female. In Denver, trained professional nurses brought suit against the city because their wages were lower than those of predominantly male tree trimmers and sign painters. Secretaries are paid less than truck drivers; librarians are paid less than traffic guards; bank tellers are paid less than stock clerks—simply, it often seems, because they are doing what society perceives as women's work. As Margaret Mead once wrote, "There are villages in which men fish and women weave and in which women fish and men weave, but in either type of village the work done by the men is valued higher than the work done by the women."

Despite the passage of the Equal Pay Act of 1963 and the Civil Rights Act of 1964, the gap between women's and men's wages has not decreased significantly in the last few decades. Women continue to earn 66 cents for every dollar earned by their male counterparts. Even when this sobering statistic is corrected for such factors as women's lesser seniority or sporadic participation in the labor force, only about half of the gap is explained away.

The remaining gap seems to be attributable to job segregation. Women are concentrated in a small number of low-paid occupations: 80 percent of all women work in only 25 of the 420 occupations listed by the Department of Labor. Secretaries are 99 percent female; registered nurses are 97 percent female; elementary schoolteachers are 84 percent female; cleaning and household service workers are 98 percent female; clerks are 86 percent female. These occupations accordingly pay less than male-dominated occupations such as truck driver, plumber, janitor, mail carrier, and meat cutter. The Bureau of Labor

Statistics reports a high inverse relationship between the percentage of women in a profession and that profession's annual earnings: Industries with a high percentage of female employees tend to have low average hourly earnings. The National Academy of Sciences summarizes its findings on the persistent wage gap between men and women in this way: "Not only do women do different work than men, but also the work women do is paid less, and the more an occupation is dominated by women, the less it pays."

This seems a clear indication that something has gone very wrong in how our society values the work women do. But what exactly *has* gone wrong? Are there serious moral problems in the way wage scales and pay rates are determined, with how we reward labor force participants for the work they do? Or do the problems arise external to the labor market, in some features of the larger society that ramify throughout our system of wages and benefits?

Free Choices in Free Markets

What principles govern the distribution of shares in our society? Are these principles just? How can we use them to account for the lesser shares that continue to accrue to women?

Ours is basically a market economy, where income is not distributed according to any set formula ("to each according to need, merit, effort"), but where individuals beginning from different starting points, with different initial bundles of aptitudes, interests, and tastes, make different choices about how to produce, consume, save, and invest. If they produce, consume, save, and invest in a way that is on balance beneficial to others, as perceived by those others, market mechanisms ideally ensure that they benefit accordingly.

Philosopher Ronald Dworkin, writing in *Liberalism Reconsidered*, believes that an idealized market economy fulfills the requirement that a just state treat its citizens as equals. Treating people equally cannot simply require giving them equal shares, for this would disregard the way individuals' choices may increase or diminish the total pool of shares, and so would essentially treat people *unequally*. Instead, people are treated equally if they have, "at any point in their lives, different amounts of wealth insofar as the genuine choices they have made have been more or less expensive or beneficial to the community measured by what other people want for their lives. The market seems indispensable to this principle."

In an actual market, however, not everyone is able to make optimal choices to work, consume, and save. Dworkin observes that people have very different socioeconomic starting points, as well as different inherent capacities and abilities. They are also differently favored by luck. These factors distort the correlation between choice and reward and so make actual markets at best imperfect instruments of distributive justice.

Does this account explain the disadvantaged financial position of women in our society? If the market is supposed to reward people according to the choices they make, then either women are making the wrong choices, for whatever reason, or something has gone wrong with the mechanisms that match choice with reward.

In the first view, some jobs are going to be low-paying, dead-end jobs whoever does them, and the problem is that women keep on choosing these jobs. Women themselves may opt for less important and valuable work, perhaps because their self-image and career expectations have been shaped by a sexist society. More likely, women may have the wrong choices made *for* them, in that their range of choice remains severely limited by employment discrimination.

In the second view, women *are* making choices "beneficial to the community, measured in terms of what other people want for their lives," but the market has failed to reward them accordingly. "Women's work" is not necessarily low-paying, reflecting its lower social value—instead, the work women do is undervalued *because* it is done by women.

Of course, some combination of the two views may be true: It may be that women are involuntarily shunted into certain professions, which then become low-paying because they are occupied by women. Both views may contain necessary components of a full explanation of the disadvantaged economic status of women, and the remedies appropriate to both may be called for if justice is to be done.

Employment Discrimination and Job Mobility

It is incontrovertible that our society channels women into certain types of work. Nurtured by an educational system that discourages girls from developing mathematical and technical skills and a culture that calls strength and assertiveness "unladylike," women at the same time confront a work force that still assigns entry positions on the basis of sex. University of Maryland economist Barbara Bergmann attributes much of the male-female pay gap to initial job assignment: "Most of the damage is done the first day a person walks into the employment office." Women, but not men, are still asked to take a typing test; women sales clerks are stationed at the candy counter, while the men are assigned the high-ticket heavy appliances, at higher wages. Given the prevailing pattern of job shunting, Bergmann concludes, "Very few employers could not be found guilty" of illegal job discrimination.

One solution to job segregation is to enhance women's job mobility by educating and training them to enter "men's" fields and legally enforcing their equal access to these fields, as well as monitoring the sexual harassment women encounter on entering previously male territory. If our society pays secretaries less than truck drivers, let the secretaries drive trucks. Move women out of women's fields into men's fields, where they can earn men's wages.

Several factors suggest, however, that this strategy cannot by itself do economic justice to women. In the first place, as Eleanor Holmes Norton, former head of the Equal Employment Opportunity Commission, notes, there just are not enough male jobs to go around. "Integration of men's occupations by women will someday reach limits beyond which it is unlikely to proceed apace if wage rates continue to offer disincentives to men to enter traditional female occupations." The one-way herding of women into male occupations only overcrowds those fields, causing a corresponding drop in wages.

Furthermore, enhanced job mobility is of little comfort to women who have already made considerable career investments in nursing, teaching, librarianship, or other fields that require long periods of education and specialized professional training. It is hard to ask such women to abandon their lifework for unskilled male work or male work that requires very different skills.

Nor would such a move be in society's best interests. Norton points out, "The vital jobs performed chiefly by women in this society—nursing, teaching, clerical work, and the like—are indispensable. Although individual women may profit personally and professionally there is no net gain for our society when people who might be nurses feel they must become doctors." Nor, one assumes, is there a gain when people who might be nurses feel they must become parking-garage attendants.

Finally, if the crucial importance of women's jobs in our society suggests that these jobs are undervalued only because they are held by women, why should women be asked to change their choices, rather than society asked to change how it rewards those choices? Why should the nurse have to park cars, rather than receive equitable recompense for the expertise she brings to the vital task of healing society's sick?

Wage Discrimination and Pay Equity

Evidence abounds that women's low pay by and large cannot be construed as a response to market forces. Labor lawyer Winn Newman says flatly, "Supply and demand appear to have little effect on the wages of female-dominated professions." The American Hospital Association's recent figures estimate hospital nursing vacancies at between sixty-five thousand and seventy thousand nationwide, while nurses' salaries remain depressed. Newman cites the example of a severe shortage of nurses at St. Luke's Hospital in Milwaukee, which resulted not in any wage increases, but in the importation of nurses from Great Britain, at considerable expense in advertising and recruitment. That nurses are paid less than (primarily male) physician's assistants, who exercise similar skill, experience, and responsibility, cannot be explained by saying that the physician's assistants made better choices than the nurses did.

If we cannot rely on the usual processes of hiring and wage-setting to alter the disparities between the wages of men and women, what is to be done?

One approach that has aroused considerable interest in the past few years attempts to tie women's wages directly to the value or worth of their work. Women should receive the same pay, it is argued, as men who are doing jobs of *comparable worth*. This approach makes the concept of job-worth its starting point. It could be applied within firms or throughout the economy, depending on the ambitions of its proponents.

The worth of a job might be conceived in a number of different ways. We might think of a job's worth as its contributory value to the employer's operation, or alternatively, to the community welfare. Jobs that contribute to the same degree would be judged of equal worth. Or jobs might be evaluated instead according to some view of their intrinsic worth. Managing people, it is claimed, is as intrinsically valuable as managing property (though the latter is generally better paid).

That worth can be conceived of in a variety of ways is, according to its opponents, the central problem with the comparable-worth approach. They claim that no philosophically nonarbitrary way exists to single out and make operational a conception of worth applicable across jobs and across firms. The effort to discover the real worth of a job is as doomed to failure as medieval efforts to construct a theory of "just price."

Proponents of the comparable-worth approach reply that two-thirds of all Americans are now paid on the basis of some kind of job evaluation plan. Ranking the worth of jobs does not seem an insuperable task. But existing intra-firm job evaluation plans provide no common, independent criteria of value. Most current plans are designed to be "policy-capturing," that is, to systematize and rationalize established features of the job and wage policies already in practice.

A less far-reaching approach to closing the gender wage gap keeps a focus on the concept of discrimination as the heart of the problem and works to apply this concept more broadly. Rather than propose new job evaluation systems that link wages with "real" worth, it attacks existing job practices that link wages discriminatorily with gender. Its initial targets are wages that are on their face discriminatory and evaluation systems tailored to achieve a discriminatory effect.

In the 1940s, for example, Westinghouse assigned point values to all company jobs on an equal basis. Where jobs filled by women had the same point value as jobs filled by men, however, the company adopted the policy of paying the women at a 20 percent lower rate. This overt and deliberate discrimination was legal when it was done. When Westinghouse revised its compensation system in the 1960s after the enactment of the Civil Rights Act, instead of revising the women's wages to bring them into accord with the evaluation scheme, it downgraded the evaluation of all women's jobs to make them match their level of pay. This is only the most egregious form of wage discrimination.

Some firms classify men's and women's jobs equally on their point scale but pay women less. On other occasions, firms' job evaluations themselves seem to betray their valuing work less just because women do it—as when female prison guards in Oregon are paid less than male guards because their duties involve, in addition to supervising prisoners, typing as well!

Bergmann suggests one approach to identifying this kind of wage discrimination without ascertaining the worth of different jobs. On the assumption that women, just like men, generally prefer more money to less, and greater rather than lesser prospects for career advancement, the suspicion of discrimination is triggered whenever women are paid less than similarly qualified men. According to Bergmann, people with the same qualifications, training, and experience should be receiving the same return on their "human capital"—"In a non-discriminatory set-up, identical people should be paid identically." The key concept here is not comparability of jobs, but interchangeability of workers. The remedy, then, to a firm's wage discrimination might appropriately be the requirement of a wage adjustment. If a nursing supervisor could do the work of the hospital's higher-paid purchasing agent, then her wages should be the same as his.

What Is It Going to Cost?

Opponents of pay equity for women frequently claim that the costs of equity will be more than our economic system is willing or able to bear. *Fortune* magazine went so far as to say that "At the extreme, to raise the aggregate pay of the country's 27.3 million full-time working women high enough . . . would add a staggering

$150 billion a year to civilian payrolls. Such a radical step, of course, seems too preposterous to be taken seriously."

Proponents of pay equity charge instead that such radical cost estimates are too preposterous to be taken seriously. Certainly, the costs incurred would vary widely depending on the scope of the approach chosen. But the economic costs of remedying overt discrimination should not prove staggering. Employers and business interests have a long history of protesting that fair treatment of workers will result in massive economic disruption. Similar claims were made preceding the abolishment of child labor and the establishment of the minimum wage, and none of the dire predictions came to pass. Furthermore, cost is simply not an acceptable excuse for breaking the law, and workplace discrimination based on sex is now, quite simply, illegal.

A related charge is that pay equity will end up harming the very women it is intended to protect—by driving up women's wages it will reduce women's employment. This charge, however, seems largely groundless. As Norton explains, "If there's work to be done, the work is still going to have to be done, even if you have to pay more for it." Women's jobs are not jobs that we as a society can easily do without. Indeed, the argument for pay equity is premised on the assumption that women are doing valuable work that just happens to be underpaid because it is done by women.

Some argue, moreover, that pay equity in the end may *save* society money, by reducing the number of women and female-headed families living on federal assistance. Social scientists in recent years have documented what they call the "feminization of poverty": One in three families headed by a woman is poor; nearly half of all poor families are headed by a woman; two out of five single mothers trying to raise a family are likely to be poor. It is estimated that if women were paid the wages that similarly qualified men earn, we could cut the number of families in poverty in half.

When we consider that 93 percent of all welfare recipients are women and their children, that 70 percent of all food stamps recipients are women, and that two-thirds of all legal services and Medicaid recipients are women, our choice seems an easy one. We can pay women fair wages for doing work that needs to be done or deny them adequate wages and pay instead through our welfare programs. Surely the first approach makes more sense for a society that prides itself on treating all its members as equals.

Sources used for this article include Women, Work, and Wages—Equal Pay for Jobs of Equal Value, *a report of the National Research Council* of the National Academy of Sciences (Washington, D.C.: National Academy Press, 1981); Comparable Worth: A Symposium on the Issues and Alternatives (Washington, D.C.: Equal Employment Advisory Council, 1981); and Pay Equity: Equal Pay for Work of Comparable Value, Joint Hearings before the Subcommittee on Human Resources, Civil Service, and Compensation and Employee Benefits of the Committee on Post Office and Civil Service, House of Representatives, September 16, 21, and 30, and December 2, 1982 (Washington, D.C.: Government Printing Office, 1983).

Views were drawn from the following sources: Ronald Dworkin, from "Neutrality, Equality, and Liberalism," in Liberalism Reconsidered, ed. Douglas MacLean and Claudia Mills, Maryland Studies in Public Philosophy (Totowa, N.J.: Rowman and Allanheld, 1983); Barbara Bergmann, from "The Economics of Compensation Claims under Title VII," by Barbara R. Bergmann and Mary W. Gray, Department of Economics and Bureau of Business and Economic Research, University of Maryland, Working Paper No. 1983-3, and from an interview conducted by the author; Winn Newman, from his congressional testimony in Pay Equity; Eleanor Holmes Norton, from her testimony in Pay Equity and from an interview with the author.

Private Clubs and Public Values

Deborah L. Rhode

In a celebrated 1959 law review article, Columbia law professor Herbert Wechsler expressed his misgivings about the Supreme Court's repudiation of "separate but equal" doctrine in racial segregation cases. At the close of the article, Wechsler put what were obviously intended as rhetorical questions: "Is there not a point . . . in the statement that 'if enforced separation stamps the colored race with a badge of inferiority' it is solely because its members chose to put that construction upon it? Does enforced separation of the sexes discriminate against females merely because it may be the females who resent it and it is by judgments predominantly imposed by males?"

More than a quarter century later, those questions no longer appear either rhetorical or adequate to capture the complexities of gender segregation. Not all females resent all forms of separatism, and the culture generally remains deeply divided over which forms count as invidious. A substantial constituency even denies, as did Wechsler, that the question involved "is one of discrimination at all." To these defenders of separatism, the preeminent issue is freedom of association, and the values of individual liberty and cultural diversity that underlie it. Moreover, some feminists have questioned women's focus on getting in, as opposed to doing in, sex-segregated clubs. In this view, the response to exclusion should be a kind of Groucho Marx stoicism. Any association that bans women is not the kind women should want to join.

For many women, however, the issues surrounding access to gender-segregated institutions are not so readily dismissed. As a practical matter, sex-segregated clubs, although their number has been gradually declining, constitute a substantial presence on the social landscape. Membership in the associations of Elks, Moose, Lions, and Eagles totals well over five million, and smaller, more elite institutions provide forums for highly significant political and commercial interchanges. As a symbolic matter, exclusion of women, like that of racial or religious minorities, carries a stigma that affects individuals' social status and self-perception. And as a conceptual matter, separatism poses questions that have been at the core of feminist legal struggles for the last century: questions about public and private, sameness and difference, and formal versus substantive equality.

Legal Challenges

Almost all of the legal challenges to gender-segregated clubs have been directed to all-male institutions. These have met with only partial success. For the most part, the practices of private organizations are not subject to constitutional scrutiny. Title II of the federal Civil Rights Act bans discrimination in public accommodations on the grounds of race, religion, or national origin, but not sex. Many state public-accommodations laws include prohibitions on gender discrimination, but virtually all of these statutes do not apply to private associations. Accordingly, their effect on sex-segregated clubs has been limited. To date, the most significant progress has occurred in states willing to give broad construction to the meaning of "public."

In 1984, the Supreme Court gave cautious approval to that approach, although the terms of its holding do not promise any fundamental assault on sex-segregated associations. The case involved a challenge to the Jaycees' policy of permitting full membership status to all males between the ages of eighteen and thirty-five, while granting only "associate" status to females, a status that conferred no power to vote, hold office, or receive awards.

Justice William J. Brennan, speaking for the majority, argued that the state's interest in eliminating discrimination outweighed the First Amendment rights of association asserted by Jaycees' members. In so holding, Justice Brennan began by noting that the Court has traditionally protected association in two senses. One line of decisions has shielded certain intimate human relationships against state intrusion in order to preserve fundamental elements of personal liberty. A second line of precedents has recognized rights to associate in order to engage in other constitutionally protected activities—speech, assembly, and religious expression. As to the first interest, the Court concluded that the Jaycees had not exemplified the kind of intimate attachments warranting constitutional protection. So, too, although a "not insubstantial" part of the Jaycees' activities constituted protected expression on political, economic, cultural, and social affairs, the Court found no basis for concluding that the admission of women as full members would alter or interfere with that expression.

Inadequacies in the Current Approach

A threshold difficulty with this approach lies in the intimate/nonintimate distinction. Under the framework endorsed in the *Jaycees* case, the ultimate question is whether an association seems more an extension of home or market. That leaves large numbers of affiliations occupying an awkward middle ground, and where any particular one will fall on a particular court's continuum is inevitably indeterminant. Certainly none of the criteria the Supreme Court has identified—size, selectivity, and exclusivity—will yield conclusive distinctions. For example, the Minnesota Supreme Court labeled the Kiwanis as "private," although that organization's size, functions, and recruiting techniques were comparable to the Jaycees'.

Missing from the Court's analysis was any acknowledgment of the values separatism might serve, independent of an association's size or exclusivity. The dynamics of mixed and single-sex organizations differ, and separatism in some contexts may present opportunities for self-expression that would be inhibited by sexual integration. Of course, in contexts like the *Jaycees* case, any interests in separatism were already compromised by the organization's policy of including female associate members in most civic and social functions. The organization was perpetuating male hierarchies, not male sanctuaries.

Equally disquieting was the Court's ready dismissal of the organization's expressive claims. Throughout the litigation, the Jaycees asserted that women might have different attitudes about various issues on which the organization had taken a public position, particularly its campaign supporting President Ronald Reagan's economic policies. Justice Brennan dismissed such claims as resting on "social stereotyping." The problem with that analysis was not simply its failure to acknowledge a wealth of gender-gap studies supporting the Jaycees' argument. A more fundamental difficulty was the implication that access to an all-male institution may depend on whether women will endorse its existing values. If the price of admission is a promise of assimilation, that strategy is not one all feminists will be prepared to embrace.

Yet the case for full female participation in associations like the Jaycees does not depend on a denial of sex-based differences or the values of single-sex affiliations. Rather, it entails a more contextual assessment of the significance of those differences and values in various cultural settings. Inclusion of members with a different perspective might enrich, rather than impair, the organization's expressive activities. One can concede that sexual integration of organizations like the Jaycees might in some measure affect their philosophical cast or social dynamics, without conceding that their basic functions would alter.

Those functions are, moreover, public in a sense neither captured by conventional public-private distinctions, nor acknowledged by most court decisions in associational privacy cases. The exclusion of women from spheres conventionally classified as private contributes to women's exclusion from spheres unquestionably understood as public.

The perpetuation of all-male enclaves has worked to women's disadvantage on several levels. The most direct harms involve lost opportunities for social status, informal interchanges, and personal contacts that men's associations have traditionally provided. In a society where men obtain almost one third of their jobs, and probably a higher percentage of prestigious positions, through personal contacts, the commercial role of social affiliations should not be undervalued. Nor should their political significance be overlooked. Elite all-male associations such as the Bohemian or Cosmos clubs have often been the locus for private discussions that later emerged as public policy. And relegating females to separate dining rooms, separate entrances, or separate organizations is an affront to individuals' dignity and sense of self-worth.

In responding to this line of argument, defenders of all-male institutions frequently maintain that women do not, in fact, experience separatism as degrading, but rather enjoy having their own clubs or dining facilities. Such rejoinders, which resemble explanations often given for excluding racial or religious minorities, obscure a fundamental distinction. Separatism imposed by empowered groups carries a different social stigma and instrumental significance from separatism chosen by subordinate groups. Exclusivity of the latter kind does not convey inferiority or serve to perpetuate existing disparities in political and economic power. By contrast, the forms of institutional separatism chosen by dominant groups tend to reinforce their privileged position and the stereotypes underlying it.

The explanations that private club members commonly advance for excluding women leave little doubt about the lingering influence of such stereotypes. According to one club manager, "If a man has a business deal to discuss, he doesn't want to sit next to a woman fussing about how much mayonnaise is in her chicken salad." Moreover, when sexist stereotypes dictate associational policy, they tend to become self-reinforcing. No women are present to counteract the assumption that males' luncheon conversations focus on mergers while females' fixate on mayonnaise. Men who are uncomfortable associating with women in such social settings will never become less so if discomfort remains a valid justification for exclusivity. And the males who have trouble treating women as equals at clubhouse lunches are unlikely to be free of such difficulties in corporate suites. As long as women do not "fit in" in the private worlds where friendships form and power congregates, they will never fully fit in in the public sectors with which the state is justifiably concerned.

The boundary between public and private is fluid in still another sense: Most "private" clubs depend heavily on public support, largely in the form of tax subsidies. Indeed, under federal and most state law, associations that discriminate on the basis of sex enjoy the anomalous status of both profit and nonprofit organizations. Clubs gain tax exemptions by claiming to be private organizations where "substantially all" activities are for pleasure, recreation, and other nonprofit purposes, while members (or their employers) deduct dues and fees as "ordinary and necessary business expenses." That the state subsidizes discriminatory associations under inconsistent theories points up the difficulties of seeking to dichotomize organizations as either commercial or noncommercial, public or private.

Alternative Frameworks

An alternative approach to single-sex organizations will require a reconceptualization of public and private. The focus should not simply be on an organization's intimate or expressive character, but also on the totality of its public subsidies and public consequences. In essence, courts and legislatures should consider the full range of governmental and commercial entanglements. Grants, licenses, and tax subsidies by the state, as well as reimbursement of expenses by employers, could serve as legitimate bases for governmental action against gender discrimination.

The state could also withdraw support in the form of tax exemptions and deductions for sex-segregated organizations, both public and private. Since employers provide an estimated $1.6 billion in annual support to private clubs, and account for 40 to 50 percent of the revenues of certain elite men's associations, the cumulative effect of such strategies might be substantial.

That is not to underestimate the price of such a regulatory approach. Subjecting associational policies to state oversight increases the risk of harassing litigation and narrows the range of private choice. In some contexts, penalizing separatism by dominant groups may undermine its legitimacy for subordinate groups. We have, however, managed to prohibit racial discrimination by private clubs and schools and sex discrimination by private employers without the disabling social consequences critics have often envisioned. Private organizations that serve public functions do not provide the only opportunities for male bonding in this society.

Of course, the more categorical any regulatory strategy, the more over- and underinclusive it will prove. Of particular concern are all-female organizations that might be inhibited by the withdrawal of preferential tax treatment. Yet a law that explicitly differentiates between men's and women's associations, while theoretically defensible, may prove politically unpalatable. The problem is not, as advocates of all-male clubs have frequently argued, that such distinctions would be unprincipled. An approach that disadvantaged men's organizations but not women's would be asymmetrical with respect to sex but not with respect to social influence. And from the point of view of reducing gender inequality, influence is what matters.

From a more prudential perspective, however, it is risky to argue for a policy that expressly grants rights to women's but not men's affiliations. Rather it makes sense to rely on strategies that differentiate all-male and all-female organizations in practice rather than in principle. That is in part the justification for an approach that focuses on commercial entanglements and public subsidies. Even if such a strategy encouraged more women's groups to adopt formal positions of gender neutrality, many would find that their composition did not actually change. Nor is it apparent that change is undesirable. As women become more fully integrated into male organizations, the need for some all-female associations may diminish. To the extent that groups like the Jaycettes or local women's networks have functioned less as communities by consent than communities by imitation or exclusion, their passing is an acceptable by-product of a more egalitarian society. Their demise would also have compensating benefits. Male involvement in female-dominant organizations can erode gender stereotypes and enlarge understanding of women's concerns. At the very least, an increase in sex-neutral admission policies would help undercut one of the most convenient current rationalizations for male separatism: that women are happy with their own institutions.

A final problem lies in the inevitable underinclusiveness of any legal assault on sex-segregated associations. The law is too crude and intrusive an instrument to reach many of the most influential separatist networks. Poker games, golfing groups, and luncheon cliques that form along gender lines doubtless play a more substantial role in limiting women's opportunities than any of the organized entities susceptible to legal intervention. Moreover, even in those formal organizations, access does not necessarily ensure acceptance; getting women into the right clubs is far easier than getting them to the right tables. But access is a necessary first step. While we cannot eliminate social segregation by legal fiats, we can at least seek to minimize its crudest form and the social legitimacy that underlies it.

Women in the Military

Claudia Mills

Women are employed more extensively in the American armed forces than in the military forces of any other nation in the world. This reliance on women for our national defense remains controversial. Congress and the armed services have never fully resolved the place of women in battle. While excluded from certain "combat" jobs (e.g., infantryman, fighter pilot, gunner's mate), servicewomen are arrayed throughout combat support positions (e.g., transportation, communications, intelligence, military police) that place them very much in the line of fire in wartime. Female soldiers suffered casualties side by side with men in the 1991 Persian Gulf war. Though Congress has generally supported the policy of letting women volunteer (within limits) for military service, it enacted a male-only Selective Service registration, which the Supreme Court upheld. Moreover, as the military grows markedly smaller in the 1990s, creating intense competition for desirable enlisted and officer jobs, renewed pressure to diminish the number of women is likely to occur. Through all the controversy surrounding this issue, the moral question remains: Should men go off to war while women weep?

This question resolves itself into several further sets of questions. First, do women have a right to serve in their nation's armed forces, and if so, what is the source of this right? Second, what limits should be placed on this right? Do sound empirical grounds exist for arguing that women's right to serve should not include a right to full participation in offensive combat? Finally, if men are drafted to serve, should women be drafted as well? Or should the female presence in the military remain voluntary? The answers we give to these questions depend on our views on the significance of sex-related differences, the purposes of the military, and the rights and responsibilities of citizenship.

The Right of Military Service

In recent years, the percentage of women in the military has risen dramatically, from 1.6 percent in 1971 to a little more than 10 percent in 1987, for a total of 220,000. But field commanders continue to complain that the increased female presence confronts the military with a host of personnel problems. These range from the provision of housing, uniforms, and adequate day care to sexual harassment and a lack of male peer acceptance.

It may seem that the recruitment of women is not worth its social and perhaps even military costs. But denying qualified women the opportunity to serve in their nation's armed forces may have still heavier moral costs. According to Sara Ruddick, a philosopher at the New School of Social Research, to deny qualified women participation in the military is to deny them a *right*, for the right to serve in one's nation's armed forces and to defend one's very way of life is a basic right of citizenship, belonging equally to all citizens. "To fight and to command fighters, when qualified to do so, is a right conferred upon citizens and cannot be denied them because of their membership in a class or group. Women claiming the right to fight are claiming full citizenship." This right, furthermore, is an especially important one for women, bearing a certain symbolic significance. Some of the military's privileges are eagerly seized by all disadvantaged groups: The military provides economic and educational opportunities for women, as it does for racial and ethnic minorities. "But there is a special point [for women] in proving our ability to fight where stakes are high and, hitherto, masculinity has prevailed. Military success would challenge the perception, common in civilian life, that women are weak, dependent, and powerless."

If military service is a right shared by all citizens, the Pentagon will have to produce weighty arguments for setting it aside. It will not suffice to cite additional expenses or inconveniences, for we ordinarily think that rights can be overridden only by considerations of special societal urgency. The difficulties of providing new uniforms for female soldiers do not tip the balance here. Seriously compromising our national security would.

Women in Combat

Those who oppose women's participation in the military frequently charge, however, that any right of women to serve is indeed overridden, or at least limited, by more urgent national security concerns. David H. Marlowe, Chief of the Department of Military Psychiatry at the

Walter Reed Army Institute of Research (speaking in a private capacity and not representing any official view), insists that the right to serve must be measured against "that potential lost war that could alter . . . the integrity of the nation and its security for decades to come." If the presence of women in the military significantly increases the likelihood of losing that war, then it may be morally permissible or even obligatory to reduce their participation, or to limit their areas of performance.

Military service can take many forms, and the right to serve need not imply a right to serve in every military capacity. While women currently serve in scores of nontraditional military positions, they are excluded from strictly combat functions, such as infantry and armor. Defenders of the exclusionary policy argue that full inclusion of women would jeopardize our fighting effectiveness. Others dispute these claims, insisting that women should have fuller access to all occupational specialties.

WOMEN IN COMBAT: NO

The case against women in combat often begins with a recounting of the physiological differences between men and women. Women average 86-89 percent of male bulk and volume, and even when size is held constant, women are only 80 percent as strong as men. These differences in scale are accompanied by differences in structure. Marlowe cites a long list of physiological traits distinguishing the sexes: "The greater vital capacity, speed, muscle mass, aiming and throwing skills of the male, . . . and his more rapid rises in adrenaline make the male more fitted for combat." Opponents of women in combat also point to anthropological evidence that women play less aggressive roles than men in all observed societies, with aggressiveness differentials manifesting themselves in very young children prior to any significant socialization. Aggression has been linked to testosterone, the male sex hormone, and has been shown to fluctuate with hormone levels.

Even if these putative sex differences turn out to be more myth than fact, the existence of the myth itself works against the inclusion of women in combat units. Marlowe cites World War II studies "[demonstrating] that the performance of military units is, in part, governed by soldiers' perception of the unit and its members." According to Marlowe, many male soldiers who currently train in sex-integrated units suffer a loss in self-esteem, feeling that they have been subjected to less intensive training than soldiers in exclusively male units, even when objective examinations show otherwise. If women could do all the things these men could do, how challenging could those things be? This self-doubt could take its toll in combat effectiveness.

Finally, the presence of women in combat units is said to have an adverse effect as well on the attitudes of our allies and enemies. Again, here the myth is as damning as the fact. University of Maryland sociologist Mady Segal points to the belief of many that: "The perception of our military effectiveness by allies and adversaries is crucial to our national security. If our military is viewed as weak because of the inclusion of women in combat roles, our international posture can be just as critically affected as if we were truly weak."

WOMEN IN COMBAT: YES

Defenders of women in combat concede many of the relevant sex differences charged by their opponents. Men *are* on average bigger and stronger. The anthropological record *does* contain unbroken millennia of male domination across widely divergent cultures. Sexual stereotypes, whether or not grounded in fact, *do* determine to some extent soldiers' self-perceptions and world attitudes toward American military effectiveness.

However, lesser female size and strength may be compensated for by the superior mental aptitude and educational background of the average female recruits. The all-volunteer force has faced severe criticism for its deteriorating personnel quality, as measured in military qualification tests. The mental and technical abilities women bring to the armed forces may on balance offset any decline in physical standards, for a net gain in fighting effectiveness. Furthermore, an elevated mental profile for our enlisted troops may favorably affect both the self-perception of units and the attitudes of allies and enemies.

Sex-linked differences in strength and physical capacity are, moreover, only differences in *average* ability. Segal cautions, "We must be careful not to confuse a difference in average physical strength between men and women with a situation in which all men are strong enough and no women are. . . . Rather than assuming that all women are incapable of performing by virtue of the average woman's lack of capability, specific requirements should serve as the selection criteria, not gender."

This emphasis on actual performance as a gender-free standard is especially important for eliminating discrimination based on unfounded prejudice. Segal reminds us that "many of the arguments currently being used to justify excluding women . . . from combat roles have been used in the past to justify excluding women from other occupations," such as medicine, law, government, and law enforcement. Many of the arguments that "prove" that women should not be fighters equally well "prove" that they should not be doctors, voters, property-owners, or, indeed, independent, strong, autonomous persons.

Such unpalatable conclusions lead us to be suspicious of the arguments that generated them.

Finally, it is important to bear in mind the wide range of tasks all falling under the common heading of combat specialties. Service in the infantry and service on board an aircraft carrier, for example, are both forms of combat service from which women are now excluded. But they require very different skills and abilities. Upper-arm strength is critical in toting heavy weapons and ammunition across jungle terrain. It is irrelevant to success in piloting fighter planes. The physiological argument against women in combat cannot justify excluding them from combat specialties where their liabilities are unimportant.

The arguments for and against excluding women from various combat specialties may seem inconclusive, with the final choice resting on our views about the essential purpose of the military. In Marlowe's view, "The primary and essential role of the armed forces is to fight and win those wars to which the nation commits them." The national security is too important for us to court the risks of possible combat ineffectiveness. For others, the military is equally important for the role it plays in our national life, as an employer of massive scale and a symbol of citizen rights and responsibilities.

Volunteers or Draftees?

It might be thought that the right to fight and the duty to fight are merely different sides of the same moral coin, that the right to volunteer for service implies the duty to serve when called on to do so. But rights do not imply duties in this way. Philosopher Sara Ruddick compares the right to fight to the right to have children. "Neither right entails that a woman in fact choose to participate in the activity to which she is entitled." These rights entail only that, having chosen, one assumes whatever responsibilities—as soldier or parent—are attendant upon one's choice.

The right to fight, then, does not itself directly imply the duty to fight. But many women claim the right to fight as a right conferred on all citizens. Perhaps in the same way the duty to fight is a duty all citizens must share. Perhaps accepting the duty to serve is a badge of full and equal citizenship. The important questions now become: Should *any* citizen be drafted? If so, do the reasons justifying such a draft apply equally well to the drafting of *all* citizens, men and women alike?

Marlowe defends a draft by arguing that the costs of losing a war are greater than the costs of coerced military service. He believes that the all-volunteer force may be incapable of successfully defending the nation, because of a skewed distribution of aptitudes and skills, and that the nation's defense is a high enough priority to justify conscription. "The costs of service as a conscriptee should be accounted . . . against the consequences to the individual and society in the event that a war vital to the national interest or national survival is lost." Against the costs of coercion he weighs "the death of a way of life."

Marlowe's argument in favor of a draft justifies drafting qualified women as well as men (though not for combat duty). An army capable of victory "requires that it have the most competent and highly skilled personnel available manning its force, its weapons, and its support systems . . . If we are to man our military force in a way that will ensure optimal competence, skill, and ability—given the approaching demographic dip of the later eighties through nineties—women will have to provide a significant part of that force."

Ruddick addresses the legitimacy of drafting women by raising questions about the sources and limits of political obligation as these bear on the coerced participation of women in the armed force. Do women and men have the same obligations to their government? Do these obligations include military service?

It can be argued that women are socially, economically, and politically disadvantaged relative to men, and that they are therefore less obligated to support their state and defend its political and economic arrangements. If benefit from and participation in the state justify a duty to serve in the military, they do not, according to Ruddick, "obligate women to the same degree and for the same reasons [as men]." Few contemporary political theorists believe, however, that such a grave duty as military service can be justified on these grounds for the vast majority of citizens.

It is more plausible, in Ruddick's view, to view political obligation generally as grounded in a "natural duty to preserve states in their justice." A citizen of a (relatively) just state accepts obligations to it "because his state is just and he is moral." If this account justifies the drafting of men, it equally justifies the drafting of women, because men and women "are the same kind of moral person." But *does* a citizen's moral obligation to a just state include military service? Ruddick thinks not: The duty entailed is a duty both to assist in just wars *and* to resist unjust wars. Individuals must be allowed in conscience to decide the justice of the wars their state chooses to wage before deciding to join in waging them; this duty of conscience is shared fully by citizens of both sexes, and for both sexes it is equally incompatible with currently proposed drafts.

For this reason, Ruddick views conventional policies of conscription as unjust and unjustified—again, for men and women alike. But if men *are* in fact unjustly drafted, should women be drafted as well? Should a burden that no one should bear be fairly shared? Ruddick believes that the answer may be yes—however socially, politically, and economically advantaged men may be as a group, coerced combat remains a terrible thing: "There is a fundamental fairness that decrees it impermissible that men, solely because of gender, bear the sole burden of combat."

Conclusion

The moral question about the role of women in the military seems in the end to resolve to a question about the rights and obligations of citizenship. If the right to fight is a citizenship right, it is a right qualified women share with qualified men. If citizenship carries with it an obligation to serve, women, as full and equal citizens, will have to accept their portion of the military burden. Segal writes: "One of the basic principles on which our nation was founded is the full participation of all citizens in all aspects of the life of the nation. The ultimate question that still remains is to what extent we are willing to treat women as equal citizens of the nation."

The services do not now accept volunteers who cannot meet established standards, and past drafts have exempted those for whom competing moral obligations—to family, church, or conscience—have forbidden military participation. There seems no reason to believe that existing standards and exemptions cannot continue to bar or excuse those men and women who cannot or ought not serve, while encouraging the full participation of all able-bodied and willing citizens, whatever their race, creed, or gender.

The views of Sara Ruddick, Mady Segal, and David H. Marlowe are drawn from their essays in Conscripts and Volunteers: Military Requirements, Social Values, and the All-Volunteer Force, *ed. Robert K. Fullinwider, Maryland Studies in Public Philosophy (Totowa, N.J.: Rowman and Allanheld, 1983).*

Gays and Civil Rights

Richard D. Mohr

When gays themselves speak of "gay rights," they generally refer to the sort of protections found in the 1964 Civil Rights Act, rather than to a host of other possible legal and constitutional protections they do not now possess (for example, the reform of sodomy and solicitation laws and the drive for domestic partner legislation). For gays, gay rights are viewed primarily as protections against discrimination in the private sphere in regard to housing, public accommodations, and especially employment—protections the Civil Rights Act currently affords racial, ethnic, gender, and religious classes.

Gays have not been particularly successful in acquiring even those limited rights. While some ninety cities and counties have such protections, only two states do—Wisconsin and Massachusetts—and a federal gay civil rights bill is nowhere on the horizon. Gays are now at about the same place blacks were in 1945.

The arguments in favor of gay civil rights cluster into three main groups. The first is a recognition that the general arguments for civil rights legislation indeed apply to gays, sometimes with special force. Second, the status of gays as an invisible minority has the practical consequence that in the absence of these protections, gays are effectively denied access to civic and political rights. Third, gays appear to be relevantly similar to classes already protected by the Civil Rights Act, so considerations of fairness call for extending its protections to gays.

General Arguments for Civil Rights

It is unfortunate that the original general motives for civil rights legislation have been forgotten in discussions of gay issues. And yet the original reasons continue to provide good and powerful engines in justifying civil rights restrictions on the private sector and apply at least as well to gays as anyone. Four such general justifications, some interrelated, arise.

First, civil rights legislation promotes human dignity. Vague as this reason may initially sound, it is the reason the Supreme Court found most compelling as a ground for state action when it unanimously upheld the constitutionality of the Civil Rights Act. No one can maintain a solid sense of self if he is, in major ways affecting him, subject to whimsical and arbitrary actions of others. Jobs, housing, and entertainment are major modes through which people identify themselves to themselves and to others. That these major vehicles of character, personality, and identity can be taken away from a person without regard to any characteristic relevant to his possessing them is an outrage against personal integrity deserving remedies from the state. To fire an employee, for instance, on the basis of some trait that has no bearing on his ability to do his job—such as his sexual preferences—is one way to degrade someone and make him feel worthless. Given widespread discrimination (actual or merely perceived) against gays, it is not surprising that gays manifest many of the same self-destructive, self-deluding, self-oppressing patterns of behavior shared by other historically oppressed minorities.

Second, a general expectation in a nonsocialist society like our own is that each person is primarily responsible for meeting his own basic needs; employment is the chief means of doing so. Civil rights legislation helps people discharge their obligation to be self-sufficient, without placing any comparable burden on those who are restricted by the legislation (employers, retailers, etc.).

Third, civil rights legislation tends to increase the overall output of goods and services in society, thus contributing to general prosperity. By eliminating extraneous factors in employment decisions, it tends to promote the best fit between a worker's capacities, talents, and skills and the bona fide occupational qualifications of his prospective work. Many gays take dead-end jobs, which do not use their full talents, in order to avoid reviews that might reveal their minority status. Such people's talents are simply wasted both to themselves and to society. Human resources are further wasted if one's energies are constantly diverted and devoured by fear of arbitrary dismissal. In the absence of gay civil rights legislation, society is squandering the human resources that closeted gays expend in the day-to-day anxiety involved in leading lives of systematic disguise as a condition for continued employment.

These three preceding general arguments can be pooled into a fourth. Government is generally recognized to have an obligation to enhance conditions that promote the flourishing of individual lives. Thus, for example, the general rationale for compulsory liberal education is that it ultimately issues in autonomous individuals capable of making decisions for themselves from a field of alternative opinions. Analogously, civil rights legislation promotes those conditions in virtue of which people can begin to lead their own lives guided by their own lights. And because the activities protected by such legislation are so central to people's lives, it achieves this result again without any comparable loss on the part of those whom it restrains. The frustrated desire (or even right) to act whimsically to a disfavored group is easily outweighed by the frustrated desire (or even right) of the disfavored minority to lead self-determining lives. This justification has special import for gays. Imagine the lives of gays who systematically forgo sharing emotional intimacy and the common necessities of life as the price for putting bread on their table. With the lessening of fear from threat of discovery, gays no longer will need to make trade-offs between components that go into making a full life.

An Invisible Minority

The status of gays as an invisible minority generates a second cluster of important arguments for gay rights. By invisible minority I mean a minority whose members can be identified only through an act of will on someone's part rather than merely through the observation of a person's appearance or his day-to-day acts in the public domain. Invisible minorities require civil rights protections as a necessary background condition for having reasonably guaranteed access to judicial or civic rights and to the political rights of the First Amendment—rights supposed to pertain equally to all.

Civil or judicial rights are rights to the impartial administration of civil and criminal law in defense of property and person. One of the greatest virtues of the American legal system is that its workings are open to scrutiny by public and press. Here trials are not star chamber affairs. But this has the unfortunate side effect that trials frequently cast the private into the public realm. Those who may face unemployment if their life-style is publicized will simply not have available to them as a live option the full remedies of justice. It is unreasonable to expect anyone to give up that by which he lives—his employment, his shelter, his access to goods and services—in order for judicial procedures to be carried out equitably.

Further, in the absence of civil rights legislation, gays as an invisible minority are in practice denied the effective use of the political rights of the First Amendment: freedom of speech, of press, of assembly, of petition, and especially the right of association—the right to join and be identified with other persons for common (political) goals.

In the absence of civil rights protections, even if gays are *free from* government interference in their political activity, nevertheless they remain effectively denied the *freedom to* act politically. All effective political strategies involve public action. And a person who is a member of an invisible minority, and who must remain invisible in respect to his minority status as a condition of maintaining the wherewithal to live, is not free to be public about his minority status or to incur suspicion by publicly associating with others who are open about their similar status. He will be denied the opportunity to express his views in a public forum and to lobby with others of like views to influence political change. By being effectively denied the public procedures of democracy, gays are incapable of defending their own interests on substantial issues of vital concern.

Treating Like Cases Alike

A third category of arguments for gay rights can be generated if gays are relevantly similar to classes already under the protection of the Civil Rights Act. Considerations of whether gays are or are not relevantly similar have made up the lion's share of the popular and political debate on this issue. The opponent of extending civil rights to gays is confronted with a dilemma here. For if it turns out that being gay is something over which one has little or no control, then being gay will be similar to having an ethnic status. And if being gay is largely a matter of personal moral choice, then it will be like having a religion. And both ethnic and religious groups are protected classes.

If sexual orientation is something over which an individual—for whatever reason—has virtually no control, then discrimination against gays is deplorable, as it is against racial and gender classes, because it holds a person accountable without regard for anything he himself has done. And to hold a person accountable for that over which he has no control is one of the central forms of prejudice.

Looking at the actual lived experience of gays in our society, it becomes fairly clear that sexual orientation is not likely a matter of choice. For coming to have a homosexual identity in our culture simply does not have the structure of decision-making.

On the one hand, the "choice" of the gender of a sexual partner does not seem to express a trivial desire that might be as easily fulfilled by substituting some other object for the desired one. Picking the gender of a sexual partner is decidedly dissimilar, that is, to picking a flavor of ice cream. If an ice cream parlor is out of one's favorite flavor, one simply picks another. And if people were persecuted and threatened with jail terms, shattered careers, and the like for eating rocky road ice cream, everyone would pick another easily available flavor. But gay sex seems not to be like that. If sexual orientation were an easy choice, no one, given society's persecution of gays, would ever be gay.

On the other hand, establishing a sexual orientation does not seem relevantly like making the central and serious life choices by which individuals try to establish who they are. We never see anyone setting out to become a homosexual, in the way we do see people setting out to become doctors and lawyers and bricklayers. We do not see gays deciding, "At some point in the future I want to become a homosexual," and then planning and acquiring the ways and means to that end, in the way we do see people deciding they want to become lawyers and then planning what courses to take, and what temperaments, habits, and skills to develop in order to practice law. Typically the gay-person-to-be just finds himself having homosexual encounters while initially resisting quite strongly the identification of being a homosexual; only with time, luck, and great personal effort—but sometimes never—does he gradually come to accept his orientation. The experience of coming out *to oneself* has for a gay person the basic structure of a discovery, not the structure of a choice.

Nevertheless, one group of self-identified homosexuals—politically motivated lesbians—holds that sexual orientation, at least in their case, is a matter of choice. If this is so, then sexual orientation becomes relevantly similar to religion, a protected category. A personal moral choice is not a reasonable ground for discrimination, even when the private belief in and practice of it has very public manifestations, as when a religious person becomes involved in politics with a religious motive. And to claim that gay sex is in some sense immoral will not suffice to establish a relevant dissimilarity here. For the nonreligious and the religious may consider each other immoral, and the various religious sects may consider each other immoral, and yet all religious belief is protected.

These various arguments have a compelling accumulative force. What is needed is more courage on the part of gays to advance them to legislators and more courage on the part of legislators to rise above popular prejudices to make minority rights against social and government coercion a realized part of our cultural ideals.

This article was adapted from papers that eventually became Part Three of Gays/Justice—A Study of Ethics, Society, and Law *(New York: Columbia University Press, 1988).*

Racist and Sexist Jokes
How Bad Are They (Really)?

Claudia Mills

In 1976 Earl Butz, President Gerald Ford's popular secretary of agriculture, fell from grace with almost unprecedented abruptness. On a flight to California after the Republican National Convention, he committed an offense so unforgivable that the public outcry drove him from office less than seventy-two hours after the story broke. The offense: telling a racist joke. Two administrations later, James Watt, the embattled secretary of the interior whom critics had unsuccessfully tried to unseat over a host of environmental issues, finally made his fatal misstep: He remarked jocularly that his coal advisory commission boasted the impeccably balanced mixture of "a black, a woman, two Jews, and a cripple." The joke precipitated Watt's forced resignation.

What did Butz and Watt do that was so terrible? How can two prominent officials lose their jobs over *jokes*? Doesn't that seem a kind of joke itself, laying bare our national oversensitivity and humorlessness? Millions of us tell racist, sexist, heterosexist, or ethnic jokes; millions of us are offended by their telling—especially if the joke hits too close to home. And when members of the target group take offense, the question comes: What's the matter? Can't you take a joke? Where's your sense of humor?

"It's Only a Joke"

Few presumably would defend racist, ethnic, sexist, and heterosexist jokes as cultural treasures, but many of the jokes are cleverly constructed, such as the infinite variations on "How many so-and-so's does it take to change a lightbulb?" that deftly caricature alleged group characteristics. "How many Jewish mothers does it take to change a lightbulb?" "None: 'Don't mind me, I'll just sit here in the dark.'" In a grim world, maybe anything to laugh about is cause for celebration.

Ronald de Sousa, professor of philosophy at the University of Toronto, asks whether humor generally can be the object of moral censure. After all, it could be claimed that humor is too trivial to merit moral condemnation; the propriety of telling or laughing at certain jokes is a matter only of good or bad taste, with the duty to refrain from racist jokes "merely a minor social duty, like the duty not to fart or burp." De Sousa concedes (which many others would not) that "laughter . . . does not have very significant consequences." But he counters that laughter—how a person laughs and what he or she laughs at—nonetheless yields insights into character. Even the sound of someone's laughter can be revelatory: "Imagine a man whose habitual sound of laughter is a *cackle*, or a *snicker*. Would you like your daughter to marry him?" But is such a reaction merely an aesthetic one? De Sousa concludes not. We judge laughter as a symptom not only of personal style but of moral character as well: "There are cases in which we say: 'If you can laugh at something like that, you must be insensitive (or) cruel.'" In the case of racist and sexist jokes, a natural judgment is "If you can laugh at something like that, you must be a racist or a sexist."

Philosopher Merrie Bergmann explains what sexist jokes show about character by appealing to one standard theory of humor: "The source of funniness in a humorous episode is the incongruous," attended to or contemplated in fun. The theory applies to sexist humor in this way: "Sexist humor is humor in which sexist beliefs, attitudes, and/or norms either must be held in order to perceive an incongruity or are used to add to the fun effect of the incongruity." She gives as an example a supposedly comic postcard, showing an attractive female sunbathing with a newspaper across her midriff; the headline reads, "Today's Sport." Bergmann observes, "Perceiving an incongruity here depends upon having a sexist attitude toward women. In our culture, there is nothing incongruous in a newspaper resting on the body of a sunbather. Nor is there anything incongruous in a newspaper's having a page headed 'Today's Sport.' What *is* incongruous is that the newspaper headline should refer to, or label, the body that is shaded by the paper, that is, that 'Today's Sport' is the female body in question. And perceiving this incongruity depends on seeing the female's body as a sex object." De Sousa argues that to laugh at such a joke is to show that one shares the underlying sexist assumptions necessary to "get" its humor. To laugh at a joke like this one, de Sousa says, "*marks you as sexist*. It's not a convincing defense to say: 'I was merely going along with the assumptions required to get the point of the joke.'" Such a joke "makes us laugh only insofar as the assumptions on which it is based are attitudes actually shared."

Is it true that people who tell racist and sexist jokes thereby show themselves to be racists and sexists? It seems, under Bergmann and de Sousa's theory, that someone truly concerned about racism and sexism can enjoy racist and sexist jokes only at a meta-level, where the laughter is directed not at the intended butt of the joke, but turned on the jokers themselves, who are ridiculed for being the kind of people who find a joke like that funny. Something is comical, for example, in a male boss who jokes to a roomful of female secretaries, "Why did God make women? Because sheep can't type!" and then wonders why no one else is laughing.

Can't derogatory jokes also be enjoyed by someone who, while no racist or sexist, nonetheless takes a sly pleasure in puncturing liberal pretensions and poking fun at societal pieties? Also, the very outrageousness of determinedly tasteless humor can be oddly refreshing. This species of pleasure in racist and sexist jokes, however, seems parasitical on a prior recognition that the jokes are morally suspect. There is no naughty fun in shouting obscenities without a prior shared recognition of what counts as obscene.

Make Jokes, Not War

One might defend racist and sexist jokes by arguing that while the jokes may express racist or sexist attitudes, in humor these are given a harmless outlet. Ethologist Konrad Lorenz, in *On Aggression*, characterizes humor as aggressive behavior held in check by reason. Laughter, according to Lorenz, "is never in danger of regressing and causing the primal aggressive behavior to break through. . . . Barking dogs may occasionally bite, but laughing men hardly ever shoot." If racist and sexist jokes are not harmful, we may welcome them as an escape valve for aggressive energies that might otherwise erupt in less socially acceptable ways.

The trouble is that racist and sexist jokes *are* in themselves harmful. They reinforce and give social legitimacy to the racist and sexist beliefs they presuppose. Philosopher Joseph Boskin, writing on the enduring comic Sambo stereotype of blacks, blames it for helping whites "in their attempt to preserve a social distance between themselves and blacks, to maintain a sense of racial superiority, and to prolong the class structure." Richard Mohr, a philosopher at the University of Illinois, charges that anti-gay jokes are similarly pernicious: "When people know few or no gays and have fag jokes as their earliest and main source of information about gays, the stereotypes which fag jokes endorse and perpetrate, by portraying and belittling gays as dizzy, flighty, unreliable, self-indulgent, sex-crazed, and plague-bearing, are especially likely to have unfortunate effects on prospective employers and on any public policy decisions affecting gays. In this way, fag jokes harm gays."

Racist and sexist jokes are vehicles not only of injury, but of insult as well. Bergmann likens the person who finds fun in sexist humor to a person who enjoys the spectacle of watching a passerby slip on a banana peel—after having first placed the banana peel on the sidewalk: "Both contribute to the stage-setting for the fun." For without the contribution of the requisite sexist beliefs, no fun is found in sexist humor. The insult of finding fun in sexist humor "is the insult of finding fun in an episode when part of the stage-setting that we have contributed to the episode, and that is necessary to the fun, hurts someone." It is an insult, Mohr explains, "for it fails to take others' pains into account as one would expect one's own pains to be taken into account by others."

Is this a special failing of racist and sexist jokes, however? Much nonracist and nonsexist humor is undeniably malicious (else why *would* we laugh when the fat man slips on a banana peel?); it might be said that the offense given by a joke is not a mark of its immorality but of its success! The distinctive wrong of racist and sexist jokes is that the stereotypes they evoke and help to maintain are so deeply implicated in our society's long history of injustice to certain disadvantaged groups. The injury and insult they cause is not an isolated or fleeting phenomenon; it is part of a pattern of systematic harms and humiliations directed by the powerful against the powerless.

Can't You Take a Joke?

A final strategy for defending racist and sexist jokes is to take the offensive against members of the target groups insulted by them (a strategy used more often with sexism than racism). An analogy is drawn to the attitude we expect an individual to have when a joke is told on him personally. It is considered a sign of good nature to be able to laugh at oneself, to appreciate a joke told at one's own expense. Those who can't are seen as stuffy, pompous, self-righteous. If how one tells a joke shows character, how one takes a joke shows character as well.

Even in the individual case, however, we draw a distinction between laughing *with* someone and laughing *at* someone, where the one grows out of affection, the other out of derision. Dignified silence, not shared laughter, is the appropriate response to being laughed *at*. And a crucial difference exists between laughter focused on an individual and laughter focused on a group. One can relish a joke on oneself if it is truly a joke on *oneself*, if it calls amused attention to one's own distinctive traits and foibles, as cartoon caricatures do. There is a pleasure in being observed carefully enough by others that teasing is possible, as long, once again, as the teasing is affectionate.

The victim of a racist joke, however, is expected to laugh at a joke allegedly about himself that he doesn't perceive as a joke about *himself* at all. The whole idea of a *racist* joke is that nothing distinctive about the individual person is involved. As Mohr observes about heterosexist humor: "The individual as distinctive is erased, dissolved into a prejudged type which determines in society's eyes all of his or her significant characteristics. The jokes . . . presume that a gay person is nothing but his sexual orientation and its efflorescences." The woman expected to laugh at a sexist joke, packaged as a joke about herself, wants to protest, "But this isn't a joke about *me*." Even this reaction is parodied in the joke where the husband says to the wife, "Women always take everything personally," and the wife replies indignantly, "*I* don't."

How are we to react, then, when a racial or ethnic joke is told by a member of that race or ethnic group? How can racist or ethnic jokes be so terrible if individuals are willing to tell these on themselves? Ethnic jokes are told on oneself in a variety of contexts. Sometimes one plugs one's own ethnic group into an all-purpose ethnic joke to be able to "get away with" telling it, without giving offense. In such cases the joke itself appeals to no distinctive stereotype of the group chosen—it satirizes, say, garden-variety stupidity—and so the punchline carries no sting. Occasionally, ethnic jokes told by ethnic-group members may provide genuine examples of affectionate self-directed humor, where the joke teasingly plays on some ethnic trait the group itself recognizes, half-affectionately, half-ruefully, as its own. But too often self-told ethnic jokes show only self-directed ethnic hatred. Boskin points to cases where blacks themselves have adopted the Sambo stereotype as self-image: "Entrapped within the illusion, the stereotyped person runs the risk of succumbing to it." That a negative stereotype, repeated and reinforced in countless ethnic jokes, can become so culturally dominant that members of the despised group at last come to internalize it is one of the most egregious wrongs such jokes perpetrate.

Conclusion

Returning now to Butz and Watt, exiled from public service for jokes that took only a moment in the telling: Did their punishment fit or exceed their crime? If racist and sexist jokes are evidence of a racist and sexist character, cause pain and harm to blacks and women, and insult and affront the dignity of blacks and women as individuals, it would seem that public administration can do without the services of those who cannot refrain from telling them.

The sources quoted in this article are Ronald de Sousa, "When Is It Wrong to Laugh?" in The Philosophy of Laughter and Humor, *ed. John Morreall (Albany: State University of New York Press, 1987); Merrie Bergmann, "How Many Feminists Does It Take to Make a Joke? Sexist Humor and What's Wrong with It,"* Hypatia *1, no. 1 (Spring 1986); Konrad Lorenz,* On Aggression *(New York: Bantam Books, 1963); Joseph Boskin, "The Complicity of Humor: The Life and Death of Sambo," in Morreall, ed.,* The Philosophy of Laughter and Humor; *and Richard Mohr, "Fag-ends and Jokes' Butts," forthcoming in a book on gays and equality.*

Privacy in the Computer Age

Claudia Mills

The odds are good that some computer somewhere knows something about you that you would rather it didn't. The databases of the federal government contain four billion separate records about American citizens—seventeen items apiece. Recently, different government files have been electronically compared to uncover telltale discrepancies: Personnel files of federal employees have been matched against state welfare rolls to flag welfare fraud; lists of eighteen-year-old male dependents generated from Internal Revenue Service records have been matched against Selective Service registrations to identify draft evaders. The Federal Bureau of Investigation's (FBI) National Crime Information Center is a massive computer network linking more than fifty-seven thousand federal, state, and local criminal-justice agencies and offering instant access to information on stolen property, missing and wanted persons, and criminal histories. This last category is of particular interest to prospective employers, who were responsible for half of the more than 200 million inquiries directed to the network last year. It is worth their while to bother checking: One in five Americans will be arrested at some time in their lives.

The federal government is joined in its computerized information gathering by behemoths in the private sector. A giant computerized credit company like TRW makes available to thousands of merchants all over the country a tidy balance sheet on any of almost 90 million Americans in a matter of three or four seconds. AT&T holds precise minute-by-minute records of the 500 million phone calls made daily from the nation's 130 million telephones, information that has been used by government investigators in a number of cases. Such information, notes David Burnham, author of *The Rise of the Computer State*, "can be extraordinarily revealing. . . . investigators can learn what numbers an individual has called, what time of day and day of week the calls were made, the length of each conversation, and the number of times an incorrect number was dialed. Considered as a whole, such information can pinpoint the location of an individual at a particular moment, indicate his daily patterns of work and sleep, and even suggest his state of mind."

In many businesses, computers are used directly and overtly for worker surveillance. A recent nationwide survey of video-display-terminal operators showed that 35 percent were monitored by computer. Computer monitoring has been used to keep a daily log of the room-tidying speed of maids at Washington's Ritz-Carlton Hotel, to clock the "average work time" of AT&T telephone operators, to see how fast the cashiers at the Giant Food Store process customers, and to tabulate the performance of United Parcel Service drivers to the hundredth of an hour.

Many charge that these cases amount to a flagrant and frightening invasion of privacy. They ask whether privacy in any recognizable form can survive the computer age. But just what kind of a threat to privacy is posed by the long memory and unblinking eye of the computer? What is privacy, and why do we value it personally and as a society? How do we weigh the threatened value of privacy against the manifold marvels the computer promises to unfold before us?

What Is Privacy?

Privacy has been defined in a number of ways. On one account, it is the measure of *control* a person has over access to information about herself, or to the most intimate aspects of her life. Privacy is a matter here, not of how much others know about the details of one's life, but of the extent to which the person herself decides what information they are to have. On another account, privacy is the *state* or *condition* of limited access to a person. In this view, someone's privacy is diminished in some measure whenever others come to know more about her.

Ferdinand Schoeman, a professor of philosophy at the University of South Carolina, favors the second account. He argues that "a person who chose to exercise his discretionary control over information about himself by divulging everything cannot be said to have lost control, although he surely cannot be said to have any privacy." And an individual can lose some control over access to personal information (if, for instance, a national security agency is authorized to monitor international phone conversations) without losing any privacy at all (if his conversations are not among those monitored). The *right* to privacy, according to Schoeman, has to do with the question of the individual's control; privacy itself concerns what the individual has control *of.*

Thus either privacy itself or certainly the right to privacy is diminished when huge databases stock vast quantities of information about us (and particularly when computerized matching programs reveal to one agency, without our authorization, information disclosed to another). Access to personal information about us is increased, and our control over who has access to this information, and what kind of access, is decreased.

Why does this matter? Why is it important that access to information about our lives remains limited, or that we control such access?

Why Privacy Matters

One reason why we might value privacy is that it carves out a space where we can do bad things without being found out. Those with criminal intentions have good reason to ward off too-close scrutiny of their affairs. But this reason for valuing privacy will not carry much weight with the rest of us, who have nothing criminal to hide. We would rather eliminate welfare fraud than shield the defrauder from a computerized matching program that would uncover his double identity.

Privacy also allows the convicted miscreant the hope that in time her past misdeeds will fade from public attention and be forgotten. The FBI's master file of computerized histories ensures, on the contrary, that memory will be steadfast and long. Legal theorist and federal judge Richard Posner argues that this is all to the good, that people should be thwarted in concealing disadvantageous information about themselves. Such concealment, he thinks, amounts to fraud in "selling" oneself to prospective employers and friends. But Richard Wasserstrom, professor of philosophy at the University of California—Santa Cruz, suggests that "there are important gains that come from living in a society in which certain kinds of derogatory information about an individual are permitted to disappear from view after a certain amount of time. What is involved is the creation of a kind of social environment that holds out to the members of the society the possibility of self-renewal and change . . . of genuine individual redemption."

Those who would have nothing to fear from the disclosure of complete and accurate information about themselves might, of course, have a good deal to fear from the disclosure of partial and false information. Unfortunately, partial and false information are just what most databases have an abundance of. Burnham reports the results of one study that found that only 45.9 percent of the records in the FBI's computerized criminal history file were "complete, accurate, and unambiguous." Anyone who has tangled with a computer over a simple billing error knows how difficult it can be to erase a faulty bit of information from the computer's elephantine memory. Furthermore, even accurate information can be subject to misinterpretation; Burnham also points to sociological experiments indicating that employers are reluctant to hire workers with arrest records, even where charges were later dropped, or where a court trial resulted in acquittal. Once arrested, one is presumed guilty even after being proved innocent! While privacy per se is not at issue in the disclosure of *false* information about ourselves, it at least reduces the sheer volume of personal information stored, thus minimizing the danger of error.

People differ in how approvingly they regard the current government, but no one has much trouble imagining some possible future government that would be far worse. It seems wise, then, to curb the power of the state over its citizens, to make sure the state doesn't come to know too much. By enhancing and fostering a clear sphere of the private, privacy helps to rein in the sphere of the public, to mark out a clear boundary that we prohibit the state from crossing. It is the crossing of this boundary that is feared when computerized databanks are likened to an Orwellian Big Brother.

These concerns, however potent, still do not seem to capture all that matters to us about preserving our privacy from computerized intrusions. If these doubts could be met in other ways—by strictly enforcing a periodical review of stored records for completeness and accuracy, say, or erecting other barriers against official abuse—we would still feel that some deeper worry was left untouched. Privacy is important not only for what it saves us from, but for what it has been argued to make possible: freedom and dignity, on the one hand, and intimate human relationships, on the other.

Freedom and Dignity

Privacy protects freedom—not only the freedom, as noted earlier, to misbehave, but also the freedom to do anything we would be inhibited in doing by the presence of external observation. Think how many actions we would feel less free to perform if someone—anyone—were intently watching us every minute of the day, taking account of every movement we made, every syllable we uttered. Such relentless scrutiny would make one reluctant to do anything commonly perceived, for whatever reason, as foolish or embarrassing; it would curtail groping, experimentation, risk taking, trial and error. Imagine trying to write a paper, a poem, a love letter, with every preliminary scribble inspected by an uninvited third party. We are less free to act, to speak, to dream in public than in private, and practices of privacy maintain the barrier between the two realms.

Do current uses of computer technology undermine privacy in a way that poses a threat to freedom? The minute-by-minute computerized surveillance of workers that is increasingly relied on as a management technique seems clearly to make workers less free. When, as in some workplaces, every keystroke is tallied electronically, every momentary respite recorded—every nose-blowing, every stretch, every bathroom break—the state of observation is too total, and too totalitarian.

To a much lesser degree, projected levels of centralized data collection and storage could also take a toll on freedom and spontaneity. With the routine storage of enormous quantities of information, Wasserstrom speculates, "every transaction in which one engages would . . . take on an additional significance. In such a society one would be both buying a tank of gas and leaving a part of a systematic record of where one was on that particular date. . . . An inevitable consequence of such a practice of data collection is that persons would think more carefully before they did things that would become part of the record. . . . we would go through life encumbered by a wariness and deliberateness that would make it less easy to live what we take to be the life of a free person."

Privacy is critical as well to the affirmation of human dignity. Jeffrey Reiman, a philosopher at American University, suggests that the cluster of behaviors that makes up the social practice of privacy has as its purpose a resonant societal declaration of respect for the dignity of the individual: "Privacy is a social ritual by means of which an individual's moral title to his existence is conferred. Privacy is an essential part of the complex social practice by means of which the social group recognizes—and communicates to the individual—that his existence is his own."

The right to privacy, in Reiman's view, "is the right to the existence of a social practice which makes it possible for me to think of this existence as *mine*." The specific nature and form of this practice may differ from society to society and may change over time. This means that the growth of computerized databanks need not undermine privacy in our society if other practices in the complex privacy ritual receive compensatory emphasis, or if new practices develop. But a danger is that the weakening of one strand in the cluster will weaken others as well. Wasserstrom warns, "If it became routine to record and have readily accessible vast quantities of information about every individual, we might come to hold the belief that the detailed inspection of any individual's behavior is a perfectly appropriate societal undertaking. We might become insensitive to the legitimate claims of an individual to a sphere of life in which the individual is at present autonomous and around which he or she can erect whatever shield is wished."

Privacy and Intimate Relationships

In one sense, privacy builds fences around persons through which others are not permitted to peer and beyond which they may not trespass. The right to privacy has been categorized as the right to be let alone. Yet here, too, it has been argued that "good fences make good neighbors"—that privacy not only protects individual freedom and dignity but is itself a necessary precondition of our entering into a wide range of diverse human relationships.

According to University of Alabama philosopher James Rachels, "There is a close connection between our ability to control who has access to us and to information about us, and our ability to create and maintain different sorts of social relationships with different people." An essential part of what distinguishes one sort of relationship from another is "a conception of the kind and degree of knowledge concerning one another which it is appropriate for [the parties] to have." Thus we disclose different amounts of information about different aspects of our lives to our doctor, employer, neighbors, children, casual acquaintances, close friends, spouse. If we could not control the level of disclosure and choose to be selective in our revelations, Rachels argues, we could not maintain an array of diverse personal and professional relationships.

Indeed, legal philosopher Charles Fried insists that without privacy, our most intimate relationships "are simply inconceivable. . . . To be friends or lovers persons must be intimate to some degree with each other. But intimacy is the sharing of information about one's actions, beliefs, or emotions which one does not share with all, and which one has the right not to share with anyone. By conferring this right, privacy creates the moral capital which we spend in friendship and love. . . . Privacy grants the control over information which enables us to maintain degrees of intimacy."

Is the possibility of genuine sharing within an intimate relationship precluded by the proliferation of centralized databanks where secrets that would be confided to the loved one are handily stored with billions of other tidbits of information on a magnetic tape? The answer would seem to depend in part on how many people in what capacity have access to the database. The Rachels-Fried view provides one argument for limiting access as far as possible—for not, for example, passing files about from one government agency to another.

Reiman argues, however, that Fried and Rachels are wrong to think intimacy is bound up with privacy in the way they propose. Their view, he feels, "suggests a market conception of personal intimacy. The value and substance of intimacy—like the value and substance of my income—lies not merely in what I have but essentially in what others do *not* have." Intimacy, in this view, is constituted by its unavailability to others—in economic terms, by its scarcity. Reiman suggests instead that "what constitutes intimacy is not merely the sharing of otherwise withheld information, but the context of caring which makes the sharing of personal information significant." He goes on to say, "It is of little importance who has access to personal information about me. What matters is who cares about it and to whom I care to reveal it. Even if all those to whom I am indifferent and who return the compliment were to know the intimate details of my personal history, my capacity to enter into an intimate relationship would remain unhindered." Computers are no threat to intimacy in this view. What matters for intimacy is not how much some computer knows, but how much some human being cares.

Computers don't care, of course, and it is likely the human beings who input intimate information into a database at so many keystrokes a minute don't care, either. This in itself can give rise to a feeling of violation—Schoeman observes that we feel defiled when information that matters deeply to ourselves is handled without recognition of its specialness. He compares intimate information, information that is of the greatest importance to our conception of ourselves, to a holy object—"something that is appropriately revealed only in special circumstances. To use such an object, even though it is a humble object when seen out of context, without the idea of its character in mind is to deprive the object of its sacredness. . . . Such an abuse is regarded as an affront."

None of this is to say that records of intimate information should not be committed to the computer. In many cases weighty societal reasons exist for collecting and storing the information that we do. But it is good for us to remember periodically that the data we collect and scrutinize are at bottom a record of people's lives. We have a charge to treat them carefully and with respect.

Conclusion

It is common to assume that technological changes inevitably pose a threat to privacy. But Schoeman notes that the industrial revolution brought in its wake a major increase in privacy, as the resultant urbanization led to heightened anonymity—"the privacy that results from the indifference of others." Generally, Schoeman suggests, "the degree to which privacy is threatened is a function of design rather than of mere consequence." The technology of the computer gives us new capabilities that would allow us to restrict the privacy of individuals in new ways, but it does not dictate how we will choose to use these capabilities. That choice depends on how important we, as a society, take privacy to be.

The views of Ferdinand Schoeman, Richard Posner, Richard Wasserstrom, Jeffrey Reiman, James Rachels, and Charles Fried are taken from their articles in Philosophical Dimensions of Privacy: An Anthology, *ed. Ferdinand Schoeman (New York: Cambridge University Press, 1984). The factual information in the article was drawn from* The Rise of the Computer State, *by David Burnham (New York: Vintage Books, 1984) and two* Washington Post *articles: "The Computer That Can Send You to Jail," by Bob Brown, September 23, 1984; and "Monitoring by Computers Sparks Employee Concerns," by Peter Perl, September 2, 1984.*

Drug Testing in Sports

Douglas MacLean

When Janis Joplin, John Belushi, and a number of other famous entertainers died of drug overdoses, many people were shocked and saddened. But the impact was not the same as when the University of Maryland's star basketball player, Len Bias, died from an overdose of cocaine. Joplin and Belushi were surely more famous, but Bias's death played on the front pages of newspapers for much longer and had a more marked policy impact, generating calls for an overhaul of athletic programs and for mandatory drug testing of athletes.

Perhaps we expect entertainers to live their lives more recklessly than the rest of us, so their drug abuse does not surprise us. But we tend to regard star athletes as more than entertainers. Nobody demands drug testing for actors or musicians, but even before Bias's death, a *Sports Illustrated* poll revealed that 73 percent of the respondents favored drug testing for athletes. Most university sports programs, along with professional baseball, football, and basketball, have instituted drug-testing programs. Such programs have been criticized on the grounds that test results are often inaccurate and that testing programs invite abuse. A more fundamental question is whether, risks of error and abuse aside, such invasions of privacy can be justified. Why should athletes be singled out for this kind of scrutiny of their private lives?

Testing Student Athletes

Many people think we should regard athletes differently from other students and be especially protective of them. Red Auerbach, general manager of the Boston Celtics, the professional basketball team that drafted Len Bias the day before he died, expresses this view clearly. "I know that it's an invasion of privacy, but there comes a time when you've got to put this altruistic civil rights stuff down the toilet, find out who's using drugs and take it from there. Athletes are targets because of their leadership. Drug sellers approach them in fifty ways, because they know that if they get an athlete hooked, other students will say, 'Hey, if my hero does it, what the hell; I may as well do it, too.'"

Singling out athletes for such invasiveness of their private lives on the grounds that they are worshiped and emulated cannot be justified. Star athletes surely enjoy the publicity they receive, but they do not ask to be made into role models. Nor should university administrators be encouraging this kind of status. It is sad if youngsters' only collegiate heroes are sports figures. Administrators inadvertently support this state of affairs by lavishly publicizing all the special requirements they place on their prominent athletes. They press on athletes a role as special representatives of their institutions. This is hardly a way to encourage kids to leave a basketball court at least long enough to attend their classes. Perhaps universities should be using drug tests to call attention to their Phi Beta Kappas instead, thus reinforcing a healthier kind of role model.

Universities in some instances are requiring their athletes to be tested for performance-enhancing drugs like steroids, amphetamines, and painkillers, as well as for recreational drugs. (The major professional sports, until recently, tested only for the latter.) Universities can thus claim that their concern is for the health and well-being of their athletes, for the athletes themselves. The pressures of competitive sports may place a heavy burden on such young adults, and they may, as Red Auerbach suggests, be a special target for campus drug pushers. No one could object to recognizing these problems, trying to avoid them, and offering help to the victims. It is surely tragic to see such gifted young people sacrifice their talents and risk their lives to drugs. But mandatory drug testing cannot be justified by compassion alone; a far better and less invasive strategy would be to de-emphasize the importance of college sports and reduce the pressures placed on student athletes.

Do any other grounds exist for singling out collegiate athletes for such invasions of privacy? Some might point to their scholarships as a justification. It is reasonable to attach certain conditions to receiving scholarships: Athletes must continue to play their sports, keep up their studies, and keep out of trouble. But these conditions should not include the kind of surveillance drug testing involves. A scholarship is an award, not a contract. Student athletes are not allowed to bargain freely for salaries or for a share of the revenues they bring to the institution for which they play. Institutions that take advantage of their financial need to subject athletes to excessive scrutiny are exploiting the very young people they claim to be trying to help. Talented young scientists do not forfeit their rights to privacy when they accept academic scholarships, and neither do athletes.

Drug Testing in the Workplace

What about drug testing for professional athletes? Team owners often sign players to multiyear contracts at astonishing salaries. They have a proprietary interest that individual performances not fall below salary-driven expectations, and so they are clearly concerned that these players perform to their full potentials. The public indirectly pays the players' salaries by their support of the games, which gives them a similar interest. Do these interests justify placing extraordinary demands on athletes? We pay the salaries of the musicians whose records we buy, too, but nobody much cares or thinks we ought to have a say in what *they* do with their personal lives.

How much intrusion into privacy and personal life is justified on economic grounds? In particular, do these reasons justify mandatory drug testing? We can begin to gain a better perspective on this issue by considering first the more general question of drug testing in the workplace.

Spurred on at least in part by public concern over Len Bias's death and drug abuse in sports, President Ronald Reagan, in September 1986, issued an "Executive Order for a Drug-Free Federal Workplace." The order announced that "The Federal Government, as the largest employer in the Nation, can and should show the way toward achieving drug-free workplaces." It expressed the government's concern for "the well-being of its employees" as well as for "the need to maintain employee productivity." The president, the vice-president, and cabinet members and their staffs all bellied up to the jar to be tested for drugs.

The government cannot order drug testing for all its employees, however. It is barred by Fourth Amendment guarantees against unreasonable search and seizure, and the Supreme Court has ruled that extracting bodily fluids is an unreasonable search. Therefore, the government must show that the conditions are exceptional, or else it must abide by due process guarantees and provide evidence showing probable cause that illegal activities are taking place. Thus, the president's Executive Order requires drug testing only for employees in "sensitive positions," where "danger to the public health and safety or national security . . . could result from failure of an employee adequately to discharge his or her position." But it invites private firms, which are not bound by Fourth Amendment restrictions, to require drug testing of all workers, whether or not their drug use might directly affect public health and safety.

The moral justification for this broader application of mandatory drug-testing programs, however, is weak, especially when weighed against the risks of allowing such invasions of privacy. Consider first the interests of the workers. Drug-testing programs are not aimed at the worst abusers; heroin and crack addicts are often not working, and those who are can likely be detected by less draconian means. Drug-testing programs are targeted at moderate and light users, whose welfare may not need protecting at all. Many occasional users of illegal drugs manage to consume in ways that are not self-destructive. Not all drug users become heroin addicts; some go on to become senators or judges.

This is not to deny that even occasional use of drugs like marijuana may be bad for people. Smoking, drinking, and even wholesome American activities like jogging or eating apple pie can lead to unhealthy abuse. But the fact that some activities are bad or unhealthy for people does not itself justify paternalistic intervention. How many people would support monitoring to detect whether we are dulling our minds in front of our television sets in the evenings? The people most likely to be detected as drug users by mandatory testing in the workplace are not leading lives that justify paternalistic intervention.

Is drug testing justified on economic grounds? Productivity losses due to drug use are hard to measure, but the available data suggest that they are significant though not critical. It is estimated that in 1980 lost productivity and work time due to drug abuse, together with treatment costs, amounted to $27.2 billion. (By comparison, the similar costs of alcohol abuse in that year were more than twice that, or $64.2 billion.) It isn't clear that workplace drug testing would reduce these costs, since it fails to reach hard-core drug users, and testing programs themselves are expensive. Several studies, moreover, including one by the National Institute on Drug Abuse, indicate that drug use appears to have peaked in the United States in 1979 and has been declining significantly since then. Historians argue that this kind of pattern is typical, that social concern about drug use increases in periods when drug use is decreasing.

But mightn't there be enormous potential for productivity gains by forcing even occasional and moderate users to adopt life-styles that would make them more alert and efficient in their jobs? This concern brings us back to the reason suggested for mandatory drug testing in professional sports. If we are paying athletes millions of dollars, don't we have a right to insist that they perform to the best of their abilities? And don't employers have this right more generally?

They do not. Imagine a striving poet who works to support herself by composing the messages in greeting cards. Can we insist she give her best creative efforts to her job? Clearly we cannot. So long as she does her job as well as expected or as well as others do it, she is giving it all we can demand. If you pay a lawyer $150 per hour to represent you, you can demand that she give you the best work she can during that time, but not that she lose sleep at night thinking about your case or exercise in the morning so she will be a little sharper in court. Employers can demand that their workers try hard and do well enough, but that is all. We still have a right to our private lives, even when what we do with our own time has some effect on our work. Consider television again. Should we prohibit workers from watching "Nightline" or David Letterman? Surely staying up late to watch these shows impairs one's job performance the next day. Of course, drug use is illegal, while television viewing is not. But this in itself should not give our *employers* any special power over us. We do not generally empower employers to serve as a volunteer police force.

Are Professional Sports Special?

Although these general economic reasons do not justify mandatory drug testing, other reasons may carry weight in particular occupations or professions. The president's Executive Order appeals to reasons of this sort in calling for drug testing for workers in "sensitive positions." We should ask, therefore, whether special reasons exist that would justify drug testing for professional athletes.

For better or worse, professional sports is a unique kind of entertainment business. It provides its customers with more than the recreational enjoyment of watching exciting matches and the exercise of great talent. Athletes are also heroes and fantasy figures. We fans spent countless hours of our own youths doing these same activities and imagining ourselves making game-winning plays in front of packed stadiums. We now find ourselves among the crowds watching those who are living out our fantasies, who succeeded in playing our childhood games better than the rest of us. We do not begrudge them their fame or their seven-figure seasonal salaries, because we are thrilled by their accomplishments. The youthful part—or the arrested development—of the typical sports fan allows him to identify with players and their teams and to relive his childhood fantasies. Sports fans care passionately, not when the home team wins, but when *our* team wins. "*We*'re number 1."

Sports league commissioners and presidents also overwhelmingly support drug testing, motivated by a concern with the economic health of the sport as a whole. They understand how fantasy and identification contribute to the popularity of professional sports. They know profits rely heavily on maintaining a culture that ensures players are suitable icons for fantasy. The image of the athlete is as important to the health of the business of sports as the excitement of play and competitive balance among the teams. Drug use is one of the many taboos of this culture. Athletes are pressured to be community spirited; open homosexuality and even political activism are culturally discouraged; and so on.

Whether enforcing this cultural code through pressure or invasive rules is morally acceptable is a vexing question. We seem to accept the propriety of holding some public figures (e.g., high government officials) to higher personal moral standards than others (e.g., musicians). We accept dress codes and restrictions on behavior in many professions, where there are good reasons for doing so. And what could be more personally invasive than the requirements imposed on those who would enter the priesthood? Perhaps enforcing the culture of the professional athlete can, after all, be shown as essential to the health and profitability of professional sports. Nobody is required to become a professional athlete, and the economic benefits of polishing the image of the athlete fall to all those involved.

Conclusion

Workplace drug testing seems to be acceptable for workers in certain "sensitive positions": The risks to the public when air traffic controllers or Amtrak engineers are impaired in their performance by drug use may outweigh concerns about privacy. Drug tests may be justified for professional athletes, too, given the enormous importance of maintaining an image to the financial health of league sports and the enormous financial rewards reaped by the players themselves. But it is hard to make out a justification for mandatory drug testing of student athletes or of workers generally. The public sector is restrained from broad-based drug testing by constitutional guarantees; the private sector should refrain by a respect for the value we place on keeping our private lives private.

FOR FURTHER READING

Boxill, Bernard R. *Blacks and Social Justice.* Totowa, N.J.: Rowman and Allanheld, 1984.

Fullinwider, Robert. *The Reverse Discrimination Controversy: A Moral and Legal Analysis.* Totowa, N.J.: Rowman and Allanheld, 1980.

Fullinwider, Robert, and Claudia Mills, eds. *The Moral Foundations of Civil Rights.* Maryland Studies in Public Philosophy. Totowa, N.J.: Rowman and Allanheld, 1986.

Mohr, Richard. *Gays/Justice: A Study of Ethics, Society, and Law.* New York: Columbia University Press, 1988.

Rhode, Deborah. *Justice and Gender.* Cambridge, Mass.: Harvard University Press, 1989.

Schoeman, Ferdinand. *Philosophical Dimensions of Privacy: An Anthology.* Cambridge: Cambridge University Press, 1984.

10

CITIZENSHIP AND POLITICS

This chapter treats a number of questions about the rights and obligations of citizenship, the proper understanding of patriotism, and the conduct of democratic politics. What is the ground of political obligation? Do citizens have rights to welfare? What rights do resident aliens have while they live in our midst? Is patriotism a value worthy of respect? How should we educate tomorrow's citizens? Does political "hardball" play a legitimate role in election campaigns? What does a candidate's private life have to do with his fitness for public office? And what place, if any, should religion occupy in American public life? These are the questions we seek here to answer, and to understand.

In "Why the Draft Is Hard to Justify," A. John Simmons attempts to determine what obligation citizens might have to serve in the military, by asking, more basically, whether citizens have any political obligations at all. He argues that all moral obligations must fall into one of three categories: requirements generated by voluntary acts, requirements based on natural moral duties, and requirements based in nonvoluntary relationships (such as filial obligations and obligations of gratitude to benefactors). In Simmons's view, an obligation of military service cannot be justified by appeal to any of these three categories.

"How Well-off Should Welfare Make You?" focuses on one relatively narrow question in welfare policy: Is it wrong for someone on welfare to end up, by means of welfare payments, better off than someone who is not on welfare at all? The article uses this question as a springboard for considering the various issues of equity, merit, and incentives that might determine our responses here.

Whatever is owed to our own welfare recipients, surely less is owed to those who are in our country illegally or on a merely temporary basis. But how much less? "Being Here: The Rights of Resident Aliens" explores the ground and extent of our societal obligations both to illegal aliens and to so-called guest-workers, those here on short-term temporary visas.

Patriotism is in fashion again, Robert Fullinwider notes in "The New Patriotism." Is this good news or bad? The cyclical waxing and waning of patriotic feeling reflects in part an enduring ambivalence about the nature and meaning of patriotism. A deep and abiding love for one's country may seem admirable—but it also conflicts with a more universal morality and with more cosmopolitan (and more local) attachments. Here Fullinwider explores the ways love of country may, and must, coexist with other loves without dominating them.

How is patriotic feeling, rightly understood, to be cultivated? How are future citizens best formed? In "Civic Education and Traditional American Values," Fullinwider looks at current controversies over inculcating "traditional American values" in the classroom, starting with the prior question of what "restoring traditional American values" *means.*

The final three articles in this chapter deal with issues regarding the conduct of electoral politics in a representative democracy, drawing examples from recent presidential campaigns. In "The Obligation to Play Political Hardball," William A. Galston provides a qualified defense of certain morally questionable political tactics, such as negative advertising and a focus on personalities rather than issues. He examines such practices by probing the broader issue of the relation between means and ends in politics more generally. Political hardball (though not "dirtyball") is not only morally permissible, Galston concludes, but also morally obligatory, if enough is at stake in the political outcome.

Judith Lichtenberg, in "Sex, Character, Politics, and the Press," takes the case study of Gary Hart's scandal-ridden withdrawal from the 1988 presidential race and uses it to illuminate a cluster of questions about the role the press should play in deciding what subjects are appropriate for political coverage. How much of a candidate's private life should rightly stay private? How much of it is relevant to judgments of his or her fitness for office?

Religion has played a larger role in presidential elections since John F. Kennedy's Catholicism became a campaign issue more than three decades ago, raising age-old questions about the proper relation-ship between religion and politics, church and state. "Religion in Public Life" tries to locate the appropriate boundaries and intercon-nections between these two domains by exploring what values separa-tion of church and state seeks to secure and how well it works to secure them.

Why the Draft Is Hard to Justify

A. John Simmons

Do we have an obligation to serve in the military? Is this one of our political obligations as citizens, along with the obligation to pay taxes and obey other kinds of laws? If so, what is the source of these other obligations? On what grounds do we have any political obligations at all? The entire justificatory program for the draft turns on these central questions.

It seems that all moral requirements fall into one of three classes, so if we have political obligations, they must fall into one of these three classes as well:

- Requirements generated by some voluntary performance, such as making a promise or signing a contract—these include obligations of fair play, which arise when persons voluntarily enter into cooperative projects

- Requirements arising simply from the moral character of the act in question, and so binding on all persons regardless of any special performances or relationships (for instance, "natural" duties not to lie or assault others)

- Requirements based in some special, but not necessarily voluntarily assumed, relationship (as obligations of children to parents and beneficiaries to benefactors)

Are political obligations requirements of any of these three kinds? If not, it seems doubtful that political obligations are really obligations at all.

Requirements Generated by Voluntary Acts

Classical political theorists such as Thomas Hobbes and John Locke argued that political obligation—and the legitimacy of all government—arises out of the voluntary consent of citizens to be governed. Realizing the great advantages of organization into a state, persons freely contract to take on the obligations of citizenship in exchange for its benefits and protections.

It is now widely recognized, however, that the political participation of the vast majority of citizens cannot be regarded as fully voluntary. Naturalized citizens are virtually the only non-officeholders who expressly consent to anything in the political sphere, and the kinds of genuine choice situations that would provide opportunities for native-born citizens to give binding consent are all but unheard of in modern political communities. Continued residence in a country need not, and routinely does not, occur in response to any fairly presented choice.

Neither does it seem plausible to characterize the average citizen as voluntarily participating in some ongoing political cooperative scheme with fellow citizens, and bound by considerations of fairness to serve in the military. While surely some persons can be taken to be voluntary participants in a fairly strong sense, many others clearly cannot—the poor, the alienated, those who are trapped and oppressed and denied opportunities for a decent life. For these citizens political participation consists of making the best of a situation where no options are worth considering. Participation of this sort will not ground obligations based on a stronger voluntariness.

Requirements Based on Natural Moral Duties

Natural duties, however, are not based in any voluntary transactions, relationships, or performances, but arise simply because of the moral character of the required act or forbearance. I am bound not to murder, for instance, not because of anything I have done (like promising not to), but because of the moral significance of murder. Similarly, duties not to steal or lie, to give aid to those in need, or to promote justice are equally shared by all persons, regardless of their voluntary acts.

Is the obligation to serve in the military a natural duty? There is good reason to think it is not. First, because these duties are binding on *all* persons, the content of any natural duty must be perfectly general: I am bound not to kill *anyone*, not just certain specified individuals. If our duty to serve in the military were a natural duty, then, it could not bind us to service in any *particular* state (specifically, our state of citizenship). Suppose, for instance, that the duty to serve were conceived as part of a natural duty to support just governments. We would then be bound by it to serve in the military of *all* just governments—certainly not a duty we should recognize as genuine. What needs to be explained is why a government's being *ours* grounds special ties to *it*, such as the requirements to pay taxes to it, obey its laws, and serve in its military. This an argument in terms of natural duties cannot do.

Requirements Based in Nonvoluntary Relationships

If political obligations must arise out of some special tie between citizens and their particular country, where this tie cannot be construed as voluntarily assumed by citizens, then this third class of moral requirements is especially promising. By understanding political obligations in these terms, we capture the spirit of the most familiar answers to questions about them. The reason we are obligated to serve the state, many argue, is that it has so effectively served us. It has provided numerous and substantial benefits at low cost, and it is the duty of those who have benefitted from the labor of others to reciprocate. Thus, in the earliest recorded discussion of political obligation (Plato's *Crito*), Socrates argues for political obligation both as reciprocation for benefits provided and as that which is due the state as "parent." Here the appeal is to two special relationships—benefactor-beneficiary and parent-child—both of which need not be entered voluntarily, and both of which are ordinarily taken to ground special obligations.

Few would deny that the state provides considerable, even essential, benefits to its citizens—benefits, furthermore, that citizens are incapable of providing for themselves. Does this mean citizens owe a debt of reciprocation to the state, to be rendered in the form of taxes, obedience, and military service?

It does not. We need to remember how an obligation of reciprocation is normally interpreted. What we owe a benefactor is almost never determined with any precision by the context, but varies with our capabilities, the benefactor's needs, and the value of and sacrifice involved in providing the benefit. We have considerable latitude in discharging such an obligation, and the best guide is only a very vague sense of what constitutes a "fitting" return. What we certainly do *not* owe a benefactor is whatever he or she demands as repayment.

Thus, even if we are obligated to reciprocate for the benefits we receive from government, we are not obligated to reciprocate in all (or perhaps any) of the ways the government demands. We are not required to serve in the military, to obey every law, or to pay precisely the amount of tax imposed on us simply because we are told to do so. The government, as benefactor, has no special claim to dictate the content of our obligation or pass final judgment on what constitutes a fitting return. The benefactor-beneficiary relationship cannot ground an obligation of military service.

Perhaps the filial obligations arising from the parent-child relationship provide a more helpful comparison. We can set aside the claim that children owe reciprocation for parental care, since the argument that obligation arises from benefaction is even less convincing in cases where the benefactors have themselves created the needs their benefits satisfy. But parent-child and state-citizen relationships have been taken to be analogous in other ways.

Socrates maintains that the citizen ought to obey the state as a child obeys his parents, "to obey in silence if it orders you to endure flogging or imprisonment, or if it sends you to battle to be wounded or die." It does not seem, however, that children do in fact owe obligations of obedience to their parents. Young children do not, because young children do not have any moral obligations, to their parents or to anyone else. Where the capacities necessary for minimal levels of moral responsibility are absent, so are moral requirements. Mature children do not owe obedience, because they have the same rights and obligations as other adults. And children of middle years may act either rightly or wrongly in obeying or disobeying parental commands. The rightness or wrongness is a function of the acts performed, not of the parental command having been obeyed or disobeyed. So, by analogy, citizens also have no obligations of obedience to the state, though it may be independently right or wrong for them to do whatever it is the state is commanding.

Filial and political relationships are also analogous in that both are routinely accompanied by strong emotional ties, of love and friendship in the one case, of loyalty and concern in the other. It is often argued that filial obligations arise from this personal intimacy—mutual caring creates the obligations, and where mutual caring ceases, the obligations cease as well. Perhaps political obligations are created and erased in the same way.

This view, however, seems to be mistaken. Moral obligations do not come in and out of existence with changes in our emotional state, and furthermore, it is precisely in the absence of emotional reasons for certain kinds of behavior that the point of ascribing moral obligations comes most clearly into focus. While children love their parents and citizens remain loyal to their country, loving and loyal behavior will be natural and unconstrained. But the love and loyalty do not make such behavior into a matter of obligation. The parent-child analogy fails as well, then, to establish an obligation of military service.

The Justifiability of Conscription

It seems, then, that there is no moral obligation to serve. The central assumption of the standard arguments for conscription is a false one. Before concluding, however, it is useful to examine the connection between political obligation and conscription more closely. It is frequently assumed that if there is an obligation to serve, conscription is thereby justified. Likewise, it is assumed that if there is no obligation to serve, conscription is thereby impermissible. Neither is the case.

IF THERE IS AN OBLIGATION TO SERVE, IS CONSCRIPTION JUSTIFIED?

Philosophers commonly claim that the existence of an obligation entails that coercion is justified in its enforcement. As stated, however, this view is too simple. It is not true that whenever someone has an obligation, someone (or everyone) else is morally justified in forcing performance. Just as it can be morally wrong, all things considered, to discharge an obligation, so it can be morally wrong to force another to discharge an obligation. For example, it would be wrong of me to ignore a drowning man in order to discharge my obligation to meet you for lunch, and it would be wrong of you to force me to discharge this obligation.

Thus, even if citizens did have a moral obligation to serve in the military, the state should not enforce this obligation under many conceivable circumstances. Some of these circumstances are in fact recognized in current practice as limits to the state's justified enforcement of the citizen's obligation to serve: Strong competing obligations, such as the obligation to support dependent family members, and the obligations of religion and moral conscience are recognized as having overriding importance, making state enforcement of the obligation to serve indefensible. Many other circumstances where state enforcement of the obligation to military service is illegitimate are not recognized in practice. These are cases where the conscript is to be used for morally unacceptable purposes, such as to wage an unjust war. Where it is wrong to serve, it cannot be right to force service.

IF THERE IS NO OBLIGATION TO SERVE, IS CONSCRIPTION IMPERMISSIBLE?

It is not, for just as obligations sometimes ought not to be discharged, so rights may sometimes legitimately be infringed. I do not act wrongly in taking your rope without permission (and so violating your property rights) in order to throw it to a drowning man.

Even if citizens have no obligation to serve, certain kinds of social or military emergencies may still make conscription (military or otherwise) morally justifiable; even if citizens have a moral right not to be conscripted, they may be justifiably conscripted. But because conscription violates many people's rights, and violates them extensively (causing prolonged loss of liberty and opportunity and risk of death), justifiable emergencies must be very real and very serious indeed. And in order to be justified, the benefits of conscription must not only outweigh its costs, but conscription must be far enough better than the next best alternative policy in reaping these benefits that its higher probability for success outweighs the infringed rights it involves. So even if conscription might otherwise be defensible, it would almost certainly be unjustifiable in virtue of the moral superiority of alternative noncoercive policies.

How Well-off Should Welfare Make You?

Claudia Mills

One hears these stories all the time. A middle-class housewife carefully clips coupons for store-brand tuna while the single man behind her in line buys sirloin steak with food stamps. A self-supporting family scrimps to meet its monthly rent, while a family in subsidized housing can afford a new television. These tales, whether fact or fiction, exert a powerful hold on the popular imagination. To many it seems wrong that someone on welfare should end up better off than someone who isn't.

A similar principle is recognized in debates over equity in welfare policy. Two different conceptions of equity are frequently cited in planning income support programs. *Horizontal equity* is the principle that those in similar circumstances should be treated similarly. *Vertical equity* is the principle that persons in different circumstances should be treated differently. Vertical equity is often considered relevant in explaining why we find the two opening examples disturbing.

According to Jodie T. Allen, formerly special assistant to the secretary of labor, vertical equity means that people in different social and economic situations ought to be treated differently. Redistributive taxes transfer income from more to less affluent individuals, and horizontal equity requires such redistribution to provide equal treatment of those with equal needs. But vertical equity limits the extent of this redistribution.

In Allen's view, "Given a distribution of income, the effect of tax or transfer policies should not be such as to reverse the position of persons in the resulting income distribution." If one family earns more than another before taxes and transfers, they should still earn more after, though the gap may be narrower. (Allen argues, however, that the gap should not be "unduly compressed.") This is not to say that the better-off should not be taxed at all to benefit others, but they should not be taxed to the point of losing their relative place in the distribution of income.

This principle, Allen points out, is persistently violated in the design of existing welfare programs, such as Medicaid, day care, and food stamps. Medicaid, for example, violates vertical equity on two scores. First, full coverage is extended to all families below a certain income (the eligibility limit for welfare), while families just slightly above the cutoff are left to fend for themselves. "If earnings on other income increase even one dollar beyond the eligibility limit for welfare, the former eligible thus abruptly loses a benefit worth on the average some $1,850 to his or her family." Thus a welfare family slightly below the limit ends up better off than a taxpaying family slightly above the limit.

Second, Allen charges that "there is an even more serious equity problem implicit in the Medicaid design. . . . At least in states providing broad-gauge Medicaid coverage, welfare recipients are assured a level of medical care beyond the financial reach of all but the most affluent. In dramatic but not unlikely terms, we may find the policeman's wife waiting in line at the clinic while the welfare mother meets her pre-arranged appointment with a Park Avenue specialist."

Welfare and Work Incentives

A clear practical reason to care about vertical equity exists. If people who do not work get just as much, or more than, people who do, incentives to work will be considerably diminished. Most jobs, particularly those available to the uneducated and unskilled, are not intrinsically rewarding or satisfying. Without extrinsic financial incentives, welfare recipients would have less reason to take such jobs, and those employed would have less reason to keep them. To put it bluntly, many of us wouldn't work, or wouldn't work as long and hard, if it weren't for the money.

Studies have shown that independent sources of income do, as expected, reduce work effort. Allen reports, "Several major field experiments have been launched to measure the impact of transfer programs on the work effort of prime age adults in families. The largest and most reliable of the experiments, the Seattle-Denver Experiment, recently [showed that] cash transfer programs of the size and design most frequently discussed in political debate do reduce work effort, and those reductions can be related to . . . the level of benefits."

Working and saving increase society's overall wealth and resources. If productivity dips, the size of the pie available for distribution is accordingly shrunk, leaving that much less for everyone. It may therefore be to the best advantage of even the least well-off that a hierarchical income structure is maintained. If income differentials provide incentives that stimulate productivity, in the long run all economic classes benefit.

However, the future benefits of trickled-down prosperity may not be great enough to offset inadequate welfare payments in the present. Vertical equity has been preserved by holding the level of welfare payments below the earnings of the poorest paid workers, and such payments may be insufficient to meet urgent human needs. Robert Fersh, formerly confidential assistant to the administrator of the Food and Nutrition Service of the U.S. Department of Agriculture, points out: "The failure to provide for adequate work incentives . . . seems to be a rather academic and distant concern in comparison to the direct effect of hunger and substandard housing on human beings. . . . A system which maximizes sensitivity to these concerns would seem to be expressive of some fundamentally important human values."

Welfare and Equity

There is another, more explicitly moral, reason to care about vertical equity. Just as it seems *fair* that people with equal needs should receive equal benefits, so it is considered *fair* that people in different economic positions should retain their different positions even after the needs of the less fortunate are met. The principle of vertical equity, after all, is supposed to be a judgment about what is *equitable*.

Why isn't it fair for the income ordering to be reversed? *Why* isn't it fair for someone who earns more to end up with less than someone who doesn't work at all? If the appeal to fairness is not just another expression of the need for work incentives, on what deeper principle is it grounded?

The underlying principle seems to be that income should be distributed on the basis of merit, where merit is measured in proportion to work. This principle can itself take various forms—for example, that income should be distributed according to effort, or according to achievement. The interpretation we choose determines our moral judgments very differently. But on this principle it certainly seems unfair for someone who works to earn less than someone who doesn't.

Philosopher Norman Daniels raises two strong objections to the application of this principle in welfare policy. First, the great majority of welfare recipients are those who are excused from the work requirement for one reason or another: the elderly, the handicapped and disabled, children, and parents solely responsible for child care. With the possible exception of the latter, these groups are not able or not expected to compete in the labor force. The able-bodied man of the opening example is hardly the typical welfare case. But if most recipients cannot be legitimately held to the merit principle, how does it violate that principle to distribute income to them on other grounds?

Writes Daniels: "If the population to whom Allen's equity principles are to apply is that part of the population which it makes no sense to hold responsible for their inability to meet their needs, then it is hard to see why it is so important not to reverse income rank orderings in order to guarantee them adequate benefit levels. Perhaps for those who fare badly because they merit little, [such principles] might be thought appropriate. But for those who are excused from merit considerations, and for whom we have some concern that their needs be met, adhering to these principles seems a misplaced scrupulosity, if not an outright contradiction."

Daniels's first objection assumes that the merit principle does indeed apply, but argues that most of the welfare population is a legitimate exception to it. His second objection challenges the principle itself, as an accurate representation of how income is in fact distributed in our society. "Do we live in a system in which, on the whole, pre-tax, pre-benefit income rank order and income distances comply with some basic meritarian principles?" he asks. He answers that we do not. Vertical equity cannot be grounded in the work ethic. Income is not generally distributed on the basis of how hard or well one works. (Consider, among others, the example of inherited wealth.) It is unjustified, then, to impose a merit principle on the distribution of income to the poor, when it does not govern the distribution of income to other classes.

Should a merit principle determine economic distribution? Before answering, we would need to reach some agreement on what is to count as merit and look more closely at the connection between merit and reward. Philosophers such as John Rawls argue that our talents and abilities—as well as our capacity for effort and discipline—are largely matters beyond our control for which we can claim no fundamental credit. To distribute wealth on such grounds seems capricious and morally arbitrary. Clearly we need a better and deeper understanding of these principles before we can elevate them into grounds for ignoring the needs of the least well-off in our society.

The views of Jodie T. Allen, Robert Fersh, and Norman Daniels are taken from their essays in Income Support: Conceptual and Policy Issues, *ed. Peter G. Brown, Conrad Johnson, and Paul Vernier, Maryland Studies in Public Philosophy (Totowa, N.J.: Rowman and Littlefield, 1981).*

Being Here
The Rights of Resident Aliens

Claudia Mills

Americans tend to be unsympathetic to complaints that illegal aliens in this country are not being treated as well as other U.S. residents or, indeed, particularly well at all. Illegal aliens by definition violated this nation's laws in order to establish their residence here; thus, it is felt, they need not be extended any special consideration as a result of that residence. For if they do not like conditions in the United States, they are perfectly welcome to go back to wherever they came from; they need not do us any favors by prolonging their illegal stay. A similar line of argument is addressed to alien workers who are here legally, under current or proposed guest-worker programs. Foreign workers are invited here on our terms—if they do not like the terms, they do not have to accept them. Other desperate unemployed foreigners will be more than willing to come in their stead. In this view, we offer prospective residents a set of terms, which they can take or leave as they choose. No minimally acceptable terms are guaranteed.

In *Plyler* v. *Doe* (1982) the Supreme Court reaffirmed that *all* U.S. residents, however they came to reside within U.S. geographical limits, are entitled at the very least to the equal protection of our laws. Writing for the majority, Justice William Brennan ruled: ". . . The protection of the 14th Amendment extends to anyone, citizen or stranger, who is subject to the laws of a state. . . . That a person's initial entry into a state, or into the United States, was unlawful, and that he may for that reason be expelled, cannot negate the simple fact of his presence within the state's territorial perimeter. Given such presence, he is subject to the full range of obligations imposed by the state's civil and criminal laws. And until he leaves the jurisdiction—either voluntarily or involuntarily . . . —he is entitled to the equal protection of the laws that a state may choose to establish." Philosopher Judith Lichtenberg calls this ruling "a benign Catch-22": "Those with no right to be here have rights in virtue of being here."

Some minimal standard, then, sets a floor on terms that legal and illegal aliens may be offered. What is this standard? What rights may aliens in our midst claim simply in virtue of the sheer fact that they are *here*?

Equal Protection and Illegal Aliens

Lichtenberg explains that equal protection means that the state may never treat a protected individual as a "moral inferior," as a non-person. "It means, first, that the state may not treat one person's or group's interests differently from the similar interests of another person or group; it cannot matter more per se that A goes hungry than that B does. . . . Second, not treating a person as a moral inferior means that one may not ignore or utterly dismiss his interests, for that would be to treat him as if he didn't matter, as if he were not a person with feelings, concerns, and projects of his own." If illegal aliens are within the pale of equal protection, then their interests, too, must be taken into consideration in establishing government policy: That a policy would affect them adversely *matters* in assessing that policy; it counts as one reason against it.

Equal protection does not mean, however, that the interests of those protected may not be overridden by the weightier interests of others; they must be placed on the scales, but they need not determine the final balance. Lichtenberg notes that legitimate governmental interests and goals may in many cases pull against the claims of individuals and groups, and where state interests are weighty and compelling, other "claims must themselves be substantial to resist the pull." The claims of illegal aliens, furthermore, must be particularly substantial to outweigh the competing claims put forward by the state. Lichtenberg recognizes that unlimited immigration to the United States may well "constitute a threat to essential features of American society." To the extent that aliens do pose such a threat, "to that extent it is legitimate to discriminate against them."

What rights emerge from this complicated balancing process of interest against interest? In which cases, if any, do the claims of illegal aliens carry the day? *Plyler* v. *Doe* gives one of the clearest examples: In it, the Court protects the rights of illegal alien children to a free public education, striking down tuition requirements imposed on them by the state of Texas. Here the children's interests at stake clearly outweighed any opposing claim of the state. The Court argued that denying these children a basic education would "impose a lifetime hardship" on them, marking them with "the stigma of illiteracy . . . for the rest of their lives." The drain placed on Texas's financial and educational resources, moreover, was negligible. And Lichtenberg doubts that a refusal to educate alien children could possibly be in the state's true interest: "It is harmful to the society itself to permit the creation or perpetuation of a 'permanent underclass' of people who make no contribution to and have no stake in the common life." Finally, even if the state has a legitimate interest in expressing its disapproval of unlawful activity, the children of illegal aliens have not chosen to break any law, and so the sins of their parents should not be set in the scales against them.

Some critics of the Court's decision in *Plyler* v. *Doe* charged that a broad array of other federal services, such as food stamps and Medicaid, would thus also have to be made available to those who enter this country in defiance of its laws. But each case must be weighed separately. It may be that other benefits represent less vital interests than education, or that providing them to illegal aliens would cost vastly more than the state is able to pay. Various benefits offered to illegal aliens might spur unlawful migration and sanction widespread lawlessness. And adults who break the law cannot claim that their illegal act should not be held against them. These are all considerations that might provide decisive reasons against treating illegal aliens on a par with legal residents. But equal protection means that reasons on the other side should always be considered as well. And sometimes, as in *Plyler* v. *Doe*, these will be reasons that determine what we, as a nation, should do.

Guest-Worker Rights

If even illegal aliens are within the pale of equal protection, how are we bound to treat legal aliens, particular workers we have expressly invited to join us as participants in the American labor force?

Thousands of foreign workers participate in temporary-worker programs, filling primarily low-level seasonal jobs. Part of the attractiveness of these programs to many employers is that foreign workers are willing to live and work on terms that would be unacceptable to most American citizens. But the terms we are required to offer them would seem to be considerably better than the worst possible terms we can get them to take.

Equal protection means that American policymaking must proceed on the assumption that, while they are on American soil, these workers matter just as citizen workers do. This has not been the case through much of the history of foreign-worker programs in this country. Manuel García y Griego gives a portrait of the importation of Mexican workers to the United States that indicates how thoroughly and systematically the interests of these workers were disregarded. Through the period of the official *bracero* program (1942-1964), and the years preceding and following, the United States consistently manipulated Mexican workers for its own interests—actively recruiting Mexican labor during times of boom, and rounding up and deporting Mexican labor during times of bust—usually with little or no regard to the effects of such recruitment and deportation on the workers themselves.

The Mexican *bracero* workers faced additional abuse and exploitation, furthermore, in substandard working and living conditions, which frequently violated even the less-than-generous terms set by the contract program. What protests were raised against this pattern of abuse, according to García, centered on the adverse effects it might be having on American labor market conditions. The interests of the Mexican workers were perceived as simply less important.

Equal protection does not exhaust the moral limits on how we may treat invited foreign workers, however. Philosopher Henry Shue has proposed three fundamental principles that should govern the design of any guest-worker program:

(1) Respect for the integrity of the family dictates that people not be required by law to live in separation from their families for any greater period of time than absolutely necessary.

(2) The principle of no taxation without representation dictates that people not be required by law to pay for the conduct of policies in which they have no voice (and from which they receive few benefits).

(3) Respect for individual liberty dictates that people not be required by law to move in and out of countries regardless of their own choices except for the strongest possible reasons.

These principles are violated by any temporary-worker program that does not provide for prompt reunification of workers with their families, that levies taxes on workers without providing any minimal system of effective self-government, or that shuttles workers back and forth from country to country without allowing them the option to apply for permanent residence in the country of employment.

Shue acknowledges that foreign workers need not be granted all the rights and privileges of full American citizenship. There are good reasons, for example, why foreigners should not be allowed to vote on certain matters of national policy, such as foreign policy toward their own country; nor is it unreasonable to believe that foreign workers need an initial period of acquaintance with their new society before they are in a position to make sound judgments about broad social issues. But Shue points to the success of Swedish experiments with allowing migrant workers to vote in local elections, and concludes that temporary residents should be allowed to help "decide the issues that most directly affect their lives."

Shue's three principles, then, set somewhat stringent conditions under which the United States is able to invite foreign workers into its labor force. If the conditions seem too exigent, we must seek other ways to meet our labor needs or reexamine the extent to which we truly need imported labor. For once people are invited onto our territory, they are able to make claims on us, claims for a decent minimum of hospitality and for a decent minimum of justice.

The positions discussed in this article are drawn from "Within the Pale: Aliens, Illegal Aliens, and Equal Protection," by Judith Lichtenberg, University of Pittsburgh Law Review, *vol. 44, no. 2 (Spring 1983), Symposium Issue on Immigration and the Constitution; "The Importation of Mexican Contract Laborers to the United States, 1942–1964: Antecedents, Operation, and Legacy," by Manuel García y Griego, in* The Border That Joins: Mexican Migrants and U.S. Responsibility, Maryland Studies in Public Philosophy, *ed. Peter G. Brown and Henry Shue (Totowa, N.J.: Rowman and Littlefield, 1983); and Henry Shue's testimony before the Subcommittee on Immigration, Refugees, and International Law of the House Committee on the Judiciary, October 14, 1981.*

The New Patriotism

Robert K. Fullinwider

Our country! In her intercourse with foreign nations may she always be right, but our country, right or wrong.—Stephen Decatur, 1816

Anyone who says patriotism is 'my country right or wrong' ought to have his head examined.—Jane Fonda, 1970

Patriotism is in fashion again. Public expressions of national pride are more abundant, participation in patriotic rituals more common than a decade ago. Renewed interest in the meaning of citizenship has arisen among educators, political leaders, and the public at large. There is more talk of "civic responsibility."

Likewise, political campaigns rely more heavily than in the recent past on patriotic themes and on direct appeals to patriotism itself. A leading motif of the Republican presidential campaign of 1984 was that Ronald Reagan had made us once more "feel good about being Americans"; and in 1988, the presidential candidates visited flag factories and played one-upmanship with the Pledge of Allegiance.

Of course, talk about patriotism is not the same thing as patriotism itself, and we might more accurately say that the rhetoric of patriotism is back in fashion. It is doubtful that people are more or less patriotic from one decade to another, but it is evident that the popularity of public appeals to patriotism waxes and wanes over time. The cyclical nature of this popularity reflects in part an enduring ambivalence about the nature and meaning of patriotism. Some have been unreserved about their rejection or embrace of patriotism. Alexander Pope declared the patriot a fool in any age; Samuel Johnson derided patriotism as a refuge for scoundrels. On the other side, Rousseau recommended that the citizen's love for the fatherland "make up his entire existence." Most of us, however, feel uncomfortable endorsing either extreme. Patriotism seems to have a good face and a bad face, and we puzzle to understand what role, if any, it can play in a moral and valuable life.

Patriotism versus Morality

Philosopher Ralph Barton Perry gave this account of the double aspect of patriotism: "The evil of patriotism, as well as its good, is embodied in the utterance 'my country, right or wrong.' Here is devotion and fidelity, but also disregard for principle. . . ." Devotion and fidelity are admirable, but if the object of the devotion is unworthy, then fidelity to its cause may require supporting wrong. If patriots must stand with their country against the morally right, then we must wonder at the price patriotism exacts.

Many seek to avoid the moral tension here by denying that patriotism and morality conflict. One argument occasionally offered is that patriotism cannot conflict with morality because the standard of right *is* the state and its ends. This line of argument is not open to anyone who holds a cosmopolitan morality, that is, to anyone—Kantian, Platonist, utilitarian, intuitionist, libertarian, Christian, Muslim, Jew—who holds universal moral principles or appeals to a moral authority beyond the state.

A more common argument is that "blind" patriotism may be morally dangerous but "enlightened" patriotism is not; enlightened patriotism does not mean our country, right or wrong. However, if "enlightened" means always conforming to the requirements of a universal morality, then the problem about patriotism seems evaded rather than avoided. Patriotism means "love of country," and to love something means to be partial toward it. To be devoted and faithful to something means to cleave to it, to stick by it, to maintain support for it through good times and bad. Morality, on the other hand, requires us to take up an impartial standpoint of judgment, to judge our country with the detachment with which we would judge any other. How could patriotism and morality *not* potentially conflict?

There seems no escaping the problematic character of patriotism. Stephen Decatur seems right about patriotism, at least in so far as "my country, right or wrong" expresses the point that patriotism cannot be detached and impartial. Nevertheless, patriotism also may be much less morally dangerous than supposed. Standing by the country, even when it is wrong, seldom will require the patriot to act against principle. Jane Fonda may be right, too. To see how this is so, we need to explore more deeply the meaning of love of country.

Love of Country

To describe patriotism as "love of country" does not advance our understanding very far because love itself is not a single, simple thing.

We do not esteem or encourage everything called love; some emotional dependencies we need to overcome or outgrow on our way to greater maturity. We value those loves that make the lover a better person and the object of love better off.

Immanuel Kant defined love as "good-will, affection, promoting the happiness of others and finding joy in their happiness." Following Kant's lead, we can define love of country as affection for and commitment to the good of the country. The patriot identifies his own fulfillment, to some extent, with the fate of his country. He is happy at its good fortune and its triumphs, disappointed at its failures. He is downcast when it is harmed and indignant when it is wronged. He is diminished when it is diminished.

Love expresses a desire for and identification with the good of particular individuals or groups. Love, whether patriotic or any other kind, can thus prompt us to disregard universal moral principle. But this threat is genuine only when the welfare of the loved one is truly at odds with morality.

The patriot must "stand by" his country, right or wrong. But this cannot mean the patriot must always support, condone, participate in, or refuse to criticize the wrongful actions and policies of his country. Where such wrongful actions and policies harm the country, to support and participate in them would be to act against, not for, the good of the country.

This point is clear enough in the parallel case of parental love. Suppose a parent, upon discovering her child is involved in a theft, insists that the child confess to the authorities and return the stolen goods. We do not see this as the parent's failing to "stand by" her child. On the contrary, the parent is acting in what she sees as the child's best interest, since she has a conception of the child's good that gives central place to honesty and acceptance of responsibility.

The patriot, likewise, must act on his conception of the good of the country. This means that quite opposed views and behavior can be equally patriotic. Since citizens may reasonably and vigorously disagree over how particular actions and policies affect the nation's welfare, patriotism cannot be identified with some "correct" or majority position on specific, contestable policies of government. A patriot may espouse courses of action as painful to his nation as the parent's strict discipline was to her child, and like the parent be acting for the ultimate good of what he loves.

The indeterminacy that inheres in patriotism is compounded by a further fact. Citizens can not only disagree about how to advance the country's good; they can disagree about the nature of that good itself. The true patriot, according to Woodrow Wilson, has a "deep ardor for what his country stands for, what its existence means, what its purpose is declared to be in its history and its policy." But the country's ideals, the meaning of its history, and the nature of its purposes are matters of considerable disagreement. If commitment to the good of the country means commitment to the flourishing of certain ideals and purposes embodied in the nation's existence, then equally good patriots can part ways on even the deepest matters.

Patriotism in Action

How should patriotism translate into action? The good patriot will be careful not to injure his country. He will respect constituted authority and give weight to authoritative justifications of national policy. He will be informed on his country's history and attentive to its ideals.

But consider what these dispositions mean. Avoiding injuring the country does not mean avoiding causing it pain. Giving weight to authoritative justifications does not mean being credulous or uncritical. Being attentive to national ideals does not mean endorsing the status quo or supporting some narrow "American way of life."

The good patriot will want to avoid two corruptions of love. First, affection can blind us to the faults of what we love. Such blindness cannot be a merit in love since to indulge or encourage its worst behavior can seldom be in the interest of what we love.

Intense identification with what we love can also corrupt the commitment to its good by inverting the direction of identification. "Living through another" can lead us not to identify our desires with his fortune but his fortune with our desires. Instead of shaping our desires to realize his good, we conceive of his good in a way that realizes our desires.

A good patriot will be wary of these corruptions of love and will want to avoid such lack of detachment as to be blinded to his country's faults or to be incapable of conceiving its good independently of his own.

A fault, but not a corruption, of love is that its partiality can exclude "outsiders" from our concern. An intense commitment to the good of some can crowd out attention to the good of others. A love can become so dominant that all other considerations get swept aside, including consideration of right or wrong. This brings us back to our original worry about patriotism and raises a question about its appropriate place. Where should love of country enter into a good life?

Patriotism—as love of country—stands uneasily between cosmopolitanism and localism. Cosmopolitanism says there are associations and causes broader than the state that deserve our loyalty; localism says there are groups and causes smaller than the state in which we should invest our love.

We naturally begin life with local attachments—to other individuals, to family, neighborhood, and community. Patriotism says: We must transcend local points of view; we must submerge parochial commitments and take up a larger point of view, the point of view of the good of the nation as a whole. Patriotism wants to dominate our other loves, so that if we have to choose between love of a friend and love of country, we will choose the latter. But why should patriotism dominate? Why is love of country a more valuable love than love of friend or family or neighborhood? E. M. Forster once wrote: "If I had to choose between betraying my country and betraying a friend, I hope I should have the guts to betray my country." This is resistance to the domination of patriotism on behalf of local attachments.

Patriotism is also pressed from the other side. Demanding as it does the enlargement of one's point of view and commitments to encompass the state, it lies in turn exposed to similar demands of enlargement. Why stop with the nation-state? Why not adopt a point of view in which the nation is but one more locality submerged in a broader community of interest? George Santayana claimed that if a man "has insight and depth of feeling he will perceive that what deserves his loyalty is the entire civilization to which he owes his spiritual life." Here is resistance to the domination of patriotism on behalf of transnational attachments.

Many jealous gods demand that we love them above all others. Do any secular gods merit such love? More important, can the nation be such a god? Rousseau wanted an identification with the fatherland so intense it excluded all other loyalties. Others find such an identification repellent.

The good patriot cannot be oblivious to the tension between national patriotism, local attachments, and cosmopolitan commitments. Does he fail to be a good patriot if he fails to accord love of country domination over every other love and commitment? Do we fail to be good parents, good spouses, good neighbors if we do not subordinate all other considerations and concerns to the claims of child, spouse, neighborhood? The answer to this question is quite evidently no. By the same token, I suggest the answer to the first question is likewise no. Love of country must be able to coexist with other loves without dominating them.

Conclusion

How do we create good patriots? How do we inculcate patriotism without creating chauvinism, false pride, and blind obedience? How do we create citizens with the sensibility, traits of character, and habits of mind to feel love, honor its demands, avoid its corruptions, and understand its place?

Part of the new patriotism is just the return to fashion of the rhetoric of patriotism, a fashion likely to be as unedifying as past such fashions. Framing political issues as matters of patriotism is almost always a shabby affair since it converts honest disagreements about policies and ideals into defamation of character and imputation of disloyalty.

But part of the new patriotism represents a renewed interest in the questions just asked about instilling patriotism and understanding citizenship. Careful reflection on these hard questions is much needed and all to the good.

The motto by Stephen Decatur is well know, that by Jane Fonda less so. Both are quoted at the front of John J. Pullen, Patriotism in America: A Study of Changing Devotions *(New York: American Heritage Press, 1971). The Ralph Barton Perry quote is from* The Citizen Decides *(Bloomington, Ind.: Indiana University Press, 1951); the Santayana quote is from* The Life of Reason, *rev. ed. (New York: Scribner, 1953); the Rousseau quote is from* The Government of Poland, *trans. by Will-moore Kendall (Indianapolis: Bobbs-Merrill, 1972). An informative history of patriotism in America is* The Roots of American Loyalty, *by Merle Curti (New York: Columbia University Press, 1946), which contains the Woodrow Wilson quote.*

Civic Education and Traditional American Values

Robert K. Fullinwider

"Something has gone tragically wrong with our society in recent years," begins a recent report of a commission on civic education. What has gone wrong, the report charges, is this: We are failing to educate future citizens for citizenship, and the core of this failure lies in a falling away from traditional American values. "A lack of honesty and integrity among ... citizens (is) directly related to the failure of our institutions to effectively transmit the values contained in our cultural heritage." This report is very much a product of its time. Countless local and national groups, study commissions, education lobbies, and reform lobbies are decrying disrespect for traditional values and advocating a rekindling of tradition as a remedy for the various public ills that assail us.

The traditionalist's argument has not met with universal assent, however. What is controversial about inculcating traditional American values? What should we conclude about the persistence of this kind of controversy? These questions force us back to a prior question: What is *meant* by "restoring traditional American values"?

Teaching Virtues

"We need to restore traditional American values in the schools" might mean that we need to work more deliberately and consciously at the training of character. We need to teach the virtues, which we can divide into four groups: (1) *the moral virtues*—honesty, truthfulness, decency, courage, justice; (2) *the intellectual virtues*—thoughtfulness, strength of mind, curiosity; (3) *the communal virtues*—neighborliness, charity, self-support, helpfulness, cooperativeness, respect for others; and (4) *the political virtues*—commitment to the common good, respect for law, responsible participation.

Now, what could be the argument against teaching some or all of these virtues in school? The moral and intellectual virtues are essential constituents to being a good human being; the communal virtues are essential constituents to being a good neighbor; and the political virtues are essential constituents to being a good citizen. As responsible parents and teachers, surely we can be committed to no less than making our children good persons, good neighbors, and good citizens.

As long as we propose teaching honesty, charity, and respect for others without specifying the operational content of such teaching, then there seems little basis for controversy and dissent. But controversy and dissent will emerge the moment we begin to specify how and what we will teach in teaching honesty, charity, respect, and so on.

Controversy necessarily emerges because of the nature of the virtues themselves. The scope of individual virtues overlaps, and on occasion the same action that will be charitable will be untruthful, and a neighborly action will be unjust. Moreover, an action that will be courageous in one situation will be foolhardy in another; a statement that is honesty in one circumstance will be inappropriate candor in another. The mature moral consciousness can make the right distinctions here, but the mature moral consciousness comes at the end, not the beginning, of moral training. At the beginning the virtues have to be taught by simple rules: Do not lie; obey the law. The rules selected and the way they will be taught can be controversial.

This is especially true when the teaching device is the institutionalization of codes of conduct. According to some university honor codes, for example, it is a violation of honesty not only to cheat on an exam but also to fail to report the cheating of others. Such a rule teaches a student about honesty. It also requires him to betray his fellows. Moreover, a fixed rule preempts the student's own judgment on the matter. Another's cheating is wrong, but sometimes the appropriate response to wrong is mercy, not punishment; support, not abandonment; silence, not accusation. Rigid adherence to rules circumscribes the student's autonomy as a moral actor. Thus, both moral and pedagogical concerns might be raised about about rules for teaching virtue.

That legitimate concerns can be raised about efforts to teach virtue does not imply that the efforts are not on balance justified, as imperfect as they may be. Given the centrality of the virtues to a worthwhile life, we may have no option but to stumble through as best we can. Controversy is endemic to the enterprise of teaching the virtues but may be contained within tolerable limits by a larger consensus about the goal of forming adults who are honest, decent, respectful, and helpful.

Restoring Customary Practices

However, where differing ideals themselves clash, controversy may become intractable. This point is illustrated by the second thing that the call for traditional American values might mean. It might mean a return to *customary practices* or *norms* of behavior. For example, it might mean a return to older norms of sexual behavior where sexual activity not confined to marriage is immoral, a matter of central concern to many of those in the back-to-traditions movement.

Controversy about sexual practices is complicated by the fact that prudential arguments and moral arguments can follow parallel lines. Sexual promiscuity can be warned against to avoid venereal disease and teenage pregnancies. Such a prudential argument would seem neutral about sexual ideals, condemning no form of consensual sexual behavior as bad in itself. In fact, it is hard to find prudential policies that are truly neutral about sexual ideals, as the persistent controversies over sex education classes demonstrate. Opponents of sex education classes argue that by their very nature they foster particular sexual ideologies. Parents may believe that when schools treat sex education in a businesslike manner, as another subject along with health, geography, and math, they convey certain attitudes about the place of sex in our lives, attitudes incompatible with the sexual ideals the parents hope to foster in their children. Even sexual knowledge itself in their children may be opposed by parents as incompatible with ideals of chastity and innocence.

When ideals clash, two strategies are available: insulation or domination. In the first, we look for arrangements that allow the conflicting ideals to coexist. In the second, we seek the triumph and domination of the "correct" ideal. The back-to-traditions movement uses both strategies on issues of sexual morality. It wants sex education out of the classroom so parents can teach their children their own sexual ideals without fear of counterteaching in the schools. In the larger national arena, however, traditionalists often want the state to give positive support to dominant sexual ideals by suppressing pornography, prostitution, and other sexual behavior at odds with those ideals.

National Identity

Both of the meanings of "returning to traditional American values" we have examined—teaching the virtues and restoring customary practices—have little to do with anything distinctively American. The virtues are virtues whether practiced in Washington, D.C., or Stockholm. And

America shares its basic sexual, cultural, and religious mores with many other countries. A distinctively American, and distinctively civic, content requires that we turn to a third meaning of "traditional American values," *national identity* and *collective aspirations*.

Here the concern is about forming a self-concept as "an American" and acquiring the patriotic attitudes appropriate to such a self-concept. We view ourselves as Americans because we share with other Americans a common history and a common understanding of what America stands for. But if this is true, how can it be that our political life consists in never-ending struggles to define the national purpose, the meaning of our common life, the content of the national interest?

We are a people because we have common icons—the Pilgrims and Thanksgiving, the Founding Fathers, Robert E. Lee giving his sword to Ulysses S. Grant, Babe Ruth pointing to right field—but only at the most shallow level do they define common goals or projects. Our central authoritative texts—the Declaration of Independence, Washington's Farewell Address, Lincoln's Second Inaugural and Gettysburg Address—declare our commitments to freedom, justice, equality. But these vague commitments are susceptible to many different plausible readings—thus, the continuous political struggles to give specific definition to Americanism and to tie American ideals to this or that policy, this or that cause. What does this say about teaching our children to be Americans?

If we are to make our children into Americans, we have to start with the teaching of national history, and such teaching has a high place in the back-to-traditions movement. But although broad agreement about the importance of teaching American history may exist, consensus soon breaks down when we turn to questions about the content and implication of history. For example, in a 1985 speech, at a time when the United States was aiding armed resistance to the Sandinista government in Nicaragua, former Secretary of Education William Bennett urged that students would have a better appreciation of current U.S. foreign policy if schools did a better job passing on a "proper sense of American values and history. . . . Our students will not recognize the urgency in Nicaragua if they cannot recognize the history that is threatening to repeat itself."

But how will history lessons instill support for U.S. policy in Nicaragua? What history lessons about the United States and its Latin neighbors are the schools failing to pass on? The Monroe Doctrine and the Good Neighbor Policy? Or dollar diplomacy and filibustering? Will students be more or less inclined to accept current American policy at face value by studying U.S. machinations to strip Panama from Colombia? Or learning of persistent U.S. interventions in the Caribbean and Gulf of Mexico to defend American financial interests?

The point is this: Lessons aplenty can be learned from American history, depending on what we select to teach. Thus, the perfectly sensible proposal to increase the teaching of American history in schools is bound to raise questions about what parts of that history to emphasize and what not. Ideological divisions about what America really stands for will be reflected in contests about the appropriate picture of the past to present to children. The fights about history in the classroom will have the same character as the fights about sex education and school prayer. They will be contests of ideals struggling for hegemony.

These contests will also have the same character as the fights about teaching virtue. We can see this by examining how the teaching of national history works in forging national consciousness. A child learns moral lessons by reading stories of moral deeds—deeds of courage and physical valor, of intrepidity and persistence against odds, of strength of character and integrity in the face of temptation. When such stories are drawn from national history, however, they connect a child to moral deeds in a special way: These were the deeds of *her* forefathers and foremothers. The child's social identity, not just her character, is formed in relation to these stories.

Thus, for young children anyway, there are things history cannot be if it is to be a vehicle of patriotism. It cannot be "debunking"; there have to be forefathers and foremothers worth admiring and emulating, and moral enterprises in which pride can be taken. Nor can it be "objective" where this means introducing the full complexity of all the issues surveyed. Just as teaching the virtues must start with simple rules, teaching national history in order to develop civic attachments must start with simple (and thus selective and distorted) accounts of the course of national development. So, once more, the quest for traditional American values leads to controversy.

Tradition and Controversy

It is not surprising that the quest to inculcate traditional values spawns controversy. The surprise would be if it didn't. Must we be dismayed that the controversies are deep and not easily dispelled? Perhaps not. After all, incessant controversy is itself a great American tradition! It is the genius of American political institutions that controversy contributes to our stability rather than our instability. The ideological struggles are valuable resources from which we sharpen our own self-understandings of our relationship to community and country, and they do not divide us to the point of political breakdown. Our political and legal practices allow controversies to be talked to death. To the strategies of insulation and domination mentioned earlier, we have to add one more: the strategy of exhaustion. No one wins big and no victory is long secure. So controversy does not undermine civic education: It is the best part of it, since the lesson the democratic citizen needs to learn is to be able to live with controversy without taking alarm. Perhaps, then, we can end on an upbeat, positive note, after all. That, of course, is itself an American tradition.

This is one way to picture the fruits of controversy. But can we really take pride in a system that dampens, defuses, and defrays controversy, co-opting every vital and vibrant dissent? Should we teach our children that the most important thing is to temper their ideals to the exigencies of co-existence and not to trample on the values of others, no matter how pedestrian or banal they may be? Should our democratic civic lessons teach future seekers after Truth, Beauty, and Justice to trim their sails so as not to unsettle what H. L. Mencken called the great "booboisie"?

The real question I mean to pose by these remarks is this: Do we perhaps buy the taming of controversy and a stable social peace at a greater cost than we think? I pose this question not because I seriously want us to rethink American institutions, but in order to deflate just a little bit that final American tradition—the propensity to pat ourselves on the back.

The Obligation to Play Political Hardball

William A. Galston

Do politicians have an obligation to play hardball? This sounds like a very odd question. It is natural to view politics as a realm where morally questionable means are particularly prevalent, and moral qualms particularly unavoidable. Hardball—the use of questionable, qualm-producing means—might be thought permissible in certain circumstances, but how can it be obligatory?

These ordinary opinions are hardly groundless. Nonetheless, I want to argue that the notion of an obligation to play hardball, far from being outlandish, is in fact implicit in a sound understanding of political practice. The basic argument is this: In most circumstances, a politician does not stand alone, but rather acts on behalf of others, or acts in ways that affect others, in pursuit of certain ends that others have good reason to expect him or her to pursue. To become a politician is in most circumstances to say to others that you take seriously the acquisition and maintenance of power and its employment to further the goals you share with them. You take upon yourself the responsibility to act effectively, which not infrequently entails the obligation to use the kinds of tactics I am calling "hardball."

The 1988 Campaign

To understand my motivation for posing the hardball question, reflect briefly on the 1988 presidential campaign. Most, I think, generally agree that Michael Dukakis failed to campaign effectively. I want to argue that this and other such failures are more than tactical blunders. To the extent that they are rooted in certain erroneous conceptions of political practice, they represent a moral failing and a failure of responsibility.

Dukakis did not want to conduct the campaign on the terrain defined by Bush, either by defending himself against Bush's charges or by responding with charges of his own. He wanted to be affirmative, not negative; he wanted to talk about what he regarded as real issues, not phony ones; and he wanted discourse to be rational, not emotional or demagogic. These are understandable desires. But my contention is that they reflected a kind of recoiling from the rigors of the combat Dukakis had willingly entered. The party that nominated him had every right to expect he would do what was necessary to maximize his chances of winning, shaping his tactics in relation to the world as it was, not as he wanted it to be.

This may strike you as the easy part of the question. What about George Bush? Did he have an obligation to campaign as he did? I am a partisan, activist Democrat, but I am compelled to answer that question in the affirmative. In accepting his party's presidential nomination, he took on the same responsibility for effectiveness that Dukakis had earlier assumed. In discharging this responsibility, moreover, he had to work within a context largely created by others; in particular, he had to overcome the "wimp factor" by projecting guts and strength. And he succeeded.

I would be the first to concede that the spectacle wasn't exactly edifying. But a reasonable person surveying the terrain in July of 1988 could well have come to the conclusion that nothing else was likely to work; the electorate was in no mood to hear a serious discussion of the long-term problems facing the country, emotional issues such as drugs and crime dominated the agenda, and the media were determined to focus on tactics and personalities.

Given our founding tradition of populist suspicion, it is natural for us to blame our leaders for these ills. I think the truth lies elsewhere. George Bernard Shaw once defined democracy as the only form of government in which the people get exactly what they deserve. Our politicians will lose all incentive to employ negative advertising when it stops being effective. They will talk to us seriously about serious things only if we give them good reason to believe they will be rewarded—or at least not punished—for it. It has been a long time since that last happened.

Means and Ends

As posed, the question of playing hardball is a subset of a larger issue—the relation between ends and means in politics. To add some particularity and bite to the hardball question, let me offer the following specifications.

First, the question as I wish to address it arises only if we assume the legitimacy of a particular politician's end or cause. We are not, for example, talking about brutal repression, mass enslavement, or genocide as policy goals to be implemented.

Second, I will make the antiutilitarian assumption that (at least) some acts, considered in themselves, above and beyond their "consequences," have intrinsic moral properties that render them distasteful or objectionable, the sort of thing a decent person would regard with aversion and hesitate to do.

Third, I want to make the antiabsolutist claim that in certain circumstances it is at least permissible to perform acts that, considered in themselves, must be judged morally distasteful.

Fourth, to say that a "politician" has a responsibility to perform such acts is not to say that nonpoliticians have that (same) responsibility, or even that it would be permissible for a nonpolitician to act in that way. That is, for the purposes of this argument I will make the familiar but by no means uncontroversial assumption that social roles affect moral rules.

Doesn't this entangle me in Aristotle's distinction between the good man and the good citizen, or (even more starkly) in Machiavelli's dictum that leaders must often choose between their fatherland and their souls? I don't think so, because I believe that a decent human being can remain decent while playing hardball if required by circumstances to do so. But (someone might retort), wouldn't it be better for individuals to avoid altogether the circumstances that continually test their sense of where to draw the line and tend over time to corrode their conviction that the line exists? I don't think that's correct either, because the effort to lead others toward legitimate goals is always permissible, and sometimes obligatory. I believe, for example, that George Washington had no choice but to accept the presidency of the infant republic and then to act effectively in that capacity.

How, then, are we to understand the nature and limits of what I have been calling "hardball"? As the term suggests, sports analogies may be illuminating.

In sports we find a threefold distinction: Hardball is understood in distinction from softball, but also from dirtyball. Consider an example from baseball. Hardball means sliding into the second baseman to break up a double play; softball means sliding around the second baseman to avoid potentially injuring him; dirtyball means sliding into him spikes up with the intention of knocking him out of the game.

It is possible to express the political import of this example in a quasi-Aristotelian formula: Playing hardball requires the political virtue of toughness, which is flanked by the opposing vices of squeamishness and brutality or cruelty. It is possible also to give an account of the vices in Machiavellian terms. Squeamishness invites the victory of evil—that is, more of the evil from which it averts its gaze. For example: The failure to apply force vigorously when necessary may open the door for greater disorder, doing greater damage or necessitating more force than would earlier have been the case. Brutality or cruelty, on the other hand, involves inflicting pain and injury beyond the minimum needed to attain an appropriate objective. At its most perverse, it can even become a kind of pleasure or end in itself. A decent political act, by contrast, is one that a morally serious and responsible person with adequate knowledge of the facts could perform in the specific circumstances in which the decision must be made.

Static Rules versus Fluid Rules

This rough-and-ready characterization of political hardball suggests two very different kinds of cases where it must be employed.

First, within a static set of rules to which all adhere, you have a responsibility to play hardball as necessary. Yes, the decision to use a brushback pitch on the other team's leading hitter appreciably raises the odds that you will hit him, a prospect you understandably view with distaste. But if you don't use the pitch, you will raise the odds that the slugger will make solid contact, and you have a responsibility to your teammates to minimize those odds, within the framework of the tactics generally specified as acceptable.

Let me offer another example from the late unlamented presidential campaign. Well before the Iowa caucuses, a now-famous "attack video" surfaced, which graphically drew the press's attention to the remarkable similarity between some of the speeches of Sen. Joseph Biden, a candidate for the Democratic nomination, and orations previously delivered by Neil Kinnock, the head of the British Labour Party. These revelations drove Sen. Biden from the race. They also led to the resignation of John Sasso, the manager of the Dukakis campaign, who had masterminded the release of the fatal videotape.

A strong case can be made that Sasso in fact did nothing wrong. After all, the video did not lie; it represented hardball but not dirtyball. Why then was Sasso compelled to resign? Early on, Dukakis had forsworn negative campaigning and had pledged to crack down hard on any member of his campaign caught indulging in it; Dukakis was thus forced to expel Sasso from his campaign to honor his own—misguided—pledge. I want to suggest that the Dukakis pledge, the refusal to play hardball, represents an instance of the political vice I have called squeamishness.

The *second* kind of hardball case involves circumstances in which the political rules are fluid rather than static. If your adversary systematically and intentionally crosses the line separating hardball from dirtyball, the location of the line may be said to shift, and you may now have a responsibility to consider the use of previously forbidden tactics, either to give your adversary an incentive to return to the status quo ante or to maintain competitive effectiveness in the circumstances your adversary has unilaterally altered to his advantage. Thus in current circumstances, for example, to forswear negative advertising, especially if one's opponent is determined to use it, is to heighten unacceptably the risk of defeat.

Where Do the Limits Lie?

At this juncture, I anticipate an anguished and perhaps angry outcry. How far can the requirements of efficacy drive us? Are there no limits? Doesn't a healthy and proper regard for our own decency at some point lead us to say *enough is enough*?

To illustrate this tension between moral self-regard and responsibility to others, I will offer a somewhat less charged example from my own life. My wife and I bicker, more or less amicably, whenever we encounter two lanes of traffic merging into one. Some people zip along the disappearing lane until the last possible moment, then wedge themselves into the surviving lane, obtaining a significant advantage over drivers who wait their turn. My wife frequently wants me to do the same thing, but I refuse. I would like to be able to say that I'm employing the categorical imperative and recoiling in horror from the world of vehicular anarchy my own lane-jumping would implicitly endorse. But in fact that's not what is going on. What really holds me back is my desire to be able to say to myself, I'm not the kind of person who engages in that kind of unfair, self-aggrandizing behavior. Because I regard the rules as fair and sensible, I want to be able to see myself as a person whose character is defined/expressed by adherence to them, even at some cost.

At least in the limit case—if I am in the car by myself, driving for personal pleasure or on some personal errand—this behavior seems morally unobjectionable. The focus on my desire to view myself in a certain way becomes steadily less defensible, however, as my responsibility to others escalates. In a case at the other extreme: If I were rushing my son to the hospital, it would be almost unimaginable to impede my progress by refusing to breach some rules of the road.

Note also that our judgment is shaped by assumptions about the nature and status of the rules. Some are purely conventional, in two senses: There is no compelling moral reason why they couldn't have been different (driving on the right versus driving on the left); and that there is a general propensity to obey them is a necessary condition of their being binding on me. Other rules are quite different in both respects: We assent to them because we regard them as rationally or morally correct, and the behavior of others may not be a necessary condition of bindingness for me, even though others' violations may impose costs on me.

Now clearly, the rules demarcating hardball from dirtyball are of the second sort. We quite properly regard an appeal to public ignorance, prejudice, or passion as wrong in itself and not merely by agreement. We would try to resist as long as possible the conclusion that such appeals by others have left us with the unpalatable alternatives of retiring from the fray or responding in kind. Nevertheless, we may ultimately be driven to confront just such a choice.

For example, in the midst of the 1984 North Carolina Senate race between Jim Hunt and Jesse Helms, the Senate took up legislation to create a national holiday honoring Martin Luther King. Helms went all out against the bill; Hunt knew that supporting it would cost him severely, but he felt he had no other morally acceptable course. One of Hunt's advisers is reported to have said to him at the time, "If the election is about race, if that's what you've got to do to win, we just won't win, and just be prepared to accept that."

Hunt's decision strikes me as defensible, for two reasons. First, it might be argued that his responsibility to his supporters was not only to win, but also to represent certain values that they cared about deeply. If the price of victory was the public abandonment of one of those values, then his victory could well be thought to lose much of its point. Second, race was not just any issue. A decent politician—and particularly a southerner—had ample reason to believe that compromise on race would be unconscionable.

Still, the result of Hunt's decision was the defeat of an intelligent and honorable man at the hands of one of the most unreconstructed race-baiters in American politics today, someone beyond the pale on a wide range of issues. If trimming on the holiday bill could have secured Helms's defeat, I believe that a decision on Hunt's part to do so would have been morally permissible. In politics (and perhaps elsewhere as well), the morality of using intrinsically attractive means is circumscribed by the ability of the political system—and in a democracy that means the people—to respond affirmatively to them. For whatever else the endeavor to pursue and exercise power may be, it is surely not a suicide pact.

Sex, Character,
Politics, and the Press

Judith Lichtenberg

When, after secretly staking out presidential candidate Gary Hart's townhouse for a weekend in the spring of 1987, the *Miami Herald* revealed that he had spent at least much of that time with a young woman, many ordinary people found themselves facing a difficult question.

Who's sleazier—Hart or the *Herald*?

After weeks of further revelations, ruminations, and reflections, some of us reached a conclusion. The press deserves the prize.

The question is harder than this glib answer suggests. Indeed, the events at that time demonstrate what a tangle of difficult issues is raised when public figures cavort and journalists report. Is a candidate's sexual behavior relevant to his fitness for the presidency? How does sexual conduct compare with other so-called character issues? Is the issue one of morality or judgment? Does the distinction matter? Even if sex is relevant, does it follow that, as far as press coverage is concerned, all's fair? What role should the press play in deciding what subjects are appropriate for coverage?

Let's begin with what seems to be the pivotal question: Is sexual behavior relevant to a person's fitness for political leadership? The question is pivotal because vindication of the press in the Hart incident requires the assumption that sex is relevant.

Surely how we conduct ourselves sexually reveals something about our moral standing as human beings—about our character. People who use other people sexually, who lead on potential sexual partners, or who deceive those with whom they purport to have an exclusive relationship are morally blameworthy. (We don't know, of course, whether Gary Hart is guilty of any of these things.) Just how harshly we judge such offenses depends on a variety of additional factors: what precautions the person takes against hurting people, how he responds when he does, how continuous the sexual failings are with the rest of his behavior.

This last question is especially important. Sexual behavior is often discontinuous with the rest of personality; sexually, people often behave "out of character." That is because of the special status of sex, the unique place it occupies in our society and our psyches. Our sexual self is powerful, often shadowy and hidden—even from ourselves. Undoubtedly this is partly a social fact about how we as a society treat sexual matters and partly an inescapable psychic truth about human beings. In any case, we cannot draw easy conclusions about character, much less leadership ability, from sexual behavior alone. People who are otherwise above suspicion can behave in strange and not altogether admirable ways sexually.

It is difficult to think of other aspects of personal conduct comparable to sex in this way. Examples presented in recent public opinion polls ("Which would you find more disturbing in a candidate: adultery or . . . ?") are heavy use of alcohol or drugs and cheating on one's income tax, behavior that may at first sight seem to be in the same boat with sex. Although not obviously political, they tell us something about a person's character. Yet the first indicates something about a person's general reliability and competence; the second tells us about his sense of civic obligation. (The public wisely deemed both more important than adultery.) Both are clearly relevant to a person's fitness to lead in a way sexual conduct is not.

For purposes of judging the qualities of leadership, the only aspect of private behavior that seems comparable to sexual habits is everyday sensitivity and decency: a set of traits we typically invoke when we call or refuse to call someone a "nice guy." There can be no question that whether a person generally treats others around him with respect and compassion reveals something important about his character. Just as clearly, alas, these traits bear little on a person's leadership qualities. It's one of life's poetic injustices that although nice guys don't always finish last, those who finish first, and should, aren't always nice guys. And this suggests perhaps the strongest evidence for the gap between sexual conduct and the virtues of leadership—call it the argument from history. Let us theorize and moralize till we turn blue, it is an undeniable fact that a catalogue of the world's most important and capable leaders— throughout history as well as in America's recent past—would include a startling proportion of adulterers and philanderers, from virtually all the English prime ministers to Franklin D. Roosevelt, the Kennedys and Martin Luther King. What else can we conclude from a hardheaded look at history but that, despite our best hopes and most noble ideals, a statesman might not be someone you would want for your friend?

This discrepancy points to the confusion lurking in all the Hart-inspired talk about character. There's character and character. Our ideal of a good person involves one set of traits, our expectations of a good leader or a good president involve a quite different set. Being a nice guy, sexually or otherwise, is far down on the list and may sometimes even get in the way of other traits we value much more in the political realm.

So sexual behavior is not, I conclude, relevant to one's fitness for political office. Part of me is sad to have to conclude this, for it would be nice if all the virtues went together, if those with sufficient drive and fortitude and whatever else it takes to lead millions were also always good mommies or daddies and faithful spouses. But it just ain't so.

Some of Hart's critics and the press's defenders will agree. Now the terms of the debate shift: It's not Hart's morals that are in question, we are told, but his judgment. Certainly his taunt to journalists to follow him was not smart. But beyond that? If it wasn't the dalliances themselves that disqualified him, it was instead, these critics say, his lack of discretion and his failure to see that "womanizing" had become an issue in his campaign, requiring careful attention to appearances.

But something is deeply wrong with this argument. At least one president, we hear, had his many women in the White House. Was that discreet? Discreet enough, apparently, because in those days reporters did not mention such things even when they knew them; it was not considered appropriate or relevant. But now, it will be said, it is thought appropriate or relevant, and Hart knew this. The standards of discretion and thus of judgment have changed.

But although this answer has some plausibility, it assigns ultimate responsibility in the wrong place. If Hart's judgment is poor, that is because the press has introduced a change in the rules; if sexual behavior and leadership ability have no connection, it has changed them for the worse. Perhaps not seeing that the rules have changed is poor judgment. But what sort of judgment is at issue here? Is it the intelligence and discernment necessary for negotiating with the Soviets or forging trade policy with Japan? Or is it merely image management—the ability to manipulate the press by acceding to its own manipulations? We ought to know better after the Ronald Reagan years than to set much store by that.

What can journalists say in defense of the new rules? One argument is that the public wants to know about the private lives of candidates and that journalists are just carrying out the public's will. But no evidence exists that people are more interested in these matters than they ever were. And even if they were, that does not amount to a license to snoop. What the public would like to know and what it has a right to know are two different things.

The more common defense of the press is slightly different: Not that the public necessarily wants to know this or that, but that the job of reporters is, simply, to publish the news and leave it up to the public to decide what is important and relevant. People may not have a right to know what goes on in the politician's bedroom, it may be said, but they have a right to vote on the basis of any damn thing they please.

So they do—legally, at least. No one can jail you for voting on the basis of shoe size. Morally, however, things are otherwise. We have a duty to do our best to purge our decisions of obvious irrationalities and irrelevancies. And—more to the present point—that goes for journalists, too. Since the press cannot cover everything, it must choose, decide, edit, omit, emphasize. Every single day journalists are confronted with the question, "What is important?"; every single day they must take responsibility for the answers they give. The idea that "the news" is something out there waiting to be appropriated like apples on the supermarket shelf is blind to the crucial processes of decision and selection behind the morning paper and the nightly newscast. And it is blind to the inescapable fact that the relationship between the public's opinions, demands, and expectations of politicians and what the press covers is not a one-way street. It is not so much that the press covers the private lives of politicians because that is now an "issue" as that the press has *made* it an issue by covering it.

After the spectacle where reporters asked Gary Hart whether he had ever committed adultery, Craig Whitney, Washington bureau chief of the *New York Times*, defended the press by asserting that "There's no question that should be regarded as out of bounds. Let's ask about it, whatever it is, and then determine whether it's news." How naive can you get? Which of the following answers to the question "Have you ever committed adultery?" would the press *not* consider news: (a) Yes; (b) No; (c) It's none of your business? In such matters, you don't "determine whether it's news" after you get the answer; you determine that it will be news *in the very act of asking the question*. That fact has as much to do with people's natural curiosity and the love of gossip as with anything. But to acknowledge this does not let the press off the hook.

It is the failure by the press to admit its own crucial and determinative role in the political process that is revealed as the gravest lapse in the Hart incident. Whether one thinks the lapse is one of "ethics" or "judgment" depends on whether one thinks that journalists understand their power, but refuse, for their own reasons, to acknowledge it, or that they are simply ignorant of the nature of their business. Either way, the lapse is inexcusable.

Religion in Public Life

Claudia Mills

In 1965 the Reverend Jerry Falwell chastised fellow clergy who were taking part in the civil rights movement for neglecting what he saw to be the only appropriate mission of a sacred calling in a profane world: "Believing in the Bible as I do, I would find it impossible to stop preaching the pure saving Gospel of Jesus Christ, and begin doing anything else—including fighting communism, or participating in civil rights reforms. . . . Preachers are not called to be politicians but to be soul winners." Today, of course, Falwell is better known as the founder of Moral Majority, a Christian activist group lobbying for a sweeping agenda of conservative legislation. Which Falwell provides a better model for the proper relationship between religion and politics?

Although ours has been derided as an age of eroding religious commitment, America remains an almost anachronistically religious society. In a recent study of religion and politics, social scientist Kenneth Wald notes that "By all the normal indicators of religious commitment—the strength of religious institutions, practices, and belief—the United States has resisted the pressures toward secularity." The proportion of church members aged fifteen and older is virtually the same today (76.9 percent) as it was in 1950 (78.5 percent), and "by overwhelming majorities, Americans have continued to endorse the core assumptions of Christianity—the existence of God, the divinity of Jesus, the reality of an afterlife—and to insist on the importance of these values in their own life." Levels of religious belief in America are higher than in Europe and Latin America, and equal to those in the Far East and sub-Saharan Africa. Indeed, abiding religious faith may be a more salient fact about the United States than attachment to democratic political institutions: "The proportion of Americans claiming to speak in tongues . . . exceeded the proportion who worked for a party or candidate in 1980."

Nonetheless, one of our bedrock assumptions as a polity is a belief in the separation of church and state. The First Amendment to the Constitution proclaims that "Congress shall make no law respecting an establishment of religion, or prohibiting the free exercise thereof," thereby establishing a "wall of separation," in Jefferson's metaphor, between religion and politics.

While almost everyone agrees that some line must be drawn between the two domains, where and how the line should be drawn is a matter of intense dispute. Almost two centuries after the ratification of the Bill of Rights, church/state wrangles are still alive in the courts and in the headlines. Controversies over school prayer and over the teaching of evolution, Rasputin-like, refuse to die. The unexpected political muscle shown by fundamentalist Protestants in recent presidential elections, as well as key political pronouncements by leading Catholic clergy, raise for some the specter of religion overstepping its rightful bounds; for others, they raise the hope of religion regaining its rightful place.

As consensus over the proper boundaries between church and state comes under increasing pressure, it may be helpful to look more closely at exactly why we want separation of church and state. What values does it seek to secure? How well does it secure them? What role do we want religion to play in American public life?

Protecting Religion from Government

Some degree of separation between church and state has been sought as a way of protecting both the church from the state and the state from the church. Ideally the principle of separation is not intended to denigrate the authority of either sphere, but to codify in legal terms the scriptural injunction to render unto God that which is God's and to render unto Caesar that which is Caesar's. Both concerns played a role in the framers' deliberations at the Constitutional Convention, and both play a role in contemporary debates.

Until recent efforts to purge the public-school curriculum of any mention of religion, schoolchildren grew up learning that the Pilgrims came to Plymouth Rock to seek freedom of worship. That our nation was settled in part by those fleeing religious persecution explains one reason for an early insistence on protecting religious faith from governmental intrusion. While many early settlers would have preferred a government that protected *their* religion and persecuted everybody else's, others recognized the danger that followed any government establishment of religion. A principle protecting all religions from state interference serves as a guarantee that one's own religion will be protected, whatever the prevailing political or theological fashion.

Separation of church and state also ensures that even the majority religion is not dominated by government interference and placed under the legislative control of secular authorities. As the price of its state support, the Church of England has been subject to Parliamentary oversight even on strictly ecclesiastical matters: Earlier in this century, a Parliament where members of the Anglican Church formed a minority twice rejected a proposal put forward by church fathers to revise the Anglican Prayer Book.

A further argument that the church should resist entanglement with the state grows out of a conviction that the church should maintain its sanctity as a sphere apart, a garden in the wilderness, a refuge and sanctuary from worldly strife. By speaking out too vehemently on the matters of this world, the church compromises its commitment to the world beyond. It espouses truths that are not timeless but trendy and runs the risk of estranging many of the once faithful. De Tocqueville, who had much to say about religion in America, cautioned, "As long as a religion rests only upon those sentiments which are the consolation of all affliction, it may attract the affections of all mankind. But if it be mixed up with the bitter passions of the world, it may be constrained to defend allies whom its interests, and not the principle of love, have given to it; or to repel as antagonists men who are still attached to it, however opposed they may be to the powers with which it is allied. The church cannot share the temporal power of the state without being the object of a portion of that animosity which the latter excites."

The institution of religion seems to be strengthened, moreover, by the diversity that flourishes in the absence of an official, state-dominated church. Wald suggests that "the persistence of religion in the United States can be related to the remarkable diversity of denominations in the country. . . . Pluralism has forced the churches to compete for members and so has encouraged them to adapt to new social realities." The vitality of American religion is striking in contrast, for example, to the lukewarm attachment of Scandinavians to the state-supported Lutheran church that all but a miniscule minority attend only to be "hatched, matched, and dispatched." A persuasive case can be made, then, that a separation of church and state invigorates religion.

Protecting Government from Religion

It has been even more widely accepted that some insulation between church and state is essential to protect government from religion. Democratic politics are based on the art of compromise, prospects for compromise are brightest if deeply held passions are given limited sway in the public arena, and no passions are more intemperate than those grounded in religious zeal. Sectarian strife in India, Lebanon, and Northern Ireland serves as a searing reminder of how religious hatred can erupt in political discord. In our own history, religious fervor against the institution of slavery fanned the flames of civil war. Today the religiously fueled abortion debate is among the most intractable issues on the public agenda.

Religious convictions are not only too intense to be safely contained within democratic debate; they are arguably inappropriate not only in degree, but in kind. Public decisions must be made by arguments that are public in character; religion, however, draws on deeply private sources of faith.

Robert Frost once observed that good fences make good neighbors. Both religion and government have been held to benefit from some clear boundary between their respective spheres. The contours of this boundary have been shaped by a doctrine of government neutrality both among competing religions and, as the First Amendment has increasingly been interpreted since the Second World War, between religion and irreligion. Reciprocally, religion has exhibited its own stance of neutrality toward government, buttressed by provisions of the tax code that bar churches from political lobbying and outright political endorsements on penalty of losing their tax-exempt status.

Of late, however, churches have chafed under this political neutrality. The Catholic church has petitioned Congress to lift tax-code restrictions on political activity by religious groups, in the wake of public chastisements by Catholic clergy of pro-abortion candidates for public office. Protestant fundamentalists have taken aggressive roles in recent presidential elections, most notably through the candidacy of television evangelist Pat Robertson. When charged with rupturing the established covenant of reciprocal neutrality, church leaders in many cases insist that they are only defending themselves against repeated governmental attacks on religion and religious values. Religion is becoming less neutral about government, they say, as government is becoming less neutral about religion. How should we understand these claims?

Neutrality as a Liberal Smokescreen

The branch of government most often accused of undermining state neutrality toward religion is the Supreme Court. Critics charge that numerous landmark decisions embody not neutrality but outright hostility toward religion. In the 1963 case of *Abington Township School District* v. *Schempp*, which barred Bible reading in Pennsylvania public schools, even several Supreme Court justices expressed worry that the trend toward secularism would be carried too far. Justices Arthur Gold-berg and John Harlan, though voting with the majority, warned against "a brooding and pervasive devotion to the secular and a passive, or even active, hostility to the religious." Justice Potter Stewart, in dissent, argued that "a refusal to permit religious exercises . . . is seen, not as the realization of state neutrality, but rather as the establishment of a religion of secularism."

Religious groups, particularly those that emphasize traditional moral values, have begun to challenge protestations of liberal neutral-ity as a smokescreen behind which the state advances liberal ends. Philosopher Thomas Nagel calls attention to doubts that professions of government impartiality "are made in good faith. Part of the problem is that liberals ask of everyone a certain restraint in calling for the use of state power to further specific, controversial moral or religious con-ceptions—but the results of that restraint appear with suspicious fre-quency to favor precisely the controversial moral conceptions that liberals usually hold." Those who argue most vociferously against school prayer often turn out to be crusading atheists; those who argue against the restriction of pornography or homosexuality on the ground that the state should not attempt to enforce religiously based standards of morality often don't think anything is in fact wrong with pornogra-phy or homosexuality. Thus the suspicion is raised "that all the pleas for toleration and restraint really disguise a campaign to put the state behind a secular, individualistic, and libertine morality—against reli-gion and in favor of sex, roughly."

William Galston, a philosopher and political analyst, likewise notes that Supreme Court decisions on pornography, school prayer, and abortion are hardly viewed by religious traditionalists as marking out a neutral government stance on the issues in question. They reject the argument that the state acts neutrally on, for example, abortion by leaving individuals to choose for themselves. "To permit a certain class of actions," as Galston explains their argument, "is to make the public judgment that those actions are not wrong. No one denies that the state should prohibit murder. To permit abortion is therefore to determine (at least implicitly) that abortion is not murder. But this is precisely the issue between proponents and opponents of abortion. Permitting abor-tion cannot be construed as neutrality, because it rests on a substan-tive moral judgment that is anything but neutral."

Religious groups thus maintain that since the state has already launched its own campaign against religious values, by taking an active political role to defend those values they do no more than redress the imbalance. But evident in their new partisan stance is also a challenge to the very ideal of religious disengagement from politics.

Religious adherents may reject the argument that their most deeply held convictions would be unduly disruptive of public debate. To insist that public debate be purged of all passion results only in a public conversation that is terminally bland. The emphasis on avoiding controversy at all costs, Galston suggests, flows from the twin liberal goals of avoiding oppression and preserving civil tranquility. But while "tranquility is an important good, . . . it is not the only good. And it is not oppression (in the eyes of the religious believer) when right conduct is commanded and wrongful acts prohibited." Even the potential for civic disruption inherent in religious controversy need not pose a definitive objection to a vital religious presence in public life. The Civil War was fueled by the religious beliefs of the abolitionist movement; Galston asks, "How many Americans believe that the Civil War was too high a price to pay for the abolition of slavery?"

Religious adherents may also challenge the argument that private faith has no legitimate place in public debate. The claim that religious conviction is essentially private seems to imply that religious truth is subjective, arbitrary, simply a "matter of opinion," not truth at all. But if religious conviction is grounded in some truth of the matter, why not give this truth expression in public as well as private spheres? Nagel asks how we can be asked to cordon off beliefs that we hold to be true in determining acceptable public policies: "If I believe something, I believe it to be *true*, yet here I am asked to refrain from acting on that belief in deference to beliefs I think are false." Government impartiality toward religion seems to rest on a skepticism about the possibility of religious truth. And that skepticism the faithful reject.

Neutrality Defended

Can we locate a rationale for keeping distinctively religious convictions out of politics that doesn't rely on dismissing the seriousness with which they are held as true by the believer—and the possibility that they may indeed *be* true? One answer, in Nagel's view, lies in looking more closely at the special features of *political* dialogue and action. Political dialogue is special, for it takes place against the background of the state's coercive power; it shapes policies that all will be compelled to support. This element of state coercion, Nagel suggests, "imposes an especially stringent requirement of objectivity in justification."

Nagel proposes that we need to draw a distinction between what justifies an individual's own beliefs and what justifies appealing to those beliefs in support of the exercise of political power. The latter requires a higher standard of objectivity, an impersonal justification that, if not universally convincing, is at least accessible to all who share a stake in the political outcome. This means that we must look at even our most deeply held convictions "from the outside," and ask of them whether they can be justified to another in impersonal terms. That some of our beliefs cannot meet rigorous tests of impersonal justification does not mean that these are not true, but only that their truth cannot be argued for impersonally.

Nagel holds that this requirement of impersonal justification calls for a "preparedness to submit one's reasons to the criticism of others" and to accept the possibility that rational consideration of the evidence will reveal that one is mistaken. "This means that it must be possible to present to others the basis of your own beliefs, so that once you have done so, *they have what you have*, and can arrive at a judgment on the same basis. This is not possible if part of the source of your conviction is personal faith or revelation. . . ." The fundamentalist insistence on a personal "born again" experience as the only avenue to religious truth, for example, limits the possibilities for dialogue between politically active fundamentalists and their adversaries.

Second, in arguing that those who do not share your views are *wrong*, one should be prepared to give an explanation of their error that goes beyond the mere assertion that they do not believe what you hold to be the truth—an explanation in terms of identifiable errors in their evidence or in their arguments from it. "A disagreement which falls on objective common ground must be open-ended in the possibility of its investigation and pursuit, and not come down finally to a bare confrontation between incompatible personal points of view. I suggest that conflicts of religious faith fail this test, and most empirical and many moral disagreements do not." Thus, Nagel concludes that religious convictions are rightfully excluded from the public stage when whatever truth they contain cannot be justified impersonally and impartially.

Conclusion

That explicitly religious arguments should not ground the claims that we make against one another does not mean, of course, that religious groups cannot join with all others in arguing about the issues of the day on their merits. But it does suggest caution in indulging openly religious rhetoric, say, in the halls of Congress or in election-year debates. Where religious convictions give rise to clearly defined moral views that can be examined in their own right, these latter should certainly be a subject of shared public scrutiny. But the principle of insulating religion from politics and politics from religion seems to remain one well worth honoring.

Sources quoted in this article are Kenneth D. Wald, Religion and Politics in the United States *(New York: St. Martin's Press, 1987); Thomas Nagel, "Moral Conflict and Political Legitimacy,"* Philosophy & Public Affairs *16, no. 3 (Summer 1987); and William A. Galston, "Public Morality and Religion in the United States,"* PS *19, no. 4 (Fall 1986).*

FOR FURTHER READING

Gutmann, Amy, ed. *Democracy and the Welfare State*. Princeton, N.J.: Princeton University Press, 1988.

Gutmann, Amy, and Dennis Thompson, eds. *Ethics & Politics: Cases and Comments*. Chicago: Nelson-Hall Publishers, 1984.

Lovin, Robin W., ed. *Religion and American Public Life: Interpretations and Explorations*. New York: Paulist Press, 1986.

Moskos, Charles C. *A Call to Civil Service: National Service for Country and Community*. New York: Free Press, 1986.

Novak, Michael. *Free Persons and the Common Good*. Lanham, Md.: Madison Books, 1989.

Simmons, A. John. *Moral Principles and Political Obligations*. Princeton, N.J.: Princeton University Press, 1979.

Thomson, Dennis F. *Political Ethics and Public Office*. Cambridge, Mass.: Harvard University Press, 1987.

Walzer, Michael. *Spheres of Justice: A Defense of Pluralism and Equality*. New York: Basic Books, 1983.

PART V

EDUCATION, THE FAMILY, AND THE COMPLEXITY OF LIFE

11

EDUCATION

S ince at least the time of Socrates, philosophers have been keenly interested in the education of the young, and in particular, in the process by which values are taught to children and so transmitted from one generation to another. This interest is now echoed in a passionate public debate over the quality of our schools—allegedly awash in a "rising tide of mediocrity" (as the National Commission on Excellence in Education bluntly charged)—and the place of moral and religious values in the public school curriculum.

"Educating Our Children: Whose Responsibility?" asks whether these concerns are best met by lodging the responsibility for education with parents, local communities, state governments, or the federal government. While persuasive arguments can be made for enhancing parental control over education via proposed voucher systems, we may doubt whether such extensive parental authority is in the best interests of children and of the wider society. What we need, the author concludes, is "a public education system that responds to parental leverage, but allows for a democratic society's interest in educating future democratic citizens." This would ideally involve government responsibility at local, state, *and* federal levels.

In "Should Public Schools Teach Virtue?" Amy Gutmann suggests that schools can hardly avoid engaging in moral education, if only by default: "The political choice facing us is therefore not whether schools should engage in moral education, but what sort of moral education they should engage in." Gutmann rejects the popular "values clarification" approach, with its ideal of liberal neutrality toward any particular values, as too indiscriminate. She opts instead for a qualified "moralist" position intermediate between the authoritarian morality often proposed by conservatives and the insistence on moral autonomy often proposed by liberals. Moral autonomy cannot be taught, Gutmann argues, but what can and should be taught is "democratic virtue"—respect among races, religious toleration, patriotism, and political judgment.

Robert Fullinwider, in "Learning Morality," offers a blueprint for moral education in the classroom. Moral education, as Aristotle says, is learning by doing. This means, according to Fullinwider, that "the central and ongoing resource for moral education is experience, real or vicarious," the latter provided by extensive exposure to history and literature, the world's great store of stories.

The most controversial values of all, in the public schools, are religious values or values held to be directly antireligious, specifically, those embodied in the teaching of evolutionary theory. In "The Case against Creationism," Allen Stairs examines the arguments for and against balancing the teaching of evolution with the teaching of "scientific creationism." He argues that, in contrast with creationism, which clearly favors a religious set of values, the theory of evolution is morally neutral in any broad secular view.

Educating Our Children
Whose Responsibility?

Claudia Mills

When the National Commission on Excellence in Education sounded the alarm in the mid-1980s that "the educational foundations of our society are presently being eroded by a risiṇg tide of mediocrity," most Americans felt vindicated rather than surprised. The commission's report, "A Nation at Risk," merely gave official voice to doubts long expressed by many that America's schools are not doing their job. As demand for highly skilled workers in technically challenging fields is accelerating, test scores are just now bottoming out of a two-decade decline. The average achievement of high school students on most standardized tests is lower today than it was when Sputnik was launched, more than three decades ago. In many international comparisons of student achievement, American students trail the rest of the industrial world. If the current state of affairs in education had been plotted by a hostile foreign power, the report concluded, we would call it an act of war.

The question is what to do about it, and critics of the Ronald Reagan and George Bush administrations charge that they are lavish with rhetoric decrying the problem, but sparing of any federal initiatives toward a solution. Federal officials counter that education is constitutionally the responsibility of the states. Far from heightening the federal government's role in education, they propose to retrench it still further, by reducing federal aid to public schools, loosening federally enforced antidiscrimination regulations, and questioning the need for a cabinet-level Department of Education.

Traditionally responsibility for education has belonged to each local community. With the demise of the little red schoolhouse, however, has come a steady trend toward state-level centralization. Local contributions to school revenues have dwindled from more than 80 percent in the 1920s to about 42 percent in 1983, with the state's share rising from less than 20 to a full 50 percent. Recent years have also seen a trend toward imposition of statewide standards of educational achievement that all students—and increasingly teachers as well—are required to meet. While many welcome these developments, others resist what they see as sterile homogenization. They would like to see responsibility for a child's education devolve to the level of the individual school, or the family.

But responsibility for education has many dimensions. Before we decide who should be responsible, we need to ask: Responsible for what? Who should set the curriculum? Certify teachers? Decide how much to spend on public education relative to other goods? Pay the bills? In each case, we have a choice of authorities—parents, school, local community, state, federal government, or even the child. Our answers to these questions will be guided in part by what interests we expect education to serve, by what we take the purposes of education in a democracy to be.

The Voucher System

If the education of adults were at issue, one might well decide that the final responsibility for any person's education should rest with the person alone. Insofar as one central purpose of education is to contribute to individual human flourishing, decisions about the nature and scope of education should be left to the individuals in question, as the best judges of their own best interests. But children are not adults. Children, at least young ones, cannot make their own decisions on how they should be educated, since a chief goal of education is precisely to enable them to make such decisions wisely.

A natural, though today quite radical, answer to where responsibility for a child's education should then be lodged is *with the parents*. The claim is that parents are, of all possible surrogates, best placed to determine what is in the best interests of their children. Thus John E. Coons and Stephen D. Sugarman, writing in *Education by Choice: The Case for Family Control*, argue the following: (1) "Beyond the broad generalization that it is good for children to be educated," no clear consensus arises on what constitutes the best interests of children generally. (2) The process of deciding what constitutes the best interests of any particular child "should always incorporate the child's own voice expressed within a decision-making community that is knowledgeable and caring about him." (3) "In its unique opportunity to listen and to know and in its special personal concern for the child, the family is his most promising champion."

How is familial responsibility for education to be translated into public policy? Almost no one suggests that the family should assume full financial responsibility for their children's education, perhaps because education is a public good that benefits all members of a society, perhaps because the resulting inequalities would be too extreme to tolerate. Nor do most proponents of parental authority call for a complete abdication of responsibility on the part of the state. Instead, what Coons and Sugarman propose, following the early lead of economist Milton Friedman, is a "voucher" system, which would turn over to parents some portion of the public education budget so they could purchase what they determine to be the best schooling for their children's particular needs—be it in competing public schools, private schools, or less traditional alternatives. While some governmental standards would remain, they would be far more attenuated than at present to encourage the maximum diversity in educational offerings. The qualifications of teachers, the content of the curriculum, and the degree and direction of moral education provided would be left to parents' choices among competing options in a free market. Regulations could be introduced, as endorsed by Coons and Sugarman (although not by Friedman's original plan), to combat racial discrimination and to equalize the amount spent on each child's education. But the driving aim of the voucher system is to facilitate parental control.

Two questions arise regarding the voucher system and the desirability of such broad parental authority over education. First, *is* such a system in the best interests of the child? And, second, are the child's and the family's interests the only relevant ones, or does the community have a legitimate and independent interest of its own—one that would be better served by some other division of educational responsibility?

In many views, a central way education benefits children is by developing their autonomy—their ability to assess intellectual and moral options and to make genuine choices among them. A liberal, pluralist society provides its citizens with a range of options; education enables them to enjoy this range to its fullest. Amy Gutmann, professor of government at Princeton University, argues, "The same principles that require a state to grant adults freedom to choose their own conception of the good life also commit it to assuring children an education that makes choice both possible and meaningful in the future."

Education enhances individual autonomy. But, according to political theorist Michael Walzer, it is also "a program for social survival." Walzer quotes Aristotle, that the purpose of education is to reproduce in each generation the character suited to the "constitution" of the society in question. In a democratic society this means, again, educating citizens to be autonomous choosers, since the legitimate exercise of government rests on their choices. It also means educating them to be tolerant of the choices of others. Without a deep-seated commitment to toleration, a pluralist society cannot endure.

Is parental control of education a good way to develop autonomy within an ongoing pluralist society? In Walzer's view, the voucher system restricts rather than widens children's horizons: "The voucher plan would guarantee that children go to school with other children whose parents, at least, were very much like their own. . . . For most children, parental choice almost certainly means less diversity, less tension, less opportunity for personal change than they would find in schools to which they were politically assigned." Gutmann argues that autonomy and toleration are fostered when children are taught "to understand and evaluate ways of life different from those of their parents." The voucher system, instead, seems likely to trap children within one parochial point of view.

Coons and Sugarman reply that a parental choice system is in fact the best way to promote autonomy and pluralism. Autonomy is better promoted, they argue, when children are exposed to intense moral commitment than to shoulder-shrugging "neutrality." Moral sensibilities must first be engaged before they can spread and deepen. And the voucher system promotes pluralism by providing an escape route from the dreary sameness of today's public schools, with their emphasis on noncontroversial views and their endorsement of majoritarian social and political norms—a sameness reinforced by the bland standardization of American mass culture: "Today the danger is not that the child will learn nothing of the world and its normalities; it is that he will learn nothing else." The voucher system, according to Coons and Sugarman, is pluralism in action: a veritable smorgasbord of options laid out for the choosing.

Gutmann observes, however, that the pluralism of the voucher system is in an important respect "illusory"—the larger society is pluralist, but it might as well not be as far as the actual educational experiences of individual children are concerned. The children themselves do not sample at will from the tempting feast of options the voucher system makes available; they are bound to the one dish preselected by their parents. The diversity the voucher system offers turns out to be "an ornament for onlookers": It is not a felt source of enrichment in the children's own lives.

Walzer suggests, furthermore, that the voucher system can be seen as actually antithetical to democratic politics. Democracy is premised on the need for citizens to work together to achieve, out of their diversity, common goals. The voucher system issues an invitation to citizens not to work together, but to walk away. Citizens avoid the necessity for debate and compromise by bailing out of the cooperative effort altogether.

Advocates of the voucher plan point out that the affluent have always been able to walk away; they aim only to provide the same freedom for all citizens. But the social effects of defection by a small minority are very different from the sweeping change in our attitude toward public education that the voucher plan would provoke. Walzer maintains that we should tolerate the recourse to private and parochial schools "so long as its chief effect is to provide ideological diversity on the margins of a predominantly public system." We should be troubled, however, when our shared commitment to a strong public system and a democratic culture is threatened. We also might wonder whether the benefits of wise parental choice in most cases would outweigh the tragic costs in some cases of parental ignorance and neglect. Gutmann also advocates that nonpublic schools should be a good deal more public-spirited than many are now; *all* schools should be required to educate their students in the moral principles essential to any democratic society, such as tolerance and respect for the rights of others. That much is within the state's prerogative "in securing its own future and the future freedom of its citizens."

Local, State, or Federal Control?

What we need is a public education system that responds to parental leverage, but allows for a democratic society's interest in educating future democratic citizens. These two concerns have combined to produce our traditional arrangement of local democratic control: School budgets are determined by local referenda and raised by local property taxes; the content of the curriculum is determined largely by a popularly elected board of education. Local democratic control is both more effective and more flexible than state-level control.

Policy analysts Denis Doyle and Chester Finn, Jr., note that bureaucracy is less intractable at local levels, and that local control leads to greater variety among educational offerings, allowing "some responsiveness both to community priorities and to the yearning of individual families to select the kind of education that their children will receive."

Few would suggest, however, that local school boards be given a blank check to write out educational policy; the underlying purposes of education in a democracy contain within them restrictions on how much authority democratic majorities, at any level of government, should be free to wield. No school board should be free to flout the basic purpose of enabling all children to make meaningful choices among good lives and to participate as equals in the democratic process. Gutmann suggests that this underlying purpose entails three restrictions on democratic control: Education must be funded at a minimum threshold level, in order to meet its objectives; the objectives must be met for *all* children; and the content of the curriculum must indeed expose children to the range of different, morally acceptable options open to them in our society and teach them the principles that make us a democratic nation.

These three conditions place clear limits on the discretion allowed to any democratic decision-making body—local, state, or federal. But they usher in special questions about local democratic control, particularly local responsibility for educational funding.

One reason for centralizing financial responsibility for education is that without outside assistance many poorer communities simply cannot afford to educate their children to the threshold level. State or federal funding is thus needed, in Gutmann's view, to ensure that the democratic threshold is met for all children.

Considerations of equity also suggest a move away from local funding. Doyle and Finn observe, "There is little relationship between the value of property in a given community and the educational needs of the children who live there." They cite one particularly egregious example of the inequities that obtained in California before the courts mandated financial reform: One poor school district reported an assessed property valuation of $100 per child; another, oil-producing district boasted for each of its handful of children an assessed valuation of one million! Such extreme differentials in the resources devoted to children's education make us rightly uncomfortable when they are based on the accidents of wealth alone and not on any variation in parental and community attitudes toward the value of education.

But even when it is corrected for inequities, local school funding, as Gutmann points out, does not provide an effective means for parents and citizens to express the value they place on education. Local citizens can decide how much to spend on schools, but they are not in a position to determine the relative priority to be given to education over comparably expensive goods such as transportation, health care, and national defense. The size of state and federal budgets, and priorities within those budgets, are matters over which local citizens have little control. Citizens who feel themselves overtaxed may end up voting against school budgets, not because they place a lower value on good schools than on highways or aircraft carriers, but because that is their only effective recourse. Gutmann concludes: "Local control over educational funding may therefore be less rather than more democratic than state control because it presents citizens and their representatives with a considerably more constrained choice."

We need, finally, some state and even national standards to ensure that the content of education is properly pluralist and that future American citizens are being prepared to participate in the American political process. "Delegating to local school boards full control over . . . education," Gutmann argues, "would reduce the United States to a collection of democratic city-states, totally neglecting our collective interest in a common moral education." The policies of local school boards, she believes, should be subject to national standards of two central kinds: "standards that are essential to any good democratic society and ones that serve to unite and distinguish us from other democratic societies." This much standardization ensures that we will pass on to our children a common heritage.

These concerns give grounds for welcoming the current shift toward state-level control of education. Why not go all the way and endorse centralization at the national level? One reason for encouraging the federal government to assume greater financial responsibility in this area is, according to Gutmann, that "federal funding would have the considerable advantage of placing education on the same level as defense, and thereby facilitating the trade-off between better minds and better missiles." But opposing considerations outweigh this advantage: "Complete federal funding of education would probably entail an equally significant decrease in its diversity, a consequence that we have good reason to fear for education, but not for defense. . . . States are small enough to preserve a degree of diversity and large enough to permit trade-offs between education and other goods." To the federal government, however, is properly assigned responsibility for ensuring equal access to an adequate education for all children. This responsibility justifies the federal government's intervention in school desegregation; Gutmann argues that it also provides a reason why the federal government should take up the often extremely expensive burden of financing special programs for the handicapped and other severely disadvantaged students.

"Education," Walzer writes, "expresses what is, perhaps, our deepest wish: to continue, to go on, to persist in the face of time." In a democratic society, education is the responsibility of democratic citizens. The sober discussion following the warnings issued by the president's commission is one hopeful sign that we may be willing as a nation to make a new effort to assume these responsibilities together.

The sources quoted in this article are John E. Coons and Stephen D. Sugarman, Education by Choice: The Case for Family Control *(Berkeley and Los Angeles: University of California Press, 1978); Amy*

Gutmann, Democratic Education *(Princeton, N.J.: Princeton University Press, 1987); Michael Walzer,* Spheres of Justice *(New York: Basic Books, 1983); and Denis P. Doyle and Chester E. Finn, Jr., "American Schools and the Future of Local Control,"* The Public Interest, *no. 77 (Fall 1984).*

Should Public Schools Teach Virtue?

Amy Gutmann

What role should public schools play in moral education? One answer is *none*: Schools should leave character development and training in moral reasoning to families and voluntary associations (such as churches). As one popular authority put it, "Personally, Miss Manners thinks that the parents of America should offer the school systems a bargain: You teach them English, history, mathematics, and science, and we [their parents] will . . . look after their souls." An apparent attraction of this solution is that public schools would thereby rid themselves of all the political controversies now surrounding moral education and get on with the task of teaching cognitive skills and factual knowledge.

But children don't leave their souls behind when they go to school, and schools cannot escape looking after children's souls in many significant and subtle ways. Even if schools avoid all courses that deal explicitly with morality or civic education, they still engage in moral education by virtue of their "hidden curriculum," noncurricular policies that serve to develop moral attitudes and character in students.

Schools develop moral character at the same time as they try to teach basic cognitive skills, by insisting students sit in their seats, raise their hands before speaking, hand in their homework on time, not loiter in the halls, be good sports on the playing field, and abide by the many other rules that help define a school's character. We become aware of some of the many ways schools shape moral character when we consider alternative school practices. Consider some common practices in Japanese elementary schools. Teachers routinely expect students who have mastered the day's lesson to help teach those who have yet to finish. Every member of the school, including the principal, shares in the chores necessary to keep the school building clean (schools have no specialized janitorial staff). These practices are lessons in egalitarianism that may never need to be taught in the curriculum if they are consistently practiced in the classroom. Most elementary schools in the United States teach different moral lessons, but they, too, engage in moral education simply by not doing what the Japanese schools do. The political choice facing us therefore is not whether schools should engage in moral education, but what sort of moral education they should engage in.

Nor would it be desirable for schools to forswear moral education, even if it were possible for them to do so. Public schools in a democracy should serve our interests as citizens in the moral education of future citizens. Our parental interests are to some extent independent of our role as democratic citizens, and hence the emphasis of moral education within the family is likely to be quite different from that within schools. Parents acting individually and citizens acting collectively both have valuable and largely complementary roles to play in the moral education of children: the former in teaching children what it means to be committed to particular people and one way of life among many; the latter in teaching responsibilities and rights within a more heterogeneous community.

Liberal Neutrality

How can public schools in a democracy best perform these functions of moral education? A popular position—which I call *liberal neutrality*—is that schools should teach the capacity for moral reasoning and choice without predisposing children toward any given conception of the good life. Just as a liberal state must leave its adult citizens free to choose their own good life, so must its schools leave children free to choose their own values. If public schools predisposed citizens by educating them as children, the professed neutrality of the liberal state would be a cover for the bias of its educational system. Liberal neutrality supports the educational method of "values clarification," which enjoys widespread use in schools throughout the United States. Proponents of values clarification identify two major purposes of moral education within public schools. The first is to help students understand and develop their own values. The second is to teach them tolerance and respect for the values of others. Values clarification is based on the premise that no teacher has the "right" set of values to pass on to other people's children.

Treating every moral opinion as equally worthy, however, encourages children in the false notion that "I have my opinion and you have yours and who's to say who's right?" This is not to take the demands of democratic justice seriously. The toleration that values clarification teaches is too indiscriminate for even the most ardent democrat to embrace. If children come to school believing that "Blacks, Jews,

Catholics, and/or homosexuals are inferior beings who shouldn't have the same rights as the rest of us," then it is criticism, not just clarification, of children's values that is needed.

Moralist Positions

What I call *moralist* positions on moral education begin where this critique of liberal neutrality leaves off, with a conception of moral education whose explicit purpose is to inculcate character. Proponents of moralist positions, both liberal and conservative, seek to shape a particular kind of moral character through their educational methods, rather than trying only to facilitate free and informed choice. They recognize that public schools are appropriate institutions of moral education because good moral character is a social, not just an individual or familial, good.

Conservative moralists emphasize teaching children to respect authority. They defend educational programs that liberals often criticize as indoctrination or at least as unduly restrictive of individual freedom: patriotic rituals, dress codes, strict discipline within the classroom, and deference to teachers' opinions. Liberal moralists, on the other hand, generally identify autonomy as the goal of moral education: Education should produce in children the desire and capacity to make conscious moral choices based on generalizable principles. They endorse nondirective methods of teaching similar to those practiced by proponents of liberal neutrality. I want to suggest that the most promising position lies between these two extremes.

Guided by Jean Piaget's work on moral development, philosopher John Rawls outlines a three-stage theory of liberal moral education that culminates in autonomy. Children begin to learn morality by following rules because their parents and other authorities issue them. Learning the "morality of authority" is an improvement over anarchy of desire. The second stage of moral development, the "morality of association," is characterized by an acceptance of rules because they are appropriate to fulfilling the roles individuals play within various cooperative associations. Children learn that students, friends, and citizens obey moral rules because they thereby benefit the association of which they are a part, and are benefitted in turn. The final stage of moral development is the "morality of principle," a direct attachment to moral principles themselves.

Nobody, however, has yet discovered a way that schools can succeed in teaching the morality of principle. The most extensive research, conducted by Lawrence Kohlberg and his associates, demonstrates that the best schools (by Kohlberg's standards and using his own set of six stages) are most successful in moving children from the morality of authority to the morality of association. But very few sixteen-year-olds reach the morality of principle, and no evidence exists to credit schools with this rare accomplishment. Although it is possible there is a way schools can teach autonomy, we have yet to find it.

But from a democratic perspective, success in teaching the morality of association marks great moral progress over the morality of authority. Children who learn the morality of association can distinguish between fair and unfair, trustworthy and untrustworthy authorities. They learn to judge the commands of professional and political authorities, along with their own actions, according to whether they live up to the cooperative virtues of democratic association. Schools that teach children these virtues—fulfilling one's obligations, respecting and making good use of the rights of citizenship, criticizing unjust and untrustworthy authorities—are uncommonly successful. Such success may be compatible with the use (at least in early stages of schooling) of many of the pedagogical practices that advocates of liberal neutrality regard as indoctrination and that Kohlberg criticizes as the "Boy Scout approach to moral education." Just as children learn filial independence after they learn to love and respect their parents, so they may learn political independence after they become patriotic toward their country. The standards of patriotism and loyalty, like those of love and respect for parents, change as children learn to think critically about politics and to recognize that their civic duties extend far beyond voting and obedience to laws. Moral education begins by winning the battle against amoralism and egoism. And it ends—if it ends at all—by struggling against uncritical acceptance of moral habits and opinions that were the spoils of the first victory.

That schools are not terribly effective in teaching autonomy should not surprise us. Since moral autonomy means doing what is right because it is right and not because any authority or law requires it, some of the most effective lessons in moral autonomy may result from the opportunity to disobey commands that are neither perfectly just nor repressive. At least we cannot assume—nor does empirical evidence suggest—that autonomy is best taught with lessons planned to develop it. So, even if the morality of association is (as Rawls suggests) a subordinate philosophical ideal, it still may be a primary political ideal for democratic moral education within schools.

If by virtue we mean moral autonomy, then the role of schools in moral education is necessarily a limited one. We know of no way that schools (or anyone else) can teach virtue in this sense. But democratic virtue can be taught in many ways—by teaching black and white students together in the same classrooms, by bringing all children up to a high minimum standard of learning, by respecting religious differences, by teaching American history not just as a series of elections, laws, treaties, and battles, but as lessons in the practice (sometimes successful, sometimes not) of political virtue. In these and other ways, schools can teach respect among races, religious toleration, patriotism, and political judgment—lessons that hold out the promise of bringing us closer to a more just democratic society.

This article is drawn from Democratic Education *(Princeton, N.J.: Princeton University Press, 1987). The quoted "Miss Manners" column appeared in the* Washington Post *on October 21, 1984; the information on practices in Japanese schools is taken from William K. Cummings,* Education and Equality in Japan *(Princeton, N.J.: Princeton University Press, 1980); John Rawls's three-stage theory of liberal moralist education is outlined in his book* A Theory of Justice *(Cambridge, Mass.: Harvard University Press, 1971); Kohlberg's studies are reported in Moshe M. Blatt and Lawrence Kohlberg, "The Effects of Classroom Moral Discussion upon Children's Level of Moral Judgment,"* Journal of Moral Education *4 (1975), and in Kohlberg and E. Turiel, "Moral Development and Moral Education," in G. Lesser, ed.,* Psychology and Educational Practice *(Chicago: Scott, Foresman, 1971).*

Learning Morality

Robert K. Fullinwider

The "ethics crisis" was box-office boffo in the 1980s. Political corruption, insider trading, racial bigotry, Abscam, the Iran-contra affair, street crime, vandalism, divorce, teenage pregnancies, Ivan Boesky, Gary Hart, drugs, selfishness, greed, pornography, Joseph Biden's plagiarism, Jim and Tammy Bakker's fall from grace—these and countless related subjects filled our headlines and dominated our airwaves. And, as usual with a crisis in our society, our first instinct was to look to education. President Ronald Reagan and his secretary of education were only the most visible of the many who urged renewed teaching of morality in the schools. Derek Bok, president of Harvard University, was in the vanguard of those who urged the colleges and universities likewise to attend to the moral growth of their students. That education must more vigorously attend to character training and moral learning is becoming the common sense of the 1990s. So we might ask: What is moral judgment, how does it develop, and how can the schools assist or retard it?

Moral Learning

Start with a simple analogy: Learning morality is like learning how to write. It is not like learning geography or mathematics. Learning how to write consists in learning a few elementary concepts—noun, verb—and a few simple pieces of grammar—subject and predicate should agree in number—and then *doing it*, that is, writing over and over and over, with the advice, recommendations, and corrections of those who already do it well.

Moral education is the same. Children in their earliest experiences and interactions on the playground and at home pick up rudimentary concepts, such as taking turns, and simple rules, such as don't hit people and don't call them names. In their interactions within this simple framework and under the tutelage of adults, children will come to attach feelings of shame and regret to bad behavior, to experience the pleasures of sharing and giving, and to feel appreciative of benefits and resentful at wrongs. With this elementary foundation, moral learning is set in motion: It is simply, as Aristotle says, learning by doing. There is no science of moral judgment any more than there is a science of writing. Instead, in both cases, we get better through increased experience and practice, which enables us to make finer and sharper discriminations. We develop the capacity to *see* a sentence or a paragraph as clumsy, graceless, plain, clear, or needed, and to *see* a moral action as ungrateful, cowardly, generous, or obligatory.

Rules and directives play a part in this development, just as "rules of good composition" aid learning to write. The young moral learner is told not to lie and not to take other people's property. The novice writer is told that every paragraph should have a topic sentence and that no sentence should end with a preposition. The point of the rules in both cases is the same. The good writer does not mechanically guide his composing by the "rules of good composition" and frequently violates them. This is because, as a result of early practice according to the rules, the good writer has come to see through the rules to the underlying values of clarity, economy, and grace the rules are meant to serve, and is able to serve them directly without mechanical guides. Likewise, moral judgment, as Aristotle observed, is not a kind of rule application but a "judging of the particular." By early training according to the simple, basic moral rules, the moral judger learns to see through them to the underlying values of respect and well-being they are meant to advance.

The Role of Stories

Now, with this extremely rudimentary sketch in place, let us ask how education can assist, or at least not seriously retard, moral development.

If moral learning is essentially learning by doing, then the central and ongoing resource for moral education is experience, real or vicarious. The school can make room for assigned responsibilities where, for example, students oversee and help other students; but limitations of time, place, resources, and structure mean that any major broadening of moral experience must come by way of vicariously living through the moral lives of others. This is accomplished principally by a curriculum in literature and history. Through stories, historical and fictional, the child enters imaginatively into the moral lives of other people and sees the various moral concepts exemplified in action.

Consider the parable that Nathan tells David in 2 Samuel 12: "There were two men in the city; the one rich, and the other poor. The rich man had exceeding many flocks and herds: But the poor man had nothing, save one little ewe lamb, which he had bought and nourished up: and it grew up together with him, and with his children; it did eat of his own meat, and drank of his own cup, and lay in his bosom, and was unto him as a daughter. And there came a traveler unto the rich man, and he spared to take of his own flock and of his own herd, to dress for the wayfaring man that was come unto him; but took the poor man's lamb and dressed it. . . . And David's anger was greatly kindled against the man; and he said to Nathan, As the Lord liveth, the man that hath done this thing shall surely die: And he shall restore the lamb fourfold, because he did this thing, and because he had no pity."

Children who read this story will have the same reaction as David, one directly responsive to the palpable ugliness of the rich man's behavior. This reaction will anchor their understanding of selfishness—of "having no pity"—and will guide their future reactions to other instances of selfish behavior. By living through a rich variety of stories, real and imagined, simple and complex, straightforward and ambiguous, young people sort out their moral emotions and acquire moral concepts that help them develop their powers of moral discrimination.

The Failure of Primary and Secondary Schools

Schools fail to provide the resources of moral learning by impoverishing their offerings of literature and history. This failure works in two ways: Schools provide little enough history and literature as it is, and what they do provide is not selected and shaped with an eye toward moral development. This problem is especially acute in the teaching of history, which for some decades now has been subordinated to a social-studies curriculum infused with the concepts of the social sciences. History as moral and political narrative is replaced by history as indirect sociology, designed to explain to students the social, economic, psychological, and cultural forces that shape their lives.

These kinds of explanations work at cross-purposes to moral education when they replace, rather than augment, moral narrative. They view human action not from the point of view of the participant's self-understanding but from the perspective of the outside observer. Your explanation of why your anger, like David's, is kindled against the rich man is that he was *without pity*; you bring your response under a justifying moral concept. The sociological or psychological explanation of your anger will leave out of the account or will explain away your own justifying point of view. History as indirect sociology is bereft of the very concepts young people need to acquire for "judging the particular."

Nor is this deficiency adequately made up by instituting explicit courses in moral reasoning. Moral reasoning is reasoning *about* experience, not a substitute *for* it. It would not make sense to set up a course in critical reflection on good writing for students who had very little experience writing, and it is generally useless, if not counterproductive, to put students with limited moral experience in courses to talk about moral reasoning. Because they are in the early stages of their moral development, students have limited capacity to "judge the particular" and will disagree about even exemplary moral cases (just as writing students may be a long way from *seeing* that George Eliot and Henry James are good writers). Teachers can try to cope with these disagreements in three ways: (1) adjudicating them by appealing to their own broader experience and maturer understanding, (2) abdicating a directive role by letting student discussions take their own course, and (3) adverting to rules and principles as effective and objective ways to get conclusions.

The first way is almost never taken. Teachers in high school lack confidence in their own moral knowledge, older students are too swellheaded to listen to anyone, and no reigning educational dogma exists to give this way support. The second way produces variations on values clarification. Students are set free to "clarify" their own experiences. Not much clarifying takes place, of course, since no more structure is brought to the discussions than what the students can bring themselves, which is very little. The third way drives courses in the direction of the intellectualist fallacy, the belief that mechanical and deductive manipulations of rules and principles will yield answers where discussion of particulars won't. Disagreement about cases is transposed to the level of disagreement about rules and principles, where it is thought that theoretical and philosophical solutions exist.

Ideally, high school students should take away from courses in moral reasoning a variety of intellectual virtues: how to listen, how to clarify a point of view, how to assess arguments, and how to respect honest differences. Instead, students come away from these courses, and from their school experience generally, not very well grounded in the practice of morality, limited in their capacity to make discriminations, and suspicious about the whole enterprise. In short, they come away ready for college.

The Failure of Higher Education

And here we wait, ready to fail them, too. What college students need is what younger students need: richer and richer experience. Now, colleges cannot help but provide great opportunities for growth. After all, students have to take charge of their own lives once in college and the curriculum is varied and broad-ranging. Even so, we hardly maximize these advantages. We take in students with limited moral concepts and experience and let them spend their college careers in the social or physical sciences or in some form or another of vocational training. At most we require them to take a shallow core of humanities.

One idea coming into vogue is to have all students take courses in ethics. This is good for keeping philosophers in business but is unlikely to do students any good. What our students need is experience; what we philosophers give them is theory.

The English department takes the middling writers it gets out of high school and sets out to improve them by making them do more writing and reading, not by introducing them to theoretical linguistics. We philosophers take *our* students, who have very limited moral experience and relatively impoverished moral concepts, and dose them up on utilitarianism, Kantianism, existentialism, and other exotic exhibits from the museum of moral theory. Why do we do this? It is because philosophy teachers are deeply wedded to the view, as one philosopher puts it, that "normative ethical theories . . . offer a means of determining in specific circumstances whether an actual or proposed course of action is right. . . . Normative theories compete as to the best general means of arriving at particular normative judgments." This view is representative of a widespread approach in introductory ethics courses. But we don't serve students well with our theory-mongering.

As moral experience develops, individuals acquire from the culture a variety of rules and principles, ideals of various stripes, knowledge of social practices, and so on, out of which they fashion reflections and arguments on moral action. Theories may help make some sense out of this welter of rules, principles, and particular experiences, but *not* by serving as decision procedures for arriving at particular normative judgments. The idea that we should throw out our acquired habits and knowledge of moral practice and guide ourselves instead by something like the principle of utility belongs right up there with the orgone box, the perpetual-motion machine, and other single-nostrum solutions to all our difficulties.

Good moral theories don't offer competing answers to moral problems, just as the contending schools in theoretical linguistics don't offer competing solutions to writing problems. Linguistic theories tell explanatory stories about the sentences all competent writers agree to be good sentences; moral theories tell explanatory stories about the moral rules and judgments that good moral-judgers accept as sound and well-established. Rights-based, duty-based, and utility-based moral theories are all trying to account for the same core moral experiences and practices. No theory will produce a different evaluation of the story of the rich man in Nathan's parable.

Students do need the intellectual substance that well-conceived ethics courses can provide. Experience without concepts is blind (someone once said), and students' grade school and high school background has given them few conceptual resources to work with. They don't have names for their moral emotions and for the virtues; they can't make elementary distinctions within moral considerations. They don't distinguish the good and the right, they confuse justifying and excusing, they conflate desert and entitlement, they commit the genetic fallacy with uncanny frequency, they can't separate attacks on a position from attacks on the person who holds the position, and on and on. Moreover, they already have their own naive theories that need contending with: their relativisms, skepticisms, nihilisms, mysticisms, religious enthusiasms, and political schemes. There is no end to their need for opportunities at analysis, reflection, systematizing, and intellectual correction, but these opportunities need to be conceived not as substitutes for moral experience but in concert with the provision of experiences profoundly rich and illuminating in their power to yield moral insight.

I have dwelt on how we fail our students in their development toward mature moral understanding. But I don't want to overstate the seriousness of the failure. The young human animal seems able to bear, without suffering too much damage, almost any educational regimen we can inflict. It always manages, somehow, to get reasonably grown up and to lead a more or less normal and productive adult life. If we educators don't contribute a great deal to this process, we probably don't retard it a great deal either, except in one respect.

If moral development is a lifelong learning through experience and reflecting on that experience, then the basic task of the schools is simple. It is not to produce sophisticated and finished moral thinkers but persons with a few basic tools and a love of reading and learning, who will continue to read and learn throughout their lives. This modest and simple goal would seem achievable without effort, but in fact it is hardly achieved at all. This is the real crime we commit against our children. It doesn't really matter very much what we teach them so long as we generate in them the joy of learning and the pleasure of reading. If we do this, we have done well enough.

This account of Aristotle and "judging the particular" leans heavily on Martha C. Nussbaum, The Fragility of Goodness *(Cambridge: Cambridge University Press, 1986), and M. F Burnyeat, "Aristotle on Learning to Be Good," in* Essays on Aristotle's Ethics, *ed. Amelie Oksenberg Rorty (Berkeley, Calif.: University of California Press, 1980). The quoted material about ethics teachers is from Bernard Rosen, "The Teaching of Undergraduate Ethics," in* Ethics Teaching in Higher Education, *ed. Daniel Callahan and Sissela Bok (New York: Plenum Press, 1980).*

Analogizing morality to language has many precedents. Plato's Protagorus *compares the state's laws to the instructions of a writing master. John Rawls, in* A Theory of Justice *(Cambridge, Mass.: Harvard University Press, 1971), compares moral theory to linguistic theory. However, my present efforts with the analogy were prompted by Adam Smith's comparison of duties and grammar in* The Theory of Moral Sentiments *(Oxford: Clarendon Press, 1976).*

The Case against Creationism

Allen Stairs

In recent years "scientific creationism" has emerged as a force to be reckoned with. Several states have passed, or contemplate passing, laws requiring "creation science" to be taught in schools where evolution is taught. Despite a successful challenge to one such bill in the federal courts, proponents continue to press the justice of their cause. It is not at all unlikely that a large percentage of the public, very possibly a majority, agree with the creationists to at least this extent: They believe that fairness requires granting the creationist point of view equal time in the classroom. Is this indeed the case? What, exactly, are the creationists maintaining? Does fairness require that we teach "creation science" in our schools?

As a minimal starting point, anyone concerned with the issue needs to understand what the creationists are saying. The first and most obvious point is that creationism goes beyond the idea that a God exists who in some way or other created the universe. Many evolutionists accept the existence of God as creator, and thus atheism is not at issue here. Scientific creationism is a particular set of doctrines that conflicts directly with evolution. Although individual creationists vary, the core position involves the following claims: (1) The universe, life, and all living "kinds" were created suddenly by a supernatural being. In particular, then, the big-bang theory, theories of the chemical origin of life, and the evolutionary account of the development of orders of living organisms are all incorrect. (2) The major geological features of the earth, including the structure of the fossil record, were the result of catastrophic processes, most notably a global flood. (3) The earth and the rest of the universe may be no more than a few thousand years old.

Although a positive doctrine is an important feature of creationism, most of its arguments are directed *against* evolutionary theory. Perhaps the most common argument offered by creationism against evolution is an attempt to discredit the fossil evidence for evolution by pointing to the relative scarcity of transitional forms. However, this is a poor argument for at least three reasons. First, in order to embarrass evolution, it would be required that evolution *predicts* the existence of numerous transitional fossils. In fact, however, there is reason to believe that major evolutionary change occurs when a *small* population becomes reproductively isolated, and that such major change occurs over a relatively *short* period of geological time. Thus, in this view, there *should* be a relative scarcity of transitional fossils. The second point is that, nonetheless, there *are* transitional fossils. The therapsids provide numerous links between reptiles and mammals, and *archaeopteryx* is a clear intermediary between dinosaurs and birds. Finally, whatever the problems associated with the fossil record, what we find does not look at all as it would be expected to if God created all varieties of life at the same time. In the very oldest layers, we find only the remains of microorganisms. Only later do we find soft-bodied animals, and hard-bodied creatures appear in still more recent layers. If creationism were true, we would expect the fossil record to have the structure of a well-stirred stew, with trilobites and tigers, dinosaurs and donkeys all side by side. This is anything but what we do find.

Two other common creationist arguments are closely related. One is that the increase in complexity required by evolution is inconsistent with the second law of thermodynamics. However, many examples in nature display spontaneous increases in complexity that are completely consistent with thermodynamics. Some of the most striking examples are to be found at the chemical level, a crucial level for evolution. The second argument is that the probability of something as complex as a living organism arising by chance is so low as to render evolution virtually impossible. But evolution is improbable only if one assumes that the processes resulting in evolution were purely random. In fact, there is no reason to make this assumption. The laws of chemistry do not operate randomly. Without this assumption, the conclusion doesn't follow.

If the creationists' direct attack against evolution fails, they next try to establish that both evolution and creationism are at least in part religious views. They concede that creationism isn't fully a science, but argue that neither is evolution. In the creationist view, the conflict between evolution and creationism is not a clash between science and religion, but between two religious views. And if the state already sanctions the teaching of one religious doctrine, it cannot consistently bar another on First Amendment grounds.

Thus, in a Jerry Falwell-sponsored debate, creationist Duane Gish denounced evolution as an opposing religious view. Although not all evolutionists may be atheists, evolution itself, in Gish's account, is atheistic. "Since evolution is a mechanistic, atheistic theory, it is a basic dogma of agnosticism, humanism, and atheism in general. The one-sided indoctrination of our students in this materialistic philosophy, in the tax-supported schools, in our pluralistic, democratic society, is a violation of academic and religious freedoms." In other words, evolution is the religion of secular humanism.

This really is the nub of the matter. What disturbs creationists most deeply is the threat they see evolution as posing to their whole way of life and their whole moral perspective. For them, evolution can only mean that there was no God to breathe the breath of life into the dust from which we rose, no moral difference between us and our brutish ancestors, and no divine ground for the moral law. As they see it, if doubt arises about some single part of the Bible, there is no reason to believe any of it. Thus they see the teaching of evolution in public schools as a tax-supported attack on their deepest religious convictions.

Occasionally one hears it argued that, properly understood, science and religion cannot conflict. Here, however, we must surely side with the fundamentalists. Some religions do make specific factual claims about the natural world, and whenever this is so, the possibility always exists that a conflict will occur between the claims of the religion and the conclusions reached by our more worldly methods of fact-finding. Here we have just such a case.

Furthermore, it is not at all uncommon nor obviously wrong for school boards and state curriculum committees to take the attitude that certain subjects are too sensitive to be included in the curriculum, largely because to include them blurs the distinction between what is properly the responsibility of the schools and what should be left up to parents. Suppose, for instance, that a school board decided not to include discussions of abortion or homosexual life-styles in the curriculum because to do otherwise would involve the school in the business of the home. It is surely not *obvious* that the authorities are wrong.

Now, the creationists are not saying that evolution is too sensitive to be taught. But they seem to be saying that evolution *is* like abortion and a number of other topics in that to include it in the curriculum is to include material of a highly value-charged nature and, in particular, to teach evolution exclusively is to favor one set of values. Thus, *if* evolution is to be taught at all, fairness requires that the opposing point of view be taught as well.

In this version, the creationists' demand sounds like a moderate one. Furthermore, it is one with which many people will agree. Nonetheless, it seems to me that it is still wrong. Recall that if blood types and the benefits of blood transfusions are discussed in the classroom, what is taught may offend Jehovah's Witnesses' beliefs. Discussions of modern medical science in general may very well lead to conflict with the beliefs of Christian Scientists. Neither group, of course, is pressing either for removal of these subjects from the curriculum or for equal time, but this isn't really to the point. If they were to, we would not be inclined to grant their request. Whether or not one agrees that there are good reasons for keeping discussions of abortion and homosexuality out of the curriculum, one might at least agree that on the face of it there is a distinction between these cases and the medical science one.

The distinction, I suggest, is this. It is virtually impossible to raise the issues of abortion and homosexuality without raising questions of personal morality. This is especially clear in the case of abortion. Whatever one's views on this question may be, it is hard to imagine someone maintaining that no moral issue arises here. We may or may not agree that the schools have no business dealing with topics that raise personal moral issues, but we don't need to adopt any special point of view to agree that if these matters *are* the province of the family, then, in particular, discussion of abortion is inappropriate at school.

This is not so for discussions of blood transfusions, not so for discussion of, say, the "germ theory" of disease, and not so for evolution. In all of these cases, it is proper to see the educator as merely presenting the best of secular knowledge, even if we include telling students that a good way to safeguard one's health during a polio epidemic is to have a booster shot. A Christian Scientist might see a moral issue here. If disease is a sort of illusion resulting from a breakdown in one's relationship with God, then perhaps it is wrong to take medications. But to see polio inoculation as a moral issue requires not just our common background of moral concepts, but a special set of religious assumptions. Without this special religious perspective, polio inoculation is morally neutral.

The same holds for evolution. From any moderately general point of view, evolution is morally neutral. It is compatible with "pro-life" or "pro-choice" sentiments, liberalism or conservatism—in short, with virtually any particular moral stance. To deny that evolution is morally neutral, one must adopt a special set of religious assumptions, as, indeed, the creationists do. Evolution, then, is *morally* neutral in any broad secular view. And while evolution is in one sense not *religiously* neutral, the same is true of medical science in exactly the same sense.

The creationists often maintain that evolution is the official view of the state, but this is a serious misdescription. If the curriculum of studies in the public schools includes a section on African history where the death of Haile Selassie is recorded, it does not thereby follow that the state's official position is that Selassie is not Jesus Christ, and hence it does not follow that the state is taking sides against some

Rastafarians, who allegedly believe Selassie *is* Christ and is still alive. The crucial point about secular knowledge is that it does not presuppose any special religious point of view. It is this, indeed, that constitutes its nonreligious nature. By restricting the contents of the public school curriculum to this realm, the state helps keep itself free of religious entanglement. If in addition the state tried to avoid having any statements in the texts that contradicted the teaching of any religion, it would set itself an impossible task. Virtually any claim whatsoever *could* in principle become part of a religion and in practice a great many unlikely ones *do*. More to the point, however, the state would misunderstand its own role if it were to undertake such a program of hygiene. The mandate the state gives the schools is to teach the best of secular knowledge *whatever* that may be. Thus the state has no stake in the correctness of evolution (or the mortality of Haile Selassie). If scientists eventually reject evolution, and texts are accordingly changed, the "official position" of the state will have altered not a whit.

In light of these remarks, it is worth noting that there is a particular inappropriateness in the "equal time" bills passed by several state legislatures. The state has a responsibility to ensure that the curriculum is based on the best of secular knowledge. However, it is obvious that constructing a sound curriculum requires expertise. Legislatures have a duty to enact legislation that will provide for an appropriate mechanism for producing a sound curriculum and to be responsive when the evidence indicates that the mechanism isn't working as it should. However, in voting for "equal time" bills not recommended by any curriculum committee nor by any body that could plausibly be thought to reflect the judgment of educators, the individual legislators were simply assuming an expertise they patently did not possess. If the integrity of the curriculum is to be preserved, it is absolutely essential that legislators not undertake to usurp the role of scholars and educators. This is not to say that those experts are infallible, but that when legislators take it on themselves to decide what does or does not constitute science or history or anything else of the sort, they are doing a service to no one.

FOR FURTHER READING

Gutmann, Amy. *Democratic Education*. Princeton, N.J.: Princeton University Press, 1987.

Neuhaus, Richard John, ed. *Democracy and the Renewal of Public Education*. Grand Rapids, Mich.: William B. Eerdmans Publishing, 1987.

Walzer, Michael. *Spheres of Justice*. New York: Basic Books, 1983. See Chapter Eight, "Education."

12

THE FAMILY

Recent decades have seen dramatic changes in the profile of the American family. Our families are getting older: Since the turn of the century, the number of Americans over the age of sixty-five has increased eightfold, with almost a tripling of their proportion in the population. Our families are increasingly falling apart: The total number of children affected by divorce has more than tripled since 1960, so that close to half of all the children in the United States are expected to experience the disruption of their parents' marriage before they reach age eighteen. Adultery, always common among men, is now on the rise among women: In one account, 54 percent of American women have had extramarital affairs. Finally, our families are forming themselves in previously all-but-unheard-of ways, with the advent of surrogate motherhood and other "unusual" avenues of procreation: Since contract surrogacy's emergence in the mid-1970s, more than five hundred children have been born through it. This chapter examines the moral and policy issues attending these developments.

"The Graying of America" asks who should bear the largest responsibility for taking care of the aged: old people themselves, their children, the government? Several reasons seem to arise for doubting that individuals can and should be held accountable for meeting the financial and health-care needs of their old age, yet the burden of caring for the elderly cannot simply fall on their children, either. For one, the duties children bear toward their parents are limited in scope; for another, parents today simply live longer, with fewer children to share the burden of their support. While certain duties fall necessarily on families simply because no one else can assume them— "duties" of love and concern—government may be required to provide direct financial assistance and to fund services that ease the strain on families' resources. The author concludes, "Intensely private and personal choices must be made by parents and children facing the aging process, choices that government cannot make for them. But there are also societal choices an aging society must make, not each of us alone, but all of us together."

"What Would King Solomon Do Today?: The Revolution in Child Custody" considers competing standards for making painful child custody decisions following a family's dissolution. The author examines policies of ruling in the child's best interest, of awarding joint custody, and of awarding custody to the "primary caretaker," and concludes that the latter is most likely to take into account both the needs of the child and the just claims of its parents.

In "Adultery" Bonnie Steinbock notes that, though many of us commit adultery, most of us disapprove of it. Her question: Does the abiding disapproval of adultery merely "give lip service to an ancient taboo" or is the prohibition against adultery rationally (and not merely religiously) grounded? While adultery often involves promise-breaking and deception, it need not do so; but Steinbock argues that nonetheless it deviates from at least one valued ideal of what marriage should be.

Surrogate motherhood may be here to stay. Our question is whether we as a society want to encourage or discourage this form of childbearing, and how strongly. "Surrogate Motherhood" assesses the concerns of the receiving parents, of the contract mother, of the child, and of society more generally, and concludes that, despite the deeply felt need to which it responds, surrogacy remains on balance morally objectionable.

The Graying of America

Claudia Mills

Americans are getting older. On the individual level, of course, the melancholy fact that every day each of us is another day older is a truism. But demographers, with a mounting urgency, have been calling attention to the aging of our society more generally. Since the turn of the century, the number of Americans over the age of sixty-five has increased eightfold, with almost a tripling of their proportion in the population. Those over the age of eighty-five—the fastest-growing group in the country—are twenty-one times as numerous as in 1900.

This dramatic change in the age structure of the United States is straightforwardly explained by two interacting social and medical developments. First, the number of children has decreased, deaccelerating precipitously in recent years as the last of the baby boomers moved into adulthood: From 1960 to 1982 the number of children younger than fifteen fell by 7 percent. Second, with improved medical care and sharply declining death rates for the elderly, the number of senior citizens has increased even more rapidly: Between 1960 and 1980 the number of people sixty-five or older grew by 54 percent. America's elderly are now facing a population explosion, demographers warn, greater than that of the population of India.

The graying of America has consequences that ramify throughout our society. McDonalds' ads portray perky oldsters slinging hamburgers, while Alzheimer's support groups multiply to help families cope with one of the tragedies plaguing the aged. But perhaps nowhere is the demographic shift more evident than in the changing contours of the federal budget. As the ranks of Medicare and Social Security beneficiaries continue to swell, the costs of administering these programs have become staggering, in an era of spiralling deficits and retrenchment in other areas of public spending. In the early 1960s, less than 15 percent of the federal budget was targeted to those over the age of sixty-five; by 1985, that percentage had almost doubled. The

$80 billion of private and government money spent on health care for the old in 1981 is expected to grow to $200 billion by the year 2000, with public expenditures alone rising to $114 billion. We now spend more on the elderly than on national defense, in 1983 some $217 billion or $7,700 per elderly person. In contrast, expenditures for child-oriented programs—Aid to Families with Dependent Children, Head Start, food stamps, child nutrition, and all federal aid to education— totaled about $36 billion in 1984, about one-sixth of federal expenditures on the elderly. Real doubts have been expressed about whether we as a society can continue to afford expenditures of this magnitude or allow programs for the elderly to dominate our public spending to such a degree.

Indeed, the question can be raised whether the support of the elderly is properly a core responsibility of government at all. It could be argued, for instance, that while the education of America's children is clearly a public responsibility, since this is an investment in the future that benefits us all collectively, health care for the elderly has no comparable dimension as a public good. Even setting aside libertarian arguments for reducing the role of the state in private life generally, special arguments can be made for centering care for the elderly in the family. Conservatives call for a return to the traditional roles and responsibilities of families, and even those who look less nostalgically at the past may worry about the values expressed by a society that increasingly consigns its elderly to institutional care.

Who should bear the largest responsibility for taking care of the aged: old people themselves, their children, the government? To what extent is it morally desirable or practically feasible to shift care of the elderly back again from the state to families? What is required in this arena by justice, by compassion, by sheer human decency?

Prudence and Self-Reliance

The elderly already shoulder much of the burden of their own care, principally by the plans they lay for their old age in their younger, working lives. Each of us tries to anticipate the financial needs of our later years, through various pension plans and saving schemes; ideally, we also try to develop other resources—hobbies, friendships, social and political commitments—that will sustain us as we retire from the work force and watch our children leave home. It seems fair to expect individuals to take the initiative in facing their own future. We have our whole lives to prepare for old age, after all. Why shouldn't the quality of our twilight years depend at least in part on the choices we made over the lifetime preceding?

But there are several reasons for doubting that individuals can and should be held accountable for meeting the financial and health care needs of their old age. For one, such long-term planning must be undertaken in the face of massive uncertainties. How long will each of us live? How healthy will we be? How will periods of inflation and recession affect our savings? The magnitude of these unknown variables as they confront individuals makes old-age planning into a gigantic crap game, where we are better served by pooling our risks through collective decision-making.

It simply seems to be the case, moreover, that in the world as we know it, individual prudence is one virtue in regrettably short supply. Daniel Wikler, a medical ethicist, argues that individual provision of finances for the elderly "would require not only adequate wealth but prudent planning, demanding in turn more discipline, self-control, and foresightedness than many individuals are normally capable of." Our best-laid plans are notorious for ganging agley; and it's difficult enough to postpone today's indulgence for tomorrow's security, let alone for the security of a tomorrow some twenty, thirty, or forty years distant. Wikler concludes that "any proposal to shift responsibility upon individuals for rationing resources in old age must address the gap that may appear between ideal or optimal allocation plans and the one that, in the many moments of actual decisions, our imperfectly rational constitution leads us to make."

Such problems might be addressed by instituting various "self-binding" mechanisms, in which a person legally commits himself to follow what he deems at the time of commitment to be the prudent course of action, but such schemes hold out little promise for financial and health-care planning across a lifetime. The binding of our future by our present selves in essence amounts to the binding of our older by our younger selves; this hardly seems likely to be the best way of securing full consideration of the interests and preferences of our twilight years. Philosopher Norman Daniels, author of *Am I My Parents' Keeper?*, reminds us that "as an individual ages, his situation changes. The passage of time erases uncertainties and alters probabilities that must affect early judgments about what it is prudent to do, even assuming preferences and values remain constant. But these are likely to change, too. . . . Adhering to the prudent choices of fully informed consumers risks biasing our health care system in favor of the prudence of the young."

Finally, perhaps through their own fault, perhaps through no fault of their own, some will simply lack the resources to sustain themselves through the vicissitudes of old age. A compassionate society cannot leave destitute even the imprudent. So the question faces us: When the elderly cannot meet their own needs, who is next in line to take up the responsibility?

The Duties of Families

A first answer is that, just as parents should take care of their young children, so adult children in turn should take care of their aging parents, in a cycle of familial reciprocity. The Chinese philosopher Lin Yutang asks: "How can any one deny that parents who have toiled for their children in their youth, have lost many a good night's sleep when they were ill, have washed their diapers long before they could talk and have spent about a quarter of a century bringing them up and fitting them for life, have the right to be fed by them and respected when they are old?"

But many do deny just this, arguing that the care given by parents to children fulfills a parental responsibility for which there is no filial analogue. Parents choose to have children and so tacitly agree to assume the obligations of parenthood; children, as teenagers are fond of reminding their parents, do not choose to be born. While children may of course *want* to provide comfort and assistance to their parents out of love and affection, this is to sidestep talk of duties altogether.

Yet it is difficult to let go of the idea that familial ties do exert a moral claim on us, however involuntarily we may have entered into them. Medical ethicist Nancy Jecker points out that we often acknowledge duties of gratitude in response to unrequested benefits, even when others are morally bound to benefit us. For example, we consider gratitude fitting if "the tasks that are required result in goods that are especially valuable" or if "discharging one's duty is especially onerous or requires substantial sacrifice or risk." Certainly parenthood often partakes of the heroic. Moreover, to have an obligation to someone other than oneself, a deep and not altogether voluntary commitment to his or her destiny, just seems to be part of how families work, what families are *for*. It seems that the explanation of why children might owe care to their aging parents may lie in some notion of what families fundamentally are all about.

Daniels argues that to the extent we believe in the institution of the family at all, as currently constituted, we may have grounds for carrying out the duties and obligations that make up family life. In our society, at least when they are functioning normally, "families are a fundamental cooperative arrangement," providing "a set of goods of mutual benefit to various family members." Legitimate expectations thus arise about "the importance of reciprocity and the importance of sustaining the kinds of interpersonal relationships which generate these benefits. . . . Filial obligations arise out of the obligation not to frustrate legitimate expectations of those with whom one intimately cooperates to produce mutual benefits of fundamental importance."

Philosopher Daniel Callahan, in *Setting Limits: Medical Goals in an Aging Society*, suggests that children may owe at least love and affection to their aging parents simply because no one else can meet these vital human needs: "In a world of strangers or fleeting casual acquaintances, of distant government agencies and a society beyond their control, elderly parents can see in their children their only hope for someone who ought to care for them." Sheer dependence can exert a powerful moral pull that is not easily escaped or evaded: "The issue, as it presents itself, may be less one of trying to discover the grounds of obligation that would require a response than one of trying to find a basis for ignoring a demand that so patently assaults the sensibilities. It is not so much 'Must I?' as it is 'How can I not?'"

Daniels, Jecker, and Callahan insist that duties of children toward parents grounded in these ways do not legitimate demands that children make major sacrifices of their own life prospects to provide financial support to their parents. Such needs, for reasons that emerge next, may be better met communally. But the need for emotional support, for love pure and simple, can often be met only by family members. Care for the elderly cannot be consigned completely to professional caregivers; we need care as persons, not merely as ciphers on an institutional roster. Jecker reminds us that we share an intimate past with our elderly parents and "the character of an earlier time imposes upon the present in a variety of ways." In their present relationship with their parents, grown children "ought not to betray the significance of a relationship that is now past." At least some duties toward the elderly seem to fall necessarily to families; they are duties no one else can assume.

The Role of Government

Some critics would like to see the government enforce a more stringent set of familial duties as a way both of reducing the public tax burden and of strengthening what they view as eroding family ties. Soaring budget deficits, as well as conservative concerns about the condition of the American family, led many state legislators in the early 1980s to propose "family responsibility initiatives" to hold family members legally responsible for costs currently paid by Medicaid. Despite strong support from the Ronald Reagan administration, these proved politically unpalatable, but calls for a renewed commitment to family-based care for the elderly continue.

It is not clear, however, that alarm about the current level of familial care is justified. While the creation of Social Security and Medicaid dramatically shifted financial burdens from the family to the state, families currently provide about 80 percent of all home health care to the partially disabled elderly. Fewer than 6 percent of the elderly at any time reside in nursing homes.

The oft-invoked good old days of multigenerational families where devoted children outdid themselves in caring for their elderly parents appear a matter more of myth than of history. One sociologist points out that, for example, in pre-industrial England, less than 10 percent of households had more than two generations in them, and levels of care within families were similar to those found today. And even if golden-tinted pictures of the family in ages past were grounded in reality, the changing demographic balance between old and young has to alter our current expectations of family-based care. Parents today simply live longer, with fewer children to share the burden of their support. Housewives once able to provide extensive home nursing are now full-time members of the labor force. No amount of wishful thinking can turn the clock back on these far-reaching demographic and social changes.

Governmental enforcement of (governmentally determined) familial duties to the elderly is promoted as a cost-saving measure, but in fact it wouldn't reduce costs; it would simply redistribute them. Daniels points out that "the overall costs of care for the elderly are not reduced through [family responsibility] initiatives, since individual families will still pick up the tab"; however, "the burden of bearing those costs will fall much more heavily on a narrower group of the young, those with frail elderly parents. For them, the burden of caring for elderly parents will intensify." Nor, Daniels observes, will shifting costs from public budgets eliminate competition between the elderly and the young for resources: "It will only shift the locus and burden of that competition—from public budgets to family budgets."

Most important, some argue that governmental intervention into the private domain of the family can only weaken rather than strengthen family ties. Philosopher Ferdinand Schoeman insists that governmental regulation of family life compromises intimacy within the family. "Such regulation," he argues, "transforms relationships into less intimate ones. . . . Practically speaking, the strength or very possibility of intimate relationships varies inversely with the degree of social intrusion into such relationships generally tolerated. . . . To give the state authority to regulate such relationships would inevitably result in a redirection or 'socialization' of [them]."

The best way to strengthen family ties, it seems, is to relieve excessive strain on them, rather than to strain them further. Parents and children are one in their fear of debilitating dependence on each other. To the extent the state assumes at least the financial burden of providing a minimal level of income and health care support, the elderly retain a sense of independence and their children are spared a festering source of resentment. Callahan suggests that "A balance is sought between that independence which enables people to have a sense of controlling their own destinies, and those ties of obligation and affection which are for each an indispensable source of solace in the face of a world that has little reason to care for them." This delicate balance would be wrenched by coercing children to make what might amount to crushing financial sacrifices for their parents.

On the positive side, government can actively assist families by funding services that make it easier for family members to continue providing home care to the elderly. According to Daniels, "Some who would provide care, or would do so for longer periods, are unable to meet the responsibilities they feel because appropriate support services are not available. This leads to frustration, guilt, and even rationalization that can undermine an individual's conviction that he or she has such family responsibilities." Thus Daniels calls for an increase in publicly funded day-care facilities for the elderly, social-support services to relieve the family, and tax incentives to reduce the stress on family obligations to younger children. Callahan concludes: "A minimal duty of any government should be to do nothing to hinder, and when possible what it can to protect, those ties which give families their power to nurture and sustain their members."

How Much? How to Decide?

None of this answers the question of how much we as a society should elect to pay for services for the elderly as opposed to meeting other pressing human needs. But it seems we can at least conclude that this is a decision we do need to make collectively, that is, as a society. We cannot escape this dilemma by delegating responsibilities in this arena to individuals or to families. Intensely private and personal choices must be made by parents and children facing the aging process, choices that government cannot make for them. But there are also societal choices an aging society must make, not each of us alone, but all of us together.

Sources quoted in this article are Daniel Wikler, "Ought the Young Make Health Care Decisions for Their Aged Selves?" The Journal of Medicine and Philosophy *13 (1988); Norman Daniels,* Am I My Parents' Keeper?

An Essay on Justice Between the Young and the Old *(New York: Oxford University Press, 1988); Nancy Jecker, "Are Filial Duties Unfounded?"* American Philosophical Quarterly *26, no. 1 (1989); Lin Yutang, "On Growing Old Gracefully," in* Philosophical Foundations of Gerontology, *ed. Patrick L. McKee (New York: Human Sciences Press, 1982); Daniel Callahan,* Setting Limits: Medical Goals in an Aging Society *(New York: Simon and Schuster, 1987); and Ferdinand Schoeman, "Rights of Children, Rights of Parents, and the Moral Basis of the Family,"* Ethics *91 (October 1980).*

What Would King Solomon Do Today?

The Revolution in Child Custody

Claudia Mills

Perhaps the first, and certainly the most famous, child custody decision was made by King Solomon, who proposed to cut the contested child in half and then awarded custody to the woman willing to renounce her claim to the child in order to save it. Solomon's decision was made swiftly and irrevocably; presumably it was not open to relitigation. And all who witnessed it rejoiced in its wisdom. Latter-day child custody disputes, by contrast, are typically prolonged and acrimonious, and few hail the wisdom of their resolution.

Lenore Weitzman's landmark study of divorce, *The Divorce Revolution*, reports that more than two million children are involved in a parental divorce in the United States each year. The total number of children affected by divorce has more than tripled since 1960, a direct result of the skyrocketing divorce rate. Close to half of all the children in the United States are expected to experience the disruption of their parents' marriage before they reach age eighteen.

The legal standard for assigning custody of minor children after divorce has evolved from a patriarchal right, based on a view of children as their father's property, to a preference for the mother to retain custody of children of "tender years," to a rule basing custody on the child's "best interest," which gained ascendancy in the 1970s and still holds a central place in family law. But the past two decades have seen not only a further evolution of child custody law, but also a veritable revolution.

The Child's Best Interest

An appeal to the child's best interest as the standard for settling custody disputes recommends itself on several grounds. Children are innocent bystanders of parental divorce, fundamentally blameless in a way neither spouse can be. Particularly vulnerable, they are in special need of the state's protection. Their interests can be seen as casting a tie-breaking vote in a deadlock between the two parents, each of whom has vital interests at stake. And a standard centered on the interests of the child avoids the sexism of either a paternal or maternal presumption.

But the standard of the child's best interest faces serious and perhaps insuperable problems of its own. First, the principle is indeterminate, requiring judges to make an often fancifully ambitious, customized prediction about which parent will prove the better custodian in the years to come. Where both parents pass a threshold of fitness, finer-grained speculations about the superiority of either are hardly clear-cut. Disputes rage over the criteria by which parental superiority should be judged—what *is* best for children? This lack of consensus motivates charges that, in applying the best-interests standard, judges unavoidably impose their own personal values.

The task of figuring out the child's best interest is also time-consuming and intrusive; the uncertainty inherent in the standard provides a spur to protracted litigation, since both parties may appear to have a plausible chance at victory. Jon Elster, professor of political science at the University of Chicago, points out that decision-making can be a costly and even self-defeating process: What might have been the best decision had it been reached quickly and effortlessly may be no longer the best, once the costs and pain of the decision-making itself are factored in. The chief victim of protracted litigation, as Elster sees it, is the child, forced into the roles of "mediator, weapon, pawn, bargaining chip, trophy, go-between, or even spy." Thus, judicial appeals to the child's best interest may end up working against those very interests, for "against the conjectural long-term effects on the child of being with the mother or the father, one must set the certain short-term pain and damage created by the custody dispute."

Jana Singer and William Reynolds of the University of Maryland Law School note that this potential for protracted and uncertain litigation also biases divorce negotiations, by weakening the bargaining power of the parent who wants custody most (usually the mother): "Uncertainty about the outcome of custody disputes creates the irresistible temptation to trade custody for lower alimony and child support payments." Such concessions "contribute substantially to the impoverishment of divorced women and their children."

Finally, Elster argues that a principle focusing exclusively on the best interest of the child is unfair to the parents, who, after all, have rights and needs, too. "If one parent, usually the mother, has devoted crucial years to child care and perhaps given up her career to do it," he suggests, "it seems prima facie right that she should get custody."

Likewise, it seems prima facie wrong—independent of any judgment about the child's future welfare—that custody should be awarded to a parent who has used illegal tactics of abduction to secure possession of the child, and so to benefit from the judicial tendency to settle custody cases in favor of the status quo. It also seems relevant if one parent would suffer far more by being deprived of custody, even if the child's best interest creates some preference for custody by the other parent. Elster concludes that, while the child needs special protection, "That protection should not . . . extend to small gains in the child's welfare achieved at the expense of large losses in parental welfare."

Joint Custody

In part for these reasons, recent years have seen a movement away from the best-interest standard. Rather than the win-lose model of naming a sole custodian, legislatures increasingly favor joint custody and shared parenting after divorce. In 1975 only one state had a statute providing for joint custody; today, more than half do, with an increasing number of statutes establishing a legislative preference for joint custody, even if imposed over the objections of one parent.

The chief arguments for joint custody are, first, that children adjust better to divorce if they continue to have meaningful relationships and frequent contact with both parents. Second, joint custody is proposed as a solution to the widespread failure of fathers to pay child support, a problem attributed partly to the tendency of divorced fathers to become estranged from their children under sole custody arrangements. Finally, joint custody is said to reflect modern changes in parental roles. Martha Fineman, director of the Family Policy Program of the Institute for Legal Studies at the University of Wisconsin, notes that proponents of joint custody find compelling the symbolic ideal of parental equality that it embodies: "Divorce is now described as a process that . . . restructures or reformulates the spouses' relationship, conferring equal or shared parental rights on both parents. . . . "

But the reality of joint custody may be less attractive than the rhetoric surrounding it. Singer and Reynolds charge that proponents of court-imposed joint custody "fail to distinguish joint *physical* custody from joint *legal* custody, in which the child resides primarily (or exclusively) with one parent—usually the mother—while the nonresidential father retains joint decision-making authority over the child's upbringing. . . . This latter category closely resembles the traditional maternal-custody-with-liberal-paternal-visitation arrangement with one essential difference: it accords the nonresidential father almost all of the rights but few of the responsibilities that raising a child entails." Thus, "the vast majority of court-ordered joint custody decrees provide for equal parental *rights*, but impose vastly unequal parental *responsibilities*."

Simply calling something "joint custody," Singer and Reynolds argue, "is neither necessary nor sufficient to ensure [parental] contact. Traditional sole custody arrangements with liberal visitation provide ample opportunity for the noncustodial parent to have significant contact with the child, *if* that parent chooses to stay in touch." And joint legal custody hardly guarantees continuing parental involvement, since the nonresidential parent has the legal option but not the legal obligation to stay involved. Moreover, virtually all the studies purportedly proving the benefits of joint custody have involved *voluntary* joint custody arrangements, providing a dubious guide to the likely success of court-ordered joint custody imposed on parents resistant to cooperation and compromise.

Nor has even voluntary joint custody been shown significantly to increase compliance with child-support awards. According to a 1985 study by Nancy D. Polikoff, even where fathers had joint legal custody, the mothers with whom the child resided received their full court-ordered support only 60 percent of the time. The same study reveals that courts awarded no child support in more than half of the cases designated as "joint residential custody," although the children in those cases were living more than two-thirds of the time with one "joint" custodian. Fineman wryly notes the irony that "the failure of divorced fathers is used as one of the major arguments for giving men more control and power over children and, through them, over their mothers' lives. . . . In no other area does the law reward those who have failed in their duties as an incentive for them to change their behavior."

Finally, a presumption in favor of court-ordered joint custody, like the best-interest standard, exacerbates inequalities in the bargaining power of the parties. Legislation skewed toward awards of joint custody increases the ability of the parent requesting joint custody to engage in extortionary bargaining over child support and alimony.

The Primary-Caretaker Presumption

An attractive alternative is the custody presumption in favor of the "primary caretaker" that recently has been adopted in several states. The primary-caretaker presumption is claimed to be far easier to implement than the best-interest-of-the-child standard, while avoiding the unfairness to the primary-caretaking parent masked by the egalitarian rhetoric of joint custody.

Fineman argues that the primary-caretaker test "implicitly recognizes that no one can confidently predict the future and that the past may in fact be the best indication we have of future care and concern. . . . The only relevant inquiry should be which parent has already adapted his or her life and interests to accommodate the demands of the child." Such an inquiry "is particularly susceptible to legal analysis because it involves fact-finding, an inquiry traditionally performed by courts."

Among the criteria for identifying the primary caretaker (taking West Virginia law as representative) are these. The primary caretaker is the person who (1) prepares and plans the meals; (2) bathes, grooms, and dresses the child; (3) provides medical care, including nursing and trips to physicians; (4) arranges babysitting and after-school activities; (5) puts the child to bed and wakes the child in the morning; (6) disciplines the child; (7) teaches elementary skills such as reading and writing. Proponents argue that lay testimony can generally demonstrate which parent performs the lion's share of these tasks, without lengthy court hearings. They maintain that the standard yields results predictable enough to decrease incentives for litigation.

Elster disagrees. Among the West Virginia criteria, he observes, "several . . . involve doing something *for* the child rather than doing something *with* the child. . . . once activities not involving interaction are taken into account, many fathers may say that through the income they earn by working they also make a contribution to primary caretaking, in the sense of doing something for the child." He acknowledges that the list of criteria could be redrawn, however, "to include only activities that are done with the child and hence either give rise to a special need of the child for the primary caretaker or a special need of the primary caretaker for the child." Elster also suggests that "it may be difficult to ascertain who is the primary caretaker when both parents are working full time." But Fineman counters, "The mere fact that both parents work does not, in the vast majority of cases, mean that both are primary caretakers (or that neither is)." Even when both parents work, mothers often make greater career sacrifices for their children and perform more caretaking functions.

The primary-caretaker presumption takes into account both the needs of the child and the claims of its parents. As Elster explains: "It is a just result that the parent who has devoted the most time to the child gets custody, and it is good for the child to be with the parent who has devoted the most time to her." In Singer and Reynolds's view, "Awarding custody to the primary caretaker furthers a child's paramount interest in stability and continuity. It preserves the child's bond with the parent who has provided daily care and nurturing during marriage and continues, to the extent possible, the childrearing arrangements in effect prior to divorce." Fineman sees it as justly assigning custody as "a reward for past caretaking behavior."

The primary-caretaker rule is explicitly gender-neutral, but in today's world it is in fact likely to favor mothers. But, as Fineman points out, "If fathers are 'left out,' they can change their behavior and begin making sacrifices in their careers and devoting their time during the marriage to the primary care and nurturing of children." Singer and Reynolds suggest that for this reason a primary-caretaker preference—and not court-imposed joint custody—"is most likely to encourage true coparenting during marriage." Whereas, "a presumption in favor of joint custody, regardless of which parent has provided care during marriage, sends a clear message to fathers that they have a right to claim their children upon divorce no matter how detached they are from the ongoing care of those children during the marriage," under a primary-caretaker regime, "parents know that only if they assume substantial parenting responsibilities during marriage will they have a realistic chance of gaining custody at divorce." In any case, the primary-caretaker presumption may be the best we can do in an imperfect world to approximate Solomonic wisdom in the painful process of awarding child custody.

The sources quoted in this article are Lenore J. Weitzman, The Divorce Revolution *(New York: The Free Press, 1985); Jon Elster, "Solomonic Judgments: Against the Best Interest of the Child,"* The University of Chicago Law Review *54, no. 1 (Winter 1987); Jana B. Singer and William L. Reynolds, "A Dissent on Joint Custody,"* Maryland Law Review *47, no. 2 (1988); Martha Fineman, "Dominant Discourse, Professional Language, and Legal Change in Child Custody Decision-making,"* Harvard Law Review *101, no. 4 (February 1988); and Nancy D. Polikoff, "Custody and Visitation: Their Relationship to Establishing and Enforcing Support,"* Clearinghouse Review *19 (1985).*

Adultery

Bonnie Steinbock

According to a 1980 survey in *Cosmopolitan*, 54 percent of American wives have had extramarital affairs; a study of 100,000 married women by the considerably tamer *Redbook* magazine found that 40 percent of the wives over age forty had been unfaithful. While such surveys are, to some extent, self-selecting—those who do it are more likely to fill out questionnaires about it—sexual mores have clearly changed in recent years. Linda Wolfe, who reported the results of the *Cosmopolitan* survey, suggests that "this increase in infidelity among married women represents not so much a deviation from traditional standards of fidelity as a break with the old double standard." Studies show that men have always strayed in significant numbers.

Yet 80 percent of "*Cosmo* girls" did not approve of infidelity and wished their own husbands and lovers would be faithful. Eighty-eight percent of respondents to a poll taken in Iowa in 1983 viewed "coveting your neighbor's spouse" as a "major sin." It seems that while almost nobody approves of adultery, men have always done it, and women are catching up.

The increase in female adultery doubtless has to do with recent and radical changes in our attitudes toward sex and sexuality. We no longer feel guilty about enjoying sex; indeed, the capacity for sexual enjoyment is often regarded as a criterion of mental health. When sex itself is no longer intrinsically shameful, restraints on sexual behavior are loosened. In fact, we might question whether the abiding disapproval of infidelity merely gives lip service to an ancient taboo. Is there a rational justification for disapproving of adultery that will carry force with everyone, religious and nonreligious alike?

Trust and Deception

Note first that adultery, unlike murder, theft, and lying, is not universally forbidden. Traditional Eskimo culture, for example, regarded sharing one's wife with a visitor as a matter of courtesy. The difference can be explained by looking at the effects of these practices on social cohesiveness. Without rules protecting the lives, persons, and property of its members, no group could long endure. Indeed, rules against killing, assault, lying, and stealing seem fundamental to having a morality at all.

Not so with adultery. For adultery is a *private* matter, essentially concerning only the relationship between husband and wife. It is not essential to morality like these other prohibitions: Stable societies exist with genuine moral codes that tolerate extramarital sex. Although adultery remains a criminal offense in some jurisdictions, it is rarely prosecuted. Surely this is because it is widely regarded as a private matter—in the words of Billie Holiday, "Ain't nobody's business if I do."

However, even if adultery is a private matter, with which the state should not interfere, it is not a morally neutral issue. Our view of adultery is connected to our thoughts and feelings about love and marriage, sex and the family, the value of fidelity, sexual jealousy, and exclusivity. How we think about adultery will affect the quality of our relationships, the way we raise our children, the kind of society we have and want to have. So it is important to consider whether our attitudes toward adultery are justifiable.

Several practical considerations militate against adultery: Pregnancy, AIDS, and genital herpes immediately spring to mind. However, unwanted pregnancies are a risk of all sexual intercourse, within or without marriage; venereal disease is a risk of all nonexclusive sex, not just adulterous sex. So these risks do not provide a reason for objecting specifically to adultery. In any event, they offer merely pragmatic, as opposed to moral, objections. If adultery is wrong, it does not become less so because one has been sterilized or inoculated against venereal disease.

Two main reasons support regarding adultery as seriously immoral. One is that adultery is an instance of promise-breaking, in the view that marriage involves, explicitly or implicitly, a promise of sexual fidelity: to forsake all others. That there is this attitude in our culture is clear. Mick Jagger, not noted for sexual puritanism, allegedly refused to marry Jerry Hall, the mother of his baby, because he had no intention of accepting an exclusive sexual relationship. While Jagger's willingness to become an unwed father is hardly mainstream morality, his refusal to marry, knowing that he did not wish to be faithful, respects the idea that *marriage* requires such a commitment. Moreover, the promise of sexual fidelity is regarded as a very serious and important one. To cheat on one's spouse indicates a lack of concern, a willingness to cause pain, and so a lack of love. Finally, one who breaks promises cannot be trusted. And trust is essential to the intimate partnership of marriage, which may be irreparably weakened by its betrayal.

The second reason for regarding adultery as immoral is that it involves deception, lying, for example, about one's whereabouts and relations with others. Perhaps a marriage can withstand the occasional lie, but a pattern of lying will have irrevocable consequences for a marriage, if discovered, and probably even if not. Like breaking promises, lying is regarded as a fundamental kind of wrongdoing, a failure to take the one lied to seriously as a moral person entitled to respect.

Open Marriage

These two arguments suffice to make most cases of adultery wrong, given the attitudes and expectations of most people. But what if marriage did not involve any promise of sexual fidelity? What if no need for deception arose, because neither partner expected or wanted such fidelity? Objections to "open marriage" cannot focus on promise-breaking and deception, for the expectation of exclusivity is absent. If an open marriage has been freely chosen by both spouses, and not imposed by a dominant partner on a dependent one, would such an arrangement be morally acceptable, even desirable?

The attractiveness of extramarital affairs without dishonesty, disloyalty, or guilt should not be downplayed. However satisfying sex between married people may be, it cannot have the excitement of a new relationship. ("Not *better*," a friend once said defensively to his wife, attempting to explain his infidelity, "just *different*.") Might we not be better off, our lives fuller and richer, if we allowed ourselves the thrill of new and different sexual encounters?

Perhaps the expectation of sexual exclusivity in marriage stems from unadmirable emotions: jealousy and possessiveness. That most people experience these feelings is no reason for applauding or institutionalizing them. Independence in marriage is now generally regarded as a good thing: Too much "togetherness" is boring and stifling. In a good marriage, the partners can enjoy different activities, travel apart, and have separate friends. Why draw the line at sexual activity?

The natural response to this question invokes a certain conception of love and sex: Sex is an expression of affection and intimacy and so should be reserved for people who love each other. Further, it is assumed that one can and should have such feelings for only one other person at any time. To make love with someone else is to express feelings of affection and intimacy that should be reserved for one's spouse alone.

This rejection of adultery assumes the validity of a particular conception of love and sex, which can be attacked in two ways. We might divorce sex from love and regard sex as a pleasurable activity in its own right, comparable to the enjoyment of a good meal. In his article "Is Adultery Immoral?" philosopher Richard Wasserstrom suggests that the linkage of sex with love reflects a belief that unless it is purified by a higher emotion, such as love, sex is intrinsically bad or dirty.

But this is an overly simplistic view of the connection between sex and love. Feelings of love occur between people enjoying sexual intercourse, not out of a sense that sexual pleasure must be purified, but precisely because of the mutual pleasure they give one another. People naturally have feelings of affection for those who make them happy, and sex is a very good way of making someone extraordinarily happy. At the same time, sex is by its nature intimate, involving both physical and psychological exposure. This both requires and creates trust, which is closely allied to feelings of affection and love. This is not to say that sex necessarily requires or leads to love, but a conception of the relation between love and sex that ignores these factors is inadequate and superficial.

Alternatively, one might acknowledge the connection between sex and love, but attack the assumption of exclusivity. If parents can love all their children equally and if adults can have numerous close friends, why should it be impossible to love more than one sexual partner at a time? Perhaps we could learn to love more widely and to accept that a spouse's sexual involvement with another is not a sign of rejection or lack of love.

The logistics of multiple involvement are certainly daunting. Having an affair (as opposed to a roll in the hay) requires time and concentration; it will almost inevitably mean neglecting one's spouse, one's children, one's work. More important, however, exclusivity seems to be an intrinsic part of "true love." Imagine Romeo pouring out his heart to both Juliet *and* Rosalind! In our ideal of romantic love, one chooses to forgo pleasure with other partners in order to have a unique relationship with one's beloved. Such "renunciation" is natural in the first throes of romantic love; it is precisely because this stage does *not* last that we must promise to be faithful through the notoriously unromantic realities of married life.

Fidelity As an Ideal

In the view I have been defending, genuinely open marriages are not *immoral*, although they deviate from a valued ideal of what marriage should be. While this is not the only ideal, or incumbent on all rational agents, it is a moral view in that it embodies a claim about a good way for people to live. The prohibition of adultery, then, is neither arbitrary nor irrational. However, even if we are justified in accepting the ideal of fidelity, we know that people do not always live up to the ideals they accept, and we recognize that some failures to do so are worse than others. We regard a brief affair, occasioned by a prolonged separation, as morally different from installing a mistress.

Further, sexual activity is not necessary for deviation from the ideal of marriage that lies behind the demand for fidelity. As John Heckler observed during his bitter and public divorce from former Health and Human Services Secretary Margaret Heckler, "In marriage, there are two partners. When one person starts contributing far less than the other person to the marriage, that's the original infidelity. You don't need any third party." While this statement was probably a justification of his own infidelities, the point is valid. To abandon one's spouse, whether to a career or to another person, is also a kind of betrayal.

If a man becomes deeply involved emotionally with another woman, it may be little comfort that he is able to assure his wife that "Nothing happened." Sexual infidelity has significance as a sign of a deeper betrayal—falling in love with someone else. It may be objected that we cannot control the way we feel, only the way we behave; that we should not be blamed for falling in love, but only for acting on the feeling. While we may not have direct control over our feelings, however, we are responsible for getting ourselves into situations where certain feelings naturally arise. "It just happened" is rarely an accurate portrayal of an extramarital love affair.

If betrayal can occur without sex, can sex occur without betrayal? In the novel *Forfeit*, by Dick Francis, the hero is deeply in love with his wife, who was paralyzed by polio in the early days of their marriage. Her great unspoken fear is that he will leave her; instead, he tends to her devotedly. For several years, he forgoes sex, but eventually succumbs to an affair. While his adultery is hardly praiseworthy, it is understandable. He could divorce his wife and marry again, but it is precisely his refusal to abandon her, his continuing love and tender care, that makes us admire him.

People do fall in love with others and out of love with their spouses. Ought they to refrain from making love while still legally tied? I cannot see much, if any, moral value in remaining physically faithful, on principle, to a spouse one no longer loves. This will displease those who regard the wrongness of adultery as a moral absolute, but my account has nothing to do with absolutes and everything to do with what it means to love someone deeply and completely. It is the value of that sort of relationship that makes sexual fidelity an ideal worth the sacrifice.

Neither a mere religiously based taboo, nor a relic of a repressive view of sexuality, the prohibition against adultery expresses a particular conception of married love. It is one we can honor in our own lives and bequeath to our children with confidence in its value as a coherent and rational ideal.

Surrogate Motherhood

Claudia Mills

"Surrogate" motherhood dates back at least as far as Genesis, to the earliest generations of recognizably human families. There Abraham's long-barren wife, Sarah, sends her husband to "lie with" the slave girl Hagar, in the hopes that through her she can "found a family." Jacob's wife Rachel makes a similar arrangement with her slave girl, Billah, "so that she may bear sons to be laid upon my knees." Despite the intense and bitter controversy surrounding contemporary cases of surrogate parenting, the practice of one woman bearing a child for another is not particularly novel.

But in the late twentieth century two dimensions to this practice *are* new. First, although traditional surrogacy is far more common, medical advances now allow for cases of what has been called "high tech" or "full-fledged" surrogacy, where the surrogate is implanted with both sperm and egg drawn from an infertile couple. The genetic material for the fetus is contributed entirely by the receiving couple, with the surrogate "loaning" her womb to carry the fetus to birth. Second, recent years have seen the advent of commercial or contract surrogacy, childbearing for a fee. Contract surrogacy emerged in the mid-1970s; by the end of 1986 some five hundred children had been born through these arrangements. The most famous, of course, is Baby M, the object of the landmark custody case that ensued when surrogate mother Mary Beth Whitehead refused to relinquish the child she had conceived and carried to term in a surrogacy contract for William Stern. Baby M's custody battle riveted public attention for months, posing in the starkest terms troubling questions about the very nature of parenthood.

The legal system's response to surrogacy can range across the spectrum from criminalizing it outright to upholding surrogacy contracts on a par with any others. Both of these extreme positions seem unpalatable alternatives. The problem with the first is that we are reluctant to ban *all* surrogacy, for sometimes one woman (a sister, or a friend) offers to bear a child for another purely out of love or an altruistic desire to relieve suffering. At most, then, we would consider banning surrogacy-for-a-fee, as an analogy to legislation against baby-selling.

The other extreme, treating surrogacy contracts as standardly enforceable, has some support in public opinion: A majority of Americans polled about the trial court's decision to enforce the surrogacy contract in *Baby M* believed that surrogate mothers should be bound by the contracts they sign. But, as the New Jersey Supreme Court later ruled, overturning the trial court's decision, this response is poorly grounded in the law. In other contexts, personal-service contracts are usually not held to be enforceable by "specific performance," that is, by forcing the reneging individual actually to perform the promised service. In an adoption situation, no state in this country binds a mother to give up her child because of a contract with prospective adoptive parents executed before the child was born; in a traditional surrogacy arrangement, the contract mother is the biological mother of the child as much as any birth mother. Thus the viable policy options involve either prohibiting commercial surrogacy altogether or else making surrogacy legal but unenforceable over the objection of the birth mother. This latter alternative is attractive to those who worry about the abuses that might attend black-market surrogacy, and so prefer the regulation of surrogacy to its criminalization.

The central question in deciding among policy options is whether we as a society want to encourage or discourage this form of child-bearing, and how strongly. To answer this we must look in turn at the concerns of the would-be receiving parents, of the contract mother, of the child, and of society more generally.

The Desire for a Biological Child

Prospective receiving parents usually come to a surrogacy arrangement after long and desperate years of infertility, when all hope of medical intervention has been reluctantly abandoned. According to the most recent data, from 1982, some 3.5 million couples—one in six couples of childbearing age—are considered infertile. Insofar as surrogacy is seen as a way of responding to the anguish of childlessness, it may seem to serve a worthy end. Yet surrogacy would hardly seem the first-choice solution to childlessness in a society where so many existing children languish in institutional care. Why surrogacy rather than adoption?

Adoption, however, is easier said than done. The number of adoptions declined from 82,000 in 1971 to 50,000 in 1982, a 38 percent drop.

In 1984 two million couples competed for the 58,000 infants placed for adoption; these couples experienced a waiting period of three to seven years. Of course, while the demand for healthy, white babies far exceeds supply, many minority babies, and certainly those with physical or mental disabilities, remain in need of loving homes. Yet it is understandable that prospective parents might not be willing to take on the challenge of a severely handicapped child or might be reluctant to cross racial lines in forming a family, given the entrenched racial prejudice of American society.

But even if adoption were more readily available, the lure of surrogacy would remain, for it promises what many parents plainly desire: a genetic link to their children. Is such a desire worthy of respect, or should it be rejected as narcissistic and egoistic? Martha A. Field, professor of law at Harvard Law School, cautions that "a desire to reproduce oneself is never the healthiest motivation for wanting to have a child." This is especially true in the traditional surrogacy situation, where the contract mother is inseminated with the father's sperm, for there the father "is focused upon only half the genes that will make up his child." The importance of the paternal genetic endowment is emphasized, that of the maternal genetic endowment is all but ignored. Yet, Field writes, "It seems odd that the couples using surrogacy should pay so little heed to the other half of the genetic material, since they are almost necessarily believers in the importance of the genetic tie."

Mary Gibson, a philosopher at Rutgers University, suggests that contract motherhood is attractive to receiving parents because of a narrow and rigid notion of the family, "consisting of breadwinning father, nurturing mother (now possibly also a career woman/supermom), and their genetic offspring (preferably, first a boy, then a girl) conceived, carried, and born the old-fashioned way. . . . Contract motherhood, if the contract mother is excluded, allows infertile couples to come as close as possible for them to the 'norm' and even appear to represent it." The desire for a child of one's "own" in such a context should have no special claim to our respect.

The desire for a genetic bond can perhaps be seen as well, however, as an expression of the need for some deep and nonarbitrary link to a child. The desire for a child of one's "own" might come down to a longing for a bond somehow stronger and more enduring than those of marriage or friendship, one that can survive, as so many other ties do not, through sickness and health, good fortune and bad, grounding a lifetime of commitment. But Robert Wachbroit, research scholar at the Institute for Philosophy and Public Policy, remains skeptical about this characterization of the longing for a genetic link, doubting both how natural it is and how noble. After all, he points out, the ancient Romans gave no importance to genetic ties; the emphasis on "blood," and its "thickness" relative to water, is hardly universal. Wachbroit sees the desire for a "special" gene-linked bond as a cousin to concerns with racial purity, and so as morally questionable.

In any case, this kind of irrevocable link is ironically just what surrogacy in practice ends up undermining. Because of the commercial nature of the exchange, as we will see, the child conceived in this way is particularly likely to be viewed as a commodity, special-ordered to fit the parents' preconceived idea of what a child of their "own" should be.

The Contract Mother

The motivations for agreeing to be a contract mother vary. They may involve a desire to help relieve the pain of childlessness in others or to work out some past psychological traumas, but certainly the desire to earn money is almost always central. In a January 1987 Gallup poll, 15 percent of the women questioned said they would consider becoming surrogates for the standard $10,000 fee. After all, working-class women still face bleak employment options. Pregnancy is work they can do either at home while caring for their other children or as the ultimate in moonlighting from another, likely low-paying, job. Some would argue that women should be as free to take on surrogacy "jobs" as any other employment; we no longer favor labor laws that, under the guise of protecting women from the rigors of the workplace, only limit their freedom to work. As Peter Schuck, professor of law at Yale Law School, argues, "A community that cherishes a woman's freedom and individuality should accord a high degree of respect to her choices, and should override them only when her decision is plainly uninformed or offends deeply and widely held social values."

Is the decision to become a contract mother fully informed and voluntary? While Schuck maintains that "the available data contradict the view that surrogates are members of an 'underclass,'" the general paucity of the financial options facing them undermines the claim that the choice of surrogacy is a fully voluntary one. And, voluntariness aside, we might nonetheless charge that the terms of the contracts are exploitative, that is, the receiving couple takes unfair advantage of the contract mother's willingness to serve or her straitened financial circumstances. The terms of Mary Beth Whitehead's contract with William Stern, for example, were appallingly disadvantageous to her. For her $10,000 fee Whitehead was obliged to "assume all risks, including the risk of death, which are incidental to conception, pregnancy, childbirth, including but not limited to postpartum complications," with no compensation whatsoever in the event of a first-trimester miscarriage, and a mere $1,000 if she were forced to submit, on Stern's demand, to an abortion. Is such a contract fair to Whitehead? Does a society like ours want to endorse it?

This poses a dilemma, however, for the better the terms of a surrogacy contract, the more its voluntariness is called into question: Higher fees make surrogacy arrangements harder to resist for women who have few other means of livelihood. But Gibson points out, "If decent pay would constitute an undue inducement, it appears that the job of contract mother cannot be offered on morally acceptable terms: it will involve either direct economic exploitation or undue inducement." She concludes, "Some kinds of jobs cannot be made good jobs, and a decent society won't countenance them even if there are people willing to do them. I suggest that contract motherhood is such a job."

The Interests of the Child

Arguments in favor of or against surrogacy on behalf of the child yet-to-be-conceived have an odd ring to them, for as yet no person exists who can be either benefited or harmed by the arrangements made. Arguments that it is good for an unborn child to be conceived, if taken seriously, would encourage a veritable population explosion in the purported interests of all those potential persons clamoring to be born. Arguments that it is bad for an unborn child to be conceived, on the other hand, face the objection that unless the child's life is particularly miserable, life on any terms seems preferable to no life at all. We do better here to step back from inquiring whether surrogacy is in the interests of the actual children born in such arrangements and to ask simply what special problems, if any, they face.

According to Schuck, far from facing special problems, such children are especially fortunate to be so wanted that their parents would go to such lengths to bring them into the world. Field points out that children produced through "unusual arrangements" can grow up feeling secure and loved, as can adopted children. One pities Baby M not because she was born of a surrogacy contract, but because of the bitter battle waged for her custody. Thus Field cautions that "if we start generalizing what kind of families or situations it is detrimental to children to be born into, and make rules accordingly, we start down a long road fraught with peril for our civil liberties."

But if Baby M suffered from being a too-wanted child, a greater peril is posed to contract children who end up being unwanted, like Christopher Ray Stiver, conceived through a surrogacy arrangement between Judy Stiver and Alexander Malahoff. The baby was born with a smaller-than-normal head, usually indicative of mental retardation. Both parents renounced care of the baby; Stiver agreed to accept him only when paternity tests revealed that her husband, and not the sperm donor, was the biological father of the child.

Of course, any child can be born with a handicap and face possible parental rejection. But Judith Areen, professor of community and family medicine at Georgetown University Law Center, argues that surrogacy increases the risk that less-than-perfect children will be abandoned at birth by both biological parents: "One parent in any surrogacy arrangement is supposed to view the child as a mere commodity, one that is to be transferred (abandoned) at birth. . . . If the child is physically or mentally handicapped, there is a real danger that both parents will view the child as a commodity, and thus abandon the infant emotionally and—if permitted by the law to do so—physically and financially. The surrogate mother will do so because that is what she is supposed to do; the father (and his spouse, if any) will do so because he is likely to feel that as a purchaser he has the right to reject 'damaged goods.' Treating children as commodities, as surrogacy does, thus poses significant risks to the children conceived." At least in the exceptional case, surrogacy can prove tragic for the children it creates.

The Interests of Society

While surrogacy has the potential to provide benefits to infertile couples and perhaps to contracting mothers, it is not clear that it promises any benefits to the rest of us. As Field points out, "We in this country, now at least, are not suffering from inadequate population; as a society we do not need more babies. There are no affirmative reasons for the state to promote surrogacy arrangements other than to fulfill the wishes of individuals who wish to use them." Does surrogacy, then, pose any dangers to society, or threaten, in Schuck's words, "any deeply and widely held social values?" It seems that it may.

One danger concerns surrogacy's possible impact on the prevalence of adoption. Some of its proponents may have done their cause a disservice by predicting that in time surrogacy will come to replace adoption, for it does not seem that the interests of society would be well served if surrogacy contributed to the neglect of existing children. But it is doubtful its impact on adoption would be significant. How many of those to whom surrogacy is attractive would choose to adopt a black baby or a baby with special needs if surrogacy were unavailable? One suspects only a few. Moreover, Field argues, "although it benefits society more for [infertile couples] to adopt an existing child than to conceive a new one, the same is true for fertile couples, who nonetheless are permitted to reproduce without any restriction by the state."

A greater danger is that surrogacy commercializes what we may feel should not be commercialized. We may cleave to the conviction that, as Field puts it, "there are some types of things that our society does not want to see measured in terms of money. Society may want to do what it can to help people keep these in a personal sphere that is distinct from the commercial; indeed it may even compel them to do so, to the extent that it can." She cites laws against prostitution and the sale of human organs—as well, of course, as laws against baby selling—as examples of our societal refusal to establish markets in certain intimate areas of life. But Schuck reminds us that we permit commercial markets in sperm and egg donation, and in child care services, although these, too, involve deeply private spheres. Our attitudes about the commercialization of childbearing will depend in part on which group of analogies seems to us more apt.

Policy Conclusions

Surrogate motherhood is unlikely to disappear as long as couples want babies and women are willing to produce them for a fee. But the laws and regulations we establish may go some way toward encouraging or discouraging its spread. While Schuck, a staunch supporter of surrogacy, calls for legal measures to facilitate surrogacy arrangements, on balance it seems that society has no compelling reason to encourage surrogacy and considerable reasons to discourage it. Gibson thus recommends that "commercial contract motherhood should be expressly prohibited. Commercial brokering should be a criminal offense. Paid private contracts should be void and unenforceable." Areen, too, would deny recognition to surrogacy contracts on the grounds that their legal recognition would in essence give a societal seal of approval to the practice.

For Wachbroit the fundamental question to ask in setting policy here is whether and to what extent "underground" or black-market surrogacy is worse than legalized surrogacy. Reasoning along these lines, Field would make surrogacy contracts legal (but unenforceable over the objection of the mother), because "it is possible that criminalizing surrogacy and thereby driving it underground would do more harm than good." This would open the way for regulation on such issues as compensation, access to surrogacy, and screening of potential surrogates. Wachbroit, however, does not see the dangers in illegal surrogacy as great enough to outweigh the affront to human dignity posed by its legalization.

Surrogacy may be here to stay, but Gibson stresses that we should work both to address controllable causes of infertility (such as venereal disease, environmental and workplace toxins, and economic pressures to postpone childbearing) and to make surrogacy increasingly less attractive as a response to infertility. She argues, "Many of the features of our society that make contract motherhood, as a response to infertility, so very attractive to many people are the same features that make it so morally and politically troubling." If working-class women had brighter employment options, if pervasive racism did not erect a bar to interracial adoptions, if we had a richer notion of what it is to be a family, surrogacy would hardly be as attractive as it is today. This is the moral paradox of surrogacy: "If there were a society in which contract motherhood would not be morally objectionable," Gibson concludes, it would also be a society in which "the practice would probably not exist."

The sources quoted in this article are Martha A. Field, Surrogate Motherhood: The Legal and Human Issues *(Cambridge, Mass.: Harvard University Press, 1988); Mary Gibson, "The Moral and Legal Status of 'Surrogate' Motherhood," address for the American Philosophical Association, December 1988; Robert Wachbroit, interview; Peter H. Schuck, "Some Reflections on the* Baby M *Case," and Judith Areen, "Baby M Reconsidered,"* The Georgetown Law Journal *76, no. 5 (June 1988).*

FOR FURTHER READING

Callahan, Daniel. *Setting Limits: Medical Goals in an Aging Society*. New York: Simon and Schuster, 1987.

Daniels, Norman. *Am I My Parents' Keeper? An Essay on Justice between the Young and the Old*. New York: Oxford University Press, 1988.

Field, Martha A. *Surrogate Motherhood: The Legal and Human Issues*. Cambridge, Mass.: Harvard University Press, 1988.

Okin, Susan Moller. *Justice, Gender, and the Family*. New York: Basic Books, 1989.

O'Neill, Onora, and William Ruddick, eds. *Having Children: Philosophical and Legal Reflections on Parenthood*. New York: Oxford University Press, 1979.

Wasserstrom, Richard. "Is Adultery Immoral?" *Philosophical Forum*, vol. 5 (Summer 1974).

13

THE COMPLEXITY
OF LIFE

None of the policy issues examined in this book has had an easy or obvious solution; indeed, some may not have any "solution" at all. The values that underlie each policy decision are complex and may conflict. No magic algorithm tells us how to weigh and measure values or tells us what to value.

This concluding section stands back from the policy arena to look more closely at some deeper questions about our values: the tension between love and justice, the relation between religion and morality, the limits of moral obligation, and, finally, on a lighter note, the competing explanations for why life so often disappoints us.

"Love and Justice" explores the seemingly fundamental opposition between these two important values: justice as impartial, blind to love, regulating the world of business and politics—the world of men; love as fiercely partisan, blind to justice, the province of hearth and home—the world of women. But this opposition, the authors suggest, is a faulty one. Although loving relationships should not be *focused* on justice, they must be *founded* on it.

"Religion and Morality" examines another complex interrelationship, that between our moral values and the religious tradition that, in some views, serves to ground them. In what ways does morality depend on religion? In what ways does it stand alone or even serve to criticize religion? On what particular "brand" of religion does morality depend? Can we pray to different gods—or no god—and still work together to revitalize a shared moral life?

The authority that moral principles exert over us has puzzled many thinkers, from Socrates onward. Why should we be moral when, so often, moral behavior gains us nothing? The next article looks at a somewhat different but clearly related question, not *why* we should be moral, but *how* moral we are in fact required to be. "How Good a Person Do I Have to Be?" analyzes what limits, if any, circumscribe our moral obligations. How moral must we be? How selfish may we be?

The final article in this section, "Why Life Is Disappointing," draws from the accumulated wisdom of theology, philosophy, economics, and psychology in an attempt to understand the gap between "hope, the thing with feathers that perches in the soul," and disappointment, "the egg that, more often than not, it lays."

Love and Justice

Douglas MacLean and Claudia Mills

Love and justice might seem to be fundamentally opposed, alike only in their blindness. Even this one similarity serves to highlight their deep differences. Justice is blindfolded so it can be meted out to persons impartially, without fear or favor, looking only to the right and wrong of an action and not to the particularity of an agent. Love, on the other hand, is blind in its cleaving to the particular loved one, despite any faults, in reckless disregard of the merits. What love is blind to is justice, one might say, just as justice is blind to love.

Love and justice have come to be associated with two spheres, and with the two genders. Love is the province of hearth and home, of the domestic sphere, presided over by women; the ideal of justice regulates the world of business and politics, the marketplace and public forum, the world of men. But even as we now challenge such gender-typing, and argue for a blurring if not an eradication of gender roles, we can also question the separateness of the two spheres, and in the context of the family, as we shall see, the opposition between love and justice themselves.

The Family: Not Just, but Better Than Just

The view that justice and love are appropriate to different spheres has a venerable pedigree. In the eighteenth century, David Hume argued that the virtue of justice is properly engaged only under certain circumstances, characterized by the scarcity of resources and the basic self-interest of human motivation. In the absence of either of these two conditions, justice would be rendered unnecessary. If we had unlimited goods to divvy up, Hume suggested, we would hardly bicker about who got what. Likewise, we would have no need of the "jealous, cautious virtue of justice" were "the mind . . . so enlarged, and so replete with friendship and generosity, that every man has the utmost tenderness for every man, and feels no more concern for his own interest than for that of his fellows; it seems evident, that the use of justice would, in this case, be suspended by such an extensive benevolence, nor would the divisions and barriers of property and obligation have ever been thought of." For Hume, the family represents an example of such enlarged affections, a sphere where justice is unnecessary.

In claiming that the need for justice arises only where feelings of friendship and generosity are insufficient, Hume reflects a strand of philosophical thought that goes back at least to Aristotle, who wrote that "if people are friends they have no need of justice." One difference between these two, however, is that where Aristotle thought it a proper goal of the state to help persons realize their virtues and develop such bonds, Hume and other—male—Enlightenment philosophers took the circumstances of justice for granted. They developed their political and moral theories against a background assumption of self-interested individuals competing for scarce resources, laying the foundation for our contemporary liberal political theory, with its emphasis on equality, individual rights, and social justice.

At the time Hume and his contemporaries were developing a conception of justice for modern public life, the institution of the family was developing into its present form. In contrast to the cheerless and bleak communal life of the Middle Ages arose the idea of home as we recognize it today, a haven in a heartless world, marked by the emergence of privacy, intimacy, and comfort—of domesticity. This development, according to architectural historian Witold Rybczynski, was primarily the work of women. The eighteenth century home "was becoming a feminine place, or at least a place under feminine control." The domesticity it introduced, which Rybczynski traces through such diverse representations as Dutch genre paintings and Jane Austen's novels, is very much part of the idea of home we hold today—a domesticity that, Rybczynski concludes, "was above all, a feminine achievement."

Men developed theories of justice, from which the family was explicitly excluded; women developed the reality of family life. And the idea of home came to be characterized by intimacy not independence, domesticity not democracy.

The Feminist Revolt: Justice, Please

Of course after a while people—that is to say, women—couldn't help but notice that home and family as a sphere apart from justice were maintained not only through the initiative of women but also largely at women's expense. The elimination of any division between mine and thine that characterized family life, however appealing in theory, in practice gave way not to "ours," but to "his." As John Stuart

Mill trenchantly observed: "The two are called 'one person in law,' for the purpose of inferring that whatever is hers is his, but the parallel inference is never drawn that whatever is his is hers."

Women were both excluded from the public sphere, on the grounds that some male representative of the indivisible family unit spoke for them, and treated unjustly within the family as well. The domesticity and comfort that Rybczynski celebrates, the cleanliness and order, didn't arise of its own accord, or by fairy hands. Someone had to wield that mop, that broom, that toilet bowl scrub brush, and almost invariably that someone was female.

In recent decades the women's movement has lobbied simultaneously for the inclusion of women in the public sphere—for equal opportunity across occupations and for greater representation of women in political life—and for justice within the family. Some feminists insist that husbands should pay cash wages to stay-at-home wives for housework and child care, which they see as work like any other and as worthy of recompense. We have seen an extension of a contractual framework to marriage, ranging from formal prenuptial agreements to job assignment lists posted on family refrigerators. Moms have gone on strike, demanding the basic protections afforded to workers in other—less demeaning?—occupations. The view of the family as providing a refuge from crass commercial and political concerns has been charged to be a sentimental facade masking a concealed tyranny: When every man's home is his castle, every man is a king and every woman a maid. It began to seem to many women not a bad idea to forswear what Hume called the "nobler virtues, and more favourable blessings" that characterized family life. Women would be willing to settle for a little less love and cherishing, in exchange for a little more fairness and respect.

Beyond Justice, to Caring

Feminism has not raised a unanimous voice, however, in favor of justice supplanting love. As some feminists have sought to remake family life on the model of the political and commercial world, others, also claiming the feminist flag, have sought to defend the importance of caring, sharing, and community as distinctively female contributions to our moral life. Their goal is not to make mothers more like businesspersons and congresspersons, but to make sure more businesspersons and congresspersons are mothers: to define and celebrate and finally to enlarge the scope of traditional feminine influence.

Looking at the distinctive contributions men and women have made to moral philosophy, philosopher Annette Baier notices a "broad brushstroke" approach in predominantly male theorizing that centers on "what has been the men theorists' preoccupation, namely obligation." But, Baier notes, there is "a lot of morality not covered by that concept." Most liberal theories contain "only hand waves concerning our proper attitude to our children, the ill, to our relatives, friends, and lovers." Baier concludes that by more or less renouncing theorizing on a grand scale in favor of a more context-situated "ethics of love," female philosophers can be seen as filling in the gaps and perhaps laying a new foundation for moral theory.

Feminist psychologists like Carol Gilligan have made respectable the notion that, in their moral reasoning, women just think differently from men. Men typically view moral problems in terms of rights, justice, and fairness; women, in contrast, tend to approach moral problems by exploring the human interrelationships at stake in them, emphasizing the importance of community and harmony. On traditional scales of moral development, the female concern with particular individuals caught in the web of actual relationships has ranked lower than the male concern with abstract moral principles. But Gilligan suggests that the two approaches to moral thinking should not be ranked as better or worse, but appreciated as complementary.

Nor are women alone in defending the importance of values other than justice. Michael Sandel, a critic of contemporary liberal political theories, writing on the relation between love and justice, asks us to consider two families. In the first, "relations are governed in large part by spontaneous affection and . . . in consequence, the circumstances of justice prevail to a relatively small degree. Individual rights and fair decision procedures are seldom invoked, not because injustice is rampant but because their appeal is pre-empted by a spirit of generosity in which I am rarely inclined to claim my fair share." Now, Sandel says, "imagine that one day the harmonious family comes to be wrought with dissension. Interests grow divergent and the circumstances of justice grow more acute. The affection and spontaneity of previous days give way to demands for fairness and the observance of rights. And let us further imagine that the old generosity is replaced by a judicious temper of unexceptionable integrity and that the new moral necessities are met with a full measure of justice, so that no injustice prevails." Would we see the second family—with its strict but sullen adherence to rules and regulations—as a moral improvement on the first? Sandel would not.

Just as academic thinkers are rediscovering the territory of love, so is family life enjoying its own renaissance. Families are "in." Headlines announce that commitment and marriage are "back," with the current baby boomlet placing concerns about family and children at the center of the national policy agenda. Both female and male workers are demanding more flexible work hours and on-site day care: some acknowledgment by employers and government that family comes— well, if not first, then at least not out of the running. Is the "me" era giving way to the "we" era, as a new "familialism" replaces the old rights-centered individualism, and love takes precedence over justice?

Love and Justice

Yet whatever central place we may give to family life, its costs are still borne primarily by women. Women still earn only sixty-six cents for every dollar earned by men—a differential explained both by discrimination in the workplace and by women's heavier share of domestic responsibilities that compromise their participation in the work force. We may give lip service to gender equality in the home, but Arlie Hochschild, professor of sociology at the University of California at Berkeley, reports that only 20 percent of couples split household tasks and childrearing equally. Squabbles over housework are beginning to replace squabbles over money as the leading subject for discord in marriage; Hochschild documents the powerful and corrosive resentment of women who find themselves stuck with the "second shift" of housework. Debates about justice in the family refuse to disappear.

Nor, of course, are most women willing to renounce concerns about justice in the wider world, whatever distinctive role they may hold in the domestic sphere. Philosopher Onora O'Neill reminds us that women's lives inescapably have political and economic dimensions, and she insists that "even if we find commonalities in women's experience, take them at face value, and use them to construct a moral voice that is to replace the voice of justice with the voice of care and concern for relationships, we will still need to say something about the political and economic context of women's lives. An ethic of caring and relationships will be adequate only if we assume lives that are confined to the nursery or the boudoir."

But what of the nursery and the boudoir? Do we want to say, with Aristotle and Hume, that when we are in a domain governed by love, we need not worry about justice? What do love and justice, in the end, have to do with each other?

In her new book, *Justice, Gender, and the Family*, Susan Moller Okin suggests that the appearance of a deep and abiding conflict between love and justice arises from our misunderstanding the way these two values might be related. Okin questions the assumption that "justice somehow takes away from intimacy, harmony, and love." She asks, "Why should we suppose that harmonious affection, indeed deep and long-lasting love, cannot co-exist with ongoing standards of justice? Why should we be forced to choose and thereby to deprecate the basic and essential virtue, justice, by playing it off against what are claimed to be higher virtues?" Okin answers that a realistic view of the family, sensitive to the long-standing gender-patterned injustices within it, allows us to conclude that we can insist on justice in families at the same time that we hope for more from them: "We need to recognize that associations in which we hope that the best of human motivations and the noblest of virtues will prevail are, in fact, morally superior to those that are just only if they are firmly built on a foundation of justice, however rarely it may be invoked."

This last seems a crucial point. The noted philosopher John Rawls, whose liberal and egalitarian theory of justice has been both praised and criticized by feminists, draws an important distinction between the basic values of political life and our ultimate personal values. The goods associated with justice, Rawls concedes, are not "anyone's idea of the basic values of human life" and are "not intended as an approximation to what is ultimately important." What we care about most, our ultimate values, have to do with family, friends, religion, and the like. But because of our historical circumstances, the pursuit of any of these values can and has led to tyranny, intolerance, and exploitation, and so our interactions, even in the domestic sphere, ought at least to conform to the demands of justice and respect, even if we may wish that they not be motivated by these concerns. We seek love when we marry and found families, not increasingly complex ways to learn to treat each other justly. We want justice to be the foundation, not the focus, of family life.

But in loving relationships people not only find intimacy, they also discover new ways to step on each other's toes, violate each other's dignity, and show a lack of respect. Not only love and justice, but also people are often blind. They are, for a variety of reasons, blind to the hurts they cause. When our partners show us how we have hurt them or acted selfishly, they are calling for justice as well as love. If justice is not the focus of loving relationships, it must still be a continuing concern: Like freedom, it requires eternal vigilance.

When Aristotle wrote that friends have no need of justice, we should recall that he took for granted that the highest form of friendship was reserved for the leisure-filled lives of aristocratic males. In our time, men and women, heirs to a long legacy of gender-based injustice both within the family and in the world beyond, have been forced to become uncomfortably specific about who owes what to whom and why. Our hope can be not that we will somehow get beyond justice, but that we can get beyond talking about it so often and so stridently. Justice should be the basis of loving relationships, not the topic for daily dinner conversations. But we may be in for a lengthy stretch of domestic strife and reorganization before our family lives can give both love and justice their due.

Sources cited in this article are David Hume, An Enquiry Concerning the Principles of Morals *(La Salle, Ill.: Open Court Publishing, 1966, reprint, 1777); Aristotle,* Nicomachean Ethics, *Book VIII, trans. Martin Ostwald (Indianapolis: Bobbs-Merrill, 1962); Witold Rybczynski,* Home: A Short History of an Idea *(New York: Viking Penguin, 1987); John Stuart Mill,* The Subjection of Women *(London: Virago, 1983); Annette Baier, "What Do Women Want in a Moral Theory?"* Nous *19 (1985); Carol Gilligan,* In a Different Voice *(Cambridge, Mass.: Harvard University Press, 1982); Onora O'Neill, "Friends of Difference,"* London Review of Books *(September 14, 1989); Michael Sandel,* Liberalism and the Limits of Justice *(Cambridge: Cambridge University Press, 1982); Susan Moller Okin,* Justice, Gender, and the Family *(New York: Basic Books, 1989); and John Rawls, "The Priority of Right and Ideas of the Good,"* Philosophy & Public Affairs *17 (1988).*

Religion and Morality

Claudia Mills

America likes to think of itself as a distinctively good country. Our founding is heralded as a great moral advance for mankind; certainly its architects articulated their purpose in rousingly moral terms. Ours was the first nation expressly "dedicated to the proposition that all men are created equal," the first to establish itself on the foundation of inalienable human rights. Despite profound national embarrassments such as slavery and the forcible removal of Native Americans, this moral vision of America has proved remarkably resilient, and in recent years "the new patriotism" has taken America's "moral superiority" as a rallying cry.

It is also a commonplace that America is a religious country. "In God We Trust" is our national motto (although it was chosen only in 1956, two years after "one nation *under God*" was inserted by an Act of Congress into the Pledge of Allegiance). Our most cherished statements of national ideals are couched in religious language, from the Mayflower Compact to Martin Luther King's "I have a dream" speech. Recent years have seen as well a resurgence of concern toward making this religious dimension of public life more explicit, particularly via the movement to reestablish some form of public school prayer.

These two facets of the American self-image may seem to be closely related. It is claimed that America's character as a moral nation depends on its character as a religious nation—indeed, that morality itself depends on religion. Such a claim was made by the first president in his Farewell Address: "Of all the dispositions and habits which lead to political prosperity, religion and morality are indispensable supports. . . . And let us with caution indulge the supposition that morality can be maintained without religion. . . . reason and experience both forbid us to expect that national morality can prevail in exclusion of religious principle." The same claim was made by Ronald Reagan: "It is only in . . . the faith that sees beyond the here and now, that we find the rationale for our daring notions about the inalienable rights of free men and women. . . . The Western ideas of freedom and democracy spring directly from the Judeo-Christian religious experience."

The claim that morality depends on religion, however, can mean very different things, and its truth or falsehood varies accordingly. In what ways does morality depend on religion and in what ways does it stand alone or even serve to criticize religion? On what particular "brand" of religion does morality depend? And what implications can we draw from the relation between religion and morality for policy issues such as prayer in public schools?

The Mount Sinai Summit

One way morality might depend on religion is that morality has religion, to some degree, as its origin. Much of our present moral code is derived historically from religious teachings—from the Ten Commandments and Jesus' Sermon on the Mount. This seems to be what President Reagan had in mind when he observed that our ideas of freedom and democracy "spring directly from the Judeo-Christian religious experience." In the words of then Secretary of Education William Bennett, "From the Judeo-Christian tradition come our values, our principles, the animating spirit of our institutions. . . . American history—the fundamental shape of the American experience—cannot be understood without reference to the Judeo-Christian tradition, a tradition which gave birth to us and which envelops us."

A good deal can be said for such claims, as a matter of historical record. But whatever their truth, they seem to imply little about any present-day connection between morality and religion. As John Stuart Mill pointed out more than a century ago, while we may be indebted to Judaism and Christianity for imparting to us various moral truths, the fact remains that they have been imparted: "This benefit, whatever it amounts to, has been gained. It has become the property of humanity, and cannot now be lost by anything short of a return to primeval barbarism." Mill's position, then, is that we can take the moral truths religion has imparted to us and leave the religion behind.

Certainly many people today seem to have done just that. Despite their differences in theology, religious and secular ethicists agree on a wide range of moral issues. Believers and nonbelievers alike join in affirming kindness, compassion, honesty, and fairness. That we can often agree on moral matters while disagreeing vigorously on religious ones suggests that moral judgments have a life of their own, whatever their long history. Given the amount and extent of religious disagreement in the world, it is fortunate that this is so.

If God Is Dead, Everything Is Permitted

A deeper claim is that morality finds in religion not only its origin, but its justification. Here the claim is not that we learn moral truths through religion, but that without religion—without God—there would *be* no moral truths.

Consider one of the most bedrock moral notions in our political discourse: the idea of fundamental human rights. Secretary Bennett quotes Thomas Jefferson's ringing proclamation that all men "are endowed by their Creator with certain unalienable rights." Without a creator, Bennett asks, "whence come these rights?" Who endows human beings with rights, if not God? If there is no God, there are no God-given rights, and maybe the notion of natural inalienable rights becomes, as Jeremy Bentham thought it was, "nonsense on stilts." Similarly, it is asked, how can there be moral commands without a commander? How can there be binding moral rules without some supreme rule-giver?

The original and still powerful objection to this argument was given by Plato in the *Euthyphro*. In modern dress, it is this. If a given action is right because God requires it, we have then to ask why God has chosen to issue that requirement. Either the reason lies in some morally desirable feature of the act, in which case God's choice depends on an external moral standard rather than itself setting that standard. Or else God's choice is essentially arbitrary—he just happened to feel like saying, "Thou shalt not kill." If the latter, morality seems hardly to have a more secure foundation than when it rested on supposedly arbitrary human desires. Moreover, it is difficult to conceive that if God had happened instead to feel like saying, "Thou shalt torture innocent children," that would be our moral law. Torture seems to be wrong because it causes undeserved suffering, not because God said so.

In fact, in one sense religion seems to depend on morality. Part of the way we recognize God as a fitting object of worship is by attention to his perfect goodness. If we do not worship God in recognition of his goodness, then, as Immanuel Kant argued, we bow down to God only as "a mighty lord whom we should have to placate . . . with flattery and incense." An omnipotent being can compel our obedience, but only a supremely good being deserves our worship. But this means, Kant concludes, that "All religion assumes morality, and morality cannot, therefore, be derived from religion."

But if morality doesn't depend on religion, what does it depend on? One answer is that it depends on what human beings collectively have decided are central rules for living together in harmony. They are grounded, not in divine commands, but in human needs, wants, loves, and fears. Compassion, respect, and tolerance are important moral virtues because they are the values that work best to preserve dignity, protect autonomy, enhance security, and make life happier and richer.

Such a foundation does not make moral rules arbitrary and subjective; it does not leave individuals free to make up the moral rules that suit them best. Moral rules are made collectively by human society and are grounded in the reality of the human condition. This is enough to justify our adherence to them. Morality, then, need not depend on religion for its justification.

You Better Be Good; You Better Watch Out

Even if morality doesn't depend on religion for its justification, it might depend on religion as a source of motivation. In the least attractive view of human psychology, people require the fear of future hellfire in order to behave toward each other with tolerable decency. But even in a more benign view of human nature, religion may be an important impetus to moral conduct. Robert Adams, a philosopher of religion, notes that most individuals have a plurality of motives for action, some self-interested, some concerned for the well-being of other people, still others concerned with values and ideals more abstractly conceived. Clearly the different springs of motivation may conflict, "but in Judeo-Christian ethics," Adams suggests, beliefs about God's will "are supposed to enable one to *fuse* these motives, so to speak, into one's devotion to God and His will, so that they all pull together." Aside from any narrow regard for one's own salvation, faith in God can make the believer simply want to be good, to please a loving Father.

Looking to society at large, the motivational claim that morality goes hand in hand with religion comes down to a sociological thesis: As religion founders, so will morality as well. But on this the historical record is at best indecisive. For one, the mere fact of correlation between religious and moral decline wouldn't of itself prove that the two were directly connected or suggest which way the connection is to be drawn. And while religious institutions have often set a shining example in ministering to the wretched, many have pointed out that religion has as often occasioned war and bigotry as peace and harmony. David Hume puts these sentiments into the mouth of Philo in his *Dialogues Concerning Natural Religion*: "If the religious spirit be ever mentioned in an historical narration, we are sure to meet afterwards with a detail of the miseries, which attend it. And no period of time can be happier or more prosperous, than those in which it is never regarded, or heard of." The Crusades, the Spanish Inquisition, the Salem witch burnings, present-day Iran—all bear no witness to the salutary moral effects of religion.

Philosopher Robert Fullinwider suggests that many who link immorality to a falling away of religious faith make their case chiefly by equating morality with "sexual decorum." William F. Buckley, for example, lambastes the absence of religious training in the schools for "its possible relationship to abandoned moral sanctions." The core of his argument is that "instruction in religion diminishes promiscuous sexual activity." Perhaps. But Fullinwider argues that a nation's morality is not a matter only of its sexual mores, but has to do as well with the development of a humane foreign policy, the decent conduct of economic life, integrity in public service, and a spirit of amiability and generosity in private life.

Nor is it surprising, he maintains, that sexual rectitude should require enforcement by religious sanctions in a way other areas of morality do not, for while other moral rules—against stealing, killing, lying—arise naturally from human needs and desires, sexual prohibitions seem to go against the grain of human nature. To the extent religious threats are required to sustain such prohibitions, this may show only that they don't fit comfortably with the rest of our moral framework.

However, religion may yet play an important role in moral life. The strongest case for this, Fullinwider suggests, begins with the observation that "religious institutions are the only institutions in our society, outside the confines of the family, in which people talk about moral values on a regular basis in a systematic way." Public schools have never rivaled religious institutions as a serious force for sustaining moral culture; it is in Sunday-school classes and Sabbath-day sermons that moral issues are most likely to be thoughtfully raised and considered. Since every society must have some institutional mechanism for transmitting moral culture, religion, in fulfilling this function, may be morality's chief ally.

Religion may be an ally of morality in another way as well. Adams raises the possibility that one danger of morality without religion is that morality then *becomes* a religion—an object of "maximal devotion." While most fear that severing morality from religion may undermine the motivational commitment to morality, a parallel danger is that it may remove any check on that commitment. This can result in an obsessive and oppressive form of moral zeal. Morality itself is "too narrow to be a suitable object of maximal devotion," since it excludes too many human excellences. But since God, for the believer, includes within him all that is true and good and beautiful, religion makes room for a richer view of human flourishing, within which morality can find its proper place.

"Religion" or My Religion?

The last two arguments give reasons to value religion for the contribution it makes to society. Do they give a reason for explicitly incorporating religion in some way into public life—perhaps by amending the Constitution to include some provision for school prayer?

The central fear involved in incorporating "religion" into public life is that religion almost inevitably comes to be narrowly identified with the religion of the dominant group. It is easy for "We are a religious nation" to slide into "This is a Christian nation," as one U.S. representative recently declared on the floor of the House—prompting Rep. Barney Frank, who was chairing the wee-hours session, to retort, "If this is a Christian nation, how come some poor Jew has to get up at 5:30 in the morning to preside over the House of Representatives?" Mr. Thwackum in Henry Fields's *Tom Jones* stipulated, "When I mean religion I mean the Christian religion; and not only the Christian religion but the Protestant religion; and not only the Protestant religion, but the Church of England." The Thwackums of this country mean by "religion" Protestantism of a fundamentalist and evangelical stripe.

Ronald Reagan and Secretary Bennett may see themselves as protecting "religion-in-general," but it is not clear that any such thing exists. The much-cited "Judeo-Christian tradition" does not represent "religion-in-general" to Buddhists, Hindus, or Moslems—nor to Jews, who resent seeing their religious heritage treated as an "Old Testament" prelude to Christianity. Within Christianity itself, Protestants and Catholics read the Bible in different translations, even say the Lord's Prayer—often viewed as a lowest-common-denominator Christian text—in different versions. And Protestants differ among themselves on how to view Christ's command to pray only in private, making no outward, public show of one's piety. Religion-in-general would have to be so bland and contentless that it is hard to see how it could count as religion at all.

Conclusion

In his August 1985 address to the Knights of Columbus, Secretary Bennett argued that "neutrality to religion turns out to bring with it a neutrality to the values that issue from religion." The choice, as the secretary presented it, is this: Either we put religion in the classroom, or we take morality out. Either we post the Ten Commandments on classroom bulletin boards, or we are left with nothing but "values clarification"—a kind of moral relativism that places all values on a par, none more right or wrong than any other. But if moral truths are truths in their own right, not just corollaries of religious principles, if some values *are* better than others, independent of any religious pedigree, then the secretary's dichotomy is a false one. We can argue directly for our moral beliefs and urge our children to adopt them, whatever our religious convictions. We can pray to different gods—or to no god—and still work together to revitalize our shared moral life.

Sources for this article include John Stuart Mill, Nature, the Utility of Religion, Theism, Being Three Essays on Religion, *3rd ed. (London: Longmans, Green, 1885); Immanuel Kant,* Religion within the Limits of Reason Alone, *trans. with introduction and notes by Theodore M. Greene and Hoyt H. Hudson (New York: Harper, 1960); Robert Merrihew Adams, "A Modified Divine Command Theory of Ethical Wrongness," in* Religion and Morality, *ed. Gene Outka and John P. Reeder, Jr. (New York: Anchor Books/Doubleday, 1973); Adams, "Saints," Journal of Philosophy 81, no. 7 (July 1984); William J. Bennett, Address to the Supreme Council Meeting of the Knights of Columbus, Washington, D.C., August 7, 1985; William F. Buckley, Jr., " . . . And Religion,"* Washington Post, *April 9, 1986; and interviews with Robert K. Fullinwider.*

How Good a Person Do I Have to Be?

Claudia Mills

How good a person am I? This is a question most of us care about being able to answer, and most of us, I suspect, know what we would like the answer to be. I, for one, would like to think that I'm a pretty good person, not saintly, but as good as most and better than some of my colleagues and friends. I'd like to be able to pat myself on the back, but also to point a finger at others; I want the requirements of morality to be lenient enough so I'll score high, but tough enough so my high score still means something. It would be nice if it turned out that however good I am is just about exactly how good a person ought to be. Contemporary moral philosophers have given a great deal of attention to these questions. What kind of a moral report card would the rest of us get from them?

Being a Good Person

If my household's gross income last year was $40,000 and I gave away $2,000 to charity, am I (a) a splendid person, (b) a good person, (c) an okay person, or (d) a bad person? A 1984 Rockefeller Brothers Fund survey reports that the average family with an income in that range donated $1,060, but while that lets me know that my hypothetical level of giving is somewhat higher than average, it doesn't tell me whether it is enough to satisfy the demands of morality. When I think of friends who probably gave less, I feel like leaving my income tax return casually lying around so they can see what a good person I am. But when I think about the amount of human suffering to be alleviated in the world, my contribution suddenly seems much less generous.

Most of us tend to decide what we owe others in part by seeing what's left over after we've secured a moderately comfortable—but not extravagant—standard of living for ourselves. We feel we shouldn't be faulted for aspiring to a middle-class lifestyle; the wealthy, on the other hand, have a good deal to apologize for. Not surprisingly, surveys show that 95 percent of Americans consider themselves middle or working class. The rich—those who ought to be "soaked" to provide benefits for the rest of us—are invariably those who have $10,000 a year more than we have.

I confess that I recently bought a $1,500 stereo system. That sum of money, as the United Nations International Children's Emergency Fund reminds me, can purchase a lot of vials of penicillin at twenty-five cents each. "But," I hasten to explain, "this is the first nice stereo I've ever bought in my whole entire life. And I know for a fact that many of my friends have stereos worth five times as much. *That's* selfish, in a world where millions of people go to bed every night hungry." Of course, someone who sold her stereo to raise money for the homeless will view me much as I view my stereophile colleagues. The difference between their lifestyle and mine is far less than the difference between my lifestyle and that of starving children sleeping on the streets in Calcutta. True enough. But a St. Francis who gives all that he has to the poor is just that: a saint. I'm not expected to be morally magnificent, but only morally decent, a middling sort of person, who does my share and then goes home to listen to *Don Giovanni* on my compact disc player. To do more is to qualify for moral extra credit.

Some philosophers define the boundaries of what we have a right to keep for ourselves more narrowly, however. Utilitarians are notorious for denying the whole category of moral extra credit. In their view, not to do a good thing is just the same morally as doing a bad thing, so every time we pass up an opportunity for a good deed, we not only forgo canonization but also invite moral criticism. Peter Singer, for one, argues that "if it is in our power to prevent something very bad happening, without thereby sacrificing anything of comparable moral significance, we ought to do it." The trouble is that, given how many very bad things are happening in the world and how very bad they are, little else is of comparable moral significance, which means we may be called on morally to give up a *lot*. Singer gives a partial list: "color television, stylish clothes, expensive dinners, a sophisticated stereo system, overseas holidays, a (second?) car, a large house, private schools for our children . . ."

Nor are utilitarians the only ones who saddle the rest of us with burdensome obligations. Rights theorists are likely to think that if somebody has a right, somebody else has a duty, and the somebody else, as often as not, turns out to be us. Henry Shue, writing in *Basic Rights*, maintains that "One is required to sacrifice, as necessary, anything but one's basic rights in order to honor the basic rights of others." It sounds suspiciously like that involves sacrificing our stereos.

These arguments suggest, moreover, that we not only ought to *have* less but also we ought to *do* more. It's true that a poet earning

$10,000 a year can give only so much before cutting into her own basic needs. But maybe she should consider a new career on Wall Street. Maybe the moral high road doesn't involve earning as little as you can, but earning as much as you can, so as to have more to give away. Philosophers who would make the rest of us feel guilty for not giving more may be at fault themselves for remaining in a nonlucrative profession when they could be more gainfully, if less happily, employed elsewhere. Whoever said you had a right to do just what you please?

Well, a number of philosophers have said, not that we have a right to do whatever we please, but that it's important to be able to make certain key choices that give meaning and coherence to our lives. In a famous argument against utilitarianism, Bernard Williams rejects the view that one is required to abandon one's own deepest commitments whenever they fail to advance the greatest good of the greatest number. To require someone to surrender his chosen life's work or his passionate creative pursuits would be "to alienate him in a real sense from his actions and the source of his actions in his own convictions. . . . It is thus, in the most literal sense, an attack on his integrity." Moreover, the project of going around all day making other people happy can only get off the ground if there are at least some "first-order projects," if at least somebody is *being* happy. After the revolution somebody has to be left to do the *living*.

One problem here is that, while we want some selfishness to turn out to be justified, we don't want *all* selfishness to turn out to be justified. The challenge, according to Shelly Kagan, philosopher at the University of Illinois at Chicago Circle, is a complex one: We want to explain why "it is sometimes permissible to refuse to perform an optimal act. But all those unwilling to embrace egoism must at the same time avoid arguments that rule out the possibility of there being any moral requirements at all. Thus the explanation must also account for the fact that sometimes a given optimal act *is* required by morality." If we try to establish some protected zone of self-interest, we will have trouble showing that this zone can ever be legitimately encroached on. And if we argue that reasons of self-interest sometimes outweigh moral reasons, then we will have to say that moral sacrifice is sometimes actually *unjustified*. But certainly we want it to be permissible, even if not required, for the moral saint to go the extra mile. Kagan concludes that it is difficult to set principled limits to what morality may demand of us.

In any case, some cold comfort may be derived from the fact that almost without exception philosophers who call for moral sacrifices fail to practice what they preach. They themselves are not rushing off to sign up with Mother Teresa. Some of them drive very nice cars. And insofar as they propose any specific guidelines for moral behavior, these tend to be calculated to reassure. Singer advocates (at minimum) giving "a round percentage of one's income like, say, 10 percent—more than a token donation, yet not so high as to be beyond all but saints." *That* isn't too bad, we might think. Shue points out that worldwide poverty could be reduced significantly with relatively modest sacrifices by affluent nations: "The affluent are expected not to enjoy less, but only to acquire more at a somewhat slower rate than they would if they maximized their own interests, narrowly construed." One feels uneasy, however, at Kagan's challenge: Why this much and no more?

Being a Saintly Person

Despite our fond wishes otherwise, it may turn out that morality is indeed uncomfortably demanding. Its bare minimum may look a lot like our maximum: Maybe Mother Teresa herself should be doing more than she is. But those of us who don't want, frankly, to be a whole lot more moral than we are, may want to reply instead: All right, morality demands a lot. But do we have to do *everything* it demands?

Susan Wolf, a philosopher at The Johns Hopkins University, suggests that being as morally good as we can be isn't in fact an admirable goal. Glad that she and her loved ones are not "moral saints," Wolf argues that "moral perfection . . . does not constitute a model of personal well-being toward which it would be particularly rational or good or desirable for a human being to strive." In a moral saint, she argues, the moral virtues (all present and all to an extreme degree) "are apt to crowd out the nonmoral virtues, as well as many of the interests and personal characteristics that we generally think contribute to a healthy, well-rounded, richly developed character." Someone who devotes all his time to raising money for Oxfam "necessarily is not reading Victorian novels, playing the oboe, or improving his backhand." Thus his is "a life strangely barren." Nor can the moral saint, it would seem, encourage in himself otherwise delightful characteristics that go "against the moral grain," such as a cynical or sarcastic wit. A moral saint, Wolf observes, "will have to be very very nice." Nice, and dreary company.

Wolf cautions, however, that "the fact that models of moral saints are unattractive does not necessarily mean that they are unsuitable ideals. Perhaps they are unattractive because they make us feel uncomfortable—they highlight our own weaknesses, vices, and flaws. If so, the fault lies not in the characters of the saints, but in those of our own unsaintly selves." But she notes that some of the qualities the moral saint necessarily lacks are *good* qualities, qualities we *ought* to admire, "virtues, albeit nonmoral virtues, in the unsaintly characters who have them."

Thus, Wolf concludes that "moral ideals do not, and need not, make the best personal ideals. . . . we have sound, compelling, and not particularly selfish reasons to choose not to devote ourselves univocally to realizing [our] unlimited potential to be morally good." In Wolf's view, we need not be defensive about the fact that our lives are not as morally good as they might be, because "a person may be *perfectly wonderful* without being *perfectly moral*." It is not always better to be morally better.

Conclusion

If Wolf is right, we can concede that morality is indeed demanding, but we can devote our lives at least in part to pursuits other than making ourselves maximally moral. Her view is not a rationalization of selfishness, however, not the view that if God hadn't meant for us to grab as much as we could, he wouldn't have given us two hands to grab it with. Instead, it is a call for a broader and more diverse ideal of human excellence, for taking the opportunity to cultivate in ourselves a rich array of both moral and nonmoral excellences.

There is little immediate danger, of course, that most of us will knock ourselves out to be too good. Whatever the optimal balance between moral and nonmoral excellences (and Wolf leaves it open how this balance should be struck), most of us err on the side of selfishness pure and simple. Nothing Wolf says gives any reason *not* to adopt, say, a policy of tithing.

But perhaps we have reason not to become overly obsessed with moral report cards. What's tiresome is not so much being good, but harping on goodness from morning to night. We could all probably stand to be a lot better morally than we are, and a lot better nonmorally as well, but maybe a first start toward progress would be simply to do more and to talk less.

Sources quoted in the article are Peter Singer, Practical Ethics *(Cambridge: Cambridge University Press, 1979); Henry Shue,* Basic Rights *(Princeton, N.J.: Princeton University Press, 1980); Bernard Williams, "A Critique of Utilitarianism," in J.J.C. Smart and Bernard Williams,* Utilitarianism: For and Against *(Cambridge: Cambridge University Press, 1973); Shelly Kagan, "Does Consequentialism Demand Too Much?"* Philosophy & Public Affairs *13, no. 3 (Summer 1984); and Susan Wolf, "Moral Saints,"* Journal of Philosophy *79, no. 8 (August 1982).*

Why Life Is Disappointing

Claudia Mills

Everyone knows that life is disappointing. We learn this early and remember it long. Or as one cheerful pundit observed: "We are born crying, live complaining, and die disappointed." Why this should be is somewhat of a puzzle, however. Any explanation must focus, not on why things generally turn out badly, but why they generally turn out so much worse than we expected. Disappointment is the gap between expectations and reality, between hope, the thing with feathers that perches in the soul, and the egg that, more often than not, it lays.

The Bible seems to suggest that a routine confounding of expectations (the first shall be last, the last first, and so on) is useful in cutting humans down to size, keeping them on their toes. The book of Job, which should have something to say about disappointment if anything does, pronounces that men are disappointed "because they were confident" (Job 6:20). Jehovah looks on Job's dashed hopes with a lofty satisfaction: "Behold, the hope of a man is disappointed" (Job 41:9). The guiding principle seems to be that man appoints, God disappoints, a perpetual reminder of our place in the scheme of things. The New Testament allows human hopes, properly directed, a somewhat brighter outlook (". . . and hope does not disappoint us"—Romans 5:5). But "hope against hope," that is, hope of the most apparently perverse sort, is the favored variety.

Enjoying a more worldly perspective, contemporary economists approach our question in a different framework. Why is it, they ask, that when we assess the projected costs and benefits of some undertaking, we end up overestimating the benefits so much more often than we end up overestimating the costs? Why do our cost-benefit analyses, measured against the subsequent unfolding of events, so often err on the side of optimism?

Harvard economists Richard Zeckhauser and Herman Leonard suggest this answer. It's not that economists are a particularly starry-eyed lot. Instead, "the crucial realization is that we do not observe a random selection of all projects analyzed. Rather, we choose to go ahead only with those projects whose net benefits are estimated to be positive. This will include some projects whose true net benefits—which we observe on completing the project—are negative, but which we over-estimated. On the other hand, some projects with true net benefits will have been estimated to yield negative net benefits and will have been scrapped." The only way to achieve parity between pleasant and unpleasant surprises would be to go ahead with *every* enterprise, what-ever its initial promise. Most of the dismal-looking ones will indeed turn out dismal, but we'll end up with a greater percentage of sleepers, as some turn out to be not quite so bad as anticipated. Disappointment is avoided, but at the price of a general increase in sorry outcomes.

Psychologists speculate that life is disappointing not because our hopes are thwarted more often than they are fulfilled, but because we feel the former more keenly than the latter. Daniel Kahneman and Amos Tversky, studying the psychology of how people form pre-ferences, found that "the threat of a loss has a greater impact on a decision than the possibility of an equivalent gain." In repeated exper-iments, people show themselves willing to take a considerable gamble to avoid a loss, but are less willing to take the same gamble to reap an analogous gain. In their terminology, "preferences between gains are risk-averse and preferences between losses are risk-seeking." Unex-pected gains, then, do not thrill in the same measure as unexpected losses gall.

The philosopher Arthur Schopenhauer explains this asymmetry by the gloomy postulate that "pleasure is only the negation of pain" and "pain is the positive element in life." In his view, "*to live happily* only means *to live less unhappily*. . . . The happiest lot is not to have experi-enced the keenest delights or the greatest pleasures, but to have brought life to a close without any very great pain." He joins with the stoics in offering this simple prescription for avoiding disappointment: "The safest way of not being very miserable is not to expect to be very happy."

But most of us would rather change the world than change our-selves. In this spirit, philosopher John Rawls offers a theory of justice motivated by the desire to produce a society that, whatever our expec-tations, will not disappoint us too deeply. He asks us to imagine we are choosing the principles that will govern society—but without knowing what our own identity in that society will turn out to be. In such a situ-ation, he proposes that we should use a "maximin" rule: Rank alterna-tives by their worst possible outcomes, and pick the one whose worst possible outcome is least awful. In other words, design a society such that, whoever you are when you emerge from behind the "veil of ignorance," your disappointment will be least unbearable. The principle points to an egalitarian theory of justice, which makes some sense: Disappointments are easier to bear if we are all disappointed equally.

Another alternative is to look on the bright side of disappointment, as a spur to run faster, stretch out our arms farther. . . . Inevitable, disappointment may be, but not necessarily without its redemptions. Mark Twain once wrote, "I believe that our Heavenly Father invented man because he was disappointed in the monkey"; feminists joke (or is it a joke?) that God created Eve because he (he?) was disappointed in Adam. Even Schopenhauer saw disappointment as the path to the highest good of experience, insight, knowledge, wisdom. A disappointing harvest, perhaps, but what else, really, should one have expected?

FOR FURTHER READING

Okin, Susan Moller. *Justice, Gender, and the Family.* New York: Basic Books, 1989.

Stocker, Michael. *Plural and Conflicting Values.* New York: Oxford University Press, 1989.

Wolf, Susan. "Moral Saints." *Journal of Philosophy* 79, no. 8 (August 1982).

CONTRIBUTORS

Charles R. Beitz is chair of the political science department of Swarthmore College. He is the author of *Political Equality* (Princeton University Press, 1989) and *Political Theory and International Relations* (Princeton University Press, 1979).

Dan W. Brock is professor of philosophy and of human values in medicine at Brown University. He served on the President's Commission for the Study of Ethical Problems in Medicine and Biomedical and Behavioral Research.

C.A.J. (Tony) Coady is Boyce Gibson professor of philosophy and chair of the philosophy department at the University of Melbourne, Australia, and also director of the Centre for Philosophy and Public Issues attached to that department. The author of *Testimony* (Oxford University Press, 1991), he has published numerous articles on epistemology, philosophy of mind, ethics, and political philosophy.

Robert K. Fullinwider is a research scholar at the Institute for Philosophy and Public Policy at the University of Maryland, College Park. He is the author of *The Reverse Discrimination Controversy: A Moral and Legal Analysis* (Rowman and Allanheld, 1980) and coeditor of *The Moral Foundations of Civil Rights* (Rowman and Allanheld, 1986).

William Galston is a professor in the School of Public Affairs and a research scholar at the Institute for Philosophy and Public Policy, both at the University of Maryland, College Park. His books include *Liberal Purposes: Goals, Virtues, and Diversity in the Liberal State* (forthcoming, Cambridge University Press), *A Tough Row to Hoe: The 1986 Farm Bill and Beyond* (University Press of America, 1985), and *Justice and the Human Good* (University of Chicago Press, 1980). From 1982 to 1984 he served as issues director of the Mondale-for-President campaign.

Samuel Gorovitz is dean of the College of Arts and Sciences and professor of philosophy at Syracuse University. He is the author of *Doctors' Dilemmas: Moral Conflict and Medical Care* (Oxford University Press, 1985) and *Drawing the Line: Life, Death and Ethical Choices in an American Hospital* (Oxford University Press, 1990).

Amy Gutmann is Andrew W. Mellon professor of politics at Princeton University, where she directs the Center for Human Values. She is the author of *Democratic Education* (Princeton University Press, 1987) and *Liberal Equality* (Cambridge University Press, 1980), editor of *Democracy and the*

Welfare State (Princeton University Press, 1988), and coeditor of *Ethics and Politics* (Nelson-Hall, 1984).

John Kleinig is professor of philosophy in the Department of Law and Political Science at the John Jay College of Criminal Justice and in the Ph.D. program in philosophy at the Graduate Center at the City University of New York.

Steven Lee is an associate professor of philosophy at Hobart and William Smith Colleges. He has written extensively on the ethics of nuclear weapons, including the forthcoming book *Morality, Prudence, and Nuclear Weapons*.

Herman B. Leonard is associate professor of public policy at the John F. Kennedy School of Government at Harvard University. He has published in the areas of policy analysis and economics.

David Lewis is professor of philosophy at Princeton University. He is the author of *Convention: A Philosophical Study* (Harvard University Press, 1969), *Counterfactuals* (Harvard University Press, 1973), *On the Plurality of Worlds* (B. Blackwell, 1986), and *Parts of Classes* (B. Blackwell, 1990).

Judith Lichtenberg is an associate professor of philosophy at the University of Maryland and a research scholar at the university's Institute for Philosophy and Public Policy. She is the editor of *Democracy and the Mass Media* (Cambridge University Press, 1990) and has written widely on philosophical issues regarding the mass media.

David Luban is a professor at the Law School of the University of Maryland and a research scholar at the university's Institute for Philosophy and Public Policy. He is the author of *Lawyers and Justice: An Ethical Study* (Princeton University Press, 1988) and the editor of *The Good Lawyer: Lawyers' Roles and Lawyers' Ethics* (Rowman and Allanheld, 1984).

Douglas MacLean is the chair of the philosophy department at the University of Maryland, Baltimore County. His many publications include *Values at Risk* (1986), *The Security Gamble* (1984), and *Energy and the Future* (1983), all published by Maryland Studies in Public Philosophy.

Claudia Mills is an assistant professor of philosophy at the University of Maryland, Baltimore County. From 1980–1989 she edited *QQ: Report from the Institute for Philosophy and Public Policy*. She is the coeditor of *Liberalism Reconsidered* (Rowman and Allanheld, 1983) and of *The Moral Foundations of Civil Rights* (Rowman and Allanheld, 1986).

Richard Mohr is a professor of philosophy at the University of Illinois, Urbana. He is the author of *The Platonic Cosmology* (E. J. Brill, 1985) and *Gays/Justice—A Study of Ethics, Society, and the Law* (Columbia University Press, 1988). He is the general editor of the book series *Between Men— Between Women: Lesbian and Gay Studies from Columbia University Press*.

Thomas Nagel is professor of philosophy at New York University. His many publications include *The View from Nowhere* (Oxford University Press, 1986), *Mortal Questions* (Cambridge University Press, 1979), and *The Possibility of Altruism* (Oxford University Press, 1970).

Derek Parfit is a fellow of All Souls College, Oxford University, and a regular visiting professor of philosophy at Princeton University. He is the author of *Reasons and Persons* (Clarendon Press, 1984).

Deborah L. Rhode is professor of law and director of the Institute for Research on Women and Gender at Stanford University. She has written widely in the area of legal ethics and gender discrimination. Recent works include *Justice and Gender* (Harvard University Press, 1989) and *Theoretical Perspectives on Sexual Difference* (Yale University Press, 1990).

Mark Sagoff is currently director of the Institute for Philosophy and Public Policy at the University of Maryland, College Park. He is the author of *The Economy of the Earth: Philosophy, Law, and the Environment* (Cambridge University Press, 1988).

Jerome Segal is a former senior adviser for agency planning at the Agency for International Development. Currently he is a research scholar at the Institute for Philosophy and Public Policy at the University of Maryland, College Park, and president of the Jewish Peace Lobby. He is the author of *Creating the Palestinian State: A Strategy for Peace* (Lawrence Hill Books, 1989).

Henry Shue is director of the Center for Ethics and Public Life at Cornell University. He is the author of *Basic Rights: Subsistence, Affluence, and U.S. Foreign Policy* (Princeton University Press, 1980) and the editor of *Nuclear Deterrence and Moral Restraint: Critical Choices for American Strategy* (Cambridge University Press, 1989).

A. John Simmons is professor and chair of the philosophy department at the University of Virginia. He is the author of *Moral Principles and Political Obligations* (Princeton University Press, 1979) and is also an editor of the journal *Philosophy & Public Affairs*.

Allen Stairs is associate professor of philosophy at the University of Maryland, College Park. He writes widely on issues in the philosophy of science, primarily on the foundations of quantum mechanics.

Bonnie Steinbock is associate professor of philosophy and public affairs at the State University of New York (SUNY), Albany, and also teaches in the Department of Health Policy and Management in SUNY's School of Public Health.

Stephen P. Stich has taught at the University of Michigan, the University of Maryland, College Park, and the University of California, San Diego. He is currently professor of philosophy and cognitive science at Rutgers, the State University of New Jersey. His publications include *From Folk*

Psychology to Cognitive Science (The MIT Press, 1983) and *The Fragmentation of Reason* (The MIT Press, 1990).

Alan Strudler has taught at Stanford University and the California Institute of Technology. He is a research scholar at the Institute for Philosophy and Public Policy at the University of Maryland, College Park, writing on philosophical issues regarding the law.

Robert Wachbroit is a research scholar at the Institute for Philosophy and Public Policy at the University of Maryland, College Park, specializing in the moral and conceptual issues surrounding new research in biotechnology.

Langdon Winner is a political theorist who specializes in social and political issues generated by modern technological change. An associate professor of political science in the Department of Science and Technology Studies at Rensselaer Polytechnic Institute, he is the author of *Autonomous Technology: Technics-out-of-Control As a Theme in Political Thought* (The MIT Press, 1977) and of *The Whale and the Reactor: A Search for Limits in an Age of High Technology* (University of Chicago Press, 1986).

Richard Zeckhauser is Frank P. Ramsey Professor of Political Economy at the John F. Kennedy School of Government at Harvard University. His research focuses on microeconomic theory, with an emphasis on incentives and uncertainty, and on policy issues related to health, the environment, human resources, and financial markets. Current projects address the role of unions in the health sector, incentive mechanisms to foster international cooperation in the control of "greenhouse" emissions, and behavioral determinants of financial market behaviors.

COPYRIGHTS AND
ACKNOWLEDGMENTS

CHARLES R. BEITZ "The Ethics of Covert Operations" reprinted from *QQ: Report from the Institute for Philosophy and Public Policy* (Fall 1988) by permission of the author and the Carnegie Council. "Should All Countries Be Democracies?" reprinted from *QQ* (Winter 1982) by permission of the author.

DAN W. BROCK "Life-Support Decisions for Newborns" reprinted from *QQ: Report from the Institute for Philosophy and Public Policy* (Fall 1984) by permission of the author.

C. A. J. COADY "Defending Human Chauvinism" reprinted from *QQ: Report from the Institute for Philosophy and Public Policy* (Fall 1986) by permission of the author.

ROBERT K. FULLINWIDER "Civic Education and Traditional American Values" (Summer 1986), "Learning Morality" (Spring 1988), and "The New Patriotism" (Spring 1985) reprinted from *QQ: Report from the Institute for Philosophy and Public Policy* by permission of the author.

WILLIAM A. GALSTON "The Obligation to Play Political Hardball" reprinted from *QQ: Report from the Institute for Philosophy and Public Policy* (Winter 1989) by permission of the author.

SAMUEL GOROVITZ "Against Selling Bodily Parts" reprinted from *QQ: Report from the Institute for Philosophy and Public Policy* (Spring 1984) by permission of the author.

AMY GUTMANN "Should Public Schools Teach Virtue?" reprinted from *QQ: Report from the Institute for Philosophy and Public Policy* (Summer 1985) by permission of the author.

JOHN KLEINIG "What Is Wrong with Entrapment?" reprinted from *QQ: Report from the Institute for Philosophy and Public Policy* (Winter 1989) by permission of the author.

STEVEN LEE "Does Nuclear Deterrence Work?" reprinted from *QQ: Report from the Institute for Philosophy and Public Policy* (Winter 1988) by permission of the author.

HERMAN B. LEONARD AND RICHARD ZECKHAUSER "Cost-Benefit Analysis Defended" reprinted from *QQ: Report from the Institute for Philosophy and Public Policy* (Summer 1983) by permission of the author.

DAVID LEWIS "Buy Like a MADman, Use Like a NUT" reprinted from *QQ: Report from the Institute for Philosophy and Public Policy* (Spring 1986) by permission of the author and from *Nuclear Deterrence and Moral Restraint*, ed. Henry Shue © 1989 by permission of Cambridge University Press.

JUDITH LICHTENBERG "Deregulating the Electronic Media" reprinted from *QQ: Report from the Institute for Philosophy and Public Policy* (Winter 1984) by permission of the author. "The Dilemma of the Journalist/Source Relationship" reprinted by permission of the author and the National Press Club *Record* ("The Journalist's Duty to Betray," Vol. 34, No. 26, July 20, 1989). And Douglas MacLean, "Is Good News No News?" reprinted from *QQ* (Fall 1988) by permission of the authors. "Sex, Character, Politics, and the Press" reprinted from *QQ* ("The Personal Is Not Political," Winter, 1987) by permission of the author.

DAVID LUBAN "Judicial Activism versus Judicial Restraint" (Fall 1987), "The Legacy of Nuremberg" (Winter 1986), "Should Lawyers Advertise?" (Summer 1988), "Should Legal Services Rise Again?" (Fall 1986), "Two Cheers for Punitive Damages" (Fall 1989), and "Why We Mistrust Lawyers" (Summer 1981) reprinted from *QQ: Report from the Institute for Philosophy and Public Policy* by permission of the author.

DOUGLAS MACLEAN "Drug Testing in Sports" (Fall 1987), "Nuclear Waste Storage: Your Backyard or Mine?" (Spring/Summer 1989), and "Why People Fear Nuclear Power" (Fall 1981) reprinted from *QQ: Report from the Institute for Philosophy and Public Policy* by permission of the author. And Judith Lichtenberg, "Is Good News No News?" reprinted from *QQ* (Fall 1988) by permission of the authors. And Claudia Mills, "Faith in Science" (Spring 1985), "Love and Justice" (Fall 1989), "Rethinking Rationality" (Winter 1988), and "Risk Analysis and the Value of Life" (Winter 1986) reprinted from *QQ* by permission of the authors.

CLAUDIA MILLS "Air Pollution: The Role and Limits of Consent" (Summer 1985), "Are We Cheating Our Children?" (Winter 1983), "Banning the Bomb: A Few Decades Too Late?" (Summer 1986), "Being Here: The Rights of Resident Aliens" (Winter 1983), "Children's Television" (Summer 1986), "Educating Our Children: Whose Responsibility?" (Winter 1985), "Exporting Hazards" (Fall 1981), "Freedom and Fairness: Regulating the Mass Media" (Fall 1986), "The Graying of America" (Spring 1988), "How Good a Person Do I Have to Be?" (Winter 1988), "How Well-Off Should Welfare Make You?" (Fall 1981), "Is Advertising Manipulative?" (Spring/Summer 1989), "Not with a Bang: The Moral Perplexities of Nuclear Deterrence" (Summer 1983), "Paying Women What They Are Worth" (Spring 1983), "Plowshares into Swords: The Political Uses of Food" (Fall 1982), "Preserving Endangered Species: Why Should We Care?" (Fall 1985), "Privacy in the Computer Age" (Fall 1984), "Racist and Sexist Jokes: How Bad Are They (Really)?" (Spring/Summer 1987), "Religion and Morality" (Spring 1986), "Religion in Public Life" (Spring/Summer 1987), "Representing Immoral Clients" (Winter 1982), "Settling Out of Court" (Fall 1988), "Surrogate Motherhood" (Winter 1989), "To Tell or Not to Tell: Conflicts about Confidentiality" (Spring 1984), "Terrorism" (Fall 1987), "'What Has Posterity Ever Done for Me?': Energy Policy and Future Generations" (Winter 1981), "What Would King Solomon Do Today?: The Revolution in Child Custody" (Summer 1988), "Why Life Is Disappointing" (Summer 1985), "Women in the Military" (Summer 1981), and "The Zealous Lawyer: Is Winning the Only Thing?" (Winter 1984) reprinted from *QQ: Report from the Institute for Philosophy and Public Policy* by permission of the author. And Douglas MacLean, "Faith in Science" (Spring 1985), "Love and Justice" (Fall 1989), "Rethinking Rationality" (Winter 1988), and "Risk Analysis and the Value of Life" (Winter 1986) reprinted from *QQ* by permission of the authors.

RICHARD D. MOHR "AIDS: What to Do—And What Not to Do" (Fall 1985), "Gays and Civil Rights" ("Gays and the Civil Rights Act," Spring 1984), and "Mandatory AIDS Testing" (Fall 1988) reprinted from *QQ: Report from the Institute for Philosophy and Public Policy* by permission of the author.

THOMAS NAGEL "A Defense of Affirmative Action" reprinted from *QQ: Report from the Institute for Philosophy and Public Policy* (Fall 1981) by permission of the author.

DEREK PARFIT "An Attack on the Social Discount Rate" reprinted from *QQ: Report from the Institute for Philosophy and Public Policy* (Winter 1981) by permission of the author.

DEBORAH L. RHODE "Private Clubs and Public Values" reprinted from *QQ: Report from the Institute for Philosophy and Public Policy* (Fall 1986) by permission of the author. Adapted from *Justice and Gender: Sex Discrimination and the Law* by Deborah L. Rhode (Cambridge, Mass.: Harvard University Press). Copyright © 1989 by the President and Fellows of Harvard College. Reprinted by permission of the publishers.

MARK SAGOFF "Animal Liberation and Environmental Ethics: Bad Marriage, Quick Divorce" (Spring 1984), "The Biotechnology Controversy" (Fall 1985), "The Limits of Cost-Benefit Analysis" (Summer 1981), and "Property Rights and Environmental Law (Spring 1988) reprinted from *QQ: Report from the Institute for Philosophy and Public Policy* by permission of the author.

JEROME SEGAL "Income and Development" reprinted from *QQ: Report from the Institute for Philosophy and Public Policy* (Fall 1985) by permission of the author.

HENRY SHUE "Are Nuclear Defenses Morally Superior?" (Spring 1985) and "Playing Hardball with Human Rights" (Fall 1983) reprinted from *QQ: Report from the Institute for Philosophy and Public Policy* by permission of the author.

A. JOHN SIMMONS "Why the Draft Is Hard to Justify" reprinted from *QQ: Report from the Institute for Philosophy and Public Policy* (Spring 1981) by permission of the author.

ALLEN STAIRS "The Case against Creationism" reprinted from *QQ: Report from the Institute for Philosophy and Public Policy* (Spring 1982) by permission of the author.

BONNIE STEINBOCK "Adultery" reprinted from *QQ: Report from the Institute for Philosophy and Public Policy* (Winter 1986) by permission of the author.

STEPHEN P. STICH "The Genetic Adventure" reprinted from *QQ: Report from the Institute for Philosophy and Public Policy* (Spring 1983) by permission of the author.

ALAN STRUDLER "Confronting the Insurance Crisis" reprinted from *QQ: Report from the Institute for Philosophy and Public Policy* (Spring/Summer 1989) by permission of the author.

ROBERT WACHBROIT "Eight Worries about Patenting Animals" (Summer 1988) and "What Is Wrong with Eugenics?" (Spring/Summer 1987) reprinted from *QQ: Report from the Institute for Philosophy and Public Policy* by permission of the author. "Who Is the Patient?" reprinted from *QQ* by permission of the author and *Maryland Medical Journal* (1989; 38 [11]: 957–59).

LANGDON WINNER "The Risk of Talking about Risk" reprinted from *QQ: Report from the Institute for Philosophy and Public Policy* (Spring 1986) by permission of the author.

RICHARD ZECKHAUSER AND HERMAN B. LEONARD "Cost-Benefit Analysis Defended" reprinted from *QQ: Report from the Institute for Philosophy and Public Policy* (Summer 1983) by permission of the authors.

A 1
B 2
C 3
D 4
E 5
F 6
G 7
H 8
I 9
J 0